ECLIPSE WEB TOOLS
PLATFORM

 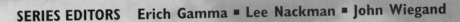

the eclipse series

SERIES EDITORS Erich Gamma ▪ Lee Nackman ▪ John Wiegand

Eclipse is a universal tool platform, an open extensible integrated development environment (IDE) for anything and nothing in particular. Eclipse represents one of the most exciting initiatives hatched from the world of application development in a long time, and it has the considerable support of the leading companies and organizations in the technology sector. Eclipse is gaining widespread acceptance in both the commercial and academic arenas.

The Eclipse Series from Addison-Wesley is the definitive series of books dedicated to the Eclipse platform. Books in the series promise to bring you the key technical information you need to analyze Eclipse, high-quality insight into this powerful technology, and the practical advice you need to build tools to support this evolutionary Open Source platform. Leading experts Erich Gamma, Lee Nackman, and John Wiegand are the series editors.

Titles in the Eclipse Series

For more information on books in this series visit www.awprofessional.com/series/eclipse

ECLIPSE WEB TOOLS PLATFORM

DEVELOPING JAVA™ *WEB APPLICATIONS*

Naci Dai

Lawrence Mandel

Arthur Ryman

✦✦ Addison-Wesley

*Upper Saddle River, NJ • Boston • Indianapolis • San Francisco
New York • Toronto • Montreal • London • Munich • Paris • Madrid
Capetown • Sydney • Tokyo • Singapore • Mexico City*

Many of the designations used by manufacturers and sellers to distinguish their products are claimed as trademarks. Where those designations appear in this book, and the publisher was aware of a trademark claim, the designations have been printed with initial capital letters or in all capitals.

The authors and publisher have taken care in the preparation of this book, but make no expressed or implied warranty of any kind and assume no responsibility for errors or omissions. No liability is assumed for incidental or consequential damages in connection with or arising out of the use of the information or programs contained herein.

The publisher offers excellent discounts on this book when ordered in quantity for bulk purchases or special sales, which may include electronic versions and/or custom covers and content particular to your business, training goals, marketing focus, and branding interests. For more information, please contact:

> U.S. Corporate and Government Sales
> (800) 382-3419
> corpsales@pearsontechgroup.com

For sales outside the United States please contact:

> International Sales
> international@pearsoned.com

Visit us on the Web: www.awprofessional.com

Library of Congress Cataloging-in-Publication Data

Dai, Naci.
 Eclipse Web tools platform : developing Java Web applications / Naci Dai, Lawrence Mandel, Arthur Ryman.
   p. cm.
 Includes bibliographical references and index.
 ISBN 978-0-321-39685-3 (pbk. : alk. paper)   1. Web site development   2. Java (Computer program language)
3. Internet programming.   I. Mandel, Lawrence.   II. Ryman, Arthur.   III. Title.

TK5105.888.D32 2007
006.7'6—dc22

2007010167

ISBN 13: 978-0-321-39685-3
ISBN 10:   0-321-39685-5

Text printed in the United States on recycled paper at Courier in Stoughton, Massachusetts.
First printing, May 2007

To my wife and best friend, Karen, who encourages and helps me in all my endeavors, and to my daughters, Maya and Ela, for letting me use their weekends and playtime for writing this book. I love you all.

—N.D.

To my wife, Elana, who inspires, encourages, and challenges me to try new things, like writing this book, and to my dad, Fred (ז״ל), who bought me my first computer and who I know would have thought this stuff was so cool.

—L.M.

To my late father, Sydney Ryman, who taught me to love books and who died peacefully at the age of 85 while I was writing this one. Dad, thank you for all those weekend trips to the public library.

—A.R.

Contents

Part II ○ Java Web Application Development   111

Foreword

The Web Tools Platform (WTP) Project is, in many ways, an Eclipse success story. The goal of the Eclipse community and the Eclipse Foundation is twofold: to cultivate both an Open Source community and an ecosystem of complementary products, capabilities, and services. Over the past two years, this project has made great progress on both fronts. WTP has been adopted by a broad cross-section of the industry as the platform for their Java EE and Web tools: BEA WebLogic Workshop, CodeGear JBuilder, Genuitec's MyEclipse, IBM Rational Application Developer, JBoss IDE, and SAP NetWeaver, to name just a few of the prominent ones. (You can read the full list in Chapter 16.) By any measure, WTP has been very successful in achieving its goal of providing a common tool infrastructure for the Java EE development world.

On the Open Source project side, WTP has garnered contributions from many organizations and companies. To list just a few of the prominent ones: WTP has active participation from ObjectWeb Lomboz developers such as Naci Dai, it has been ably led by Tim Wagner from BEA, it has seen contributions of code and committers from Oracle in both the JavaServer Faces (JSF) and object-relational persistence (Dali ORM), and—last but not least—has had major support from IBM in terms of code, committers, and leadership from Lawrence Mandel, Arthur Ryman, David Williams, and others. For the full story, I highly recommend reading the WTP Is Born section in Chapter 2.

In short, Web Tools has been a wonderful community effort, an effort that has been rewarded with many shipped products. And in the Eclipse community, this is truly the measure of a successful project.

The simple fact that so many organizations—many of them fierce competitors in the marketplace—cooperate on the development of WTP and ship products on top of it is a testament to the WTP project leadership. It is also one of the strongest proof-points that the Eclipse community's model of "collaborate on the platform and compete on the product" is the correct one for today's world of highly complex software, faster time-to-market requirements, and shrinking development budgets. Each of the products listed earlier (WebLogic Workshop, RAD, JBuilder, NetWeaver, and so forth) is highly differentiated, yet they share the same Eclipse Web Tools Platform base.

Since the project's inception, the WTP team has been working toward creating both a strong set of tools for developer productivity and a stable platform on top of which tool builders can ship products. Neither of these are simple goals, and that WTP has been successful on both fronts speaks volumes about the hard work of the committers on the project. Both topics are covered in the book, with Part II focusing on using the tools, and Part III describing how to extend WTP for additional servers, filetypes, and the like.

I hope *Eclipse Web Tools Platform: Developing Java Web Applications* will make you a more productive Java developer. Please pay special attention to the Contributing to WTP section in Chapter 2. Eclipse is all about active community involvement, and we hope to welcome you soon as an active contributor to WTP and other projects at Eclipse. As you work with WTP and the capabilities described in this book, I'd encourage you to communicate your successes back to the community, and perhaps consider contributing any interesting extensions you may develop. The WTP Web site may be found at

http://www.eclipse.org/webtools/

It includes pointers to the WTP newsgroup, where you can communicate and share your results with other WTP developers, and pointers to the Eclipse installation of Bugzilla, where you can contribute your extensions.

—*Mike Milinkovich*
Executive Director
Eclipse Foundation

Preface

Our goal in writing this book was to help build the community around the Eclipse Web Tools Platform (WTP) Project. We decided to write this book soon after WTP was approved by the Eclipse Foundation. At that time, the project was in its formative stages and there was virtually nothing written about WTP. We believed that a book on how to use and extend WTP would help promote its adoption.

We naively hoped that we would have this book finished soon after WTP 0.7 was released in July 2005. However, since we were all actively engaged in developing WTP, work on this book got delayed. Also, many significant changes in the design of WTP were planned, so we felt it was better to have the book describe the next major version, WTP 1.5, which was part of the Eclipse 3.2 Callisto simultaneous release in June 2006.

Allowing WTP to mature also gave us more time to develop and refine the material in this book. Much of the material in this book has been test-driven at several major software development conferences including EclipseCon, EclipseWorld, Rational Software Development Conference, and Colorado Software Summit. Attendees at those events provided valuable feedback that has improved the content of this book.

Since the WTP 1.5 release, there has been increasing adoption of WTP by both commercial and Open Source tool developers. This activity has generated a stream of maintenance releases. As we went into production, this book accurately reflected the content of WTP 1.5.2, but by the time it appears in print, the latest release should be WTP 1.5.3. However, each maintenance release should only contain bug fixes and not affect the user interface. This book should therefore also be accurate for WTP 1.5.3 and future maintenance releases. And although WTP 2.0, which is planned for June 2007, will certainly contain many enhancements, we expect that most of the content of this book will still be valid.

About This Book

This book is divided into four parts: Getting Started, Java Web Application Development, Extending WTP, and Products and Plans.

In Part I, Getting Started, we introduce you to WTP. We give a brief overview of the history and architecture of the project and discuss how you can contribute to its development. By being an active contributor as well as a user, you can help improve WTP and ensure its long-term success. We also introduce you to League Planet, a fictitious amateur sport Web site, which serves as the inspiration for the programming examples in the rest of the book. Next we take you on a Quick Tour of WTP in which you build a simple Web application that includes dynamic content generated by servlets and JSPs running on Tomcat, JDBC database access to Derby, and Web services running on Axis. We conclude with a detailed discussion of how to install WTP and tailor it to your needs using its many preferences. At the end of this part, you'll be able to start building your own Java Web applications with WTP.

Part II, Java Web Application Development, is for Java Web application developers. We describe the architecture of Java Web applications and how to build them using WTP. We start with a discussion of how to set up your project, including the use of Maven for automated builds. We then discuss architecture in some detail. Java Web applications have a multi-tiered architecture, and each of the presentation, business logic, and persistence tiers is addressed in its own chapter. The presentation tier chapter covers tools for HTML, CSS, JavaScript, XML, DTD, and XSLT. The business logic tier chapter discusses tools for EJBs and XDoclet. The persistence tier chapter describes tools for SQL. Next we focus on developing Web services, including tools for SOAP, WSDL, XSD, and UDDI. We close with a discussion of testing, including JUnit, Cactus, HttpUnit, and the Eclipse Test and Performance Tools Platform (TPTP).

In Part III, Extending WTP, we shift attention to developing Eclipse plug-ins that extend WTP. This part of the book is aimed at tool developers. WTP contains many plug-ins and extension points, so the coverage here serves mainly to illustrate the process. A comprehensive treatment of all the APIs in WTP would itself fill several books. We start with the important example of adding a new server runtime to WTP, and illustrate this by adding support for GlassFish, the reference implementation for Java Enterprise Edition 5 (Java EE 5). Next, we show how to add support for new file types and do so for DocBook, the XML format used for authoring books (such as this one). We follow that by describing how to support new WSDL extensions and add a new SOAP binding as an example. We conclude this subject by extending the URI resolution framework, which enables XML processors to locate resources.

The book wraps up with Part IV, Products and Plans. We begin with a brief survey of commercial and Open Source Eclipse-based Web development products that can be used with WTP. Although WTP contains a core set of useful tools, it is also a platform intended to be built on by others. After you master WTP, you may find that your tool needs are not fully satisfied. Perhaps you want to develop with Struts, Hibernate, or Spring. Or you may want to use a different Web development language, such as PHP, Python, or Ruby, in conjunction with Java. Fortunately, there are many products available to round out your Web development IDE. We end the book with a preview of functions we expect to be added to WTP in future releases. WTP is currently hosting subprojects for JavaServer Faces (JSF), Java Persistence Architecture (Dali), and AJAX (ATF). In addition, WTP is planning tighter integration with other Eclipse projects, as well as support for Java EE 5. Of course, the future of WTP largely depends on you. By becoming an active user and contributor, you will influence the continuing support and evolution of WTP.

Audience

This book is primarily written for Java Web application developers. We assume that you have a working knowledge of Java programming and some experience using Eclipse. There are many excellent books available that cover both topics. Some experience in Java Web application development is also desirable. We have made an attempt to introduce the subject of Java Web application development in addition to describing the tools available in WTP. Although this book deals with WTP, it will also be of use to users of products built on WTP. And remember, one of the best ways you can contribute to WTP is by reporting bugs. If you hit a bug while using WTP, please report it to the Eclipse Bugzilla system at

```
https://bugs.eclipse.org/bugs/enter_bug.cgi?product=Web+Tools
```

This book also includes material for Eclipse plug-in developers who want to extend WTP. Experience in plug-in development is assumed. Several available books cover the topic of Eclipse plug-in development for those who need some background information. Although we expect commercial and Open Source projects to extend WTP, we also expect individuals to do so. If you develop a cool plug-in that fits within the scope of the WTP charter, please consider contributing it to WTP. To do so, start by sending a note to the WTP developers mailing list at

```
<wtp-dev@eclipse.org>
```

Sample Code

The Web site for this book is located at

```
http://www.eclipsewtp.org
```

All of the example code used throughout this book can be downloaded from there. The site will also provide an errata list, and other news related to the book.

The following Eclipse components are required to run the examples in this book:

- ○ Eclipse Software Development Kit (SDK), Version 3.2
- ○ Eclipse Modeling Framework (EMF), Version 2.2
- ○ Graphical Editing Framework (GEF), Version 3.2
- ○ Java Edit Model (JEM), Version 1.2
- ○ Web Tools Platform (WTP), Version 1.5

All of the above are available from

`http://www.eclipse.org/webtools/downloads`

Conventions

We use a sans serif font for user interface elements such as menu items, buttons, and labels. We use a monospace font for programmatic elements such as file names, source code listings, URLs, package names, and XML content. Examples of these conventions are listed below.

- ○ buttons, e.g., **Submit**
- ○ class names, e.g., `LoginServlet`
- ○ code, e.g., `out.println("Hello, world");`
- ○ email addresses, e.g., `<feedback@eclipsewtp.org>`
- ○ file names, e.g., `web.xml`
- ○ labels, e.g., **Servers**
- ○ menu items, e.g., **File ► New ► Project**
- ○ method names, e.g., `getParameter()`
- ○ URLs, e.g., `http://eclipse.org`

Feedback

We've set up an e-mail address to receive feedback about this book. Please send your comments on this book to

`<feedback@eclipsewtp.org>`

Acknowledgments

We'd like to begin by thanking the people who directly contributed to the preparation of this book. Our technical reviewers, Simon Archer, John Arthorne, Michael Elder, Jane Fung, Daniel Holt, and Kimberley Peter, gave us highly valuable, in-depth comments that greatly improved the contents of this book. Mike Milinkovich graciously provided us with an inspiring Foreword. We received authoritative feedback on the accuracy of the project and product descriptions contained in Chaper 16, Other Web Tools Based on Eclipse, from Jens Eckels, Matthew Gammie, Axel Kramer, Jochen Krause, Kyle Shank, Greg Stachnick, and Fabio Zadrozny. And, of course, Greg Doench and Michelle Housely, our wonderful editors at Addison-Wesley, were a continuous source of support and encouragement. We are grateful to you all.

We would also like to acknowledge our fellow members of the WTP development project, since their contributions gave us something well worth writing about.

WTP was created as the result of a three-way collaboration between IBM, ObjectWeb, and the Eclipse Foundation. From IBM, we'd like to thank the executive team of Lee Nackman, Hayden Lindsey, and Karen Hunt for approving the contribution of part of Rational Application Developer V6.0 and supporting its ongoing development in WTP. Also at IBM, we'd like to thank Dave Thomson, John Wiegand, and Scott Rich for contributing to the initial formulation of the project. At ObjectWeb, we'd like to thank Christophe Ney for leading the project creation effort. Christophe was instrumental in enabling the contribution of Lomboz from eteration, a member of ObjectWeb. At Eclipse, we'd like to thank Mike Milinkovich for supporting the creation of WTP, and John Wiegand and Bjorn Freeman-Benson for shepherding WTP through the creation process.

Next, we'd like to thank the WTP leadership team. Bjorn Freeman-Benson, Christophe Ney, and Tim Wagner co-led the Project Management Committee (PMC); Dominique de Vito, Jochen Krause, Mitch Sonies, Raghu Srinivasan, and

David Williams served on the PMC; Chris Brealey, Chuck Bridgham, Der-Ping Chou, Tim de Boer, Craig Salter, Sheila Sholars, and David Williams led component teams; and Jeffrey Liu was the lead release engineer.

Finally, we would like to thank all of the many committers and contributors who have made WTP such a memorable experience and huge success. For the complete list, see

```
http://www.eclipse.org/webtools/people/
```

About the Authors

Naci Dai, eteration

Naci is a founder of the WTP project, a member of its Project Management Committee (PMC), and the leader of the J2EE Standards Tools (JST) subproject. Naci is the Chief Scientist and Managing Director of eteration, a.s. Turkey. eteration is a member of the ObjectWeb Consortium. Naci is an object mentor and an educator. He is the founder of ObjectLearn and one of the initiators of the eteration network. He wrote Lomboz, a tool for J2EE development. Prior to eteration, he was with BEA Systems Inc. and The Object People as a managing director with their professional services organizations. He teaches object technology, Web development, and distributed computing. His background is in applied engineering and computational physics. He received his Ph.D. from Carleton University, Ottawa, Canada.

Lawrence Mandel, IBM

Lawrence is a WTP committer and was the leader of documentation and ecosystem development until the release of WTP 1.5.2. Lawrence is a software architect and developer at the IBM Toronto Lab. He is currently the Web Subsystem Architect for a new Enterprise Portfolio Management product under development at IBM Rational. Up until accepting his current position, Lawrence worked on Java Web application development tools including WebSphere Studio Application Developer and Rational Application Developer. Throughout this time his development efforts focused on building XML and Web services tools for Eclipse. In addition, he is leading the Apache Woden project, which is developing a reference implementation of WSDL 2.0. Lawrence holds an Hon. B.Sc. in computer science and human biology from the University of Toronto.

Arthur Ryman, IBM

Arthur is a founder of WTP, a member of its PMC, and was the leader of the Web Standard Tools (WST) subproject up until the release of WTP 1.5. Arthur is a software development manager and architect at the IBM Toronto Lab where he has worked since 1982. He led the IBM contribution to WTP from the inception of the project until the release of WTP 1.5. He is currently the Chief Architect for a new Enterprise Portfolio Management product under development at IBM Rational. Arthur was previously responsible for Web Service, XML, Java Connector tools, and performance analysis for Rational Application Developer. Prior to that, he worked on WebSphere Studio Application Developer and VisualAge for Java. Arthur is a member of the W3C Web Service Description Working Group and an editor of the WSDL 2.0 Specification and Test Suite. He is a committer on the Apache Woden project, which is developing a reference implementation of WSDL 2.0. He is a member of the IBM Academy of Technology, an adjunct professor of computer science at York University in Toronto, and a senior member of the IEEE. Arthur received his B.Sc. in mathematics and physics from York University, his M.Sc. in mathematics from London University, and his Ph.D. in mathematics from Oxford University.

PART I

Getting Started

Our goal in Part I of this book is to get you started using the Eclipse Web Tools Platform (WTP) project to develop Java Web applications. We begin with an overview of the structure of the book and then introduce you to the fictitious League Planet Web site, which serves as the inspiration for the programming examples used throughout. We follow this with some background information on WTP, including its genesis and architecture. Next, we give you a Quick Tour of WTP, which touches on most of its main tools. After taking the Quick Tour, you should be able to start using WTP in your development projects. We conclude this part with a more in-depth discussion of how to download and configure WTP.

CHAPTER 1

Introduction

Nobody will ever need more than 640K RAM!

—Bill Gates, 1981

Java Web Application Development and Eclipse

We are living in a Golden Age of software development. The Internet has opened up fantastic new opportunities for applications. There is an abundance of powerful, inexpensive personal computers and mobile devices that can access the Internet and run these new applications. And, to fuel their creation and deployment, the Open Source movement has created an unprecedented array of high-quality, freely available middleware and tools. It is truly a great time to be a software developer. We are limited only by our imagination and our ability to master the skills demanded by this rich environment.

Java technology and the Java 2 Enterprise Edition (J2EE) have emerged as one of the dominant platforms on which to build Web applications. Numerous Open Source and commercial products support and extend J2EE middleware. And, in the tool arena, Eclipse has emerged as one of the most popular Java integrated development environments (IDE). The main focus of this book is the Web Tools Platform (WTP), a top-level Eclipse project. As the name implies, WTP extends Eclipse into the domain of Web applications. WTP includes both a set of core tools for Web application developers and a set of platform application programming interfaces (API) for tool vendors.

The purpose of this book is to assist you in your quest to become a highly productive Java Web application developer. In the following chapters, we'll describe all the tools that make up WTP and discuss how they can be extended. We'll also talk about Java Web application architecture and the pragmatics of how to run your development project.

3

If you're a typical programmer, you probably want to dive right in and start developing your first Web application with WTP. The best way for you to get a feel for WTP is to take the Quick Tour (see Chapter 3). By all means, feel free to skip ahead and take the Quick Tour now. You can return here to get more background information later.

What This Book Contains

One of our guiding principles in selecting content for this book was to not reproduce standard reference material that was easily obtained elsewhere. We wanted this book to provide substantial added value above and beyond that which you can derive from reading the WTP online Help or the articles, tutorials, and presentations that are available on the WTP Web site. After all, why would anyone read a book if it simply duplicated available material? And even if we wanted to include extensive reference information in this book, it would soon be out-of-date since WTP, like all healthy Open Source projects, undergoes constant improvement and refinement. Programmers really want reference information while they are programming, so the best place for it is in the Help system where it can be retrieved in the correct context with a few keystrokes.

There are a couple of immediate consequences of this decision. First, this book does not contain an exhaustive list of every menu, command, keyboard shortcut, view, editor, perspective, or preference. Check the online Help for that information. If it isn't there, open a bug or, better yet, contribute a nice write-up yourself! Second, this book does not contain Javadoc listings for API information. The Javadoc listings are included in the online Help. If you find the Javadoc unclear, open a bug or, better yet, submit a source code patch. The online Help and source code are the definitive sources of reference information.

Having decided not to write a reference book, we instead wrote a book that presented WTP in the context of developing actual Web applications. As each element of Web application development is introduced, we discuss the corresponding parts of WTP in enough depth to accomplish some small amount of real work. In general, we do not discuss any part of WTP in exhaustive detail. You'll have to consult the online Help or source code for the full story.

Another of our guiding principles was to use realistic examples for purposes of illustration. Many programming books adopt the practice of using examples that have names like foo and bar in them. However, if a programming topic is worth discussing at all, then there must be some realistic situation that motivates it, so why not use that? The one exception to this rule is the "Hello, world" example in Chapter 3, which follows the long-standing tradition honored in many programming books. We have therefore created a realistic, albeit fictitious,

Web site named "League Planet" at the domain `leagueplanet.com` to serve as the source of inspiration for our examples. We'll describe League Planet at the end of this chapter.

The programming examples within a chapter are as self-contained as possible. We provide the source code files (see "Source Code Examples") required to start each chapter so that you can work through the chapters independently and in the order you desire. However, you may need some of the skills developed in earlier chapters, such as how to add a server or create a project, to proceed. Within a chapter, the programming examples are broken down into a sequence of *iterations* that build on each other. Each iteration consists of a sequence of steps that result in running code. You should work through the iterations sequentially.

How This Book Is Organized

This book is divided into the following parts:

- ○ Part I, Getting Started
- ○ Part II, Java Web Application Development
- ○ Part III, Extending WTP
- ○ Part IV, Products and Plans

Part I, Getting Started, introduces you to WTP. Its goal is to quickly give you an overview of the tools in WTP, both as an IDE for Java Web application development and as an Eclipse Open Source development project. Part I contains the following chapters:

- ○ Chapter 1, Introduction, describes the contents of each part and chapter of the book and introduces League Planet, the fictitious Web site used as the inspiration for examples throughout the book.

- ○ Chapter 2, About the Eclipse Web Tools Platform Project, discusses the history, goals, and economics of the project; its division into the Web Standard Tools (WST) and Java Standard Tools (JST) subprojects; and ways in which you can contribute to WTP.

- ○ Chapter 3, Quick Tour, gives you an overview of the core tools in WTP by walking you through the creation of a simple "Hello, world" Java Web application.

- ○ Chapter 4, Setting Up Your Workspace, describes how to obtain and install WTP and how to customize your workspace by setting preferences. These tips will help you optimize WTP performance.

Part II, Java Web Application Development, is really the heart of the book. It presents the WTP tools from the point of view of developing a Java Web application. Part II contains the following chapters:

- Chapter 5, Web Application Architecture and Design, gives some guidance on how to structure a Web application into multiple tiers that implement presentation, business logic, and persistence. It also includes a discussion of Web services and Service Oriented Architecture (SOA). These design principles provide a roadmap for building Web applications.

- Chapter 6, Organizing Your Development Project, introduces Best Practices for organizing your code into projects that can be developed in a team environment, built automatically, and tested automatically. CVS, Subversion, Ant, Maven, and CruiseControl are discussed here.

- Chapter 7, The Presentation Tier, focuses on your application's user interface and the Web and J2EE technologies used to implement it. These include HTML, CSS, JavaScript, XML, servlets, JSP, and JSF.

- Chapter 8, The Business Logic Tier, describes how to develop your application's business rules and processes, including guidance on when and how to use EJBs as well as techniques, such as XDoclet, for developing them.

- Chapter 9, The Persistence Tier, describes how to persistently store the data in your Web application, including how to configure and access databases. JDBC and Apache Derby are discussed here.

- Chapter 10, Web Services, describes how to expose your application's functions via Web services and how to create clients that access them. XSD, WSDL, JAX-RPC, UDDI, WSIL, and Apache Axis are covered here.

- Chapter 11, Testing, outlines testing techniques, including JUnit, Apache Cactus.

Part III, Extending WTP, addresses the topic of developing Eclipse plug-ins that extend WTP. As previously stated, one of the main goals of WTP is to be a platform that can be extended by both commercial vendors and other Open Source projects, either at Eclipse or elsewhere. We have already seen early versions of WTP appear in several products (see Chapter 16, Other Web Tools Based on Eclipse), and some major vendors, including IBM and BEA, have plans to release IDEs based on WTP. We have already seen WTP appear in several products (see Chapter 16), including the products of some major vendors, such as IBM and BEA, which have released IDEs based on WTP. Although creating an IDE based on WTP is a major undertaking, WTP does provide several extension points that allow some degree of customization by individuals. In general, however, writing extensions boils down to understanding the APIs provided by WTP. The chapters in this part go into some detail for several extension points and APIs. This information should help you get started developing WTP extensions. Part III contains the following chapters:

- Chapter 12, Adding New Servers, describes how to extend WTP to support new Web and J2EE application servers using the Server Tools extension points and API.

- Chapter 13, Supporting New File Types, discusses how to create editors and validators for new file types using the Validation Framework and Eclipse Platform APIs.

- Chapter 14, Creating WSDL Extensions, outlines how to extend the WSDL editor and validator to support WSDL extensions such as bindings for alternate Web service invocation protocols.

- Chapter 15, Customizing Resource Resolution, explains how to extend the URI Resolution Framework with new resource resolution strategies.

Finally, Part IV, Products and Plans, concludes the book with an overview of other Eclipse-based products for Web application development. Some of these tools currently extend WTP or plan to do so in the future. WTP provides a core set of tools, and these will be complemented by a wide variety of commercial and Open Source extensions. The time you invest in becoming a skilled WTP user will give you a solid foundation for using these more advanced IDEs. Part IV also gives you a glimpse into the future releases of WTP. There are many new specifications, such as Java EE 5 and WSDL 2.0, on the horizon, and WTP will continually strive to keep current. In addition, as Eclipse grows as an Open Source community, new projects, such as the Data Tools Platform (DTP), will affect the architecture of WTP. Part IV contains the following chapters:

- Chapter 16, Other Web Tools Based on Eclipse, is a brief survey of other Web application development IDEs that are based on Eclipse. Many of these are currently based on WTP or will be in future releases.

- Chapter 17, The Road Ahead, gives you a sneak preview of what is being planned in upcoming WTP releases.

The book includes some useful reference material. The glossary defines many of the acronyms and terms used in this book. If you can't find a definition there, try Wikipedia at

```
http://www.wikipedia.org
```

The reference section lists useful articles, books, and standards. If you can't find a particular reference there, try Google at

`http://www.google.com`

or your favorite search engine.

Source Code Examples

Source code examples are the lifeblood of programming books. We have taken great care to ensure that all source code listings actually work. In fact, the source code listings are automatically generated from working source code files as part of the book production process.

As you go through the programming iterations in this book, you will be asked to create files and write code at various steps. By all means, do this. You should try your hand at implementing the examples. However, before you go on to the next step, you should import the working example code that is provided.

We decided to not include the example code on a CD with the book so that we'd have the opportunity to constantly improve it. Instead, we created a Web site where you can obtain the code and other information related to this book. You can obtain the example code from

`http://www.eclipsewtp.org`

Follow the links to download the `examples.zip` archive and unzip it to a convenient directory.

The examples are organized by chapter, iteration, and Eclipse project. For example, the examples for Chapter 3, Iteration 1, in the project `web1` are located in the directory

`examples/ch03/iteration1/Web1`

The directory layout of each example exactly matches that of the corresponding project, so you can simply import the file. For example, to import the example `hello-world.jsp` file into the `webContent` directory of the `web1`, do the following:

1. Select the `web1` project in the workspace and execute the **Import** command. Select **File System** from the **General** category as the source of the import.

2. Select the directory

   `examples/ch03/iteration1/Web1`

   as the source of the import.

3. Select the file

`WebContent/hello-world.jsp`

as the file to import. The file `hello-world.jsp` will then be imported correctly to the `WebContent` directory of the `web1` project.

Introducing League Planet

As just mentioned, the examples throughout this book are inspired by the fictitious, yet realistic League Planet Web site. This section will introduce you to it.

One approach to creating a successful Web business is to first think of some interesting content that will attract large numbers of visitors, and then develop a business model for deriving profit from it. If the content is compelling and the business model is sound, the next step is to design the application and build it. Here we'll just discuss the content and business model. We'll work on the design and implementation in the following chapters.

The simple idea behind League Planet is to serve the many people who are interested in sports, both as players and as fans. League Planet offers the facilities to set up amateur or recreational sports leagues. Anyone can go to the League Planet Web site and create a new league where they can record their teams, players, schedules, venues, scores, statistics, and other kinds of information. The Web site will be visited by players, their friends, and their family members. Since amateur and recreational sports are played in every country by people of all ages, there is a potentially huge user community for League Planet.

The business model behind League Planet is that use of the site is completely free to players and fans. Anyone can set up a league at no cost. Revenue is generated by leveraging the content in many ways. Here are some of the potential applications and opportunities for profit.

The most obvious way to generate profit is via merchandising. Much information is available about the visitors to the site, for example, what sports they are interested in, their age group, and where they live. This provides us with the information required to do targeted marketing. We can place ads on the site according to the profile of the visitors. For example, a page that displays Little League baseball scores for a team in New York City might display ads for baseball video games, tickets to New York Yankee games, and books about famous New York Yankee players. The ads would link to sites such as Amazon or eBay via Web services, and League Planet would get commissions on sales. The site could also host ads that were paid for by sponsors.

The player and team information on the site can be exploited in many ways. For example, lists of player names and clothing sizes can be sent to uniform manufacturers or T-shirt companies. Teams can benefit from this information through fundraising activities. For example, teams can be sponsored by local businesses. The site can help match up teams and sponsors. In return for a sponsorship fee, the team can place the sponsor's name and logo on its uniforms and Web pages. Individual player statistics can also be used for fundraising. For example, personalized baseball cards can be created and sold to raise money for team activities. What child wouldn't want his or her picture on a baseball card? Proud parents can also purchase the cards and hand them out to friends and relatives. The site can also provide game program printing services, coordinate team photos, and help schedule award banquets at the end of the season, with tie-ins to banquet halls and trophy companies.

The site provides opportunities for many novel applications. For example, the site can send out e-mail or text messages to subscribers when games get rained out or moved to different venues. Parents generally appreciate any service that helps them stay on top of their children's schedules, so they will certainly appreciate this type of service. The site can provide real-time score notifications. Imagine a scorekeeper sending in results via a PDA and the site then relaying them to parents away on business trips. Cell phone companies will undoubtedly be interested in sponsoring such an application.

The site can expand into a service for professional sports clubs. In addition to hosting league information, the site can be used for booking courts, arranging games, and running tournaments. Professional sports clubs would pay a fee for this type of service.

There is also the potential to get seed money to start League Planet from government grants. Fitness is a major concern today, yet the Internet and personal computers have been blamed for creating a generation of inactive, out-of-shape children. With League Planet, children should be highly motivated to play sports and achieve their own personal Web presence. The site can run pilot programs with schools to host their sports house leagues and probably qualify for public funds from government education and health departments.

We hope you find this description of League Planet both realistic and interesting. We'll develop parts of the League Planet Web site in the following chapters.

Summary

The goal of this book is to provide you with information about WTP that complements the online Help, source code, and Web site. In particular, this book does not reproduce reference information. Rather, you are encouraged to refer to and contribute to the online sources of reference information.

All source code examples listed in this book are working code and are provided for your use. You can obtain the example code from the Web at

```
http://www.eclipsewtp.org
```

This book is organized into four parts. Part I provides a quick introduction to WTP and some background information. Part II describes how to use WTP for Java Web application development. Part III describes several ways that WTP can be extended. Part IV concludes with a survey of related products and a sneak preview of future WTP enhancements.

The examples used in this book are based on the development of the fictitious League Planet Web site that possesses many aspects of real Web sites.

CHAPTER 2

About the Eclipse Web Tools Platform Project

WTP Is Born

Those who cannot remember the past are condemned to repeat it.

—George Santayana

If you are just interested in developing Web applications, feel free to skip this section. However, if you're mildly curious about how Open Source projects get created, or you're wondering why software vendors think it's a great idea to give away millions of dollars worth of tools, read on.

WTP formally began life in the spring of 2003 as a proposal from IBM to Eclipse.org. At that time IBM was working on the Eclipse-based WebSphere Studio product family and had already shipped several releases of it. IBM proposed to contribute a core set of plug-ins from WebSphere Studio Application Developer. The thinking behind this proposal was that the time had come to take Eclipse to the next level of support for Java development. Eclipse had achieved a good level of maturity and success for J2SE development, but the killer application for Java is J2EE development. However, the J2EE tool space was very fragmented. Although there was a vibrant ecosystem of Eclipse plug-in providers, no other major J2EE application server vendor had adopted Eclipse as its primary IDE platform.

From a customer perspective, having lots of vendors to choose from can be either a good or a bad thing. It's a good thing if it means that competition between vendors produces better quality at lower prices. It's also a good thing if it means that niche vendors can cheaply enter the market and fill gaps. However, it's a bad thing if it means that vendors waste resources reinventing the wheel by implementing the same base functionality for each IDE platform. It's also a bad thing if customers can't integrate tools from different vendors into a complete solution.

In 2003, there were many excellent J2EE IDEs. J2EE developers could choose from IBM WebSphere Studio Application Developer, BEA WebLogic Workshop, Borland JBuilder, Oracle JDeveloper, Sun NetBeans, and many others. In many respects, J2EE developers never had it so good. However, there was no common tool infrastructure. This meant that vendors spent a lot of resources keeping up with the continually evolving J2EE specifications and reproducing the basic function that was expected by all customers. The situation was equally awkward for vendors who wanted to extend the IDEs. Which IDEs should they support? Obviously, supporting five different IDEs is a lot more expensive and time-consuming than supporting one. The result was less innovation. The situation was also difficult for Web application developers who wanted to target multiple J2EE application servers. Learning to use a different IDE for each application server increased cost and reduced productivity. Life would be much simpler if one IDE could target any server.

Now compare the J2EE world to the .NET world. Visual Studio .NET is the single, dominant tool infrastructure for .NET development. This results in a much more efficient market for development tools since vendors only have to support integration with Visual Studio .NET. Of course, the downside is that Microsoft uses its monopoly position to control both the .NET programming interfaces and tool infrastructure, so other vendors are at a disadvantage. The .NET playing field is definitely not level. Microsoft always has the inside track on supporting new .NET programming interfaces and can exploit deeper integration with Visual Studio .NET to gain an advantage in any application development tool domain that it decides to enter. Nevertheless, Visual Studio .NET is an excellent IDE and supports a thriving and loyal developer community. Microsoft is expert at developer relations. The company understands that developers create applications and applications drive sales of operating systems. Microsoft's traditional focus on developers is certainly one of the factors that has led to its remarkable success.

The problem then was how to achieve the substantial benefits of a common tool infrastructure for J2EE in a market that enjoyed healthy competition among many vendors. The solution was to ensure that WTP was a true partnership right from the start. The Eclipse Management Organization (EMO) approved the creation of WTP in June 2003. However, work on the project did not begin immediately for two closely related reasons. First, IBM recognized that for Eclipse to become the dominant J2EE tool infrastructure, Eclipse.org itself would first have to become an independent legal entity. The Eclipse Foundation was therefore created and officially launched in time for the first ever Eclipse developers conference, EclipseCon, in February 2004. IBM also realized that WTP could not begin without significant commitment from other partners. Months of discussions led up to a very successful WTP Birds-of-a-Feather (BOF) session at EclipseCon where many vendors expressed support for the proposal. Among the vendors who supported WTP were ObjectWeb, eteration, Innoopract, Exadel, Thales, Frameworx, and Genuitec. ObjectWeb, an Open Source middleware consortium based in Europe, agreed to lead WTP through the new Eclipse Foundation project creation process and bring in many of its members as contributors.

In the weeks following EclipseCon, IBM and ObjectWeb worked together to hammer out the WTP charter. ObjectWeb then hosted a three-day meeting at the Institut National de Recherche en Informatique (INRIA) in Grenoble, France, in June 2004, where the architecture of WTP was mapped out and the code contributions were reviewed. The meeting was attended by IBM and many members of ObjectWeb. The result of the meeting was that WTP would be based on code contributions from IBM and ObjectWeb. The IBM contributions were a subset of Rational Application Developer V6.0, which was the follow-on to WebSphere Studio Application Developer V5.1. The ObjectWeb contributions came from eteration Lomboz, a popular Eclipse plug-in for J2EE development. The initial code contributions were posted on the Eclipse Web site in July 2004, and development of WTP officially began.

As WTP development progressed, other vendors became involved. JBoss.org soon joined the project and contributed an adapter for the JBoss Application Server. WTP received a major boost in February 2005 when BEA joined the project and agreed to co-lead the Project Management Committee (PMC). BEA also announced that it would create a version of WebLogic Studio based on WTP and contribute resources to the project. In June 2005, Oracle joined WTP and agreed to lead the development of JSF tools. Although not officially project members, both Borland and SAP have announced plans to adopt WTP. With many major vendors adopting WTP, the center of gravity for J2EE development tools has clearly shifted to Eclipse.

WTP Economics

In the long run, we're all dead.

—John Maynard Keynes

We hope you found the preceding history lesson informative. However, as the fine print on mutual funds prospectuses reads, "Past performance is no guarantee of future results." Yes, WTP, and Eclipse, have a nice head of steam, but they will only succeed in the long run if they make economic sense. Both Eclipse and WTP were seeded with large initial investments by IBM. Other vendors are now committing significant resources to WTP and other Eclipse projects. But vendors cannot and will not continue to contribute resources unless there is a fair return on investment. We believe that WTP does make a lot of economic sense. WTP will therefore be guided by principles that promote its sustainability as an open, multi-vendor development project.

The problem of sustainability applies to all Open Source projects. How can vendors profit from giving away software? In his essay "The Magic Cauldron" [Raymond2001], Eric Raymond likened Open Source economics to the Welsh myth about the goddess Ceridwen who could command an empty cauldron to produce nourishing food. How can vendors command the Open Source cauldron to generate profit? Raymond discusses many business models for doing just that. We'll explore how these ideas apply to WTP next.

Reducing Development Expense

Vendors can increase their profit by reducing their development expense or increasing their revenue. WTP affects both of these variables. Vendors can reduce their development expense by cooperating on the development of common infrastructure components, such as source code editors, validators, and debuggers. These are the components that are necessary but do not differentiate one vendor from another. Vendors can also reduce their development expense by relying on the community to contribute. The benefits of early user testing are widely acknowledged. The cost of correcting a defect strongly depends on when it is discovered. Defects found early in the development cycle are much cheaper to remove than ones found later. Like most Open Source projects, WTP practices continuous integration and produces stable milestone releases that are suitable for user testing. The large and diverse user communities that are the norm in Open Source also have the benefit of giving code much wider platform and configuration test coverage than would be affordable in typical commercial projects. The user community can also help correct defects by submitting patches. Very active users become part of the extended development team and further reduce development expense. The user community becomes an active participant in the development of the code. In exchange for free software, the user community helps develop it.

Let's explore the cost-saving benefits in more detail for J2EE IDE vendors. A vendor may decide to enter this market for a variety of reasons. Some vendors, such as BEA, Oracle, JBoss, and SAP, create J2EE IDEs to drive sales of their application servers. For them, tools are a necessary evil. These vendors really only want to sell their application servers, but they realize that they need good tools. J2EE is a complex programming model, and application servers may implement proprietary extensions on top of it, so tools are absolutely necessary to make J2EE development productive when compared with competing technologies. Other vendors, like Borland, are primarily tool vendors and may add J2EE tools to an existing repertoire of tools for other programming languages and technologies. IBM, the founder of Eclipse, has both of these IDE requirements since it needs J2EE tools to drive sales of the WebSphere application server and also needs a platform to integrate the many tools that make up the Rational portfolio.

Adopting Eclipse in general, and WTP in particular, makes sense for both types of vendor. IDEs have been around a long time, and most of the user interface design principles have been worked out. There is now a definite convergence in IDE design. In fact, if you look quickly at a screenshot of a typical IDE, you'll probably have trouble identifying it. The general layout of the screen varies little from vendor to vendor. Typically you'll see a tree view that displays the files in your development project, a source code editor with syntax highlighting and code assist, some property sheets, and a console for displaying build process output. There will also be a debugger, integration with a source code control system, and some visual user interface designers. These features are no longer differentiators. They are table stakes for entering the IDE market.

Adopting Eclipse makes a lot of sense for vendors that derive most of their revenue from tool sales, since it is a generic tool integration framework and can be used as the common infrastructure for IDEs for any programming language. This was in fact the primary motivation for the creation of Eclipse. Although IBM had VisualAge IDEs for C++, Smalltalk, Java, and other languages, they were independent products and were usually based on completely different technologies. Even when they shared technology, as in the case of VisualAge Smalltalk and Java, they were mutually exclusive. While mixed language development may not have been a factor in the 1980s, it was the norm in the 1990s with the advent of Web applications that mixed source code written in Java, HTML, JavaScript, and others. IBM needed a new, language-neutral IDE technology, built from the ground up, that would *eclipse* its aging VisualAge family and provide the basis for the next generation. Eclipse was designed to be language-neutral so that no programming language was a second-class citizen. All key IDE services are exposed to plug-ins via well-defined APIs. All languages play by the same rules.

Adopting WTP makes even more sense for vendors that derive most of their revenue from application server sales, because developing IDE infrastructure is expensive and not their core competence. Although these vendors are J2EE experts, it is very expensive to maintain standards currency. J2EE is a moving target. So far, we've had J2EE 1.2, 1.3, and 1.4, and the latest version, which Sun is calling Java EE 5.0, is becoming the default choice for new development. But customers don't port all their existing applications whenever a new J2EE version appears. Application development is also very expensive, and customers need to focus on developing new applications that yield business value rather than redoing running applications. WTP provides core support for J2EE, tracks the standards, and ensures that support for the different versions can coexist within the IDE. When WTP is upgraded to support a new version of J2EE, you'll still be able to use it to maintain your existing applications.

The value proposition for J2EE tool vendors is that WTP lets them share the development expense for creating a high-quality, standards-compliant, and standards-current infrastructure so they can focus on those value-added features that differentiate their products and services from the competition.

WTP is also very well aligned with one of the core principles of J2EE, application portability. J2EE is a set of APIs and file formats that allow Web applications to run on any compliant server. This is the extension of the Java "Write once, run anywhere" (WORA) principle to Web applications. WTP promotes the WORA principle for J2EE by focusing on standards and employing the well-known quality benefits of Open Source development to find and fix errors in implementation. WTP adheres to the principle of vendor-neutrality and hosts the development of server adapters for many J2EE application servers, including IBM WebSphere, BEA WebLogic, JBoss Application Server, Apache Tomcat and Geromino, ObjectWeb Jonas, Oracle Application Server, and others. Additional vendors are adopting WTP and could contribute more server adapters in the future. This large variety of application servers using WTP means that the test coverage is excellent—far more than any single tool vendor could afford. The result is that the standards compliance, and therefore portability, of applications developed with WTP is second to none.

There are also additional costs in Open Source development. Fostering an active user community requires that developers devote a significant amount of time to responding to questions on newsgroups, answering bug reports, reviewing patches, writing tutorials, speaking at user groups, presenting at conferences, and even writing books like the one you're reading now. Many of these activities are also part of proprietary software development, but they acquire a much greater significance for Open Source projects given the key role that the user community plays. On balance, the extra development expense associated with maintaining a healthy user community is more than compensated for by the cost-sharing benefits.

Generating Revenue

The preceding discussion addressed the cost half of the equation. It should be clear now that vendors can reduce development expense by adopting WTP, and that for WTP to be sustainable, vendors will also have to contribute resources to WTP. How can vendors generate revenue from WTP? The following revenue streams are some of the main opportunities: commercial products, commercial plug-ins, application servers, customer support, application development services, training, mentoring, tool development services, and tool management services. Let's now explore these in more detail.

Commercial Products Based on WTP

The simplest way for a vendor to generate revenue from WTP is to create a commercial product based on it. This is the approach that most vendors will adopt initially because it is the traditional way to generate revenue. Commercial products that are based on Open Source software are often referred to as *distributions*. The vendor packages the software in a convenient form, and often adds components and customer support to it. Vendors can differentiate themselves along many dimensions, such as the additional components they add, the quality of their customer support, the price, the range of the operating systems they cover, their sponsorship of the Open Source community, and so forth.

Of course, vendors will have to add significant value to compete with the freely available version of WTP. Also, users may want to combine plug-ins from different vendors in a common installation of WTP rather than having multiple stand-alone installations. Nevertheless, many customers are used to buying fully integrated products and may be more comfortable dealing with a vendor in the traditional way. Such customers may not even be aware that their vendor has adopted WTP as the base.

Commercial Plug-Ins That Extend WTP

Many customers will be satisfied with WTP as a starting point but require additional plug-ins to complete the solution. The scope of WTP is restricted to Web and J2EE standards, so support for popular technologies such as Struts, Spring, and Hibernate must come from elsewhere. The decision to focus on standards in WTP was intended to encourage vendors to innovate in the nonstandard areas. Vendors can generate revenue by developing commercial plug-ins that extend WTP.

Individual plug-ins will undoubtedly command a much lower price than traditional IDEs. This is a high-volume, low-margin business model. Vendors will probably sell their plug-ins through online stores in order to reduce sales expenses. Eclipse includes an Update Manager that allows additional plug-ins to be easily installed. Vendors can exploit the Update Manager to deliver extensions on top of existing WTP installations. Imagine finding some cool new plug-in at a vendor's Web site, entering your credit card number, and clicking a link to download and install it in your WTP installation. The benefit to developers is that they can easily buy and install exactly what they need, when they need it, and from the supplier of their choice.

J2EE Applications Servers and Middleware

As mentioned previously, many vendors derive more of their revenue from the sale of J2EE application servers and related middleware such as databases, message brokers, and so forth than from tools. Such vendors have a vested interest in the success of J2EE as a programming technology. If the market adoption of J2EE increases, then the pie grows and each vendor can grab a correspondingly larger slice of it. This is sometimes referred to as the *drag* effect. Vendors will invest in a low-profit product, such as a J2EE IDE, if it drags along the sale of high-profit products, such as J2EE middleware.

The market adoption of a technology such as J2EE depends on many factors, but among the most important are the availability of applications and a skilled labor pool for developing them. Customers often consider the cost and availability of skilled labor when selecting a programming technology. Some excellent technologies have literally priced themselves out of the market because the small developer pool could command very high wages. The free availability of development tools is a key contributor to the growth of the developer community. By funding the development of WTP, J2EE vendors are investing in the growth of the developer pool. Ideally, WTP will even be used in universities and community colleges to teach J2EE development. This will result in an abundant source of J2EE professionals. WTP can therefore, in part, be cost-justified as an extension of the developer relations program of J2EE vendors.

Customer Support for WTP

Vendors will of course sell customer support for their own commercial IDEs and plug-ins, but there is also an opportunity to sell this service for WTP itself. As mentioned, many customers may be satisfied with the capabilities of WTP, possibly extended by some third-party plug-ins. Such customers may be willing to pay for WTP customer support.

Selling customer support is perfectly consistent with the spirit of Open Source. There is virtually no cost associated with making a copy of a piece of software, so the software itself should be free. However, there is cost associated with customer support. Responding to customer problems requires employing skilled people who demand salaries, and therefore any company prepared to provide support for Open Source software is more than entitled to charge for this service.

It is very difficult to provide good customer support due to the complexity of software. There is a lot of scope for vendor differentiation here. The best providers will probably use sophisticated knowledge bases to quickly diagnose and correct problems. However, although a customer support company may keep its knowledge-base technology a trade secret, it is in everyone's best interest if they contribute fixes back to WTP. After all, they are profiting from WTP, so they too should contribute to its success. Furthermore, by contributing fixes back to WTP they will avoid redoing work when a new version is released. By contributing fixes they will earn the right to become committers, thereby improving their credibility and knowledge of WTP internals. Customers are more likely to buy support from providers who are good WTP citizens.

J2EE Application Development Services

Many vendors provide consulting services to customers who want to develop new J2EE applications. In fact, consulting services are one of the largest revenue components of the information technology industry. WTP has the potential to become the standard IDE for consultants because of its free availability, extensibility, and support for multiple application servers. Customers display a lot of diversity in their selection of application servers and third-party components. It would be very expensive for consultants to acquire and become skilled in a different IDE for each customer engagement. By standardizing on WTP as the basis for their IDE, consultants can reduce training costs and improve their productivity.

When consultants finish development, they leave the application in the hands of the customer for future maintenance and enhancement. If the application was developed using WTP, then customers can continue to use WTP after the consultants leave without the burden or expense of acquiring a matching tool set. Furthermore, since WTP has a large user community, customers will be able to find developers for future work. WTP in a sense future-proofs the application and could therefore give consultants who adopt it a competitive advantage. Of course, since WTP focuses on standards, customers are free to continue development using their tools of choice.

WTP Training

Vendors provide training for all aspects of J2EE application development, including object orientation; Java programming; basic J2EE concepts; advanced frameworks such as Struts, Spring, and Hibernate; and tool use. Adding WTP to their curriculum is an obvious source of additional revenue. Creating material based on WTP has many benefits for vendors due to its free availability, focus on standards, and role as a platform for third-party extensions. As more enterprises adopt WTP or its commercial incarnations, the demand for WTP training services will increase.

J2EE Development Project Mentoring

Many vendors provide mentoring services to help customers adopt new technologies. Mentoring services are a good way for customers who have in-house development organizations to quickly come up to speed. As the WTP user base grows, many customers will seek mentoring services for WTP-based J2EE development. Vendors who are active contributors to WTP will have a competitive advantage in acquiring business in this market.

WTP Tool Development Services

As more customers adopt WTP, they will generate a demand for custom tool development services to extend WTP for their unique requirements. For example, customers may have in-house coding standards or proprietary middleware that they want supported by WTP. Developers who contribute to WTP will be viewed as experts and be preferentially hired by such customers.

Tool Management Services

As WTP changes the J2EE IDE landscape, many customers will seek technology that helps them manage the contents of their developers' desktops. Many customers will want to provide their developers with a controlled tool environment that consists of approved versions of WTP or its commercial derivatives, additional third-party plug-ins, and updates to these components. For example, when a new version of a plug-in becomes available, a customer may want to run it through a quality assurance process first, and then have it automatically deployed overnight to everyone's desktop. This creates an opportunity for servers that automatically deploy approved updates to developer's desktops, possibly with license management capabilities.

The Structure of WTP

The structure of a system reflects the organization that designed the system.

—Melvin Conway

The Eclipse Foundation is run by the EMO, who approves the creation of top-level projects, such as WTP. Each top-level project has a charter and is run by a

Project Management Committee (PMC). The charter defines the scope of the project and divides the work into subprojects. Each subproject has a lead who becomes a member of the PMC. Therefore, the first major organizational decision WTP faced was to define its scope and to create its subprojects.

The Scope of WTP

Defining the scope of an Open Source project is very important since it stakes out turf, defines boundaries, and thereby avoids duplication of effort. Clearly advertising the scope of a project lets interested developers know where they can find like-minded individuals who want to share the effort. In his essay "Homesteading the Noosphere" [Raymond2001], Eric Raymond described this process in detail. Raymond used the term *noosphere* to describe the conceptual sphere of ideas that gets populated with software development projects. After a project lays claim to a set of ideas, interested developers can join it rather than set up competing projects that would dilute the scarce developer resources. There are only a finite number of skilled developers available, so it makes sense for them to work together. As long as there is good cooperation, the project remains intact. However, dissatisfied developers always have the right to fork the project and start up an independent, competing effort. Forking a project is generally viewed as a sign of failure, but the existence of this escape clause is one of the features that make Open Source development attractive.

As the name implies, the scope of WTP is Web application development. However, Web application development is too broad since there are many competing development technologies, including the three major platforms: J2EE, .NET, and Linux-Apache-MySQL-Perl/PHP/Python (LAMP). Instead, the scope of WTP is currently limited to J2EE-based Web application development. This scope includes the common underlying standard Web technologies such as HTML, XML, and Web services, but excludes the Java frameworks built to extend or compete with J2EE, such as Struts, Spring, and Hibernate.

However, if a vendor wanted to develop tools for .NET or LAMP at Eclipse, then they could propose the creation of a new subproject of WTP, or even a new top-level Eclipse project. In fact, this has already started to happen with the creation of the PHP IDE project (see Chapter 17). But for now, all development resources at WTP are devoted to J2EE and the underlying Web standards that it is based on.

Within the J2EE world, there are the core standards defined by the JCP as well as many Open Source and commercial extensions. Since J2EE is itself a very broad area, WTP focuses on just its standard aspects as defined by the JCP.

However, we need to make a distinction between the runtime standards for J2EE and tools for developing J2EE applications. Support for popular J2EE development tools, such as XDoclet and Cactus, is within the scope of WTP. As long as the tools do not require the use of nonstandard runtime libraries in the J2EE application, their support is within the scope of WTP. Furthermore, although the nonstandard runtime extensions are outside the scope of WTP, it is the mission of WTP to enable the third-party development of tools that support these extensions.

There are many economic and pragmatic reasons for restricting WTP to standards-based J2EE Web application development. All projects have limited resources and need to establish a solid foundation for future extensions. It therefore makes sense to start with the core building blocks of J2EE. Also, vendors are interested in reducing development expense by sharing the cost for common components. All vendors must support the core J2EE standards and so they form a solid basis for cooperation. Finally, WTP needs to leave room for innovation. By limiting the scope of WTP to standards, vendors are given a clear signal that they can invest in the development of commercial products to support popular Open Source J2EE extensions such as Struts, Spring, and Hibernate.

WTP has the dual goals of providing a core set of J2EE tools for Web application developers and platform APIs for tool vendors. There are two main reasons why WTP includes both tools and APIs. The first is that users are the most important factor for the success of an Open Source project. Users contribute to the quality of the code by testing it, reporting bugs, and providing enhancement requests. They also validate the project in the eyes of vendors. A large user community tells vendors that the code is useful and that there is a large market for tools that extend it. If a project only provided APIs and not tools, then it would have a much smaller user community. The second reason is that APIs are hard to get right, and the best way to assess the quality of an API is to develop a tool that uses it. This process is sometimes referred to as "eating your own dog food." The goal is to ensure that WTP is rather tasty. Clearly, if WTP did not include a set of tools that used its own APIs, then there would be little assurance that any vendor could build high-quality tools on top of it.

WTP Subprojects

Having settled on the scope of WTP, the next decision to make was how to divide the project into subprojects. One approach would be to have a single subproject. That would certainly be simple, but it would not promote one of the main goals of WTP: extensibility. A key part of the project name is *platform*, which means that WTP is intended to be extended by vendors. The Web is based on open standards that do not dictate how systems should be implemented. Web standards in general specify protocols and formats rather than APIs for specific implementation languages. As was mentioned, J2EE is only one of three major programming technologies that are in widespread use for developing Web applications. It was therefore natural to divide WTP into two main subprojects: Web Standard Tools (WST) that supports Web standards that are independent of any implementation technology, and J2EE Standard Tools that supports J2EE as the implementation technology.

We can therefore view the WTP noosphere as being divided into four quadrants by the orthogonal axes of implementation technology and standards (see Figure 2.1). The horizontal axis is implementation technology and indicates the J2EE content. The left side is completely independent of J2EE while the right side conforms to the J2EE specification. The vertical axis is standards formality and indicates the official standing of the specification.

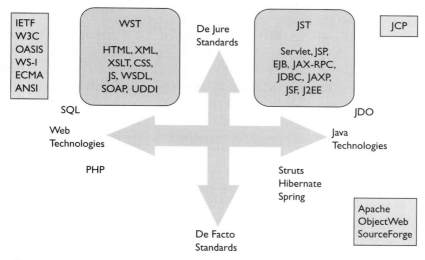

Figure 2.1   WTP Subproject Scopes

The bottom half is completely informal. These are the *de facto* standards that acquire their weight based solely on market adoption. The de facto standards are often created by Open Source projects such as Apache, SourceForge, and ObjectWeb, and by commercial vendors. The top half is the domain of

Standards Development Organizations (SDO), which are industry consortia or government organizations. These standards acquire their weight through industry consensus or government legislation. In the latter case, the standards have the force of law and are called *de jure* standards. The International Organization for Standardization (ISO), the International Electrotechnical Commission (IEC), and the International Telecommunication Union (ITU) are examples of de jure SDOs; however, they have played virtually no role in the standardization of the Internet or the Web. Instead, the standardization of the Internet and Web has been driven by industry consortia. Although not actually enforced by legislation, standards developed by credible industry consortia are often referred to as de jure standards to contrast them with de facto standards. These SDOs have well-defined processes for developing standards and use a consensus-building approach based on vendor input and community feedback. There are many important SDOs, such as the World Wide Web Consortium (W3C), the Internet Engineering Task Force (IETF), the Web Services Interoperability Organization (WS-I), the European Computer Manufacturers Association (ECMA), and the Organization for the Advancement of Structured Information Standards (OASIS) in the technology-neutral space, but only one, the Java Community Process (JCP), in the Java space.

WST and JST are the main subprojects of WTP, but additional subprojects will be created in the future. One of the main reasons for the creation of new projects is to incubate new work. The Eclipse Foundation is taking the approach of putting new proposals through an incubation phase to ensure that the proposed work is viable. Formerly, new proposals were created as subprojects of the Eclipse Technology or Tools projects. The idea was that when the subproject showed useful results it would be absorbed by the most appropriate top-level project. In fact, the Web Service Interoperability (WS-I) Test Tools component of WST started life as the Web Service Validation Tools (WSVT) subproject of the Technology project before becoming part of WTP. However, now with the creation of many new domain-specific top-level projects such as WTP, new proposals will be incubated as subprojects of their target top-level project. For example, Oracle recently proposed the creation of JavaServer Faces (JSF) tools. Since JSF is part of Java EE 5.0, this proposal was incubated as a subproject of WTP. When the JSF subproject exits its incubation phase, it will become a component of the JST subproject.

As was mentioned, WTP may expand in the future to include other permanent subprojects if vendors come forward with proposals to populate the bottom two quadrants. However, that would require significant additional resource commitments, and any such proposal would have to go through the normal Eclipse Foundation creation process. The decision to initially focus on standards was based on availability of resources and a desire to build the ecosystem. Support for .NET, LAMP, and the Open Source extensions to J2EE is consistent with the principles of the Eclipse Foundation and could be hosted within WTP if that made sense to the participants.

The Architecture of WTP

> *Explanations should be as simple as possible, but no simpler.*

> —Albert Einstein

No explanation of the structure of a software system would be complete without the obligatory architectural box diagram. Therefore, we present to you the structure of WTP (see Figure 2.2). This type of diagram is meant to convey the high-level organization of the software. WTP is a moderately complex system, approximately half the size of the Eclipse platform itself. To be useful, an architectural diagram must omit much detail; otherwise, it would simply be an incomprehensible clutter of boxes. The trick, of course, is to not oversimplify the description. For the purposes of this section, descriptions of the high-level layering of the plug-ins that comprise WTP are appropriate.

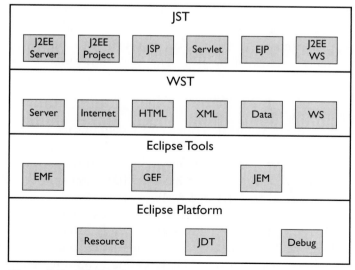

Figure 2.2 WTP Architecture

Like all Eclipse projects, WTP is built from a collection of plug-ins. However, the plug-ins are not organized in a flat structure. Instead, they depend on each other in a very controlled way. The plug-ins can be organized into layers such that plug-ins in one layer do not depend on plug-ins in the layers above them. This layering of plug-ins is an important design characteristic since it decouples the layers from each other. Lower layers can be built and used independently of upper layers. Ideally, the dependencies between layers are through well-defined, stable, platform APIs so that the implementation of lower layers can be changed without affecting the upper layers. The definition of platform APIs in WTP is a major goal and will be achieved incrementally in future releases.

The bottom layer is the Eclipse Platform. WTP uses many APIs in this layer, but has notable dependencies on the Java Development Tools (JDT) and the Debug APIs. J2EE projects are Java projects with additional structure, so the dependency on JDT is clear. The dependency on the Debug APIs comes through the need to debug J2EE components in application servers and to source debug JSPs. WTP supports JSP debugging through JSR 45, which is the standard for debugging non-Java source in a JVM.

Next is the Java Tools layer. WTP makes use of three components: Eclipse Modeling Framework (EMF), Graphical Editing Framework (GEF), and Java Edit Model (JEM). EMF is used as the basis for defining the models provided by WTP. For example, JST provides EMF models for all J2EE deployment descriptors, such as `web.xml` and `application.xml`. The graphical tabs in the XSD and WSDL editors use GEF. JEM was part of the Visual Editor (VE) subproject and provides a higher-level API for accessing Java source code. JEM extends the Java model provided by JDT. The WTP download page contains links to the correct versions of EMF, GEF, and JEM for each WTP build. Final WTP releases also include an all-in-one zip that bundles these three components and the Eclipse platform.

The third layer is WST. As just described, WST contains no J2EE dependencies. It can be used for Web page, XML, Data, and Web service development. The WTP development team plans to define Eclipse features for each of these functional groupings. WST is suitable as a basis for IDEs that support other programming technologies such as .NET or LAMP.

The top layer is JST, which extends WST. For example, the JSP editor extends the HTML editor, the J2EE Web services tools extend the XML Web service tools, and the J2EE application server support extends the core server support. The WTP development team plans to define Eclipse features for J2EE functional groupings such as JSP, servlet, EJB, and Web services.

The WST Subproject

This section gives a brief outline of the main subsystems and components of the WST subproject. For more information, see

`http://eclipse.org/webtools/wst/components.html`

The WST subproject includes tools and APIs that support Web application development based on standards that are independent of implementation technology. The JST subproject is the primary consumer of these APIs. However, it is a goal of WST to be usable as a basis for tools that support non-J2EE-based Web application development. For example, WST should be usable for tools that support LAMP or .NET. Now let's look under the covers and examine some of the major subsystems in WST.

Server Tools

The defining characteristic of Web application development is that code, such as server side includes (SHTML), PHP, and CGI, runs on a Web server. This is especially true for J2EE, where we use the term *Web application server* to denote that the server manages the application as opposed to simply serving up Web pages. However, servers are a key part of all Web application development, so the core support for servers is part of WST. The first subsystem we'll discuss is therefore the Server Tools.

WST introduces servers as a new first-class object into Eclipse. The Server Tools let you add server runtime environments to your workspace. WST does not include any server runtime environments. Instead, you have to obtain server runtimes from their developers. All Open Source server runtimes can be freely downloaded from their Web sites, although you may have to buy a license for product support or advanced features. Many commercial server runtimes have trial or developer versions that can also be freely downloaded.

WST provides APIs so that you can add new server runtime environments to Eclipse. We refer to a plug-in that supports a server runtime environment as a *server adapter*. A server adapter lets you control the server. It lets you configure, start, stop, restart, and debug the server, and publish your Web application to it. At present, WTP includes server adapters for many popular commercial and Open Source J2EE servers, but none for non-J2EE servers such as the Apache Web server. If you'd like to contribute one, just send a note to the WST developer mailing list and outline your proposal. Database servers could also be integrated into Eclipse using server adapters, for example, to support Java stored procedure development.

A server can be associated with a Web application development project. This lets us extend the **Run As** command to execute HTML files and other artifacts on the server. When you select an HTML file and invoke the **Run As ▶ Run on Server** command, the file gets published to the associated server, the server gets started, and the Web browser gets opened with the URL of the file on the server.

Internet Tools

WST includes an Internet subsystem that adds several useful tools. Obviously, when working with Web applications it is handy to have a Web browser. Of course, you can configure Eclipse to open an external Web browser, but having one that is integrated into Eclipse as a editor component is simpler and more convenient. WST originally contained a Web browser plug-in, but since this component was useful in other contexts, the Help system for example, WTP contributed this to the Eclipse platform.

In the course of developing Web applications, tools may have to access URLs on the Internet. For example, you may want to search external Universal Description, Discovery, and Integration (UDDI) registries for Web services, or you may want to validate XML files using remote Document Type Definitions (DTD) or XML Schemas (XSD). This poses a problem for Eclipse because Eclipse is itself a Java application, and Java applications access remote URLs using classes in the `java.net` package that must be configured properly to negotiate any proxies that may come between you and the Internet. WST contributes a **Preference** page that lets you specify the proxy settings used by Eclipse.

Debugging Web applications adds some new complexities such as HTTP sessions, cookies, and XML Web service messages. You may need to view the HTTP traffic that you send or receive in order to understand what's happening or going wrong. WST provides a TCP/IP monitor that lets you capture and view the messages sent to and received from a specified port and host. The TCP/IP monitor also lets you save the messages in an XML log file that can be analyzed by the WS-I Test Tools.

Another notable feature of Web applications is that they contain many XML artifacts, such as XHTML documents and J2EE deployment descriptors, whose structure is defined by schemas (DTDs or XSDs). Some of these schemas are provided with WTP, but others must be retrieved from remote servers. Clearly, retrieving a schema from a remote server is a costly operation, so the WTP Internet tools include a cache, technically referred to as a caching URI resolver, that stores retrieved schemas locally. The cache is preconfigured with some key schemas and you can add others to it.

Structured Source Editor Framework

Web application development involves many source formats in addition to Java. WST provides the Structured Source Editor (SSE) framework for developing new editors and includes source editors for HTML, XHTML, Cascading Stylesheets (CSS), JavaScript, XML, DTD, XSD, and Web Service Description Language (WSDL).

SSE is primarily designed to simplify the creation of source editors for languages in the HTML and XML families. It provides an extended Document Object Model (DOM) that is tailored for the requirements of editors. SSE provides all the usual forms of programmer assistance that Eclipse users have become accustomed to for editing Java source files. These include syntax coloring, code completion, error highlighting (red squiggles), error markers, and formatting.

Web Page Tools

As mentioned in the preceding section, WST contains a full set of source editors for Web page development. All the main source formats used in Web page development are supported—HTML and XHTML, JavaScript, and CSS. These editors are built on the SSE framework and are designed to be used as the source tab of multi-tab editors or to be further extended. For example, the JSP editor provided in the JST subproject extends the HTML editor. Other projects could extend the HTML editor to support additional source formats such as PHP.

Web pages are treated as executable artifacts and can be launched using the **Run As ▸ Run on Server** command. Web pages are also subject to validation. For example, link checking will be added in future versions of WTP.

XML Tools

WST contains a core set of XML tools. These include a multi-tab editor for XML documents that contains a source tab and a design tab. The design tab provides a form-based outline view of the document. The XML editor provides code assistance based on the grammar of the document. The editor uses the DTD or XSD if one is associated with the document, or it infers a grammar from the document if none is provided.

WST includes a simple source editor for DTDs and a high-function multi-tab editor for XSD. The XSD editor includes a source tab and a graphical tab. The graphical tab provides a tree view of the structure of the XSD that lets you drill down into detail by incrementally expanding nested structures. The XSD editor is also tightly integrated with the WSDL editor.

WST provides validators for XML, DTD, and XSD documents. It also provides utilities for generating XML documents from DTD or XSD, which can give you a useful kick start to the editing process. The generated XML documents contain a skeleton with the correct structure but synthetic content. Simply replace the synthetic content with real data.

Web Service Tools

WST provides an extensive set of Web service tools. The reason for including such a complete set of tools was to help establish J2EE as the preferred platform for Web service development. J2EE has often been criticized, with some justification, as being more complex than alternatives such as .NET and LAMP. The goal was to make J2EE more accessible and attractive to Web service developers by including a powerful set of tools in WTP.

WST includes the Web Service Explorer that lets you search registries and Web sites for Web services, dynamically test remote Web services without generating any code, and register descriptions of your own Web services. Searching for Web services is referred to as *discovery*, and the explorer supports two standards: UDDI and Web Service Inspection Language (WSIL). UDDI is a standard for sophisticated registries, while WSIL is a simple XML document format that you can add to your Web site. The end result of the discovery task is locating the WSDL document that describes the Web service you are interested in accessing. The explorer can dynamically interpret WSDL documents and present you with a user interface for invoking the available operations. The explorer captures the SOAP messages and presents them to you so you can understand the behavior of the Web service. And when you have completed development of your own Web service, the explorer lets you register the WSDL document that describes it in a UDDI registry. This task is referred to as *publishing*.

WSDL is one of the central artifacts involved in Web service development. WST provides a high-function WSDL editor that can be used for creating new WSDL documents and viewing existing ones. The WSDL editor contains a source tab that is based on the SSE framework and a graphical tab that provides an overview of the structure of the document. The WSDL editor is also tightly integrated with the XSD editor since WSDL documents can contain inlined XSD.

WST provides a powerful, extensible wizard that ties together all the tasks involved in Web service development. These include the discovery and publishing tasks just described, as well as creation, deployment, testing, and client access. JST extends the **Web Service** wizard to support J2EE Web services.

Finally, WST includes WS-I Test Tools that let you test Web services for compliance with the WS-I profiles. The test tools include a SOAP message analyzer that works with the log files generated by the TCP/IP monitor and a WSDL validator that is integrated with the WSDL editor. WST provides a **Preference** page that lets you control the level of WS-I compliance on a per project basis.

Data Tools

Virtually all Web applications involve database access. WST therefore includes a core set of data access tools. These tools are aimed at application developers rather than database designers or administrators. The assumption is that a database exists and that the application developer is given the task of accessing it. WST provides the **Database Explorer** and **Data Output** views for working with databases, and an **SQL Scrapbook Editor** for developing queries.

The **Database Explorer** lets you connect to databases, view their structure, and sample their contents. A powerful connection wizard is provided to help you create new connections. All major databases, including DB2, Informix, Oracle, Sybase, SQL Server, MySQL, and Derby, are supported, and with a little Eclipse plug-in development you can add others.

The **SQL Scrapbook Editor** lets you create and execute SQL statements. Each scrapbook page is associated with a database connection and provides code assistance based on the tables and columns available in the database. You can select any SQL statement in the page and immediately execute it against the associated database. The results are displayed in the **Data Output** view.

Since data is a rich subject in its own right and is useful in many other contexts besides Web applications, a new top-level Eclipse project, Data Tools Platform (DTP), has been created for it. The Data tools in WST will be moved into DTP in the next major release.

Utility Components

WST also includes a collection of utility components that are of interest to both users and tool developers. The WST utility components are not necessarily only useful in the context of Web applications, so we expect that most of these will be contributed to the Eclipse platform in future releases. We'll describe some of the main WST utility components next.

WST provides a **Snippets** view that lets you define useful code snippets that you can drag and drop into source editors. This can save you from repeatedly keying in the same code block. WST also provides a **Tabbed Properties** view, generally a useful component for displaying and editing the properties associated with any resource.

Validation is the general task of checking the consistency or compliance of a resource or a set of related resources. Web application development introduces many new types of artifacts and relations between them. While validators can provide useful error detection, there is a performance cost in running them, so users need a way to manage them. WST provides the Validation Framework for registering and controlling the execution of all the validators that are active within the workspace.

Although Eclipse provides an excellent user interface, in many cases it is very desirable to run commands in batch mode. For example, you may want to run a command as part of an automated Ant build script, or you may simply want to execute the command from a command shell where Eclipse is not running. Clearly, it is highly desirable to share commands between Eclipse and other environments, both to eliminate duplication of effort and to ensure that you get the same results everywhere. WST provides the Environment Command Framework for providing an abstraction layer that isolates commands from their environment.

Eclipse provides support for simple wizards, but powerful wizards such as the Web Service wizard need to be highly extensible, configurable, and dynamic with respect to user selections. For example, the next page the wizard displays might depend on the selections that a user has made on previous pages. WST provides the Dynamic Wizard Framework for creating sophisticated wizards.

The JST Subproject

This section gives a brief outline of the main subsystems and components of the JST subproject. For more information, see

```
http://eclipse.org/webtools/jst/components.html
```

The JST subproject includes tools and APIs that support Web application development based on core J2EE standards. Direct support for commercial or Open Source frameworks that build on J2EE is explicitly out of scope. However, it is a goal of JST to enable the development of tools that support commercial extensions and popular Open Source frameworks such as Struts, Spring, and Hibernate.

Server Tools

JST extends the WST Server Tools with support for J2EE application servers. Server adapters can be developed using either Java APIs or the XML-based *generic* server support. A generic server adapter is defined by an XML configuration file that specifies commands that implement the server control functions. Generic server adapters trade looser coupling for potentially less capability than Java adapters, but are attractive alternatives to plug-in developers since they require less development effort. Generic server adapters are especially useful for integrating commercial J2EE application servers that do not provide public Java APIs.

Although JST does not include any server runtime environments, it does include server adapters for many popular commercial and Open Source servers. These server adapters provide a good out-of-the-box experience for users and act as examples for tool developers who want to create their own adapters. JST treats all servers equally and will host the development of an adapter for any server provided that there are developers who are prepared to maintain it. The current list of server adapters includes Apache Tomcat and Geronimo, ObjectWeb Jonas, JBoss, IBM WebSphere, and BEA WebLogic.

Server control is being standardized by the JCP. JSRs 77 and 88 define the use of Java Management Extension (JMX) for server control and deployment. JST plans to add support for server adapters based on JSR 88 in a future release.

J2EE Tools

JST provides support for J2EE development in several ways. JST defines the structure for J2EE projects and provides APIs for accessing the artifacts that make up J2EE modules. The J2EE project API is sometimes referred to as the *flexible project API* since it lets you arrange the development artifacts and folders in a very flexible manner. JST extends the Project Navigator to display J2EE components, such as servlets, EJBs, and Web services, as first-class objects instead of collections of related resources. JST also provides Eclipse Modeling Framework (EMF) models for all the J2EE deployment descriptors and configuration files. These EMF models are part of the JST platform API.

J2EE defines a complex programming model that consists of many Java and XML artifacts. Annotation-based programming is becoming an increasingly popular way to simplify J2EE development. Rather than maintain all the artifacts, developers add annotations to Java source files and generate the artifacts using a processor. The most popular form of annotations are Javadoc tags that are processed using XDoclet. JST currently supports this form of annotation. With JDK 5.0, Java has standard support for annotations based on JSR 175. Future releases of JST will support JSR 175-based annotations for J2EE.

Servlet and JSP Tools

The simplest and most popular form of J2EE Web application is based on a servlet container that hosts servlets and JSPs. These artifacts are deployed as a Web module and packaged as a Web Archive (WAR). JST refers to Web modules as *dynamic Web applications* to distinguish them from collections of static Web pages. JST has wizards for creating Web modules, servlets, and JSPs. Servlets may optionally use code annotations.

JST has a high-function JSP source editor that extends the HTML editor. The JSP source editor provides code assistance for HTML tags, JSP tags, and imbedded Java scriptlets. JSPs are typically translated by the application server into servlets for execution. This introduces a complexity for debuggers since developers normally prefer to debug the JSP source that they have written rather than the generated Java source. J2EE includes JSR 45, which defines the standard for debugging non-Java sources, and JST supports this for JSP via the Eclipse debugger.

Although JSP is currently the J2EE norm for dynamic Web pages, Java EE 5.0 adds support for JSR 127 JavaServer Faces, which extends JSP with a richer user interface programming model. Oracle is leading the JSF Tools incubator project, which will become part of JST in a future release.

EJB Tools

JST includes wizards for creating EJB modules and EJBs, optionally using code annotations. There are several types of EJB: Session Beans, Entity Beans, and Message-Driven Beans. At present, JST mainly supports Session Beans, the most commonly used type. Session Beans are also the recommended way to deploy enterprise Web services. Support for the other types of EJB will come in future releases.

JSR 220, which is part of Java EE 5.0, defines the EJB 3.0 standard. JSR 220 contains many programming model simplifications such as improved APIs, a new object-relational persistence specification, and JSR 175-based code annotations. Oracle and Versant initiated projects that support different aspects of JSR 220. This support is being developed in the Dali incubator project, which will become a component of JST in a future release.

Web Service Tools

J2EE includes several Web service standards, including JAX-RPC and JSR 109. JAX-RPC defines the Java binding for WSDL and the associated client programming model. JSR 109 specifies how Web services are deployed as Session EJBs. As mentioned earlier, enterprise Web services are displayed as first-class objects in the Project Navigator.

JST extends the **Web Service** wizard with support for JAX-RPC and JSR 109. JST also includes out-of-the-box support for Apache Axis 1.3, which is a reference implementation for JAX-RPC. The wizard supports the creation and deployment of Web services and the generation of JAX-RPC-compliant client access to Web services. Web services may be created using either a top-down or bottom-up approach. In the top-down approach, a WSDL document that describes the Web service interface is created first, and a Java Web service implementation skeleton is generated from it. In the bottom-up approach, a Java Web service implementation class is created first and the WSDL is generated from it. In general, the top-down approach leads to cleaner and more interoperable Web service interfaces, and we highly recommend its use. The WSDL editor is designed to simplify the creation of well-designed Web service interfaces.

Java EE 5.0 includes JSR 181, which defines JSR 175 code annotations for Web services. The WTP development team plans to support JSR 181 in a future release of JST. Many advanced Web service specifications dealing with security, reliable delivery, and other qualities of service are currently being implemented in the Apache Axis 2.0 project, and you can expect to see support for them in future releases.

Contributing to WTP

One of our motives for writing this book is to encourage developers like you to contribute to the ongoing development of WTP. WTP will only be a success if it attracts a large and active user community that helps make it better. There are many ways to contribute. This section explores some of them.

Become a User

The easiest way to contribute is to become a WTP user. If you've downloaded WTP, you've already helped the project. You've increased the user community by one. A large user community helps the contributing vendors justify their ongoing investment. You've also encouraged other vendors to build extensions to WTP. If WTP helps you do your job, please tell your colleagues and help grow the user base further.

Monitor the Newsgroup

While using WTP, you're sure to have questions. There are many sources of help for you. Start with the built-in Help system. Next go to the WTP Web site and try the articles, tutorials, and FAQs. If you're still stuck, try the newsgroup

```
news://news.eclipse.org/eclipse.webtools
```

You'll need a newsreader such as the freely available Mozilla Thunderbird to access the newsgroup. The newsgroup is the place where users can ask each other questions and share their knowledge. WTP developers also monitor the newsgroup and offer advice. After you become an experienced WTP user, please check the newsgroup periodically and see if you can help other less-experienced users.

Report a Problem

Your next level of contribution is to help the development team by reporting errors. No piece of software is perfect and, although the WTP developers have tried to make WTP defect-free, it does have its fair share of bugs. Like most Open Source projects, WTP uses a publicly available bug tracking system so users can report problems. WTP uses Bugzilla, which you can access at

```
https://bugs.eclipse.org/bugs/enter_bug.cgi?product=Web+Tools
```

Before you enter a new bug report, you should search Bugzilla to see if the problem you are experiencing has already been reported. If the problem has already been reported, you can still comment on it and add yourself to the cc list to keep track of the progress. However, don't worry if you report a known problem; the responsible developer will simply mark it as a duplicate. Even if the problem is known, you may be able to provide new information such as how to recreate it. Your bug report will get the most attention if it occurs in the version currently under development. Try to reproduce your bug on a recent build (see the WTP Build Types section in Chapter 4, Setting Up Your Workspace).

Writing good bug reports takes practice. The most helpful thing you can do is to provide instructions that let the developer reproduce the problem. Most bugs that can be easily reproduced can be easily fixed. To enter a new bug, or add information to an existing bug, you'll need to register your e-mail address with Bugzilla.

Entering a bug report is just the start of your contribution. As the bug is being worked on, you'll receive e-mail notifications of its progress. The developer assigned to fix the bug may ask you for more information. Please respond in a timely fashion. If you don't, the developer may simply close the bug with no action if he can't reproduce the error. When the developer fixes the problem, your next contribution will be to verify that the fix is correct. You'll need to download the fixed version and attempt to recreate the error. If you can no longer recreate the error, report that the fix has been verified. Otherwise, report that the error still exists so the developer can continue work.

Suggest an Improvement

WTP uses Bugzilla for requirements in addition to errors. As far as Bugzilla is concerned, the only difference between a requirement and an error is that requirements use a special value for the *severity* of the bug. Errors have severities such as *normal*, *major*, *critical*, and *blocker*. Requirements use the special value *enhancement*. A requirement is also referred to as a *Request for Enhancement*, or RFE. If you have an idea for how to improve WTP, please enter an RFE in Bugzilla.

Fix a Bug

Reporting bugs is an extremely valuable contribution, but fixing them is even more valuable. If you have Eclipse plug-in development skills, please consider helping to fix WTP. You are probably most motivated to fix bugs that affect your personal use of WTP, but if you are looking for areas to work on, simply query Bugzilla and look for unassigned bugs. You can also search Bugzilla for the special keyword *helpwanted,* which indicates that the development team is especially looking for help on some bugs. There is also a Help Wanted page on the WTP Web site. As you work on bugs you'll communicate with the other WTP team members using one of the WTP developer mailing lists. The general developer mailing list is

```
<wtp-dev@eclipse.org>
```

There are also specialized mailing lists for the subprojects.

To get started with WTP plug-in development, try the tutorial *Developing the WTP with Eclipse* [Hutchinson2005], which is available on the WTP Web site. You can contribute both fixes and JUnit tests. Like most Open Source projects, WTP practices automated testing. Whenever a bug is found, it is highly desirable to create a JUnit test that recreates the problem. This test is then added to the test suite that is run whenever WTP is built. Having the test case in the test suite guards against future regressions. JUnit tests are also highly desirable for enhancements. When you contribute an enhancement, include some JUnit tests that verify its correct operation. This protects the enhancements against future breakage.

Both fixes and JUnit tests must be contributed through Bugzilla. Use Eclipse to package your code contribution as a patch and attach it to the bug report. A committer will then assess your contribution and commit it to the code base. Contributing your code through Bugzilla is very important since all code that goes into any Open Source project must be carefully accounted for. One of the goals of WTP is to provide a platform for commercial products, so the authorship of all code that comprises it must be recorded.

Write an Article or Tutorial

If you like writing, please consider contributing an article or tutorial that describes your experience. Let other users know how you solved your problem. You can get your article published on the WTP Web site. If your article points out a particularly clumsy feature of WTP, it may even inspire the developers to improve the user interface.

Become a Committer

After you establish a track record of valuable code contributions, you may want to become a committer. You become a committer by earning the respect of the other committers who contribute to WTP. They must formally vote you commit rights. When you become a committer you will be responsible for designing new features, fixing bugs, and assessing the patches submitted by other contributors.

Grow the Community

You can contribute to WTP in many other ways. For example, consider sharing your expertise at local user groups, write articles for trade journals, or submit papers to conferences. You might even want to start a new Open Source project that extends WTP into some new domain, or start your own company and sell the next great WTP plug-in! These are all important contributions to the WTP ecosystem.

Summary

In this chapter, you learned how WTP got started as a multi-vendor project at the Eclipse Foundation and how Open Source is changing the old business models and creating new ones for the software industry. You then explored the scope of WTP with its focus on open standards, and the architecture of its subprojects, WST and JST. Finally, you learned the many ways that you can contribute to WTP and participate in its community.

You are now ready to explore WTP in greater depth. Chapter 3 describes how the rest of this book is organized. You can read the remaining chapters sequentially, or just focus on your areas of interest.

CHAPTER 3

Quick Tour

A journey of a thousand miles begins with a single step.

—Confucius

Overview

Following the long-standing tradition used in programming books, our first Web application will be "Hello, world." The purpose of "Hello, world" is to get your development environment set up and to go through one complete edit-compile-debug iteration that results in running code. Accomplishing this means that you have solved most of the problems that are unique to a new development environment or programming language. You can then focus on your programming tasks and incrementally learn new features of the tools as you need them. However, Java Web application development has many facets, so we'll develop "Hello, world" in four iterations, each of which focuses on one group of tools in WTP. This will give you a good cross section of the capabilities of WTP. The four iterations are as follows:

- ○ In Iteration 1 you configure an application server, create a Web application, develop a simple JavaServer Pages (JSP) document that prints a greeting, and run it on the server.

- ○ In Iteration 2 you add a login JSP, write Java scriptlets to display the user name, create a Java servlet that controls the application page flow, and debug the servlet and JSPs.

- ○ In Iteration 3 you create a database to store user information, develop an SQL query to access it, and add Java Database Connectivity (JDBC) calls to your servlet to invoke the query and retrieve the user information.

❍ In Iteration 4 you deploy the database query as a Web service, generate a JSP test client that invokes the Web service, and monitor the Simple Object Access Protocol (SOAP) message traffic.

After completing the Quick Tour, you'll have a fair understanding of the fundamentals of Java Web application development with WTP. You should then be comfortable enough with WTP to begin developing simple Web applications and to explore the other features of the environment. So power up your computer and get ready to code. The tour is about to begin!

To get the most out of the Quick Tour, you should set up Eclipse and WTP, and follow along. The first thing you'll need is a J2SE Development Kit (JDK). You need this to run both Eclipse and a J2EE servlet container like Tomcat. See the Getting a JDK sidebar for instructions on how to get a JDK.

Getting a JDK

In this book we do not explain how to program in Java. We assume that you have some Java development experience. You probably already know how to get a JDK. We are including a brief discussion of this topic here for completeness.

The following instructions just give a high-level description of how to install a JDK. Refer to the installation instructions that come with the JDK for more details. Do the following:

❍ Download a J2SE Development Kit (JDK). Strictly speaking, only a Java Runtime Environment (JRE) is needed for running Eclipse since it contains its own Java compiler. However, you will be doing JavaServer Pages (JSP) development that requires a Java compiler, so you need a JDK. We use the JDK 1.4.2 in this book. You can download a JDK from IBM, Sun, and other vendors.

Download the IBM JDK from

```
http://www.ibm.com/developerworks/java/jdk/
```

Download the Sun JDK from

```
http://java.sun.com/j2se/1.4.2/download.html
```

Select a JDK for the operating system you are using.
❍ After you download the JDK, follow its installation steps.
❍ To verify that you correctly installed the JDK, open a command window and enter the following command:

```
java -version
```

The Java virtual machine should run and print out its version number.

After you have a JDK installed, you'll need Eclipse and WTP. See the Getting Eclipse and WTP sidebar for brief instructions on how to do this. This topic is covered in much more detail in the Installing and Updating WTP section in Chapter 4.

Getting Eclipse and WTP

In this book we do not explain the fundamentals of using Eclipse. We assume you have some experience using Eclipse and are now interested in learning how to use WTP for Java Web application development. You probably already know how to install Eclipse. However, adding WTP requires some extra steps.

There are several ways to install WTP. In fact, since many other products are built on top of WTP, you might already have it installed (see Chapter 16 for a list of products that include WTP), in which case, you are done. If you need to install WTP, read on.

The following instructions just give a high-level description of how to install the software. Refer to the installation instructions that come with each component for more details. Install WTP and its Eclipse prerequisites as follows:

○ The easiest way to install WTP is to download the "all-in-one" zip file from the WTP 1.5 download page, and unzip it in a convenient directory. The all-in-one zip includes WTP and all of its Eclipse prerequisites, including Eclipse itself. You can download the all-in-one zip from

```
http://download.eclipse.org/webtools/downloads/
```

On the WTP downloads page, select the most recent Released Build, e.g., WTP 1.5.2, to open its page. Then download and unzip the `wtp-all-in-one-sdk-...` zip file for your operating system (Windows, Linux, or MacOS).

○ If you already have Eclipse 3.2 installed, then you can install WTP 1.5 and its other Eclipse prerequisites using the Update Manager. For detailed instructions, search the Eclipse online Help for the topic "Installing new features with the update manager."

WTP 1.5 is part of the Callisto simultaneous release that includes ten Eclipse projects. Invoke the menu command **Help ▶ Software Updates ▶ Find and Install...** to run the **Feature Updates** wizard. Select **Search** for new features to install and check the **Callisto Discovery Site**. When you are presented with a list of features to select, choose the **Web and J2EE Development** category to get WTP. Note that WTP requires some other features, so be sure to click the **Select Required** button before you start the installation.

○ Finally, if you are a do-it-yourself kind of person, do the following

○ Install Eclipse. We use Eclipse 3.2 in this book. You can download the Eclipse Platform from http://www.eclipse.org/downloads/

After you download the Eclipse zip file, unzip it in a convenient directory.

○ Install WTP. We use WTP 1.5 in this book. You can download WTP from

http://download.eclipse.org/webtools/downloads/

The WTP download page also lists the following prerequisite components from a few other Eclipse projects:

○ the Eclipse Modeling Framework (EMF),

○ the Graphical Editing Framework (GEF), and

○ the Java Edit Model (JEM).

Download these too. After you download WTP and its prerequisites, install them on top of Eclipse by extracting each one to the directory in which you extracted Eclipse.

○ After you have installed WTP, verify the installation by opening Eclipse. Select an existing workspace or create a new one. Then invoke the menu command **Help ▸ About Eclipse SDK** to open the **About Eclipse SDK** dialog box. Click the **Feature Details** button and verify that there are J2EE Standard Tools and Web Standard Tools features installed.

Iteration 1: J2EE Web Applications

WTP extends Eclipse in two dimensions: *development artifacts* and *runtime environments*. A development artifact is any source code or configuration file that you need to develop in order to build and deploy your application. A runtime environment is the software context in which your development artifacts execute. For example, consider normal Java 2 Standard Edition (J2SE) development. Here the primary development artifact is the Java source file and the primary runtime environment is the J2SE Runtime Environment (JRE). The simplest J2SE component is a Java main program composed of a public class that has a public main method with the standard signature for passing in command line arguments. Java main programs are design to run in a command shell. In addition to Java main programs, J2SE also defines applets and JavaBeans. Java applets are designed to run in a JRE that is embedded in a Web browser. JavaBeans are designed to be composed with other Java components and have both design-time and runtime programming interfaces.

In J2EE, the situation is much more complex. Several additional kinds of Java components, such as servlets, Enterprise JavaBeans, and Web services, are defined. New development artifacts types, such as JSP, Extensible Markup Language (XML) deployment descriptors (e.g., web.xml for Web applications), and archives (e.g., Web Application Archive [WAR] for Web applications), are introduced. These new Java components and artifacts run in J2EE application servers. The simplest J2EE application servers are servlet containers. More advanced containers support Enterprise JavaBeans (EJB) and offer a wide variety of application services such as transactions, method-level authorization, and object pooling.

In addition to the development artifact types associated with J2EE, there are many more associated with Web application development in general. JSPs are used to generate Web pages, which typically contain Hypertext Markup Language (HTML) or Extensible HTML (XHTML), Cascading Style Sheets (CSS), and JavaScript. CSS and JavaScript can be placed inline in JSPs or in separate source files. Modern Web browsers also have the ability to display XML documents and apply Extensible Stylesheet Language Transformations (XSLT) to them. XSLT can also be applied on the server. Web service development involves the creation of Web Service Description Language (WSDL) and XML Schema (XSD) documents. Web applications often access relational databases using Structured Query Language (SQL). Database access can also be performed by invoking stored procedures that execute in the database.

As you can see, J2EE Web application development involves many more kinds of artifacts and execution environments than J2SE development. One of the main goals of WTP is to seamlessly extend all the capabilities that Eclipse developers currently enjoy for Java development into the domain of Web development. Java source editing functions such as code completion, syntax coloring, error highlighting, and quick fixes all have direct analogs for Web artifacts. Semantic search and refactoring also have their extensions to Web applications. For example, the Java refactoring operation of renaming a class should be extended to include any JSPs or deployment descriptors that refer to the class. The initial releases of WTP have taken the first steps toward implementing this goal, but much work remains to bring Web development up to the same level of maturity as Java development.

The purpose of this iteration is to create and execute the simplest possible J2EE Web application, namely a Web application that contains a single Web page that displays the message "Hello, world." You'll perform the following development tasks in this iteration:

1. Add a Server Runtime Environment.

2. Create a J2EE Web Application Project.

3. Create and Edit a JSP.

4. Run the JSP on the Server.

Refer to Chapter 7 for more detail.

Add a Server Runtime Environment

By analogy with the Eclipse support for JREs, WTP adds support for *Server Runtime Environments*. You'll be developing servlets and JSPs in this Quick Tour, so you need a J2EE servlet container such as Apache Tomcat, the popular Open Source reference implementation of the Servlet and JSP specifications. We use Tomcat 5.0.28 in this book. Tomcat 5 implements the Servlet 2.4 and JSP 2.0 specifications, which are part of J2EE 1.4. If you already have Tomcat or another supported servlet container installed, feel free to use it in the Quick Tour. Otherwise install Tomcat now (see the Getting Tomcat sidebar for instructions).

Getting Tomcat

In this book we assume that you are new to Java Web application development and might never have installed a servlet container before. The following instructions are a brief introduction to how to install and run Tomcat. However, a complete description is beyond the scope of this book. If you run into problems or require more information, consult the resources available on the Tomcat Web site.

Download and unzip the Tomcat 5.0.28 binary distribution in a convenient directory. Note that WTP supports many other versions of Tomcat too. We are using Tomcat 5.0.28 for illustration purposes. The startup and shutdown commands for other versions may differ.

You can download Tomcat from

```
http://tomcat.apache.org
```

Verify that Tomcat is installed correctly before proceeding. Tomcat includes commands for starting and stopping the server. Do the following:

1. The startup command requires that the environment variable JAVA_HOME be set to the installation directory of the JDK. If the JDK installation process did not set JAVA_HOME correctly, set it now to the directory where you installed the JDK (see the Getting a JDK sidebar).

2. To start Tomcat, open a command window and change the current directory to the bin subdirectory of the Tomcat installation directory. Then invoke this command:

```
startup
```

A second command window opens and launches Tomcat on port 8080 by default.

3. After the startup process completes, verify that Tomcat is running by opening this URL in a Web browser:

```
http://localhost:8080/
```

You should see the Tomcat home page displaying this message:

```
If you're seeing this page via a web browser, it means you've setup
Tomcat successfully. Congratulations!
```

4. To stop Tomcat, enter this command in the first command window:

```
shutdown
```

Tomcat should stop and the second command window should close.

Ports Already in Use

Be sure to stop the server. Otherwise, when WTP tries to start it you will receive an error message telling you that several ports may already be in use (see Figure 3.1). If you want to keep Tomcat running outside of WTP, you'll have to use a different set of port numbers in WTP.

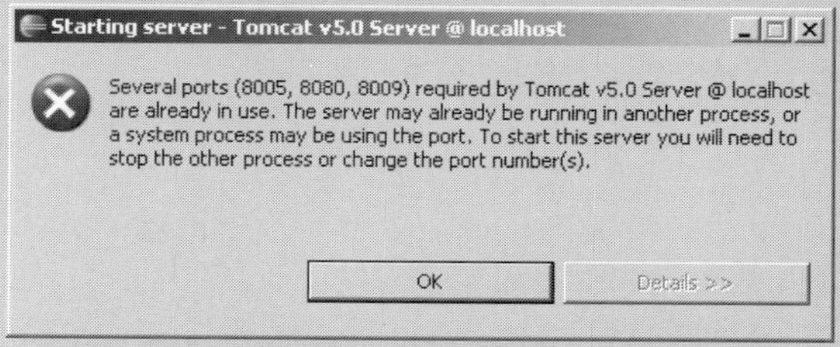

Figure 3.1 Starting Server Error

Do the following to extend Eclipse with the Tomcat server runtime environment:

1. Launch Eclipse and invoke the command **Window ▸ Preferences** from the menu bar to open the **Preferences** dialog. Expand the **Server** preferences category and select the **Installed Runtimes** page (see Figure 3.2). Note that initially there are no server runtime environment definitions.

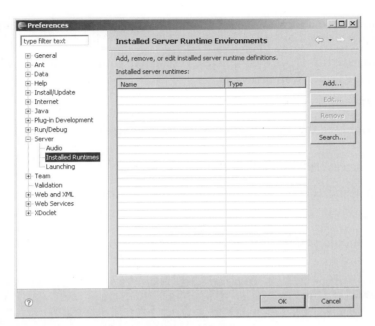

Figure 3.2   Installed Server Runtime Environments

2. Click the **Add** button to open the **New Server Runtime** wizard. Expand the
   Apache category and select **Apache Tomcat v5.0** (see Figure 3.3).

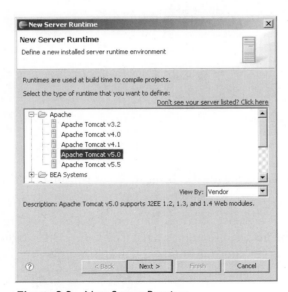

Figure 3.3   New Server Runtime

3. Click the **Next** button to display the **Tomcat Server** page. Click the **Browse** button to select the directory where you installed Tomcat (see the Getting Tomcat sidebar), for example,

```
E:\jakarta-tomcat-5.0.28
```

The **Tomcat installation directory** field should now show the selected directory (see Figure 3.4).

Figure 3.4   Tomcat Server

4. The **JRE** field is initialized to the **Workbench default JRE,** which is the JVM you used to launch Eclipse.

JDK Required for JSP Development

Part of the server runtime environment setup process involves specifying the JRE to use for launching Tomcat. Be sure to specify a full JDK instead of just a JRE because you'll be doing JSP development. If you do not currently have a JDK defined to Eclipse, add the one you previously installed (see the Getting a JDK sidebar). JSP development requires a Java compiler, which is included in the JDK but not the JRE. JSP compilation will fail if you specify a JRE. Note that you can precompile your JSPs in order to use a JRE in your production server environment.

Click the **Installed JREs** button to open the **Installed JREs** wizard. This wizard lets you define additional JREs to Eclipse. Click the **Add** button and select the directory where you installed the JDK (see the Getting a JDK sidebar), for example,

```
E:\ibm-java2-142
```

The JDK is added to the **Installed JREs** page. Select its checkbox to make it the default JRE (see Figure 3.5), and click the **OK** button to return to the **Tomcat Server** page.

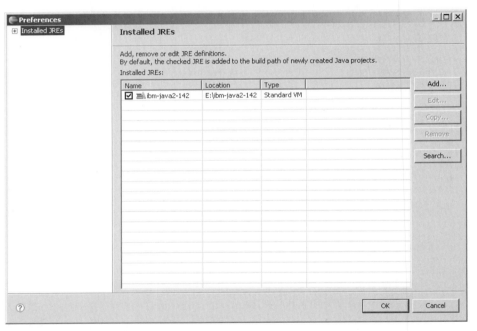

Figure 3.5 Installed JREs

5. Select the JDK from the drop-down list of the **JRE** field (see Figure 3.4). When WTP launches Tomcat later, it will use the specified JDK. Click the **Finish** button to complete the definition.

Tomcat is now listed on the **Installed Server Runtime Environments** page (see Figure 3.6). You have now extended Eclipse with a J2EE servlet container and are ready to create your first Java Web application development project.

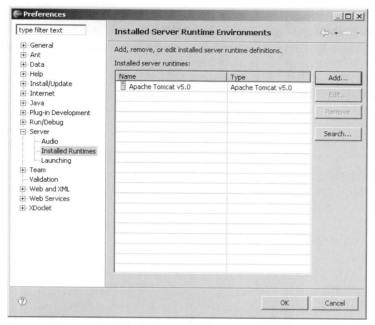

Figure 3.6   Installed Server Runtime Environments with Tomcat Added

Create a Dynamic Web Project

We assume you are familiar with the Eclipse concepts of *workspace, project,* and *builder*. Recall that an Eclipse workspace contains a set of projects. You typically put projects that are related to each other in the same workspace. For example, in J2EE development, you would put related Web, EJB, and utility projects in the same workspace. Each project has a set of builders associated with it. Builders are what give the project its intelligence. Builders know how to process the artifacts in a project. The most common example of a builder is the Eclipse incremental Java compiler, which knows how to compile your Java source files into class files. WTP provides builders for Java Web applications. These builders know, for example, how to package the artifacts in J2EE modules so that they can be deployed to J2EE application servers.

In general, a J2EE application will contain several modules. For example, you might want to use a Web module for the presentation logic and an EJB module for the business logic. Here you'll just develop a Web module. Do the following to add a Web module to your workspace:

1. To begin development, create a new dynamic Web project by invoking the
   File ▸ New ▸ Project menu command to open the **New Project** wizard.
   Select **Web ▸ Dynamic Web Project** as the project type (see Figure 3.7).

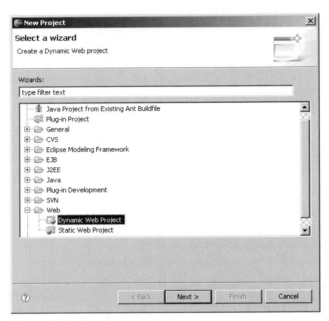

Figure 3.7   New Project

2. Click the **Next** button. The **Dynamic Web Project** page is displayed (see
   Figure 3.8). Enter web1 in the **Project Name** field. Note that Apache Tomcat
   is selected as the **Target Runtime** since it is the only server runtime environment you have defined. The **Configurations** field lets you select a predefined
   configuration of *project facets*. Leave the setting as **<custom>** for now. You
   can also ignore the checkbox to add the Web module to an EAR project
   since Tomcat is just a servlet container and doesn't support EARs.

3. Click the **Next** button to advance to the **Project Facets** page (see Figure 3.9). A
   facet is part of the runtime configuration of a project, such as the version of
   Java or J2EE. Facets will be discussed in more detail in Chapter 6. For now,
   simply accept the selections.

4. Click the **Next** button to advance to the **Web Module** page (see Figure 3.10).
   You can change some of the project settings here. For example, the Context
   Root of the Web application defaults to its project name, web1. Accept the
   defaults for now.

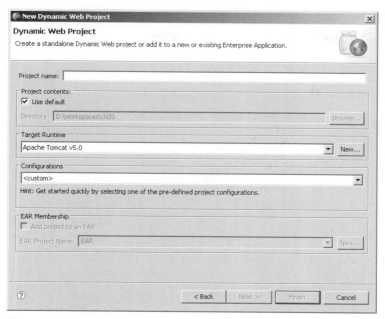

Figure 3.8   Dynamic Web Project

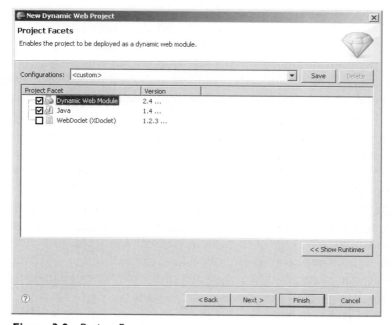

Figure 3.9   Project Facets

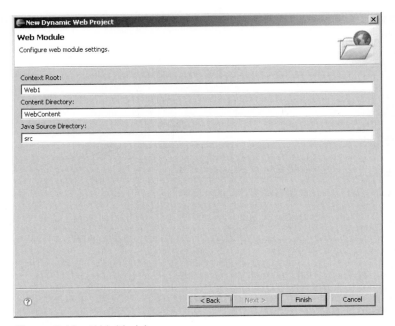

Figure 3.10 Web Module

5. Click the **Finish** button to create the Web project. Since this is the first time you have created a Web project, you are prompted to accept the J2EE license from Sun (see Figure 3.11). WTP will next attempt to download the J2EE schemas from the Sun Web site, so you must accept the license before WTP proceeds. Products built on top of WTP may have obtained the right to redistribute the J2EE schemas, in which case you won't see this dialog.

6. Click the **I Agree** button to accept the license. Note that if you do not accept the license, then WTP will be unable to validate the J2EE XML artifacts, such as the deployment descriptors (e.g., web.xml), you create.

   WTP has a special J2EE perspective and will attempt to switch to it when you create any J2EE project, such as a dynamic Web project or an EJB project. One of the user interface design guidelines of Eclipse is to not switch perspectives without asking the user if they want to. You are therefore prompted to switch perspectives (see Figure 3.12).

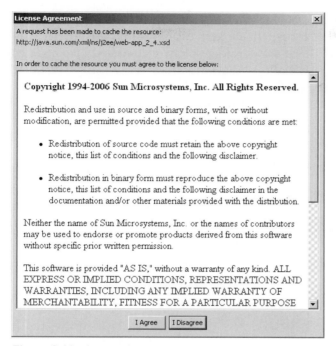

Figure 3.11 License Agreement

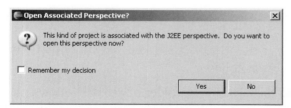

Figure 3.12 Open Associated Perspective

7. Click the **Yes** button to agree to the switch. The wizard opens the **J2EE** perspective for you so you can see the logical structure of your modules. The J2EE **Project Explorer** view (see Figure 3.13) now shows the project structure after web1 has been created. Note that the wizard created some folders and files under the web1 module. These items are defined by the J2EE specification. For example, the webContent folder is the root of the Web application and is where the normal Web content, such as HTML

pages, JSPs, and images, go. The webContent folder contains a special folder named WEB-INF, which contains items that are not accessible by a Web browser. The WEB-INF folder is where compiled Java code goes. It also contains a special file, web.xml, which is the J2EE Web deployment descriptor; more on that later (see Chapter 7). Now you are ready to start creating the content of the Web application.

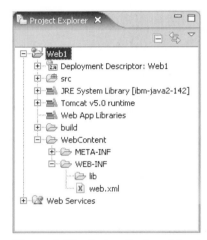

Figure 3.13   Project Explorer View

Create and Edit a JSP

Add a JSP file to your project as follows:

1. Add a new JSP file to the webContent folder of web1 as follows. In the **Project Explorer** view, expand web1, right click on webContent, and invoke the **New ▸ JSP** command to open the **New JavaServer Page** wizard. Give the new file the name hello-world.jsp. The wizard lets you pick a template for the new JSP. Select the template for JSP with HTML markup, and click the **Finish** button.

2. The wizard creates the JSP file with the content filled in from the template and opens it in the JSP editor. The JSP editor provides full content assist on HTML tags, JSP tags, and Java code scriptlets. Edit the JSP to say "Hello, world" using HTML tags (see Figure 3.14). The Web application is now ready to run.

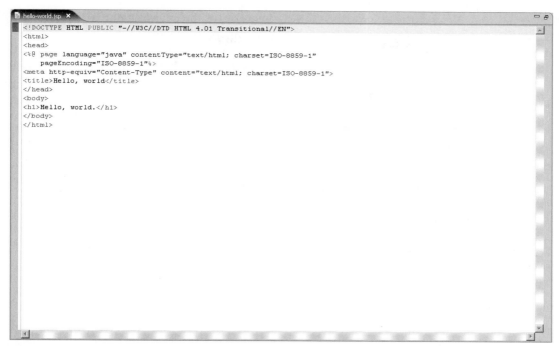

Figure 3.14   JSP Editor

Run the JSP on the Server

The Eclipse Java Development Tools (JDT) lets you run a Java main program (i.e., a Java class that has a standard main method) by selecting its source file and invoking the **Run As ▸ Java Application** command. WTP extends the **Run As** command to Web artifacts such as HTML and JSP files. Simply select the file and invoke the **Run As ▸ Run on Server** command from the context menu. In WTP, a server runtime environment plays the role that a Java runtime environment plays in JDT. Another difference between JDT and WTP is that in JDT, the input and output of the Java application is displayed in the **Console** view, but in WTP, the user interface of a Web application is hosted in a Web browser.

Run your JSP file as follows:

1. Select hello-world.jsp and invoke the **Run As ▸ Run on Server** command from the context menu. Since this is the first time you have tried to run any artifact from the web1 project, WTP will prompt you to define a new server (see Figure 3.15). WTP defaults the server runtime environment to Apache Tomcat, which you previously associated with the project. However, in

WTP a *server* consists of both a server runtime environment and configuration information such as the port numbers to use and the set of projects to deploy or publish on it. Note that a project may be deployed on several servers, which is handy when you are testing a Web application for portability to different vendors.

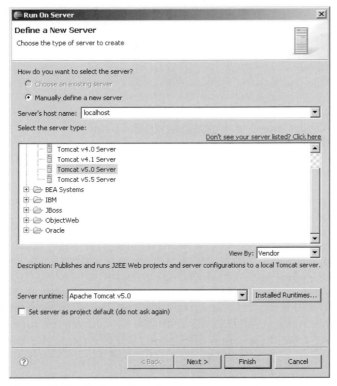

Figure 3.15   Define a New Server

2. Click the **Next** button to advance to the **Add and Remove Projects** page (see Figure 3.16).

3. Click the **Finish** button to confirm that you want WTP to add the web1 module to the server configuration. WTP then starts the server and opens a Web browser with the Uniform Resource Locator (URL) of the JSP file (see Figure 3.17).

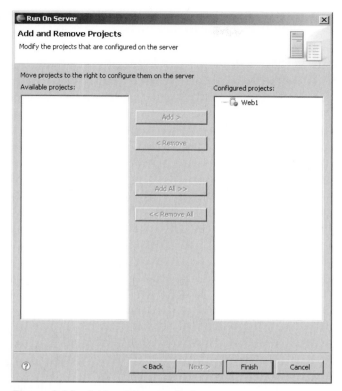

Figure 3.16 Add and Remove Projects

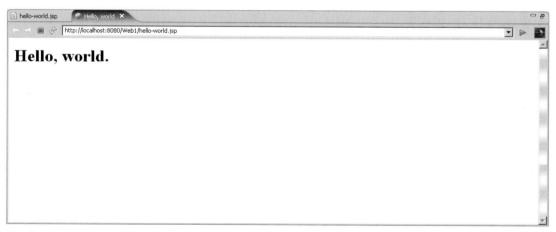

Figure 3.17 Web Browser—hello-world.jsp

WTP Launches Tomcat in a New JVM Process

WTP starts Tomcat in a new process using the JVM that you specified when you defined its server runtime environment. If you have another Tomcat process currently running, you will be unable to start Tomcat from WTP unless you use a different set of port numbers (see the Ports Already in Use sidebar earlier in this chapter).

Summary of Iteration 1

In this iteration you added Tomcat to Eclipse as a server runtime environment, created a dynamic Web project, added a JSP file to it, and ran the project on Tomcat.

Congratulations! You have just created your first Web application with WTP. You're now ready to add some Java code and do a little debugging.

Iteration 2: Servlets and Scriptlets

The Web application you have created so far is rather boring since it is static. There is no way to interact with this application. You could have achieved the same behavior using an HTML page. To liven things up, you will add some Java code. You'll add a Java scriptlet to your JSP. This scriptlet will look for a query parameter in the request and display its value. You'll also create another JSP to prompt the user to enter this parameter, and you'll add a Java servlet to control the application flow between these JSPs. In this process, you'll use the debugger to step through both the JSP and the servlet code. You'll perform the following development tasks in this iteration:

1. Add a Java Scriptlet to a JSP.

2. Debug a JSP.

3. Create a Servlet.

4. Debug a Servlet.

Refer to Chapter 7 for more detail.

Add a Java Scriptlet to a JSP

The simplest way to add dynamic behavior to a JSP is to insert a Java *scriptlet*. A Java scriptlet is a block of Java code that gets executed when the JSP is requested. Java scriptlets are placed inside of <% and %> delimiters. Within a scriptlet, the Java code has access to several predefined variables. For example, the HTTP request is represented by a `request` variable. The scriptlet can retrieve the HTTP query parameters from the `request` variable.

You'll now make your JSP display the name of the user that is passed in on the request URL as a query parameter. Query parameters are specified after the "?" in the URL. For example, to greet Alice, you request the JSP using the URL

```
http://localhost:8080/web1/hello-world.jsp?user=Alice
```

Do the following to add dynamic behavior to your JSP:

1. Edit the `hello-world.jsp` file in the JSP editor and add the scriptlets (see Example 3.1). Here, the Java scriptlet gets the value of the `user` query parameter from the request, checks if it's null, and creates a `person` string that is then displayed on the page.

Example 3.1   Listing of hello-world.jsp

```
<!DOCTYPE HTML PUBLIC "-//W3C//DTD HTML 4.01 Transitional//EN">
<html>
<head>
<%@ page language="java" contentType="text/html; charset=ISO-8859-1"
    pageEncoding="ISO-8859-1"%>
<meta http-equiv="Content-Type" content="text/html; charset=ISO-8859-1">
<title>Hello, world</title>
</head>
<body>
<h1>Hello, world.</h1>
<%
  String person = "?";

  String user = request.getParameter("user");
  if (user != null) person = user;
%>

Welcome to WTP, <%= person %>!

</body>
</html>
```

2. The JSP editor provides full Java code assist within the scriptlet. Experiment with code assist as you edit the JSP file.

Debug a JSP

You now have some executable code to try out. However, rather than simply run it, you'll debug it. Do the following to debug your JSP:

1. Setting a breakpoint in a JSP file is just like setting one in a Java file. Simply double-click in the left-hand margin on the line where you want execution to halt. Set a breakpoint now in `hello-world.jsp` on the following line of the scriptlet:

```
String user = request.getParameter("user");
```

2. Select `hello-world.jsp` and invoke the **Debug As** ▸ **Debug on Server** command from the context menu. Since you have modified the JSP, WTP will prompt you to update the Web application (see Figure 3.18).

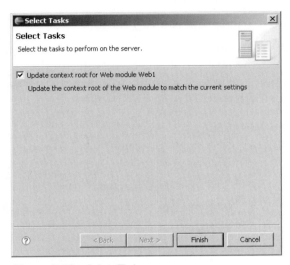

Figure 3.18   Select Tasks

3. Check the box to update the context root of `web1` and click the **Finish** button. WTP will update `web1` and restart the server in debug mode. Since the server is currently not in debug mode, WTP will prompt you to confirm the mode change (see Figure 3.19).

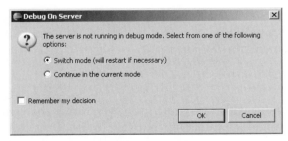

Figure 3.19   Debug On Server

4. Select the **Switch mode** radio button and click the **OK** button. WTP will restart the server in debug mode and request the JSP in a Web browser as

before. Execution will now halt at the breakpoint and WTP will attempt to open the **Debug** perspective. Since this is a perspective switch, WTP will prompt you to confirm the switch. Accept the perspective switch and view the JSP halted at the breakpoint. Use the **Debug** perspective as usual to explore the halted state. Click the **Resume** button to continue execution.

5. To debug the query parameter handling, go to the Web browser, append the query string

```
?user=Alice
```

to the end of the URL, and refresh the browser. Execution will halt again at the breakpoint (see Figure 3.20). Click the **Step Over** button to execute the line of code that assigns the value `Alice` to the user variable. Note that the **Variables** view shows the value of the `user` variable set correctly.

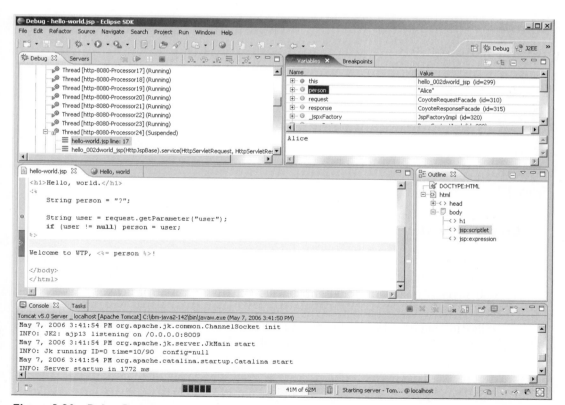

Figure 3.20   Debug Perspective

6. All of the usual Java debugging functions are available for JSPs. Continue to explore the variables and step through the code. Click the **Resume** button to complete the processing of the HTTP request (see Figure 3.21). Note that the greeting is now "Welcome to WTP, Alice!"

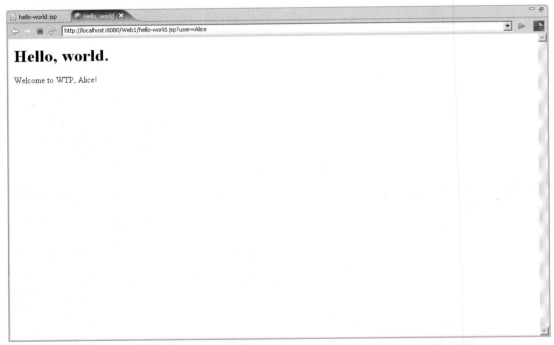

Figure 3.21   Web Browser—hello-world.jsp?user=Alice

Create a Servlet

The code for a Web application includes business logic, application logic, and presentation logic. Business logic implements business rules such as how to compute prices and taxes. Application logic implements the flow of control between Web pages. Presentation logic implements how the data is rendered in the Web browser. Since JSPs can contain arbitrary blocks of Java code, it is tempting to put all of the logic in the JSPs. However, when designing a Web application, it is good practice to limit the code in JSPs to just the presentation logic. Application logic should be put in servlets that invoke Java business objects, get the results, and pass them back to JSPs as presentation objects. Business logic should be put in Java classes that are independent of the presentation and application logic so they can be easily reused and maintained.

You'll modify your example to illustrate this design pattern. Your example currently consists of a single JSP, `hello-world.jsp`, which checks for the presence of the `user` query parameter and displays its value. Users do not normally tack query parameters on to the end of URLs by hand. Instead, users enter parameters into HTML forms, and then click a submit button to send the parameters to the server for processing. To implement this servlet design pattern, you'll add the following files:

○ `login-user.jsp`—a JSP that presents an HTML form to the user and sends the input to the `HelloServlet` servlet for processing. This JSP also displays an error message if one is present. The error message lets `HelloServlet` communicate with the user.

○ `HelloServlet.java`—a servlet that checks for the presence of the `user` query parameter. If the query parameter is present and contains a nonempty user id, the servlet forwards the request on to `hello-world.jsp` for presentation to the user. Otherwise the servlet generates an error message for the user and forwards the request back to `login-user.jsp`.

Do the following to implement the servlet design pattern in your project:

1. Begin by creating `login-user.jsp` using the **New JSP** wizard. Enter its code (see Example 3.2).

Example 3.2   Listing of login-user.jsp

```
<!DOCTYPE HTML PUBLIC "-//W3C//DTD HTML 4.01 Transitional//EN">
<html>
<head>
<%@ page language="java" contentType="text/html; charset=ISO-8859-1"
   pageEncoding="ISO-8859-1"%>
<meta http-equiv="Content-Type" content="text/html; charset=ISO-8859-1">
<title>Login User</title>
</head>
<body>
<h1>Login User</h1>
<%
   String error_message = "";
   Object error = request.getAttribute("error");
   if (error != null) error_message = error.toString();
%>
<form action="HelloServlet">
<table cellspacing="4">
   <tr>
     <td>Enter your user name:</td>
     <td><input name="user" type="text" size="20"></td>
     <td style="color: red"><%= error_message %></td>
   </tr>
   <tr>
     <td></td>
     <td><input type="submit" value="Login"></td>
     <td></td>
```

```
    </tr>
  </table>
  </form>
</body>
</html>
```

login-user.jsp checks for the existence of an optional error message and, if present, displays it on the page. Note that the action attribute of the **Login** button is set to HelloServlet. When the user clicks the **Login** button, the value of the input field gets sent to HelloServlet as the value of the user query parameter. Your next step is to create the HelloServlet.java class that will process the request.

2. Create the HelloServlet.java servlet as follows: Select the Web1 project and invoke the **New ▸ Servlet** command from the context menu. This opens the **New Servlet** wizard. Create the servlet in the src directory of the Web1 project and give it the package name

   org.example.ch03

   and the class name

   HelloServlet

   (see Figure 3.22).

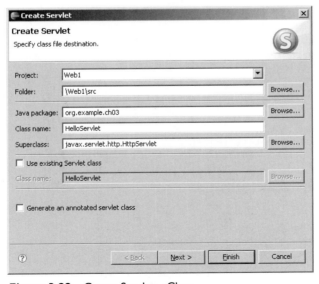

Figure 3.22   Create Servlet—Class

Note that the **Generate an annotated servlet class** checkbox gives you the option of using XDoclet. Uncheck this option for now. We'll discuss XDoclet in Chapter 6.

3. Although you could finish here, click the **Next** button to view the next page. The wizard lets you modify the default servlet name and URL mapping. Accept the default servlet name `HelloServlet` and URL mapping /`HelloServlet` (see Figure 3.23). The servlet name is used for internal bookkeeping in `web.xml`. For example, the servlet name links the servlet class with the URL mapping. The URL mapping determines how the servlet is invoked. This value must match the value you specified in the action attribute of the HTML form element in `login-user.jsp`. Although you use the URL mapping /`HelloServlet`, it is a better practice to use a value that doesn't expose the implementation details, such as the fact that you are using a servlet. In practice, you may change the implementation, so it is a good idea to minimize the number of URLs that are affected.

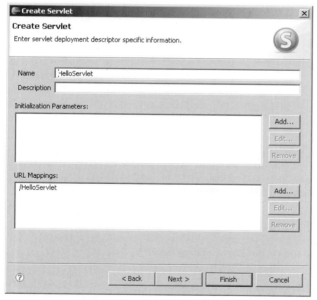

Figure 3.23   Create Servlet—Deployment Descriptor

4. Click the **Finish** button. The wizard creates the skeleton of the servlet. All you need to do is fill in the application logic in the body of the `doGet` method. Enter the code for the servlet (see Example 3.3).

Example 3.3   Listing of HelloServlet.java

```java
package org.example.ch03;

import java.io.IOException;

import javax.servlet.RequestDispatcher;
import javax.servlet.ServletContext;
import javax.servlet.ServletException;
import javax.servlet.http.HttpServletRequest;
import javax.servlet.http.HttpServletResponse;

/**
 * Servlet implementation class for Servlet: HelloServlet
 *
 */
public class HelloServlet extends javax.servlet.http.HttpServlet implements
    javax.servlet.Servlet {
  /**
   *
   */
  private static final long serialVersionUID = 1L;

  /*
   * (non-Java-doc)
   *
   * @see javax.servlet.http.HttpServlet#HttpServlet()
   */
  public HelloServlet() {
    super();
  }

  /*
   * (non-Java-doc)
   *
   * @see javax.servlet.http.HttpServlet#doGet(HttpServletRequest request,
   *        HttpServletResponse response)
   */
  protected void doGet(HttpServletRequest request,
      HttpServletResponse response) throws ServletException, IOException {

    String url = "/hello-world.jsp";

    String user = request.getParameter("user");
    if (user == null || user.length() == 0) {
      url = "/login-user.jsp";
      request.setAttribute("error", "User name must not be empty.");
    }

    ServletContext context = getServletContext();
    RequestDispatcher dispatcher = context.getRequestDispatcher(url);
    dispatcher.forward(request, response);
  }
}
```

The `HelloServlet` class implements the `doGet` method, which handles HTTP GET requests. The purpose of the servlet is to decide which JSP should handle the request. The servlet computes the URL of the appropriate JSP and forwards the request to it using the `forward` method of the `RequestDispatcher` class. The servlet grabs the `user` query parameter from the request using the `getParameter` method. If the `user` query parameter is absent, or it is an empty string, the servlet generates an error message, stores it as an attribute of the request using the `setAttribute` method of the `HttpServletRequest` class, and sets the URL to `login-user.jsp`. If the `user` query parameter is present and non-empty, the servlet sets the URL to `hello-world.jsp`.

Debug a Servlet

Debugging a servlet is very similar to debugging an ordinary Java class, except that you use the **Debug As ▸ Debug on Server** command, just as you did for JSPs. You'll now debug the application control flow. Debug the servlet as follows:

1. Set a breakpoint in `HelloServlet.java` on the line of the `doGet` method that contains the code

   ```
   String user = request.getParameter("user");
   ```

2. Select `HelloServlet.java` in the **Project Explorer** view and invoke the **Debug As ▸ Debug on Server** command from the context menu. This command starts the server in debug mode and opens a Web browser with the URL of the servlet, which in this case is

   ```
   http://localhost:8080/Web1/HelloServlet
   ```

> ### What do I do if I get a 404?
>
> Sometimes when you run or debug a servlet or JSP, you might get a 404 in the Web browser. This problem is caused by the Web browser requesting the resource before the server has fully deployed it. WTP detects when resources have changed and republishes them to the server. However, there may be a time delay as the server restarts. If you run into a 404, manually restart the server from the **Servers** view and try again.

3. Step through the code and verify that there is no value set for the `user` query parameter. The servlet therefore generates an error message and forwards the request to the `login-user.jsp`. Click the **Resume** button in the debugger to allow execution to proceed. `login-user.jsp` is displayed in

the Web browser, with the error message prompting the user to enter a user id (see Figure 3.24).

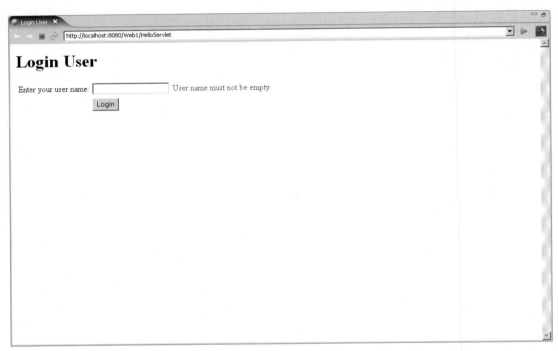

Figure 3.24   Web Browser—login-user.jsp

4. Do a little testing now. If you click on the Login button, control is passed back to the servlet, which generates the error message again and forwards the request back to `login-user.jsp`. This time enter a user id and click Login. Now the servlet forwards control to `hello-world.jsp`.

Summary of Iteration 2

In this iteration you created and debugged a servlet that controlled the presentation logic of your Web application. For simple Web applications, you can code this logic manually. However, for complex applications, you should consider using a Web application framework, such as JSF, Struts, or Spring MVC.

In Struts, the control flow logic is externalized into an XML configuration file so that you can easily modify it. Struts also provides a framework for many common Web application programming tasks, such as parameter passing and error handling. Although Struts enjoys widespread popularity among Java Web application developers, it is not part of J2EE. The ideas behind Struts have been standardized in JSR 127: Java ServerFaces, which is now part of Java EE 5. WTP 1.5 includes the JavaServer Faces Tools incubator subproject, which will become a component of JST in WTP 2.0.

Iteration 3: Database Access

Virtually every Web application takes input from users and stores it on the server. Relational databases are by far the most popular technology for storing data. XML promises to become another popular storage format since it is more convenient for semi-structured data than relational tables. In fact, relational databases are now being updated to store and query XML data. XML data can be queried using SQL extensions, XPath, XSLT, and the new XML query language, XQuery. We'll discuss XML more later in Chapters 7 and 10, but for now we'll focus on relational databases.

You'll extend your Web application by adding some very simple database access. Rather than greet users by their user id, you'll update your application to greet users by their full names. You'll create a relational database to store a table of full names, and you'll develop a Java class to access the database using JDBC. You'll develop the SQL query using the Data tools in WTP.

The Data tools in WTP use JDBC to access databases. WTP has out-of-the-box support for many databases and, with a little Eclipse plug-in development effort, others can be added. Virtually all databases have JDBC drivers, so you have lots of choices available, but for purposes of illustration you'll use Apache Derby. Derby is very suitable for development with WTP because it is Open Source, pure Java, and can be embedded easily in Web applications. If you have another supported database already installed, feel free to use it. Just modify the following instructions accordingly.

Getting Derby

If you'd like to use Derby, download it from

```
http://db.apache.org/derby/derby_downloads.html
```

The Derby project has packaged the code as an Eclipse plug-in, so download that and install it in your Eclipse directory. We use version 10.1.2.1 here. You can download the zip file

```
derby_core_plugin_10.1.2.zip
```

from

```
http://apache.mirror99.com/db/derby/db-derby-10.1.2.1/
```

To install Derby, exit from Eclipse, unzip the plug-in into your **eclipse** installation directory (see Figure 3.25), and then restart Eclipse. Note that when you exit Eclipse, WTP will automatically stop any of your running servers.

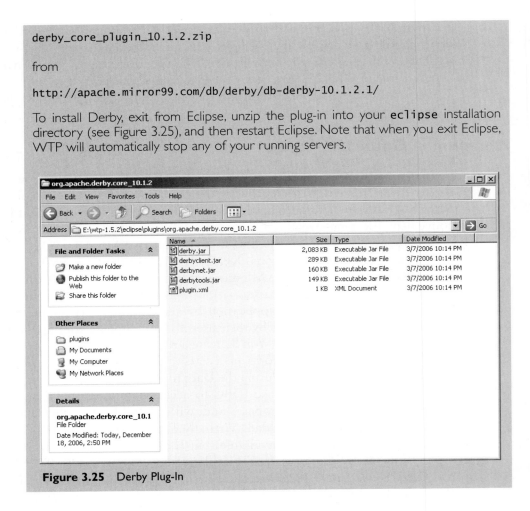

Figure 3.25   Derby Plug-In

You'll perform the following development tasks in this iteration:

1. Connect to a Database.

2. Execute SQL Statements.

3. Add Database Access to a Web Application.

   Refer to Chapter 9 for more detail.

Connect to a Database

Add a database connection to your project as follows:

1. WTP provides two views for working with databases: **Database Explorer** and **Data Output**. The **Database Explorer** view lets you connect to databases and examine their contents. The **Data Output** view lets you see the results of executing SQL statements on a database. Add these views to the J2EE perspective as follows:

    a. Invoke the **Window ▸ Show View ▸ Other** command from the menu bar to open the **Show View** dialog.

    b. Expand the **Data** category (see Figure 3.26), select the **Database Explorer** and **Data Output** views, and click the **OK** button.

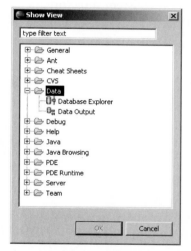

Figure 3.26 Show View—Data Views

2. WTP adds these views to the **J2EE** perspective (see Figure 3.27). Feel free to rearrange these views according to your personal tastes.

3. To work with a database, you need to add a new connection to the **Database Explorer** view. In the **Database Explorer** view, select the **Connections** folder, right click, and invoke the **New Connection** command from the context menu. This opens the **New Connection** wizard. Create a new connection to Derby as follows:

    a. Select **Derby 10.1** as the database manager.

    b. Select **Derby Embedded JDBC Driver** as the JDBC driver.

    c. Enter a convenient directory, for example, c:\web1db, as the **Database location**. This should either be a nonexistent directory or a directory that contains a previously created Derby database. If the directory is nonexistent, make sure that the **Create the database if required** checkbox is checked. To delete a Derby database, simply delete its directory.

Enter the location of `derby.jar` as the **Class location.** If you installed the Derby plug-in (see Figure 3.25 in the previous sidebar), then `derby.jar` is located in the `plugins` directory in the

`org.apache.derby.core`

directory.

Click the **Test Connection** button to verify that your connection is configured correctly. If you specified a nonexistent directory, then testing the connection will create the database (see Figure 3.28).

Click the **Finish** button to create the connection.

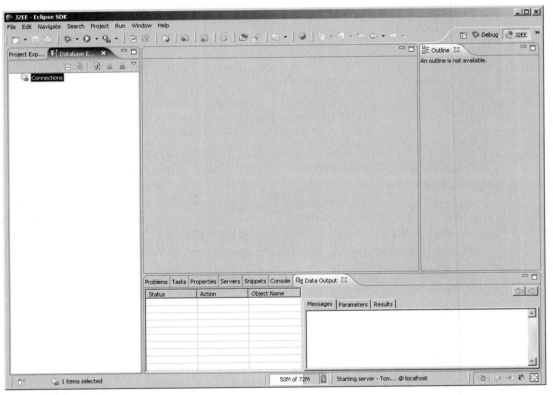

Figure 3.27 J2EE Perspective with Data Views

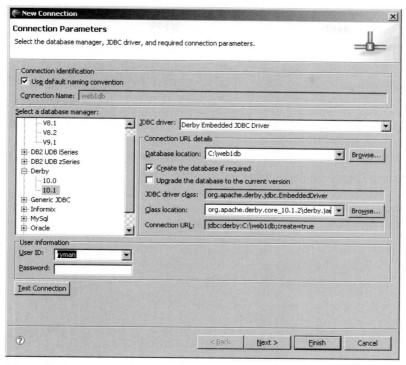

Figure 3.28 New Connection Wizard

4. When the **New Connection** wizard completes, a new connection appears in the **Database Explorer** view. You can now explore the database by expanding the connection to see its schemas, tables, columns, and other database components. You can view the contents of a table as follows: Select a table and invoke the **Data ▸ Sample Contents** command from the context menu. The contents of the table will appear in the **Data Output** view. You're now ready to create a table for your Web application and populate it with some data.

Execute SQL Statements

WTP lets you interactively execute SQL statements in a database using the SQL Scrapbook editor. The **SQL Scrapbook** editor is associated with files that have extension `*.sqlpage`. Do the following to execute some SQL statements:

1. Open the **SQL Scrapbook** editor on a new page by clicking the **Open SQL Scrapbook** icon 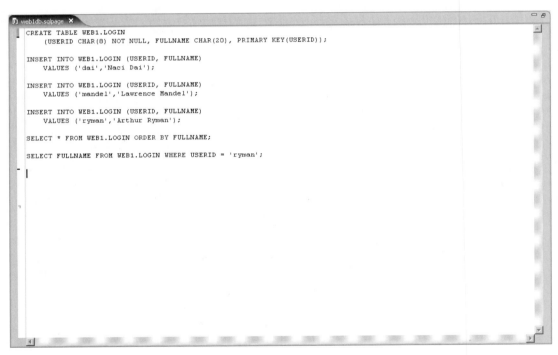 in the **Database Explorer** view. When prompted, create the new SQL scrapbook page in the web1 directory, give it the name web1db, and associate it with the web1db connection you previously created.

   Note that you can also open the editor by running the **New** wizard and selecting the **SQL Scrapbook Page** file type from the **Data** category.

2. Enter the SQL statements as shown in the editor (see Figure 3.29). These statements create a table, populate it with three rows of data, and query it. The last query is what you'll use in your Web application to look up the full name for a given user id.

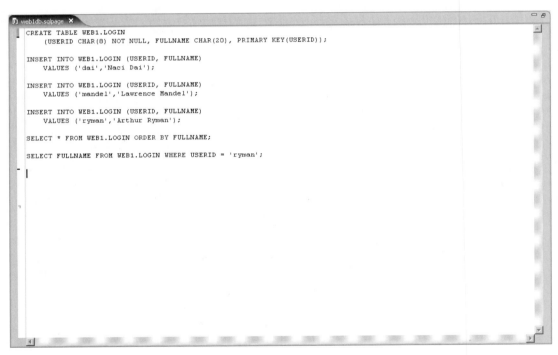

```
web1db.sqlpage  X
CREATE TABLE WEB1.LOGIN
    (USERID CHAR(8) NOT NULL, FULLNAME CHAR(20), PRIMARY KEY(USERID));

INSERT INTO WEB1.LOGIN (USERID, FULLNAME)
    VALUES ('dai','Naci Dai');

INSERT INTO WEB1.LOGIN (USERID, FULLNAME)
    VALUES ('mandel','Lawrence Mandel');

INSERT INTO WEB1.LOGIN (USERID, FULLNAME)
    VALUES ('ryman','Arthur Ryman');

SELECT * FROM WEB1.LOGIN ORDER BY FULLNAME;

SELECT FULLNAME FROM WEB1.LOGIN WHERE USERID = 'ryman';
```

Figure 3.29   SQL Editor—web1db.sqlpage

Note that SQL scrapbook pages are actually XML files. They contain the database connection information as well as the SQL statements that are wrapped in a CDATA section (see Example 3.4). If you see the XML tags when editing, then you have not opened the file in the SQL editor. To remedy this, simply close the editor and reopen the page with the SQL editor.

Example 3.4 Listing of web1db.sqlpage

```
<?xml version="1.0" encoding="UTF-8"?>
<SQLPage nameConnection="web1db">
<Statement><![CDATA[CREATE TABLE WEB1.LOGIN
  (USERID CHAR(8) NOT NULL, FULLNAME CHAR(20), PRIMARY KEY(USERID));

INSERT INTO WEB1.LOGIN (USERID, FULLNAME)
  VALUES ('dai','Naci Dai');

INSERT INTO WEB1.LOGIN (USERID, FULLNAME)
  VALUES ('mandel','Lawrence Mandel');

INSERT INTO WEB1.LOGIN (USERID, FULLNAME)
  VALUES ('ryman','Arthur Ryman');

SELECT * FROM WEB1.LOGIN ORDER BY FULLNAME;

SELECT FULLNAME FROM WEB1.LOGIN WHERE USERID = 'ryman';

]]></Statement>
</SQLPage>
```

3. In the **SQL Scrapbook** editor, click anywhere and execute all the statements by invoking the **Run SQL** command from the context menu. You can also execute individual statements by selecting them and invoking the command. Note that the statements are delimited by the semicolon character. You can change this using a menu command. When each statement is executed, an entry is made in the **Data Output** view. For the SELECT statement, you can view the result set by clicking on the **Results** tab (see Figure 3.30).

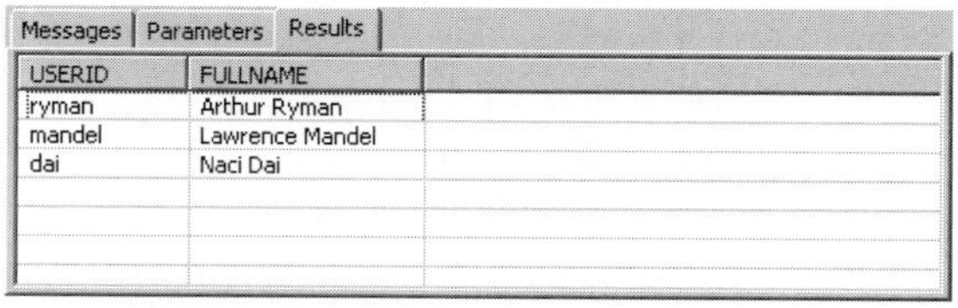

Figure 3.30 Data Output View Results Tab

4. You have now created and populated the database, and executed some queries against it. You are ready to add the lookup query to your Web application.

Before proceeding, you need to disconnect from the Derby database. Select the web1db connection in the **Database Explorer** view and invoke the **Disconnect** command from the context menu. This cleanly shuts down the connection and lets other applications connect to the Derby database.

Disconnect Derby from Data Tools

Derby only supports connections from one process at a time. The Data tools establish a connection to the Derby database, and this locks out the Web application from concurrently connecting to it. Be sure to disconnect from Derby when you are finished using the Data tools so you can access Derby from your Web application.

Add Database Access to a Web Application

In order to add database access to your Web application you need to make the database driver available to it. Do the following to add Derby access to your Web application:

1. The simplest way to add Derby access to a Web application is to copy `derby.jar` into the `WEB-INF/lib` directory. The `WEB-INF/lib` directory of a J2EE Web application is precisely intended to hold any JAR files that the application needs. Copy `derby.jar` into `WEB-INF/lib` now.

Using Derby with Multiple Web Applications

Although this technique for adding Derby support is simple, it is limited to cases where only one Web application needs Derby access. If more than one application needs Derby access, Derby must be configured differently. In that case a shared copy of Derby must be used, and it must be initialized and shut down properly by Tomcat. Refer to the tutorial *Apache Derby Fortune Server Tutorial* [Anderson2006] by Jean Anderson or the article *Integrating Cloudscape and Tomcat* [Bader2004] by Lance Bader for instructions on how to configure a shared copy of the database.

2. You'll add the lookup query to your Web application by creating a new Java class, `Database.java`. Create a new Java class in the same package as `HelloServlet` and enter its code (see Example 3.5). When entering this code, be sure to update the database connection URL string

   ```
   "jdbc:derby:C:\\web1db"
   ```

   to match the location of your database.

Example 3.5   Listing of Database.java

```
package org.example.ch03;

import java.sql.Connection;
import java.sql.DriverManager;
```

```java
import java.sql.PreparedStatement;
import java.sql.ResultSet;
import java.sql.SQLException;

public class Database {

  /**
   * Looks up the full name of a user in the database.
   *
   * @param userid
   *            the user id string
   * @return the full name string
   * @throws SQLException
   *             if a database problem occurs
   */
  public String lookupFullname(String userid) throws SQLException {

    Connection connection = null;
    PreparedStatement statement = null;
    ResultSet resultset = null;
    String fullname = "";
    String DRIVER = "org.apache.derby.jdbc.EmbeddedDriver";
    String URL = "jdbc:derby:C:\\web1db";
    String QUERY = "SELECT FULLNAME FROM WEB1.LOGIN WHERE USERID = ?";

    try {
      Class.forName(DRIVER);
      connection = DriverManager.getConnection(URL);
      statement = connection.prepareStatement();
      statement.setString(1, userid);
      resultset = statement.executeQuery(QUERY);

      if (resultset.next())
        fullname = resultset.getString("FULLNAME").trim();

    } catch (Exception e) {
      e.printStackTrace();
    } finally {

      if (resultset != null)
        resultset.close();

      if (statement != null)
        statement.close();

      if (connection != null)
        connection.close();
    }

    return fullname;
  }
}
```

The Database class has a single method, lookupFullname, that takes the user id as input and returns the full name as output. This method performs direct database access using JDBC calls.

In general, the business logic of your application should not directly access the database since that makes maintenance difficult. Here the Database class is the data access layer that isolates the rest of the application from the details of the database.

However, JDBC is a low-level API, and its use is error prone. It is preferable to use a higher-level persistence framework such as Java Persistence API (JPA), Hibernate, JDO, or Entity EJBs. JDBC is used here for simplicity and purposes of illustration.

3. Now modify your Web application to use the Database class. Update HelloServlet to call the Database class and add the full name to the request (see Example 3.6, which has modified lines in bold font).

Example 3.6   Listing of Modified HelloServlet.java

```java
package org.example.ch03;

import java.io.IOException;
import java.sql.SQLException;

import javax.servlet.RequestDispatcher;
import javax.servlet.ServletContext;
import javax.servlet.ServletException;
import javax.servlet.http.HttpServletRequest;
import javax.servlet.http.HttpServletResponse;

/**
 * Servlet implementation class for Servlet: HelloServlet
 *
 */
public class HelloServlet extends javax.servlet.http.HttpServlet implements
    javax.servlet.Servlet {
    .
    .
    .
    protected void doGet(HttpServletRequest request,
        HttpServletResponse response) throws ServletException, IOException {

        String url = "/hello-world.jsp";

        String user = request.getParameter("user");
        if (user == null || user.length() == 0) {
            url = "/login-user.jsp";
            request.setAttribute("error", "User name must not be empty.");
        } else {
            try {
```

```
            String fullname = new Database().lookupFullname(user);
            request.setAttribute("fullname", fullname);
        } catch (SQLException e) {
            e.printStackTrace();
        }
    }

    ServletContext context = getServletContext();
    RequestDispatcher dispatcher = context.getRequestDispatcher(url);
    dispatcher.forward(request, response);
  }
}
```

4. Finally, modify hello-world.jsp to display the full name. Add the scriptlet (see Example 3.7; modified lines are in bold font). Here the scriptlet checks for the presence of an attribute named fullname in the request. If the attribute is present, it is displayed to the user.

Example 3.7   Listing of Modified hello-world.jsp

```
<!DOCTYPE HTML PUBLIC "-//W3C//DTD HTML 4.01 Transitional//EN">
<html>
<head>
<%@ page language="java" contentType="text/html; charset=ISO-8859-1"
    pageEncoding="ISO-8859-1"%>
<meta http-equiv="Content-Type" content="text/html; charset=ISO-8859-1">
<title>Hello, world</title>
</head>
<body>
<h1>Hello, world.</h1>
<%
    String person = "?";

    String user = request.getParameter("user");
    if (user != null) person = user;

    Object fullname = request.getAttribute("fullname");
    if (fullname != null) person = fullname.toString();
%>

Welcome to WTP, <%= person %>!

</body>
</html>
```

5. With these modifications, you're ready to run the application. Select login-user.jsp and run it on the server. Enter one of the defined user ids, for example, ryman, click the **Login** button, and verify that the correct full name, for example, Arthur Ryman, is displayed (see Figure 3.31).

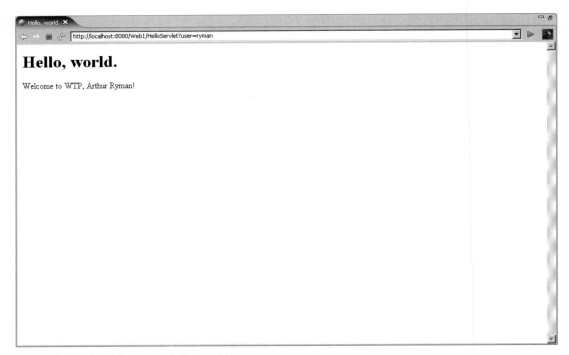

Figure 3.31   Web Browser—hello-world.jsp

Summary of Iteration 3

In this iteration you added the Data tools views to your perspective, created a connection to the Derby database, used the SQL Scrapbook to interactively execute SQL statements and view the results, created a Java class to access the database using JDBC, and added this class into your Web application to look up user names.

Although JDBC access was used here, you should consider using a persistence framework, such as JPA, in your Web application. WTP 1.5 includes the Dali JPA Tools incubator subproject, which will become a component of JST in WTP 2.0.

Iteration 4: Web Services

Web services are a way to let your Web application become integrated into other applications. The topic of Web services is covered in much more detail in Chapter 10. A brief discussion is given here.

Web services are like ordinary Web pages except that instead of HTML, Web services return pure data in XML and other formats so other applications can use it. Web services often use SOAP to format and process messages. The capabilities of a Web service are described by a WSDL document that software toolkits can process, typically to generate client access code. J2EE contains Web services specifications such as *JSR 101: Java APIs for XML-based RPC (JAXRPC)* [JSR101] and *JSR 109: Implementing Enterprise Web Services* [JSR109].

You'll conclude the development of your Web application by deploying the Database class as a Web service. This will let other applications programmatically get the full name of a user, given their user id. WTP contains a very complete set of extensible Web service tools. You'll use the **Web Service** wizard to deploy the Web service, generate a client proxy for it, create a JSP test client application that uses the proxy, and set up a TCP/IP monitor so you can view the SOAP traffic that flows between the client and service. The **Web Service** wizard performs all these tasks for you without requiring you to write any code.

Deploying a Web service requires that a suitable Web service runtime, sometimes referred to as a *SOAP engine*, be available for your application server. WTP comes with out-of-the-box support for Apache Axis 1.3 and will support Axis2 1.0 in the future. Axis is very suitable for development with WTP because it is an Open Source, pure Java, lightweight SOAP engine that works well with Tomcat and that implements JAX-RPC. However, the **Web Service** wizard is extensible, so with a little plug-in development work, other SOAP engines can be added.

You'll perform the following development tasks in this iteration:

1. Deploy a Web service.

2. Use a Test Client.

3. Monitor SOAP Messages.

Refer to Chapter 10 for more detail.

Deploy a Web Service

Do the following to deploy your Java class as a Web service:

1. Deploying your Java class as a Web service is simple. Just select Database.java and invoke the **Web Services ▸ Create Web service** command from the context menu. This opens the **Web Service** wizard (see Figure 3.32).

   The **Web Service** wizard is very powerful and extensible. It brings together many of the tasks you normally perform in the course of Web service development.

   The wizard has two sliders. The top one controls the service and the bottom one the client. Both the service and client are deployed as Web applications. When you create a service, you often also want to test it using a client, so you use both sliders. When you want to access a service that was previously created, you just use the bottom slider.

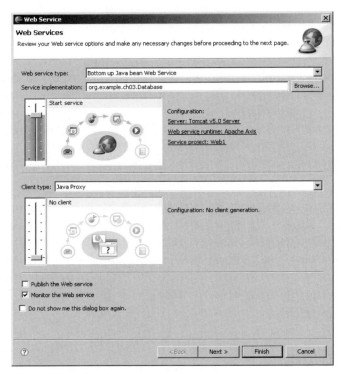

Figure 3.32   Web Service Wizard

The wizard also lets you set up a monitor that sits between the service and the client and records the message traffic between them. This is handy when you are trying to understand what the service is sending or if you want to test it for compliance with a Web Service Interoperability (WS-I) profile. Finally, the wizard lets you publish a service to a UDDI registry. Refer to Chapter 10 for more detail.

Since you opened the wizard by selecting a Java class, the wizard is set to perform the **Bottom up Java Bean Web Service** scenario. The term *bottom up* describes the development approach where you start with an implementation class and deploy it as a Web service. In this approach, the WSDL for the service is automatically generated from the implementation class. The term *top down* describes the approach of designing the WSDL first and generating the skeleton of an implementation class from it. Designing the WSDL first also requires that you have some skill with XML Schema, but the extra effort can result in much cleaner and interoperable Web services. As you might guess, the wizard also supports the top-down approach. Both the bottom-up and top-down approaches can be used with ordinary Java classes or EJBs.

2. You will now use the wizard to deploy the Java class as a Web service, generate a Java client proxy to access it, generate a JSP test client application to exercise the client proxy, and monitor the SOAP messages.

The wizard lets you set up both a service and a client, each of which goes through a life cycle consisting of these steps: *develop, assemble, deploy, install,* and *test.* Sliders let you control how many of these steps the wizard performs. The wizard also lets you optionally publish the service to a registry and monitor its message traffic.

Move the service slider to its topmost position (**Test service**). This starts the application server after the Web service is deployed, making it ready to handle requests.

Move the client slider to its topmost position (**Test client**). This generates a Java client proxy and a JSP test client application, deploys it, and starts it, making it ready to send requests.

Check the **Monitor the Web service** checkbox. This configures and starts a TCP/IP monitor since we want to monitor the SOAP messages. This option also configures the JSP test client to send requests to the TCP/IP monitor, which then forwards them to the Web service.

Click the **Finish** button. The wizard is smart enough to do all the right things.

If you are really curious about the steps that the wizard performs, then click the **Next** button instead of **Finish** and look at all the pages that comprise the wizard.

The wizard does a lot of work for you. It installs the SOAP engine, for example, Axis 1.3, in the application if this is the first Web service you are deploying. The SOAP engine is responsible for sending and receiving XML messages over HTTP, and converting them into calls on your Java objects. Installation of the SOAP engine involves copying the required JAR files into the Web module and updating the Web deployment descriptor with entries for servlets that handle both Web service requests and administration.

The wizard generates a WSDL file that describes the Web service, and then generates and updates all the configuration files. The wizard starts or restarts the application server to complete the deployment step. At this point you have a running Web service. The next step is to generate client code to access it.

The wizard next creates a new project for the client Web application and generates a Java client proxy from the WSDL. Using a separate project for the client application is highly advisable since you probably don't want to deploy the test client along with the Web service. Also, using a separate project avoids potential name conflicts between the generated client code and the Web service code. The wizard then generates a JSP test client application that accesses the Web service using the client proxy. This client application is mainly for test purposes, but you can also look at the generated code for examples of how to invoke Web services using the client proxy.

The wizard configures and starts a TCP/IP monitor to forward requests to and responses from the Web service. The TCP/IP monitor therefore behaves just like the Web service, but in addition it captures the SOAP messages and presents them in a handy view. The wizard configures the JSP test client to use the URL of the monitor instead of the Web service. Finally, the wizard runs the test client so you can begin exercising the Web service.

Use a Test Client

The test client is created in the web1Client Web project. It consists of a set of generated JSP pages that use a Java proxy to access the Web service. Unlike the general-purpose **Web Service Explorer** tool provided by WTP, it is designed specifically to test the Web service you just created. Do the following to test your Web service:

1. WTP opens the generated JSP test client application in a Web browser (see Figure 3.33). The test client lists all the operations in the Web service in the **Methods** frame on the left-hand side of the Web browser. The test client also lets you view and modify the URL of the Web service endpoint using the getEndpoint and setEndpoint methods.

2. Your Web service has a single operation, lookupFullname, which takes as input a user id and returns as output the user's full name. Click the lookupFullname link to open an input form in the **Inputs** frame in the top right corner of the Web browser. Enter a valid user id, ryman for example, and click the **Invoke** button. This sends the user id in a SOAP request message to the Web service. The test client receives the SOAP response message and displays the result in the **Results** frame at the bottom right corner of the Web browser.

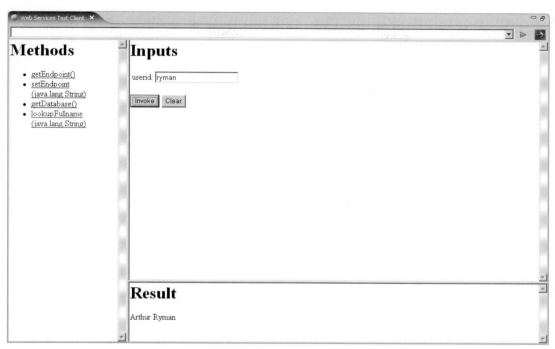

Figure 3.33 Web Browser—TestClient.jsp

Monitor SOAP Messages

Do the following to monitor the SOAP messages:

1. When you invoked the `lookupFullname` operation, the request and response were captured and displayed by the TCP/IP monitor (see Figure 3.34). The TCP/IP monitor can be used to display general HTTP traffic in addition to Web services. Web services use XML for both requests and responses, so select **XML** from the drop-down menus. You can see the SOAP message envelopes used to send the user id and return the full name. The TCP/IP monitor normally filters out the HTTP headers, but these can be displayed by selecting **Headers** from the drop-down menu at the top right corner of the view.

2. Invoke the `lookupFullname` operation a few more times to generate more messages in the TCP/IP monitor. Feel free to experiment with the other options in the **TCP/IP Monitor** view.

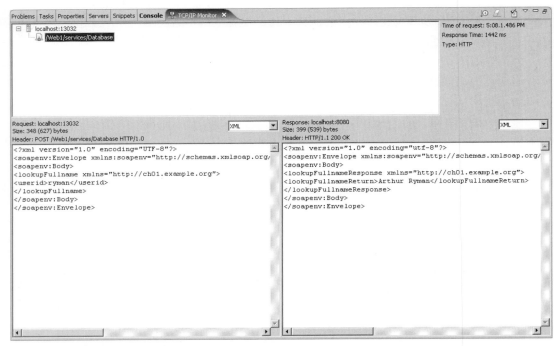

Figure 3.34   TCP/IP Monitor View

Summary of Iteration 4

In this iteration, you used the **Web Service** wizard to deploy your Java class as a Web service. The wizard also generated a JSP test client and set up a TCP/IP monitor for the SOAP messages. You used the test client to exercise the Web service and viewed the SOAP messages in the TCP/IP monitor.

Summary

In this chapter you were given a brief introduction to WTP and then dove right in to using it. You learned how to download and install WTP. You then took a Quick Tour through many of its key areas. You created and debugged a simple "Hello, world" JSP page, added a login servlet for it, accessed a database to look up user names, and then deployed the lookup class as a Web service.

This formally concludes the Quick Tour. By now you should be starting to feel comfortable with WTP. You might even feel confident enough to start developing your own Web applications without reading any further. If this describes you, then we encourage you to dive in and start kicking the tires. In an ideal world, the user interface and online Help in WTP would be so easy to use that no one would need to read a book about it. However, the reality is that Java Web application development is a very rich subject and WTP is a very capable environment, so we're sure you'll get a lot of benefit from reading the rest of this book.

The following chapters will explore WTP in more detail. If you are new to Java Web application development, you'll find some valuable guidance about architecture and project organization. And if you are interested in extending WTP with some new tools, you'll find helpful tips and examples about that too. The chapters do follow a logical progression, but they do not have to be read sequentially. Feel free to read them in any order.

We hope you find WTP to be a valuable addition to your toolbox. However, we acknowledge that WTP is a relatively new project and there is still much work to be done to bring it up to the high standards of other Eclipse projects. Remember that WTP is an Open Source project and that it relies on the contributions of its user community to make it better. We are especially interested in your contributions. As you use WTP and read this book, please seriously consider becoming a contributor. We discussed how you can contribute to WTP previously (see the Contributing to WTP section in Chapter 2).

CHAPTER 4

Setting Up Your Workspace

There is a third option!

—The Cat in the Hat–The Movie

An Eclipse workspace is where you keep your development resources and settings. Your resources are organized into projects. Your settings provide configuration information and options that control the way the tools work. Some settings are global to the workspace while others are scoped to individual projects.

A WTP workspace contains Web projects that contain static resources such as HTML, CSS, JavaScript, and XML files, and dynamic resources such as JSP, servlet, and EJB components, and their deployment descriptors. A WTP workspace also contains settings such as server runtime environment definitions, server configurations, and options for the many WTP tools.

Preparing a workspace is your first task in starting to use WTP. If you took the Quick Tour (see Chapter 3), you have already performed many of the steps required to set up your workspace. However, in the Quick Tour, you only did enough setup to get started. In this chapter we go into more depth about how to install, update, and configure WTP. Consult the WTP online Help for the full details.

Installing and Updating WTP

Obviously, you have to install WTP before you can use it, and since it is being continually improved you'll want to keep it up-to-date (see Getting Eclipse and WTP in Chapter 3 for a quick introduction to this topic). Although you can accomplish this task easily, it will help you to have a basic understanding of what goes into WTP.

The Installable Components of WTP

This section looks at WTP from the installation point of view. For the architectural view of WTP, refer to The Structure of WTP section in Chapter 2. WTP consists of the following installable components:

○ *Java Development Kit (JDK)*. Eclipse is a Java application, so you need to install a JDK. Technically, you only need a Java Runtime Environment (JRE), but since you will also probably be developing JSPs you should install a JDK. See the Getting a JDK sidebar in Chapter 3 for more information.

○ *Eclipse Platform*. WTP is a set of Eclipse features and plug-ins, so you need to install Eclipse.

○ *Prerequisite Eclipse Features*. WTP requires features from the following Eclipse projects:

   ○ *Eclipse Modeling Framework (EMF)*. WTP uses EMF to model J2EE deployment descriptors, relational databases, and other objects.

   ○ *Graphical Editing Framework (GEF)*. WTP uses GEF in its graphical XSD and WSDL editors.

   ○ *Java Edit Model (JEM)*. WTP uses JEM in its JSP editor. JEM provides an EMF model for Java code. JEM was developed as part of the Eclipse Visual Editor (VE) project. Starting with WTP 2.0, JEM will move to WTP.

○ *WTP Features*. WTP consists of Eclipse features and plug-ins. Its main features are Web Standard Tools (WST) and J2EE Standard Tools (JST). At a minimum, you need to install WST. JST requires WST. WTP also has incubating features for JavaServer Faces (JSF), Java Persistence (Dali), and AJAX (ATF). Both JSF and Dali require JST. ATF is independent of J2EE, so it only requires WST.

○ *Optional Third-Party Content (3PC)*. WTP includes optional support for many other third-party products, such as Tomcat, Derby, and XDoclet, but does not redistribute them. To use this support you must acquire and install these products (see the Getting Tomcat and Getting Derby sidebars in Chapter 3 for some quick pointers).

○ *WTP Extensions*. WTP is a platform and defines many extension points that other products can build on. These range from additional server adapters to complete commercial IDEs. See Chapter 16 for a discussion of products built on WTP. To round out your installation, you may want to install some of these. Most of the commercial IDEs built on WTP bundle together many of the components you need, so the installation process is greatly simplified.

WTP Build Types

There are two main approaches to installing and updating WTP. You can use the Eclipse Update Manager, or you can directly download and unzip files from the

Eclipse Web site. Note that although the following discussion refers to the Windows *zip* format, everything applies equally to the *tar* format that WTP provides for Linux and Mac OS X systems.

In practice, you will use a combination of these approaches, since to use Update Manager you need to start with a base Eclipse installation. You create the initial installation by downloading zip files. And even if you completely installed WTP from zip files, you might want to get the latest maintenance updates via the Update Manager.

There is also another pragmatic consideration when deciding which approach to use. The Update Manager is typically only refreshed with official releases, whereas the zip files are created continuously. This means that if you need to test a fix during development, you'll have to download the zip files. This leads us into a discussion of the WTP build types and how they affect your installation choices. The WTP downloads page lists the downloads by build type (see Figure 4.1).

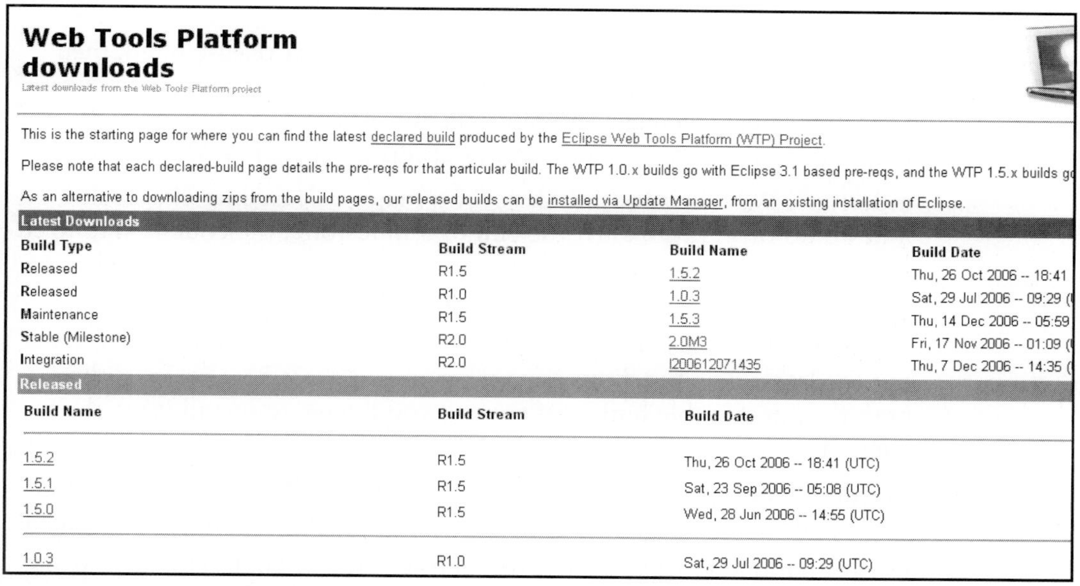

Web Tools Platform downloads
Latest downloads from the Web Tools Platform project

This is the starting page for where you can find the latest <u>declared build</u> produced by the <u>Eclipse Web Tools Platform (WTP) Project</u>.

Please note that each declared-build page details the pre-reqs for that particular build. The WTP 1.0.x builds go with Eclipse 3.1 based pre-reqs, and the WTP 1.5.x builds g̶

As an alternative to downloading zips from the build pages, our released builds can be <u>installed via Update Manager</u>, from an existing installation of Eclipse.

Latest Downloads

Build Type	Build Stream	Build Name	Build Date
Released	R1.5	1.5.2	Thu, 26 Oct 2006 -- 18:41
Released	R1.0	1.0.3	Sat, 29 Jul 2006 -- 09:29 (
Maintenance	R1.5	1.5.3	Thu, 14 Dec 2006 -- 05:59
Stable (Milestone)	R2.0	2.0M3	Fri, 17 Nov 2006 -- 01:09 (
Integration	R2.0	I200612071435	Thu, 7 Dec 2006 -- 14:35 (

Released

Build Name	Build Stream	Build Date
1.5.2	R1.5	Thu, 26 Oct 2006 -- 18:41 (UTC)
1.5.1	R1.5	Sat, 23 Sep 2006 -- 05:08 (UTC)
1.5.0	R1.5	Wed, 28 Jun 2006 -- 14:55 (UTC)
1.0.3	R1.0	Sat, 29 Jul 2006 -- 09:29 (UTC)

Figure 4.1   Web Tools Platform Downloads

Like most Eclipse projects, WTP produces the following types of builds:

○ *Release* builds (or R-builds) are fully tested and ready for use in day-to-day work by Java Web application developers. Major releases are typically built annually and are made available at the same time as major Eclipse releases. For example, WTP 1.5 was made available with Eclipse 3.2 as part of the

Callisto simultaneous release of ten Eclipse projects (Callisto was the first simultaneous release of Eclipse). Major releases introduce new functions and APIs.

Minor releases are made available more frequently and only include bug fixes. They are typically made available at the same time as Eclipse minor releases. For example, WTP 1.5.1 was released with Eclipse 3.2.1. Minor releases are also referred to as maintenance releases, not to be confused with maintenance builds.

From an installation point of view, release builds give you the most options. You can obtain release builds via Update Manager or zip files. In fact, release builds are also packaged as convenient *all-in-one* zips, which include the Eclipse platform, the prerequisite Eclipse features, and WTP itself.

❍ *Maintenance* builds (or M-builds) are tested versions of minor releases. They incorporate the latest available fixes and are a step on the road toward an official minor release build.

If you urgently need a fix and can't wait for the next release build, then install the latest maintenance build by downloading the component zips. Sorry, no Update Manager or all-in-one for these.

❍ *Stable* builds (or S-builds) are tested builds produced at the end of a milestone. WTP divides the work for a major release into six-week-long milestones or iterations. At the end of a milestone, the code is stabilized so that other projects can pick it up and use it as the base for their next iteration.

Stable builds are also of interest to adventurous users who want to try out the latest new functions. If you are one of these heat seekers, then grab the latest stable build. Of course, you'll have to install it via the component zips.

❍ *Integration* builds (or I-builds) are produced weekly. They are *smoke tested*, which essentially means that they won't burst into flames when you use them.

Integration builds are primarily of interest to the WTP development team, which is itself divided into component development teams. The integration builds are a way for all the component development teams to catch up with each other and get on a common code base for the coming week. These are only made available in component zips.

❍ *Nightly* builds (or N-builds) are produced continuously and are more properly called *continuous* builds. Unlike the other build types, which are produced via map files that point to officially released versions of the code, continuous builds are produced from the latest committed code, that is, from CVS HEAD.

Continuous builds are mainly of interest to WTP committers and early testers who want to work with code that is under active development. This code is only guaranteed to build. It may actually burst into flames when executed. These builds are only made available as component zips.

Installation via Update Manager

Installation via the Update Manager is the recommended way to get WTP releases. The Update Manager will install WTP and all its prerequisite plug-ins and features with minimal effort on your part. Update Manager will also update existing installations to new releases. However, to use the Update Manager you need an existing installation of Eclipse and a functioning Internet connection.

Do the following to install WTP via the Update Manager:

1. Invoke the Help ▸ Software Updates ▸ Find and Install command from the menu bar.
2. The Install/Update wizard opens. Select the Search for new features to install radio button (see Figure 4.2). Click the Next button.

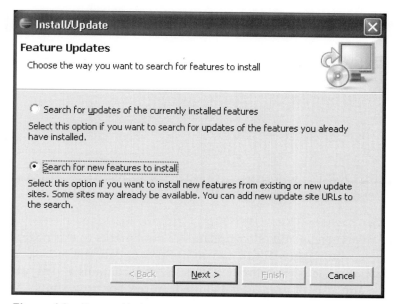

Figure 4.2   Feature Updates

3. The Install page is displayed. WTP updates are available as part of Callisto, the first coordinated release of Eclipse projects. Select the **Callisto Discovery Site** (see Figure 4.3).

> **Note:** Future coordinated Eclipse releases will likely have their own unique names. The upcoming coordinated release is named Europa. Upon the release of Europa, the latest discovery site name will likely change to something like Europa Discovery Site.

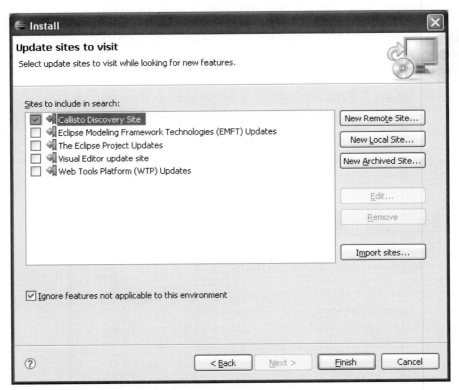

Figure 4.3   Update Sites to Visit

4. Note that you can add other update site bookmarks to this page. For example, you might want to add an intranet update site mirror. An Eclipse Update Manager site is simply a Web site that contains a `site.xml` descriptor file and a set of installable Eclipse features. For now, simply click the **Finish** button to search the Callisto site.

5. The **Updates** page is displayed. Expand the **Callisto Discovery Site** item, then expand and select its **Web and J2EE Development** item, where WTP is located. Note that it is also possible to select a subitem such as the **Web Standard Tools**. An error message is displayed indicating that the selected features require other features. In this case the message tells us that WST requires GEF (see Figure 4.4).

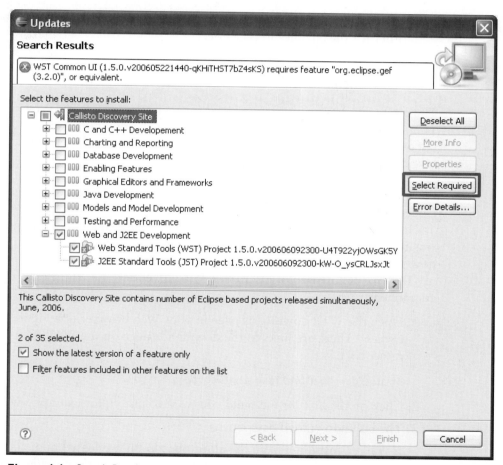

Figure 4.4   Search Results

6. Click the **Select Required** button. This will select prerequisite features such as EMF, GEF, and JEM if they have not been installed already. Click **Next** to proceed with the installation.

7. The Update Manager displays the licenses of each selected feature. Review the license agreements and accept the terms if you agree to them. Do not proceed to download the features if the license terms are not acceptable to you.

8. Next, choose the install location for the features. Click **Finish** to begin the download.

9. Once the download and installation is complete, a confirmation prompt will be displayed. You will be advised to exit and restart the workbench in order for the changes to take effect.

Installation via Zip Files

The alternative to using the Update Manager is to install WTP from zip files. This involves selecting the desired build from the downloads page, downloading one of the WTP distributions and its prerequisites, and then extracting them to a directory.

This method is prone to human error, but it is the only way to get any build other than a release build. Recall that only the release builds are published on an Update Manager site.

In the early days of WTP, users complained that installing the component zips was too difficult. To address this concern, all-in-one zips were created. These are now provided for the release builds along with the Update Manager alternative.

Do the following to install WTP from either the all-in-one zip or the component zips:

1. Open the WTP downloads page in your Web browser (see Figure 4.1 earlier). There are links to the downloads page on the WTP Web site. The direct URL is

   `http://download.eclipse.org/webtools`

2. Click on the link for the build you want to install, for example, WTP 1.5.2.

3. The build download page opens.

   If you are installing from the all-in-one zip for a release build, click on the link for your desired operating system. WTP currently provides all-in-one zips for Windows, Linux, and Mac OS X. For example, the link for the WTP 1.5.2 Windows all-in-one zip is labeled

   `wtp-all-in-one-sdk-R-1.5.2-200610261841-win32.zip`

Otherwise, download all the required component zips to some convenient directory. The complete list of requirements is given on the WTP build download page (see Figure 4.5). Typically this list contains the Eclipse SDK, as well as the Eclipse EMF, GEF, and JEM project distributions. Of course, a WTP distribution is also needed, so download that too.

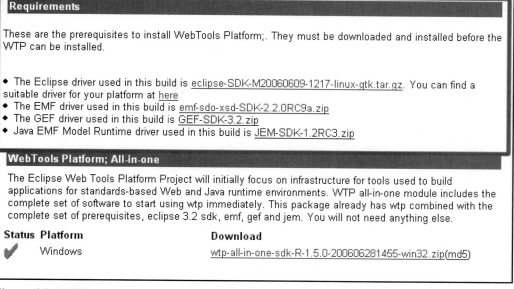

Requirements

These are the prerequisites to install WebTools Platform;. They must be downloaded and installed before the WTP can be installed.

* The Eclipse driver used in this build is eclipse-SDK-M20060609-1217-linux-gtk.tar.gz. You can find a suitable driver for your platform at here
* The EMF driver used in this build is emf-sdo-xsd-SDK-2.2.0RC9a.zip
* The GEF driver used in this build is GEF-SDK-3.2.zip
* Java EMF Model Runtime driver used in this build is JEM-SDK-1.2RC3.zip

WebTools Platform; All-in-one

The Eclipse Web Tools Platform Project will initially focus on infrastructure for tools used to build applications for standards-based Web and Java runtime environments. WTP all-in-one module includes the complete set of software to start using wtp immediately. This package already has wtp combined with the complete set of prerequisites, eclipse 3.2 sdk, emf, gef and jem. You will not need anything else.

Status	Platform	Download
✔	Windows	wtp-all-in-one-sdk-R-1.5.0-200606281455-win32.zip(md5)

Figure 4.5 WTP Build Download Page

4. WTP downloads are handled by the standard Eclipse download mirror network. Select a mirror site near you.

5. When you have finishing downloading, create a directory where you want to install WTP, for example,

   ```
   c:\webtools
   ```

6. Extract the contents of all the zip files into this directory. The contents of the zips will be extracted under a common folder named `eclipse` (see Figure 4.6), for example:

   ```
   c:\webtools\eclipse
   ```

7. To start WTP, run the executable named `eclipse.exe` in this directory, for example,

   ```
   c:\webtools\eclipse\eclipse.exe
   ```

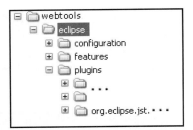

Figure 4.6 Program Folder

Installing Third-Party Content

In general, WTP avoids redistributing third-party content (3PC). For example, WTP does not come with a Java Web server runtime. To test a simple dynamic Web application, a runtime such as Tomcat is needed. Setting up a complete development environment typically involves downloading and installing server runtimes such as Tomcat, JOnAS, Geronimo, WebSphere, and WebLogic among others (see the Getting Tomcat sidebar in Chapter 3 for instructions on how to install Tomcat).

Web development may require other types of runtimes, such as Web service engines like Axis and databases like Derby (see the Getting Derby sidebar in Chapter 3 for installation instructions). Note that WTP includes Axis since it is used internally for the **Web Service Explorer** tool. This means you don't have to install Axis yourself. In general, unless a third-party component is used internally by WTP, you'll have to install it yourself. The XDoclet runtime is typically used to simplify EJB and Web development using attribute-oriented programming style with annotations. Application frameworks such as Struts, Spring, and Hibernate are other examples of popular Java Web runtimes. If you plan to use them, you'll need to install them. Follow the instructions provided with these components to perform their installation.

There are many reasons behind the WTP policy to avoid redistributing 3PC. For example, each third-party component has its own licensing terms, and the Eclipse Foundation may have to obtain the right to redistribute it. In the case of Open Source components, the Eclipse Foundation would also have to review the pedigree of the code to ensure that it conforms to Eclipse policy. In fact, one of the benefits of purchasing a commercial product built on WTP is that the vendor provides this added value. Another reason not to redistribute 3PC is fairness. WTP wants to remain vendor-neutral and not give any vendor an advantage by redistributing its content in preference to another's. For example, if WTP redistributed Tomcat, then it would be morally obligated to redistribute JOnAS, Geromino, GlassFish, and so on, and this would result in a bloated WTP distribution. Finally, by not redistributing 3PC, WTP is not tied to their release schedules. If you want the latest version, you get it directly from the supplier.

Of course, the downside to this policy is that users have to do more work. Typically this involves downloading and installing the 3PC using the instructions provided by the supplier and then configuring WTP to use the downloaded code. Configuration is usually just a matter of telling WTP where you installed the code. WTP project and workspace settings are used to describe these runtimes. After you install the 3PC, follow the instructions in the **Preferences** pages to tell WTP about them.

WTP is working on ways to improve the situation for users. For example, third-party server adapters can now be registered with WTP. Rather than redistributing the 3PC server adapter and runtime environment, WTP only redistributes a pointer to where you can obtain them. To see how this works, do the following:

1. Open the **Preferences** dialog, expand the **Server** category, and select the **Installed Runtimes** page (see Figure 4.7).

2. Click the **Add** button. The **New Server Runtime** dialog opens (see Figure 4.8).

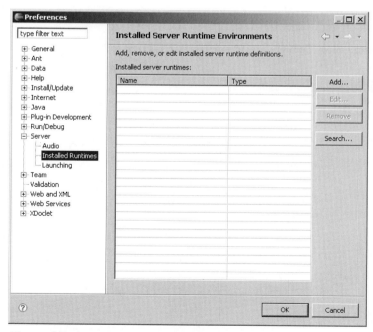

Figure 4.7   Installed Server Runtime Environments

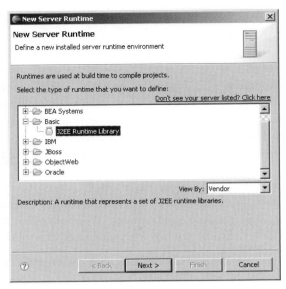

Figure 4.8   New Server Runtime

3. Click the link labeled:

  `Don't see your server listed? Click here.`

  The **Install New Server** dialog opens (see Figure 4.9).

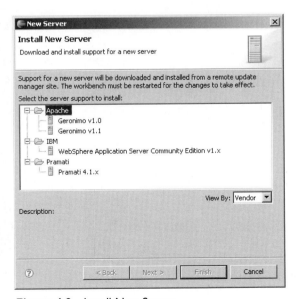

Figure 4.9   Install New Server

This dialog lists the server adapters that are registered with WTP and hosted on remote Update Manager sites. After you install one of these server adapters, you can then add a new server runtime environment. The wizard provided for configuring the server runtime environment may also link to a remotely hosted server runtime that you can also download. For an example of this capability, try installing the Geronimo adapter.

JDK Setup

For Java Web application development, the JRE you select should be a JDK. A JDK contains a Java compiler and other development tools. These tools are typically found in the JAR named `tools.jar`. A Java compiler is required for JSP development.

The JDK version should also be compatible with the server runtime you are planning to use. For example, Tomcat versions 5 and above require a JDK that is version 1.4 or higher, IBM WebSphere requires an IBM JDK, BEA WebLogic comes with a high-performance VM called JRockit, and so forth. Some server runtimes come with their own JDK.

You can add a suitable JDK to Eclipse via opening the **Preferences** dialog, expanding the **Java** category, and selecting the **Installed JREs** page. Click the **Add** button to add the new JRE definition to the workbench (see Figure 4.10).

Specify the JRE type, a name, and select the root directory for this JRE installation.

Verifying the Installation

After you have installed WTP, there are a few things you can check to verify that all is well.

First, check that the WTP features are present. Invoke the **Help ▸ About Eclipse SDK** command from the menu bar and click the **Feature Details** button. You should see features named **J2EE Standard Tools** and **Web Standard Tools** listed. Of course, this list should also contain the prerequisite EMF, GEF, and JEM features. If these features are not present, there is no point in starting development. Try reinstalling.

If the features are present, then you should see user interface contributions from WTP. Open the **Preferences** dialog and verify that the following WTP contributed categories are present: **Data**, **Internet**, **XDoclet**, **Server**, **Validation**, **Web and XML**, and **Web Services**. Expand the **Internet** category, select the **Cache** page, and check the item:

```
Prompt me for agreement of licenses for whose terms I have already disagreed
```

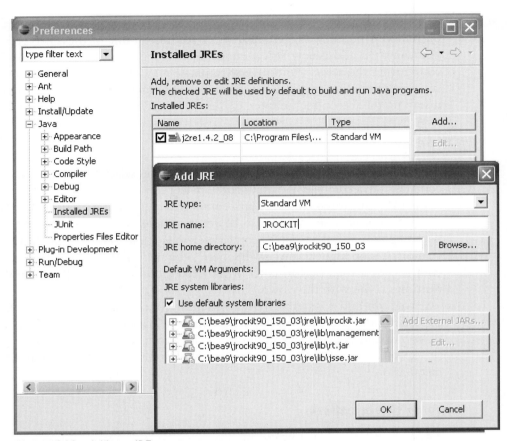

Figure 4.10 Adding a JRE

This will allow WTP to display license terms dialogs for those components to which you might have accidentally disagreed.

Finally, you can try the Quick Tour (see Chapter 3). At this point things are ready to go. The following sections describe how you can use settings to tailor the behavior of WTP to your tastes. However, before leaving the topic of installation we'll briefly discuss updating WTP to new versions.

Updating WTP

Updating from an older version of WTP to a newer release is simple with the Update Manager. However, the Update Manager only updates Eclipse features and plug-ins. You also need to update your configuration settings and development projects.

Workspaces contain both development artifacts such as Java source files, which are completely independent of Eclipse, and setting files, which are specific to Eclipse. In general, workspaces are not guaranteed to be fully compatible between major releases. For example, new views may be added and old ones deprecated, eventually to be completely removed. Such is the price of progress.

The safest way to move up to a new major release is to check in your projects to a source code repository before you update and then check them back out into new workspaces after you update. You can also preserve global workspace settings by exporting them before the update and then importing them back into your new workspace after the update.

However, creating new workspaces does take time, so WTP supports workspace migration. If you open an existing workspace with a new version of WTP, then any downlevel settings will be automatically updated. This is a one-time process and may mean that you can no longer use the updated workspace with an older version of WTP. Note that you may also have third-party settings that need to be updated.

> **Tip:** You should always make a backup of your workspace before updating. Typically, once a workspace is updated, it cannot be used with the older version again. Your backup will always give you the ability to revert to the older version if anything goes wrong.

If you do back up your workspace and later have trouble locating it, you can always start Eclipse with the -data option, for example,

```
eclipse -data c:\webtools\myworkspace
```

When you use the -data argument at startup, it clearly specifies the location of your workspace.

Configuring WTP

WTP has many settings for validators, Web projects, editors, server runtimes, and so forth. Some settings are scoped to an individual project while others are global to the workspace. You use workspace **Preferences** and project **Properties** pages to create and modify these settings. In this section we'll review some of the common WTP preferences that you might like to change (see Table 4.1).

Table 4.1   Summary of WTP Preferences

Preference	Description
Data	These settings are for the Data tools. These tools allow you to explore relational databases and run SQL queries.
Internet	Some WTP features require a connection to the Internet. Here you can set parameters, such as the Web proxy settings, and caching policy that enable you to work offline.
Java	This is a JDT preference, but it must have a proper Java Development Kit (JDK) set up for WTP to work properly. Most WTP users will change the Installed JRE to the one that is required by their server runtime environment.
Run/Debug	Here you will set your preferences for Run/Debug extensions. WTP adds notable extensions to the base Run/Debug facilities for Web development. For example, it has a TCP/IP monitor that is very useful for debugging and monitoring Web applications.
Server	To run and debug most Web applications you need a server runtime environment. These preferences will allow you to install and configure many popular runtimes that can be used for Web development.
Validation	WTP has an extensive validation system. It can validate many artifacts, such as XML, HTML, and XSD files, for correctness. These preferences allow you to control which validators will be enabled in your environment.
Web and XML	WTP tools extend Eclipse standard editing capabilities, such as coloring, content assist, syntax checking, etc., to Web and XML files. These preferences will allow you to change the preferences, such as default encoding, styles, formatting, and default cached XML catalogs that are used for validation and content assist.
Web Services	WTP can create Java Web services and create Java clients for existing ones. Web Services preferences allow you to change the settings for Web service wizards, Web service runtimes, testing, project layouts, etc.
XDoclet	Annotations enable you to use attribute-oriented programming for Web development. Here you will choose and set the preference for the runtime engines that WTP uses for annotations. For example, this is the place where you will set the preferences for `xdoclet`, which can be used to develop servlets and EJBs with WTP.

The following sections describe these preferences in more depth. Consult the WTP online Help for full details.

Data Preferences

This preference set is for the Data tools. The defaults are suitable for most development activities. Data preferences contain the following pages:

❍ **Label Decorations** sets the labels for database table metadata displayed in the **Database Explorer** view.

❍ **Output** sets the limits for query results shown in the **Data Output** view. This view displays messages, parameters, and results related to database objects.

Internet Preferences

The Internet preferences contain the following pages:

❍ **Cache** sets the download cache preferences. Some WTP tools need to access the Web. For example, the XML editor may download schema files to validate a document. Downloaded documents may come with click-to-accept licenses. Internet preferences enable caching for these documents for offline development.

❍ **Proxy Settings** set the network parameters used by WTP tools. If you work behind firewalls and Web proxies, you can configure WTP here.

Server Preferences

These preferences configure the Server tools. The Server preferences contains the following pages:

❍ **Audio** sets sounds associated with various server events. These can be handy for processes that may take a long time, such as server startup or publishing. By setting a sound here you'll be alerted when these processes are complete.

❍ **Installed Runtimes** lets you add new server runtime environments. For example, see the Add a Server Runtime Environment section in Chapter 3.

❍ **Launching** sets behavior associated with server processes such as publishing, starting, restarting, and switching the debug mode.

Validation Preferences

WTP tools will process Web artifacts such as XML, HTML, JSP, and EJBs that are invalid or even not well formed. Tools do their best to understand the contents of the files. As files are edited, tools can incrementally validate them. Many syntax errors are easy to catch with highlighting. There will be other times when it will be beneficial to perform formal validation on these artifacts. Validation preferences allow you to control the types of artifacts that will be validated and when these artifacts will be validated.

Web and XML Preferences

WTP has source editors and visual tools for creating and editing Web files. It can handle CSS, DTD, HTML, JavaScript, JSP, WSDL, XML, and XML Schema files. You can set the following preferences for each editor:

- ○ **Encoding and Line Delimiters** set the default character encoding and the line delimiters.
- ○ **Source** sets the typical features of the source editors, such as formatting and content assist.
- ○ **Styles** sets the preferences for syntax highlighting and source coloring.
- ○ **Templates** sets the templates used for file creation. You can modify existing templates and create new ones.

   XML Catalog preferences are also defined here. An XML catalog entry is used by WTP to resolve XML entity references. Each entry specifies a rule that redirects an Internet resource reference. By adding entity mappings, WTP can use locally stored schemas rather than downloading them from the Internet. For example, adding a mapping such as

```
http://www.leagueplanet.com/schemas/team.xsd
```

that points to the locally stored

```
file:///C:/myschemas/team.xsd
```

on your machine will tell WTP to resolve this entity using the local schema. This way a connection to access resources on the Internet is not needed. (We'll cover the XML catalog in detail in Chapter 15.)

Web Services Preferences

Web services preferences modify options used in the Web services wizards, resource creation, servers, testing, and interoperability.

- ○ **Axis Emitter** sets the parameters used by the Axis WSdl2Java and Java2Wsdl code emitters.

○ **Popup Dialog Selection** lets you control the pop-up dialogs that are available in the Web services wizards. Leaving all of the dialogs hidden results in a wizard that will create services and clients with default assumptions. If these assumptions are not suitable, make the pop-up dialogs visible. Changing the settings presented in these dialogs alters the behavior of the Web service wizard operations.

○ **Profile Compliance and Validation** sets the level of compliance checking and enforcement with the Web Service Interoperability (WS-I) profiles and when WSDL validation is performed during wizard operations.

○ **Project Topology** sets the preferred project types for creating Web services and clients. These preferences just set the default selections, which can later be changed by the user in the wizard.

○ **Resource Management** sets the defaults for file and folder creation, overwriting, checkout, and merging during wizard operations.

○ **Scenario Defaults** sets the default scenarios in the wizard.

○ **Server and Runtime** sets the default server runtime environment and Web service runtime used by the wizard.

○ **Test Facility Defaults** sets the default test facility selection for Web services and whether it is launched after the creation of the Web service.

XDoclet Preferences

This set of preferences is for configuring XDoclet, a popular Open Source technology for attribute-oriented programming using annotations to develop servlets and EJBs. An XDoclet runtime must be downloaded separately. Here you can set the version and location of the XDoclet runtime. Choose the location where you have installed XDoclet, and select the version number that corresponds to it. WTP validates the selected location as a valid XDoclet runtime. This preference is required for XDoclet to work. The XDoclet preference contains the following pages:

○ **ejbdoclet** is an xdoclet task that processes Java code with XDoclet annotations and generates EJB code. In this page, attributes for most common tasks are defined. To include a task, check its includes box. To edit tasks with attributes, click **Edit**.

○ **webdoclet** is an xdoclet task that processes Java code with XDoclet annotations and generates servlet code. In this page, attributes for most common tasks are defined. To include a task, check its **include** box. To edit tasks with attributes, click **Edit**.

Sharing Settings

Some developers have it easy—they can use the settings shared by someone else in their team. Just as we share projects using resource-oriented mechanisms like CVS, you can also share your project and workspace settings.

WTP provides preferences that can be workspace or project scoped. Some tools, such as Servers and XDoclet, can define preferences at the project level. Project scoped preferences are stored in a file located inside the project (in an invisible folder, appropriately called .settings). This makes it easy to store a set of preferences and exchange them with other users using resource-oriented methods such as file sharing or a version control system.

Global preferences, the preferences that are stored with the workspace, are not easily shared. These settings can be lost with a product update, or if the workspace is switched. To save and share these preferences within a team, the import/export facility is used. To export workspace preferences, invoke the File ▶ Export command. In the Export wizard, select Preferences and save the desired preferences to a file. The saved preferences file will only include settings that are different than the defaults. The resulting file can be imported to another workspace using the File ▶ Import command.

As a best practice, teams often create a standard default configuration that can be used as the starting point for new workspaces. These are archived in a common area and used to speed the startup for similar setups. To start fresh, developers simply copy and extract the contents. During development things can go wrong, so it is very helpful to be able to make a quick clean start.

Summary

In this chapter we discussed how to set up a WTP workspace for Web development. We discussed the use of the Eclipse Update Manager to install and update WTP and its prerequisites as well as how to download and install WTP directly. We also discussed many of the preferences available for configuring the WTP tools.

This concludes Part I. You should now be able to set up a WTP development environment and tailor it to your needs. You are now ready to proceed to Part II and dive into the topic of developing Java Web applications with WTP.

PART II

Java Web Application Development

Our goal in Part II of this book is to help you become an expert WTP user. We start by reviewing the multi-tier structure of Java Web applications. Next, we give you an in-depth discussion of the best practices for organizing your application development work into WTP projects, including tips for using Maven to automate your builds. In the next three chapters, we focus on the WTP tools for developing the presentation, business logic, and persistence tiers. We conclude Part II with a discussion of how to perform unit, integration, system, and performance testing, as well as how to profile your application.

CHAPTER 5

Web Application Architecture and Design

Mistakes are the portals of discovery.

—James Joyce

In this chapter we'll describe two kinds of Web systems: application infrastructures and service infrastructures. Many of us build applications that have Web front-ends. These front-ends access business layers and persist their data in databases. Application infrastructures provide the basic layered architecture for these types of systems. In contrast, service infrastructures collaborate with each other using the Web, in addition to interacting with users. They have Service-Oriented Architectures (SOA).

There are issues common to both types of systems; we would like to have a foundation for creating large, well-structured Web systems that are based on sound object-oriented (OO) principles. We'll review the lessons learned from the OO technologies and discover how these should be applied to the Web.

The Web Landscape

The Web is evolving from being a medium that gives users worldwide information access to becoming the preferred medium for communication and collaboration between people and applications (see Figure 5.1).

The Web has standard and open protocols. It is heterogeneous, distributed, and widely available. The Web is the perfect platform for communication and cooperation. Building Web applications and integrating these applications are not separate tasks anymore. The basic premise of SOA is that Web systems should be composed from services that expose well-defined interfaces that enable both application-to-application and user-to-application communication.

114

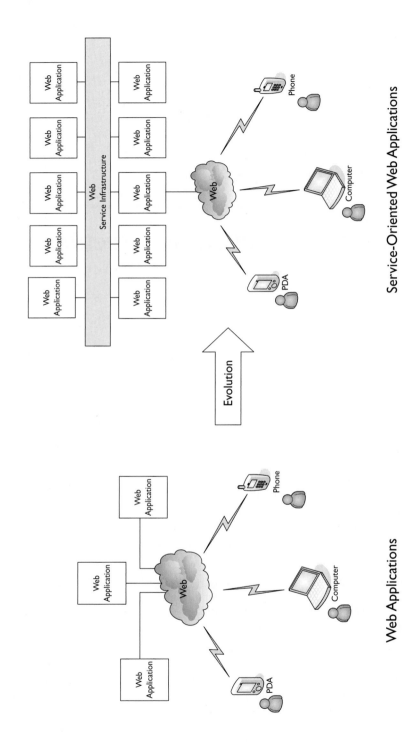

Web Applications

Service-Oriented Web Applications

Figure 5.1 Web Applications and Services

A service-oriented world has many applications distributed over the Web: payment applications running on mainframes, photo printers that make paper copies of your digital snapshots, and news feeds that provide up-to-the-minute information on any conceivable topic. These applications are all examples of service providers. Each service provider exposes its capability using a public interface that defines the service. New applications consume these services and orchestrate them into new capabilities, which themselves may be exposed as new services. This simple provider-consumer model enables the creation of the next generation of Web applications with unbounded new capabilities.

Web Applications

A simple Web application has three basic logical tiers or layers: Presentation, Business Logic, and Data (see Figure 5.2). More layers can be defined to abstract different parts of the architecture. The physical architecture is an orthogonal concern; all layers can run on the same application server on a single machine, or on three or more application servers on separate machines. J2EE allows you to manage the physical layer independent of the application layers.

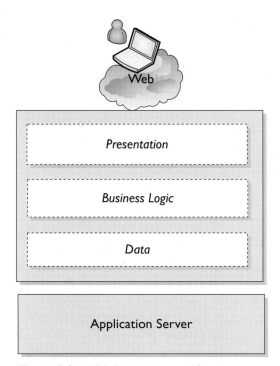

Figure 5.2   Web Applications and Services

The top layer is for presentation. This user interface layer is often built using HTML. Rich Internet Applications (RIA) and AJAX introduce other client technologies, such as Flash and JavaScript, to this layer. If the user interface does not require anything more than a Web browser to run, it is called a thin client.

> **Adobe Flash**
>
> Although Flash is best known as a rich media client technology, it is also often used to create multi-tiered applications. Flash has its own OO programming language, ActionScript 2.0, and components for interfacing with Web services and databases. For more information about the Flash platform, see
>
> `http://www.adobe.com/platform/`

The middle layer is where you implement the business logic. For example, this would be the layer with the objects that know how to add a team to a league. Typically, this layer is not specific to Web applications. A well-designed system can reuse the business model.

The bottom layer is where you keep the data in a persistent store. Databases are the most common choice. However, you can keep the data in any place you like. They can be kept in a file or a mainframe.

We will talk about the concerns addressed in each layer later in this chapter. You can find many examples of this type of application on the Web; they provide business services and information to end users. Although these Web applications are hyperlinked, they are not really integrated. They form a loosely coupled ecosystem where users act as the binding agent. In a service-oriented system, applications are integrated using services; the users are replaced by other Web applications, and the presentation layer is replaced by the service layer.

Java Web Applications

Java Web applications use technologies described in the J2EE specification and the more general standards such as HTML, XML, and Web Services.

Layered architectures and client-server designs have been around longer than Java and Web technologies. Probably the most significant architectural contribution of J2EE has been to provide a practical and standardized specification. There are many commercial and Open Source application servers that support this standard.

J2EE provides the standard for the programming and runtime models used for Java Web applications. J2EE has components for client sessions, presentation, application and business logic, and business operations. It has services such as distribution, transaction, and data management to run these components in an enterprise environment.

J2EE Web applications are portable between compliant application servers. Portability is provided by defining a complete standard that includes how clients interact with the systems, how components are implemented, and how the components use the service APIs to integrate with other enterprise systems. The J2EE model splits the presentation tier into client- and server-side presentation layers. EJB components can be used to model business logic, and they are typically used to implement the business tier. The persistence tier can also be implemented using EJBs and J2EE services that are available to access enterprise information systems.

J2EE has containers for Web components and business components (EJB) (see Figure 5.3). Containers provide standard services such as distribution, security, sessions, and transactions. Clients can be thin client applications, like the Web browser, or rich desktop applications. All Web protocols are supported by the runtime engines.

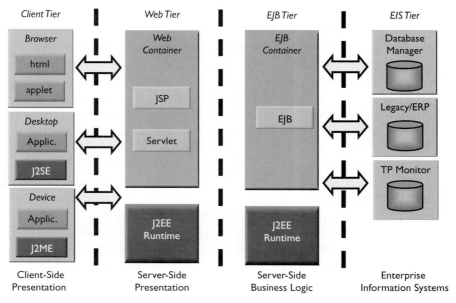

Figure 5.3 J2EE Containers

The Web container runs components such as JSPs and servlets. These components are typically used to implement the presentation layer.

The EJB container provides the runtime environment for business components, business façades, and access to enterprise information systems.

The runtime environment has an extensive set of standard services, such as Java database connectivity (JDBC), Java Transaction API and transaction service (JTA/JST), Java 2 connector architecture (J2CA), Java authentication and authorization service (JAAS), Java naming and directory interface (JNDI), and other APIs that provide the connectivity and extensibility for J2EE-based systems.

Designing Java Web Applications

We are sometimes so excited about new technologies and systems that we forget the lessons of the past. Applying software engineering principles, particularly OO techniques, with these new technologies is challenging [Knight2002]. These new technologies are as dangerous as they are powerful. They lend themselves to, or even encourage, bad practices. JSPs can encourage cut-and-paste reuse, direct-to-database coding, and poor factoring. EJBs are the building blocks for business components, but are criticized for complexity. XML emphasizes reuse and sharing, but can be abused to substitute for a programming environment.

Java Web applications use JSPs and servlets as their building blocks. You can use JSPs and servlets to build layered architectures. There are two popular designs for Java Web applications built this way. These application patterns are usually referred to as Model 1 and Model 2 architectures. In Model 1, requests are sent directly to JSPs, whereas in Model 2 they are sent to a controller servlet, which forwards requests to JSPs. For a description of these models see Section 4.4 of *Web-Tier Application Framework Design* of *Designing Enterprise Applications with the J2EE™ Platform, Second Edition* [Singh2002] by Inderjeet Singh et al. Model 1 is used for very simple Web applications. Model 2 is an adaptation of the Model View Controller (MVC) pattern to Web applications. We will talk about MVC in detail later in this chapter (see the Model View Controller (MVC) for the Web section).

In Model 1, the primary objective is to move all presentation code out of Java classes and put them into JSPs. JSPs are popular because they can manage Web content—such as HTML, CSS, JavaScript, and XML—and Java code in one place. In a JSP, you can process HTTP requests and generate an HTML response. JSPs are easy to understand for Web programmers. In the Model 1 architecture, the JSP is responsible for everything. Some claim that there is a separation of presentation from content, because all data access is performed using Java beans. Although the Model 1 architecture is a quick solution for simple applications, for anything beyond a few pages of code, it is just a bad design. JSPs are not good places to encapsulate business or application logic. Model 1 quickly leads to repetition and complexity. Model 1 compresses all the layers in our architecture to a single component.

Considering JSPs and Model 1 from an OO and layering perspective, the most immediate problem is that a single script has been assigned responsibilities spanning several layers. In Model 1, the JSP must

1. Accept input

2. Handle application logic

3. Generate output (presentation logic)

This design couples all the layers together, making it difficult to modify or test any particular aspect in isolation. In addition, there are significant issues related to handling these responsibilities. We will describe them next. For servlets used alone, the same issues apply (because we can consider a servlet as a script with some additional embedded text, such as XML or HTML), and mixing code with the text also presents code management and debugging issues.

Accepting Input

When accepting input, a script receives an `HttpServletRequest` object, which is a minimally parsed representation of the HTTP input stream. HTTP supports three different mechanisms for passing parameters (encoding into the URL, query parameters, and form data), and all of these pass the data as simple strings. Each script must know or determine the parameter-passing mechanism, convert the parameters to appropriate types, and validate them. The lack of common handling code causes developers to duplicate code between scripts.

Handling Application Logic

Another issue, which affects both input and application logic, is the lack of information hiding when accessing request and session data. The script must retrieve input data from the request by name. HTTP is a stateless protocol, so data used in multiple JSPs must be either stored in a session associated with the user or reread from an external data source in each script requiring the data.

For example, if a script passes login information as form data, the code to store that information in the session might look like that shown in Example 5.1.

Example 5.1 Storing HTTP Request Parameters in the Session

```
password = request.getParameter("passwordField");
decrypted = this.decode(password);
request.getSession().setAttribute("password", decrypted);
```

Both storage in the session and storage in an external data source are effectively global in scope, and the application accesses the data in a dictionary-like fashion using strings as keys. Normal programming mechanisms for controlling variable access do not apply to this data, and any scripts or server pages that wish to use this data must be aware of the naming conventions. You cannot easily find all accesses to the variables using programming-language mechanisms, so modifications become more difficult. If the JSP does not encapsulate these conventions, knowledge of them and details of the HTTP protocol can spread throughout the application, greatly hindering adaptation to new uses. Furthermore, this is a potential source of errors because of both spelling mistakes and reuse of a parameter name for different purposes in different scripts. As the number of JSPs increases, these problems can become overwhelming.

When using JSPs for application logic, you are adding potentially significant amounts of code to the page. Code management techniques are minimal and awkward for code inside JSPs. Debugging code inside the server pages is difficult due to the mix of text with code. Although WTP provides features for code authoring and interactive debugging, for precompiled JSPs you may need to debug inside complex server-generated code. For these reasons, it is a good idea to minimize the amount of code in JSPs and to keep application logic out of them.

Handling Business Logic

A JSP has all its code in a single, monolithic structure. Although business logic may be delegated into Java objects, it is still mixed into the application and presentation logic. Unlike unit testing methods in a Java class, it is not possible to test and run JSP fragments independently. JSPs can quickly become overloaded with code, sacrificing manageability and comprehensibility.

Generating Output

In producing output, simple scripts mix the text, HTML, or XML encoding of the result with the dynamic data. This couples the page's markup, its look and feel, with the other layers. Changing the Web site's look or adapting the application to multiple output devices becomes extremely difficult. The latter is becoming increasingly important as the Web expands to include mobile devices such as Internet-connected mobile phones and other embedded devices. JSPs help address this last issue by letting Web designers create and maintain the look and feel of the pages, letting Java programmers provide presentation logic in annotations. This is generally considered the most appropriate use for server pages.

Layered Web Application Design

A layered architecture is a system containing multiple, strongly separated tiers (layers) with minimal dependencies and interactions between the layers. Such a system has good separation of concerns, meaning that you can deal with different areas of the application code in isolation, with minimal or no side effects to different layers. By separating the system's different pieces, you make the software adaptable so that you can easily change and enhance it as requirements change. The layers include input and output logic for presentation, application logic, business logic, and persistence. These layers can be related back to the basic three-tier structure we described earlier; the input layer is a part of the presentation layer.

The application logic is typically split into page flows that are in the presentation tier, and the business processes and workflows that are in the business tier. The business logic and persistence logic are in the corresponding tiers.

Input Layer

The input layer contains the code concerned with processing and syntactically validating input such as SOAP, HTTP, and SMTP, and extracting parameters from the request. In the Model-View-Controller (MVC) framework, this corresponds to the input controller.

You have servlet components and APIs that provide support for the HTTP protocol to build such a layer. You will discover later in the chapter that these components and APIs provide the plumbing to build an input layer.

Application Logic

The application logic code is concerned with the Web application's overall flow. We often refer to this layer as the glue layer, separating business logic from input and output logic and managing the interface between the two. This requires some knowledge of both layers. For example, this layer will be involved in converting between presentation-level inputs and outputs as strings and the corresponding business object messages or state. In a Web application, this layer might also manage a multipage Web interaction as a sequence of steps (Web page flows). In the MVC framework, this corresponds to the application controller.

The J2EE standard does not directly provide components for implementing application logic. This layer is typically implemented inside the J2EE Web container and uses similar components and APIs to those found in the input layer. However, this situation is improving with the addition of JavaServer Faces (JSF) to Java EE 5.

Business Logic

The business logic code, referred to as business objects, is concerned only with the underlying business functionality. This code should be entirely unaware of the output layer (presentation). In a complex application, business logic is likely to be the largest component and is strongly related to the code that accesses external systems such as databases, Enterprise Information Systems (EIS) such as Enterprise Resource Planning (ERP) and Customer Relationship Management (CRM), and other related services. In the MVC framework, this corresponds to the model.

Objects handling the business logic should not depend on any other layer. This makes it easy to implement the core business, and it enables the use of these objects with or without a J2EE application server or other application frameworks. Our recommendation about designing the business layer is to keep them as simple as possible using ordinary Java objects, sometimes referred to as Plain Old Java Objects (POJO), and make them independent of all other architectural layers. For example, it would be bad design to refer to a view component, such as a JSP, or a Web-specific J2EE API, such as the HTTP request object, in a business model object. Equally, you would not want to refer to database APIs of the persistence layer directly from the business object itself. What would happen to the business object if you decided to change the persistence technology later? Managing the dependencies properly frees you to make these decisions and changes independently.

Business logic implemented in this form allows it to be managed via a J2EE EJB container or any other method. The point is that this layer should not depend on J2EE.

Persistence

Business logic that is implemented as objects in Java needs to store the business data kept in the objects in a persistent store. Most applications use relational databases for data storage. It is also possible to use alternative technologies such as XML databases or object databases to achieve the same goal. The purpose of the persistence layer is to provide this functionality. The business logic should not depend on the persistence layer, and you should not refer to datastore APIs in the business model.

There are various approaches to object persistence. These range from Data Access Objects (DAO), which are usually dependent on database access APIs and query languages like SQL. This approach is more suitable for a small set of simple objects but may provide greater flexibility. Other approaches include Java Persistence API (JPA), sophisticated Object-Relational Mapping (ORM) frameworks like Hibernate and TOPLink, and Object database approaches, among others. Object persistence has been the focus of extensive work. A detailed discussion of object persistence is beyond the scope of this book.

Presentation

This layer contains code and non-code resources (such as HTML, XML, and images) used to present the output of the application. It typically contains little code, and this code is concerned only with formatting and presenting data. For example, a JSP can contain Java code fragments that print the balance of a bank account into a dynamically generated Web page. In the MVC framework, this corresponds to the view.

The J2EE standard provides JSP and servlet components for implementing a presentation layer. These components are supported by a rich set of APIs for HTML and XML processing, creating images, managing URLs, and basically handling all needs related to building user interfaces for the Web.

Model View Controller (MVC) for the Web

The MVC framework provides a clean conceptual model to separate the concerns in a server-side Web application. You can use a combination of servlets, services, JSPs, and application code to implement an application. The approach presented here is part of a family of possible approaches to properly partition responsibilities and overcome weaknesses in the underlying technologies. MVC concepts originated in the Smalltalk-80 system to promote a layered approach when developing graphical user interfaces. The main concepts in MVC are as follows:

❍ The *model* handles application and business logic.

❍ The *view* handles presentation logic.

❍ The *controller* accepts and interprets keyboard and mouse input.

The motivation behind MVC was to separate the model code (meaning non-user interface (UI) code) from its presentation. The model code does not contain any UI information, but it broadcasts notification of any state changes to dependents, which are typically views.

This scheme provides a good separation between these three layers but suffers from two weaknesses. First, it has a simplistic view of the model and does not account for any difference between application logic (for example, flow of control and coordination of multiple Web pages) and business logic (for example, payment processing). Second, most rich-client libraries and windowing systems combine the view and controller functions in a single widget, making the logical separation into view and controller less useful.

The common understanding of the MVC framework has evolved. The term *controller* now refers to the object handling application logic, and the term *model* is reserved for business objects. We use *model* to refer to business objects, and we use *input controller* and *application controller* to refer to the two types of controllers.

Java frameworks, such as JSF, Struts, and Spring, build on the concepts of MVC by using a combination of Java code, JSPs, servlets, and POJOs to implement the various components. These frameworks primarily focus on the separation of the view from the controller, but do not necessarily suggest a solution to separate the controllers, or the application logic, from the business logic. In the Web context, the dual uses of the term *controller*, both as an input controller and an application controller, are valid. For HTTP applications, input and presentation are entirely separate, so it is useful to have an input controller distinct from the view. For applications of any complexity, you also need an application controller to separate the details of application flow from the business logic.

In the following sections, we discuss the basic object structure of Web MVC frameworks (see Figure 5.4). This architecture is implemented by many of the previously mentioned frameworks.

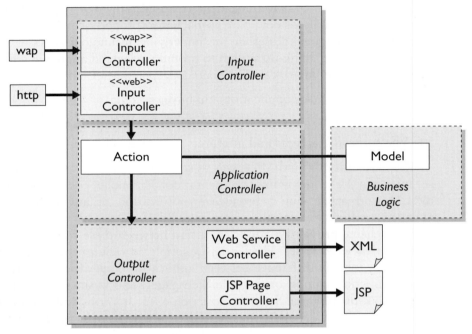

Figure 5.4   MVC for the Web

Input Controller

The input controller is a central feature. There is a single input controller for all pages in a Web application. The input controller parses input, determines the parameter-passing mechanisms, extracts any necessary information from the request, cooperates with the application controller to determine the next operation (typically called an *action*), and invokes that action in the correct context. By having a single component as an input controller, any knowledge of HTTP or naming conventions is localized at the request level. This reduces the amount of code duplication and the total size of code. This also makes it easier to modify any of the input processing functions because there is a single point of modification. Note that the input controller component is typically a servlet, and there may be one instance for accessing the applications over HTTP via a regular Web browser and another instance for mobile applications using a Wireless Application Protocol (WAP) enabled device.

Application Controller

The application controller is typically a regular Java object. It coordinates logic related to the application flow, handles errors, maintains longer-term state (including references to the business objects), and determines which view to display. The application controller needs to understand requests, and how they participate in the organized flow of the application, and forward these requests to the planned responses. Web requests are HTTP encoded, string, and string-based key-value pairs. Application controllers typically need a mapping of these input keys to the application objects that manage the flow. Most frameworks maintain these mappings in complex XML configuration files, such as the `struts-config.xml` file used in Struts. For example, URI sequences like the following are known by the input controller,

```
/leagueplanet/addPlayer.do
```

This relies on a naming convention, with the disadvantages described earlier, but because this is the only component used in this way, the impact is minimized. In a better design, a single application controller is typically responsible for multiple Web pages and activities. In a simple application, a single application controller might be responsible for all pages. In a complex application, there are typically multiple application controllers for the different areas of the application. By using a single, well-encapsulated object as the central point of reference for encapsulating information, the application controller resolves the issues of information hiding and naming conventions. Rather than storing isolated pieces of information in the session, the information can be stored in business objects and accessed using messages from the application controller. Programming language mechanisms let you track the use of the application controller and business objects, making it easier for you to modify your code. You also get static type checking as an additional validation of data usage.

There are several designs for application controllers. The Struts framework refers to them as *actions* while JSF calls them *managed backing beans*. In Struts there can be many actions. For example, if your application has two use cases that support creating teams and adding players to these teams, you may perform these using two corresponding actions. The program listing in Example 5.2 is a summary of how these action classes might look in a Struts application.

Example 5.2   Struts Action Class Example Code

```
public class CreateTeamAction
{
  public void execute(..){}
}
```

```
public class AddPlayerAction
{
  public void execute(..){}
}
```

Clearly, these team and player actions are related. For example, you add players to teams. However, Struts does not have a mechanism to group the actions. For example, multiple actions that are a part of the same flow, like an online registration process, cannot be grouped.

This shortcoming in Struts is addressed by other Struts-based frameworks, such as the Eclipse Pollinate project, where the application controller is a Java object called the *page flow*. The page flow is a class that encapsulates a group of actions as methods and defines a structure for describing the flow between them. In Pollinate, you would have implemented the same use case using a single page flow class. The action classes and their behavior shown in Example 5.2 would have been implemented as methods in a page flow.

The program listing in Example 5.3 demonstrates the ability to group actions and associate them with an object, such as the page flow. Having an application controller for a related group of actions increases your ability to express the application logic. Additionally, you can maintain state for this flow in an object rather than using HTTP specific request and session APIs.

Example 5.3   Page Flow Class Example Code

```
public class LeaguePlanetPageFlow extends PageFlowController
{
  public Forward createTeam(){..}
  public Forward addPlayer(){..}
}
```

The two most popular MVC implementations for Java Web applications, Struts and JSF, are very similar in concept. Some claim that JSF is closer to MVC than Struts due to the availability of a rich stateful component set at the view layer and support for an event-based model to manage controller interactions (e.g., button-clicked events). JSF also provides an extensive standard tag library to reduce the amount of Java code in JSPs (see Example 5.4).

Example 5.4   JSF JSP Tags

```
<h:panelGroup>
  <h:commandButton id="submitCreateTeam"
    action="#{JsfLeaguePlanetBean.createTeam}" value="Create Team" />
  <h:commandButton id="submitAddPlayer"
    action="#{JsfLeaguePlanetBean.addPlayer}" value="Add Player" />
</h:panelGroup>
```

However, one must always keep in mind that these frameworks exist on top of the stateless HTTP protocol. JSF has the concept of an application controller in the form of managed backing beans (see Example 5.5). These beans can encapsulate a group of related activities, a capability that Struts lacks. Finally, the concept of page flow does not exist in either JSF or Struts. This information is implicit in the controllers and XML-based configuration files.

Example 5.5   JSF-Managed Backing Bean

```
public class JsfLeaguePlanetBean
{
  public String createTeam(...){}
  public String addPlayer(...){}
}
```

The input controller will invoke one of many possible actions on each request. One of its responsibilities is to determine the correct action to invoke. This decision depends on both the input from the client and the application's current state, so it is determined by the application controller. We represent the result of this determination as the ApplicationController object (ApplicationController is an implementation of the Command pattern described in [Gamma1995]).

Business objects are plain Java objects that contain only business logic. They should have no knowledge of any other layers. The application controller is the only component that manipulates the business objects (see Figure 5.4 earlier). These characteristics make it much easier to develop and test the business logic in isolation from the Web infrastructure. If the application is designed properly, the business objects are isolated, allowing you to use the same implementation for a thin-client Web application, a more rich-client implementation, or even a traditional desktop UI.

View

In a J2EE application, views are typically JSPs that can access the application controller and business objects. Views should contain as little code as possible, delegating most functionality to the application controller or business objects. Only code directly related to presentation in the current page should be used in a page. The JSP specification also defines tag libraries (taglibs) for defining customized JSP tags that encapsulate complex view layer behavior. It is preferable to use taglibs to create custom tags to remove complex code from the pages altogether. Figure 5.4 (earlier) shows two different view mechanisms. The JSP Page Controller uses a JSP implementation appropriate for a Web browser or WAP device. The Web Service Controller responds to the same request and produces an XML response suitable for consumption by other applications, such as a .NET system, or a rich-client application.

Java Application Frameworks

There are a number of Open Source Java frameworks that help implement Web application best practices. In this section we'll quickly review some of them (see Figure 5.5). These frameworks simplify development of Java Web applications. They provide capabilities that improve the testability and maintainability of the code and simplify development. They separate architectural concerns and integrate well with application servers.

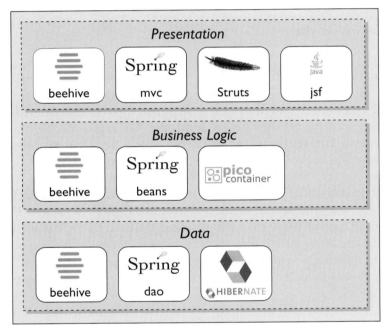

Figure 5.5   Java Application Framework

OSGi

The OSGi Alliance (formerly the Open Services Gateway Initiative) defines a standard for providing Java-based service platforms. The specification defines a framework for an application life cycle model and a service registry.

OSGi implementations such as Eclipse Equinox, Felix, and Knoplerfish provide complete and dynamic component models, something that has been missing in standard Java runtime environments. This means applications or components, which are called OSGi bundles, can be installed, started, stopped, updated and uninstalled, even remotely, without requiring a reboot.

OSGi is gaining momentum as a general service platform because it can scale from embedded devices to enterprise systems. Eclipse, and therefore WTP, is an example of an OSGi-based system. IBM and BEA are building their next-generation application servers using OSGi platforms. What is more interesting is that we can also use OSGi to develop simple business components and services that are assembled in runtime to provide business services. For example, you can run Spring 2.0-based applications on OSGi runtimes.

Apache Beehive

The Beehive project provides a framework for lightweight, metadata-driven components that reduce the coding necessary for J2EE. Beehive addresses all three layers of Web applications. The framework is based on annotations, particularly JSR 175 metadata [JSR175]. It uses other Apache projects such as Struts and Axis. It has NetUI for presentation, Controls framework for lightweight components and Web Service Metadata (WSM), an implementation of JSR 181, and an annotation-driven model for building Java Web services [JSR181].

Apache Struts

Apache Struts is a framework to provide a control layer based on standard Java Web technologies, like JSPs and servlets, and other Apache projects. It is a variation of the MVC design pattern.

JavaServer Faces

JSF is a JCP standard, JSR 127 [JSR127], that defines a set of JSP tags and Java classes to simplify Web UI development. It is hoped that JSF will standardize tools and components by providing a single-component framework for JSP and servlets. JSF provides a framework for the presentation layer and also draws on the MVC concepts. JSF is a part of the Java EE 5 specification.

Spring

Spring offers a framework that covers the complete stack of the layers in a Java Web application. The framework implements the Inversion of Control and Dependency Injection design patterns uniformly across all components. It provides Spring MVC and Web flows for the presentation layer. It provides a light-weight container to implement the business logic using POJOs, and therefore claims to eliminate the need for EJBs. It also provides solutions to manage the application data.

Pico Container

Pico Container is a light-weight framework that is also based on the Inversion of Control and Dependency Injection patterns. Similar to Spring, it also grew as a reaction to the complexity of J2EE development, specifically against the difficulties associated with EJB development.

Hibernate

Hibernate is an Object Relational Mapping (ORM) framework. It allows developers to implement object relational persistence and query services for POJOs without any modifications to Java code.

The EJB3 Entity Beans specification, and specifically the Java Persistence API (JPA) that has evolved from it, increases the attractiveness of Hibernate and ORM frameworks alike to solve this difficult problem.

Service-Oriented Architecture (SOA)

SOA is about separating parts of your business into meaningful units, called services, and building applications that are integrated using services. Service orientation is encapsulation of business logic. A service is an application of a fundamental OO concept, separating the implementation from the interface. Combined with standard languages such as XML, common protocols for transport such as HTTP, and the capability of searching and binding to a service provider at runtime, SOA has rapidly become the preferred integration technology for a diverse set of systems. SOA and Web services are based on many standards such as XML; XML Schema; Web Service Description Language (WSDL); Universal Description, Discovery, and Integration (UDDI); SOAP; JAX-RPC; and many WS-* specifications. A detailed description of SOA is beyond the scope of this book. However, we will describe how you can use WTP to build service-oriented Web applications, primarily using Web service technologies.

Providing Services: The Service Layer

The purpose of the service layer in your application is to expose your business and application capabilities as services. Your applications are only as interesting as the clients that use them. The classic question, if a tree falls in the forest and no one is there to hear it, does it make a sound? applies here.

Many types of clients can use services:

❍ Rich Client Applications that consume services from many providers

❍ Embedded Systems, such as mobile phones

○ Portals and Web applications, ranging from remote portals and Web applications to the controller layer of a vertical system that uses a service layer to access the business model in an extended MVC with a service layer as described next

○ Integration solutions using Business Process Execution Language (BPEL) to automate business processes

○ Systems providing services by orchestrating others around a new business model

Adding a Web service layer to your previous architecture (see Figure 5.6) allows you to create an application that is interoperable with many other systems. The additional layer will have entities such as Web services, service registries (UDDI), service contracts (WSDL), and proxies that bind these services to our applications. The service layer exposes well-defined interfaces to the same underlying business model. The service interface is defined by a service contract described using WSDL. Your business may have processes and logic that use services from external systems. The service consumers are not exposed to the details of the business model. All the technical details needed to consume a service are described in WSDL.

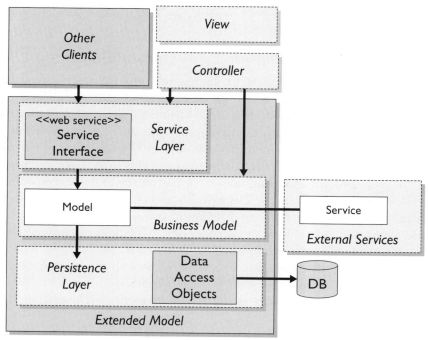

Figure 5.6 Adding a Service Layer

Where does SOA fit?

It is useful to discuss how SOA fits with the traditional layers in our application. Some immediate questions to answer are: Is SOA a part of the presentation layer? Does SOA replace the presentation layer with a service layer? What about the business logic, where does it belong?

A service does not have a view; therefore, there is no need to have a presentation layer. This is typically replaced with a service layer. A useful analogy is to think about the service layer as a form of the presentation layer; a service is a presentation of the business logic in a form that can be used by applications.

The harder question is whether services are a part of the model and the business logic tier. The simple answer is no, but there is more to it. Business logic is not always modeled in a form that immediately can be made available as services: a good object model is fine-grained—lots of small, easy-to-understand objects with easy-to-understand methods. These objects encapsulate significant business concepts and data, but they are not very useful for creating services. Services are typically designed based on business use cases; they capture behavior for a flow of the events, such as "Pay for a reservation." Fine-grained objects do not capture such flows. Services are a mix of business and application logic that capture processes and workflows. For example, in the League Planet application, the service layer would have an object that handles the creation of a new league. We'll discuss the business logic tier in Chapter 8.

Consuming Services: Orchestration

Applications consume services to aggregate content or services from service providers. You can provide new business processes by integrating services from a variety of providers and adding new business logic, rules, and capabilities. Existing content is recomposed and mapped into the business model of the client application, and it is presented in a new and unique way that is not necessarily available from any of the individual providers. This is the basic premise of SOA.

Business process modeling and service orchestration can consume business services in a standard way by using Web services. The service layer provides an abstraction over a wide range of different business systems, and you can leverage these services to assemble business processes. WTP does not have tools for service orchestration, but vendors such as IBM, BEA, and Oracle have extended WTP to support the design and execution of these business processes. Business Process Execution Language (BPEL) is an OASIS standard to provide what is essentially an XML programming language for service orchestration.

Case Study: League Planet

In this section, we develop the architecture of our fictitious League Planet Web site (see the Introducing League Planet section in Chapter 1). From an architectural viewpoint, League Planet is a multifaceted system with many different user profiles.

First, there are the people who provide the content of the system. These are the people who are interested in sports and use League Planet to set up amateur sports leagues. They visit the Web site and create new leagues where they can record their teams, players, schedules, venues, scores, statistics, and many other kinds of information. League Planet needs to provide a highly dynamic Web front-end that will allow these users to interact with our system directly.

As people use the system they navigate the pages in the Web site and perform actions such as viewing the information presented, filling in forms, and ordering goods offered by League Planet business partners. To support these users, League Planet will have a presentation layer. The presentation layer will be implemented using JSPs. To reduce the amount of Java code required to describe the UI, standard Java tag libraries will be used. The presentation layer will be limited to code that displays information and accepts user input. Application flow and control will be delegated to a control layer.

The control layer is responsible for tasks such as input validation, page flow and navigation, and collaborating with the business model layer to perform business tasks and to provide content to the view layer.

The next profile for League Planet is the applications, such as the corporate sponsors, that will need services. League Planet generates an important part of its revenue from sponsored advertisements. The information about the teams, players, visitors, and their user profiles can be used for targeted marketing. These profiles are used to generate advertising banners and links to business partner sites. League Planet uses services to share this information. League Planet provides a service layer for its services and can access services from sponsors to show ads.

Finally, League Planet supports partner organizations by providing most of its content and services online. Free and subscription-based information about the leagues, players, teams, visitor profiles, announcements, flash news, and latest real-time game results are only some of the services available. As a provider of services, League Planet is the source of unique content and services available for consumption by other applications.

To implement this system, you use the architecture described in the previous section (see Figure 5.6 earlier). To demonstrate how this would work, consider the scenario described in the sequence diagram shown in Figure 5.7.

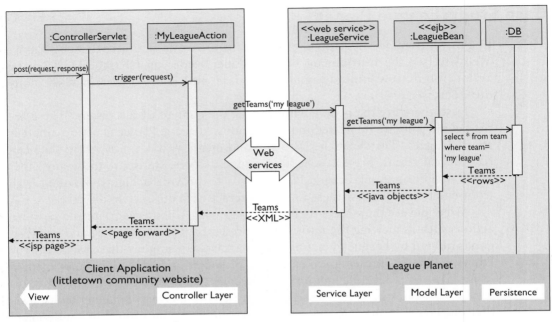

Figure 5.7   Providing a Service Layer

A client application, similar to your Web application, consumes services provided by League Planet. The service consumer will use one of your Web services, using SOAP as the protocol. These systems have completely different business models and application logic, but they will be able to collaborate using this SOA architecture. The client sends a service request to get information about the team playing in a league. This request is sent using SOAP. The service layer at League Planet receives the request. The Web service runtime resolves the request and maps the inputs that are described as XML data to corresponding Java classes. The Java bindings in the LeagueService receive the message as if it were sent from a Java object. The service layer sends Java messages to the model layer to access the team data stored in the database. The teams represented by Java objects are returned to the service layer. The service layer serializes the Java objects into the XML representation defined by the types in the WSDL that describe the server. The response is returned to the client application as XML. The service consumer client uses similar technologies to map the response to its internal business model and displays the team content on its Web pages.

Summary

The concepts discussed in this chapter should help you build Web applications that have the right architecture. We have presented a variety of different architectural approaches and different frameworks. Following the patterns presented here, we showed how better software quality can be achieved because good OO principles follow naturally from them. These frameworks are even more important for the inexperienced OO developer because they provide a starting point for high-quality code without knowing the details of these systems. The MVC frameworks mentioned in this chapter could be extended in several different areas, addressing different Web application requirements such as validation, security, and others. We recommend experimenting with these technologies to understand the architectural trade-offs and suitability for a particular domain.

You are now ready to continue learning how to use WTP to develop your Web application. In Chapter 6 you will get an understanding of several styles of Java Web development and project organization.

CHAPTER 6

Organizing Your Development Project

All right, guys! It's time to clean up this town!

—Homer Simpson

In this book we describe how to build applications that are defined by the J2EE specification. When you build an application, you create one or more projects that correspond to J2EE modules. You also use these same projects to organize your development work; that is, you use these projects

- ○ to manage the source code and files that make up the application,
- ○ to divide the work between the teams, and
- ○ to set up an automated process that builds the application, runs tests, and creates project reports.

This chapter starts with a basic description of the types of applications and projects that are supported in WTP. We will show you how to create different kinds of projects to build applications.

In the second part of the chapter, we will describe some of the advanced project features that are available with WTP. There is very little available in terms of standards to guide you in the organization of project artifacts and source code for Web projects. Project best practices achieve a balance between the concerns that drive a particular development project:

- ○ How many teams and developers are there?
- ○ What are the subsystems?
- ○ What components are tested, and how are they tested?
- ○ Who builds the code?

❍ How is it integrated?

❍ How is it released?

Naturally, each concern is a different dimension of the project. We will use advanced WTP features to create project templates and apply best practices that are helpful to organize your development work. We use the generic term *Web project* to describe the WTP project types that are provided for J2EE development.

Web Project Types and J2EE Applications

A project is used to develop modules such as J2EE Web applications and EJBs. Typically, each module is a project, but this is not a strict requirement (see Figure 6.1).

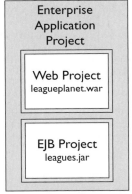

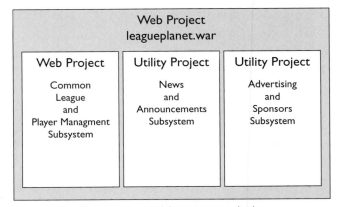

An enterprise application project that contains a Web project and an EJB project with components for leagues and players.

For better manageability, a team can divide a large Web project into many projects. Each project is used to develop a subsystem.

Figure 6.1   J2EE Applications and Web Projects

For example, in a complete J2EE enterprise application, one project might consist of a Web application module for the presentation logic while another would be used to develop the EJB module for the business components. In this case, the complete application consists of three projects for the modules: one for the enterprise application, one for the Web application, and one for the EJBs. It is also possible to split the development of a single module into multiple projects. For example, a basic module like a Web application might be built from utility modules built in other projects. You will learn how to organize your projects and modules using similar patterns later in this chapter.

Web Projects

Projects organize your source code and modules. WTP provides Web projects that are sophisticated Eclipse projects that know about J2EE artifacts. In addition to having basic Java project capabilities, a Web project can be used to organize J2EE artifacts into buildable, reusable units (see Figure 6.2).

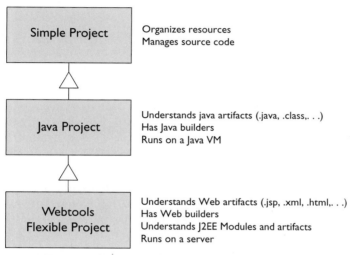

Figure 6.2 Web Projects

An Eclipse *simple project* (or general project) provides the basic infrastructure to organize and build resources. The structure of a general project is very open; resources such as files and directories can be organized in any arbitrary form that makes sense for a particular purpose.

A JDT *Java project* contains Java elements such as packages, types, methods, fields, and property files for creating Java programs. A Java project knows how to build and run Java programs. Each Java project has a Java builder that can incrementally compile Java source files as they are edited.

You can change the properties of a Java project, such as the Java build path. The build path is the classpath that is used for building the project. There are alternative ways of structuring the sources in a Java project; examples include using a single source folder that is the project root or multiple source folders for organizing complex Java projects.

A WTP Web project has more than just Java code. It contains sources that are used to build Web applications, EJBs, and enterprise applications. A Web application can be as simple as a bunch of HTML files, or it can have servlets,

JSPs, tag libraries, and Web services. These artifacts make the Web application. A Web project knows how to build, publish, and run J2EE modules and artifacts on application servers.

Web projects have builders, validators, and code generators. Builders produce standard publishable modules from complex development layouts. Validators help identify and catch coding errors at development time. J2EE validators are very valuable, because the sooner you find a problem the easier it is to fix. In J2EE, there are many deployment descriptors that have references to Java code and each other. These are interrelated in complex ways. Failure to catch a problem at development time could lead to a runtime error that might be very difficult to diagnose and fix. Generators create components from annotations in source code (for example, using XDoclet or JSR 175).

J2EE Modules

The output of the development activities are discrete J2EE components (EJBs, servlets, application clients), which are packaged with component-level deployment descriptors and assembled into J2EE modules. Web application modules, EJB modules, enterprise application modules, and Java 2 Connector Architecture (J2CA) resource modules are typical J2EE modules. A module contains code, resources, and deployment descriptors. A J2EE module forms a stand-alone unit, which can be deployed and run on a J2EE application server. Figure 6.3 provides an overview of the J2EE structure associated with common J2EE modules, such as Web, EJB, and EAR, as described by the specification.

Creating Applications

WTP provides projects and wizards to help you get started quickly with different types of Web and J2EE applications. You can use these wizards to create most standard Web and J2EE artifacts. Additional tools will help you create, build, validate, and run your applications on servers.

To get started, we will review the steps involved in creating different types of applications. The simple steps provided in this section will help you acquire the skills you will need to work with the examples in this book. More specifically, you will learn how to create these types of projects:

❍ Dynamic Web project, where the output artifact is a WAR file

❍ EJB project, where the output artifact is an EJB JAR file

❍ EJB client project, where the output artifact is a JAR file that contains client-side classes for accessing an EJB module

○ Enterprise application project, where the output artifact is an EAR file containing Web, EJB, and other modules

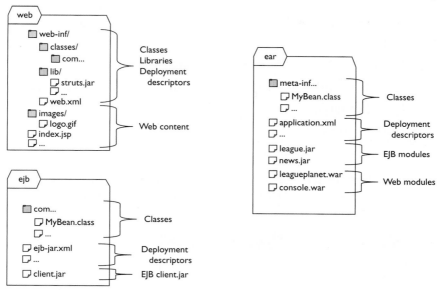

Figure 6.3 J2EE Modules

Creating Web Applications

To build a Web application you need a project that contains a Web module. There are two types of Web projects: static and dynamic.

Static Web projects contain resources that provide static content. You can use a static Web project to develop Web applications that contain many of the standard Web resources, such as HTML, images, CSS, and XML, and test them using a Web browser. These projects can be deployed to a conventional Web server, such as the Apache HTTP Server, that has no J2EE capabilities.

Dynamic Web projects are for J2EE Web applications that contain servlets, JSPs, and filters, in addition to static content. A dynamic Web project can be used as a stand-alone Web application, or it can be combined with other modules to create a J2EE enterprise application.

The J2EE specification defines a standard for Web application directory structure. It specifies the location of static Web files, JSPs, Java class files, Java libraries, deployment descriptors, and supporting metadata. The default dynamic Web project layout resembles the structure of a J2EE Web application module. In the workbench, you can use the **New Web Project** wizard to create a new Web project. WTP has support for other types of project layouts and can automatically build a J2EE Web application archive (WAR) structure defined by the standard.

When you want to create a dynamic Web project, you will typically do the following:

1. Invoke the **Dynamic Web Project** wizard.

2. Provide parameters such as project name and locations for Web artifacts.

3. Choose a target runtime.

4. Choose project facets.

You can try these steps by repeating the following:

1. Switch to the **J2EE** perspective. In the **Project Explorer** view, right click, and invoke the **New** ▸ **Dynamic Web Project** menu item (see Figure 6.4).

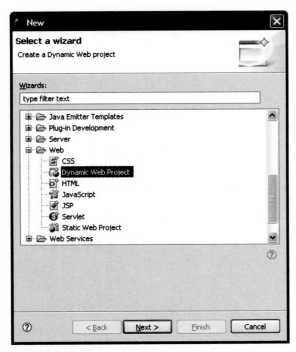

Figure 6.4   Select Wizard

Click **Next**. The **New Dynamic Web Project** wizard opens (see Figure 6.5).

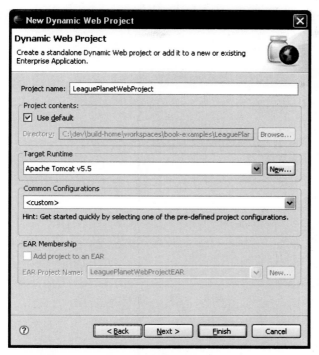

Figure 6.5　New Dynamic Web Project

2. Enter LeaguePlanetWebProject for the project name. A dynamic Web project contains J2EE components such as JSPs and servlets. It is necessary for J2EE APIs to be a part of the project classpath. This is done for you automatically when you associate a J2EE server runtime with the project. The runtime provides a set of libraries that will also contain JARs such as the servlet.jar. If you switch the runtime at a later time, the classpath is also updated. If your prefer not to use a runtime to provide these libraries, you can create a folder that contains the J2EE libraries and point to it as your runtime library. However, this method will require you to obtain appropriate libraries for the J2EE APIs from

   http://java.sun.com

   Assuming you have defined a server runtime such as Tomcat, select it as the target runtime. We will revisit servers and runtimes in other chapters.

   Configurations allow you to choose a set of project facets for common styles of Web projects. For example, if you choose the WebDoclet configuration, WTP will set up the project to enable XDoclet.

Click the **Next** button. The **Project Facets** selection page is displayed (see Figure 6.6).

Figure 6.6   Select Project Facets

3. A project facet describes some runtime aspect of the Web module. For Tomcat 5.0, you can specify the J2EE version, the Java version, and, optionally, the XDoclet version. Each server defines a set of supported facets and their allowed values. WTP configures the Web module and sets up the classpath for the project so that it matches the specified facets. Accept the defaults here and click the **Next** button. The **Web Module** page is displayed (see Figure 6.7).

4. The **Web Module** page lets you specify its context root name and the directories for its Web and Java resources. The context root is the name that appears in the URL for the Web application. Specify LeaguePlanetWebProject as the context root and accept the defaults for the directory names. Click **Finish**. WTP creates the project and populates it with configuration files such as the J2EE Web deployment descriptor, web.xml (see Figure 6.8).

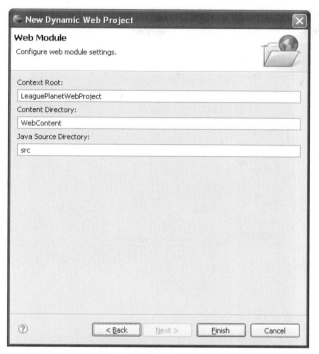

Figure 6.7 Web Module

You have now created a dynamic Web project named `LeaguePlanetWebProject` and targeted it to Tomcat.

The **Dynamic Web Project** wizard creates folders and files under the project (see Figure 6.9). Open the project you have just created and browse its contents. For example, the `WebContent` folder contains a special folder named `WEB-INF`, which holds items that are defined by the J2EE specification and are not accessible by a Web browser. The `WEB-INF/classes` folder is where compiled Java code goes. It also contains a special file, `web.xml`, which is the J2EE Web deployment descriptor.

The `WebContent` folder contains Web resources such as JSP and HTML files, and other types of supporting resources (see Figure 6.9). The contents of `WebContent` will be accessible from the Web application context root.

The following default elements are created with a dynamic Web project:

○ `WebContent/WEB-INF/web.xml`: This is the Web deployment descriptor.

○ `src`: This is the Java source code for classes, beans, and servlets. The publisher will copy the compiled class files into the `WEB-INF/classes` folder of the final application.

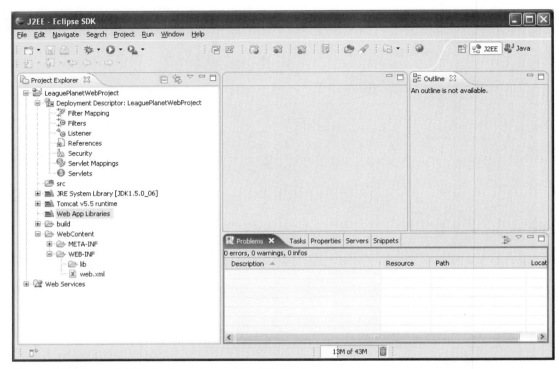

Figure 6.8   Dynamic Web Project—LeaguePlanetWebProject

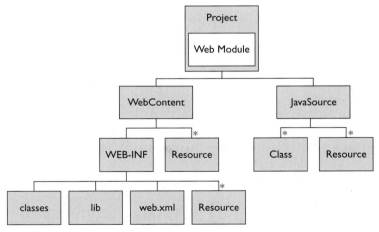

Figure 6.9   Elements of a Dynamic Web Project

○ webContent: This is the Web application root. All Web artifacts placed in this folder will be available to the client. The publisher will copy the complete contents of this folder into the root of the final WAR file. It is possible to choose a different name for the webContent folder or rename it.

○ WebContent/WEB-INF/classes: Sometimes code and libraries will be delivered to you in the form of class files (in comparison to those that are provided to you as JAR files, which you would put into the WEB-IF/lib folder). To add them to the classpath of the final Web application, you can place them in this folder.

○ WebContent/WEB-INF/lib: We will place all libraries that are provided to use in the form of JAR files here. They will be added to the build path of the project. The publisher will copy them into the WAR file, and they will be available to the class loader of the Web application.

A dynamic Web project can publish its contents as a Java Web application archive (WAR) file (see Figure 6.10). Publishers assemble the artifacts in a Web project, such as Java sources; Web content, such as JSPs, HTML, and images; and metadata, such as Web deployment descriptors, in a form that can run on a J2EE application server.

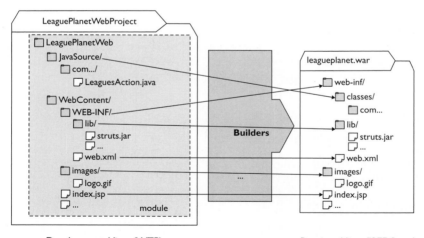

Development View (WTP)   Runtime View (J2EE Spec.)

Figure 6.10 Publisher

WTP wizards simplify the tasks involved in creating J2EE modules. We have just shown how to create a Web module. WTP online documentation at

`www.eclipse.org/webtools`

provides detailed information about these wizards and the project structure. The process of creating an EJB application is equally simple. The next section describes how to create an EJB project that contains an EJB module.

Creating EJB Applications

An EJB project contains an EJB module. This project can be used to assemble one or more enterprise beans in a single deployable unit. EJBs are deployed in a standard Java archive (JAR) file. An EJB project can be used to build stand-alone components, or it can be combined with other modules in a J2EE enterprise application (EAR).

Recall the structure of an EJB module (see Figure 6.3 earlier). EJB modules have a simple structure that contains EJB classes and deployment descriptors. In the workbench, we can use the **New EJB Project** wizard to create a new EJB project with an EJB module in it.

Getting an EJB Container

EJB projects require a server runtime environment that supports EJBs. You will need an application server such as Geronimo, JBoss, or JOnAS to develop EJBs with WTP. You should obtain the application server first, and use the WTP preferences to define a new server runtime environment.

You can obtain Geronimo from

`http://geronimo.apache.org`

or you can download and install it via WTP (see the Installing Third-Party Content section in Chapter 4). JBoss can be obtained from

`http://www.jboss.org`

and JOnAS can be obtained from

`http://jonas.objectweb.org`

You will not be able to use Apache Tomcat for EJB development. Tomcat only supports J2EE Web modules, not EJBs or enterprise applications.

When you want to create an EJB project, you will typically do the following:

1. Switch to the **J2EE** perspective. In the **Project Explorer** view, right click, and invoke the **New ▶ EJB Project** menu item (see Figure 6.11).

Figure 6.11   Select Wizard

Click **Next**. The **New EJB Project** wizard opens (see Figure 6.12). Enter LeaguePlanetEJB for the project name and select a target runtime that supports EJBs such as JBoss. We will discuss EJBs in more detail later in Chapter 8.

Configurations allow you to choose a set of project facets for common styles of EJB projects. For example, if you choose the EJB Project with XDoclet configuration, WTP will set up the project to enable XDoclet. Click the **Next** button to proceed to the **Project Facets** selections page.

2. Project facets describe aspects of J2EE modules (see Figure 6.13). For an EJB module, you can specify the J2EE version, the Java version, and, optionally, the XDoclet version. Each server defines a set of supported facets and their allowed values. For example, you will not be able to set an

Figure 6.12   New EJB Project

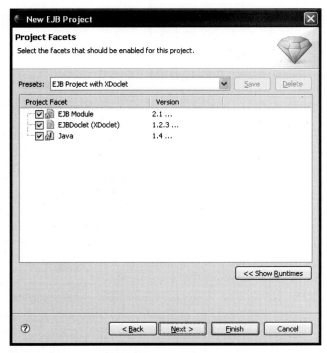

Figure 6.13   EJB Project Facets

EJB facet using a Tomcat server because it does not have an EJB container. WTP configures the EJB module and sets up the classpath for the project so that it matches the specified facets. Here, you will use XDoclet to develop EJBs. Add the XDoclet facet by checking it. Accept the defaults for the EJB and Java facets and click the **Next** button to proceed to the EJB module settings.

3. The **EJB Module** page (see Figure 6.14) lets you specify the directory for Java resources. Optionally, you can create a Java utility module that will contain EJB classes and interfaces, which will be required by EJB clients. Click **Finish**.

Figure 6.14   EJB Module

4. WTP creates the EJB project and populates it with configuration files such as the EJB deployment descriptor, `ejb-jar.xml` (see Figure 6.15).

You may notice some errors in the new EJB project. For example, if your EJB project does not contain any EJB components, this is considered an error according to the J2EE specification. If you chose the XDoclet facet and an XDoclet runtime is not yet configured, this will show up in the problem markers. These errors are normal and will be removed when you fix the preferences and add EJBs to the project.

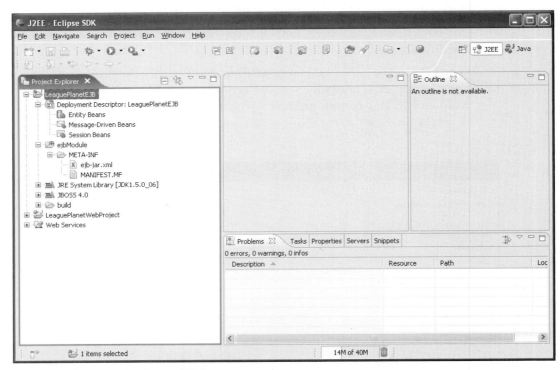

Figure 6.15   Project Explorer—EJB Project

The `ejbModule` folder contains Java and EJB resources such as the deployment descriptor (see Figure 6.16).

Similar to Web application modules, an EJB project has a publisher for EJB applications (see Figure 6.17). This publisher creates a deployable EJB module from the contents of the project with all the classes and deployment descriptors.

EJB Client Projects

There is another EJB related project type called the **EJB Client Project**. These projects are used to share common classes between EJB modules and their clients such as a Web application. Typical classes that are found in these modules are the EJB interface types and models. EJB project wizards can create an EJB client project. This option can be selected only when the EJB module is added to an EAR module. It is also possible to add the client project to an existing EJB module by using the context menu in the **Project Explorer** view.

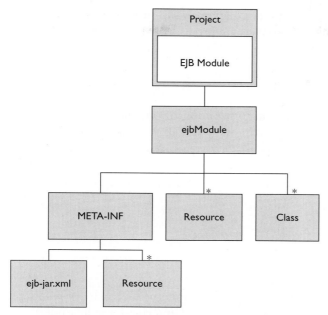

Figure 6.16 Elements of an EJB Project

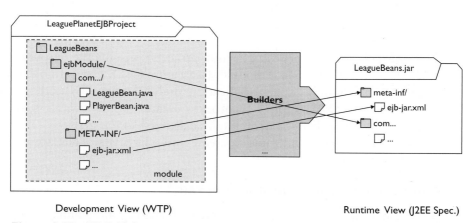

Figure 6.17 EJB Publisher

This completes the process of creating an EJB project. The next section describes how to create an enterprise application project that can combine EJB and Web modules in a J2EE Enterprise Application (EAR) module.

Creating Enterprise Applications

The most interesting J2EE enterprise applications have more than one module. They have several Web applications and EJB modules. The J2EE specification provides a basic application packaging structure called an *enterprise application*. Enterprise application archives are packaged as Java archives with the .ear suffix. Therefore, they are also known as *EARs*. An EAR can contain one or more

- ❍ EJB modules
- ❍ Web application modules
- ❍ J2CA resource adapter modules
- ❍ Application client modules

An enterprise application project contains the hierarchy of resources that are required to deploy these modules as a J2EE enterprise application.

An enterprise application module contains a set of references to the other J2EE modules that are combined to compose an EAR. In addition to the modules, an enterprise application module also includes a deployment descriptor, application.xml.

Publishers for enterprise application projects consume the output of the publishers from their component modules (see Figure 6.18). For example, the builder of an EAR that contains a Web application module and an EJB module waits until the builder for the Web and EJB projects creates the deployable structures for these modules, and then it assembles these artifacts in the EAR.

WTP has wizards and tools to create and edit EARs. They are described in the following use cases.

Create a New Web or EJB Module in an EAR

When a new J2EE module project is created, such as a dynamic Web project or an EJB project, it can be associated with an enterprise application project (see Figure 6.19). The project wizards let you specify a new or existing enterprise application. You can also choose the project in which you would create the enterprise application module. Finally, the EAR is updated to include the new J2EE module in it.

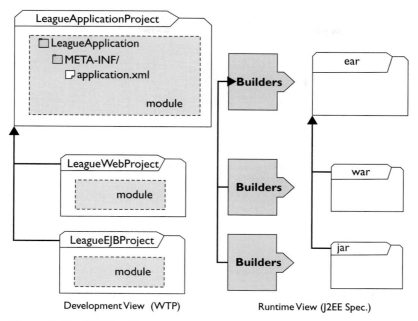

Figure 6.18 EAR Publisher

Adding Existing Web and EJB Modules to an EAR

In the second scenario there are existing J2EE modules, which are to be added to a new enterprise application. You create a new EAR project and add your existing modules to it. The **Enterprise Application** wizard creates a new project and allows you to choose the modules to be included in it.

When you want to create an EAR project, you will typically do the following:

1. Switch to the **J2EE** perspective. In the **Project Explorer** view, right click, and invoke the **New ▸ Enterprise Application Project** menu item (see Figure 6.20).

2. Click **Next**. The **New Enterprise Application Project** wizard opens (see Figure 6.21).

3. Enter LeaguePlanetEar for the **Project name**. Click the **Next** button to proceed to the **Project Facets** selection page.

Figure 6.19 Adding a Module to an EAR

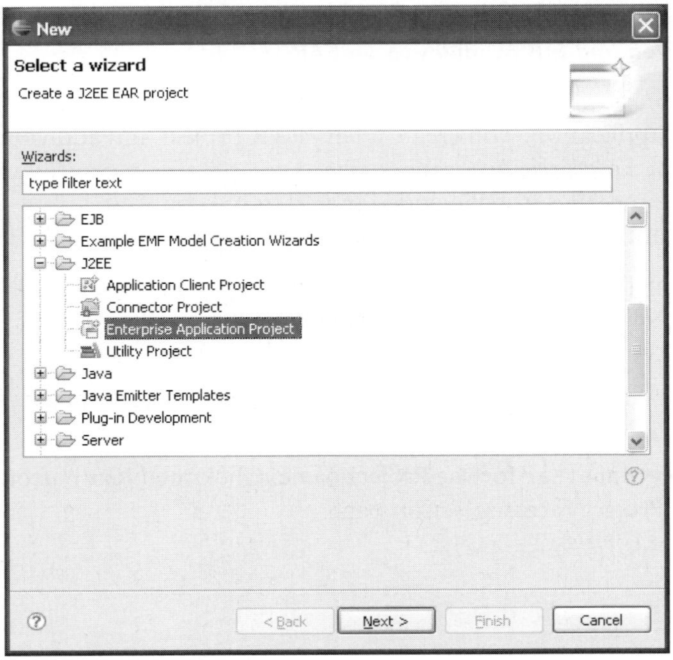

Figure 6.20 Select Wizard

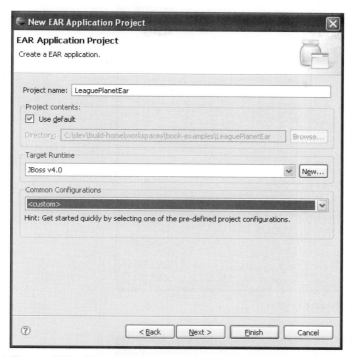

Figure 6.21   New Ear Project

4. Project facets describe aspects of enterprise applications (see Figure 6.22). For the EAR module, there is only the EAR facet. Each server defines a set of supported facets and their allowed values. For example, you will not be able to set an EAR facet using a Tomcat server because it does not support EARs. Click the **Next** button to proceed to the EAR module settings.

5. The **J2EE Module** page (see Figure 6.23) lets you select the modules that will be included in the application. Select the `LeaguePlanetEJB` and `LeaguePlanetWebProject` modules. Note that you can also make the wizard generate new empty modules by clicking the **New Modules** button. Click **Finish**.

6. WTP creates the EAR project and its deployment descriptor, `application.xml` (see Figure 6.24).

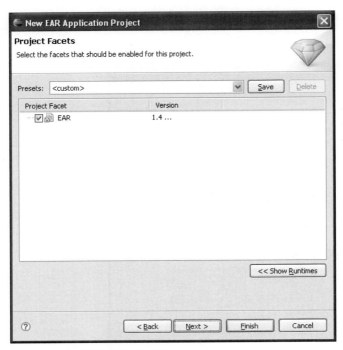

Figure 6.22 EAR Project Facets

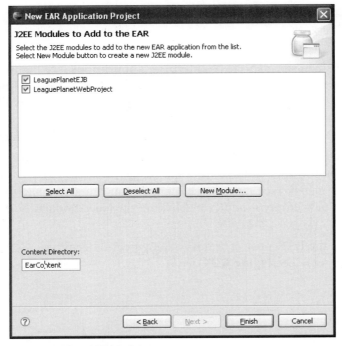

Figure 6.23 J2EE Modules

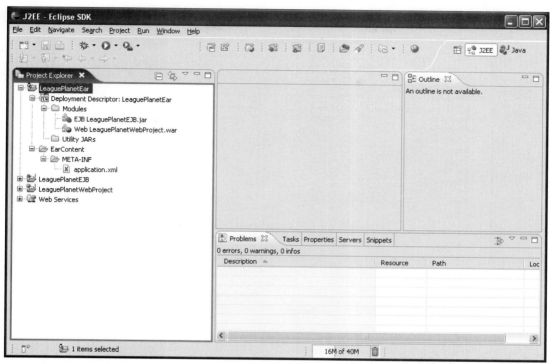

Figure 6.24　Project Explorer—EAR Project

Editing EARs

In the final scenario, you modify the modules in an EAR. You can add new modules to an EAR or remove existing ones by using the J2EE Module Dependencies property page.

When you want to modify an EAR project, you will typically do the following: In the **Project Explorer**, highlight the enterprise application LeaguePlanetEar, right click, and select **Properties**. As Figure 6.25 shows, you can then choose the modules to be included in the EAR.

EAR modules have a simple structure. When modules are added or removed from an EAR, WTP automatically updates the module and the contents of the EAR deployment descriptor, application.xml, which is stored in the META-INF directory.

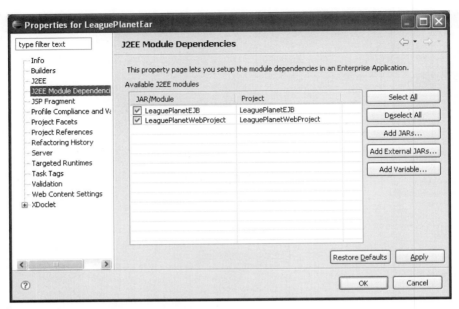

Figure 6.25   J2EE Module Dependencies

Advanced Web Projects

The default project types and layouts cover many of the common application and development needs. Sometimes you need to do more with a Web project; you can use it to improve your development process, organize your code, and share your work with other team members.

Here are some development considerations that can determine the organization of a project:

❍ *Project Deliverables:* These are the concrete outputs of the development activities. For example, in a J2EE development project, deliverables are the standard modules such as Web application archives (WARs), EJB component archives (JARs), Enterprise application archives (EARs), and so forth. Architecture also influences the design of deliverables. You may use a single EAR project if all the containers run on the same application server. However, it will be better to divide the projects if the Web and EJB containers are on different servers.

Some projects are simple Web applications while others involve multiple modules and components. An application may group many Web applications and EJBs together. The J2EE specification describes a structure for these deliverables.

○ *Team Organization:* Team organization determines who will do what in the project. A team can be one person or it can have groups of developers. The structure of the project is a significant factor in determining the productivity of the team and the management of the overall software engineering process.

○ *Change Control, Configuration and Release Management:* Software can be viewed in terms of components that are assembled and configured to form an application. It is important to track the changes to these components using a version control system. The organization of these components determines the units that are used to control the changes in the scope of the project. The configuration and version of components that make an application are very important to the release process.

○ *Testing:* Test plans, test cases, and execution of the tests must be regular and continuous parts of the development process. Test objectives and responsibilities are determined based on the modules. Unit and integration tests are part of the development for each module.

When the WTP project was started, the development team had long discussions on how to extend the basic Java projects to handle different styles of custom projects. A key requirement for Web projects was to enable the separation of the two fundamental view points to help manage resources in a project, for example, the *developer view* and the *runtime view*.

The runtime view is defined by the J2EE specification. The developer's view is most often modeled using the J2EE specification. Mimicking the structures defined in the specification creates valid J2EE applications, but this is not always suitable for all development projects.

In WTP, the developer's view of a project is captured by a model that maps the contents of the project to the runtime view. Each WTP Web project has a *structural model* that is used to describe how developers lay out the resources. Publishers and WTP tools use the structural model to create J2EE artifacts. This mapping gives you flexibility to create projects in ways that you could not do before. For that reason, WTP developers sometimes also refer to these projects as *flexible projects*. We'll use the term *Web project* in this book.

Technically speaking, an Eclipse project that has the Module Core Nature is a Web project. This nature indicates that these projects have a structural model for the modules and will support WTP tools. We will start with a short description of this advanced project capability, and then give examples demonstrating its use. Power users can employ these capabilities to create many different layouts for their projects.

Modeling the Developer View

The structural model of a Web project tells publishers how to compose a runtime artifact (see Figure 6.26).

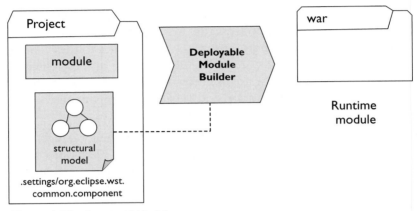

Figure 6.26   Structural Model

This model is defined in an XML component file stored with the other project settings. The project settings and component files are normally invisible in the **Project Explorer** view. However, they are visible in the Eclipse **Navigator** view that is included in the **Resource** perspective. The structural model is stored in a file named

```
org.eclipse.wst.common.component
```

inside the .`settings` folder of any Web project (see Figure 6.27).

The model file listed in Example 6.1 is for a typical dynamic Web application module. The module is named `LeaguePlanetWebProject`. The model specifies how resources in the development view map to resources in the runtime view. Here, you map the complete contents of the `webContent` folder to the module root. The `source-path` is relative to the project root and the `deploy-path` is relative to the module root at the destination. You can have as many resource mappings as you like for each module. The module also has type-specific properties such as `context root`, which defines the context root of the Web application module. The `java-output-path` property tells the publisher where to find the compiled classes.

Example 6.1   Web Module Definition

```
<?xml version="1.0" encoding="UTF-8"?>
<project-modules id="moduleCoreId" project-version="1.5.0">
    <wb-module deploy-name="LeaguePlanetWebProject">
```

```
            <wb-resource source-path="/WebContent" deploy-path="/"/>
            <wb-resource source-path="/src" deploy-path="/WEB-INF/classes"/>
            <property name="context-root" value="LeaguePlanetWebProject"/>
            <property name="java-output-path" value="build/classes"/>
        </wb-module>
    </project-modules>
```

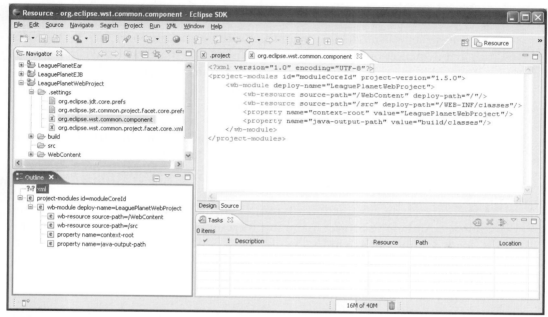

Figure 6.27   Structural Model Definition

Another example is the model of an enterprise application (see Example 6.2). Here the interesting parts are the dependent modules. In this example, the EAR uses an EJB module and a Web module. A dependent module is referenced using a handle, which is a module URL. A module URL starts with the prefix `module:`, and is followed by a workspace-relative path to determine the project and the name of the module within that project.

Example 6.2   EAR Module Definition

```
<?xml version="1.0" encoding="UTF-8"?>
<project-modules id="moduleCoreId" project-version="1.5.0">
  <wb-module deploy-name="LeaguePlanetEar">
    <wb-resource source-path="/EarContent" deploy-path="/" />
    <dependent-module deploy-path="/"
      handle="module:/resource/LeaguePlanetEJB/LeaguePlanetEJB">
      <dependent-object>EjbModule_1147426182270</dependent-object>
```

```
        <dependency-type>uses</dependency-type>
    </dependent-module>
    <dependent-module deploy-path="/"
     handle="module:/resource/LeaguePlanetWebProject/LeaguePlanetWebProject">
        <dependent-object>WebModule_1147426182290</dependent-object>
        <dependency-type>uses</dependency-type>
    </dependent-module>
  </wb-module>
</project-modules>
```

The structural model is a mapping for the organization of files that are distributed over a set of Web projects. A publisher uses this model and can construct a deployable, runtime Web artifact as described in the J2EE specification.

When you create projects and modules using a project creation wizard, the model is automatically added to a project. Wizards create a model based on a default template. However, you can easily modify the default mapping as shown in the next sections. Some of the common types of artifacts used in model definitions are resources, modules, and dependent modules.

Resource

A *resource* is an abstraction of project artifacts such as files, folders, and libraries. An Eclipse project maintains its resources, ensuring that each resource is loaded only once within the workspace. Resources are referenced with resource URIs, which are relative to the projects that contain the resource. WTP has additional URI converters that can resolve URIs to their underlying physical resource, such as the module URI we discussed earlier.

Module

A *module* represents a deployable artifact, such as a WAR, EJB JAR, or EAR. A WTP project can be associated with only one module, but it can refer to others. This makes it possible to distribute the code for a module over a set of projects.

A J2EE module has a standard layout and is targeted to some J2EE runtime container. J2EE projects generate archives as JARs or as exploded archives. These archives must contain compulsory files, such as deployment descriptors, and must conform to the J2EE specification. There are five core types of J2EE modules and a general-purpose utility module:

○ Enterprise application (EAR)

○ Enterprise application client (JAR)

○ Enterprise JavaBean (JAR)

○ Web application (WAR)

○ Resource adapter for J2CA (RAR)

○ Utility modules (JAR)

Dependent Module

As its name suggests, a *dependent module* is used to define dependencies between modules. It can also help define a module with its code split into several projects. For example, we can maintain the Web applications that are in an enterprise application as dependent modules. Another common pattern is to maintain basic utility JAR modules, which contain the extracted contents of the archive, as separate projects. The benefit of using extracted modules is that all the artifacts can be modified, and Web projects assemble them into a deployable form.

Example Projects

It is time to discover how you can create some interesting projects. These best practices provide different styles of projects for Web and J2EE development. You can extend and customize these examples to fit your needs. The examples we'll discuss are a basic enterprise application, dividing a Web module into multiple projects, and using Maven for Web application development.

Basic Enterprise Application

Using the J2EE application deployment specification as a template, you will create an enterprise application with multiple modules. This is recommended if you do not have a compelling reason to do it another way. These projects map to the J2EE specification in a straightforward way and can be created using wizard defaults. Adherence to standards reduces the behavioral discrepancies between the runtime and the development environments.

In this example, each architectural application layer will correspond to a project. For example, the presentation layers will correspond to a dynamic Web project with a Web application module and the business logic layer to an EJB project with an EJB module. The enterprise application project will be used to assemble the modules as a single coherent unit.

To create this structure, you will use a **J2EE Enterprise Application Project** (see Figure 6.28). The EAR project has two modules: `LeaguePlanetWebProject`, a Web application module; and `LeaguePlanetEJBProject`, an EJB module. The Web application module is going to be a dynamic Web project with the same name. The EJB module is divided into an EJB project and the EJB client project. The EJB client JAR is a Java utility project named `LeaguePlanetEJBClientProject`.

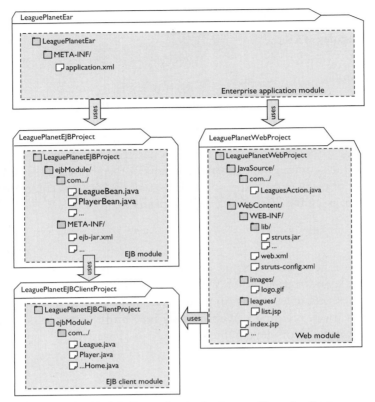

Figure 6.28 Module Dependencies for League Planet Application

To demonstrate the use of Web application libraries, the Web application will use the Struts MVC framework. In order to use Struts, all Struts and supporting libraries, that is, `struts*.jar`, `commons*.jar`, `jakarta*.jar`, `log4j.jar`, and `antlr.jar`, are kept in the `WEB-INF/lib` directory. The Struts configuration file, `struts-config.xml`, is in the `WEB-INF` directory. The business model for League Planet is provided by the EJBs. The Web application delegates the business behavior to this layer.

Clean Workspace

In the first part of this chapter, we described how you can create different types of projects. In this example we will use the same names. If you have tried the earlier examples and are using the same workspace, you should delete those projects before starting this one. If you would like to keep the old work, remember to back up.

To create an EAR project with this structure, do the following:

1. Start as we described earlier in this chapter to create a new **Enterprise Application Project**. Name it `LeaguePlanetEar`. Select the default facets, continue to the **J2EE Modules** page, and click **Finish** to create an empty EAR. In the next steps you will create the Web and EJB projects.

2. Repeat the steps we described earlier in this chapter to create a new **Dynamic Web Project**. Name it `LeaguePlanetWebProject`. Choose the `LeaguePlanetEar` as the EAR for the Web project (see Figure 6.29). Continue to the other pages to select the default facets, and click **Finish** to create the Web project. The EAR project will be automatically updated to reflect the addition of the new Web module.

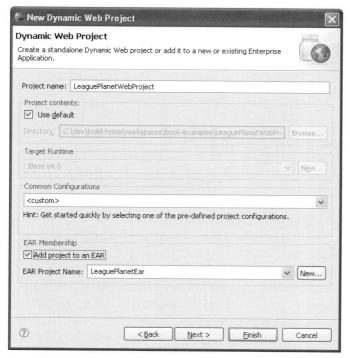

Figure 6.29 Web Project Added to an EAR

3. To do this step, you must have the Struts framework installed someplace on your machine. You can obtain Struts from

   `http://struts.apache.org`

Import all the Struts libraries and their supporting libraries into

`WebContent/WEB-INF/lib`

Refer to the Struts documentation for the exact list of libraries. Once the JARs are copied into the `lib` folder, they will be automatically added to the build path under the `Web App Libraries` category (see Figure 6.30).

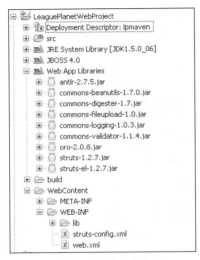

Figure 6.30   Web App Library

4. Repeat the steps we described earlier in this chapter to create a new EJB project. Name it `LeaguePlanetEJBProject`. Choose the `LeaguePlanetEar` as the EAR for the EJB project (see Figure 6.31). You can choose one of the default facet configurations for development, such as the **EJB Project with XDoclet**. You do not need to change the default choices. If you do choose one, you should make sure that your workspace is set up to use it (that is, the XDoclet settings are valid). Click **Next** to go to the other pages to select the default facets. Click **Next** to go to the **EJB Module** page.

5. The Web application will be a client of the EJB module. Create an EJB client module named `LeaguePlanetEJBClientProject` (see Figure 6.32). Click **Finish** to create the EJB and EJB client projects. The EAR project will be automatically updated to reflect the addition of the two new modules.

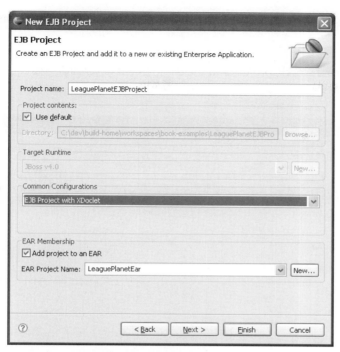

Figure 6.31 EJB Project Added to an EAR

Figure 6.32 EJB Client Module

6. WTP updates the EAR project and the deployment descriptor, `application.xml` (see Figure 6.33).

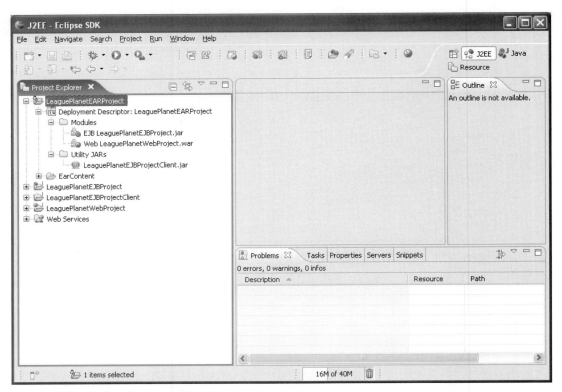

Figure 6.33   Project Explorer—EAR Project

To create these projects, you used the same wizards described earlier in this chapter.

Web Application Module Uses EJB Client

You need to make sure that the dependency between the Web application module and the EJB client is set. The Web application is a client of the EJB module. You need to describe this dependency. Remember that you created an EJB client module named `LeaguePlanetEJBClientProject`. You will add this module to the J2EE dependencies in the Web project. Select the Web project in the **Project Explorer,** right click and invoke the **Properties** menu item. Select the **J2EE Dependencies** page. In this tab, select `LeaguePlanetEJBClient` from the list (see Figure 6.34).

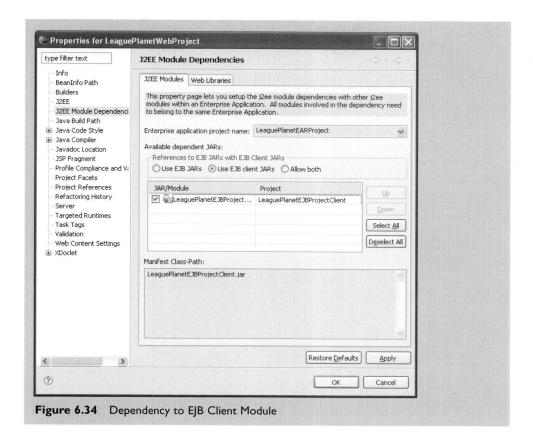

Figure 6.34 Dependency to EJB Client Module

Later, you can extend this model by adding more Web projects—an administration site, for example. The business model can be extended with more EJBs.

Dividing a Web Module into Multiple Projects

Size, structure, and the geographical and sociological aspects of a development team are significant factors in determining the project layout. When these are important to a project, they can determine the structure. The key constraints for this template are the manageability and divisibility of work. Manageability relates to aspects such as ownership of code, development responsibilities and tasks, configuration and version control, integration, and release management. Divisibility relates to dividing the work between members of the development team.

In this example, you will extend the project structure described in the previous example. `LeaguePlanetWebProject` is a large Web application module. It will contain many large, loosely coupled subsystems. League management, player management, sponsorship, and advertising are some of these subsystems that will be developed by different teams. You will divide and manage subsystems as separate projects. Each subsystem can be released on different schedules. You will therefore start by dividing the Web module into two projects (see Figure 6.35). You can increase the number of subsystems following the same pattern later on. The dynamic Web project in the previous example contains the Web application module and will have common Web components such as menus, navigation bars, and so forth. There is a new subsystem for league management. This is a Java utility project on steroids. The league management module has its own presentation layer with JSPs and Struts configuration files in addition to its own Java classes.

To create this structure, you will need to create a new basic **Java Utility Project** named `LeaguePlanetManagementWebProject`. Java utility projects can be used to refactor reusable components of applications into separate projects. J2EE module dependencies will help assemble these components automatically.

To create the **Java Utility Project** and divide the module, the following steps must be performed:

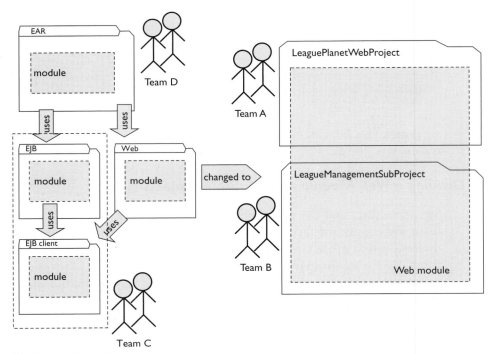

Figure 6.35 Dividing a Web Module into Multiple Projects

1. Create a new **Java Utility Project** using the wizard.

2. Add the Web application libraries to its build path.

3. Add the utility project to the list of J2EE dependencies for the Web project.

4. Create a new `webContent` folder in the utility project and add this to the structural model.

Do the following:

1. In the **Project Explorer** view, right click and invoke the **New** ▸ **Other** ▸ **J2EE** menu item (see Figure 6.36). Select **Utility Project**.

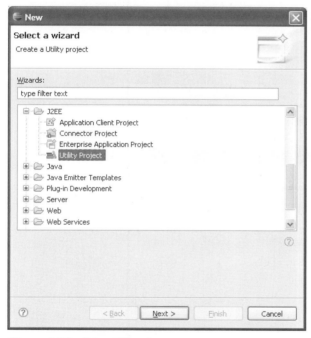

Figure 6.36 Select Wizard

Click **Next**. The **New Java Utility Project** wizard opens (see Figure 6.37).

2. Enter `LeaguePlanetManagementWebProject` for the project name. Use the same target runtime for all your projects. Use the default configuration. Click the **Next** button. The **Project Facets** selection page is displayed (see Figure 6.38).

Accept the defaults here and click **Finish**. WTP creates the empty utility project.

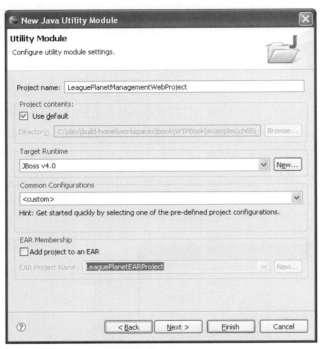

Figure 6.37 New Java Utility Project

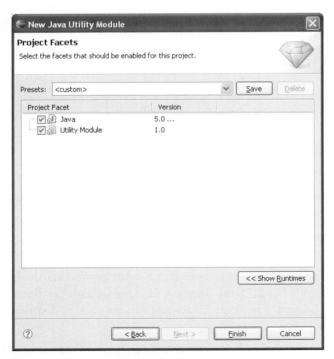

Figure 6.38 Select Project Facets

3. You need to add this submodule to the J2EE dependencies of the Web project. To do this, select `LeaguePlanetWebProject` in the **Project Explorer**, right click, and invoke the **Properties** menu item. Select the **J2EE Dependencies** page. In this page, go the **Web Libraries** tab and add `LeaguePlanetManagementWebProject` from the list (see Figure 6.39).

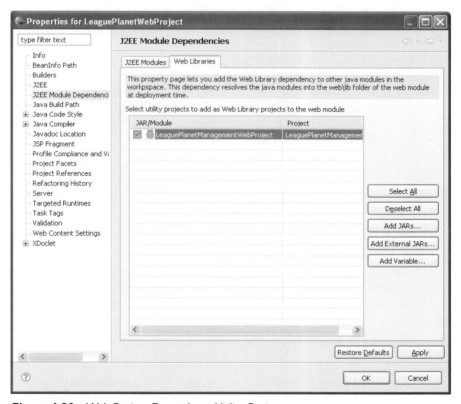

Figure 6.39 Web Project Depends on Utility Project

Managing the Web Application Classpath

When you add a dependency to a utility project, it is automatically added to the final WAR and to the **Web App Libraries** section of the build path of the Web project. However, the reverse is not true. The utility project has no knowledge of the Web application. If you have dependencies to external libraries, like Struts, in the original Web module, all JARs that are inside the `WEB-INF/lib` are available in the class loader of `LeaguePlanetWebProject`.

However, things can get a bit complicated if your new utility project needs classes from the Web application. For example, you may want to add new Struts actions to the utility project module or use Struts taglibs in the JSP files.

You can try to add `LeaguePlanetWebProject` to the build path of the utility project but this would create a circularity, so Eclipse will not allow it.

The best solution is to create other utility projects for common subsystems. These common utility projects can be added to the build path of the Web application as J2EE module dependencies and can also be included in the build path of the other utility projects as Java project dependencies. This approach avoids circularities.

Finally, some development teams prefer to maintain the binaries for external libraries, such as Struts or Hibernate, in a common folder but not in the Web project. For example, some use Maven repositories to maintain project dependencies to these JARs. You will learn about Maven in the next section. WTP allows you to maintain libraries externally and automatically assembles them into the final WAR file before publishing it to the server. If these libraries are added as J2EE dependencies, they are also automatically added to the build path. You can use the project **Properties** window and add them as an external JAR dependency on the **J2EE Module Dependencies** tab.

4. This is an optional step. The league management module is a part of the Web module, but it may need some external libraries to be on its build path. You can do this by adding the external JARs to the build path of the Java utility project. Select `LeaguePlanetManagementWebProject` in the **Project Explorer**, right click, and invoke the **Properties** menu item. Select the **Java Build Path** page. Click on the **Libraries** tab. In this tab, click **Add External JARs** (see Figure 6.40).

   The **JAR Selection** wizard will open (see Figure 6.41). This wizard allows you to browse your local file system for JARs.

   Select all the same external libraries, like Struts, that you have used for the Web project here, too. Click **Finish**. Apply and close the **Properties** window.

5. Next you will create a new `WebContent` folder in the league management project. In the **Project Explorer**, select `LeaguePlanetManagementWebProject`, right click, and invoke the **File ▸ New ▸ Folder** menu item. The **New Folder** wizard will open (see Figure 6.42).

6. Enter `WebContent` as the folder name. Repeat the same process to create a new `WEB-INF` folder inside the `WebContent` folder.

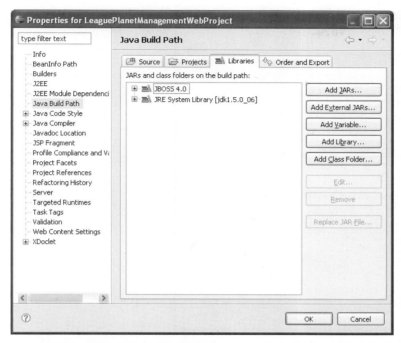

Figure 6.40 Utility Project Java Build Path

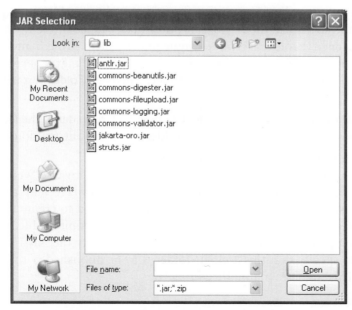

Figure 6.41 Add External JARs Library

Figure 6.42   WebContent Folder

7. Next you will link the new webContent folder to the main Web project and add it to the structural model so that publishers will assemble the contents of the webContent folder from the league management project into the overall project. In the **Project Explorer**, select LeaguePlanetWebProject, right click, and invoke **File ▸ New ▸ Folder**. The **New Folder** wizard will open (see Figure 6.43).

8. Enter Management as the folder name. Click on **Link to folder in the file system**. Click **Browse** to select the webContent folder created in the previous step.

   You will need to specify that the webContent folder in LeagueManagementWebProject gets copied into the deployable Web application module. Currently, there are no nice graphical tools to map these resources, so you will need to edit some files. You need to create the link to the webContent folder before editing the module definition file. You already completed this step. Therefore, you can modify the XML component file to specify that this content folder is to be published with the Web module. This involves manually editing the

   ```
   org.eclipse.wst.common.component
   ```

   definition in the .settings folder. Edit the file as shown in Example 6.3.

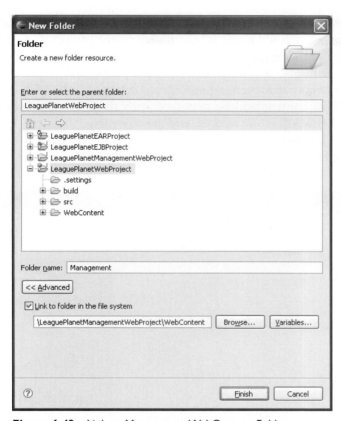

Figure 6.43 Link to Management WebContent Folder

Example 6.3 Modified Web Module Definition

```xml
<?xml version="1.0" encoding="UTF-8"?>
<project-modules id="moduleCoreId" project-version="1.5.0">
  <wb-module deploy-name="LeaguePlanetWebProject">
    <wb-resource source-path="/WebContent" deploy-path="/" />
    <wb-resource source-path="/Management" deploy-path="/" />
    <wb-resource source-path="/src" deploy-path="/WEB-INF/classes" />
    <dependent-module deploy-path="/"
      handle="module:/resource/LeaguePlanetEJBProject/
      LeaguePlanetEJBProject">
      <dependency-type>uses</dependency-type>
    </dependent-module>
    <dependent-module deploy-path="/WEB-INF/lib"
      handle="module:/resource/LeaguePlanetManagementWebProject/
      LeaguePlanetManagementWebProject">
      <dependency-type>uses</dependency-type>
    </dependent-module>
    <property name="context-root" value="LeaguePlanetwebProject" />
    <property name="java-output-path" value="build/classes" />
  </wb-module>
</project-modules>
```

You have now split a Web module into multiple projects. The publisher will add the Java classes developed in the league management project as a JAR in the WEB-INF/lib folder to the original Web application module.

The publisher will also assemble any JSPs and additional Struts configuration files from the league management module, as well as all the Web content in this submodule. This content will be deployed with the Web application automatically. After the WAR is created, it will be assembled into the enterprise application as usual. When you are done, the workbench will have projects that look like Figure 6.44.

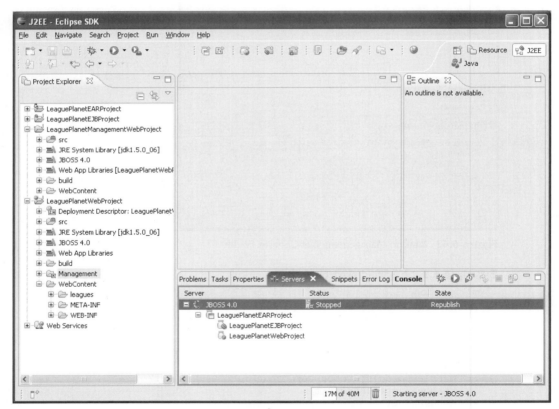

Figure 6.44   Dependent Module in the Project Explorer

Using Maven for Web Application Development

Maven is a software project management and comprehension tool. It started as a tool developed to build the Turbine project at apache.org and quickly spread to other Apache projects. Today, it is used as the main build tool for many of the

Java projects at Apache. For an in-depth description of how to use Maven on your project, refer to *Maven: A Developer's Notebook* [Massol2005] by Vincent Massol and Timothy O'Brien.

Maven is more than a Java build tool. It provides capabilities to make your life easy as a developer. Some of these capabilities are a well-defined project structure, a well-defined development process to follow, and a coherent body of documentation that keeps developers and users informed of what's happening in the project. This is essential in many team projects where there aren't enough people dedicated to the task of building, documenting, and propagating the information about the project. Maven captures the knowledge embedded in people's heads to do these tasks. For example, the development processes of Eclipse and Apache are evolutionary and resulted from the experiences gained from running many projects. This body of knowledge is typically captured in the tools that are used in building projects. Maven provides a standard environment that encourages the use of development and project best practices, and it disseminates this information to project stakeholders.

Following the success of Maven in Apache projects, many teams adopted Maven for their own use, including some J2EE projects. There is a set of J2EE-specific development best practices and processes captured in Maven. The use of Maven to develop a J2EE project enables the transfer of this knowledge. When a new J2EE project starts, it can immediately copy the build tasks and project know-how. The new project reuses the existing tools and conforms to the established practices. Maven does this by providing a framework and templates. For example, by having a common directory structure, developers are instantly familiar with a new project. To quote Aristotle, "We are what we repeatedly do. Excellence is not an act, but a habit."

There are other, less well-known approaches, such as JOFFAD, that also provide generic development frameworks to facilitate, speed up, and normalize J2EE projects. You can read about JOFFAD at

`http://joffad.sourceforge.net/structure.html`

In Example 6.4 you will use the advanced WTP Web project features to develop a Web application using Maven. Maven has a default, but customizable, process that gets a project started using these J2EE best practices quickly. Although both are named a project, a Maven project is conceptually very different from a WTP project.

Maven and Eclipse have overlapping functionality such as compiling, building, and testing. However, Eclipse is normally used for developer-centric coding, testing, and debugging activities, whereas Maven is used for team-centric build management, reporting, and deployment. The primary purpose of Maven is to create a documented, repeatable, and modeled build process that is inclusive of all these activities. It complements the development activities in Eclipse.

You will start by defining a new Web project and organizing the resources in this project according to the best practices suggested by Maven. See

`http://maven.apache.org/reference/conventions.html`

for a description of Maven conventions. Maven recommends a standard project directory structure, which is referenced in the Maven Project Object Model (POM). The directory structure of your project will follow Maven conventions (see Example 6.4).

Manual Operation

At the time of writing this book, neither WTP nor Maven had tools to create a Maven-style Web project. Therefore, you will manually prepare the project files to make WTP work with the resource structure of Maven-style projects.

Example 6.4　Maven Project Layout

```
/LeaguePlanetWebProject
+- src/
|   +- main/
|   |   +- java/
|   |   |   +- ...[classes and packages]
|   |   +- resources/
|   |       +- ...
|   |   +- webapp/
|   |   |   +- web-inf/
|   |   |   |   +- classes/
|   |   |   |   |   +- ...[compiled classes]
|   |   |   |   +- lib/
|   |   |   |   |   +- ...[external libraries]
|   |   |   |   +- web.xml
|   |   |   |   +- ...
|   |   |   +- ...[other web files]
|   +- test/
|   |   +- java/
|   |   |   +- ...[test classes and packages]
|   |   +- resources/
|   |       +- ...
|   +- site/
|       +- xdoc/
|           +- ...
+- target/
|   +- ...
+- pom.xml
```

All sources are grouped under the `src` directory. `src/main/java` contains your primary Java classes and packages. `src/test/java` contains your classes and packages for unit tests. src/main/webapp, similar to the WTP webContent folder, contains your Web content, such as the JSP and HTML files, and their supporting resources. src/site/xdoc has sources for the project Web site.

To create the Maven project, do the following:

1. Repeat the steps described earlier in this chapter to create a new dynamic Web project named LeaguePlanetWebProject. Select a target runtime and default configuration for facets. Click the **Next** button to proceed to the Web module settings (see Figure 6.45).

Figure 6.45 Maven Web Module

2. The **Web Module** page lets you specify the directory for Java resources. This is where you will define locations for the Java sources and Web content. Enter src/main/webapp for **Content Directory** and src/main/java for **Java Source Directory**. Click **Finish**.

3. WTP creates the Web project, configuration files, deployment descriptor, and so forth.

Once the project is created, the structural model for the Web project is defined as Example 6.5.

Example 6.5 Structural Model for Maven-Style Web Project

```xml
<?xml version="1.0" encoding="UTF-8"?>
<project-modules id="moduleCoreId" project-version="1.5.0">
  <wb-module deploy-name="LeaguePlanetWebProject">
    <wb-resource source-path="/src/main/webapp" deploy-path="/" />
    <wb-resource source-path="/src/main/java"
      deploy-path="/WEB-INF/classes" />
    <wb-resource source-path="/src/test/java"
      deploy-path="/WEB-INF/classes" />
    <property name="context-root" value="LeaguePlanetWebProject" />
    <property name="java-output-path" value="build/classes" />
  </wb-module>
</project-modules>
```

Classpath Management with Maven and WTP

WTP requires that the `webContent` folder contain the J2EE specification directories `WEB-INF`, `WEB-INF/classes` for the compiled Java classes, and `WEB-INF/lib` for the JARs. All JARs inside this folder are automatically added to the classpath of the project under the **Web App Libraries** category. WTP manages the build path of the project automatically based on the contents of the `WEB-INF` folder.

Maven does not know about your WTP project classpath. It uses dependencies to manage external libraries and code that your project needs. Dependencies are defined in the POM and used to automatically construct a classpath for the Java compiler. Selected libraries are also included in the `WEB-INF/lib` folder. Maven encourages the use of repositories to store and share external libraries, and does not keep them with the project. Instead, Maven retrieves them from a repository when needed. Repositories provide a very consistent and manageable method for maintaining libraries. There is a default Internet-based central Maven repository that keeps most popular Java libraries, served from `ibiblio.org` at

http://www.ibiblio.org/maven/

On the other hand, WTP requires that these libraries be kept inside the `WEB-INF/lib` folder. There is code duplication here. In Maven 1.0, dependencies and WTP can coexist in a number of ways. One such method is to use a mechanism to override dependencies per project. This allows you to maintain your external libraries inside the `WEB-INF/lib` folder and override the JAR dependencies. Maven will then retrieve these libraries from your project location instead of the repository. In Maven 2.0, dependencies are always retrieved from a repository.

Let's review what you accomplished so far. You have created a dynamic Web project using the project layout conventions suggested by Maven (see Figure 6.46).

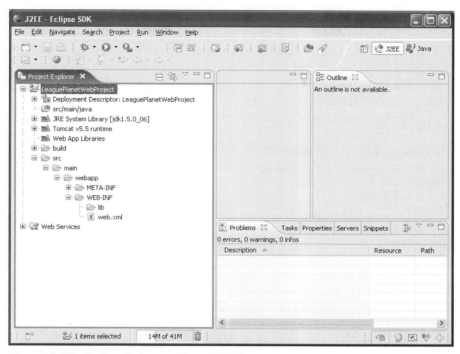

Figure 6.46 Project Explorer—Maven Web Project

Mavenizing the Project

The next step is defining the Maven POM that will automate builds, unit tests, documentation, project reporting, and so on.

The POM is defined by an XML file named pom.xml (see Example 6.6). This file tells Maven everything that it needs to know about your project. Maven has tools that can create skeleton POMs, but we will create the POM from scratch. The snippet shown in Example 6.6 is the start of a POM for your Web application.

Example 6.6 Content of POM

```xml
<?xml version="1.0" encoding="UTF-8"?>
<project>
  <modelVersion>4.0.0</modelVersion>
  <artifactId>leagueplanet</artifactId>
  <groupId>com.leagueplanet</groupId>
  <name>LeaguePlanet.com Web Project</name>
  <version>1.0-SNAPSHOT</version>
  <packaging>war</packaging>
  <build>[...]</build>
  <dependencies>[...]</dependencies>
</project>
```

The project `artifactId` corresponds to the Web application module in your project. Dependencies will define external libraries needed by your Web application. You will use the Struts framework, so `struts*.jar` and `commons*.jar` libraries must be present in this list. The build section tells Maven how the Java sources and other resources are organized. Maven project definition allows you to define filters for including or excluding source files.

The build section is quite simple to set up, as shown in Example 6.7.

Example 6.7 Maven Build Section

```
<?xml version="1.0" encoding="UTF-8"?>
<project>
  [...]
  <build>
    <finalName>${artifactId}-${version}</finalName>
  </build>
</project>
```

The build section can be used to customize your project. Since you used the default location, you do not have to modify anything here. The `finalName` element automatically constructs the name of the exported WAR from other information provided in the POM.

The dependency section is probably the longest (see Example 6.8).

Example 6.8 Maven Dependencies Section

```
<?xml version="1.0" encoding="UTF-8"?>
<project>
  [...]
  <dependencies>
    <dependency>
      <groupId>junit</groupId>
      <artifactId>junit</artifactId>
      <version>3.8.1</version>
      <scope>test</scope>
    </dependency>
    <dependency>
      <groupId>struts</groupId>
      <artifactId>struts</artifactId>
      <version>1.2.7</version>
    </dependency>
    <dependency>
      <groupId>struts</groupId>
      <artifactId>struts-el</artifactId>
      <version>1.2.7</version>
    </dependency>
    <dependency>
      <groupId>commons-validator</groupId>
      <artifactId>commons-validator</artifactId>
```

```
            <version>1.1.4</version>
        </dependency>
        <dependency>
            <groupId>commons-logging</groupId>
            <artifactId>commons-logging</artifactId>
            <version>1.0.3</version>
        </dependency>
        <dependency>
            <groupId>commons-fileupload</groupId>
            <artifactId>commons-fileupload</artifactId>
            <version>1.0</version>
        </dependency>
        <dependency>
            <groupId>antlr</groupId>
            <artifactId>antlr</artifactId>
            <version>2.7.5</version>
        </dependency>
        <dependency>
            <groupId>commons-digester</groupId>
            <artifactId>commons-digester</artifactId>
            <version>1.7</version>
        </dependency>
        <dependency>
            <groupId>commons-beanutils</groupId>
            <artifactId>commons-beanutils</artifactId>
            <version>1.7.0</version>
        </dependency>
        <dependency>
            <groupId>oro</groupId>
            <artifactId>oro</artifactId>
            <version>2.0.8</version>
        </dependency>
        <dependency>
            <groupId>servletapi</groupId>
            <artifactId>servletapi</artifactId>
            <version>2.3</version>
            <scope>compile</scope>
        </dependency>
    </dependencies>
</project>
```

Each entry corresponds to an external JAR that is needed by your project. The Struts framework requires a few of these dependencies to be set. Some of these JARs are needed to compile your code; others, such as JUnit, are for testing. The JARs have a scope tag that defines when they are used. For example, by default all Struts JARs will be included with the Web application module, but JUnit has the scope test, so it will not be included.

Remember that Maven gets the libraries defined in the dependencies from a repository. However, for WTP to function properly, you need to keep a copy of these libraries inside the src/webapp/WEB_INF/lib folder instead of the repository. Unfortunately, there is no tool to synchronize the dependencies and libraries.

You have defined the minimal Maven POM to build your Web application. Maven is typically run from the command line. Maven commands are also called *goals*. Goals are high-level tasks that can include other subtasks. Mevenide is an Eclipse plug-in for Maven that allows you to run Maven goals from the Eclipse IDE. Here you will use the command line. You can build a deployable Web module and a project site by running the maven clean package site goals. The package goal depends on other goals such as compile and test, so Maven will run them automatically. During the build, Maven creates a folder named target to store the generated files. The name and location of the generated files can be modified by additional settings. When you run Maven, you will get an output like that shown in Example 6.9.

Example 6.9 Maven Console Output

```
C:\workspace\LeaguePlanetWebProject>mvn clean package site
[INFO] Scanning for projects...
[INFO] ------------------------------------
[INFO] Building LeaguePlanet.com Web Project
[INFO]     task-segment: [clean, package]
[INFO] ------------------------------------
[INFO] [clean:clean]
[INFO] Deleting directory
  C:\workspace\LeaguePlanetWebProject\target
[INFO] Deleting directory
  C:\workspace\LeaguePlanetWebProject\target\classes
[INFO] Deleting directory
  C:\workspace\LeaguePlanetWebProject\target\test-classes
[INFO] [resources:resources]
[INFO] Using default encoding to copy filtered resources.
[WARNING] While downloading servletapi:servletapi:2.3
  This artifact has been relocated to javax.servlet:servlet-api:2.3.

[INFO] [compiler:compile]
Compiling 1 source file to
C:\workspace\LeaguePlanetWebProject\target\classes
[INFO] [resources:testResources]
[INFO] Using default encoding to copy filtered resources.
[INFO] [compiler:testCompile]
Compiling 1 source file to
  C:\workspace\LeaguePlanetWebProject\target\test-classes
[INFO] [surefire:test]
[INFO] Setting reports dir:
  C:\workspace\LeaguePlanetWebProject\target/surefire-reports


-------------------------------------------------------
 T E S T S
-------------------------------------------------------
[surefire] Running com.leagueplanet.tests.LeaguePlanetBVTTest
[surefire] Tests run: 2, Failures: 0, Errors: 0, Time elapsed: 0.01 sec
[INFO] [site:site]
[INFO] Generate "Continuous Integration" report.
[ERROR] VM #displayTree: error : too few arguments to macro. Wanted 2 got 0
[ERROR] VM #menuItem: error : too few arguments to macro. Wanted 1 got 0
[INFO] Generate "Dependencies" report.
```

```
[INFO] Generate "Issue Tracking" report.
[INFO] Generate "Project License" report.
[INFO] Generate "Mailing Lists" report.
[INFO] Generate "Source Repository" report.
[INFO] Generate "Project Team" report.
[INFO] Generate "Maven Surefire Report" report.
[INFO] Generate an index file for the English version.
[INFO] ------------------------------------------------------------
[INFO] BUILD SUCCESSFUL
[INFO] ------------------------------------------------------------
[INFO] Total time: 11 seconds
[INFO] Finished at: Sat May 13 15:48:09 EEST 2006
[INFO] Final Memory: 9M/17M
[INFO] ------------------------------------------------------------
```

That is all there is to building a WAR with Maven. You will see from the log that package is a composite goal. In addition to assembling a Web application module using the war goal, it runs the java goal to compile the classes and the test goal to compile and run the tests. Once the build is complete, you can browse the results of the build in the target folder (see Figure 6.47).

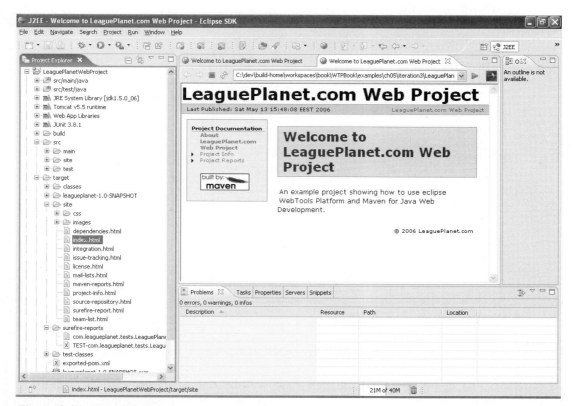

Figure 6.47   Project Site

So far, you could have done most of this using WTP, without the hassle of setting up Maven in the project. Building Web application modules is something
WTP does well, and it does it automatically with minimal effort. But you can get
more out of Maven. The next section shows you how to automate testing and
reporting on the League Planet project using Maven.

Getting More Out of Maven

Now that you can build the Web application module using Maven, you can add tests
and more project information to the POM to find out what more Maven can do.

Unit Tests with Maven

To run unit tests with Maven, you will create JUnit test cases and define required
libraries, including JUnit in the project dependencies. Since you defined the JUnit
dependencies in the previous section, you can start writing a test in the src/tests/
java source folder. In the **Project Explorer**, select LeaguePlanetWebProject, right
click, and invoke the **File ▶ New ▶ Source Folder**. The **New Source Folder** wizard
will open (see Figure 6.48).

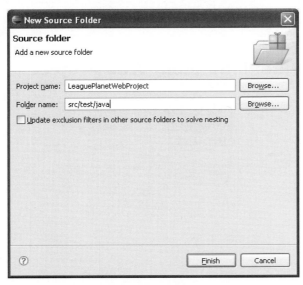

Figure 6.48   Source Folder for Tests

Enter src/test/java as the folder name. Click **Finish**. A new source folder
will be added to the project.

To create a new JUnit test case, invoke the **JUnit test case** wizard using
File ▶ New ▶ JUnit Test Case, and then enter package and class names, for example,

com.leagueplanet.tests and LeaguePlanetBVTTests. Click **Finish**. The wizard will prompt you to add junit.jar to the project build path if it is not included there already. Accept it to add the JAR.

JUnit JAR Is Defined Twice

Remember that Maven does not know about your project classpath. Therefore it will not know about the JUnit JAR unless it is added to the POM dependencies. You add JUnit to the dependencies as shown in Example 6.10.

Example 6.10 Maven JUnit Dependency

```
<dependency>
  <groupId>junit</groupId>
  <artifactId>junit</artifactId>
  <version>3.8.1</version>
  <scope>test</scope>
</dependency>
```

This is inconvenient, but it is something that you will have to live with if you want to use Maven.

A new test class will be created at the location shown in Example 6.11.

Example 6.11 Maven Test Directory

```
/LeaguePlanetWebProject
+- src/
|   +- test/
|   |   +- java/
|   |   |   +- com
|   |   |   |   +- leagueplanet
|   |   |   |   |   +- tests
|   |   |   |   |   |   +- LeaguePlanetBVTTests.java
|   |   |   |   |   |   +- [...] other unit tests
|   [...]
```

Execute the Maven package site goals to run the tests. If you want to run the tests only, you just execute the test goal. Running the Maven test goal creates output as shown in Example 6.12.

Example 6.12 Maven Test Output

```
[INFO] Scanning for projects...
[INFO] ------------------------------------
[INFO] Building LeaguePlanet.com Web Project
[INFO]    task-segment: [test]
[INFO] ------------------------------------
[INFO] [resources:resources]
```

```
[INFO] Using default encoding to copy filtered resources.
[WARNING] while downloading servletapi:servletapi:2.3
  This artifact has been relocated to javax.servlet:servlet-api:2.3.

[INFO] [compiler:compile]
[INFO] Nothing to compile - all classes are up to date
[INFO] [resources:testResources]
[INFO] Using default encoding to copy filtered resources.
[INFO] [compiler:testCompile]
[INFO] Nothing to compile - all classes are up to date
[INFO] [surefire:test]
[INFO] Setting reports dir:
  C:\workspace\LeaguePlanetWebProject\target/surefire-reports


------------------------------------------------------------------

  T E S T S
------------------------------------------------------------------

[surefire] Running com.leagueplanet.tests.LeaguePlanetBVTTest
[surefire] Tests run: 2, Failures: 0, Errors: 0, Time elapsed: 0.03 sec
[INFO] ------------------------------------------------------------
[INFO] BUILD SUCCESSFUL
[INFO] ------------------------------------------------------------
[INFO] Total time: 2 seconds
[INFO] Finished at: Sat May 13 15:58:43 EEST 2006
[INFO] Final Memory: 3M/6M
[INFO] ------------------------------------------------------------
```

You will find the Maven JUnit test reports under the target/surefire-reports folder. Of course, XML reports can be transformed into a more human-readable format, but you will see in the next section that Maven also does this for you (see Figure 6.49).

Project Information and Reports

The Maven project model can also contain information about the developers, configuration and version control systems, issue tracking, mailing lists, and other process-related project information. This information is used by Maven plug-ins to generate project information and reports. The listing shown in Example 6.13 provides the complete code for a typical Maven project model.

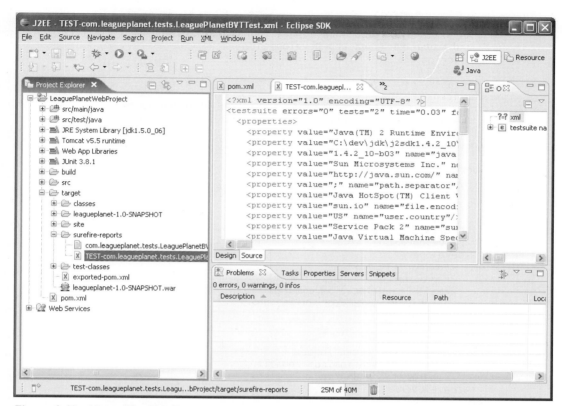

Figure 6.49 Maven JUnit Test Reports

Example 6.13 Listing of pom.xml

```xml
<?xml version="1.0" encoding="UTF-8"?>
<project xmlns="http://maven.apache.org/POM/4.0.0"
  xmlns:xsi="http://www.w3.org/2001/XMLSchema-instance"
  xsi:schemaLocation="http://maven.apache.org/POM/4.0.0
    http://maven.apache.org/maven-v4_0_0.xsd">
  <modelVersion>4.0.0</modelVersion>
  <artifactId>leagueplanet</artifactId>
  <groupId>com.leagueplanet</groupId>
  <name>LeaguePlanet.com Web Project</name>
  <version>1.0-SNAPSHOT</version>

  <packaging>war</packaging>

  <organization>
    <name>LeaguePlanet.com</name>
    <url>http://www.leagueplanet.com/</url>
  </organization>
```

```xml
<description>
    An example project showing how to use eclipse WebTools Platform
    and Maven for Java Web Development.
</description>

<licenses>
  <license>
    <comments>Eclipse Public Licence (EPL)v1.0</comments>
    <url>http://www.eclipse.org/legal/epl-v10.html</url>
  </license>
</licenses>

<developers>
  <developer>
    <id>ndai</id>
    <name>Naci Dai</name>
    <email>naci.dai@eteration.com</email>
    <organization>Eteration</organization>
  </developer>
  <developer>
    <id>lmandel</id>
    <name>Lawrence Mandel</name>
    <email>lmandel@ca.ibm.com</email>
    <organization>IBM</organization>
  </developer>
  <developer>
    <id>ryman</id>
    <name>Arthur Ryman</name>
    <email>ryman@ca.ibm.com</email>
    <organization>IBM</organization>
  </developer>
</developers>

<build>
  <finalName>${artifactId}-${version}</finalName>
</build>
<dependencies>
  <dependency>
    <groupId>junit</groupId>
    <artifactId>junit</artifactId>
    <version>3.8.1</version>
    <scope>test</scope>
  </dependency>
  <dependency>
    <groupId>struts</groupId>
    <artifactId>struts</artifactId>
    <version>1.2.7</version>
  </dependency>
  <dependency>
    <groupId>struts</groupId>
    <artifactId>struts-el</artifactId>
    <version>1.2.7</version>
  </dependency>
  <dependency>
    <groupId>commons-validator</groupId>
```

```
            <artifactId>commons-validator</artifactId>
            <version>1.1.4</version>
          </dependency>
          <dependency>
            <groupId>commons-logging</groupId>
            <artifactId>commons-logging</artifactId>
            <version>1.0.3</version>
          </dependency>
          <dependency>
            <groupId>commons-fileupload</groupId>
            <artifactId>commons-fileupload</artifactId>
            <version>1.0</version>
          </dependency>

          <dependency>
            <groupId>antlr</groupId>
            <artifactId>antlr</artifactId>
            <version>2.7.5</version>
          </dependency>
          <dependency>
            <groupId>commons-digester</groupId>
            <artifactId>commons-digester</artifactId>
            <version>1.7</version>
          </dependency>
          <dependency>
            <groupId>commons-beanutils</groupId>
            <artifactId>commons-beanutils</artifactId>
            <version>1.7.0</version>
          </dependency>
          <dependency>
            <groupId>oro</groupId>
            <artifactId>oro</artifactId>
            <version>2.0.8</version>
          </dependency>
          <dependency>
            <groupId>servletapi</groupId>
            <artifactId>servletapi</artifactId>
            <version>2.3</version>
          </dependency>
        </dependencies>
        <reporting>
          <plugins>
            <plugin>
              <groupId>org.apache.maven.plugins</groupId>
              <artifactId>
                maven-project-info-reports-plugin
              </artifactId>
            </plugin>
            <plugin>
              <groupId>org.apache.maven.plugins</groupId>
              <artifactId>maven-surefire-report-plugin</artifactId>
            </plugin>
          </plugins>
        </reporting>
      </project>
```

The project reports are generated using the Maven site goal. This goal builds a local copy of the project site for reports, documentation, and reference. The result is generated into the target/site directory in the project's base directory, which contains an entire Web site of documentation (see Figure 6.50).

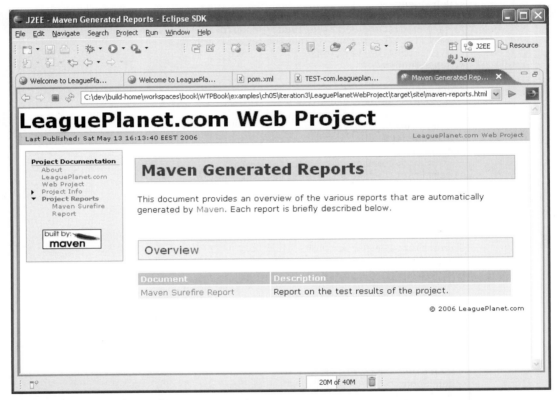

Figure 6.50 Maven Project Reports

Summary

We have described how modules and projects are managed in WTP. You now should have enough knowledge to start exploring these project styles and customizing them as you see fit.

Web projects are very flexible, but they can't model every style of project that you can imagine or that is in use somewhere. Our advice to you is to use one of the more popular templates, such as the default ones created by WTP, or widely published conventions such as Maven. You can build on top of existing know-how and make use of the experience that is readily available. When you are organizing your development, the last thing you want to be is surprised, so do take advantage of well-established best practices.

You can now proceed to either Chapter 7, which covers the presentation layer, or Chapter 8, which covers business logic, depending on the type of development you want to start.

CHAPTER 7

The Presentation Tier

The inmates are running the asylum.

—Alan Cooper

Introduction

Software architecture and design is largely a process of taking a complex system and dividing it into smaller, more manageable subsystems. One of the most important lines of division is that which separates the user interface of a system from its core. The core of a system is often referred to as its *business logic* and the user interface as its *presentation logic*. We discussed the architectural aspects of this division previously in Chapter 5. We discuss WTP support for presentation logic in this chapter and for business logic in the next, Chapter 8.

The division between presentation and business logic is especially important in Web applications for two reasons. First, the user interface is likely to change very frequently to improve its usability and to take advantage of new presentation technologies, but the core is likely to be stable. For example, in a banking system the core operations of transferring money between accounts or paying bills don't change much from year to year, but the bank is very likely to continually improve its ease of use. If there is a clear separation between the presentation logic and the business logic, then the presentation logic can be changed and tested much more quickly, cheaply, and reliably. Second, if the business logic is independent of the presentation logic, then it can be reused in other contexts and made available via other channels. For Web applications, this means that the same business logic can be accessed, for example, by Web browsers, voice response units, and Web services. The set of components that implements the presentation logic of a Web application is referred to as the *presentation tier*. This chapter describes the structure of the presentation tier for Java Web applications and the tools in WTP for developing it.

A large number of powerful technologies, such as HTTP, HTML, CSS, JavaScript, XML, XSLT, servlets, JSP, and JSF, are available for constructing the presentation tier of Java Web applications. The fact that you are reading this book means that you are probably a programmer and are therefore very capable of mastering these technical aspects of user interface development. However, most programmers lack the training to design the nontechnical aspects of the user interface. By nontechnical aspects, we mean things like the way in which the user interacts with the application, and its graphical look and feel. If your development project can afford it, bring in some trained professionals to help you with those aspects. However, adding experts to your team is not always an option, and in any case a basic understanding of these issues is very useful. So before we launch into a discussion of Web technologies, let's spend a little time talking about interaction design and graphic design.

Interaction Design

In his book *The Inmates Are Running the Asylum* [Cooper2004], Alan Cooper defines the concept of *interaction design*, which, simply put, is the process of viewing the application through the eyes of the intended users and designing it accordingly. As the title suggests, this process is not the norm in software development. Instead, the user interaction typically is designed by developers who are focused on the internal structure of the application, with the result that the application frequently has an abominable user interface. How often have you heard the excuse, "We can't do it that way because the code doesn't allow it." when you suggested an improvement to an awkward user interface? Interaction design avoids those problems by putting the users first and designing the application to support the desired user experience.

The main tool of interaction design is the *persona*. A persona is a fictitious user of the application, described in graphic detail. You should define one or more personas for each major user role that the application supports. Each persona is given a name and a lifelike description. The goal is to make the development team start thinking about the personas as if they were real people. It is especially important to describe the skill set of each persona to ensure that the user interface does not make incorrect assumptions.

Let's define the personas for League Planet now. We'll begin with a description of the user roles. All users of League Planet are expected to be comfortable on the Web. They'll have e-mail accounts and know how to use typical Web applications such as Google or Amazon. The main user roles in League Planet are, in order of increasing sophistication: fan, player, manager, and administrator.

○ A *fan* is a user that follows some sports. Since League Planet is for amateur sports, a fan is typically a family member or friend of one of the players. A fan can browse the site for information about leagues, teams, players, and games without signing in. However, when fans sign in, they are shown information according to their interest profile and are given additional capabilities. Fans can register interest in specific items and request notification of certain events, for example, when the location or time of a game changes, when the score of a game changes, or when a specific player scores. Fans can also participate in discussions, communicate with each other, and arrange transportation to and from games.

○ A *player* is a user who participates in some sports. Players are typically school children, teenagers, or young adults. Each player is assigned an account and has all the fan capabilities. Players can control the display of their statistics and can update their own biographical and contact information.

○ A *manager* is a user who registers and sets up the leagues, teams, players, games, and so forth. Managers are expected to have actual experience in managing amateur sports leagues and teams. Managers need to keep accurate records and enter this information into League Planet.

○ Finally, an *administrator* is a user who runs League Planet. An administrator creates and deletes accounts, and monitors the operation of the Web site. League Planet is a geographically distributed organization, so its employees need a Web user interface that allows them to administer the site from any location and at any time. Administrators are information technology professionals.

Now let's create some personas for these roles:

○ *Anne French, Fan:* Anne is a 42-year-old mother of two teenage boys, Max and Jason, who both play hockey. Max is 14 and Anne drives him to practices and games. Jason is 18 and drives a car, but Anne likes to attend his games. Anne has her own personal computer and uses it mainly for e-mail and shopping online. Although Anne can install and update software, she dreads doing so since something always goes wrong and she has little patience for troubleshooting. Anne is especially interested in the car-pooling application available in League Planet since Max's hockey practices are at odd hours. She'd also like to receive text message notifications about schedule changes on her cell phone. She hopes the League Planet user interface will be a no-brainer.

○ *Kenny Pau, Player:* Kenny is a 12-year-old baseball player. He uses the family personal computer mainly for playing Doom, Quake, and Halo. However, he is also very adept at using Google to do research for his homework assignments. Although he thinks it would be very cool to have his own Web page for baseball stats at League Planet, he is not prepared to learn HTML like those loser geeks who belong to the computer club at school.

○ *Sheila MacPherson, Manager:* Sheila is a 21-year-old university student, majoring in psychology. She's the captain of her college's Ultimate Frisbee team and thinks it would be great to use League Planet to coordinate both the regular schedule and playoffs. Sheila uses her laptop computer for all her university assignments. She is very comfortable with spreadsheet software, which she uses for her psychology labs and personal finances. She hopes League Planet will be as easy as that.

○ *Peter Alverez, Administrator:* Peter is a 26-year-old Webmaster. He obtained a bachelor of computer science degree from a state university where he picked up UNIX system administration skills in his spare time by running one of the labs. After graduating, he did Web development for a small start-up that went broke after two years. He recently has been hired by League Planet as an administrator. Peter lives thousands of miles and several time zones away from the League Planet main office and will work remotely.

The astute reader will notice that we have employed the mnemonic device of starting the last name of each persona with the same letter as their user role. However, after a while these personas should become so familiar to us that no mnemonic will be necessary. The personas should come alive to us. For example, when we design the player user interface we should be asking ourselves what Kenny would think of it. If we are tempted to introduce some Wiki-like syntax for marking up the player biographies, then we should quickly reject it on the grounds that Kenny would think it was turning him into a geek. On the other hand, if we think that managers might like to import and export team information in comma-separated value format, then we should tell ourselves that Sheila, the spreadsheet expert, would probably appreciate that.

Graphic Design

Graphic design includes the layout of Web pages and the selection of colors, typography, and images. Creating a pleasing graphic design requires both talent and training and is best left to a skilled professional. Although some programmers do possess artistic ability, they are the exception. The rest of us can, however, take some steps to improve the situation.

If you cannot employ the services of a professional graphic designer, then you can at least learn how to avoid the most obvious errors. In their classic book, *Web Pages That Suck* [Flanders1996], Vincent Flanders and Michael Willis teach good design principles by looking at bad examples. Their book is both informative and highly entertaining.

For a very accessible introduction to the principles of visual design and typography, see *The Non-Designer's Design Book* [Williams1994] by Robin Williams. This book discusses the use of proximity, alignment, repetition, and contrast in design and also explains how to select and combine typographic elements. Although this book was written for print media, it applies equally well to the Web. For specific guidelines for Web design, see the sequel, *The Non-Designer's Web Book* [Williams1998], by Robin Williams and John Tollett.

If you are interested in acquiring UI design skills, there are excellent resources available. *Designing Interfaces* [Tidwell2005] by Jennifer Tidwell takes an overall look at Web usability, but is for people who already know basic UI terminology and core UI design concepts. You can also find professional advice on the Web at sites such as Luke Wrobleski's LukeW Interface Designs at

```
http://www.lukew.com/
```

Even if you are an expert graphic designer, you should separate the graphic style elements from the presentation logic as much as possible so they can be changed independently. In the extreme case, you might want to allow the end user to change the graphic design elements while the application is running. One of the simplest techniques you can use is stylesheets. A *stylesheet* lets you separate the presentation of a Web page from its content. There are two standard stylesheet technologies in common use on the Web: CSS and XSLT. We'll discuss the tools available in WTP for developing CSS and XSLT later (see the sections Iteration 2: CSS and Iteration 4: XML and XSLT).

CSS is the most widespread stylesheet technology. CSS lets you control the color, font, alignment, spacing, and other display properties of HTML tags. The presentation logic of your Web application should avoid directly specifying these display properties in the HTML. Instead, HTML tags should include a `class` attribute that abstractly defines their content, and the display properties of each class should be specified in a CSS document. Although CSS is very powerful, it is limited in that it cannot change the order in which the page content is presented. If you need to rearrange the content, use XSLT.

XSLT allows very general rearrangements and transformations of the page content. However, to use XSLT the page content must be well-formed XML. While CSS is applied in the Web browser, XSLT may be applied either in the Web browser or the Web server. Applying XSLT on the Web server is generally a safer option in practice since not all browsers support XSLT, and those that do support it may have subtle differences.

CSS and XSLT are in fact complementary technologies. Although it is possible to include display properties in the output of XSLT, it is generally a better design to limit XSLT to rearranging and transforming the page content into HTML with class attributes so that CSS can be applied to it in the Web browser. XSLT is a much more complex format than CSS, so it is therefore easier to make changes to display properties if they are specified in CSS.

In summary, good graphic design requires talent and training. The presentation logic should therefore use stylesheets to separate the page content from its graphic design elements so they can be more easily changed by a skilled professional. However, if you have to create the graphic design yourself, at least be aware of the basic principles and try to avoid the most common errors.

The Structure of the Presentation Tier

The first Web browsers were fairly simple, being limited to presenting HTML pages and handling fill-in forms. However, as desktop computers became more capable, Web browsers evolved to include many powerful processing technologies, including scripting languages such as JavaScript; plug-ins for Flash, Java, PDF, and so forth; and XML languages such as XSLT, SVG, and MathML. This increase in client-side processing power enabled a new architecture for the presentation tier. Rather than do all the processing on the server, processing could now be done either on the server or the client, wherever it made the most sense.

Consider the problem of data entry. Many Web applications contain fill-in forms that may have dozens of data entry fields. In this situation, there is much scope for user error. Some fields may be required, some may be numeric values that must lie within a certain range, while others, such as e-mail addresses and telephone numbers, may need to obey certain syntax rules. The server side of the application should be bulletproof. It should assume that it will receive bad data and always perform a complete set of validity checks. However, if the validity checks are only performed at the server, then the user experience will be poor. If the data contains several errors, the user may have to repeatedly submit the form to resolve all the problems. Each time the user submits the form there will be the usual network and server processing delays. A better design is to perform as many validity checks as possible on the client. This will improve the responsiveness of the application and produce a better user experience. It will also have the benefit of reducing the load on the server. Of course, there will always be a cost-benefit trade-off when deciding what validations can be done on the client. For example, checking that a street address matches a zip code requires a database that is too large to be sent to a client.

Another excellent use of client-side processing is data presentation. For example, consider the result of a database query presented as a multi-column table. The user may want to view the data sorted by different columns or as a chart in different styles. With client-side processing, the raw data can be sent to the Web browser once and then redisplayed many times according to the user's selections. Again, the benefit is improved response time and reduced server load.

In traditional multi-tiered distributed applications, the presentation tier is called *Tier-1*, the business logic tier is *Tier-2*, and the persistence tier is *Tier-3*. Tier-1 is traditionally a desktop computer with a windowing user interface. However, the presentation tier in modern Web applications is in fact physically split between the Web browser client and the Web application server. The client side is sometimes referred to as *Tier-0*, although this term is often used for limited capability wireless devices such as cell phones and PDAs.

In J2EE parlance, a multi-tiered distributed application is spread over a *client tier*, a *middle tier*, and an *Enterprise Information System (EIS) tier*. The client tier is the end-user device such as a desktop computer or cell phone. The middle tier consists of several modules such as *Web containers* and *EJB containers*. The EIS tier consists of databases, Enterprise Resource Planning (ERP) systems, and other legacy applications. Refer to section 1.2.1.1 in *Multitier Model* of *Designing Enterprise Applications with the J2EE Platform, Second Edition* [Singh2002], for more details. Thus in J2EE, the presentation tier physically consists of the client tier and a Web container on the middle tier. WTP currently supports development for a presentation tier that consists of a Web browser on the client tier and a Web container on the middle tier.

One of the hottest new Web browser technologies is Asynchronous JavaScript and XML (AJAX). In this approach, the Web browser makes asynchronous requests for XML data from the server. The use of asynchronous requests means that the user interface is not blocked waiting for the server to respond. Instead, when the response is received, a user-supplied callback function is invoked to process the data. XML is used here as a data interchange format. Clearly, Web services are an important potential source of AJAX data. For more information on using AJAX with J2EE, see *Asynchronous JavaScript*

Technology and XML (AJAX) With Java 2 Platform, Enterprise Edition [Murray2005] by Greg Murray.

The ability to make asynchronous HTTP requests was introduced via the XMLHTTP ActiveX object in Internet Explorer 5. Compatible implementations of an XMLHttpRequest object were later added to Mozilla and other browsers, making the development of cross-browser applications feasible. Google then exploited this capability in some highly successful Web applications such as Google Maps and Google Suggest, thereby generating a wave of interest in the AJAX approach. Refer to *Ajax: A New Approach to Web Applications* [Garrett2005] by Jesse James Garrett for a more complete description.

Although WTP does not currently include any explicit support for AJAX development, aside from JavaScript editing, there is a new Eclipse project, the AJAX Toolkit Framework (ATF), in the works that extends WTP for this purpose. Watch for a full-fledged JavaScript debugger that is seamlessly integrated with WTP in a future release.

AJAX development can be simplified through the use of a JavaScript framework or toolkit. One of the most popular AJAX toolkits is Dojo. You can obtain the Dojo toolkit from

```
http://dojotoolkit.org/
```

For a good introduction to Dojo development, refer to "Develop HTML Widgets with Dojo" [Kusakov2006] by Igor Kusakov.

Although it is possible to use Java applets in Web browsers, we will not be discussing them here. Java applets are part of J2SE, and tools for developing them are available in the Eclipse JDT and Visual Editor (VE) projects. WTP supports Tier-0 development via the HTML, CSS, JavaScript, and XML editors.

Historically, Java burst onto the Web landscape via Java applets. However, Java applets had many problematic aspects and today are not the dominant technology for implementing browser-based interactivity. In contrast, when Java servlets were introduced, they had many advantages over traditional server-side Common Gateway Interface (CGI) programs. This led to the rapid growth of Java as an important server-side development technology. Today, the real sweet spot for Java in the presentation tier lies in the Web container, not the browser. WTP includes tools for developing servlet, JSP, and JSF components, which are part of J2EE (and Java EE 5).

The presentation tier is an extremely fertile ground for innovation. In addition to J2EE, the other main technologies are LAMP and .NET, both of which are outside the scope of WTP. However, WTP is the base for the new Eclipse PHP project, which is aimed at LAMP development. There are also a large number of Java frameworks based on J2EE. These include Struts, Velocity, Tiles, Tapestry, Cocoon,

Spring MVC, and many more. There are Eclipse-based tools for many of these frameworks, and some of them either currently extend WTP or have plans to do so. For example, the Eclipse Lepido project, which contains tools for Cocoon, is based on WTP. Similarly the Spring IDE project is also based on WTP.

No discussion of presentation tier structure would be complete without mentioning portal and edge servers. A *portal server* provides user interface integration for multiple small applications called *portlets*. Commercial and Open Source portal servers are available in many technologies, including Java. The Java specification for portlets is defined by JSR 168. Commercial portlet development tools based on WTP are under development.

An *edge server* provides user interface scalability by off-loading the main application server. A network of edge servers is distributed geographically to move the presentation tier closer to the end users. The use of an edge server, such as that offered by Akamai, requires some special HTML markup. Edge server support is outside the scope of WTP.

We'll explore WTP support for presentation tier development by building part of the League Planet Web site using the following sequence of iterations:

○ In Iteration 1 you use the HTML editor to create a schedule of games for an ice hockey league. We'll also discuss static Web projects and the general features of the WTP Structured Source Editors, including content assist, templates, and snippets.

○ In Iteration 2 you add some style to the game schedule using the CSS editor.

○ In Iteration 3 you add some client-side processing to the schedule using the JavaScript editor. You also create an HTML fill-in form to enter game scores. You use JavaScript to perform e-mail address obfuscation and form validation.

○ In Iteration 4 you convert the schedule into XML using the XML editor and create an XSLT stylesheet to transform it to HTML.

○ In Iteration 5 you generate a DTD for the schedule, modify it using the DTD editor, and validate the schedule data against the DTD.

○ In Iteration 6 you add some server-side processing by creating a servlet to apply the XSLT to the XML data for the schedule. We'll also discuss dynamic Web projects and the Server tools.

○ In Iteration 7 you add a JSP to generate the HTML fill-in form for entering game scores using the JSP editor. We'll also discuss user authentication, HTTP sessions, and Web browser cookies.

○ In Iteration 8 you monitor the HTTP traffic using the TCP/IP Monitor to understand how HTTP sessions are maintained.

Iteration 1: Static Web Projects, HTML, and the Structured Source Editors

In this iteration, you are going to start work on the part of the League Planet Web site that displays the game schedules for ice hockey leagues. These Web pages will be viewed by all users, including fans, so they must be very simple and easy to use. In the actual League Planet Web site, these pages will probably be dynamically generated from a database. However, to start the design process, you can develop the page layout using static HTML pages.

Static Web Projects

WTP supports both *static* and *dynamic* Web projects. A static Web project is simply a collection of resources, such as HTML, CSS, and JavaScript, that can be sent directly to Web browsers without any J2EE server-side processing. In contrast, a dynamic Web project contains additional J2EE resources, such as JSPs and servlets, that require server-side processing. This terminology is somewhat misleading, since there are many other ways to generate dynamic Web content besides J2EE. For example, dynamic Web content can also be generated using server-side includes, CGI scripts, and PHP. Although WTP has attempted to move all J2EE dependencies into the J2EE Standard Tools (JST) subproject, the separation is not perfect, and there are still a few J2EE remnants, such as the static terminology, lurking in the WST subproject. The situation will undoubtedly improve as more Web tools, especially those for PHP, are based on WTP.

Since you are only concerned with the client tier for the first few iterations, you'll start by creating a static Web project, as follows:

1. Launch Eclipse, and invoke the File ► New ► Project command to open the New Project wizard (see Figure 7.1).

2. Open the Web folder, select the Static Web Project item, and click the Next button to open the New Static Web Project wizard (see Figure 7.2).

3. The first page of the wizard lets you specify the project name and target runtime. Enter the name icehockey for the Project name. Leave the Target Runtime blank. WTP does not currently include any server adapters for purely static Web projects; however, as WTP is used by more projects, we expect some adapters to be contributed, such as for the Apache Web server. Click the Next button to proceed to the Select Project Facets page (see Figure 7.3).

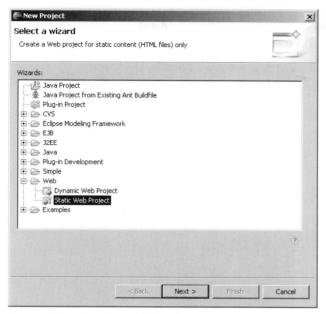

Figure 7.1   New Project Wizard

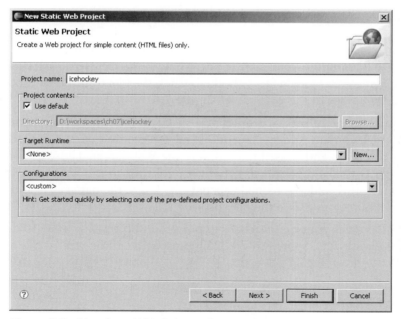

Figure 7.2   New Static Web Project—Project Name

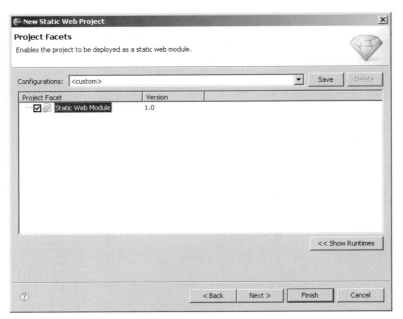

Figure 7.3   New Static Web Project—Facets

4. The second page of the wizard lets you specify the project facets. We'll discuss project facets more in the context of dynamic Web projects. Briefly, a *project facet* specifies what you want to develop in your project. The wizard will configure your project according to the facets you select. Leave the **Static Web Module** facet checked. Click the **Next** button to proceed to the final page of the wizard (see Figure 7.4).

5. The last page of the wizard lets you specify a context root and a name for the Web content folder. The context root is the first part of the URL path for resources and is used to configure the Web server. The Web content folder contains the resources that get published to the Web server. By default, this folder is named webContent. Leave the name as is and click the **Finish** button to create the new project.

6. WTP creates your new icehockey project and the webContent folder in it (see Figure 7.5). Switch to the J2EE perspective if the wizard did not do so.

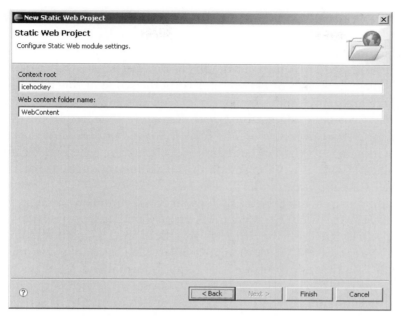

Figure 7.4   New Static Web Project—Web Content Folder

Figure 7.5   Project Explorer

HTML

You've now created your Web project and are ready to create an HTML file. As a Web application developer, you will need to have a good knowledge of HTML, especially if you are using vanilla WTP. Although there are many other tools that do support visual (a.k.a. "What You See Is What You Get," or WYSIWYG) editing, WTP currently only supports source editing. However, even if WTP did include a visual HTML editor, you, as an application developer, would still need to understand HTML for many other purposes, for example, to write JavaScript code that produced Dynamic HTML (DHTML) effects.

A detailed discussion of HTML is beyond the scope of this book, but fortunately there are many other excellent books on this topic. See part two of *Web Design in a Nutshell: A Desktop Quick Reference* [Niederst1999] by Jennifer Niederst for a short overview or *The HTML Sourcebook: A Complete Guide to HTML* [Graham1995] by Ian Graham for a more comprehensive treatment. Of course, since HTML is a W3C standard, the definitive source of information is the *HTML 4.01 Specification* [HTML401].

In addition to classic HTML, there is an XML-compliant version, XHTML. Refer to *XHTML™ 1.0 The Extensible HyperText Markup Language (Second Edition)* [XHTML10] for the complete specification. The main reason for using XHTML instead of HTML is to enable other XML technologies, most importantly, XSLT. In the following, we'll be rather informal and use the generic term HTML to mean HTML 4.01, XHTML 1.0, or any other member of this family.

You'll begin work on the League Planet presentation tier by developing the HTML to display ice hockey schedules. A schedule is simply a list of games showing their date, time, location, teams, and—if the game has already been played—the result. A league will typically have a regular season schedule and a play-off schedule. There might also be schedules for tournaments. In ice hockey, the location is called an arena, and one team is designated as the home team and the other as the visitor. The home team has certain advantages, such as the ability to make the last line change before a face-off.

When designing HTML pages, it's a good idea to have some realistic content. You'll create the 2005–2006 Regular Season Schedule for the fictitious Rosehill Girls Hockey League. This league consists of four high school teams named the Foxes, Ladybugs, Snowflakes, and Vixens. The teams play at the Hillview High School and Maple Community Centre arenas. Create the schedule as follows.

1. Since you are going to use the HTML editor, confirm that it is the default editor associated with files named *.html. In the main menu bar, select the **Window ▸ Preferences** menu item to open the **Preferences** dialog (see Figure 7.6). Expand the **General** category and its **Editors** subcategory, then open the **File Associations** page and select *.html in the **File types** list. Select **HTML Editor** in the **Associated editors** list and click the **Default** button to make it the default if it is not currently the default. Click the **OK** button to close the dialog.

2. In the **Project Explorer** view, expand the icehockey project folder. Right click on the webContent folder and invoke the **New ▸ HTML** menu item to launch the **New HTML Page** wizard (see Figure 7.7).

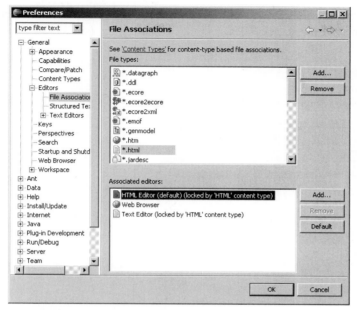

Figure 7.6   HTML File Associations

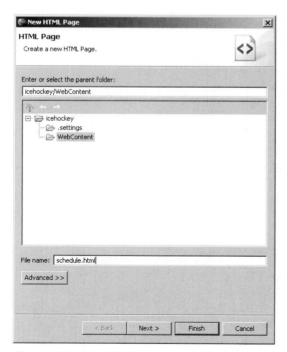

Figure 7.7   New HTML File—Enter Name

3. In the **File name** field, enter the name `schedule.html` and click the **Next** button to proceed to the **Select HTML Template** page (see Figure 7.8).

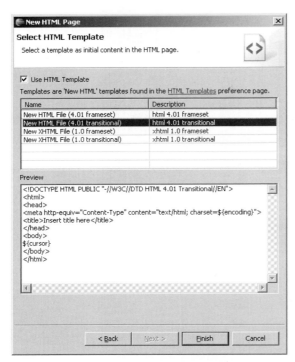

Figure 7.8   New HTML File—Select Template

4. The **Select HTML Template** page lists templates for typical HTML pages. A *template* is a boilerplate document that contains both fixed text and variable slots that get filled in with data when the document is created. WTP provides a few built-in templates and you can add your own. We'll discuss templates in more detail later in the Templates section. For now, accept the default selection of `HTML 4.01 transitional` and click the **Finish** button. The wizard creates a new HTML file and opens it in the HTML source editor (see Figure 7.9).

You've now created the new HTML file, `schedule.html`, and are ready to enter content. The HTML editor has many of the features of a Java editor, such as content assist. Invoke content assist as usual by typing `Ctrl+Space` to get a list of suggestions. Enter some of the content for `schedule.html` (see Example 7.1), and then import the complete file from the examples (see the Source Code Examples section in Chapter 1 for a description of how to import examples).

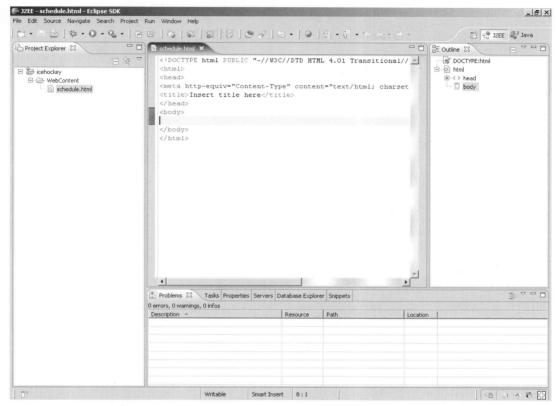

Figure 7.9 HTML Editor

Example 7.1 Listing of schedule.html

```html
<!DOCTYPE HTML PUBLIC "-//W3C//DTD HTML 4.01 Transitional//EN">
<html>
<head>
<meta http-equiv="Content-Type"
  content="text/html; charset=ISO-8859-1">
<title>Rosehill Girls Hockey League 2005-2006 Regular Season
Schedule</title>
</head>
<body>
<h1>Rosehill Girls Hockey League</h1>
<h2>2005-2006 Regular Season Schedule</h2>
<table>
  <thead>
    <tr>
      <th>Date</th>
      <th>Time</th>
      <th>Arena</th>
      <th>Visitor</th>
```

```
          <th>Home</th>
          <th>Score</th>
        </tr>
      </thead>
      <tbody>
        <tr>
          <td>Jan. 7, 2006</td>
          <td>7:00 PM</td>
          <td>Hillview High School</td>
          <td>Ladybugs</td>
          <td>Vixens</td>
          <td>3-7</td>
        </tr>
        <tr>
          <td>Jan. 7, 2006</td>
          <td>9:00 PM</td>
          <td>Hillview High School</td>
          <td>Snowflakes</td>
          <td>Foxes</td>
          <td>5-2</td>
        </tr>
          .
          .
          .
        <tr>
          <td>Jan. 22, 2006</td>
          <td>7:30 PM</td>
          <td>Maple Community Centre</td>
          <td>Snowflakes</td>
          <td>Vixens</td>
          <td>2-6</td>
        </tr>
      </tbody>
    </table>
  </body>
</html>
```

schedule.html is a very simple HTML document. The <h1> element contains the name of the league, the <h2> element contains the name of the schedule, and the <table> element contains the list of games with one game per row and one field per column. To view this document in a Web browser, select it in the **Project Explorer**, right click, and invoke the **Open With Web Browser** menu item. The document will be opened in the currently selected Web browser (see Figure 7.10).

Here the currently selected Web browser is the Eclipse **Internal Web Browser**, which is integrated into the editor window. Eclipse also lets you select an external Web browser. You can select the **Default system** Web browser, which is the Web browser the operating system uses by default to open HTML files, or you can explicitly select any registered Web browser. You can select the Web browser using the **Window ▸ Web Browser** submenu of the **General** category **Web Browser** preference page (see Figure 7.11).

Figure 7.10   Web Browser—schedule.html

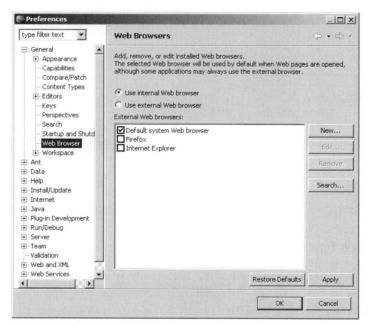

Figure 7.11   Web Browser Preferences

The Eclipse **Web Browser** preferences are very handy, but they limit you to using one Web browser at a time. This can be a problem in some situations. For example, suppose you want to do a side-by-side comparison of a more advanced DHTML version of schedule.html in two or more Web browsers to ensure that it displays correctly. The solution is to use the **File Association** preferences (see Figure 7.6). Simply associate each externally installed Web browser as an editor for the file extension *.html by clicking the **Add** button. Depending on how you installed each Web browser, it may be listed as an external program or you may need to click the **Browse** button to find it (see Figure 7.12).

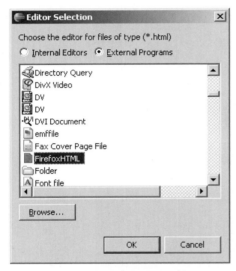

Figure 7.12   Editor Selection—*.html

schedule.html contains all the information a League Planet user needs, but it is rather drab and has no hyperlinks to related information, such as the teams or the league (see Figure 7.10). However, it is a good starting point for further development. We'll address the drabness issue by using CSS. However, before doing that we'll look at some general features of the WTP family of structured source editors.

Structured Source Editors

One of the major contributions of WTP is that it extends the Eclipse platform with source editors for many of the formats used in Java Web application development. WTP has source editors for HTML, CSS, JavaScript, XML, DTD, XSD, WSDL, JSP, and the family of J2EE XML deployment descriptors including web.xml, ejb-jar.xml, and application.xml. The design goal for these editors was to make them as similar as possible to the Java source editor in the Eclipse Java Development Tools so that Eclipse users would feel at home in WTP. This goal is a work in progress. It will take a few more releases before all the WTP source editors achieve the polish of JDT, but many of the key features are already implemented. If you are an aspiring Eclipse plug-in developer and are interested in source editors, the WTP project would welcome your contributions!

For more information about the structured source editors, refer to the *Editing markup language files* section of the *Web Application Development Guide* of the WTP Help. In the Help documentation, the term *structured text editor* is used instead of *structured source editor*.

The structured source editors provide a collection of features that help developers edit files that contain markup and programming languages. These languages define a structure that the files must adhere to. The structured source editors provide menu commands, visual cues, and prompts that help developers create well-structured files. Some of the major features of the structured source editors are:

- ❍ Undo and Redo: The editor provides the ability to undo and redo an unlimited number of editing operations.

- ❍ Syntax Highlighting: Keywords and syntax elements can be assigned different colors that are specified by user preferences.

- ❍ Formatting: Source can be reformatted using indentation and line widths that are specified by user preferences.

- ❍ Content Assist: A list of suggested completions can be displayed by typing `Ctrl+Space`.

- ❍ Error Highlighting: Invalid text is indicated by a wavy red underline.

- ❍ Marginal Indicators: The editors display useful information in the right and left margins. The range of the currently selected structure is displayed in the outer left margin. Quick diff information is displayed in the inner left margin. Error information is displayed in the right margin.

- ❍ Templates and Snippets: User-defined text fragments that contain variable slots can be used in file creation and content assist. We'll discuss these in detail in the following sections.

Many of the features of the structured source editors are controlled by user preferences. The structured source editors inherit the **Text Editor** preferences, which are found under the **General** category, **Editors** subcategory. Settings that apply to all the structured source editors are made in the **General ▸ Editors ▸ Structured Text Editors** preferences (see Figure 7.13).

Settings for specific types of structured source files, HTML for example, are made in the **Web and XML** preferences (see Figure 7.14).

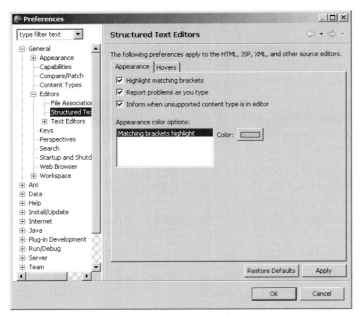

Figure 7.13   Structured Text Editor Preferences

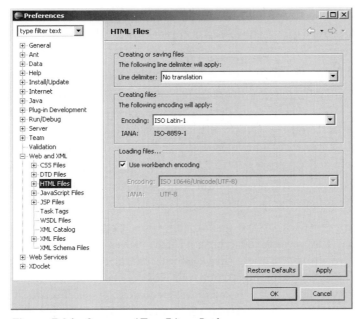

Figure 7.14   Structured Text Editor Preferences

There are too many preferences to describe here. The best way to understand the effect of a preference is simply to try it. Go ahead and explore the various preferences. If you are trying to control some specific aspect of editor behavior, be sure to search the **Preferences** dialog for it. You can filter the display of preferences by entering the keyword you are interested in. More than likely, you'll find what you're looking for.

For example, suppose you are trying to change the tab width. Do the following:

1. Open the **Preferences** dialog and enter the keyword `tab` (see Figure 7.15).

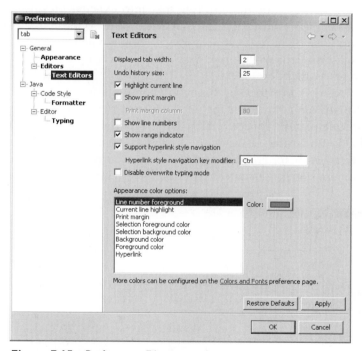

Figure 7.15   Preferences Filtering—tab

2. Select the **General ▸ Editors ▸ Text Editors** page and enter the desired value, for example, 2, in the **Displayed tab width** field.

3. Click the **Apply** button and watch any open text editor redisplay your file with the new tab width.

Templates

Recall that when you created an HTML file, the wizard offered you the choice of a template on which to base your document (see Figure 7.8 earlier). A *template* is a text pattern that acts as a boilerplate for a document or some part of a document. A template contains a combination of static text and variables. Variables are denoted by the syntax ${name}, where name is the variable name. There are a few predefined variables, such as date and user, and you can add custom variables. The variables are replaced by values when the template is instantiated. The values of the predefined variables are automatically generated. The values of the custom variables are initialized to the variable name, and you are placed in a special variable entry mode in which each custom variable is surrounded by a box and you can move from one variable to another using the Tab key. A template can be used for either creating new files or for inserting text into existing files using content assist. Template-enabled editors typically provide some built-in templates and allow you to add your own. You can export the template definitions to a file and import them back into your workspace. This lets you back up template definitions and share them with other developers.

Template support is provided by the base Eclipse platform, and the Java and Ant editors take advantage of this capability. Most of the WTP structured source editors support templates. To see which editors support templates, open the **Preferences** dialog and filter it using the keyword template (see Figure 7.16). Templates are very handy for creating new structured source files that require hard-to-remember content such as document type and XML namespace declarations.

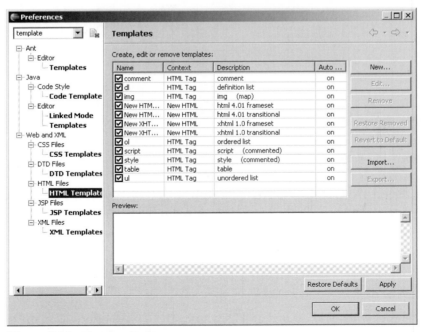

Figure 7.16   Template Preferences

For example, suppose you want to create and use a template for the HTML `<a>` element that prompts you for the URL value of the `href` attribute. Do the following:

1. Open the **Preferences** dialog and select the HTML templates page (see Figure 7.6 earlier). Click the **New** button to add the new template.

2. Enter a for the template **Name** and `anchor with href` for its **Description**. Enter `<a href="${url}">${cursor}</a>` as the **Pattern**. Here `${url}` is a custom variable. `${cursor}` is a predefined variable. It specifies where the cursor should move after you enter the last custom variable value. Click the **OK** button to create the new template (see Figure 7.17).

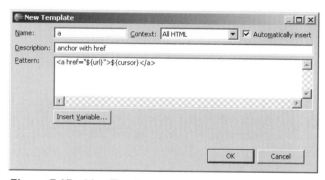

Figure 7.17   New Template

3. The new template has now been added to the HTML templates. Close the **Preferences** dialog by clicking its **OK** button.

4. The template is now ready to use. Open `schedule.html` in the HTML editor and place the insertion cursor after the `<body>` tag. Press `Ctrl+Space` for content assist and type the letter a to filter the list of suggestions (see Figure 7.18).

5. Select the `# a - anchor with href` item from the list of suggestions and press `Enter` to insert the template. The HTML editor goes into template variable entry mode (see Figure 7.19).

6. The editor is now prompting you to enter a value for the `url` variable. Type the URL

   `http://leagueplanet.com`

   and press `Tab` to move the insertion point.

7. The editor moves the insertion point to the content of `<a>` element that was specified using the `cursor` predefined variable (see Figure 7.20).

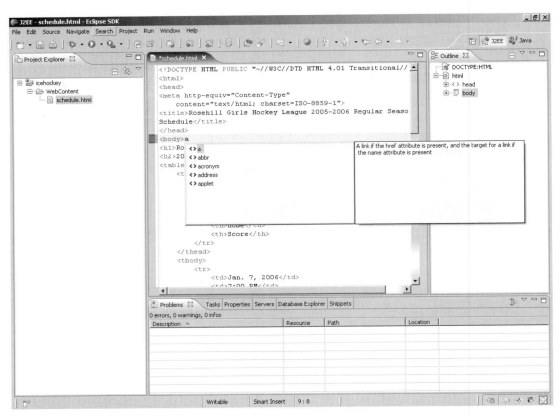

Figure 7.18   Content Assist—a Template

Snippets

Snippets, like templates, are also text patterns that consist of static text and variables. Snippets may contain HTML, JSP, Java, or any other type of text. Snippets have their own view that presents them as a palette of drawers, each containing a specific category. You insert snippets into source code using the **Snippets** view instead of using content assist. After inserting a snippet, you supply values for variables using a special dialog instead of using the editor variable entry mode. You can easily create new snippets by selecting code in an editor and invoking the **Add to Snippets** pop-up menu item or by pasting code into the **Snippets** view. You customize snippets using a special dialog instead of the **Preferences** dialog. Like templates, you can import and export snippet definitions. Unlike templates, snippets cannot use the predefined variables, nor can they be used for new file creation.

Figure 7.19 Template Variable Entry Mode

Figure 7.20 End of Template Variable Entry

Snippets are a WTP feature and are not currently available in the base Eclipse platform. However, snippets are useful for text editing in general and do not have any specific dependencies on Web applications. In view of the more general applicability of snippets and the many similarities between snippets and templates, it would seem to make sense to move snippets into the base Eclipse platform and to unify them with templates.

To illustrate the similarities and differences between templates and snippets, you'll redo the preceding HTML <a> element template example as a snippet. Do the following

1. With `schedule.html` still open in the HTML editor, select the complete `<a>...</a>` element contents that you just inserted as a template, right click, and invoke the **Add to Snippets** item from the pop-up menu (see Figure 7.21). Alternatively, copy the selected text to the clipboard, then select the **Paste as Snippet** item from the **Snippets** view's pop-up menu.

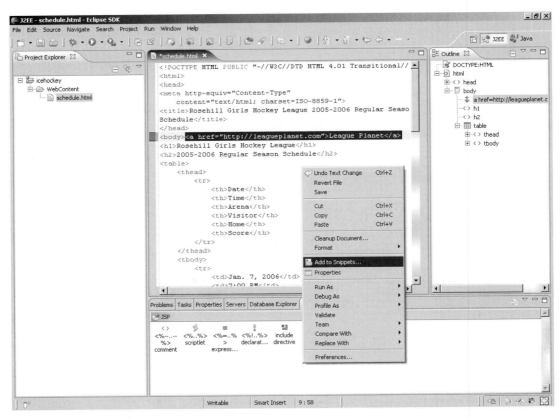

Figure 7.21 Add to Snippets

2. Since this is your first snippet, you need to create a new category for it. WTP comes with a predefined JSP category, but you can't add your snippet to that. The **New Category** dialog opens. Enter the category name HTML and press the **OK** button (see Figure 7.22).

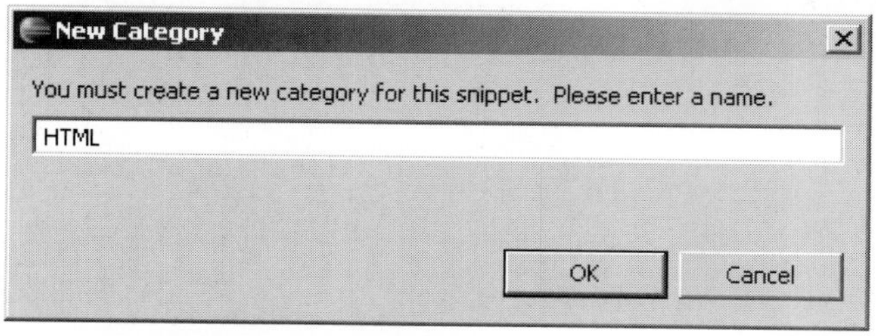

```
New Category                                        [x]

You must create a new category for this snippet.  Please enter a name.

HTML

                              OK            Cancel
```

Figure 7.22   New Category

3. The **Customize Palette** dialog opens. Enter anchor tag as the **Name** and HTML anchor with href as the **Description**. Click the **New** button twice to add two variables. Name the variables content and url, give them the descriptions Link Content and Link URL, and the default values League Planet and

   http://leagueplanet.com

   Edit the **Template Pattern** to be

   ```
   <a href="${url}">${content}</a>
   ```

   To insert the variables in the pattern, click the **Insert Variable Placeholders** button and select the variable name from the list. Click the **OK** button to save the new snippet (see Figure 7.23).

4. The **Snippets** view now contains the new anchor tag snippet (see Figure 7.24).

5. You are now ready to use the new snippet. In the HTML editor, select the content of the <h1> element, Rosehill Girls Hockey League, and cut it to the clipboard. Cutting the league name to the clipboard both removes it from the file and makes it available to paste back in the next step after you insert the anchor tag snippet. Double-click the anchor tag snippet to insert it into the HTML editor. Alternatively, drag and drop the snippet to the content of the <h1> element using the mouse. The **Insert Template** dialog opens.

6. You can now enter values for the snippet variables. Paste the league name, which is on the clipboard, into the value of the content variable and edit the url variable to be

`http://leagueplanet.com/rghl`

Click the **Insert** button to insert the snippet into the HTML document (see Figure 7.25).

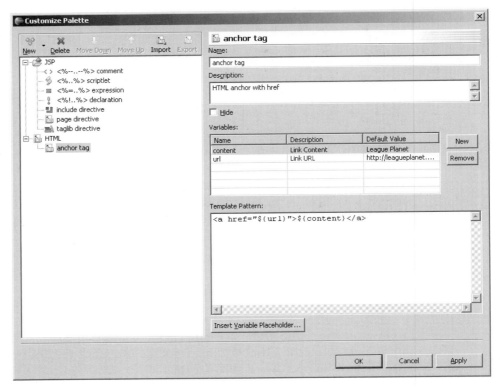

Figure 7.23   Customize Palette

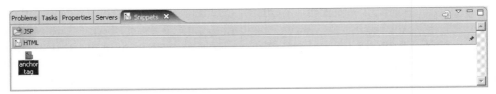

Figure 7.24   anchor tag Snippet

7. The HTML document now contains the snippet with the variables replaced by the values you entered (see Figure 7.26).

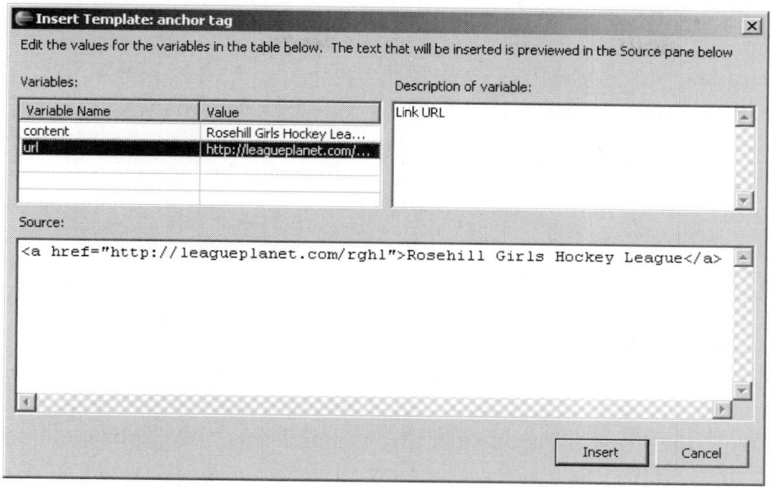

Figure 7.25   Insert Template—anchor tag

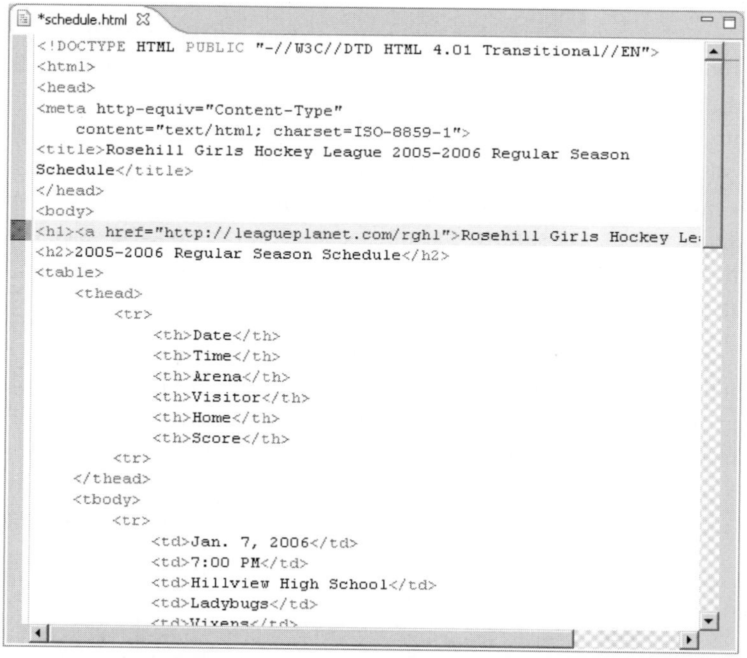

Figure 7.26   HTML Document with anchor tag Snippet Inserted

Summary of Iteration 1

In this iteration you created a static Web project and added an HTML page to it. You edited the page using the HTML source editor, which is a member of the WTP structured source editor family. You learned about the features common to members of this family. These include content assist, templates, and snippets. You are now ready to liven up your HTML page by adding CSS styles to it.

Iteration 2: CSS

Now that you understand the basics of HTML editing, it's time to move on to the CSS editor. As mentioned previously, schedule.html contains the information we want, but it is rather drab. Brightening it up is a perfect job for CSS. A detailed treatment of CSS is beyond the scope of this book, but we'll cover a few basic concepts here. For a brief overview of CSS, see Chapter 23 of *Web Design in a Nutshell* [Niederst1999] by Jennifer Niederst. CSS is a W3C standard, so the definitive source of information about CSS is *Cascading Style Sheets, level 2, CSS2 Specification* [CSS2].

CSS lets you specify *styles* for elements. A *stylesheet* contains a list of *style rules*. A style rule consists of a *selector* and a set of *properties*. The selector specifies the elements that the rule applies to. A selector can specify an element name, a path of element names, a class, or an id. A property consists of a *name* and a *value* that specifies display characteristics like color, font, alignment, and position. Styles can be specified for the document, for a class of elements, or for individual elements. Styles are said to *cascade* because more specific selectors override the properties specified in more general selectors.

In this iteration you'll develop a stylesheet for schedule.html. Do the following:

1. Open schedule.html in the HTML editor and save it as schedule-css.html. Edit schedule-css.html (see Example 7.2, modified lines are in bold font). schedule-css.html differs from schedule.html in two respects. First, there is a <link> element that refers to the schedule.css stylesheet. Second, the <tr> elements in the table body have been modified to include a class attribute. Even-numbered rows have the class even-row and odd rows have odd-row.

Example 7.2   Listing of Modified schedule-css.html

```
<!DOCTYPE HTML PUBLIC "-//W3C//DTD HTML 4.01 Transitional//EN">
<html>
<head>
<meta http-equiv="Content-Type"
  content="text/html; charset=ISO-8859-1">
<title>Rosehill Girls Hockey League 2005-2006 Regular Season
Schedule</title>
```

```
<link rel="stylesheet" href="schedule.css" type="text/css">
</head>
<body>
<h1>Rosehill Girls Hockey League</h1>
<h2>2005-2006 Regular Season Schedule</h2>
<table>
  <thead>
    <tr>
      <th>Date</th>
      <th>Time</th>
      <th>Arena</th>
      <th>Visitor</th>
      <th>Home</th>
      <th>Score</th>
    </tr>
  </thead>
  <tbody>
    <tr class="odd-row">
      <td>Jan. 7, 2006</td>
      <td>7:00 PM</td>
      <td>Hillview High School</td>
      <td>Ladybugs</td>
      <td>Vixens</td>
      <td>3-7</td>
    </tr>
    <tr class="even-row">
      <td>Jan. 7, 2006</td>
      <td>9:00 PM</td>
      <td>Hillview High School</td>
      <td>Snowflakes</td>
      <td>Foxes</td>
      <td>5-2</td>
    </tr>
      .
      .
      .
    <tr class="odd-row">
      <td>Jan. 22, 2006</td>
      <td>7:30 PM</td>
      <td>Maple Community Centre</td>
      <td>Snowflakes</td>
      <td>Vixens</td>
      <td>2-6</td>
    </tr>
  </tbody>
</table>
</body>
</html>
```

2. Select the WebContent folder and invoke the **New ▸ Other** command. The **New** wizard opens. Expand the **Web** category, select **CSS**, and click **Next**. The **New CSS File** wizard opens (see Figure 7.27). Enter the filename **schedule.css** and click **Finish**.

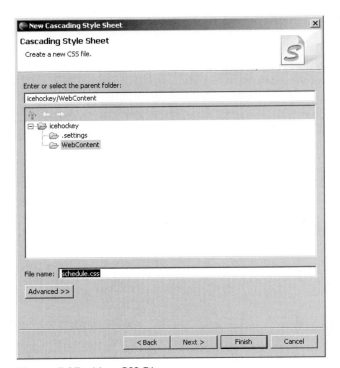

Figure 7.27   New CSS File

3. The CSS editor opens on schedule.css. Edit it (see Example 7.3). As a member of the WTP structured source editor family, the CSS editor supports content assist. Experiment with content assist as you enter properties' names and values, for example, the color property. Although you are editing a CSS file here, CSS content assist is also available when editing the values of style attributes of HTML tags using the HTML editor.

Example 7.3   Listing of schedule.css

```
body {
  font-family: sans-serif;
}

h1 {
  background: blue;
  color: white;
}

h2 {
  color: blue;
}
```

```
thead {
  background: red;
}

td {
  padding: 4pt;
}

.odd-row {
  background: rgb(200, 200, 200);
}

.even-row {
  background: white;
}
```

4. schedule.css specifies a font for the <body> element using the font-family, and foreground and background colors for the <h1>, <h2>, and <thead> elements using the color and background properties. It also specifies background properties for the even and odd table row classes, which are specified using the selectors .even-row and .odd-row. To see the effect of these style rules, open schedule-css.html in a Web browser (see Figure 7.28).

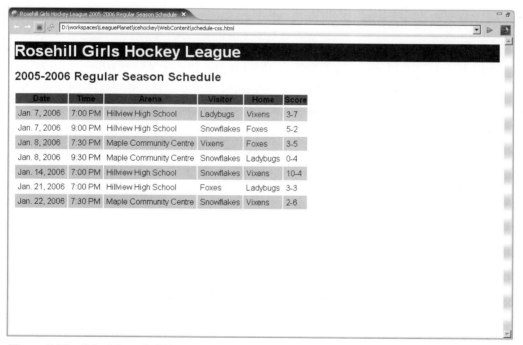

Figure 7.28   Schedule with CSS

Summary of Iteration 2

In this iteration, you added style to your HTML page using the CSS editor. You added class attributes to elements on your HTML page and linked it to a CSS stylesheet. Your page now looks better, but it is still non-interactive. You're now ready to add some interactivity to your HTML page using JavaScript.

Iteration 3: JavaScript

In this iteration you'll explore client tier processing by using JavaScript in the Web browser. JavaScript is itself a very rich topic and requires much more space than is available here to do it justice. However, if you are a Java programmer, then its syntax will feel familiar. Most of the complexity of JavaScript comes from its API for accessing the browser and HTML document. See Chapter 22 of *Web Design in a Nutshell: A Desktop Quick Reference* [Niederst1999] by Jennifer Niederst for an introduction or *JavaScript: The Definitive Guide, Fourth Edition* [Flannagan2002] by David Flannagan for a complete treatment.

First you'll update the schedule page by adding an e-mail link. Then you'll develop a form to update game scores and include some form validation logic.

E-Mail Address Obfuscation

By now your schedule Web page is starting to look fairly respectable. As a final touch, you'll add an e-mail link to the League Planet Webmaster so users can report problems. Of course, you could simply add a hyperlink using the URL

```
mailto:webmaster@leagueplanet.com
```

but the problem with doing this is e-mail spam. Spammers use programs that crawl the Web and extract e-mail addresses. These crawlers scan Web pages for strings that look like syntactically valid e-mail addresses, both in the content of the page and in any mailto: URLs in hyperlinks. Very soon after you published the Webmaster's e-mail address, spammers would have it and inundate him with spam. Since the Webmaster is unlikely to know all the users of the League Planet site, it would be very difficult to set up an effective spam filter. A better course of action is to obfuscate the e-mail address to defeat the Web crawls. Do the following:

1. Open schedule-css.html in the HTML editor and save it as schedule-js.html. Edit schedule-js.html (see Example 7.4, modified lines are in bold font).

Example 7.4 Listing of schedule-js.html

```
<!DOCTYPE HTML PUBLIC "-//W3C//DTD HTML 4.01 Transitional//EN">
<html>
<head>
<meta http-equiv="Content-Type"
  content="text/html; charset=ISO-8859-1">
<title>Rosehill Girls Hockey League 2005-2006 Regular Season
Schedule</title>
<link rel="stylesheet" href="schedule.css" type="text/css">

</head>
<body>
<h1>Rosehill Girls Hockey League</h1>
<h2>2005-2006 Regular Season Schedule</h2>
<table>
  <thead>
    <tr>
      <th>Date</th>
      <th>Time</th>
      <th>Arena</th>
      <th>Visitor</th>
      <th>Home</th>
      <th>Score</th>
    </tr>
  </thead>
  <tbody>
    <tr class="odd-row">
      <td>Jan. 7, 2006</td>
      <td>7:00 PM</td>
      <td>Hillview High School</td>
      <td>Ladybugs</td>
      <td>Vixens</td>
      <td>3-7</td>
    </tr>
      .
      .
      .
    <tr class="odd-row">
      <td>Jan. 22, 2006</td>
      <td>7:30 PM</td>
      <td>Maple Community Centre</td>
      <td>Snowflakes</td>
      <td>Vixens</td>
      <td>2-6</td>
    </tr>
  </tbody>
</table>
<br>
<hr>
<script language="JavaScript">
var protocol = "mailto";
var user = "webmaster";
var server = "leagueplanet.com";
```

```
function contact() {
  window.open(protocol + ":" + user + "@" + server, "_self");
 }
</script>

<p>For questions about this Web page, please contact <a
   href="javascript:contact()">webmaster at leagueplanet dot com</a></p>

</body>
</html>
```

2. schedule-js.html differs from schedule-css.html by the addition of some JavaScript code in a <script> element and HTML markup, including a hyperlink after the table. Experiment with content assist as you enter the JavaScript code. There are a few points worth discussing here. First, note that content of the hyperlink contains the obfuscated text

   webmaster at leagueplanet dot com

   instead of the true e-mail address

   webmaster@leagueplanet.com

   Second, the href of the hyperlink contains the special URL

   javascript:contact()

   instead of

   mailto:webmaster@leagueplanet.com

   When you click the hyperlink, the Web browser executes the JavaScript. The JavaScript function contact dynamically constructs the correct mailto: URL from variables that contain the Webmaster's user id and mail server, and it opens a new browser window using that URL as its location. This action opens the default e-mail program. Open schedule-js.html in a Web browser to view the hyperlink (see Figure 7.29).

3. Click the hyperlink. Your e-mail program should open on a new message with the Webmaster's e-mail address filled in (see Figure 7.30).

Data Entry Form Validation

You'll continue this iteration by developing an HTML form that lets League Planet managers enter game scores. You'll only develop the client side of the form processing now. The client-side processing will demonstrate the use of JavaScript to validate the data entered in the form before it is submitted to the League Planet server. Do the following:

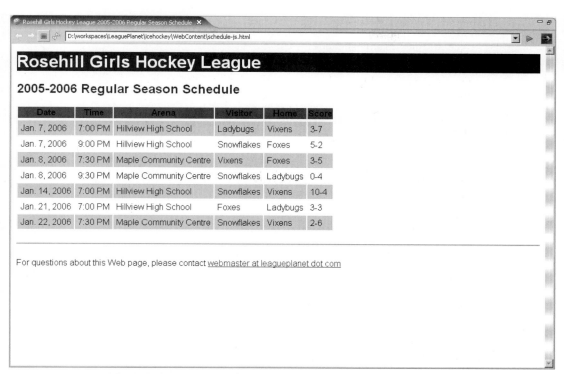

Figure 7.29 Schedule with E-mail Hyperlink

1. Use the **New HTML File** wizard to create `score-form.html`, the game score entry form, and edit it (see Example 7.5).

Example 7.5 Listing of score-form.html

```html
<html>
<head>
<title>Enter Score</title>
<link rel="stylesheet" href="schedule.css" type="text/css">
<link rel="stylesheet" href="validator.css" type="text/css">
<script type="text/javascript" src="score-validator.js">
</script>
</head>

<body onload="validateFields()">
<h1>Please enter the score for the game:</h1>

<form name="enterScore" action="confirmation.html" method="get"
  onsubmit="return submitScore()" onreset="resetValidators()">
```

```html
<table>
  <tr>
    <th align="right">League:</th>
    <td>Rosehill Girls Hockey League</td>
  </tr>

  <tr>
    <th align="right">Schedule:</th>
    <td>2005-2006 Regular Season</td>
  </tr>

  <tr>
    <th align="right">Date:</th>
    <td colspan="3">Jan. 7, 2006</td>
  </tr>

  <tr>
    <th align="right">Time:</th>
    <td>7:00 PM</td>
  </tr>

  <tr>
    <th align="right">Arena:</th>
    <td>Hillview High School</td>
  </tr>

  <tr>
    <th align="right">Visitor:</th>
    <td><input id="visitorId" name="visitor" value="0" size="2"
      maxlength="2" onchange="validateVisitor()"> Ladybugs</td>
    <td><span id="visitorValidator" class="validator" /></td>
  </tr>

  <tr>
    <th align="right">Home:</th>
    <td><input id="homeId" name="home" value="0" size="2"
      maxlength="2" onchange="validateHome()"> Vixens</td>
    <td><span id="homeValidator" class="validator" /></td>
  </tr>

  <tr>
    <td colspan="2"> </td>
    <td>
    <button type="reset">Reset</button>
     
    <button type="submit">Submit</button>
    </td>
  </tr>

</table>

</form>

</body>
</html>
```

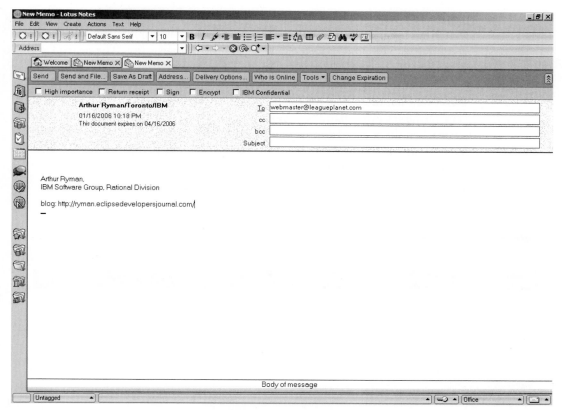

Figure 7.30   E-mail Program with New Message Addressed to the Webmaster

In the actual Web application, this page would be dynamically generated. The user would, say, select a game from the schedule and click an **Enter Score** button. The server would then generate this page, filling in the known game details. JSP is a great way to generate HTML pages, and an easy way to create a JSP is to start from an example of the desired HTML result. Therefore, the HTML page you develop here feeds naturally into the server-side development task.

`score-form.html` contains links to the `schedule.css` and `validator.css` stylesheets. You created `schedule.css` in the previous iteration. Using it here makes the score entry form have the same style as the schedule page, and it gives the League Planet Web site a consistent look and feel. You'll create `validator.css` later in this iteration.

`score-form.html` contains a script element that loads JavaScript code used in the form from the `score-validator.js` file. You'll create score-validator.js later in this iteration. Notice how JavaScript code is associated with various browser events. For example, when the browser finishes loading the page, the <body> element fires the onload event. The onload event handler invokes the validateFields JavaScript function, which ensures that the data entry fields have accurate error messages. The <form> element has two event handlers, one for the onsubmit event and one for the onreset event. The onsubmit event handler explicitly returns a result. If the handler returns true, then the form action is invoked; otherwise, the action is canceled. This is the heart of form validation. If the handler finds an error, it displays an error message and returns false to allow the user to correct the error.

2. Open score-form.html in a Web browser to see what it looks like (see Figure 7.31).

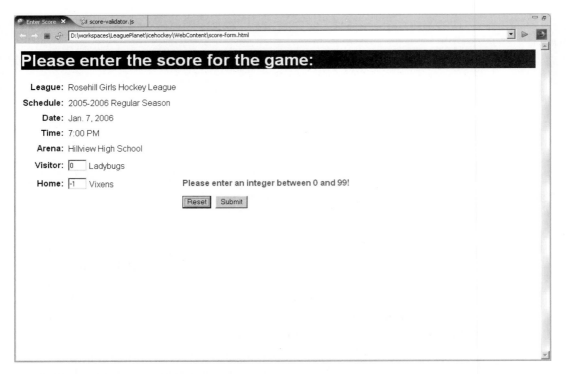

Figure 7.31   Game Score Entry Form

3. Each data entry field in the form has an associated validator element that displays error messages. For example, the data entry field

```
<input id="visitorId" name="visitor" ...>
```

is associated with the element

```
<span id="visitorValidator" class="validator" />
```

which is a placeholder for error messages. You want these error messages to be visually distinct, so you have given them the class attribute `valida-tor`. You define the style for the `validator` class in `validator.css`. Use the **New CSS File** wizard to create `validator.css` and edit it (see Example 7.6).

Example 7.6   Listing of validator.css

```
.validator {
  color: red;
  font-weight: bold;
}
```

4. Creating JavaScript files is just like creating CSS files. Use the **New JavaScript File** wizard to create `score-validator.js` (see Figure 7.32).

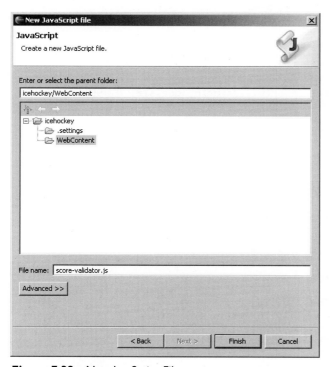

Figure 7.32   New JavaScript File

5. The wizard opens `score-validator.js` in the JavaScript source editor. Edit it (see Example 7.7). Experiment with content assist as you edit the file.

Example 7.7 Listing of score-validator.js

```
// Validate an integer input value

function validateInteger(validatorId, valueId, minValue, maxValue) {

  var validatorElement = document.getElementById(validatorId);

  var valueElement = document.getElementById(valueId);
  var value = Number(valueElement.value);

  // validate the value
  if (isNaN(value) || (value != Math.round(value)) ||
    (minValue > value) || (value > maxValue)) {

    validatorElement.innerHTML =
      "Please enter an integer between " + minValue +
      " and " + maxValue + "!" ;
    return false;
  }

  // the value is valid
  validatorElement.innerHTML = "";
  return true;
}

function validateGoals(validatorId, goalsId) {

  // the number of goals must be an integer between 0 and 99
  return validateInteger(validatorId, goalsId, 0, 99);
}

function validateVisitor() {

  return validateGoals("visitorValidator", "visitorId");
}

function validateHome() {

  return validateGoals("homeValidator", "homeId");
}

// Validate all the input fields

function validateFields() {

  var visitorValid = validateVisitor();
  var homeValid = validateHome();

  return visitorValid && homeValid;
}

// Submit the score

function submitScore() {

  var valid = validateFields();
```

```
  if (!valid) {

    window.alert(
      "You entered an invalid score.\n" +
      "Please correct the errors and resubmit.");
  }

  return valid;
}

// Reset the validator messages

function resetValidators() {

  document.getElementById("visitorValidator").innerHTML = "";
  document.getElementById("homeValidator").innerHTML = "";
}
```

6. Switch to the Web browser displaying `score-form.html`, and refresh the window to load the newly created `score-validator.js` file so you can test the validators. The validators check that the game scores are integer values between 0 and 99. Enter an invalid value, say `-1`, in the **Home** field and press `Tab`. The onchange event fires, the field is validated, and the error message

   `Please enter an integer between 0 and 99!`

   is displayed to the right of the **Home** input field (see Figure 7.33).

7. Leave the error uncorrected and press the **Submit** button. The browser displays an error message dialog (see Figure 7.34).

8. To complete development, use the **New HTML File** wizard to create `confirmation.html` and edit it (see Example 7.8). For prototyping purposes, you use a static HTML page as the form action. In the real Web application you would use a servlet or JSP.

Example 7.8   Listing of confirmation.html

```html
<!DOCTYPE HTML PUBLIC "-//W3C//DTD HTML 4.01 Transitional//EN">
<html>
<head>
<meta http-equiv="Content-Type"
  content="text/html; charset=ISO-8859-1">
<title>Confirmation</title>
<link rel="stylesheet" href="schedule.css" type="text/css">
</head>
<body>
<h1>Thank you for submitting the score.</h1>

</body>
</html>
```

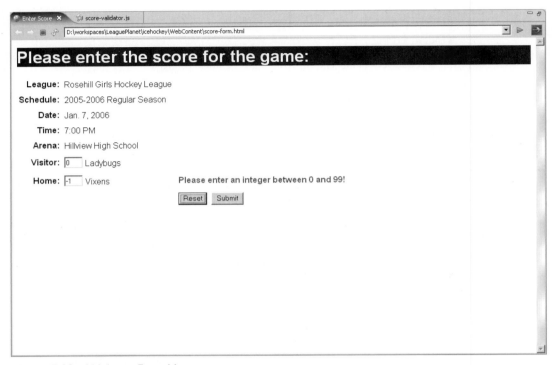

Figure 7.33   Validation Error Message

Figure 7.34   Submit Error Message

9. Switch to the Web browser and enter a valid game score, say Visitor 2, Home 4. Click the **Submit** button. The validators are invoked again, but this time they return `true` and the form action is invoked. The confirmation page opens in the Web browser (see Figure 7.35).

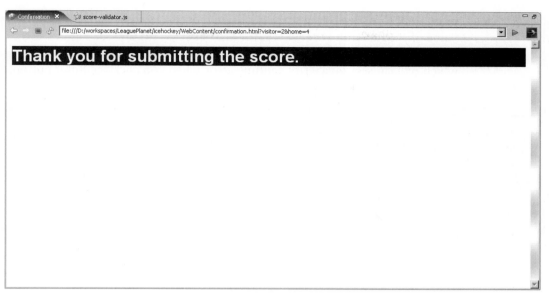

Figure 7.35 Confirmation Page

10. The JavaScript code you entered was fairly complex, so it's easy to make coding errors when writing it. Web browsers normally silently ignore JavaScript errors to avoid exposing users to cryptic error messages. While this is good for users, it makes debugging JavaScript difficult for developers. Unfortunately, WTP does not currently include a JavaScript debugger. However, there is a simple alternative. Some Web browsers, such as Firefox, include a JavaScript console that displays runtime error messages.

To conclude this iteration, you'll need Firefox (or some other Web browser that has a JavaScript console). If Firefox is not currently installed, download it from

```
http://www.mozilla.com/firefox/
```

install it, and restart Eclipse. You should then see Firefox listed in the **Window ▸ Web Browser** submenu.

Select the **Window ▸ Web Browser ▸ Firefox** menu item to make Firefox your current Web browser and open `score-form.html` in it.

11. In Firefox, select the **Tools ▸ JavaScript Console** menu item to open the **JavaScript Console** window.

12. In Eclipse, edit score-validator.js to introduce an error by changing the name of the function resetValidators to resetValidator (see Figure 7.36). Now the onreset handler of the form refers to a nonexistent function, which will cause a JavaScript runtime error when you click the **Reset** button.

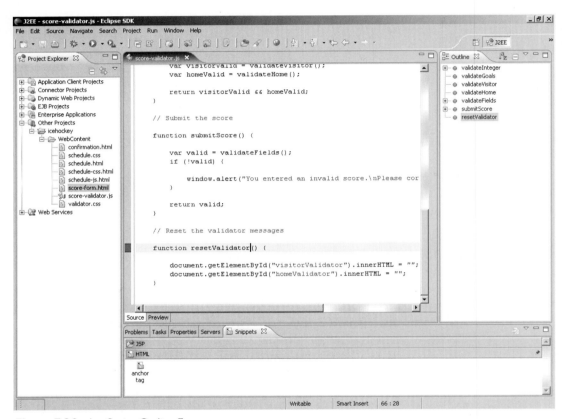

Figure 7.36   JavaScript Coding Error

13. In Firefox, refresh the score-form.html browser window to load the modified version of score-validator.js. Click the **Reset** button to trigger the error. The browser window silently ignores the error, but the JavaScript console displays the following error message (see Figure 7.37):

```
Error: resetValidators is not defined
```

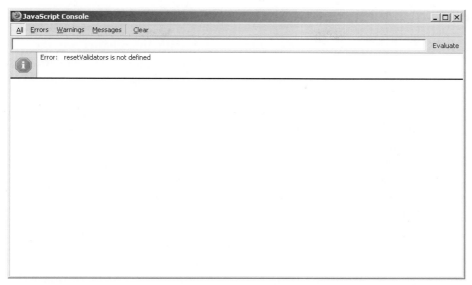

Figure 7.37 JavaScript Console Error Message

14. Go back to Eclipse and correct the JavaScript error. Then return to Firefox, clear the JavaScript console, refresh the browser window to load the correction, and retest the **Reset** button on the form. This time the form works properly and no error is displayed in the JavaScript console. In practice, you'll repeat this edit-refresh-test cycle many times as you develop your own JavaScript code.

Summary of Iteration 3

In this iteration you used the JavaScript editor to add interactivity to your HTML page. You used JavaScript to perform e-mail address obfuscation and data validation. You also used the Firefox JavaScript console to help debug your code.

JavaScript development is a deep topic and has received much interest recently due to the popularity of AJAX. See Chapter 17 for a brief discussion of planned WTP JavaScript tool improvements coming in the ATF project.

In the next iteration, you'll extract the data from your HTML page and put it into an XML file. You'll also develop an XSLT stylesheet to transform the XML data back into an HTML page.

Iteration 4: XML and XSLT

XML has emerged as the standard for data interchange on the Web. While HTML lets you describe the content of Web pages, XML lets you describe any structured or semi-structured data. Instead of using a fixed vocabulary for marking up content, XML lets you define your own vocabulary for each problem domain. Refer to *XML: A Primer* [StLaurent1998b] by Simon St. Laurent for a good introduction. The definitive reference for XML is the W3C standard *Extensible Markup Language (XML) 1.0 (Third Edition)* [XML10].

As discussed earlier, CSS allows you to separate the style properties of an HTML document from its content, but it cannot alter the order in which the content is presented. If you need to reorder the content of a document, or combine its content with that of other documents, then XSLT is an excellent choice. XSLT allows you to transform well-formed XML documents into XML, HTML, or arbitrary text formats. See *XSLT* [Tidwell2001] by Doug Tidwell for an excellent treatment of this powerful programming language. The definitive reference for XSLT is the W3C standard, *XSL Transformations (XSLT) Version 1.0* [XSLT10]. For an extremely useful online reference, see *XSLT Reference* [Nic2000] by Miloslav Nic.

Consider the League Planet game schedule you have been developing. It contains all the required information but presents it in a rather boring tabular arrangement. A fan, like Anne French, would most likely prefer the schedule presented as a calendar page. That kind of arrangement is beyond the ability of CSS, but is an easy job for XSLT. To enable this type of reordering of the schedule, you will redo the HTML schedule as XML data plus an XSLT stylesheet.

XML

Since XSLT requires XML input documents, your first task is to convert the game schedule data into XML. Do the following:

1. Right click on the webContent folder and select the **New ▸ Other** menu item to open the **New** wizard. Select the **XML ▸ XML** item and click the **Next** button to open the **New XML File** wizard (see Figure 7.38).

2. The **Create XML File** wizard gives you the option of creating the file from an existing DTD or XSD grammar, or from scratch. When you create an XML file from a grammar, the wizard populates the file with sample data. Since there is no grammar available, select the option to create the file from scratch, and then click the **Next** button (see Figure 7.39).

Figure 7.38 New XML File

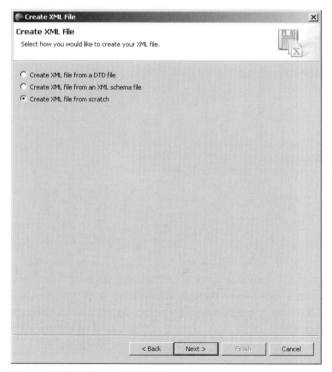

Figure 7.39 Create XML File

3. Name the file `schedule.xml`, and click **Finish** to create the file.

4. The wizard opens `schedule.xml` in the XML editor. The XML editor has two tabs: **Design** and **Source**. The **Design** tab contains a form-based editor. The **Source** tab contains a member of the structured source editor family that supports the usual functions, including content assist. If the file has an associated grammar, then content assist uses the grammar to provide suggestions. If the file is not associated with a grammar, then the editor infers a grammar based on the file's content, and content assist uses the inferred grammar. Open `schedule.html` in the HTML editor, select its content, and then copy and paste it into the **Source** tab of `schedule.xml` as a starting point. Edit `schedule.xml` (see Example 7.9).

Example 7.9   Listing of schedule.xml

```
<?xml version="1.0" encoding="UTF-8"?>
<?xml-stylesheet type="text/xsl" href="schedule.xsl"?>
<schedule>
   <league>Rosehill Girls Hockey League</league>
   <name>2005-2006 Regular Season</name>
   <games>
     <game>
       <date>Jan. 7, 2006</date>
       <time>7:00 PM</time>
       <arena>Hillview High School</arena>
       <visitor>Ladybugs</visitor>
       <home>Vixens</home>
       <score>3-7</score>
     </game>
       .
       .
       .
     <game>
       <date>Jan. 22, 2006</date>
       <time>7:30 PM</time>
       <arena>Maple Community Centre</arena>
       <visitor>Snowflakes</visitor>
       <home>Vixens</home>
       <score>2-6</score>
     </game>
   </games>
</schedule>
```

5. WTP includes an XML validator. For this exercise, turn off autobuilds by toggling the **Project ▸ Build Automatically** menu item to the unchecked state. To validate `schedule.xml`, select it in the **Project Explorer** view, right click, and invoke the **Validate** menu item. Any errors will be listed in the **Problems** view and marked with error markers in the **Source** tab of the editor.

Validation

WTP contains a sophisticated validation framework, which lets you control when validators run. You can include individual validators in the manual **Validate** command or when the project is built. You make these settings for the workspace using the **Validation** preference page (see Figure 7.40). You can also allow projects to override the workspace preferences, in which case you make the settings on the project properties page.

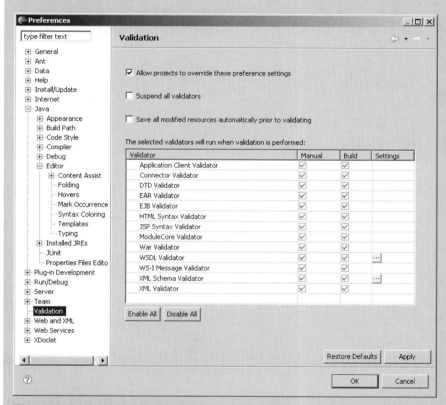

Figure 7.40   Validation Preferences

If you include a validator in project builds and you have set the project to build automatically, then the validator will run whenever you edit and save a file.

In this iteration you disabled the autobuild setting, in which case you must run the **Validate** command manually.

6. Finally, click the **Design** tab and invoke the **XML ► Expand All** menu item from the main menu bar to view the file as a form (see Figure 7.41). Note that the file contains an `<?xml-stylesheet?>` processing instruction that refers to `schedule.xsl`. You'll create that file next.

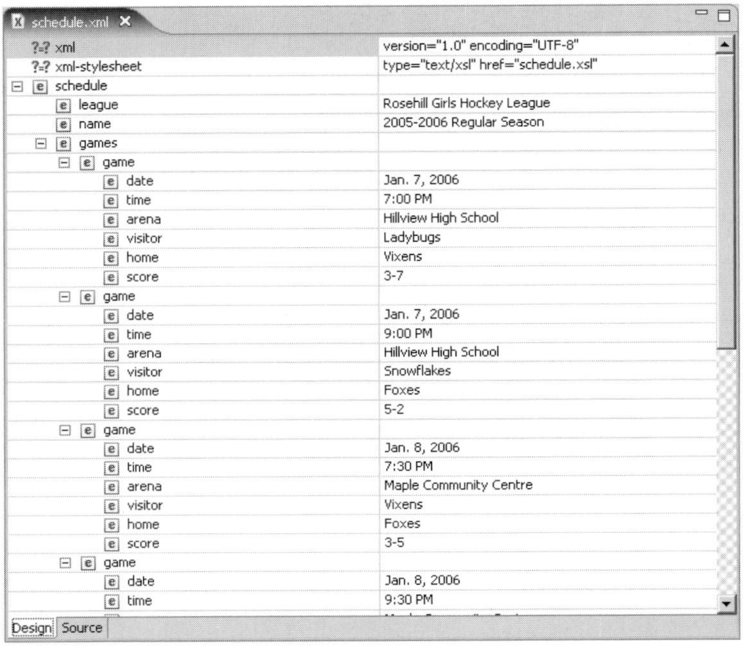

Figure 7.41   XML Editor Design Tab

XSLT

The schedule data is now ready to be transformed. Create the XSLT stylesheet as follows:

1. WTP does not currently have any explicit support for XSLT. WTP does recognize the file extension `*.xsl` as being an XML content type and will therefore edit files with that extension in the XML editor. Use the **New XML File** wizard to create the XSLT file. Right click the `webContent` folder and invoke the **New ► Other** menu item. Then expand the **XML** category, select **XML**, and click **Next**. Select the **Create XML file from scratch** radio button and click **Next** again. Name the file `schedule.xsl` (see Figure 7.42).

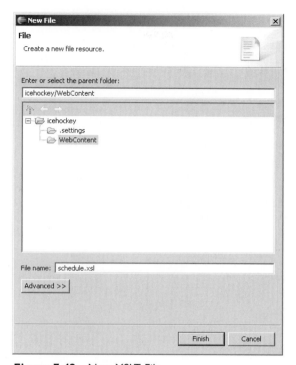

Figure 7.42 New XSLT File

2. The wizard opens `schedule.xsl` in the XML editor. Edit it
   (see Example 7.10).

   The stylesheet copies the XML data into the HTML file, replacing the
   XML tags with suitable HTML tags. One interesting feature is the

   ```
   <xsl:for-each ...>
   ```

   loop, which processes each game and copies it into a row of the table,
   assigning the row a class attribute of either `odd-row` or `even-row` based on
   the position of the game within the table.

Example 7.10 Listing of schedule.xsl

```
<?xml version="1.0" encoding="UTF-8"?>
<xsl:stylesheet xmlns:xsl="http://www.w3.org/1999/XSL/Transform"
  version="1.0">

  <xsl:output method="html" />

  <xsl:template match="/schedule">
    <html>
      <head>
```

```
        <title>
          <xsl:value-of
            select="concat(league,' ', name,' Schedule')" />
        </title>
        <link rel="stylesheet" href="schedule.css"
          type="text/css" />

      </head>
      <body>
        <h1>
          <xsl:value-of select="league" />
        </h1>
        <h2>
          <xsl:value-of select="concat(name,' Schedule')" />
        </h2>
        <xsl:apply-templates select="games" />
        <xsl:call-template name="email" />
      </body>
    </html>
  </xsl:template>

  <xsl:template match="games">
    <table>
      <thead>
        <tr>
          <th>Date</th>
          <th>Time</th>
          <th>Arena</th>
          <th>Visitor</th>
          <th>Home</th>
          <th>Score</th>
        </tr>
      </thead>
      <tbody>
        <xsl:for-each select="game">
          <tr>
            <xsl:attribute name="class">
              <xsl:choose>
                <xsl:when test="position() mod 2 = 1">
                  <xsl:text>odd-row</xsl:text>
                </xsl:when>
                <xsl:otherwise>
                  <xsl:text>even-row</xsl:text>
                </xsl:otherwise>
              </xsl:choose>
            </xsl:attribute>
            <td>
              <xsl:value-of select="date" />
            </td>
            <td>
              <xsl:value-of select="time" />
            </td>
            <td>
              <xsl:value-of select="arena" />
            </td>
```

```
          <td>
            <xsl:value-of select="visitor" />
          </td>
          <td>
            <xsl:value-of select="home" />
          </td>
          <td>
            <xsl:value-of select="score" />
          </td>
        </tr>
      </xsl:for-each>
    </tbody>
  </table>
</xsl:template>

<xsl:template name="email">
  <br />
  <hr />
  <script language="JavaScript">
    <![CDATA[
var protocol = "mailto";
var user = "webmaster";
var server = "leagueplanet.com";
function contact() {
  window.open(protocol + ":" + user + "@" + server, "_self");
}
]]>
  </script>

  <p>
    For questions about this Web page, please contact
    <a href="javascript:contact()">
      webmaster at leagueplanet dot com
    </a>
  </p>
</xsl:template>
</xsl:stylesheet>
```

3. Major Web browsers such as Internet Explorer and Firefox are able to apply XSLT stylesheets to XML documents. The stylesheet is specified by the <?xml-stylesheet?> processing instruction. To see the effect of schedule.xsl on schedule.xml, you simply open schedule.xml in an XSLT-capable Web browser. Unfortunately, WTP does not come configured to open XML files in Web browsers, but this is a simple matter to correct. Open the **File Associations** preference page, click the top **Add** button, and add *.xml as a new file type. Then select the *.xml file type, click the bottom **Add** button, and add the internal Web browser as an associated editor (see Figure 7.43).

4. Finally, select schedule.xml in the **Project Explorer** and open it in the Web browser. The Web browser opens and transforms schedule.xml into HTML that is visually identical to that in schedule.html (see Figure 7.44).

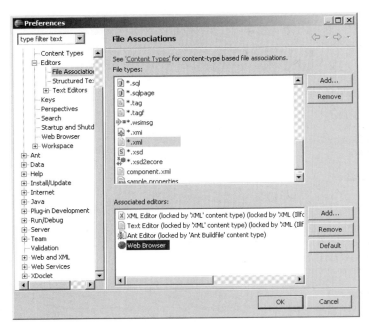

Figure 7.43   Associating the Web Browser with XML Files

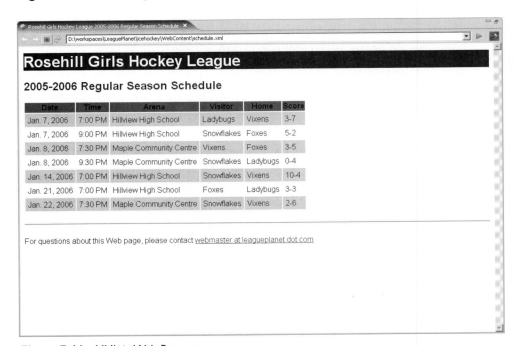

Figure 7.44   XML in Web Browser

Summary of Iteration 4

In this iteration you used the XML editor to create the data file for the content of your HTML page. You also developed an XSLT stylesheet that transformed the XML data into HTML. Next, you'll develop a DTD to help validate the XML data file.

Iteration 5: DTD

There are two levels of correctness checking defined for XML documents: well-formedness and validity. An XML document is said to be *well formed* if it obeys a certain set of general syntax rules. These rules are constraints, such as: Every element must have an end tag that matches its begin tag, all elements must be properly nested, all attributes must have values, and all attribute values must be properly quoted. The well-formedness rules can be stated independently of the specific vocabulary of tags present in a document. A well-formed XML document is said to be *valid* if it obeys an additional set of constraints specified by some *grammar*. The XML specification defines grammars based on DTDs; however, other grammar definition languages, such as XSD and RelaxNG, exist. WTP includes support for DTD and XSD. We'll discuss DTD here and defer coverage of XSD until we discuss them in the context of Web services. Refer to *XML: A Primer* [StLaurent1998a] by Simon St. Laurent for an introduction to DTDs.

Although there is a clear distinction between well-formedness and validity, common practice is to be a little sloppy with these terms and refer to both types of checking as *validation*. WTP provides a **Validate** menu command, which performs a well-formedness check and, if a grammar is specified, a validity check. Validating XML files is an important part of development. For example, if you accidentally misspell a tag name in an XML data file and apply an XSLT stylesheet to it, the stylesheet would most likely silently ignore the error and mysteriously omit data from the output.

Defining a grammar for your XML documents has other benefits. The grammar acts as a form of documentation for human authors. Grammars can also be processed by other tools. For example, the WTP XML editor uses the grammar to drive content assist. There are many tools that perform XML data binding to programming languages such as Java based on the grammar. For example, in the context of Web service development, tools can read the XSD grammar that describes the messages and generate a Java API that lets you access their content. The Java standard for XML data binding is *JSR 31: XML Data Binding Specification* [JSR31], also known as *The Java Architecture for XML Binding* (JAXB).

In this iteration, you'll develop a DTD to check the correctness of the League Planet game schedule. Do the following:

1. Select `schedule.xml` in the **Project Explorer**, right click, and invoke the **Validate** command. No errors should be reported in the **Problems** view.

2. To perform true validation, you need to create a DTD. Select the `WebContent` folder, right click, and select the **New ► Other** menu item. The **New** wizard opens. Select **XML ► DTD File** and click the **Next** button (see Figure 7.45).

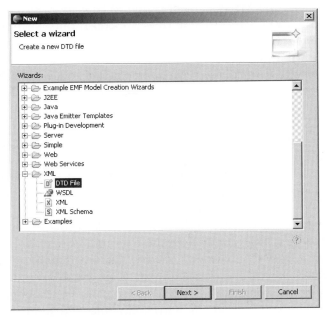

Figure 7.45   New DTD File

3. Name the DTD `schedule.dtd` and click **Finish**. The wizard creates the file and opens the DTD editor on it. The DTD editor is a member of the structured source editor family and supports some of the standard editing features, such as syntax highlighting. Edit the DTD (see Example 7.11). This is a fairly simple DTD since it only contains ELEMENT definitions. DTDs can also contain ATTRIBUTE and ENTITY definitions.

Example 7.11   Listing of schedule.dtd

```
<!ELEMENT schedule (league, name, games)>
<!ELEMENT league (#PCDATA)>
```

```
<!ELEMENT name (#PCDATA)>
<!ELEMENT games (game*)>
<!ELEMENT game (date, time, arena, visitor, home, score)>
<!ELEMENT date (#PCDATA)>
<!ELEMENT time (#PCDATA)>
<!ELEMENT arena (#PCDATA)>
<!ELEMENT visitor (#PCDATA)>
<!ELEMENT home (#PCDATA)>
<!ELEMENT score (#PCDATA)>
```

4. You now have to associate the DTD with the XML file. Insert the *document type declaration* statement

```
<!DOCTYPE schedule SYSTEM "schedule.dtd">
```

into `schedule.xml` on the line preceding the `<schedule>` element, and save the new version as `schedule-dtd.xml` (see Figure 7.46). The document type declaration associates the DTD `schedule.dtd` with the XML document and asserts that its root element is `<schedule>`.

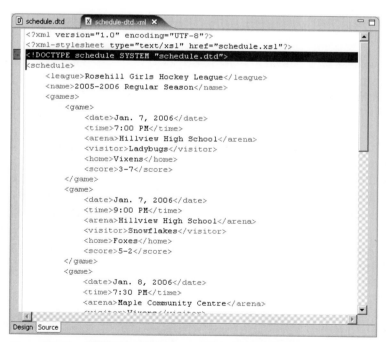

Figure 7.46 XML File with Document Type Declaration

5. Validate `schedule-dtd.xml`. No errors are reported in the **Problems** view.

6. Now create an error in `schedule-dtd.xml` by commenting out the `<league>` element (see Figure 7.47).

Figure 7.47 XML File with Invalid Content

7. Validate `schedule-dtd.xml` again. As expected, an error marker is placed in `schedule-dtd.xml` and is listed in the **Problems** view (see Figure 7.48). In this case, the error marker has been placed on the `</schedule>` tag because its content is invalid. This is not very helpful because the offending line is actually immediately after the `<schedule>` tag. Unfortunately, the XML validator is not clever enough to produce a more informative error message. To resolve the error, you'll have to inspect the definition of the `<schedule>` element in the DTD and compare it with the actual content of the `<schedule>` element in `schedule-dtd.xml`.

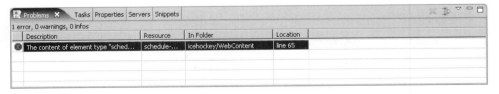

Figure 7.48 XML Validation Error in the Problems View

WTP provides a validator that checks the correctness of DTDs. To validate a DTD, select it, right click, and invoke the Validate menu item.

WTP also provides a code generator that can generate a sample XML file based on a DTD. To generate a sample XML file, select the DTD, right click, and select the Generate ▸ XML File menu item.

Summary of Iteration 5

In this iteration you used the DTD editor to develop a DTD that helped validate the XML data for your HTML page. Although DTD has been largely superseded by XML Schema (XSD) for data validation, it is a simpler technology and is still needed in order to define XML entities, even if you use XSD for validation. You will learn about WTP support for XSD in Chapter 10.

In the next iteration, you will start to look at the server side of the presentation tier. You'll add a server and create dynamic content using servlets.

Iteration 6: Servers, Dynamic Web Projects, and Servlets

It's now time to move away from the client tier and onto the middle tier. WTP uses the term *dynamic Web project* to describe projects that let you develop Web applications that make use of a middle-tier *Web application server*. At present WTP includes support for J2EE Web application servers in the JST subproject. In this iteration you'll:

1. Add Apache Tomcat to your workspace

2. Create a dynamic Web project that uses Tomcat

3. Develop a servlet that dynamically generates HTML using server-side XSLT

Servers

The main feature that distinguishes Web applications from ordinary Web sites is that Web applications generate dynamic content. Rather than seeing unchanging content on Web pages, users sees content that changes in response to their requests. Web application servers are Web servers that have been extended with additional capabilities for hosting Web applications. Although Web servers have almost always supported the generation of dynamic content through technologies such as server-side includes and CGI scripts, Web application servers go above and beyond ordinary Web servers by providing additional services for hosting and managing applications. Web applications become first-class objects that can be configured, deployed, started, and stopped. One of the most important application services provided by Web application servers is session management, which layers the notion of sessions on top of the inherently sessionless HTTP.

Shortly after Netscape embedded a Java virtual machine in its Web browser to support applets, they proposed Java servlets as a superior alternative to CGI. Servlets had the advantage of using threads instead of the more costly processes used by CGI. Servlets are what really started the use of server-side Java, which has become the sweet spot for Java development. Sun then standardized the API for Java servlets and added them to J2EE. In J2EE, the presentation functions are hosted in a *Web container* or, as it is sometimes called, a *servlet engine*. Sun provided an initial implementation of servlets in the Java Servlet Development Kit, which they subsequently contributed to the Apache Jakarta project. This contribution resulted in the Tomcat servlet engine. Although there are many other servlet engines available now, Tomcat remains very popular and you'll be using it here.

WTP extends Eclipse with *server runtime environments,* which are similar in spirit to the familiar *Java runtime environments* supported by JDT. Just as with JDT you can select a Java main class and run it as a Java application using an installed Java runtime environment, with WTP you can select Web resources, such as HTML, JSP, and servlets, and run them on an installed server runtime environment. The WTP concept of server is not restricted to Web resources, though. For example, database servers could be treated this way too. It would make perfect sense to select a Java stored procedure class and run it on a database server.

Using a server with WTP is a three-step process:

1. Obtain and install the server runtime environment.

2. Add the server runtime environment to your workspace.

3. Create a server configuration, and add dynamic Web projects to it.

If you've already added Tomcat to your workspace in the Quick Tour (see Chapter 3), you can skip ahead to the Dynamic Web Projects section. Otherwise, do the following.

First, you must obtain and install the server runtime environment. Like the Eclipse Platform, WTP does not include any runtimes. You must obtain the server runtime from elsewhere and install it on your machine. WTP does include an extension point that server providers can use to simplify the process of installing the runtime.

Second, you add the server runtime environment to your workspace. To add the server runtime environment, you need a *server adapter* for it, which is a special plug-in that lets you control a server using the server tools provided by WTP. WTP comes with a respectable list of server adapters, and you can obtain others from commercial vendors and other Open Source projects. WTP includes an extension point where other server adapter providers can advertise the availability of server adapters and have them added to your Eclipse installation. Configuring the adapter involves telling WTP where to find the server runtime installation and setting other parameters, such as what JVM to use.

Although at present you need a specific server adapter for each type of server, the situation may change in the future. The task of server control is in the process of being standardized using the Java Management Extension (JMX). JSR 77 defines J2EE Management APIs [JSR77], and JSR 88 defines J2EE Deployment APIs [JSR88]. As these aspects of server control become more widely supported, it should be possible to create a common server adapter that works with servers from many providers.

Finally, you create a *server configuration* and add dynamic Web projects to it. A server configuration is a list of dynamic Web projects, and other configuration parameters, such as port numbers. When you select a Web resource to run, it gets deployed to a server that includes its project, the server gets started, and a Web browser is launched on a URL for the selected resource.

Do the following to add Tomcat to your workspace:

1. Open the **Preferences** dialog and select the **Server** page (see Figure 7.49). The main server preferences page lets you control how WTP reacts to various events that affect servers. For example, you can have WTP automatically publish changed resources to servers. Leave these settings as is and explore them later at your leisure.

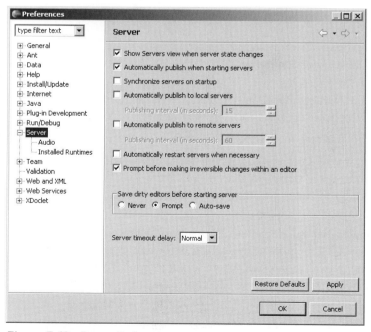

Figure 7.49   Server Preferences

2. Select the **Audio** preferences page (see Figure 7.50). This page lets you associate sounds with various server events. For example, you can associate a sound to play after the server has completed its startup sequence. This is handy for servers that take a long time to start. Play with these settings later.

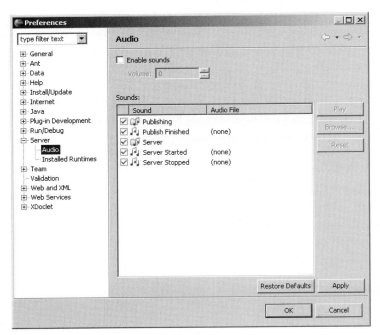

Figure 7.50   Server Audio Preferences

3. Select the **Installed Runtimes** preferences page (see Figure 7.51). This is where you add server runtime environments to your workspace.

4. Click the **Add** button. The **New Server Runtime** wizard opens (see Figure 7.52).

   Note that you can also add server runtimes by means of the **Search** button. The server tools will then search your hard disk for installed server runtimes and add them automatically. If you do that, be patient since it takes a few minutes.

5. The **New Server Runtime** dialog lists all of the server adapters that are currently installed. WTP includes server adapters for many popular servers. WTP also provides an extension point where server adapter providers can list additional ones. Any provider is welcome to contribute an extension to WTP to advertise their adapters. To see the list of other available adapters, click the link labeled

   `Don't see your server listed? Click here.`

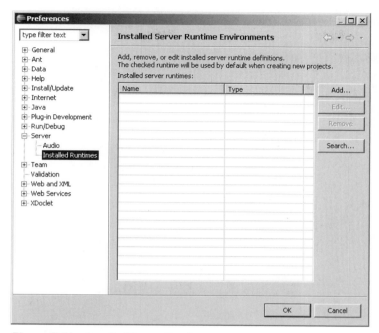

Figure 7.51 Installed Server Runtimes

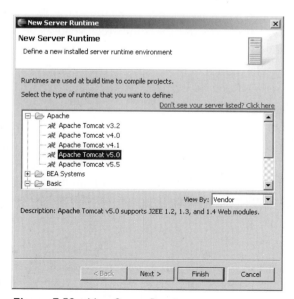

Figure 7.52 New Server Runtime

The Install New Server wizard opens (see Figure 7.53).

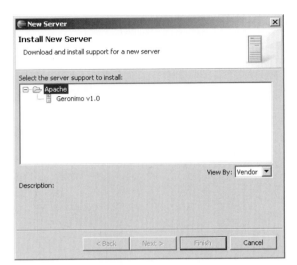

Figure 7.53   Install New Server

6. The downloadable server adapters advertised here are simply Eclipse Features hosted on remote Update Manager sites. Hosting the server adapter at the site where the server is developed lets it evolve independently of the WTP release schedule. This capability is also attractive for commercial vendors who may not want to contribute their adapters to WTP.

   You won't be installing Geronimo here, so simply click the **Cancel** button to return to the **New Server Runtime** wizard.

7. Back in the **New Server Runtime** wizard, select **Apache Tomcat v5.0**, and click the **Next** button. The **Tomcat Server** wizard opens (see Figure 7.54).

8. If you do not currently have Tomcat installed on your machine, you must install it now. Tomcat 5.0.28 is used in this example. If you prefer to use a version of Tomcat 5.5 instead, be sure to also use a matching JDK. Download and install Tomcat to any convenient directory. You can download Tomcat from

   ```
   http://tomcat.apache.org/
   ```

   WTP provides an extension point for server adapters to simplify the process of downloading and installing server runtimes. A server runtime provider can package their runtime as an Eclipse Feature, and the server adapter can advertise the location of the Update Manager site.

Figure 7.54 Tomcat Server

The **Tomcat Server** wizard requires you to specify the location of the Tomcat installation directory. Enter the location or select it using the **Browse** button. You also need to specify a JRE. Be sure to specify a full JDK instead of a JRE since later you will be developing JSPs (see the Iteration 7: JSP section). JSP development requires a Java compiler that is not included in JREs. You can also specify a descriptive name for the server runtime environment. Accept the default for now. Click the **Finish** button. The **Installed Runtimes** preference page now lists Tomcat (see Figure 7.55). Click the checkbox to make Tomcat the default server runtime environment.

You have now added Tomcat to your workspace and are ready to use it to run a dynamic Web project.

Dynamic Web Projects

WTP provides dynamic Web projects to host the development of J2EE modules. Since J2EE modules contain Java code, each module is developed in a separate dynamic Web project so it can have its own Java classpath as defined by JDT. Within a dynamic Web project, you can freely arrange the Web resources in separate folders, just as JDT lets you arrange Java sources in separate source folders. When you are ready to run your Web resources, WTP assembles them into the format specified by

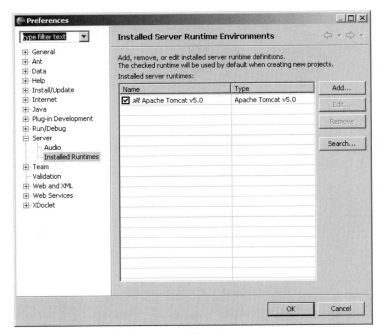

Figure 7.55   Installed Runtimes—Tomcat

J2EE and deploys them to the server associated with the project. In fact, one dynamic Web project can be associated with one or more server configurations. You can select one of the server configurations as the project default.

Here you create a Web module for League Planet ice hockey schedules. Do the following:

1. In the **Project Explorer** view, use the **New Dynamic Web Project** wizard to create a project named IceHockeyWeb (see Figure 7.56). For detailed information on creating Web projects, refer to the Creating Web Applications section. Select Tomcat as the **Target** runtime, and enter icehockey as the context root. The context root is the name that appears in the URL for the Web application.

2. Accept defaults for other options. Click **Finish**. WTP creates the project and populates it with configuration files such as the J2EE Web deployment descriptor, web.xml (see Figure 7.57).

   You have now created a dynamic Web project named IceHockeyWeb and targeted it to Tomcat. Next you'll add a servlet to it.

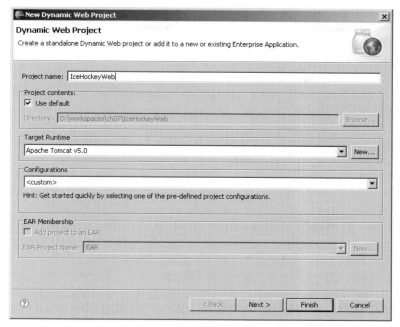

Figure 7.56 New Dynamic Web Project

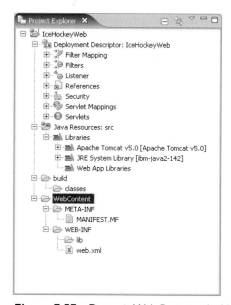

Figure 7.57 Dynamic Web Project—IceHockeyWeb

Servlets

The first server-side component defined by J2EE was called a *servlet* as the counterpart to the J2SE client-side *applet* component. Since the introduction of the servlet, J2EE has expanded to include JSPs, EJBs, and Web services. In practice, you will develop these more specialized components rather than servlets. However, servlets still have their uses, and a knowledge of servlets will help you understand JSPs, which are compiled into servlets.

In the previous iterations, you developed schedule.xml, an XML version of the hockey schedule, and schedule.xsl, an XSLT stylesheet for transforming it to HTML. You included a processing instruction in schedule.xml so that Web browsers could apply schedule.xsl to it and display the result as HTML. Although client-side XSLT is appealing, it has a few drawbacks.

First, not all Web browsers support XSLT, and those that do support it have some minor differences. If you want to reach the maximum number of browsers and ensure the highest possible fidelity on them, then you can't rely on client-side XSLT support. However, the situation is sure to improve over time as users upgrade to modern Web browsers and the minor bugs are corrected.

Second, and more seriously, Google doesn't index XML files. This is a real showstopper at the moment. As more users come to rely on Google to find information, your site is at a major disadvantage if its pages are not being indexed. The inability to index XML seems like a temporary oversight on the part of Google. Surely the Google Web crawlers could apply the stylesheets and index the resulting HTML. Perhaps there is not enough XML on the Web to make this enhancement of interest to Google. It's probably just a matter of time before Google does support XML.

Fortunately, there is an easy workaround. In this iteration, you will develop a servlet that applies XSLT on the server using the *Transformation API for XML (TrAX)*, which is part of *JSR 63: The Java API for XML Processing (JAXP)* [JSR63]. TrAX is included in J2EE. When Google follows a link to your servlet, it will receive an HTML document and index it as usual. Do the following:

1. The new project has no Web resources. Copy schedule.xml, schedule.xsl, and schedule.css from the icehockey static Web project you previously created into the webContent folder of IceHockeyWeb. This completes project setup.

2. In the **Project Explorer**, select the IceHockeyWeb project, right click, and invoke the **New ▸ Servlet** menu item. The **Create Servlet** wizard opens.

3. Ensure that IceHockeyWeb is selected as the **Project** and \IceHockeyWeb\src is selected as the **Folder**. Enter com.leagueplanet as the **Java package** and ScheduleServlet as the **Class name**. As Figure 7.58 shows, the **Superclass** should be set to

Figure 7.58   Create Servlet

```
javax.servlet.http.HttpServlet
```

4. Click the **Next** button. The next page of the wizard is displayed. This page lets you specify information that goes in web.xml, the Web module deployment descriptor. Accept the default **Name** and enter a brief **Description**. You'll modify the URL mappings next. A URL mapping defines how the server runtime maps URLs to servlets. The default mapping uses the prefix /ScheduleServlet. However, this is a bad choice since it exposes the implementation technology. You may want to change the implementation technology later, but not break any existing URLs. A better choice is to use a prefix that doesn't expose the implementation technology. Select the /ScheduleServlet URL mapping and click the **Remove** button. Then click the **Add** button and enter the mapping /schedule (see Figure 7.59).

5. Click the **Next** button to continue. The final wizard page appears. This page lets you specify details about the servlet class. The superclass contains methods that handle some of the most common HTTP methods, such as GET and POST. The wizard lets you select the methods that you want to handle in your servlet and will create stubs for these. You will only handle the GET method, so just leave the doGet method checked (see Figure 7.60).

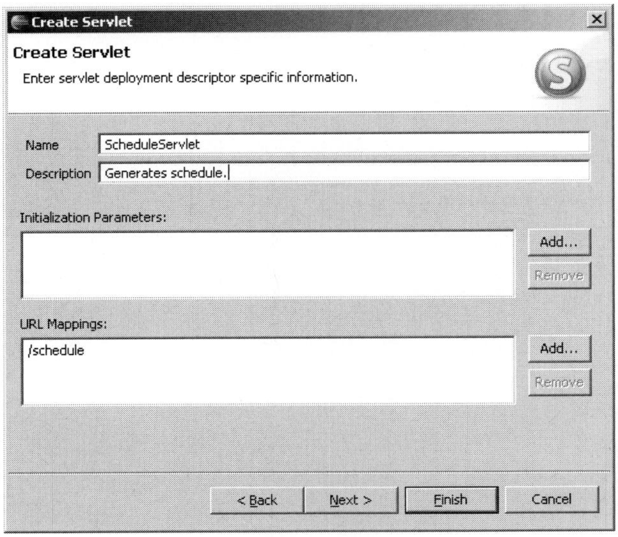

Figure 7.59   Create Servlet—URL Mappings

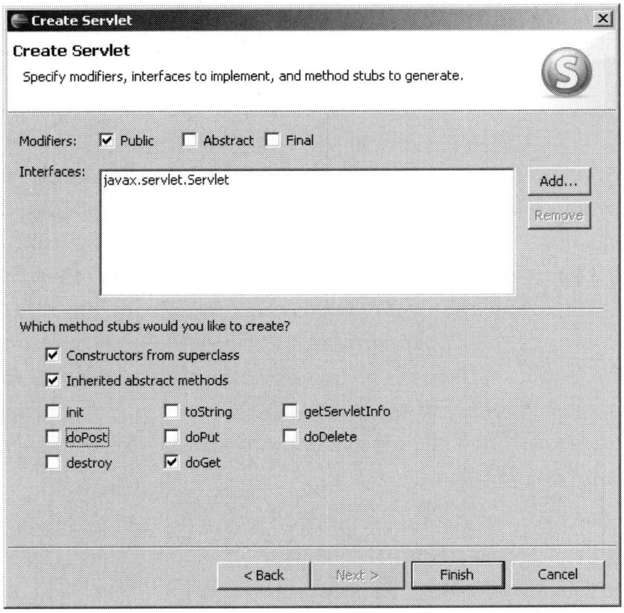

Figure 7.60   Create Servlet—Method Stubs

6. Click the **Finish** button. The wizard adds the new servlet information to
web.xml, generates the Java source file for the servlet, and opens it in the
Java source editor (see Figure 7.61).

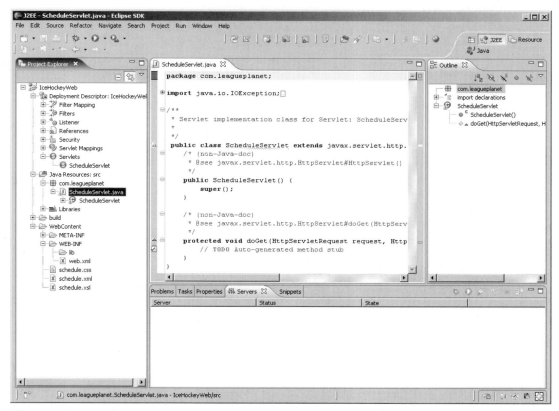

Figure 7.61   ScheduleServlet Created

7. Edit ScheduleServlet.java (see Example 7.12).

Example 7.12   Listing of ScheduleServlet.java

```
package com.leagueplanet;
import java.io.IOException;
import java.io.InputStream;
import java.io.PrintWriter;

import javax.servlet.ServletContext;
import javax.servlet.ServletException;
import javax.servlet.http.HttpServlet;
import javax.servlet.http.HttpServletRequest;
import javax.servlet.http.HttpServletResponse;
```

```
import javax.xml.transform.Result;
import javax.xml.transform.Source;
import javax.xml.transform.Templates;
import javax.xml.transform.Transformer;
import javax.xml.transform.TransformerException;
import javax.xml.transform.TransformerFactory;
import javax.xml.transform.stream.StreamResult;
import javax.xml.transform.stream.StreamSource;

/**
 * Servlet implementation class for Servlet: ScheduleServlet
 *
 */
public class ScheduleServlet extends HttpServlet implements
    javax.servlet.Servlet {

  private static final long serialVersionUID = 1L;

  protected void doGet(HttpServletRequest request,
      HttpServletResponse response)
        throws ServletException, IOException {

    try {
      ServletContext context = getServletContext();
      InputStream xsl = context.getResourceAsStream("schedule.xsl");
      Source xslSource = new StreamSource(xsl);

      TransformerFactory factory = TransformerFactory.newInstance();
      Templates templates = factory.newTemplates(xslSource);
      Transformer transformer = templates.newTransformer();

      InputStream xml = context.getResourceAsStream("schedule.xml");
      Source xmlSource = new StreamSource(xml);

      PrintWriter out = response.getWriter();
      Result htmlResult = new StreamResult(out);

      transformer.transform(xmlSource, htmlResult);

      response.flushBuffer();
      out.flush();
    } catch (TransformerException e) {
      throw new ServletException(e);
    }
  }
}
```

The servlet uses TrAX to apply schedule.xsl to schedule.xml. TrAX uses
the AbstractFactory creational pattern as described in Chapter 3 of *Design
Patterns* [Gamma1995] by Erich Gamma et al. This pattern lets you create
a transformer without specifying the concrete implementation class. There
are several Java XSLT implementations, such as Xalan and Saxon, so using
the AbstractFactory pattern lets your code be independent of the particular

implementation that is configured in your JDK. Using TrAX therefore makes your code more portable.

The servlet uses the servlet context to get input streams for `schedule.xml` and `schedule.xsl`. This technique is preferred to directly accessing the file system since these resources might not be available as loose files. For example, the servlet engine may be executing the Web application without unzipping its WAR file. The servlet wraps these input streams as TrAX source streams. The servlet gets the output writer from the HTTP response and wraps it as a TrAX result stream.

The servlet creates a transformer from the `schedule.xsl` source stream and then applies it to the `schedule.xml` source stream, writing the HTML output to the response result stream.

8. Select the servlet, right click, and invoke the **Run As ▸ Run on Server** menu item. The **Run On Server** wizard opens (see Figure 7.62).

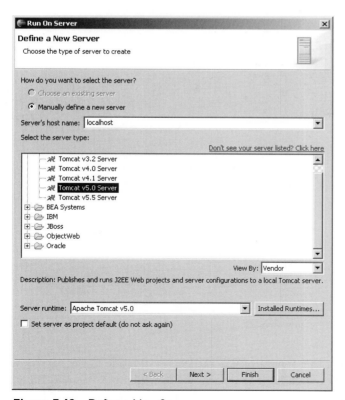

Figure 7.62   Define a New Server

9. You now must create a new server. Although you already added Tomcat to your workspace, that just specifies where the server runtime is installed. Now you have to create a configuration for it. A *configuration* is a list of dynamic Web projects, which will be deployed to the server, and other information, such as port numbers. WTP uses the term *server* to mean a configuration.

The **Define a New Server** page of the wizard lets you select the server runtime to use. Since you only have Tomcat installed, leave that as the selected runtime. You can also set this server to be the default associated with the project. Click **Next** to continue. The **Add and Remove Projects** page is displayed (see Figure 7.63).

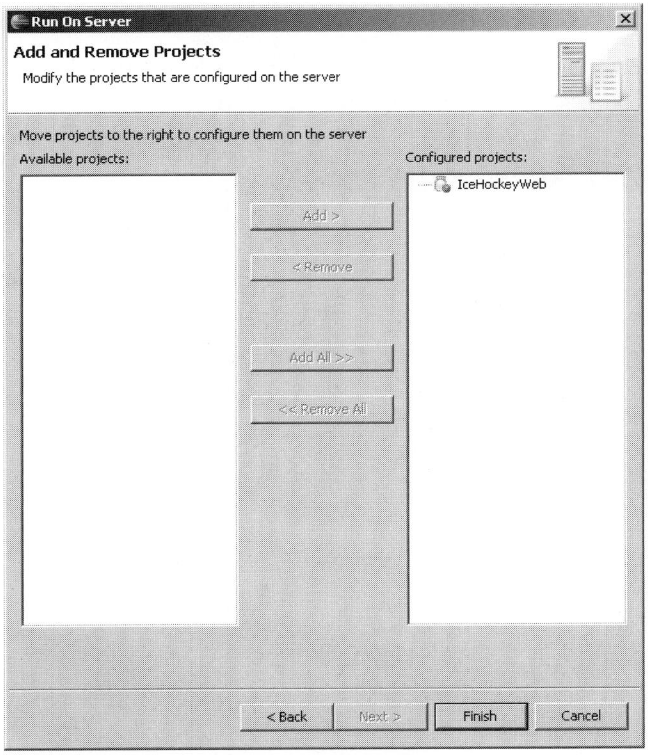

Figure 7.63   Add and Remove Projects

10. You can select the dynamic Web projects to include in the server. You only have one project available, IceHockeyWeb, which has been automatically added for you since it contains the servlet you want to run. Click the **Finish** button. The wizard creates the server, starts it, publishes the IceHockeyWeb

project to it, and launches the Web browser using the URL mapping for the servlet (see Figure 7.64). As the server starts, startup messages are displayed in the **Console** view.

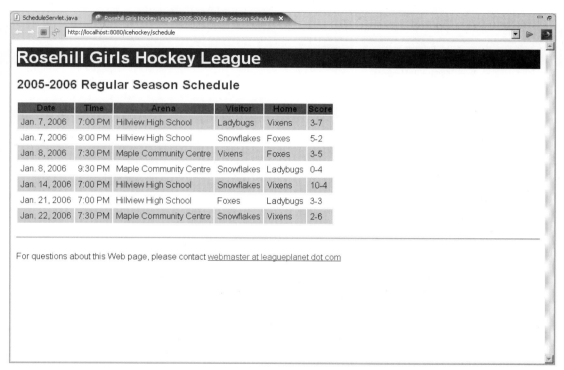

Figure 7.64   Run On Server—ScheduleServlet.java

11. The wizard created a special new project named `Servers` to hold the server you just created (see Figure 7.65). The new server is named

    ```
    Tomcat v5.0 Server @ localhost-config
    ```

    The server configuration files are normal project resources, so you view and edit them using the WTP editors. Doing so, however, requires a knowledge of server administration. Many of the Tomcat configuration files contain detailed comments to assist you. Consult the Tomcat documentation for more details.

12. The new server is also displayed in the **Servers** view, where you can control it using pop-up menu items (see Figure 7.66). The **Servers** view lets you start, stop, and restart servers, optionally in debug mode. You can also create new servers, as well as add and remove their projects.

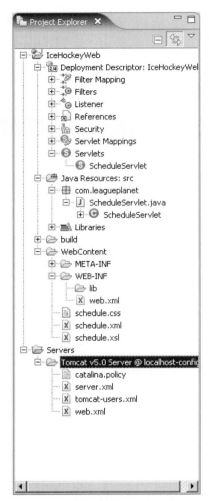

Figure 7.65 Servers Project

Figure 7.66 Servers View

Summary of Iteration 6

In this iteration you added a server, created a dynamic Web project, and generated some dynamic content using a servlet. Although it is possible to generate HTML from a servlet, this practice is discouraged since modifying servlet code requires the skills of a Java programmer. Instead, HTML should be generated by JSPs since they can be more easily modified by Web developers. In the next iteration, you'll generate HTML using a JSP.

Iteration 7: JSP

JSP is the J2EE recommended way to dynamically generate Web pages. You will normally use JSP to generate HTML; however, you can generate any textual content, XML for example. JSP is a template language. A JSP document consists of template text and JSP markup. The template text is sent back to the client unchanged, but the JSP markup is executed on the server and the results are inserted into the output stream.

A JSP document has access to Java objects that live in various *scopes*, including application, session, request, and page. *Application-scoped objects* are accessible by all pages in the Web application. These are like global variables. *Session-scoped objects* are accessible by all pages within a single HTTP session. Recall that an HTTP session consists of a sequence of requests from a Web browser. A Web application will typically maintain many concurrent sessions. You'll explore session objects in the next two iterations. Request-scoped objects are accessible by all pages within a single request. Typically a servlet will set up request objects and forward the request to a JSP. Page-scoped objects are accessible only within a single JSP. These are like local variables.

Server-side Web scripting languages are often interpreted. This means the server reads and parses the script file on every request, which can result in poor performance. When a Web browser requests a JSP, the server translates it into a Java servlet, compiles it, and then executes it. The compilation is only done when the JSP is first requested or if the JSP has been modified since the last request. The fact that JSPs are compiled instead of interpreted makes them very efficient at runtime. You can also precompile JSPs into servlets to avoid the overhead of compilation in production.

JSP markup consists of directives, tags, and scriptlets. Directives control aspects of the page. For example, the page directive can specify that the JSP has access to the Java session object. Tags are like HTML markup and are suitable for use by non-programmers. Scriptlets consist of arbitrary Java source code fragments and are suitable for use by programmers. In general, scriptlets should be kept to a minimum so that the pages can be easily modified by non-programmers. The recommended design pattern for JSP is to use servlets, which should handle the requests, perform detailed computations, generate results to be displayed, and then forward the request to a JSP for presentation. Another reason to minimize the amount of Java code in JSP scriptlets is that it can't be easily reused elsewhere. You'll have to copy and paste useful scriptlets from one JSP to another. Copy and paste is a bad development practice since it increases code bulk and makes maintenance difficult. If you need to correct an error or make an enhancement, you'll have to locate every JSP that contains the scriptlet. If you find yourself copying and pasting scriptlets, you should refactor the common code into Java source files so it can be reused across multiple JSPs.

A more complete discussion of JSP markup is beyond the scope of this book. See *JavaServer Pages* [Whitehead2001] by Paul Whitehead or *JSP: JavaServer Pages* [Burd2001] by Barry Burd for good treatments of this topic.

WTP includes a JSP creation wizard and a JSP structured source editor. JSP is actually a very complex source format since it combines HTML, JavaScript, and CSS in the template text with the JSP directives, tags, and scriptlets. The JSP editor provides many advanced features, including syntax highlighting and content assist for JSP tags as well as full content assist for Java scriptlets.

You can set breakpoints in JSP source files and debug them just like you debug Java code. You can step from the JSP source code into any Java source code called by scriptlets and tags. In fact, since JSPs are compiled into servlets, you are debugging Java code. However, the debugger shows you the JSP source code instead of the translated Java servlet code. The mapping from the Java bytecodes back to the original JSP source code has been standardized in *JSR 45: Debugging Support for Other Languages* [JSR45].

In this iteration you'll develop JSPs that allow League Planet users to log in and out of the Web site. Users are not required to log in, but if they do, then additional function is available to them. For example, fans can set up interest profiles, and managers can update game schedules and scores. These functions require that users identify themselves to the League Planet Web application. The login state of each user is held in a session variable. We'll discuss how J2EE manages sessions in the next iteration. Next we describe how to develop the login and logout JSPs.

For the GET method, the servlet simply forwards the request to either `login.jsp` or `logout.jsp`, which you'll create next. The servlet determines the correct JSP by examining the `User` object in the session. The `getUser` method retrieves the session object from the request. The boolean `true` argument on the `getSession` method causes a new session object to be created if one doesn't already exist. The `forward` method selects `login.jsp` if the user is not logged in, and `logout.jsp` if the user is logged in. Note that you make these methods `protected` so you can test them later using Cactus (see Iteration 2: Integration Testing with Cactus section in Chapter 11).

For the POST message, the servlet looks for an action parameter. If the action is `Logout`, the servlet logs out the user. If the action is `Login`, the servlet looks for the `userId` and `password` parameters and validates them. The validation logic here is trivial. The `userId` must be at least two characters long and the `password` must be `guest`. In practice, the login request would come over a secure connection and the password would be checked against a database. If a validation error occurs, the error message is attached to the request so `login.jsp` can display it. The `userId` is also attached to the request so it can be redisplayed. This illustrates the technique of using request-scoped objects.

1. In the **Project Explorer**, select the `src` folder of the `IceHockeyWeb` project, right click, and select the **New ▸ Class** menu item to create a Java class named `User` in the `com.leagueplanet` package. This class will be used to hold the login state of a user. Edit `User.java` (see Example 7.13). `User` is a simple JavaBean. It contains two properties: a boolean flag that indicates whether the user is logged in, and a string that holds the user id. The class also has two methods: one to log in and another to log out.

Example 7.13   Listing of User.java

```java
package com.leagueplanet;
public class User {

  private boolean loggedIn = false;

  private String userId = "";

  public boolean isLoggedIn() {
    return loggedIn;
  }

  public void setLoggedIn(boolean loggedIn) {
    this.loggedIn = loggedIn;
  }

  public String getUserId() {
    return userId;
  }

  public void setUserId(String userId) {
    if (userId == null) {
      this.userId = "";
    } else {
      this.userId = userId;
    }
  }

  public void logIn(String userId) {
    setLoggedIn(true);
    setUserId(userId);
```

```
    }

    public void logOut() {
      setLoggedIn(false);
      setUserId("");
    }
}
```

2. Create a new servlet class named `LoginServlet` in the `com.leagueplanet` package using the steps you learned in the previous iteration. Map this servlet to the URL `/login`. Edit `LoginServlet.java` or import it from the examples (see Example 7.14). This servlet handles GET and POST methods.

Example 7.14   Listing of LoginServlet.java

```
package com.leagueplanet;
import java.io.IOException;

import javax.servlet.RequestDispatcher;
import javax.servlet.ServletContext;
import javax.servlet.ServletException;
import javax.servlet.http.HttpServletRequest;
import javax.servlet.http.HttpServletResponse;
import javax.servlet.http.HttpSession;

/**
 * Servlet implementation class for Servlet: LoginServlet
 *
 */
public class LoginServlet extends javax.servlet.http.HttpServlet implements
    javax.servlet.Servlet {

  private static final long serialVersionUID = 1L;

  protected User getUser(HttpServletRequest request) {

    // get the current session or create it
    HttpSession session = request.getSession(true);

    // get the user or create it and add it to the session
    User user = (User) session.getAttribute("user");
    if (user == null) {
      user = new User();
      session.setAttribute("user", user);
    }

    return user;
  }

  protected void forward(HttpServletRequest request,
      HttpServletResponse response) throws ServletException, IOException {
```

```
    User user = getUser(request);
    String url = user.isLoggedIn() ? "/logout.jsp" : "/login.jsp";

    ServletContext context = getServletContext();
    RequestDispatcher dispatcher = context.getRequestDispatcher(url);
    dispatcher.forward(request, response);
}

protected void doGet(HttpServletRequest request,
    HttpServletResponse response) throws ServletException, IOException {
    forward(request, response);
}

protected void doPost(HttpServletRequest request,
    HttpServletResponse response) throws ServletException, IOException {

    User user = getUser(request);

    String userId = request.getParameter("userId");
    if (userId == null)
      userId = "";
    request.setAttribute("userId", userId);

    String password = request.getParameter("password");
    if (password == null)
      password = "";

    String action = request.getParameter("action");
    if (action == null)
      action = "Login";

    if (action.equals("Logout")) {
      user.logOut();
    } else {
      if (userId.length() < 2) {
        request.setAttribute("userIdMessage",
            "User id must have at least 2 characters!");
      } else {
        if (!password.equals("guest")) {
          request.setAttribute("passwordMessage",
              "Wrong password! Try using: guest");
        } else {
          user.logIn(userId);
        }
      }
    }

    forward(request, response);
  }
}
```

3. Select the webContent folder, right click, and select the **New ▶ JSP** menu item. The **New JSP** wizard opens (see Figure 7.67).

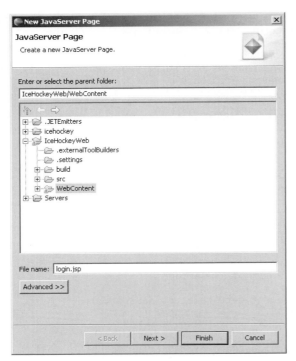

Figure 7.67   New JSP

4. Enter the name login.jsp and click the **Next** button. The **Select JSP Template** page of the wizard is displayed (see Figure 7.68).

5. The wizard lets you select a template for the style of JSP you want. You can select templates that use the traditional JSP markup syntax and that generate HTML or XHTML pages, or the newer XML-compliant syntax for use with XHTML. Select the **New JSP File (html)** template and click the **Finish** button. The wizard creates login.jsp and opens it in the JSP source editor. Edit it (see Example 7.15). Experiment with content assist as you edit.

Note the first line of login.jsp, which contains a page directive with the session="true" attribute. This enables HTTP session tracking. login.jsp also contains a scriptlet that retrieves the userId and error messages for the request object. The remainder of the login.jsp is HTML template text, except for the small scriptlets that write the userId and error messages into the HTML form. This illustrates the technique of server-side validation.

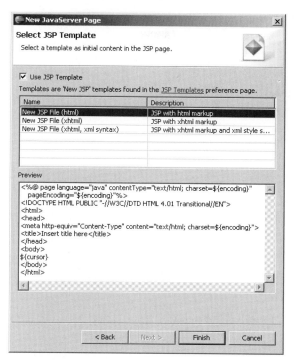

Figure 7.68   Select JSP Template

Example 7.15   Listing of login.jsp

```
<%@ page language="java" contentType="text/html; charset=ISO-8859-1"
pageEncoding="ISO-8859-1" session="true"%>
<!DOCTYPE HTML PUBLIC "-//W3C//DTD HTML 4.01 Transitional//EN">
<html>
<head>
<meta http-equiv="Content-Type" content="text/html; charset=ISO-8859-1">
<title>League Planet Login</title>
<link rel="stylesheet" href="schedule.css" type="text/css">
<link rel="stylesheet" href="validator.css" type="text/css">
<%String userId = (String) request.getAttribute("userId");
    if (userId == null)
      userId = "";

    String userIdMessage = (String) request
        .getAttribute("userIdMessage");
    if (userIdMessage == null)
      userIdMessage = "";

    String passwordMessage = (String) request
        .getAttribute("passwordMessage");
    if (passwordMessage == null)
```

```
            passwordMessage = "";
%>
</head>
<body>
<h1>League Planet Login</h1>

<form action="login" method="post">
<table>
  <tr>
    <th align="right">User id:</th>
    <td><input name="userId" type="text" value="<%= userId %>"></td>
    <td><span class="validator"><%= userIdMessage %></span></td>
  </tr>
  <tr>
    <th align="right">Password:</th>
    <td><input name="password" type="password" value=""></td>
    <td><span class="validator"><%= passwordMessage %></span></td>
  </tr>
  <tr>
    <td colspan="2"> </td>
    <td><input name="action" type="submit" value="Login">  <input
      name="reset"s type="reset" value="Reset" /></td>
  </tr>

</table>
</form>

</body>
</html>
```

6. Create a second JSP named `logout.jsp` and edit it (see Example 7.16).
   `logout.jsp` also contains a page directive that enables HTTP session tracking. The user session object is retrieved in the HTML <head> element using
   the <jsp:useBean> tag. The userId is written into the page using the
   <jsp:getProperty> tag.

Example 7.16   Listing of logout.jsp
```
<%@ page language="java" contentType="text/html; charset=ISO-8859-1"
    pageEncoding="ISO-8859-1" session="true"%>
<!DOCTYPE HTML PUBLIC "-//W3C//DTD HTML 4.01 Transitional//EN">
<html>
<head>
<meta http-equiv="Content-Type" content="text/html; charset=ISO-8859-1">
<jsp:useBean class="com.leagueplanet.User" id="user" scope="session" />
<title>League Planet Logout</title>
<link rel="stylesheet" href="schedule.css" type="text/css">
</head>
<body>
<h1>League Planet Logout</h1>

<form action="login" method="post">
```

```
<table>
  <tr>
    <th align="right">User id:</th>
    <td><jsp:getProperty name="user" property="userId" /></td>
  </tr>
  <tr>
    <td colspan="2"></td>
    <td><input name="action" type="submit" value="Logout" /></td>
  </tr>
</table>
</form>

</body>
</html>
```

7. In the **Project Explorer**, select the LoginServlet in either the src folder or under the **Servlets** category of the IceHockeyWeb item, right click, and select the **Run As ► Run on Server** menu item. The project is published, the server starts, and the Web browser is opened on the URL

   ```
   http://localhost:8080/icehockey/login
   ```

   Note that occasionally the server may not have completely started before the browser requests the servlet, in which case you'll get a 404 error. To fix this, restart the server and try again (see the sidebar in Chapter 3, What Do I Do If I Get a 404?).

   The LoginServlet receives the GET request and forwards it to login.jsp. The Web browser displays the **League Planet Login** page (see Figure 7.69).

8. Enter an invalid userId and password, and click the **Login** button to test the server-side validation logic. Enter a valid userId, anne for example; and password, guest for example; and click the **Login** button. The Web browser displays the **League Planet Logout** page (see Figure 7.70). Note that logout.jsp correctly retrieved the userId from the session object and displayed it in the Web page.

9. Experiment with debugging by setting breakpoints in the servlet and JSP scriptlets, and repeat the above testing. This time select the **Debug As ► Debug on Server** menu item instead of **Run As ► Run on Server**. The familiar Java debugging perspective opens.

Figure 7.69   League Planet Login

Figure 7.70   League Planet Logout

Summary of Iteration 7

In this iteration you used the JSP source editor to generate dynamic Web content. You also used the JSP debugger to step through your JSP code. You are now ready to develop both the server and client sides of your presentation layer.

In the next iteration, you'll use the TCP/IP monitor to view HTTP message traffic. This tool will help you debug Web applications and understand HTTP topics such as cookies and sessions.

Iteration 8: Monitoring HTTP Sessions

HTTP Sessions

In the preceding iteration, you explored the use of HTTP session tracking in servlets and JSPs. HTTP is actually a sessionless protocol, so it is something of an abuse of terminology to talk about HTTP sessions. In reality, Web application servers layer *virtual* HTTP sessions on top of the HTTP protocol. There are several techniques for accomplishing this. They all boil down to the server sending a session id in some form to the browser so that the browser sends it back to the server in the subsequent requests. The server maintains state information associated with the session id and retrieves that information when it receives a request that contains the session id.

One way to implement session tracking is through URL rewriting and hidden form variables. In this approach, every URL that the server sends in a response is rewritten to include the session id. Also, every HTML form that gets sent to the server includes a hidden input field that contains the session id. This ensures that any request back to the server will contain the session id. Using this approach requires extra steps for the application developer. For example, every URL must be explicitly rewritten when the response is generated.

A much simpler approach is to use client-side *cookies*, which were introduced by NetScape Communications. In this approach, the server sends the session id using an HTTP Set-Cookie response header, and the browser returns it using a Cookie request header. For a thorough treatment of cookies, see *Cookies* [StLaurent1998a] by Simon St. Laurent.

J2EE includes support for session tracking. If the user has enabled cookie support, then cookies are used. Otherwise, URL rewriting is used. The servlet runtime automatically detects whether cookies are enabled and selects the correct method. However, if cookies are disabled, your application won't work correctly unless you explicitly rewrite your URLs using the `encodeURL` method of the `HttpServletResponse` class.

The TCP/IP Monitor

WTP contains a very useful tool called the *TCP/IP Monitor* that lets you peek into the HTTP traffic and see what's going on. The TCP/IP monitor is especially useful for understanding Web services and is a central tool for performing WS-I validation. We'll discuss that topic later (see Iteration 4: Testing Web Services for Interoperability section in Chapter 10). Here you'll use the TCP/IP monitor to explore session tracking.

It is natural to think of the end product of your work when building a Web application as the pages that are displayed in a Web browser. However, in a real sense the true end product of your work is TCP/IP packets of HTTP information that are sent over the network. You do not normally see these packets in their raw form, but they carry the content of your Web application. When you deploy an application that doesn't necessarily have a client that renders this information visually, it can be difficult to understand what's going on and diagnose problems. This is especially true of Web services where the client is typically another application that may not directly display the information to an end user.

The TCP/IP monitor sits between a client and a server, playing the role of a "man-in-the-middle." The TCP/IP monitor accepts requests from clients, forwards those requests to a server, receives the responses, and sends those responses back to the clients (see Figure 7.71). The TCP/IP monitor records the messages and allows you to view, modify, resend, and save them.

Figure 7.71   TCP/IP Monitor as a Man-in-the-Middle

The TCP/IP monitor can display the messages either as raw bytes or using special renderers for XML and image content (for example, so you can view images and not their binary representation). You can view each message in the format best suited to it. You can also optionally show or hide the HTTP message headers.

The TCP/IP monitor can also serve as a handy test client since it allows you to modify and resend requests. This can save you time while testing since you don't have to modify the client to try different data.

You can configure the TCP/IP monitor to work with either local or remote Web servers. This comes in handy when you are trying to debug a client for an external Web service. When you use the wizard to create your own Web services, you can have it automatically configure the TCP/IP monitor for you.

Viewing HTTP Sessions with the TCP/IP Monitor

The developers of League Planet have decided that users must enable cookies to use the advanced functions of the Web site. Calling the URL rewriting API is too much work for the developers and is too error prone. In this iteration, you'll monitor the HTTP traffic for the LoginServlet to ensure that session tracking is working correctly. Do the following:

1. In the **Servers** view, select the **Tomcat** server, right click, and select the **Monitoring ▶ Properties** menu item. The **Monitoring Ports** dialog opens (see Figure 7.72). If you have any monitors defined from previous work, remove them now by selecting each one and clicking the **Remove** button.

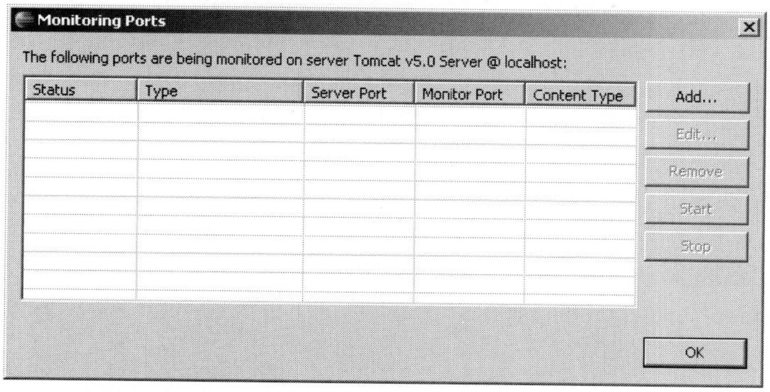

Figure 7.72   Monitoring Ports

2. Click the **Add** button to add a TCP/IP monitor to Tomcat. The list of available ports is displayed (see Figure 7.73).

3. Select the HTTP port. Accept the entries for the **Monitor Port (8081)** and the **Content type filter (All)**. The monitor port is the port that the monitor listens to. It forwards requests to Tomcat and relays replies back the client. In the process, it records the requests and responses so you can view them. The content type filter controls the type of content that gets recorded. Click the **OK** button. The monitor is created, and the **Monitoring Ports** dialog is redisplayed with the new monitor added (see Figure 7.74).

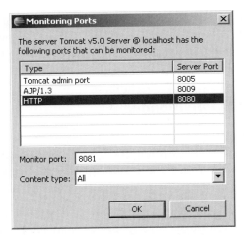

Figure 7.73   Monitor HTTP Port **8080**

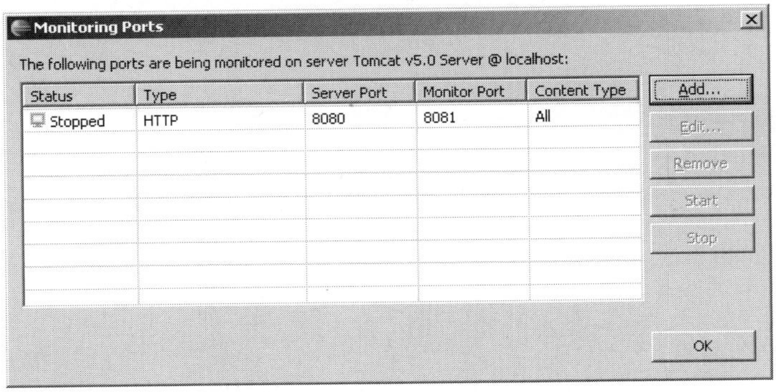

Figure 7.74   Monitor Added on Port 8081

4. Select the newly created monitor and click the **Start** button. The monitor is now listening to port 8081 and will forward requests received there on to port 8080. Open a new Web browser window outside of Eclipse to ensure that a new session will be started. Enter the following URL:

```
http://localhost:8081/icehockey/login
```

The **TCP/IP Monitor** view opens and displays three entries (see Figure 7.75). Select the **TCP/IP Monitor** view pull-down ▽ menu (down arrow) in the top right-hand corner, and then select the **Show header** menu item to display the HTTP headers. Select the first entry, which is the request for `/icehockey/login`. Look at the **Response** pane and notice the `Set-Cookie` header, which contains the new session id. This sends the session id to the Web browser.

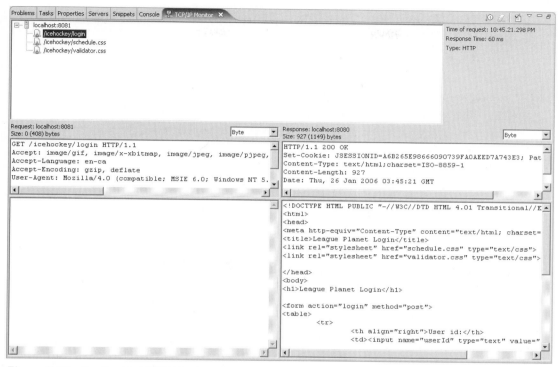

Figure 7.75 Set-Cookie HTTP Header

5. Now select the second entry, which is for /icehockey/schedule.css (see Figure 7.76). Look at the **Request** pane and scroll down the header widget to locate the Cookie header that contains the session id. This sends the session id back to the server, which then correlates the request with the session. All subsequent requests will contain the session id in a Cookie header until the Web browser closes. The server will invalidate the session id if the Web browser is inactive for a preset period of time. If this happens, the server discards the current session and creates a new one when the Web browser sends the next request.

6. To stop the TCP/IP monitor, open its preference page, select the monitor, and click **Stop** (see Figure 7.77).

Modifying and Resending a Message

As a man-in-the-middle, the TCP/IP monitor simply listens to a conversation. However, the TCP/IP monitor can also directly participate in a conversation and send its own requests to a server. This ability to act as a client can help in diagnosing problems since it allows you to quickly test different requests.

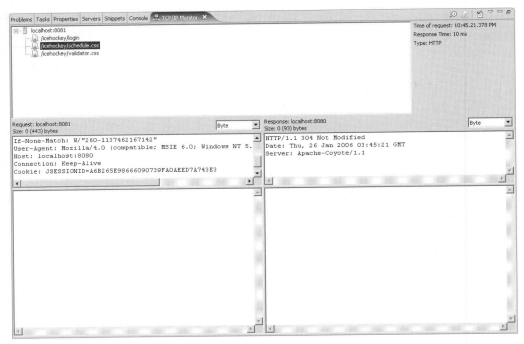

Figure 7.76   Cookie HTTP Header

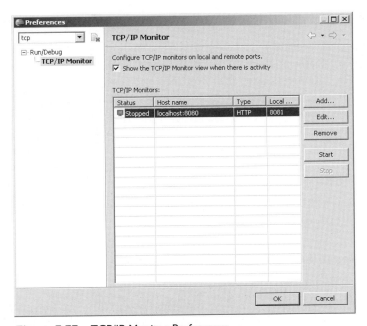

Figure 7.77   TCP/IP Monitor Preferences

There are two options for resending requests from the TCP/IP monitor. You can either resend a request exactly as it was sent earlier, or you can modify and resend the request. Resending an unmodified request is useful when you are debugging a server problem or if you want to see the effect of a change to the server. Resending a modified request is useful when you want to understand the behavior of a server and correct the behavior of a client.

To modify and resend a request, do the following:

1. Right click on the message in the TCP/IP monitor message tree.

2. Invoke the **Modify request** menu item. A new request appears as a child of the existing request.

   Note that if you want to resend the unmodified request, simply invoke the **Resend request** menu item at this point.

3. Edit the request in the **Request** pane, for example, by changing one of the input parameters.

4. Right click on the modified message in the message tree and invoke the **Send Modified Request** menu item. Your modified request is re-sent and the result is displayed in the **Response** pane.

Summary of Iteration 8

In this iteration you used the TCP/IP monitor to view HTTP traffic. This is a powerful tool for understanding and debugging Web applications. You'll also use the TCP/IP monitor in Chapter 10 to validate that Web service messages comply with Web Service Interoperability (WS-I) profiles.

Summary

In this chapter we have discussed the structure of the presentation tier and the tools that WTP contains for developing both the client and server portions of it. Of course, there is much more to the presentation tier than we have gone into here. For example, we have not touched on the vast subject of J2EE application frameworks such as Struts, Spring, and JSF. We will discuss WTP plans for JSF tools at the end of the book (Chapter 17).

At this point you should be comfortable with creating HTML, CSS, JavaScript, XML, DTD, JSP, and servlets in both static and dynamic Web projects. You should also be able to control servers and monitor HTTP traffic. You're now ready to move on to developing the business logic tier.

CHAPTER 8

The Business Logic Tier

The business of everybody is the business of nobody.

—Thomas Babington Macaulay

The term *business logic tier* is suggestive enough—this is the layer where the business objects and rules are modeled. It is common practice to build applications with three layers, with each layer hosted on one tier of a three-tier architecture. The business layer lies between the persistence layer, which stores the data, and the presentation layer, which provides the user interface. In this chapter, we'll discuss some of the best practices for developing a business tier and show how WTP can be used to do this.

Although we offer advice here, you should be aware that there is much debate over how to build the business tier. Component architectures, the use of plain (Naked) objects, and service-orientation are some of the most popular approaches (see [Sessions1997], [Pawson2002]).

Component architectures are a natural evolution of OO concepts. They offer coarse-grained business-level functions that are easier to understand, have clear interfaces, and can be distributed over a network. However, component architectures are not without problems. The large variety of component protocols, component interoperability problems, multiple interface languages, and heavyweight runtime infrastructures, and the complexity of standards and technologies have long been causes for concern. Service-Oriented Architecture (SOA) addresses some of the interoperability and integration problems by offering common standards and protocols, such as XML and HTTP (see Chapter 10). Consult the large number of excellent resources available elsewhere for patterns related to business models, uses of component architectures, SOA, and EJBs. We will skip the history here and briefly outline what we believe works.

We believe in OO architectural principles and that objects must be at the core of components and services. Therefore, our business model, sometimes referred to as the *domain model* [Fowler 2003], will be an object model. Obviously, given the title of this book, we will implement the business model in Java. Objects capture the business data and rules by encapsulating them as attributes and behavior. A simple business model may look like a reflection of the data model. However, as models evolve and get richer, the business layer contains much more than a representation of a database. The real strength of objects is how they collaborate using their relationships to accomplish business behavior.

A good object model is fine-grained with lots of small, easy-to-understand objects that have easy-to-understand methods. There should be objects encapsulating significant business concepts and data. Specific extensions and interfaces should be modeled by subclasses with fine-grained object interfaces. Domain relationships should be captured in objects by explicit object-to-object relations and not with database-like primary and foreign key mappings. OO presents a rich set of strategies and techniques to design a model for your business [Gamma1995]. Domain complexity is a fundamental aspect of many business systems. You should not expect OO to make something that is complex simple. That would be like expecting mathematics to make physics simple. If the business is complex, the object model will also be complex. OO will not make the domain simple, but it will help you model it faithfully. OO is definitely not a bed of roses. Object models have their associated difficulties but, fortunately, there are also ways to deal with them [Fowler1999].

Fine-grained domain models impose challenges from two primary perspectives: distribution and application logic.

Domain models built using Plain Old Java Objects (POJO) work well until you need to distribute the objects. In a fine-grained model, objects make a lot of small calls to each other. In a distributed system, this causes problems. Remote calls are expensive. This is where components and services come in handy. They present course-grained interfaces, or *façades*, to clients. You also need to handle security, transactions, reliability, multiple protocols, and heterogeneous environments. J2EE runtime environments take care of those details. In this chapter, we solve the distribution problem by using EJBs.

It is important to distinguish between the two aspects of systems that are captured in the business tier: the domain model and the application logic. Martin Fowler explains this very nicely in his book [Fowler2003]. The domain model represents the core business concepts and their behavior. This is different than the business use cases or the flow of the events. Application logic captures the latter. Application logic objects capture processes and workflow logic. These usually correspond to use case scenarios. For example, in the League Planet application, the service layer would handle the process of creating a new league. This might include sending data to an external system, e-mailing the league owner, and saving the league data in a database. Without application logic objects, finding the objects for a particular use case, which could involve literally thousands of objects, is a daunting task. More importantly, the process is not captured. Application logic is typically captured in a service layer with façades. Façades provide a unified interface to the objects contained in the domain model, making the domain model easier to use in applications.

Distinguishing the application logic from the domain model makes it easy to introduce the service layer. Services are coarse-grained objects with coarse-grained interfaces. Services can provide façades to the domain model, or they can implement processes. The operations provided by the service layer are defined by the requirements of the consumers of these services. *Remoting capability*, which is the enablement of objects in different processes to communicate with one another, is needed for most service objects since their clients are distributed. Remoting capability of the service layer also deals with serializing the domain objects over the network. The service layer provides the functionality of the business layer to other applications, which are integrated with it in an SOA world. This design is illustrated in Figure 8.1. A deeper discussion of these patterns can be found in [Fowler2003].

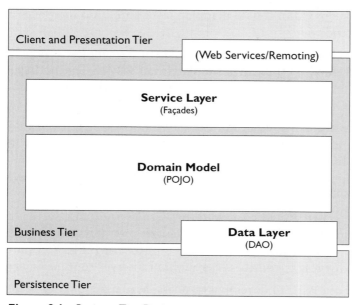

Figure 8.1 Business Tier Design

Last but not least, data must be kept in a datastore, and we will discuss this layer in the next chapter. The interface to the persistence layer is typically considered to be a part of the business tier. The objects that implement the interface to the persistence layer are typically referred to as Data Access Objects (DAO) or, in the case of JPA, the Persistence Manager. This interface uses domain objects as its parameters. The data access interface abstracts the details of the datastore, storage technology—such as SQL—and object-relational mapping technology from the business tier.

A Common Business Tier Design

Let's describe a business tier layered design to demonstrate the concepts just introduced. This scenario is guided by the following principles:

○ The business tier contains a service layer that provides and implements business logic. This tier is accessed by the presentation layer, service consumers, and other types of clients. The presentation layer can call the business tier directly in process, or it can use remote interfaces provided by EJBs. Other clients can call the business tier using Web services. The business tier can thus support clients with different protocol and access requirements.

○ Business data or enterprise information is maintained in a separate layer called the persistence tier. Data is kept in datastores and enterprise information systems (EIS). A data mapping layer and DAO interfaces abstract the persistence tier.

○ Objects are back! The domain is modeled in the simplest way possible. POJOs are good. POJOs are a simpler, faster way to develop business models. The domain model is easier to organize, encapsulate, and test using POJOs. Business interfaces should also be plain Java interfaces.

○ POJOs are not distributed, nor do they support transactions or security. Transactions, security, and concurrency are services needed by most applications. These services are available in J2EE server runtime environments. Often they are needed even when there is no application server to provide them.

○ The business tier should be able to run with or without a server container. A server runtime environment should not be a requirement for the business layer. This tier should not depend on EJBs, or J2EE. You should be able to use or test the business tier without a server runtime environment.

You'll use WTP to develop a business layer based on this scenario in the following iterations:

❍ In Iteration 1, you build the model, service, and data objects as POJOs. You also use Java Utility projects and define J2EE module dependencies.

❍ In Iteration 2, you use EJBs. You use stateless session beans to provide remote interfaces for services. You develop EJBs using XDoclet annotations, and run and debug EJBs on servers. To test your EJBs, you use a simple Web application. You use an enterprise application to organize and share common components.

❍ In Iteration 3, you implement reliable, asynchronous calls using message-driven beans (MDB).

Iteration 1: The Domain Model

You will start building a domain model for League Planet using POJOs. The model has objects such as leagues, teams, and players. The presentation tier sends messages to these objects via the service layer and displays the results. The service layer captures application logic and flow, such as requests for scheduling games or resolving schedule conflicts with the aid of an administrator. External systems, like the local news Web site, can use the service layer and Web services to get information about the games.

Obviously, the domain model is a core layer of the complete application. The presentation layer and service consumers need to access it. The classes in the business tier can be referenced by Web modules, EJB modules, and Web services. The persistence tier uses the domain model to populate lists as responses to queries or to save information to a database. As you can see, the domain model must be carefully designed so that it can be used in many parts of the overall application.

J2EE Utility Projects

WTP provides J2EE Utility Projects for the development of Java libraries that can be shared between modules. Utility projects behave much like plain Java projects, but they know about J2EE modules. Refer to Chapter 6 to learn more about creating utility projects. The contents of a utility project can be packaged as a JAR. Other J2EE projects—Web, EJB, and EAR modules, for example—can refer to utility projects, and WTP automatically packages the utility project with these modules so that it is available at runtime.

For these reasons, you will use a utility project to hold the domain model. Create a utility project as follows:

1. Launch Eclipse, and invoke the **File ▸ New ▸ Project** command to open the **New Project** wizard (see Figure 8.2).

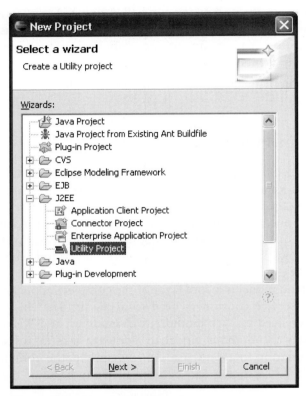

Figure 8.2   New Project Wizard

2. Open the **J2EE** category, select the **Utility Project** item, and click the **Next** button to open the **New Utility Project** wizard (see Figure 8.3).

3. The first page of the wizard lets you specify the project name and target runtime. Enter the name `LeaguePlanetModel` for the project name. You can also set the target runtime for a utility project. This is only meaningful if you refer to classes, such as

```
javax.naming
```

that are provided by a server runtime environment. Your business tier will be independent of a server runtime environment, so your choice of a

runtime is irrelevant. Choose a default runtime environment, and click the
Next button to proceed to the **Select Project Facets** page (see Figure 8.4).

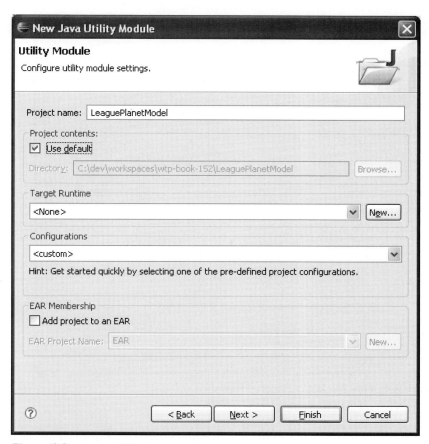

Figure 8.3   New Utility Project—Project Name

4. The second page of the wizard lets you specify the project facets. The
wizard will configure your project according to the facets you select. For
example, if there was a Spring Beans facet, the wizard would add libraries
for the Spring application framework to your project. Simply accept the
default facets. Make sure that **Java** and **Utility Module** are checked. Click the
Finish button to create the new project.

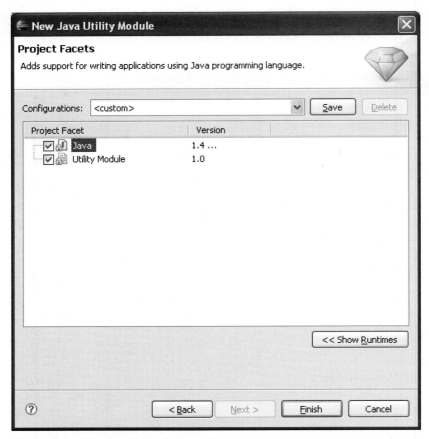

Figure 8.4   New Java Utility Project—Facets

5. Utility projects are normally associated with the **J2EE** perspective even though they do not contain J2EE resources. The wizard will prompt you to switch to the J2EE perspective after it creates the project. Click the **OK** button to switch to the **J2EE** perspective.

The Object Model

League Planet users can define leagues. Each league can have multiple teams, which can have multiple players. There will be game schedules for each league. Games are events between two opposing teams. It is possible to enrich the domain with many additional use cases, but the simple model shown in Figure 8.5 will be sufficient to demonstrate WTP.

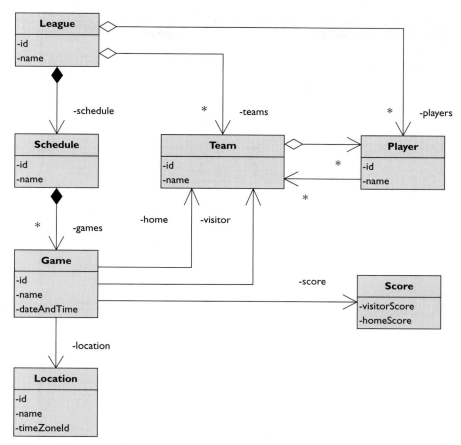

Figure 8.5   League Planet Object Model

Your model for League Planet will use POJOs. You will use the standard **New Class** wizard provided in JDT to create these classes. Implement the League Planet model as follows:

1. To start, create the League class. Select the source folder named src in the utility project named LeaguePlanetModel that you just created. Invoke the **File ▸ New ▸ Class** command to open the **New Class** wizard (see Figure 8.6).

2. Enter com.leagueplanet.model as the package and League as the class name. Click the **Finish** button to create the class.

3. Try to code the League class. Your implementation should look like Example 8.1.

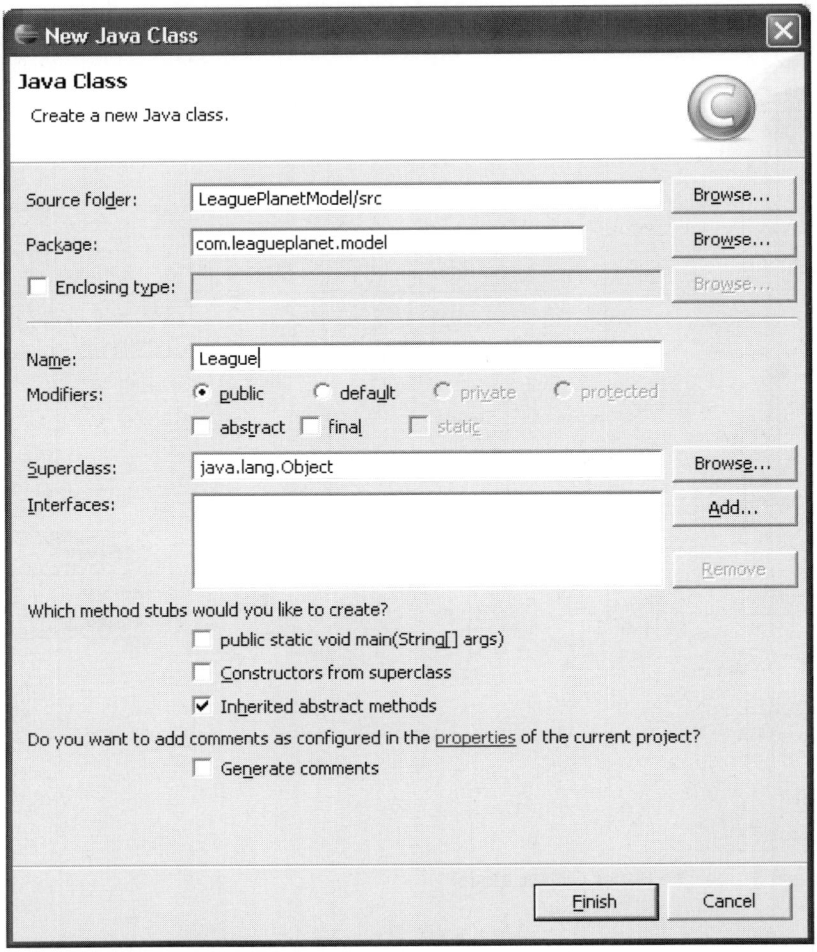

Figure 8.6   New Class Wizard

Example 8.1   Listing of League.java

```
package com.leagueplanet.model;

import java.io.Serializable;
import java.util.HashSet;
import java.util.Set;

public class League implements Serializable {
  private static final long serialVersionUID = 1L;

  private long id;
```

```
    private String name;
    private Set teams = new HashSet();
    private Set players = new HashSet();
    private Set schedules = new HashSet();
    public League() {
      this(0, "");
    }
    public League(long id, String name) {
      setId(id);
      setName(name);
    }
    public long getId() {
      return id;
    }
    public void setId(long id) {
      this.id = id;
    }
    public String getName() {
      return name;
    }
    public void setName(String name) {
      this.name = name;
    }
    public Set getPlayers() {
      return players;
    }
    public void setPlayers(Set players) {
      this.players = players;
    }
    public Set getTeams() {
      return teams;
    }
    public void setTeams(Set teams) {
      this.teams = teams;
    }
    public Set getSchedules() {
      return schedules;
    }
    public void setSchedules(Set schedules) {
      this.schedules = schedules;
    }
  }
```

4. Repeat the same process to create the Game class. Your implementation
   should look like Example 8.2.

Example 8.2   Listing of Game.java

```java
package com.leagueplanet.model;

import java.io.Serializable;
import java.text.ParseException;
import java.text.SimpleDateFormat;
import java.util.Calendar;

public class Game implements Serializable {

  private static final long serialVersionUID = 1L;

  private long id;

  private String name;

  private Location location;

  private Calendar dateAndTime;

  private Schedule schedule;

  private Team home;

  private Team visitor;

  private Score score = new Score();

  public Game(long id, String name, Calendar dateAndTime) {
    setId(id);
    setName(name);
    setDateAndTime(dateAndTime);
  }

  public Game(long id, String name, String dateAndTime)
      throws ParseException {
    Calendar gameDateAndTime = Calendar.getInstance();
    SimpleDateFormat dateFormat = new SimpleDateFormat(
        "yyyy-mm-dd hh:mm:ss");
    gameDateAndTime.setTime(dateFormat
        .parse(dateAndTime));
    setId(id);
    setName(name);
    setDateAndTime(gameDateAndTime);
  }

  public Game() throws ParseException {
    this(0, "", "1970-01-01 00:00:00");
  }

  public Game(long id, String dateAndTime)
      throws ParseException {
    this(id, "", dateAndTime);
  }
```

```
public Game(long id, Calendar dateAndTime) {
  this(id, "", dateAndTime);
}

public long getId() {
  return id;
}

public void setId(long id) {
  this.id = id;
}

public String getName() {
  return name;
}

public void setName(String name) {
  this.name = name;
}

public Location getLocation() {
  return location;
}

public void setLocation(Location location) {
  this.location = location;
}

public Schedule getSchedule() {
  return schedule;
}

public void setSchedule(Schedule schedule) {
  this.schedule = schedule;
}

public Team getHome() {
  return home;
}

public void setHome(Team home) {
  this.home = home;
}

public Score getScore() {
  return score;
}

public void setScore(Score score) {
  this.score = score;
}

public Team getVisitor() {
  return visitor;
}
```

```
  public void setVisitor(Team visitor) {
    this.visitor = visitor;
  }

  public Calendar getDateAndTime() {
    return dateAndTime;
  }

  public void setDateAndTime(Calendar dateAndTime) {
    this.dateAndTime = dateAndTime;
  }

}
```

5. The complete source code for the com.leagueplanet.model package is located in the directory examples/ch08/iteration1/LeaguePlanetModel/src. Import this package into your LeaguePlanetModel project source folder now.

The Service Layer

The service layer defines the interfaces for clients. These interfaces are determined by the types of requests made by the clients and their use cases. The service layer captures the application logic and flow described in these use cases. This logic is distinct from the domain model you wrote in the previous section. The domain model is shared, whereas the interfaces in the service layer are typically designed to meet client specifications.

For example, your presentation tier will have administrative pages, which will be used to create leagues, teams, and players. Other pages will display schedules for the leagues. These use cases will require interfaces in the business tier. You will need services to create leagues, find leagues, find teams, get game scores, and so forth.

Consider the following use case to define a new league. Recall the personas we defined for League Planet (see the Interaction Design section in Chapter 7). Sheila MacPherson, the psychology student, manages her college ultimate frisbee team and decides to use League Planet to coordinate the league. Here's how she creates the league:

1. Sheila logs in.

2. Sheila navigates to the league admin page.

3. Sheila clicks the **Create New League** button.

4. Sheila enters a name for the league, the type of sport, and the location, then clicks the **Submit** button.

5. The League Planet system makes sure the name of the league is unique and presents a summary page to Sheila to confirm the information.

6. Sheila clicks the **Confirm** button.

7. The system creates the league, saves the data to a database, and returns a page to Sheila to show that the operation has completed successfully.

To realize this use case, the presentation tier must call the business tier multiple times. It needs to check that a league with the same name does not exist. Another call is made to create the league. The creation operation must validate the information again, create the model objects, and save them to a database using the persistence layer. These calls and the sequences must be captured in a service layer. The design pattern that uses a service interface in front of a domain model is called a *façade*. The service façades will be implemented by Java interfaces that define the business calls and Java implementation classes that provide the services. This design enables you to choose among calls to Web services, EJBs, or local components transparently. Therefore, it gives you the ability to separate the interface of a service from the technology that invokes it, increasing your alternatives for different solution architectures and runtimes. The following diagram summarizes this design (see Figure 8.7).

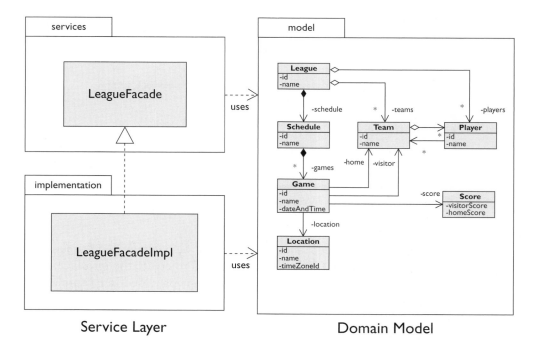

Figure 8.7 Service Layer Design

To create the service interfaces, do the following:

1. Select the source folder named src in the utility project as before. Invoke
   the File ▸ New ▸ Interface command to open the New Interface wizard
   (see Figure 8.8).

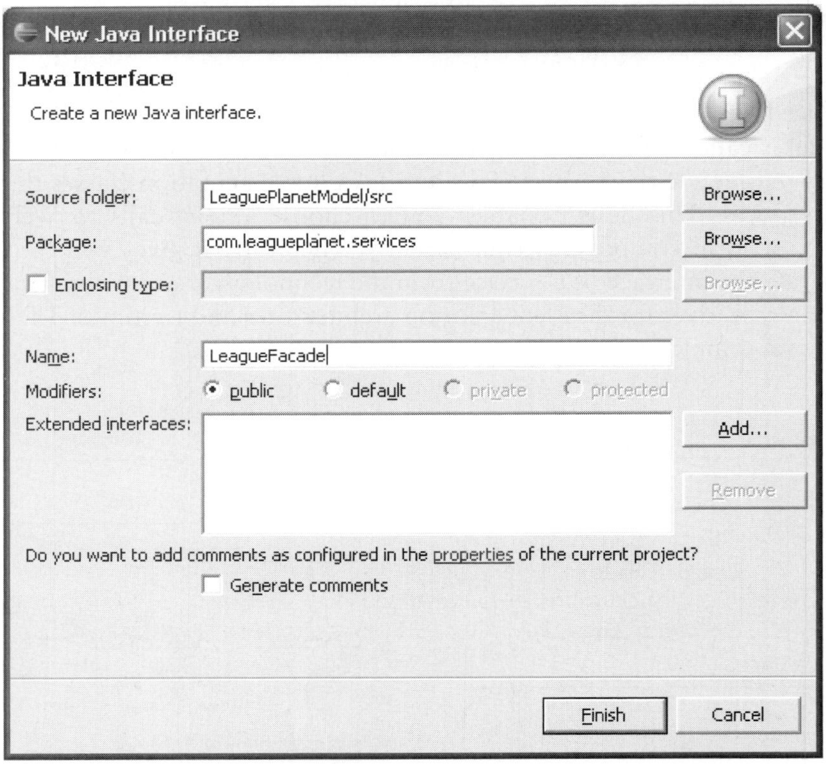

Figure 8.8   New Interface Wizard

Enter com.leagueplanet.services as the package and LeagueFacade as the
interface name. Click the Finish button to create the interface. The complete program listing for this interface is provided in Example 8.3. Import
the code now.

Example 8.3 ▸ Listing of LeagueFacade.java

```
package com.leagueplanet.services;

import java.util.Set;
```

```java
import com.leagueplanet.model.Game;
import com.leagueplanet.model.League;
import com.leagueplanet.model.Location;
import com.leagueplanet.model.Player;
import com.leagueplanet.model.Schedule;
import com.leagueplanet.model.Team;

public interface LeagueFacade {

    public Game findGame(long id);

    public League findLeague(long id);

    public Location findLocation(long id);

    public Player findPlayer(long id);

    public Schedule findSchedule(long id);

    public Team findTeam(long id);

    public Set getSchedulesForLeague(String league);

    public boolean doesLeagueExist(String name);

    public boolean createLeague(League newLeague);

}
```

2. The code for the façade implementation, which provides the service object that implements the LeagueFacade interface, is provided in Example 8.4. This class delegates persistence to the data layer (see Example 8.5 in the next section).

Example 8.4   Listing of LeagueFacadeImpl.java

```java
package com.leagueplanet.services.impl;

import java.util.Set;

import com.leagueplanet.dao.LeagueDAO;
import com.leagueplanet.model.Game;
import com.leagueplanet.model.League;
import com.leagueplanet.model.Location;
import com.leagueplanet.model.Player;
import com.leagueplanet.model.Schedule;
import com.leagueplanet.model.Team;
import com.leagueplanet.services.LeagueFacade;


public class LeagueFacadeImpl implements LeagueFacade {
    private LeagueDAO leagueDAO;
```

```java
  public LeagueDAO getLeagueDAO() {
    return leagueDAO;
  }

  public void setLeagueDAO(LeagueDAO leagueDAO) {
    this.leagueDAO = leagueDAO;
  }

  public boolean doesLeagueExist(String name) {
    Set allLeagues = leagueDAO
        .findLeaguesWithName(name);
    return allLeagues.size() > 0;
  }

  public boolean createLeague(League newLeague) {
    if (doesLeagueExist(newLeague.getName()))
      return false;
    leagueDAO.save(newLeague);
    return true;
  }

  public Set getSchedulesForLeague(String league) {
    return leagueDAO.getSchedulesForLeague(league);
  }

  public Game findGame(long id) {
    return leagueDAO.findGame(id);
  }

  public League findLeague(long id) {
    return leagueDAO.findLeague(id);
  }

  public Location findLocation(long id) {
    return leagueDAO.findLocation(id);
  }

  public Schedule findSchedule(long id) {
    return leagueDAO.findSchedule(id);
  }

  public Team findTeam(long id) {
    return leagueDAO.findTeam(id);
  }

  public Player findPlayer(long id) {
    return leagueDAO.findPlayer(id);
  }
}
```

The Data Access Layer

This layer provides an abstraction between the business tier and the persistence tier. The business tier must be independent of the persistence mechanism and the mapping tools that store the objects in the database. The interface with the data layer is defined by the LeagueDAO interface (see Example 8.5).

Example 8.5 Listing of LeagueDAO Interface

```
package com.leagueplanet.dao;

import java.util.Set;

import com.leagueplanet.model.Game;
import com.leagueplanet.model.League;
import com.leagueplanet.model.Location;
import com.leagueplanet.model.Player;
import com.leagueplanet.model.Schedule;
import com.leagueplanet.model.Team;

public interface LeagueDAO {

  public Game findGame(long id);

  public League findLeague(long id);

  public Location findLocation(long id);

  public Player findPlayer(long id);

  public Schedule findSchedule(long id);

  public Team findTeam(long id);

  public Set getSchedulesForLeague(String league);

  public Set findLeaguesWithName(String name);

  public void save(League newLeague);

}
```

Let's skip the implementation details as they will be covered in Chapter 9. To test your code, you can use a simple in-memory implementation. This class will maintain an example set of objects such as ice hockey leagues, teams, and players. When you implement a full-scale persistence layer, the example can be transparently replaced by the real implementation. The example façade is provided in Example 8.6.

Example 8.6   Listing of IceHockeyFacade.java

```
package com.leagueplanet.services;

import com.leagueplanet.dao.LeagueDAO;
import com.leagueplanet.dao.example.IceHockeyDOAImpl;
import com.leagueplanet.services.LeagueFacade;
import com.leagueplanet.services.impl.LeagueFacadeImpl;

public class IceHockeyFacade {

  private static LeagueFacade facade = null;

  public static LeagueFacade getLeagueFacade() {
    if (facade == null) {
      init();
    }
    return facade;
  }
  private static void init() {
    // create a new facade implementation
    LeagueFacadeImpl facadeImpl = new LeagueFacadeImpl();
    // point the facade at the dao for the ice hockey league
    LeagueDAO dao = IceHockeyDOAImpl.getLeagueDAO();
    facadeImpl.setLeagueDAO(dao);
    facade = facadeImpl;
  }

}
```

The example DAO is provided in Example 8.7.

Example 8.7   Listing of IceHockeyDAOImpl.java

```
package com.leagueplanet.dao.example;

import java.text.ParseException;
import java.util.HashMap;
import java.util.HashSet;
import java.util.Iterator;
import java.util.Set;

import com.leagueplanet.dao.LeagueDAO;
import com.leagueplanet.model.Game;
import com.leagueplanet.model.League;
import com.leagueplanet.model.Location;
import com.leagueplanet.model.Player;
import com.leagueplanet.model.Schedule;
import com.leagueplanet.model.Score;
import com.leagueplanet.model.Team;

public class IceHockeyDOAImpl implements LeagueDAO {

  // singleton DAO
```

```java
    private static IceHockeyDOAImpl leagueDAO = null;

    // in-memory copy of data
    private HashMap leagues = new HashMap();

    private HashMap schedules = new HashMap();

    private HashMap locations = new HashMap();

    private HashMap teams = new HashMap();

    private HashMap games = new HashMap();

    private HashMap events = new HashMap();

    private HashMap players = new HashMap();

    public Set getSchedulesForLeague(String league) {
      return new HashSet(schedules.values());
    }

    public Set findLeaguesWithName(String name) {

      Set results = new HashSet();
      Iterator leagueIterator = leagues.values()
          .iterator();
      while (leagueIterator.hasNext()) {
        League aLeague = (League) leagueIterator.next();
        if (name.equals(aLeague.getName()))
          results.add(aLeague);
      }
      return results;
    }

    public void save(League newLeague) {
      // TODO Auto-generated method stub

    }

    public static LeagueDAO getLeagueDAO() {
      if (leagueDAO == null) {
        leagueDAO = new IceHockeyDOAImpl();
        try {
          leagueDAO.init();
        } catch (ParseException e) {
          e.printStackTrace();
        }
      }

      return leagueDAO;
    }

    private void init() throws ParseException {
```

```
League league1 = new League(1,
    "Rosehill Girls Hockey League");
leagues.put(new Long(1), league1);

Location location1 = new Location(1,
    "Hillview High School", "Canada/Eastern");
locations.put(new Long(1), location1);

Location location2 = new Location(2,
    "Maple Community Centre", "Canada/Eastern");
locations.put(new Long(2), location2);

Team team1 = new Team(1, "Ladybugs");
teams.put(new Long(1), team1);
league1.getTeams().add(team1);

Team team2 = new Team(2, "Vixens");
teams.put(new Long(2), team2);
league1.getTeams().add(team2);

Team team3 = new Team(3, "Snowflakes");
teams.put(new Long(3), team3);
league1.getTeams().add(team3);

Team team4 = new Team(4, "Foxes");
teams.put(new Long(4), team4);
league1.getTeams().add(team4);

Schedule schedule1 = new Schedule(1,
    "2005-2006 Regular Season");
schedules.put(new Long(1), schedule1);
schedule1.setLeague(league1);
league1.getSchedules().add(schedule1);

Game game1 = new Game(1, "2006-01-07 19:00:00");
events.put(new Long(1), game1);
games.put(new Long(1), game1);
game1.setLocation(location1);
game1.setVisitor(team1);
game1.setHome(team2);
game1.setScore(new Score(3, 7));
game1.setSchedule(schedule1);
schedule1.getEvents().add(game1);

Game game2 = new Game(2, "2006-01-07 21:00:00");
events.put(new Long(2), game2);
games.put(new Long(2), game2);
game2.setLocation(location1);
game2.setVisitor(team3);
game2.setHome(team4);
game2.setScore(new Score(5, 2));
game2.setSchedule(schedule1);
schedule1.getEvents().add(game2);

Game game3 = new Game(3, "2006-01-08 19:30:00");
events.put(new Long(3), game3);
```

```
        games.put(new Long(3), game3);
        game3.setLocation(location2);
        game3.setVisitor(team2);
        game3.setHome(team4);
        game3.setScore(new Score(3, 5));
        game3.setSchedule(schedule1);
        schedule1.getEvents().add(game3);

        Game game4 = new Game(4, "2006-01-08 21:30:00");
        events.put(new Long(4), game4);
        games.put(new Long(4), game4);
        game4.setLocation(location2);
        game4.setVisitor(team3);
        game4.setHome(team1);
        game4.setScore(new Score(0, 4));
        game4.setSchedule(schedule1);
        schedule1.getEvents().add(game4);
        Game game5 = new Game(5, "2006-01-14   19:00:00");
        events.put(new Long(5), game5);
        games.put(new Long(5), game5);
        game5.setLocation(location1);
        game5.setVisitor(team3);
        game5.setHome(team2);
        game5.setScore(new Score(10, 4));
        game5.setSchedule(schedule1);
        schedule1.getEvents().add(game5);

        Game game6 = new Game(6, "2006-01-21   19:00:00");
        events.put(new Long(6), game6);
        games.put(new Long(6), game6);
        game6.setLocation(location1);
        game6.setVisitor(team4);
        game6.setHome(team1);
        game6.setScore(new Score(3, 3));
        game6.setSchedule(schedule1);
        schedule1.getEvents().add(game6);

        Game game7 = new Game(7, "2006-01-22   19:30:00");
        events.put(new Long(7), game7);
        games.put(new Long(7), game7);
        game7.setLocation(location2);
        game7.setVisitor(team3);
        game7.setHome(team2);
        game7.setScore(new Score(2, 6));
        game7.setSchedule(schedule1);
        schedule1.getEvents().add(game7);
    }

    public Game findGame(long id) {
        Object x = games.get(new Long(id));
        return (Game) x;
    }

    public League findLeague(long id) {
```

```
    Object x = leagues.get(new Long(id));
    return (League) x;
  }

  public Location findLocation(long id) {
    Object x = locations.get(new Long(id));
    return (Location) x;
  }

  public Schedule findSchedule(long id) {
    Object x = schedules.get(new Long(id));
    return (Schedule) x;
  }

  public Team findTeam(long id) {
    Object x = teams.get(new Long(id));
    return (Team) x;
  }
  public Player findPlayer(long id) {
    Object x = players.get(new Long(id));
    return (Player) x;
  }
}
```

Import the complete `LeaguePlanetModel` source code now from

`examples/ch08/iteration1/LeaguePlanetModel`

Testing

One of the nice things about building the business tier with POJOs is that you can test it without a server runtime environment.

It is good practice to keep your tests in a separate place, and even better practice to keep them in a separate project. (See Chapter 11.) To test your implementation, you will create an ordinary Java project and add JUnit tests to it. You will add your utility project to the build path of the tests project. Do the following:

1. Choose the **File ▸ New ▸ Project** command to open the **New Project** wizard. Expand the Java category, select the **Java Project** item, and click the **Next** button to open the **New Java Project** wizard (see Figure 8.9).

2. The first page of the wizard lets you specify the project name. Enter the name `LeaguePlanetModelTests` for the project name. Click the **Next** button to proceed to the next page.

3. Using the **Projects** tab, select the `LeaguePlanetModel` project to add it to the build path. Click the **Finish** button to create the new project.

4. Next you will add a JUnit test. Choose the **File ▸ New ▸ JUnit Test Case** command to open the **New JUnit Test Case** wizard (see Figure 8.10).

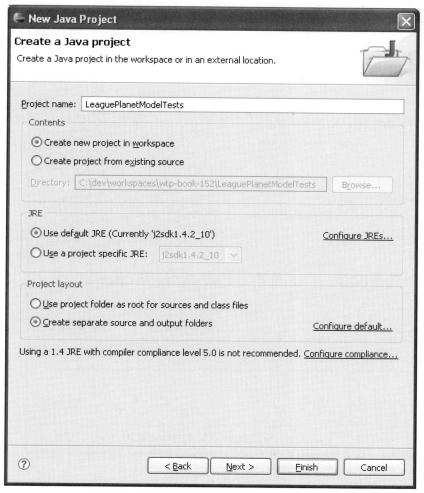

Figure 8.9 New Java Project—Project Name

5. Enter `com.leagueplanet.tests` as the package name. Name the test `LeagueFacadeTest`. Choose `LeagueFacadeImpl` as the class under test. JUnit JARs are not added to your build path yet, so you will receive a warning. Click on the `Click Here` link if you want the wizard to help you add JUnit to the project. Click the **Next** button.

6. Choose business methods such as `createLeague` and `doesLeagueExist` to test (see Figure 8.11). Click the **Finish** button to create the test.

7. The code in Example 8.8 describes the complete test.

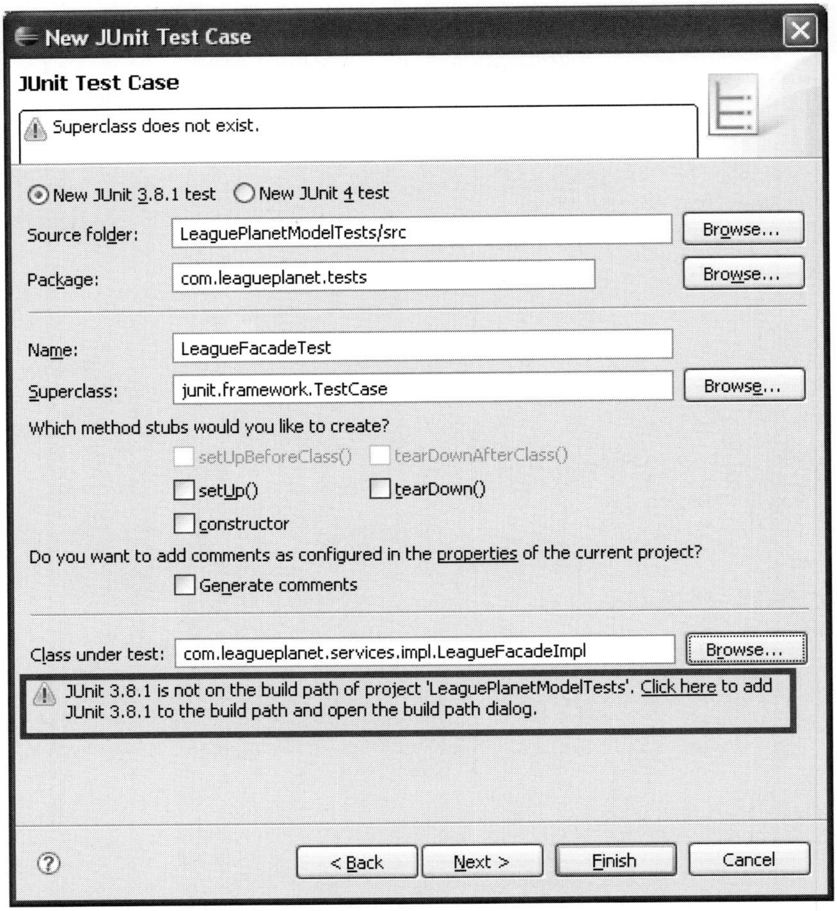

Figure 8.10   JUnit Test Wizard—Test Class

Example 8.8   Listing of LeagueFacadeTest.java

```
package com.leagueplanet.tests;

import com.leagueplanet.dao.example.IceHockeyDOAImpl;
import com.leagueplanet.model.League;
import com.leagueplanet.services.LeagueFacade;
import com.leagueplanet.services.impl.LeagueFacadeImpl;

import junit.framework.TestCase;

public class LeagueFacadeTest extends TestCase {
  LeagueFacade facade;

  public void setUp() throws Exception {
    super.setUp();
    facade = new LeagueFacadeImpl();
```

```
        ((LeagueFacadeImpl) facade)
            .setLeagueDAO(IceHockeyDOAImpl
                .getLeagueDAO());
    }

    public void testDoesLeagueExist() {
        assertFalse(facade.doesLeagueExist("A random name"));
    }

    public void testCreateLeague() {
        League league = new League();
        league.setName("Test League");
        assertTrue(facade.createLeague(league));
    }

}
```

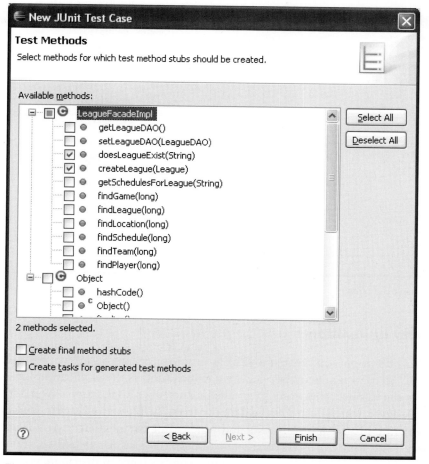

Figure 8.11   JUnit Test Wizard—Test Methods

8. Choose the test class using the **Package Explorer** and select **Run As ▸ JUnit Test** from the menu.

9. The **JUnit** view will display the results of your test (see Figure 8.12).

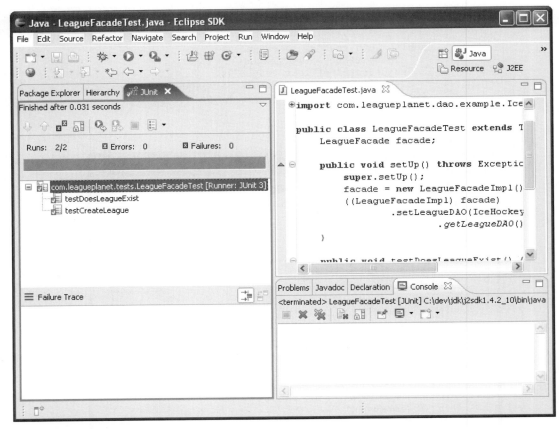

Figure 8.12   JUnit Run View

Summary of Iteration 1

In this iteration you created a J2EE utility project and added your POJO domain model to it. You added a service layer, which models the application logic and provides the business functionality to clients and other applications. You added a data access layer, which abstracts the data tier from the object model. Finally, you created a separate project for your tests and tested your business layer. You learned about using J2EE utility projects to create common libraries for shared components. You are now ready to add EJBs to the business tier so you can distribute your objects.

Iteration 2: Developing Session EJBs

Building distributed business applications has been a long-standing development challenge. EJBs help by tackling many of the hard problems such as distributed objects, transactions, security, component architectures, and message-oriented systems, to name a few. A comprehensive treatment of EJBs is beyond the scope of this book. We will, however, get you started with using WTP to develop EJBs for your business tier. To learn more about EJBs, see the excellent book *Enterprise JavaBeans* [Monson-Haefel1999] by Richard Monson-Haefel.

Recall the three-tier Web application architecture, which consists of logical layers for presentation, business logic, and persistence (see Chapter 5). These logical layers can be physically distributed in many ways. They can run in the same process, in different processes on the same machine, or on different machines. An EJB is a distributed object, which means it can be called by objects in other processes as easily as it can be called by objects in the same process. For example, a JSP can run in a Web container on one machine and call EJBs running on another machine. The EJB programming model makes this distribution transparent; the same interfaces are used for both local and remote calls. An EJB client uses the same code in either case (see Figure 8.13).

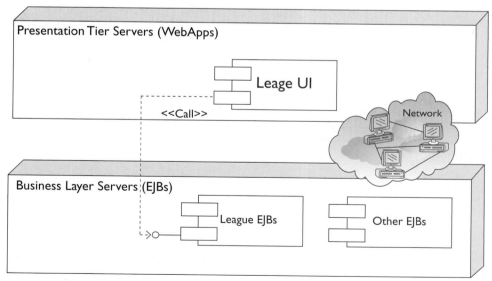

Figure 8.13 Distributed Application Using EJBs

Although JPA introduces a lightweight programming model for persistence, which can be used by desktop client applications, EJBs are primarily used for server-side applications that run in an application server container. EJB containers support complex business processes, high transaction volumes, high availability, transactions, and security. Using the EJB programming model, you do not write code for distribution, transactions, security, and other services provided by the container. Instead, you declaratively specify these runtime policies in XML deployment descriptors. The use of deployment descriptors results in a clean separation between the application logic and the runtime policies. Moreover, an administrator can change the runtime policies without having to modify the Java code. Java EE 5 introduces code attributes that let you specify these runtime policies in the code, but you can override the values you set there by providing deployment descriptors.

There are three types of EJBs: session beans, message-driven beans, and entity beans. *Session beans* and *message-driven beans* are coarse-grained components designed to model business processes. In contrast, *entity beans* are used to model fine-grained data objects. Client applications typically call session beans or message-driven beans instead of entity beans. Session beans and message-driven beans are often a part of the service layer in the business tier.

Session beans are designed to act as the interface between client and business tiers. In this iteration, they will implement the service façades. There will be a session bean for each service façade, and it will act as a wrapper for the underlying façade implementation.

By using session beans to wrap your service façades, you add transaction management, remoting, and security to your business functionality. Consult references such as *Mastering Enterprise JavaBeans* [Roman2005] by Ed Roman et al., *EJB Design Patterns* [Marinescu2003] by Floyd Marinescu, and *Core J2EE Patterns* [Alur2003] by Deepak Alur et al. for examples of many other scenarios where EJBs provide value to your applications.

Are there EJB alternatives?

EJBs are sometimes criticized as being complex to develop and heavyweight to run [Johnson2004]. As a result, a number of Open Source frameworks have been developed as alternatives. For example, both the Spring Framework and PicoContainer seek to provide lightweight containers for the business tier. In response to these criticisms, the EJB 3.0 specification [JSR220] addresses most of the shortcomings found in previous versions. The main theme of EJB 3.0 is ease of development. EJB 3.0 provides significant improvements in developer productivity and even provides the ability to use EJBs without a server runtime container. Metadata and Java 5 annotations are used for the development of EJBs. Annotations remove the need for the large number of interfaces and invasive coding requirements that were a part of the earlier specifications. The new specification supports persistence of POJOs, provides inversion of control (IOC) and dependency injection, removes the requirement to use remote exceptions, and makes many other simplifications. Although WTP 1.5 does not support EJB 3.0, JPA support is currently being developed in the Dali incubator project, which will be part of WTP 2.0 (see the Eclipse Dali Java Persistence Architecture (JPA) Tools Project section in Chapter 17).

The EJB 3.0 programming and deployment model is significantly different from previous versions of the specification. Ease of development is the primary goal of these changes. The EJB 3.0 specification is backward compatible with EJB 2.1, the previous version of the specification, which means that you can continue to use existing EJBs. The changes are only to the programming model, not the requirements; EJBs continue to support the same needs. WTP 2.0 will have tool support for Java EE 5 and the new EJB (see the Java Enterprise Edition 5 section in Chapter 17). However, you don't have to wait for WTP 2.0 to start. Hints for using JDT to develop EJB 3.0 applications follow. In the remainder of the chapter, we will continue to use the EJB 2.x style programming model and tools.

OSGi is also gaining momentum as an alternate service platform. It is a standardized, lightweight, and extensible alternative that can scale from enterprise applications to embedded systems.

In this iteration you will use an EJB to execute a complete business scenario for League Planet. You want this EJB to run a scenario in a single transaction with a single remote invocation to ensure good performance. Business scenarios typically involve multiple server-side objects, and sending multiple messages over the network is prohibitively expensive.

Imagine a Web page showing a table of game information. If the page accessed fine-grained business objects directly, it could easily send thousands of messages to the business tier and, as a result, perform very poorly. A session EJB solves this problem by returning all displayed objects in a single call.

The integrity of a scenario is also very important. For example, when displaying the game information, you don't want to show a partially updated game, which could result when making many calls to fine-grained objects. An EJB can run a scenario as a single transactional unit of work. EJBs can be used to manage the transaction boundary for calls to multiple server-side objects that participate in a scenario.

These are all good things: you can use EJBs to reduce the coupling between the client and the server, get better performance, and improve concurrency by reducing transaction times. This EJB design pattern is referred to as the *Session Façade* [Marinescu2003].

You will start by building a stateless session bean that provides distributed access to your service layer using the LeagueFacade interface, which uses the Session Façade pattern. The complete implementation includes:

○ The EJB component class that wraps the façade object

○ The component interface that extends EJBObject and replicates the LeagueFacade interface

○ The home interface

You repeat the interface because EJB component interfaces must include EJB specific types and you do not want to build this dependency into your model classes (see Figure 8.14). If you were using EJB 3.0 you could have avoided this duplication. There are many mechanical steps in creating an EJB. Luckily, you can use WTP to simplify your job. To do this, you will use XDoclet to generate some of this code for you because most of the information, such as component interface methods, can be deduced from the EJB component class.

WTP provides EJB projects that can build, test, and package EJBs and run them on J2EE application servers. This support is provided in the JST subproject. The following is a typical order of steps for defining and testing an EJB 2.x component:

1. Create an EJB project, an EJB Client project and an Enterprise Application project. You will use the last two projects to develop EJB components in a manageable and reusable manner.

2. Create the Java types that are needed for the EJB: the component interfaces that specify the business methods, the EJB home interface that is used to create and access EJB components, and the EJB bean class that implements the business methods. The EJB bean class will use the model you developed in the previous section to define its behavior.

   The EJB class must implement the methods defined by the component interfaces. You can develop the interfaces and classes by hand. However, the task of keeping these classes and interfaces in sync can create maintenance problems in large systems. Therefore, you will use XDoclet to automatically update interface definitions each time an EJB class is modified. XDoclet is useful for EJB 2.1 style development, but it will become obsolete with increased use of EJB 3.0.

3. Create the deployment descriptor to define container attributes such as JNDI names, transactions, and security parameters. Deployment descriptors need tool support for editing. They are typically XML files with complex schemas. You can also use tools such as XDoclet to generate deployment descriptors.

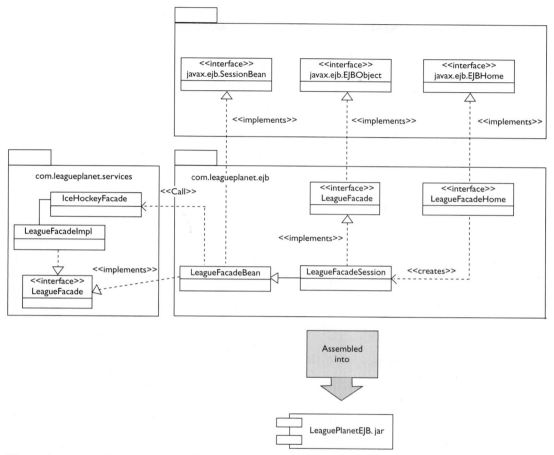

Figure 8.14 The Class Diagram for the EJB Component

4. Assemble the EJBs in an EJB-JAR file and deploy it to a server. You may need to define additional configuration information, such as JDBC connection pools or JMS destinations, to run EJBs.

Adding JBoss

Before you start building EJBs, you will need to add a server runtime environment that supports EJBs. This iteration contains instructions for using JBoss. However, if you have another J2EE application server that supports EJBs—Apache Geronimo, for example—feel free to use it instead. Also, XDoclet will speed your coding but you will need to configure it before you can use it.

Just as you use a JRE to run Java applications, WTP uses installed server runtime environments to run EJBs. The JBoss application server is one of the many available runtime environments that support EJBs.

To use JBoss with WTP you must:

1. Obtain and install the JBoss server runtime environment

2. Add the server runtime environment to your workspace

3. Create a server configuration, and add EJB projects to it

WTP does not include any runtimes. You must obtain the JBoss server runtime from

```
http://www.jboss.org
```

and install it on your machine. To add the JBoss server runtime environment to your workspace, you will use the Generic Server Adapter for JBoss, which is provided with WTP. This adapter can start and stop the server and publish your projects to it. You can easily replace JBoss with any other server runtime environment that has support for EJBs, such as ObjectWeb JOnAS, Apache Geronimo, IBM WebSphere, BEA WebLogic, Oracle AS, and others. After you install the server, you configure the adapter with the installation location and other parameters, such as passwords.

Do the following to add JBoss to your workspace:

1. Open the **Preferences** dialog and select the **Server** page. Select the **Installed Runtimes** preferences page. Click the **Add** button. The **New Server Runtime** wizard opens (see Figure 8.15).

2. The **New Server Runtime** dialog lists all of the server adapters that are currently installed. Select **JBoss v4.0** from the **JBoss** category and click the **Next** button. The **JBoss Server** wizard opens (see Figure 8.16).

3. JBoss must be installed on your machine at this point in order to proceed. You will use JBoss v4.0.5 GA in this example. The **JBoss Server** wizard needs the location of the JBoss installation directory. Enter the location or select it using the **Browse** button. You also need to specify a JRE. A full JDK is needed, because it has the required Java compiler. Click the **Finish** button. The **Installed Runtimes** preference page now lists JBoss (see Figure 8.17). Click the checkbox to make JBoss the default server runtime environment.

JBoss is now added to your workspace. Next you will add XDoclet to your workspace.

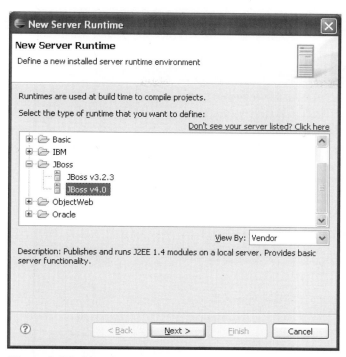

Figure 8.15   New Server Runtime

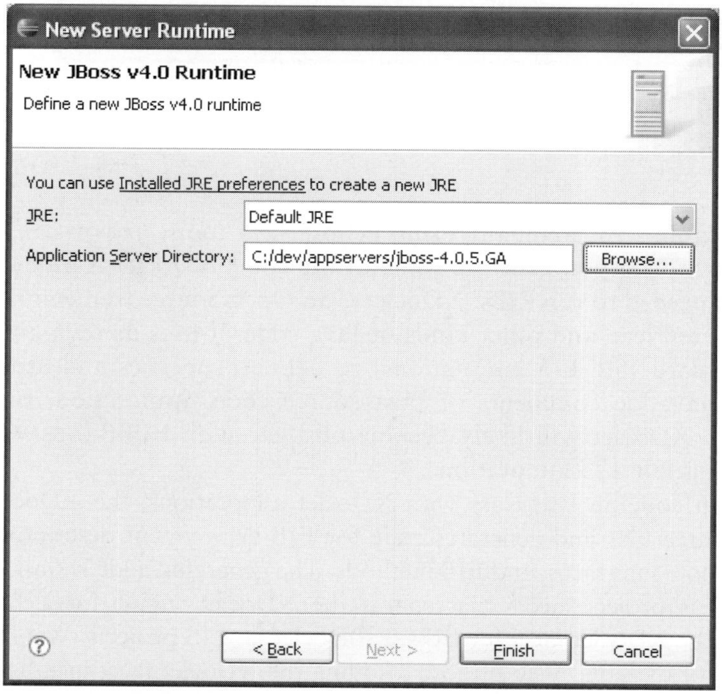

Figure 8.16   JBoss Server

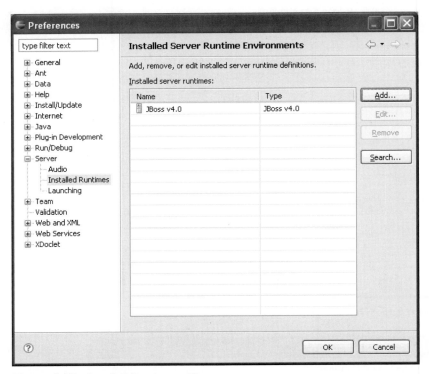

Figure 8.17   Installed Runtimes—JBoss

XDoclet

You can program EJBs manually using Eclipse Java tools, or you can use tools like XDoclet to help you generate some of the code. XDoclet is a development tool; it is not needed to run EJBs. XDoclet is an Open Source framework for generating EJBs, servlets, and other kinds of Java code. It uses its own annotations (not the standard JSR 175 annotations) to define properties and attributes of EJBs in the Javadoc comments of Java source code. Annotations are special Javadoc tags. XDoclet will likely become obsolete with EJB 3.0 as we will all switch to using JSR 175 annotations.

When you code an EJB class with XDoclet annotations, the XDoclet engine parses the source files and generates code for EJB deployment descriptors; home, local, and remote interfaces; and EJB methods. The generated code is standard J2EE code. WTP has project facets that enable the XDoclet engine for EJB projects. You can add the XDoclet facet for EJBs, EJBDoclet, to EJB projects. WebDoclet is a similar facet for dynamic Web projects. Adding the XDoclet facet installs a builder that automatically generates EJB code from the annotated source code.

WTP does not come with an XDoclet runtime. Before you can add XDoclet facets to projects, you must install it and add it to your workspace. XDoclet can be obtained from

`http://xdoclet.sourceforge.net`

To use XDoclet in your workspace, do the following:

1. Open the **Preferences** dialog and select the **XDoclet** page. The main **XDoclet** preferences page lets you set the default location and version of XDoclet for your workspace. You can override your global workspace settings and use different XDoclet settings for each project in your workspace.

2. XDoclet must be installed on your machine at this point to proceed. WTP needs the location of the XDoclet installation directory. Enter the location or select it using the **Browse** button (see Figure 8.18). Choose the correct version of the XDoclet runtime. You will use XDoclet v1.2.3 here. The XDoclet builder checkbox should be checked for the builder to call the XDoclet engine when the Java source code for an annotated bean is modified. Click the **Apply** button.

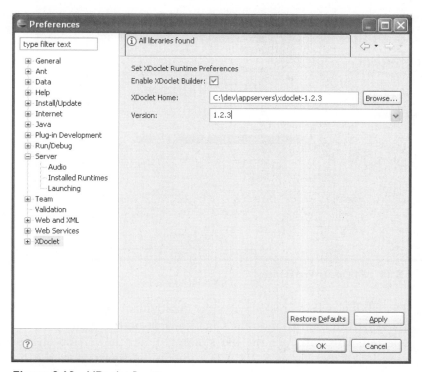

Figure 8.18 XDoclet Runtime

3. Select the **ejbdoclet** preferences page (see Figure 8.19). The ejbdoclet engine does the work for generating code for EJBs. To change how ejbdoclet generates Java code, you modify the properties in this page. The list enumerates all ejbdoclet subtasks that are currently supported by WTP. The subtasks required by most projects are selected by default. You can include or exclude a subtask by checking or unchecking it in the list. Subtasks also have properties of their own. To edit subtask parameters, select the subtask in the list and click the **Edit** button. In this iteration, you will use JBoss for your development. Therefore, check the JBoss subtask, which will instruct ejbdoclet to generate the required JBoss-specific deployment descriptors. Click the **Apply** button to apply your changes.

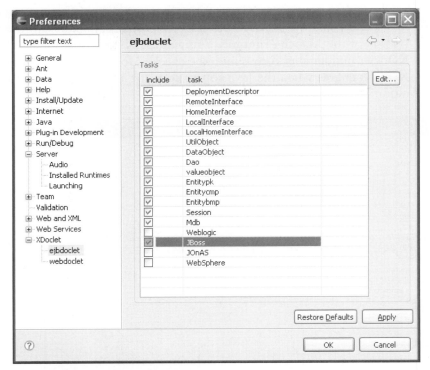

Figure 8.19   EJBDoclet Preferences

4. The ejbdoclet JBoss task creates the deployment descriptor named `jboss.xml` in the EJB module. Click the **Edit** button while the JBoss task is selected. This will open the JBoss dialog. Enter the version of JBoss as version 4.0 (see Figure 8.20). Click the **OK** button to close the dialog. Click the **Apply** button to save the ejbdoclet preferences.

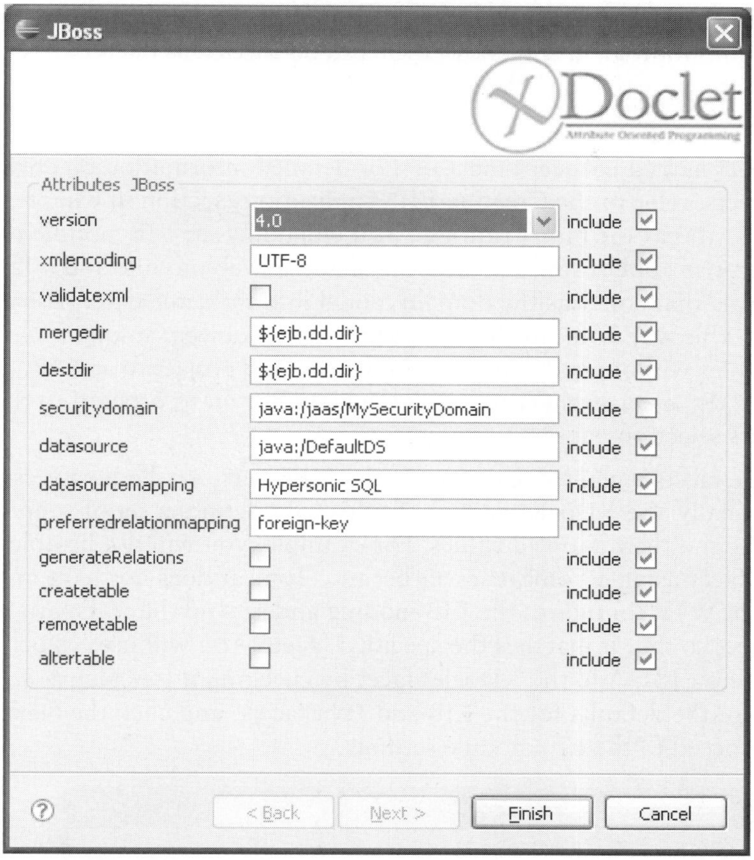

Figure 8.20   JBoss Subtask

XDoclet is added to your workspace. You are now ready to develop and run your EJBs.

EJB Projects

WTP provides EJB projects for the development of EJB components. An EJB module can contain the Java code for multiple EJB components. EJBs contained in the same project are packaged as a single archive. An application can have multiple EJB projects. An EJB module is mapped to a single project so that the Java classpath of the project has the same rules as the class loaders used by the server. Typically, an EJB module contains Java resources for EJB classes and deployment descriptors. These classes and resources can be arranged in separate folders. EJB projects know how to assemble them into the format specified by the J2EE specification before the module is deployed to a server. As usual, an EJB project can be targeted to multiple server configurations for testing, and one of them can be selected as the project default.

To create the EJBs for League Planet, do the following:

1. In the **Project Explorer** view, select the **New EJB Project** wizard to create a project named LeaguePlanetEJB. For detailed information on creating EJB projects, refer to the Creating EJB Applications section in Chapter 6. Select JBoss v4.0 as the target runtime. You will add your EJB module to a J2EE enterprise application. Later, you will add a Web module and a Java utility module that contains the domain model into the same enterprise application. This way you can share the same model objects among multiple J2EE modules without code duplication. Check **Add project to an EAR**, and name the EAR LeaguePlanetEAR. Click the **Next** button to proceed to the **Project Facets** selection page.

2. In the facets page, you can specify the J2EE version, the Java version, and, optionally, the XDoclet version. Each server defines a set of supported facets and their allowed values. For example, you will not be able to set an EJB facet using a Tomcat server because Tomcat does not have an EJB container. WTP configures the EJB module and sets up the classpath for the project so that it matches the specified facets. You will use XDoclet to develop EJBs. Add the XDoclet facet by checking it (see Figure 8.21). Accept the defaults for the EJB and Java facets, and click the **Next** button to proceed to the EJB module settings.

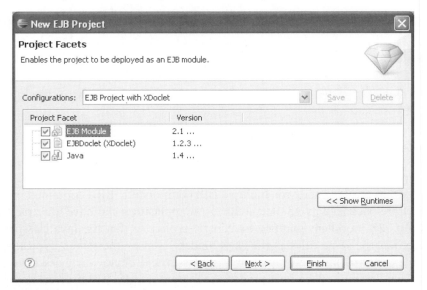

Figure 8.21 EJB Project Facets

3. The **EJB Module** page lets you specify the directory for Java resources and, optionally, create a Java utility module that will contain EJB classes and interfaces required by EJB clients (see Figure 8.22). It is good practice to create a client module because it simplifies the development of client-side applications. They can simply refer to the client JAR to find all the necessary code needed to call the EJBs. Check the **Create an EJB client** module box. Enter `LeaguePlanetEJBClient` and `LeaguePlanetEJBClient.jar` as the name and URI for the EJB client JAR, respectively. Click **Finish**.

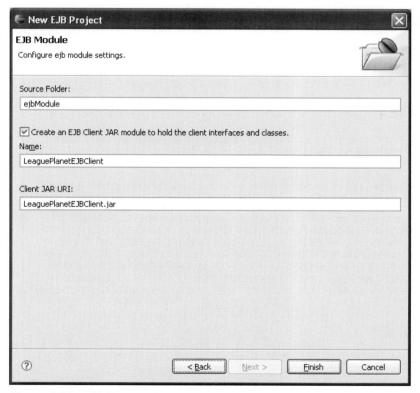

Figure 8.22   EJB Client Module Page

4. WTP creates the EJB project and populates it with configuration files such as this EJB deployment descriptor: `ejb-jar.xml`.

WTP also validates the EJB project. During this process you may be asked to approve licenses from Sun Microsystems (see Figure 8.23). Read the terms of the license, and if you agree with them click **I Agree**. If you accidentally click

I Disagree, you can use the Internet Cache preferences page to be prompted again for the license the next time it is needed.

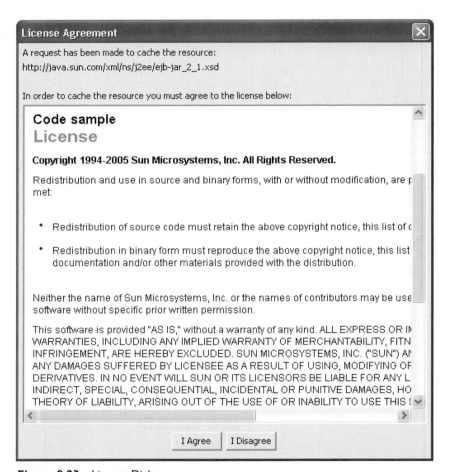

Figure 8.23   License Dialog

Let's review the projects that have been created. You previously created a Java utility project that holds the domain model. You created a new EJB project that will hold the code for your EJB components, and an EJB client project that will contain the EJB classes needed by clients. Finally, you asked for an enterprise application project to assemble all these modules into an integral J2EE application. When the wizard finishes its work, it creates three new projects: LeaguePlanetEJB, LeaguePlanetEAR, and LeaguePlanetEJBClient (see Figure 8.24).

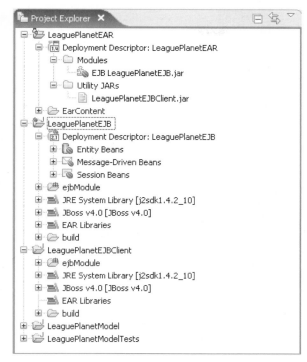

Figure 8.24   League Planet Projects—EJB, EJB Client, and EAR Projects

Creating Session Beans

Arguably, the most common and useful type of EJB is the *stateless session bean*. These EJBs have no conversational state associated with any specific client. Since they have no state, server runtimes can be very efficient in running stateless session beans. Client state is typically maintained in the presentation tier or another layer of components. In this example, you will create stateless session beans for your service façades.

To create a stateless session bean, do the following:

1. Select the `LeaguePlanetEJB` project in the **Project Explorer**. Right click, and select the **New ▶ XDoclet Enterprise JavaBean** menu item. The **Create EnterpriseJavaBean** wizard opens (see Figure 8.25).

2. In the first page of the wizard, you are presented with three choices for EJB types. Click the **Session bean** button. The link for the provider will take you to the **XDoclet** preferences page. Since you already set up XDoclet, you do not have to do anything else in this page. Click the **Next** button to go to the **Enterprise JavaBean Class** page (see Figure 8.26).

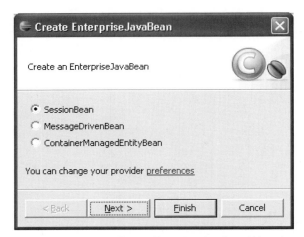

Figure 8.25   New Create EnterpriseJavaBean Wizard

Figure 8.26   Create EnterpriseJavaBean Class

3. Ensure that LeaguePlanetEJB is selected as the project and /LeaguePlanetEJB/ ejbModule is selected as the folder. Enter com.leagueplanet.ejb as the Java package and LeagueFacadeBean as the class name. XDoclet uses naming conventions for bean names. It uses the suffix Bean for class names. You should avoid using other suffixes such as Session, Entity, CMP, and BMP, since they are used by XDoclet for the generated code. Leave the superclass as Object. Click the **Next** button. The next page allows you to enter initial attributes of the stateless session bean (see Figure 8.27).

Figure 8.27 Stateless Session Bean Properties

4. In this page you can review and modify EJB parameters. These parameters are reflected as settings in the deployment descriptors. Ensure that the State Type is `stateless`. You will leave the other settings as defaults. Click the **Next** button. The next page allows you to choose interfaces for the EJB (see Figure 8.28).

Figure 8.28 Stateless Session Bean Interfaces

5. A stateless session bean must implement both the `javax.ejb.SessionBean`
   interface and the required business scenario interfaces. Accept the defaults
   here. Click **Finish** to generate the EJB. The wizard will create the new stateless session bean, and the XDoclet engine will generate the code for its EJB
   interfaces, methods, and deployment descriptors. Note that the wizard puts
   the server runtime EJB classes in the EJB project and those that are needed
   by clients in the EJB client project. After the generation is complete, you
   can browse these classes using the **Project Explorer** view (see Figure 8.29).

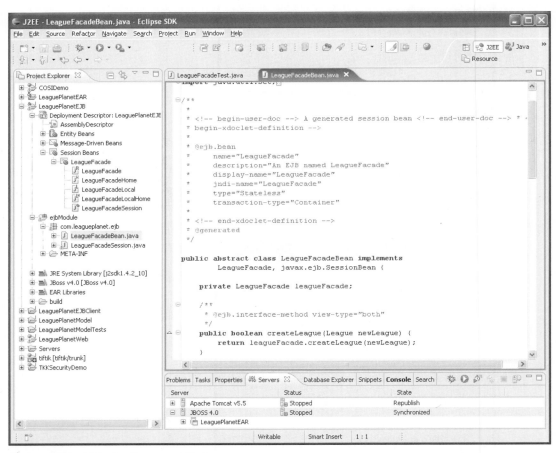

Figure 8.29   XDoclet Generated Code

6. The **EJB** wizard created a bean class that is already annotated with XDoclet tags for a stateless session bean. The XDoclet engine uses these tags to determine the type of the EJB, its JNDI name, the business methods, and the bean's transaction and security attributes. WTP extends the Java source editor to provide code assist support for XDoclet annotations (see Figure 8.30).

Figure 8.30   Code Assist for XDoclet

You can design the work done by the bean into units called *transactions*. All EJBs are transactional by default unless you explicitly make them non-transactional. You can either explicitly handle transactions in your business methods or you can delegate this responsibility to the EJB container. These alternatives are referred to as *bean-managed* and *container-managed transaction demarcation*. In container-managed transaction demarcation, the container ensures that a unit of work either fully completes or is fully rolled back. We prefer container-managed transactions because you do not have to deal with issues such as failure recovery and concurrent access in your code. Although session and message-driven beans can use either bean-managed or container-managed transactions, entity beans must use container-managed transactions. You will modify the generated code to add an annotation for the transaction attribute. Use the XDoclet code assist to add the `@ejb.transaction` tag and set its type to `Supports` (see Figure 8.31).

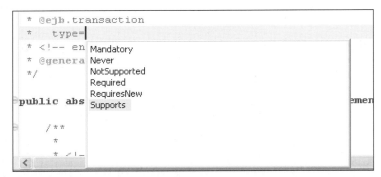

Figure 8.31   Transaction Demarcation with Annotations

If the client calls the EJB with a transaction context, the container invokes the EJB in the client's transaction context. This means your EJB can participate in a transaction if the caller has already initiated a transaction. However, if there is no transaction, it will execute the method without a transaction. The `Supports` type therefore allows the EJB to operate in both cases.

Next you will implement the business methods described in the `LeagueFacade` interface. To do this you must implement the interface in the `LeagueFacadeBean` class and add the methods. But wait! The domain model is in a different project. To use it, you need these classes to be on your classpath. You need to compile the EJB classes with them, but you do not want to include the model classes in the EJB module. They should be deployed to the server runtime environment separately. WTP allows you to describe the dependencies between J2EE modules. With module dependencies, WTP can automatically maintain the project classpaths and assemble them to deploy a complete application to a server environment. To set dependencies you will:

1. Include all EJB modules in the `LeaguePlanetEAR` enterprise application.

2. Add the `LeaguePlanetModel` utility module to `LeaguePlanetEAR`.

3. Make the `LeaguePlanetEJB` and `LeaguePlanetEJBClient` modules dependent on `LeaguePlanetModel` because you will use these types in your business methods.

To make these changes, do the following:

1. In the **Project Explorer,** select the LeaguePlanetEAR project. Right click, and invoke the **Properties** menu item. The project properties dialog opens. Click on the **J2EE Module Dependencies** to open the module dependencies page (see Figure 8.32).

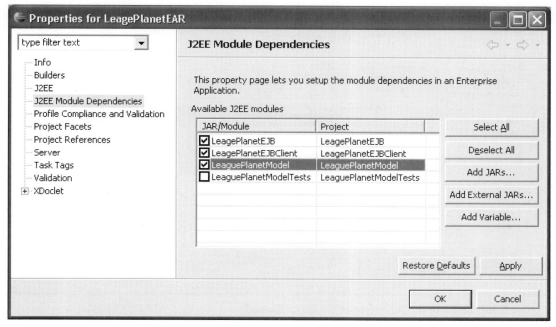

Figure 8.32 Properties for LeaguePlanetEAR

2. In this page you can add existing J2EE modules to LeaguePlanetEAR. You can also add binary JARs, such as struts.jar, to an EAR. Check LeaguePlanetModel to add it to the enterprise application. Click the **OK** button to accept your changes.

3. Next select the LeaguePlanetEJB project in the **Project Explorer,** right click, invoke the **Properties** menu item as before, and navigate to the **J2EE Module Dependencies** page (see Figure 8.33).

4. You can now define the module dependencies among the modules that are contained in the same enterprise application. Notice that the EJB module is already dependent on the EJB client module. Check LeaguePlanetModel to add it to the list. Click the **OK** button to accept your changes.

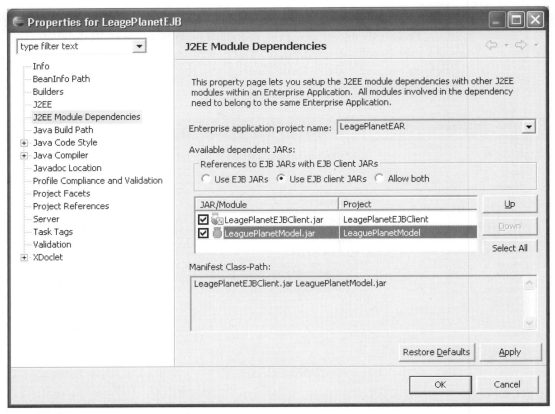

Figure 8.33   J2EE Module Dependencies for LeaguePlanetEJB

5. Next select the `LeaguePlanetEJBClient` project in the **Project Explorer**, right click, and repeat the same process to add a dependency to `LeaguePlanetModel` (see Figure 8.34).

Now you can use the model objects to finish the implementation of your stateless session bean. Your stateless session bean will use your service façade implementation to call League Planet services. The first thing to do is to initialize the stateless session bean. The `ejbCreate` method is the correct place to do this. Edit `LeagueFacadeBean.java` so that it matches Example 8.9. Save your code. You have completed programming your EJB. Note that the XDoclet engine updates all generated classes according to your new implementation.

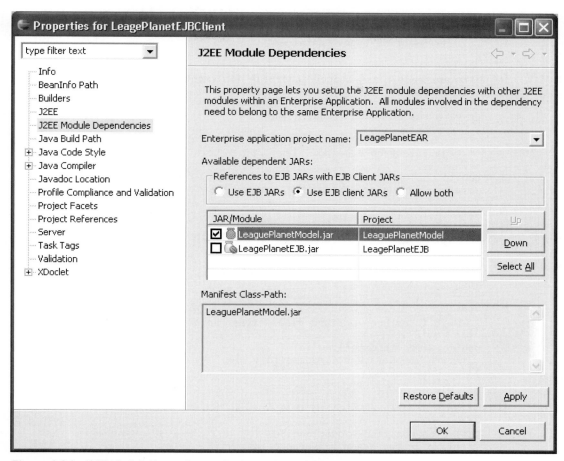

Figure 8.34   J2EE Module Dependencies for LeaguePlanetEJBClient

Example 8.9   Listing of LeagueFacadeBean.java

```
package com.leagueplanet.ejb;

import java.util.Set;

import com.leagueplanet.model.*;
import com.leagueplanet.services.IceHockeyFacade;
import com.leagueplanet.services.LeagueFacade;

/**
 * @ejb.bean
 *      name="LeagueFacade"
 *      description="An EJB named LeagueFacade"
 *      display-name="LeagueFacade"
```

```
 *       jndi-name="LeagueFacade"
 *       type="Stateless"
 *       transaction-type="Container"
 */
public abstract class LeagueFacadeBean implements
    LeagueFacade, javax.ejb.SessionBean {

  private LeagueFacade leagueFacade;

  /**
   * @ejb.interface - method view - type="both"
   */
  public boolean createLeague(League newLeague) {
    return leagueFacade.createLeague(newLeague);
  }

  /**
   * @ejb.interface - method view - type="both"
   */
  public boolean doesLeagueExist(String name) {
    return leagueFacade.doesLeagueExist(name);
  }

  /**
   * @ejb.interface - method view - type="both"
   */
  public Game findGame(long id) {
    return leagueFacade.findGame(id);
  }

  /**
   * @ejb.interface - method view - type="both"
   */
  public League findLeague(long id) {
    return leagueFacade.findLeague(id);
  }

  /**
   * @ejb.interface - method view - type="both"
   */
  public Location findLocation(long id) {
    return leagueFacade.findLocation(id);
  }

  /**
   * @ejb.interface - method view - type="both"
   */
  public Player findPlayer(long id) {
    return leagueFacade.findPlayer(id);
  }


  /**
   * @ejb.interface - method view - type="both"
```

```
   */
  public Schedule findSchedule(long id) {
    return leagueFacade.findSchedule(id);
  }
  /**
   * @ejb.interface - method view - type="both"
   */
  public Team findTeam(long id) {
    return leagueFacade.findTeam(id);
  }


  /**
   * @ejb.interface - method view - type="both"
   */
  public Set getSchedulesForLeague(String league) {
    return leagueFacade.getSchedulesForLeague(league);
  }


  /**
   * @ejb.create - method view - type="remote"
   */
  public void ejbCreate() {
    leagueFacade = IceHockeyFacade.getLeagueFacade();
  }
}
```

Building a Web Client

A component with no clients is not very useful. Here you will modify the Web
module from Chapter 7 to use your EJBs. The Web application will be assembled
into the same enterprise application and will be deployed to the same server for
testing. Since you already know how to create dynamic Web projects, quickly do
the following to create the Web module for League Planet:

1. In the **Project Explorer** view, use the **New Dynamic Web Project** wizard to create a project named LeaguePlanetweb. For detailed information on creating
   projects, refer to the Creating Web Applications section in Chapter 6. Select
   JBoss as the target runtime. Add the Web module to the LeaguePlanetEAR.

2. Accept the defaults for the other options and click **Finish**. WTP creates the
   project and populates it with configuration files such as the J2EE Web
   deployment descriptor, web.xml.

3. Next define the module dependencies so that your Web module can call
   EJBs and use model objects. Select the LeaguePlanetweb project in the
   Project Explorer, right click, and invoke the **Properties** menu item as
   before. Navigate to the **J2EE Module Dependencies** page (see Figure 8.35).

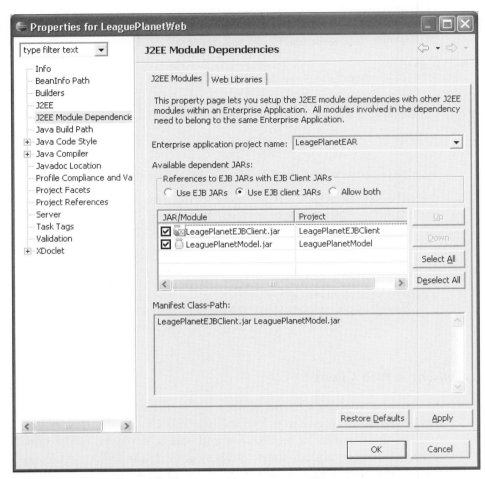

Figure 8.35   J2EE Module Dependencies for LeaguePlanetWeb

4. Check `LeaguePlanetModel` and `LeaguePlanetEJBClient` to add them the list. Click the **OK** button to accept your changes.

5. Next you will add a JSP that displays information about the leagues by calling your EJBs. To do this you must add a JSP to your Web module and write some code. The first thing to do is to add the JSP. In the **Project Explorer,** navigate to the `WebContent` folder in the `LeaguePlanetWeb` project, right click, and invoke the **New ▸ JSP** menu item.

6. Use the **New Java Server Page** wizard to create the JSP. Enter `schedule.jsp` as the name, and make sure that the file is created inside the `WebContent` folder. Click **OK** to create the file.

7. Edit schedule.jsp so that it looks like Example 8.10. You can copy
schedule.css from the examples you have done in Chapter 7.

Example 8.10   Listing of schedule.jsp

```jsp
<%@ page language="java" contentType="text/html; charset=ISO-8859-1"
    pageEncoding="ISO-8859-1"%>
<%@page import="com.leagueplanet.ejb.LeagueFacade"%>
<%@page import="com.leagueplanet.ejb.LeagueFacadeUtil"%>
<%@page import="com.leagueplanet.model.League"%>
<%@page import="com.leagueplanet.model.Schedule"%>
<%@page import="com.leagueplanet.model.Game"%>
<%@page import="java.util.Iterator"%>
<%@page import="java.text.SimpleDateFormat"%>
<html>
<%
        LeagueFacade leagueFacade = LeagueFacadeUtil
                .getHome().create();
        League league = leagueFacade.findLeague(1);
        Iterator schedules = league.getSchedules()
                .iterator();
%>
<head>
<title><%=league.getName()%></title>
<link rel="stylesheet" href="schedule.css" type="text/css" />
</head>
<body>
<h1><%=league.getName()%></h1>
<%
        while(schedules.hasNext()){
        Schedule schedule = (Schedule)schedules.next();
 %>
<h2><%=schedule.getName()%></h2>
<br />

<table>
  <thead>
    <tr>
      <th>Time</th>
      <th>Arena</th>
      <th>Home</th>
      <th>Visitor</th>
      <th>Score</th>
    </tr>
  </thead>
  <tbody>
<% Iterator events = schedule.getEvents().iterator();
  int i = 0;
  while (events.hasNext()) {
    i++;
    Game game = (Game) events.next();
    SimpleDateFormat dateFormat = new SimpleDateFormat(
    "MMM d, yyyy - HH:mm ");
%>
```

```
    <tr class="<%= (i%2 == 0 ? "even-row" :"odd-row") %>">
      <td><%=dateFormat.format(game.getDateAndTime()
                   .getTime())%></td>
      <td><%=game.getLocation().getName()%></td>
      <td><%=game.getHome().getName()%></td>
      <td><%=game.getVisitor().getName()%></td>
      <td><%=game.getScore().getHome()%>-
         <%=game.getScore().getVisitor()%></td>
    </tr>
<%
      }
%>
  </tbody>
</table>
<%
      }
%>
</body>
</html>
```

XDoclet EJB Utility Class

XDoclet generates a utility class that encapsulates some of the standard tasks for accessing the EJB home object from the JNDI tree, creating a remote stub for the EJB, and so forth. In Example 8.10, you replaced all that work with a simple call to the utility object

```
LeagueFacadeUtil.getHome().create();
```

Running the Application

At this point, you have created all the code for the application and are ready to run it. Running the application involves deploying it to the application server. Do the following:

1. Select schedule.jsp, right click, and invoke the **Run As ▸ Run on Server** menu item. The **Run On Server** wizard opens (see Figure 8.36).

2. You must now add your modules to a new server configuration. You already have JBoss added to your workspace, so select it as the server runtime. You can also set this server as the default server associated with the project. Click **Next** to continue. Accept the defaults, and click **Next** again. The **Add and Remove Projects** page is displayed (see Figure 8.37).

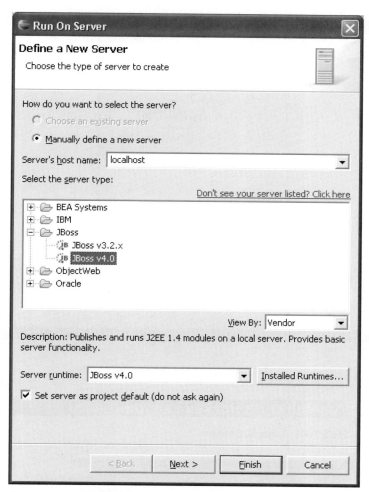

Figure 8.36　Define a New Server

3. Select the EAR project to include in the server. Since the enterprise application already includes all the modules, you do not have to add them individually. You only have one EAR project available, `LeaguePlanetEAR`, and it contains the EJB, Web, and utility modules you want to run. Click the **Finish** button. The wizard creates the server, starts it, publishes the projects to it, and launches the Web browser using the proper URL for `schedule.jsp` (see Figure 8.38).

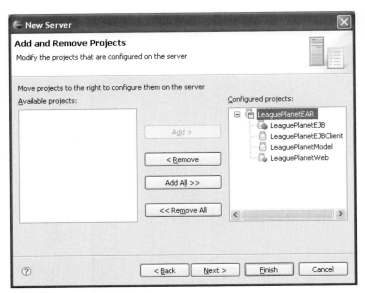

Figure 8.37   Add and Remove Projects

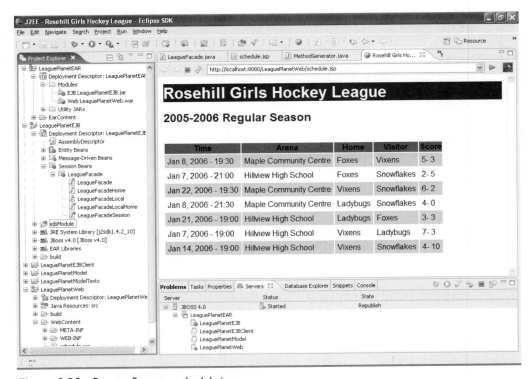

Figure 8.38   Run on Server—schedule.jsp

Server Delays

Sometimes the Web browser will request the URL before the deployment process is complete. This is because as soon as the server starts, the browser will get a chance to send the request. However, it takes a few seconds for the server to complete the deployment process. If you experience problems testing the EJB, check the server console for messages (see Example 8.11). The console will indicate when the deployment process is complete. After the EJBs are deployed, you can refresh your browser. You should get the proper response.

Example 8.11 JBoss Console Output

```
INFO   [EARDeployer] Init J2EE application: LeagePlanetEAR.ear
INFO   [EjbModule] Deploying LeagueFacade
INFO   [BaseLocalProxyFactory]Bound EJB LocalHome 'LeagueFacade' to jndi
INFO   [ProxyFactory]Bound EJB Home 'LeagueFacade'to jndi 'LeagueFacade'
INFO   [EJBDeployer]Deployed: LeagePlanetEAR.ear/LeaguePlanetEJB.jar
INFO   [EARDeployer]Started J2EE application: LeagePlanetEAR.ear
```

4. When you modify any of the modules, you will need to publish them again before you can test your changes. In addition to publishing, the **Servers** view lets you start, stop, and restart servers (see Figure 8.39).

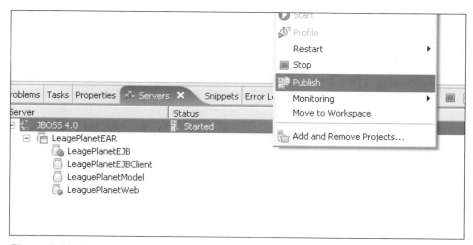

Figure 8.39 Servers View

Developing EJB 3.0 with WTP

WTP 1.5 does not have many tools for EJB 3.0. These will be available with WTP 2.0. You can try using an early WTP 2.0 build that provides EJB 3.0 projects if you are really keen (see the WTP Build Types section in Chapter 4). In fact, you'll be making a valuable contribution to WTP 2.0 by evaluating the planned EBJ 3.0 support and providing feedback.

However, there is no need to wait for WTP 2.0. If you are willing to get your hands a little dirty, you can still build EJB 3.0 application using WTP 1.5. In this section we give you some hints as to how you can use WTP 1.5 for EJB 3.0 development.

In EJB 3.0, you still need to build a bean, you still need a container, and clients still call EJBs, but the programming model becomes a lot simpler. EJB 3.0 beans are still packaged in EJB-JAR files, so you can use a basic J2EE utility project to package them. Deployment descriptors are optional for EJB 3.0, so you can skip creating them for now.

You can take any POJO and make it an EJB 3.0 bean. You can use the same business class and the same business interface. For example, you do not have to change the classes in your model to make them EJB 3.0 beans or create component and home interface types like you have already done. You make your POJOs EJB 3.0 beans by adding JSR 175 annotations. However, these annotations are only available if you use Java 5 and above. To create an EJB 3.0 bean for League Planet, do the following:

1. Use a JDK that is 1.5 (that is, Java 5) or above as the Java runtime environment for your projects and servers.

2. Use a server runtime environment that supports EJB 3.0. For example, Sun Microsystems provides GlassFish that can run EJB 3.0. GlassFish also provides a WTP server adapter plug-in. You can download this plug-in from

   `https://glassfishplugins.dev.java.net/`

3. Use a J2EE utility project (for example, the `LeaguePlanetModel` project you used in this chapter) and target it to a server that supports EJB 3.0.

4. Add EJB 3.0 JARs that are provided with the server to the build path of the project so you can use EJB 3.0 annotations.

5. Add annotations to your classes and interfaces so that they are marked as EJB 3.0 beans. For example, you can easily use the classes in your `com.leagueplanet.services` package by adding EJB 3.0 annotations (see Example 8.12).

Example 8.12   LeagueFacade EJB 3.0 Stateless Session Bean

```java
package com.leagueplanet.ejb3;

import java.util.Set;
import javax.ejb.*;
import javax.annotation.*;

import com.leagueplanet.model.*;
import com.leagueplanet.services.IceHockeyFacade;
import com.leagueplanet.services.LeagueFacade;

/**
 * Stateless session bean.
 */

@Stateless
@Remote(LeagueFacade.class)
public class LeagueFacade implements LeagueFacade {

  private LeagueFacade leagueFacade;

  @Init
  public void init() {
    leagueFacade = IceHockeyFacade.getLeagueFacade();
  }

  public boolean createLeague(League newLeague) {
    return leagueFacade.createLeague(newLeague);
  }
  public boolean doesLeagueExist(String name) {
    return leagueFacade.doesLeagueExist(name);
  }
  public Game findGame(long id) {
    return leagueFacade.findGame(id);
  }
  public League findLeague(long id) {
    return leagueFacade.findLeague(id);
  }
  public Location findLocation(long id) {
    return leagueFacade.findLocation(id);
  }
  public Player findPlayer(long id) {
    return leagueFacade.findPlayer(id);
  }
  public Schedule findSchedule(long id) {
    return leagueFacade.findSchedule(id);
  }
  public Team findTeam(long id) {
    return leagueFacade.findTeam(id);
  }
  public Set getSchedulesForLeague(String league) {
    return leagueFacade.getSchedulesForLeague(league);
  }

}
```

6. Export the project as a JAR file, and use the application server tools to deploy the EJBs.

That is it. Isn't this much better than EJB 2.1?

Summary of Iteration 2

In this iteration, you added a stateless session EJB to your business tier using WTP wizards. You added LeagueFacadeBean to support access to your service layer from distributed clients. You also used a Web application to test your EJB. The JSP in your Web application used the EJB to get game information and display it. Your Web application could run on a different server than the EJB.

You're now ready to move on and build reliable messaging systems that use asynchronous communication via message-driven EJBs.

Iteration 3: Message-Driven Beans

Some processes in an application can be long running. For example, a loan application may involve manual review processes. Similarly, when you create a new league, it might go through a manual approval process. It is unreasonable to expect the client application to wait for the response to a message that may take hours or days to complete. For these types of scenarios you will use Java Message Service (JMS) and Message-Driven Beans (MDBs). In this iteration you will learn how to develop J2EE messaging applications in WTP. Since you're already familiar with building EJBs and Web modules, this will be a relatively simple task.

Messaging is an alternative to making remote calls to distributed objects. The JMS server is the message-oriented middleware (MOM). MOM gets the messages from the client and sends them to the receiver. Once the client gives the message to the MOM, it continues its work and does not wait for the server to receive and process the message. This allows the client and the server to work asynchronously. MOMs are very reliable systems. They can provide guarantees to message producers and consumers that the messages are delivered. This makes them very attractive for many critical business operations.

A Brief Introduction to MDBs

Before you start coding, let's do a crash course in MDBs. JMS provides asynchronous messaging for J2EE. MDBs are a combination of session beans and JMS. On the server side, MDBs behave like session beans. The client of an MDB is just a JMS client. JMS has *publish-and-subscribe*, or simply *pubsub*, in which a single message can be received by many consumers, and *point-to-point* (PTP) messaging, in which each message can be received by only one consumer. These two styles of messaging are managed by different types of JMS destinations. Pubsub messages are sent to *topics,* while PTP messages are sent to *queues.* Okay, we admit this is not really enough to understand JMS, but bear with us and use the example code to try to understand how it works. You should, as always, refer to other resources for MOM and JMS.

Create an MDB

The example code in this iteration is very simple. You will add two new components, a servlet for the Web module, and an MDB for the EJB module. The Web client will publish messages to a JMS queue to create a league, and the MDB will handle it. The messages will be of type `javax.jms.ObjectMessage`, which can transfer your domain objects as message payloads. When the MDB receives the message, it will simply call the service façade to create the new league.

MDBs are not much different from any JMS message consumers in the messaging system. What makes them different from other JMS clients is that they are EJBs. This means the container takes care of security, concurrency, and transactions. Now that you know just enough to be dangerous, you will start with creating a new message-driven bean. Do the following:

1. In the **Project Explorer,** select the `LeaguePlanetEJB` project, right click, and invoke the **New ▸ XDoclet Enterprise JavaBean** menu item. The **Create Enterprise JavaBean** wizard opens (see Figure 8.40).

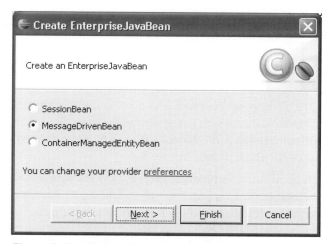

Figure 8.40   New EJB Wizard

2. Select the **MessageDrivenBean** radio button. Click the **Next** button to proceed to the **EnterpriseJavaBean** class page (see Figure 8.41).

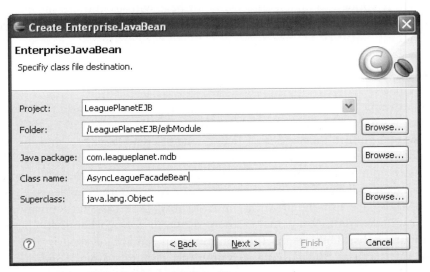

Figure 8.41   Create EnterpriseJavaBean Class

3. Ensure the `LeaguePlanetEJB` project is entered as the project and `/LeaguePlanetEJB/ejbModule` is selected as the folder. Enter `com.leagueplanet.mdb` as the Java package and `AsyncLeagueFacadeBean` as the class name. Click the **Next** button. The next page allows you to enter initial attributes of the message-driven bean (see Figure 8.42).

4. In this page you can review and modify MDB parameters. These parameters are reflected as settings in the deployment descriptors. Ensure that the destination type is `Queue`, since in this example you only want one MDB to ever receive a given message. Change the destination JNDI name to `queue/AsyncLeagueFacade`. Leave the other settings with their default values. Click the **Next** button. The next page allows you to choose interfaces for the EJB (see Figure 8.43).

5. A message-driven bean must implement the `javax.ejb.MessageDrivenBean` and `javax.jms.MessageListener` interfaces in addition to its business interfaces. Proceed with the defaults, and click **Finish** to generate the MDB. The wizard will create a new MDB, and the XDoclet engine will generate the rest of the code.

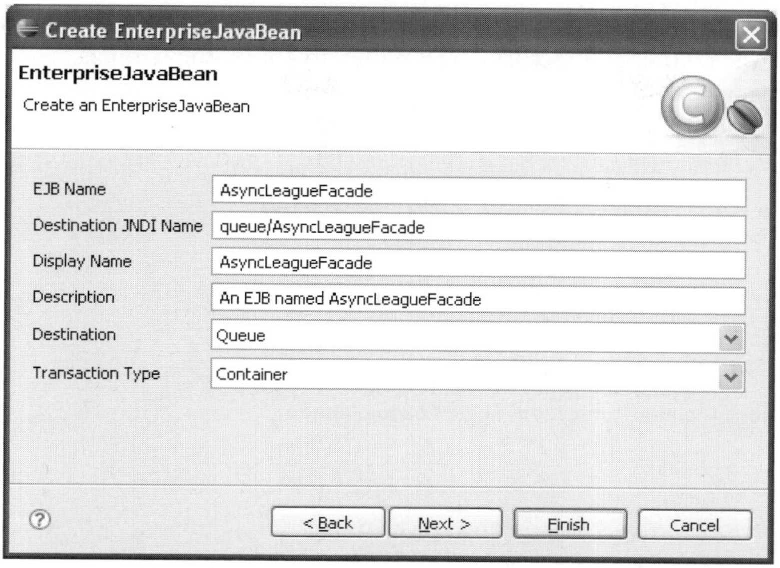

Figure 8.42 MDB Properties

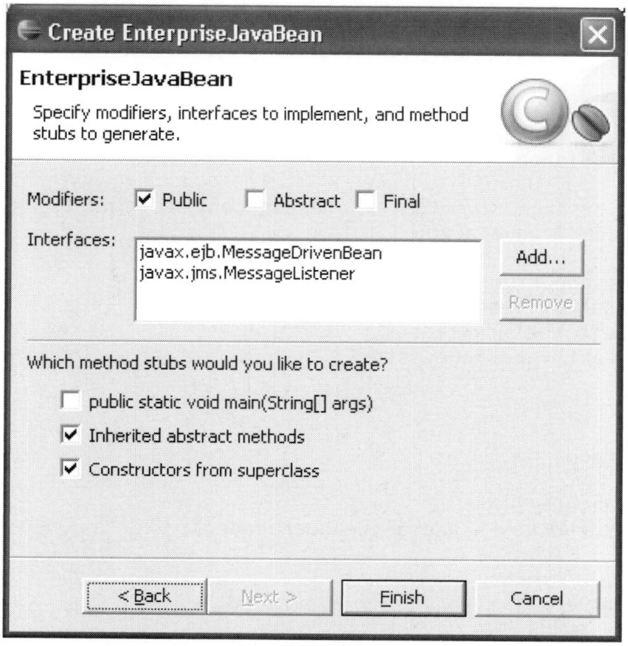

Figure 8.43 MDB Interfaces

6. Open the `AsyncLeagueFacadeBean` class, and add an XDoclet annotation for the connection factory JNDI name. In JBoss, the name is `Connection Factory`. Also modify the contents of the `ejbCreate` and `onMessage` methods to match what you see in Example 8.13.

Example 8.13   Listing of AsyncLeagueFacadeBean.java

```
package com.leagueplanet.mdb;

import javax.jms.JMSException;
import javax.jms.ObjectMessage;

import com.leagueplanet.model.League;
import com.leagueplanet.services.IceHockeyFacade;
import com.leagueplanet.services.LeagueFacade;

/**
 * @ejb.bean
 *        name="AsyncLeagueFacade"
 *        acknowledge-mode="Auto-acknowledge"
 *        destination-type="javax.jms.Queue"
 *        transaction-type="Container"
 *        destination-jndi-name="queue/AsyncLeagueFacade"
 *        connection-factory-jndi-name="ConnectionFactory"
 *
 * @ejb.transaction="Supports"
 */
public class AsyncLeagueFacadeBean implements
    javax.ejb.MessageDrivenBean,
    javax.jms.MessageListener {

  private javax.ejb.MessageDrivenContext messageContext = null;
  private LeagueFacade leagueFacade;

  public void setMessageDrivenContext(
      javax.ejb.MessageDrivenContext messageContext)
      throws javax.ejb.EJBException {
    this.messageContext = messageContext;
  }

  /**
   * @ejb.create-method
   */
  public void ejbCreate() {
    leagueFacade = IceHockeyFacade.getLeagueFacade();
  }

  public void ejbRemove() {
    messageContext = null;
  }

  public void onMessage(javax.jms.Message message) {
```

```
try {
  League aNewLeague = (League) ((ObjectMessage) message)
      .getObject();
  leagueFacade.createLeague(aNewLeague);
  System.out.println("New League:"
      + aNewLeague.getName());
} catch (JMSException e) {
  e.printStackTrace();
}

  }

}
```

It is this simple. Next you add a new message destination to JBoss.

Add a Queue to JBoss

All that's left is to use some administrative magic to define a new message destination in JBoss named `queue/AsyncLeagueFacadeQueue` and write a simple Web application that will send messages to your MDB.

JBoss defines JMS topics and queues using *MBeans*. (Refer to JBoss documentation for detailed information on MBeans.) There are two ways to create them: adding your queue to the appropriate XML configuration file or using the JBoss console. The configuration file is fairly simple, so you will use that method. Locate the file named `jbossmq-destinations-service.xml` in the JBoss `server/default/deploy/jms` folder. It contains a list of JMS destinations and sets up a list of test topics and queues. You can follow the example to add a queue. Add a definition like what is shown in Example 8.14.

Example 8.14 Configuration of the JBoss MQ Destination

```
<mbean code="org.jboss.mq.server.jmx.Queue"
  name="jboss.mq.destination:service=Queue,name=AsyncLeagueFacade">
  <depends optional-attribute-name="DestinationManager">
    jboss.mq:service=DestinationManager
  </depends>
</mbean>
```

Create a JMS Web Client

1. The EJB module is now ready. Next you will add a servlet and an HTML form to your Web module. Create a new servlet named `CreateLeagueAction` in the `LeaguePlanetWeb` project. The servlet URL mapping should direct

all requests to `CreateLeagueAction`. Use the servlet wizard to add this servlet to the Web module. The deployment descriptor for the Web module should now have definitions for this servlet (see Example 8.15).

Example 8.15   Listing of web.xml

```xml
<?xml version="1.0" encoding="UTF-8"?>
<web-app id="WebApp_ID" version="2.4"
  xmlns="http://java.sun.com/xml/ns/j2ee"
  xmlns:xsi="http://www.w3.org/2001/XMLSchema-instance"
  xsi:schemaLocation="http://java.sun.com/xml/ns/j2ee
    http://java.sun.com/xml/ns/j2ee/web-app_2_4.xsd">
  <display-name>LeaguePlanetWeb</display-name>
  <servlet>
    <description></description>
    <display-name>CreateLeagueAction</display-name>
    <servlet-name>CreateLeagueAction</servlet-name>
    <servlet-class>
      com.leagueplanet.servlet.CreateLeagueAction
    </servlet-class>
  </servlet>
  <servlet-mapping>
    <servlet-name>CreateLeagueAction</servlet-name>
    <url-pattern>/CreateLeagueAction</url-pattern>
  </servlet-mapping>
  <welcome-file-list>
    <welcome-file>index.html</welcome-file>
  </welcome-file-list>
</web-app>
```

2. Implement the servlet code. Make sure that the code for your servlet looks like what is shown in Example 8.16.

Example 8.16   Listing of CreateLeagueAction.java

```java
package com.leagueplanet.servlet;

import java.io.IOException;

import javax.jms.*;
import javax.naming.NamingException;
import javax.servlet.*;
import javax.servlet.http.*;

import com.leagueplanet.mdb.AsyncLeagueFacadeUtil;
import com.leagueplanet.model.League;

public class CreateLeagueAction extends HttpServlet
    implements Servlet {
  private final static int SESSIONTYPE = Session.AUTO_ACKNOWLEDGE;
```

```java
  public CreateLeagueAction() {
    super();
  }

  public void doGet(HttpServletRequest request,
      HttpServletResponse response)
      throws ServletException, IOException {
    try {

      String leagueName = request
          .getParameter("league.name");
      sendMessage(leagueName);
      forward(request, response);

    } catch (Exception e) {
      e.printStackTrace();
    }

  }

  private void sendMessage(String leagueName)
      throws NamingException, JMSException {
    QueueConnection qConnection = AsyncLeagueFacadeUtil
        .getQueueConnection();
    Queue queue = AsyncLeagueFacadeUtil.getQueue();
    QueueSession qSession = qConnection
        .createQueueSession(false, SESSIONTYPE);
    QueueSender qSender = qSession.createSender(queue);

    League league = new League();
    league.setName(leagueName);

    ObjectMessage objectMessage = qSession
        .createObjectMessage(league);
    qSender.send(objectMessage);
    qSession.close();
    qConnection.close();
  }

  private void forward(HttpServletRequest request,
      HttpServletResponse response)
      throws ServletException, IOException {
    this.getServletContext().getRequestDispatcher(
        "/schedule.jsp").forward(request, response);
  }

}
```

3. It is now easy to create a simple HTML form to submit league creation requests to this servlet (see Example 8.17).

Example 8.17   Listing of form.html

```html
<html>
<head>
<title>Add League</title>
</head>
<body>

<form action="CreateLeagueAction" method="get">
<table>
  <tr>
    <th>League name:</th>
    <th><input type="text" name="league.name" value=" /></th>
  </tr>
  <tr>
    <td colspan="2"><input type="submit" name="add" value="add" /></td>
  </tr>
</table>
</form>
</body>
</html>
```

When the servlet receives a request, it will connect to the JMS queue to send a message. Your servlet does not have to wait until the message is processed. You can easily continue your work and request the MDB to create more league objects before the previous messages are processed.

4. You are done. Save your work and publish the enterprise application to the JBoss server. To test your MDB, select form.html and run it on the server (see Figure 8.44). When you enter a name and submit, the servlet will send a message to your MDB.

Figure 8.44   New League Form

Summary of Iteration 3

Messaging and JMS are rich, mature technologies that have been applied to enterprise-level integration for a very long time. In this iteration you used an MDB to create a reliable, asynchronous Web application that implemented the new league creation function at League Planet. By using asynchronous communication, you allowed for these creation requests to go through a manual approval process. You created an MDB and used XDoclet to simplify the programming work. You added a message queue to JBoss, and you developed a servlet to send messages to this queue using JMS. The MDB received messages from the queue and processed the requests to create new leagues.

Summary

In this chapter you have seen how you can build a business tier using POJOs, which can serve as the basis for EJB-based enterprise components. You also used your experience gained in building the presentation tier to build a Web application that called the business tier using both synchronous session beans and asynchronous MDBs.

In the next two chapters, you will see how to use WTP to build the persistence tier and Web services for the service layer.

CHAPTER 9

The Persistence Tier

*I paint to systematize confusion and thus to help discredit completely
the world of reality.*

—Salvador Dali, About *The Persistence of Memory*

Java objects live in computer memory and normally vanish when the program
that created them terminates. The lifecycle of most objects ends then. However,
some objects must survive for a longer period of time. Databases and files are
common datastores that you can use to keep these objects around for extended
periods of time. The application layer that deals with mapping objects from
memory to datastores is called the *persistence layer*, and the place where these
objects are stored is called the *persistence tier* (see the Persistence section in
Chapter 5).

The simplest type of persistence in Java is serialization, which supports
writing and reading objects using streams. Java serialization is used to temporarily
store inactive stateful session beans on disk when memory gets full. Java serialization
is also used in Remote Method Invocation (RMI), which EJBs use for
object distribution. When a remote EJB is called, the Java objects in the parameter
list are serialized into a stream and sent over the network where they are
deserialized by the receiving object. However, Java serialization is not a good
approach for long-term persistence since it can only be used in practice by other
Java applications. Programming-language-neutral file formats and databases are
better alternatives.

Modern applications have many options to store data, but it is probably safe
to say that most Web applications use relational databases to persist objects.

Let's start with restating some of the more important principles for building
a data layer.

Presentation and business tiers should not depend on the persistence mechanism. You should keep the business model and the presentation independent of the internal details of the persistence. Ideally, you should be able to replace the persistence mechanism or the database without affecting the other tiers.

In a classical distributed architecture, the persistence layer of a Web application separates the model objects from the datastore. The business tier uses the persistent layer to access the data. By using this layer, the business tier does not need to know whether a database or a file is used to store objects. The implementation of the persistence tier will differ for a relational database, an XML store, or an object database. The persistence layer accesses these datastores without exposing the details of their technology to the rest of the application. The details of datastore-specific mechanisms and languages, such as SQL, are cleanly abstracted away from the business logic. This way you can change the persistence implementation without affecting the rest of the application.

Persistence layer APIs must be transparent and simple to access. Recall the discussion in Chapter 8. The data layer interfaces abstract the datastore (see the section, The Data Access Layer) from the details of storage technologies, such as SQL, and object-mapping technologies from the business tier.

A simple persistence layer API can be summarized as having the following set of operations:

○ Create, read, update, and delete (CRUD) operations for persistent objects defined in the business layer

○ Create and run queries; encapsulate query languages

○ Manage connections, transactions, caching, performance, and object identity

Designs for the Persistence Layer

In this chapter we will look at the most common type of persistence mechanism used for Java objects: relational databases. When you use relational databases, you need to translate Java objects into database tables, columns, and records as well as translate relationships, such as inheritance, dependencies, and references, into additional columns or tables.

The following practical designs are available for building a persistence layer (see Figure 9.1).

○ Use JDBC APIs to map objects to a database

○ Use entity beans to map objects to a database

○ Use object-relational frameworks to map objects to a database

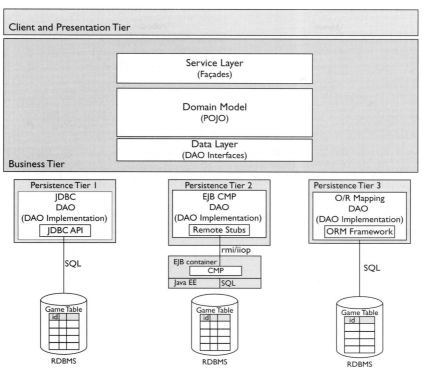

Figure 9.1 Kinds of Persistence Designs

The object-relational (O/R) design is the one most recommended for building a persistence layer. However, in this chapter we will use a simpler approach and show how to use WTP for developing the persistence layer using both JDBC and entity beans.

Use JDBC APIs to Map Objects to a Database

In this design, Java classes in the data layer embed SQL code using JDBC to implement the persistence API. This approach allows you to write code very quickly and encapsulate persistence logic in one place. The JDBC APIs are simple, but they require a good understanding of relational databases and SQL technology. Since SQL is exposed, they offer very little in terms of transparency. This approach is useful for building quick and small applications. The most important disadvantage is the strong coupling between the database schema and Java classes. Any change in the database requires a change in the Java code.

The JDBC API provides Java applications with standard access and manipulation of data stored in relational databases. It is a call-level API for SQL-based database access and includes interfaces for establishing connections to a database, accessing tabular data sources, executing SQL statements, and processing the results.

The JDBC architecture provides interfaces for both application developers and database vendors. Database vendors implement drivers using these interfaces to support their own database protocols and servers. This architecture allows developers to write applications that are independent of the database servers.

A simple JDBC application typically connects to a database, executes queries, and retrieves and processes the results (see Example 9.1).

Example 9.1   JDBC Example

```
Connection connection
 = DriverManager.getConnection("jdbc:derby:league", "user","pwd");
Statement statement = connection.createStatement();
ResultSet result = statement.executeQuery("SELECT * FROM APP.GAME");
while (result.next()) {
      int x = result.getDate("DATE");
      String s = result.getString("ARENA");
      ...
}
```

Use Entity Beans to Map Objects to a Database

This is a variation of the previous design where you use EJBs instead of JDBC to implement the persistence API. An EJB, more specifically an entity bean, is responsible for inserting, updating, selecting, and removing data from the database. When you use the EJB 2.1 specification, this approach has disadvantages similar to the first design. However, as you will see with the next design, the Java Persistence API (JPA) introduced with EJB 3.0 helps you create a more robust persistence layer.

EJBs are executed within a managed container on a server environment. Therefore, this design allows you to create a data layer that can be distributed across many machines and accessed remotely as if it were on a local server. You get the full benefits of EJB persistence when you start using session beans and MDBs integrated with the persistence tier. An EJB-based persistence tier is highly available, secure, and transactional by virtue of the EJB container.

J2EE provides several types of services, APIs, and component architectures to access data. Persistence with entity beans can be managed by the EJB container. This is called *container-managed persistence* (CMP). Alternatively, an entity bean can directly access the persistent data. This is called *bean-managed persistence* (BMP).

In EJB 2.1 and earlier specifications, entity beans had a number of design and performance shortcomings, and introduced significant overhead in terms of code maintenance and performance. For these reasons, many Web application developers preferred alternatives to entity beans.

JPA is a complete specification for object-relational mapping supporting the use of Java language metadata annotations (JSR 175) and XML deployment descriptors to define the mapping between Java objects and a relational database. JPA provides a rich query language extended from EJB-QL for defining static and dynamic queries. Persistence is transparently provided by pluggable providers such as Hibernate or TOPLink, which has been donated to Eclipse to seed the new Eclipse Persistence Platform Project.

Use Object-Relational Frameworks to Map Objects to a Database

In this design, Java classes in the data layer use one of the many available excellent O/R mapping frameworks, such as Hibernate or TOPLink, to implement a robust and loosely coupled persistence layer. With this approach, changing the database schema and the object model is easier, and their dependencies are more manageable. This kind of persistence is more suitable for large business-critical applications. The main disadvantage is that it can have a steep learning curve and a potential runtime performance hit.

Most O/R mapping frameworks offer consistent, simple APIs and reasonable transparency, but they are proprietary. There is nothing wrong with proprietary APIs, but mapping technologies can be quite different, so porting between frameworks is a significant task. Fortunately, JPA is a standardization of O/R mapping interfaces and provides for greater portability between implementations. JPA is part of Java EE 5 and is usable with or without an EJB container.

In OO programming, programmatic objects are used to represent real-world objects. When you want to save these objects to a relational database you immediately face the problem of translating objects to forms that can be stored in database tables. This is a nontrivial problem, especially with complex object models. Objects and tables in a database are very different things, so either the programmer or a framework is expected to bridge this *semantic gap*. Although simple objects can be directly mapped to tables, typical objects need more work. Some relationships, such as those with 1-1, 1-*n* or *n-n* multiplicity, apply equally well to both objects and tables. For example, a team can have many players. This is a 1-*n* relationship, which can be modeled using object references and collections or database primary and foreign keys. Other relationships, like inheritance, can be expressed naturally in an object model but must be grafted onto a relational database. This problem is known as the O/R *mapping problem*.

O/R mapping frameworks, such as Hibernate, TOPLink, and iBatis, simplify storing objects in databases and the associated SQL programming details, and therefore help close the semantic gap. They provide libraries of classes that can do the mapping automatically using declarative descriptions. These mapping descriptions are typically provided by the programmers in the form of annotations or XML files. For example, when you send a message to a data layer object to get the game information, the framework will automatically create the proper query, execute it, and then process the SQL results to translate them into game objects. From the business layer perspective, the persistence layer looks like an object store.

You should not let this simple description mislead you about the complexity of the more general object-relational mapping problem. This subject has been studied in great detail, and you should consult references that are available elsewhere.

Overview of Iterations

The Data Tools component of the Web Standard Tools (WST) subproject of WTP lets you work with relational databases from many vendors (see the Data Tools section in Chapter 2). With these tools you can browse database schemas and tables, sample the data, run SQL queries, and edit the contents of tables. Shortly after the creation of WTP, the Eclipse Data Tools Platform (DTP) project was created and seeded with the WTP Data Tools and contributions from Sybase. Future releases of WTP will depend on features of DTP instead of the Data Tools component (see the Eclipse Data Tools Platform (DTP) Project section in Chapter 17).

The EJB Tools component of the J2EE Standard Tools (JST) subproject of WTP lets you create EJB 2.1 entity beans (see the EJB Tools section in Chapter 2). These beans can be either created from scratch or generated from tables. With EJB 3.0, the entity bean specification has changed significantly. JPA has evolved out of this work. Persistence with JPA can be as simple as adding a few annotations to a Java class. The resulting class can be used without an EJB container. The Dali incubator project of WTP lets you develop JPA-based Java applications (see the Eclipse Dali Java Persistence Architecture (JPA) Tools Project section in Chapter 17).

This chapter describes how to develop the persistence tier of League Planet using WTP in the following iterations:

❍ In Iteration 1 you create a database and a table that stores League Planet schedule information. You design, create, and query a table using the SQL editor. You enter game data using the **Database Explorer**.

○ In Iteration 2 you develop a persistence layer with Java Data Access Objects (DAO) that use JDBC APIs to read and write the objects to the League Planet database. You then develop a simple Web application that uses this layer to display game information.

○ In Iteration 3 you develop a persistence tier with CMP entity beans to read and write objects. You use the XDoclet wizard to generate these EJBs.

At the end of this chapter you will be able to create, modify, and query databases using the Data Tools, access databases using JDBC, and develop CMP entity beans using XDoclet.

Iteration I: Creating a Database

The League Planet database stores information about leagues, teams, players, and games in an organized fashion so that users can enter and query their data. In this iteration you will create a database and a table that stores League Planet schedule information. To create a database you will need a database management system (DBMS). This chapter assumes you are using Apache Derby; however, any relational database supported by WTP should also work.

You'll perform the following tasks:

○ Install Apache Derby.

○ Use the **Database Explorer** and **New Connection** wizard to connect to the database.

○ Use the **Database Explorer** to display and browse the contents of a database. Save the database state to work in the offline mode.

○ Use the **SQL Scrapbook** page to run SQL code, create a new table, and review results of SQL execution using the **Data Output** window.

○ Use the **Table** explorer to browse tables.

○ Use the **Table** editor to enter new games and edit data in the tables.

1. WTP supports many databases, including Apache Derby. Install Derby on your machine (see the Getting Derby sidebar in Chapter 3). The project Web site includes excellent documentation to get you started. You can also refer to [Zikopoulos2005] for more insight.

Derby is a pure Java, embeddable database, which means that the database runs in the same JVM process as the rest of the application. For example, Derby can be embedded in a single-user stand-alone Java application or a multi-user Web application server. It is also possible to use Derby as a network server using the Network Client driver.

Enough said about Derby. Now that you have it ready to go, open a **Database Explorer** and start working with it.

2. WTP has a view called the **Database Explorer**, which allows you to connect to databases, browse, and edit their contents. In the J2EE perspective, invoke the **Window ▸ Show View ▸ Other** menu item (see Figure 9.2). In the **Show View** window, select **Data ▸ Database Explorer** and then click **OK**.

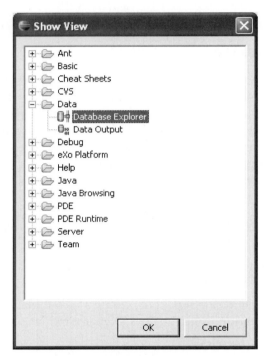

Figure 9.2   Show View—Database Explorer

The **Database Explorer** view, by default, will appear in the bottom right part of the workspace. Right click anywhere in this view and invoke the **New Connection** menu item (see Figure 9.3).

3. The **New Connection** wizard opens. At this point, you must have an RDBMS already installed in order to proceed. Select **Derby** as the database manager and choose the proper version. This will cause the wizard to display a Derby-specific connection dialog (see Figure 9.4).

Figure 9.3 New Connection

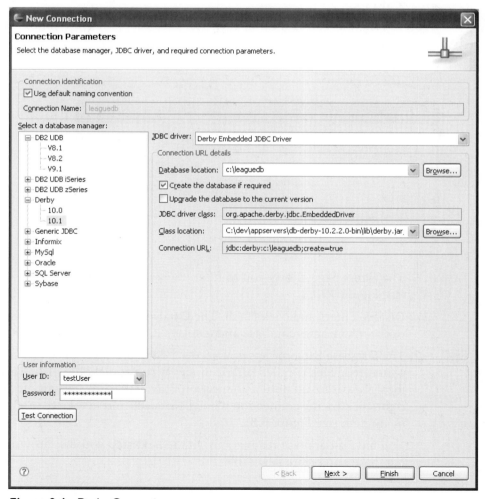

Figure 9.4 Derby Connection

4. Select the database location, for example:

`c:\leaguedb`

Check **Create the database if required.** Derby will create a new database at this location if the database does not exist yet. You will need to choose the JAR that contains the Derby JDBC drivers. This file is typically named `derby.jar`, and you can find it under the `lib` folder of the Derby installation directory. Set the user and password as `testUser` and `testPassword`. The JDBC URL is automatically generated based on your choices. If you feel comfortable editing the URL directly, you can choose to do so.

5. To test your configuration, click **Test Connection.** If everything was done properly, you should see a message prompt (see Figure 9.5).

Click **Next.**

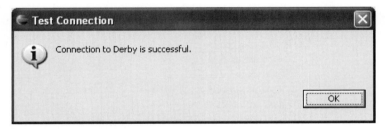

Figure 9.5   Test Connection

6. The **Filters** page allows you to filter items shown by the **Database Explorer** (see Figure 9.6).

Disable Filters and click **Finish.** The **Database Explorer** opens a connection to the new league database and displays its contents (see Figure 9.7).

7. The **Database Explorer** lets you access a database even when you are not connected. This is called *offline* mode. When you choose offline access, a local view is saved until a connection is available. To save an offline view, right click on the connection named `leaguedb` and invoke the **Save Offline** menu item (see Figure 9.8).

You have a database ready to go. In the next step you will browse the database and create new tables.

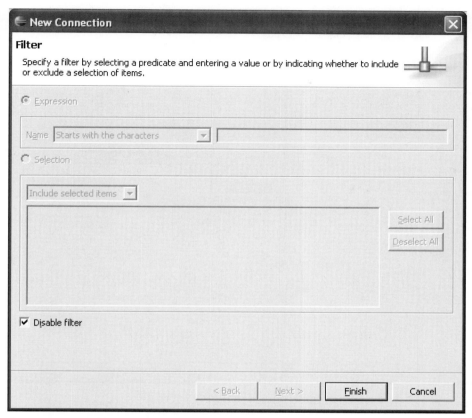

Figure 9.6   Connection Filters

8. Tables are where data is stored in the database. You will need to create tables to store the objects in League Planet. The WTP tools will help you create these tables. To do this you will need to write SQL code and run it. We will not explain the details of SQL programming in this book. You can find plenty of good books written on the subject, such as *Using SQL* [Groff1990] and *Understanding the New SQL: A Complete Guide* [Melton1993].

   To work with SQL you will use an SQL scrapbook. Using the **Database Explorer,** right click on the leaguedb database connection and invoke the **Open SQL Scrapbook** menu item (see Figure 9.9).

9. The **New SQL Scrapbook Page** wizard opens. Choose a project and name the file, then click **OK** (see Figure 9.10).

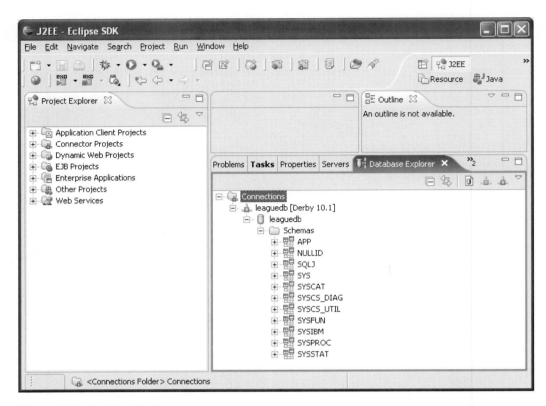

Figure 9.7   Database Explorer

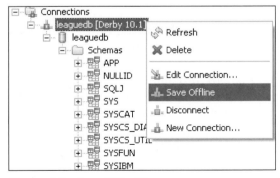

Figure 9.8   Save Offline View

Figure 9.9 Open SQL Scrapbook—Database Explorer

Figure 9.10 New SQL Scrapbook Page

10. WTP opens the SQL page in the SQL editor. The SQL editor provides syntax highlighting and content assist for SQL code. In the SQL editor you can write and run the SQL code to manipulate databases.

Before you write the code, let's briefly review what goes into a table. Tables are divided into rows and columns. Each row represents one piece of data, and each column can be thought of as representing an attribute of that piece of data. For example, if you have a table for games, then the columns will contain information such as id, date, time, arena, home and visitor teams, scores, and so on. As a result, when you specify a table, you will define the column headers and their data types.

SQL has many data types. For your tables, you will use date and time expressions (such as '2006-APR-13' '09:54:00') and string formats (such as 'Snowflakes'). When you specify a table, you will need to specify the data type associated with each column. For example, 'arena' is of type varchar(40), meaning that it is a string up to 40 characters. Note that different databases may support different data types, so you should consult their documentation to avoid portability problems.

Enter the following code in the SQL editor (see Example 9.2).

Example 9.2   Listing of createtables.sqlpage

```
DROP TABLE APP.LEAGUE ;
DROP TABLE APP.SCHEDULE ;
DROP TABLE APP.GAME ;

CREATE TABLE APP.LEAGUE (
     ID INT NOT NULL,
     NAME VARCHAR(40) );

CREATE TABLE APP.SCHEDULE (
     ID INT NOT NULL,
     LEAGUEID INT NOT NULL,
     NAME VARCHAR(40) );

CREATE TABLE APP.GAME (
     ID INT NOT NULL,
     SCHEDULEID INT NOT NULL,
     DATE DATE NOT NULL,
     TIME TIME NOT NULL,
     ARENA VARCHAR(40),
     HOME VARCHAR(40),
     VISITOR VARCHAR(40),
     HOMESCORE VARCHAR(40),
     VISITORSCORE VARCHAR(40) )
```

11. In the SQL editor, right click, and invoke the **Run SQL** menu item. The SQL editor will use the current database connection to run the SQL. You can switch the database by changing the connection. Use the **Use Database Connection** context menu item to do this. After you run the SQL, you will see the results in the **Data Output** view (see Figure 9.11).

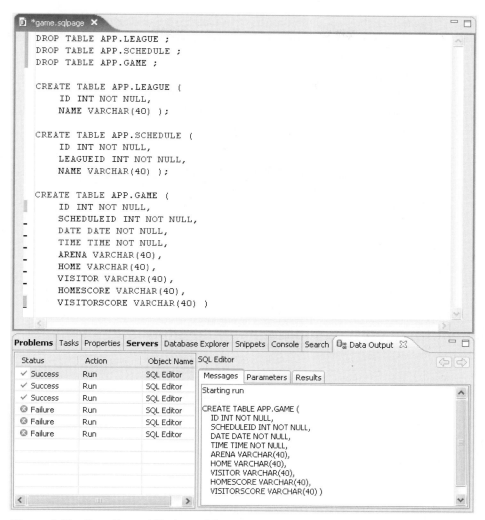

Figure 9.11 Data Output Window—SQL Run

Notice that the DROP statements resulted in an error because, to begin with, there were no tables to delete. The CREATE statements completed successfully. In the next step you will browse the database and the new tables, and edit table data to add new games.

12. Select the leaguedb database in **Database Explorer**, right click, and invoke the **Refresh** command. This action retrieves the new table information from the database.

Expand the **Schemas** item and the APP schema within. Expand the **Tables** item, and select the GAME table and expand its contents. The **Database Explorer** view allows you to browse the tables, columns, and other useful information (see Figure 9.12).

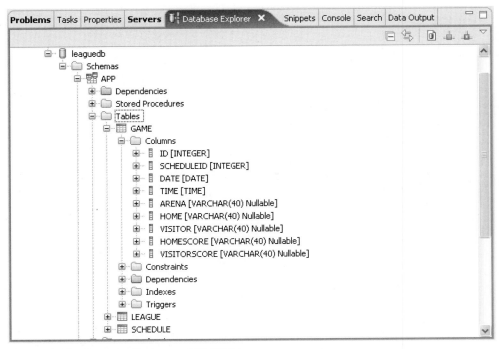

Figure 9.12   Database Explorer—GAME Table

13. Using the **Database Explorer** you can browse and directly update data in the database. To do this, right click the GAME table and invoke the **Data ► Edit** menu item. A table editor opens (see Figure 9.13).

14. Click <new row> to enter new games. For example, enter 1, 1, 01/07/2006, 6:30:00 PM, Hillview High School, Ladybugs, Vixens, 3, 7 for the ID, schedule id, date, time, arena, home team, visitor team, and scores, respectively. Repeat the same steps to enter other game data (see the example listings in the section The Data Access Layer in Chapter 8). Hit Ctrl+S to save and commit the data to the database.

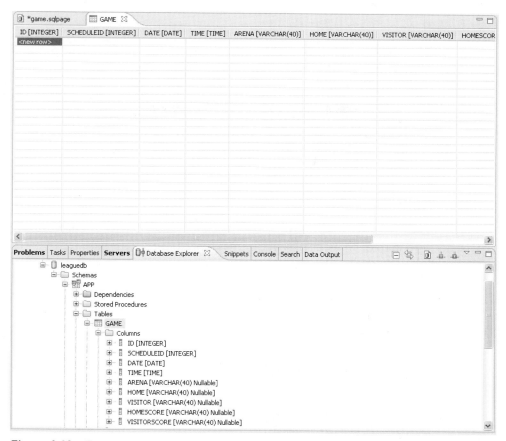

Figure 9.13 Table Editor

15. In embedded single-user mode, Derby only supports a connection to a given database from one process. You will need to disconnect from Derby before using the database in your Web application. Right click on leaguedb in the **Database Explorer** and invoke the **Disconnect** menu item.

Summary of Iteration I

In this iteration you created a database connection to Apache Derby using the **Database Explorer** view. You added tables to the database by executing SQL statements using the SQL scrapbook. Finally, you added some sample data to the table using the table editor. You are now ready to develop Java classes that insert and query data from these tables.

Iteration 2: Data Layer

Recall the layered architecture that was introduced in Chapter 8; the data layer provides an abstraction between the business tier and the persistence tier. The business tier must be independent of the persistence mechanism and the mapping tools that save the objects to the database. This goal was achieved by defining a set of interfaces for DAO. In this iteration, you will implement the data layer API as described in the Use JDBC APIs to Map Objects to a Database section.

In this iteration, you'll perform the following tasks:

❍ Use JDBC APIs to implement the `LeagueDAO` interface (see The Data Access Layer section in Chapter 8) and replace the example DAO implementation with this new class.

❍ Test `LeagueDAO` with the previously developed Web application (see Chapter 8) to display the games stored in the database.

1. Recall the `LeagueFacade` interface and `LeagueFacadeImpl` from the `LeaguePlanetModel` utility project (see The Service Layer section in Chapter 8). The façade object provides game information as a service. This object delegates persistence-related tasks to the classes that you will now implement.

DAO interfaces provide the API to the data layer. This is the interface that your new DAO will implement (see Example 9.3).

Example 9.3 Listing of League DAO Interface

```
package com.leagueplanet.dao;

import java.util.Set;

import com.leagueplanet.model.Game;
import com.leagueplanet.model.League;
import com.leagueplanet.model.Location;
import com.leagueplanet.model.Player;
import com.leagueplanet.model.Schedule;
import com.leagueplanet.model.Team;

public interface LeagueDAO {
  public Game findGame(long id);
  public League findLeague(long id);
  public Location findLocation(long id);
  public Player findPlayer(long id);
  public Schedule findSchedule(long id);
  public Team findTeam(long id);
  public Set getSchedulesForLeague(String league);
  public Set findLeaguesWithName(String name);
  public void save(League newLeague);
}
```

2. The DAO implementation for the game objects is prototypical of any Java application that uses JDBC. The DAO connects to the `leaguedb` database, creates an SQL query, and executes it. It then processes the result set to convert rows into game objects. Finally, it closes the connection and returns the results. This example only maps the game object. Mappings for others, such as schedule and league objects, are left incomplete (see Example 9.4).

Example 9.4 Listing of IceHockeyJdbcDAOImpl.java

```
package com.leagueplanet.dao.example;

import java.sql.Connection;
import java.sql.DriverManager;
import java.sql.ResultSet;
import java.sql.SQLException;
import java.sql.Statement;
import java.sql.Time;
import java.text.ParseException;
import java.util.Calendar;
import java.util.HashSet;
import java.util.Set;
import com.leagueplanet.dao.LeagueDAO;
import com.leagueplanet.model.Game;
import com.leagueplanet.model.League;
import com.leagueplanet.model.Location;
import com.leagueplanet.model.Player;
import com.leagueplanet.model.Schedule;
import com.leagueplanet.model.Score;
import com.leagueplanet.model.Team;

public class IceHockeyJdbcDAOImpl implements LeagueDAO {

  // singleton DAO
  private static IceHockeyJdbcDAOImpl leagueDAO = null;

  public static LeagueDAO getLeagueDAO() {
    if (leagueDAO == null) {
      leagueDAO = new IceHockeyJdbcDAOImpl();
    }
    return leagueDAO;
  }

  private Connection openConnection() throws ClassNotFoundException,
      SQLException {
    Connection connection;
    Class.forName("org.apache.derby.jdbc.EmbeddedDriver");
    connection = DriverManager
        .getConnection("jdbc:derby:C:\\leaguedb");
    return connection;
  }

  private void closeConnection(Connection connection) {
    if (connection != null)
```

```
      try {
        connection.close();
      } catch (SQLException e) {
      }
  }

  public League findLeague(long id) {
    // TODO: Add mappings for leagues and schedules
    League league = new League(id, "Rosehill Girl's Hockey League");
    league.getSchedules().add(findSchedule(1));
    return league;
  }

  public Schedule findSchedule(long id) {
    // TODO: Add mappings schedules
    Schedule schedule = new Schedule(id, "2005/6 Regular Season");
    Connection connection = null;
    Statement statement = null;
    ResultSet resultset = null;
    try {
      connection = openConnection();
      String QUERY = "SELECT * FROM APP.GAME WHERE SCHEDULEID="
          + id;
      statement = connection.createStatement();
      resultset = statement.executeQuery(QUERY);
      while (resultset.next()) {
        Game game = createGameFromResultSet(resultset);
        schedule.getEvents().add(game);
      }
    } catch (Exception e) {
      e.printStackTrace();
    } finally {
      closeConnection(connection);
    }
    return schedule;
  }

  private Game createGameFromResultSet(ResultSet rs)
      throws SQLException, ParseException {
    Game game = new Game();
    game.setId(rs.getInt("ID"));
    Calendar dateAndTime = Calendar.getInstance();
    Time time = rs.getTime("TIME");
    dateAndTime.setTime(rs.getDate("DATE"));
    dateAndTime.set(Calendar.HOUR_OF_DAY, time.getHours() + 1);
    dateAndTime.set(Calendar.MINUTE, time.getMinutes() + 1);
    game.setDateAndTime(dateAndTime);
    game.setLocation(new Location(0, rs.getString("ARENA")));
    Team homeTeam = new Team();
    homeTeam.setName(rs.getString("HOME"));
    game.setHome(homeTeam);
    Team visitorTeam = new Team();
    visitorTeam.setName(rs.getString("VISITOR"));
    game.setVisitor(visitorTeam);
```

```
        Score gameScore = new Score(Integer.parseInt(rs
            .getString("HOMESCORE")), Integer.parseInt(rs
            .getString("VISITORSCORE")));
        game.setScore(gameScore);
        return game;
    }

    // TODO: Add mappings later
    public Set getSchedulesForLeague(String league) {
        return null;
    }

    public Set findLeaguesWithName(String name) {
        return null;
    }

    public void save(League newLeague) {
    }

    public Game findGame(long id) {
        return null;
    }

    public Location findLocation(long id) {
        return null;
    }
    public Team findTeam(long id) {
        return null;
    }

    public Player findPlayer(long id) {
        return null;
    }
}
```

3. To complete the persistence layer, replace the example DAO from Chapter 8, which provides in-memory samples, with the class just defined. Your data layer abstracts persistence properly, so this change will be transparent to the business and presentation tiers. In the IceHockeyFacade class, find the line where the DAO is set and replace it with the singleton from the new IceHockeyJdbcDAOImpl class (see Example 9.5).

Example 9.5   Listing of the IceHockey Jdbc DAO Implementation

```
package com.leagueplanet.services;

import com.leagueplanet.dao.LeagueDAO;
import com.leagueplanet.dao.example.IceHockeyDAOImpl;
import com.leagueplanet.dao.example.IceHockeyJdbcDAOImpl;
import com.leagueplanet.services.LeagueFacade;
import com.leagueplanet.services.impl.LeagueFacadeImpl;
```

```
public class IceHockeyFacade {
  private static LeagueFacade facade = null;

  public static LeagueFacade getLeagueFacade() {
    if (facade == null) {
      init();
    }
    return facade;
  }

  private static void init() {
    // create a new facade implementation
    LeagueFacadeImpl facadeImpl = new LeagueFacadeImpl();
    // point the facade at the dao for the ice hockey league
    LeagueDAO dao = IceHockeyJdbcDAOImpl.getLeagueDAO();
    facadeImpl.setLeagueDAO(dao);
    facade = facadeImpl;
  }

}
```

4. Now you can test your persistence tier with the Web application from Chapter 8. If you do not have it available, import the source code to create the dynamic Web project named LeaguePlanetWeb or refer to the instructions in Building a Web Client in Chapter 8.

5. Before testing, the Derby libraries that contain the JDBC drivers must be added to the Java classpath of the application server. Copy derby.jar and derbyclient.jar from your Derby installation to JBOSS_HOME/server/default/lib. If you are not using JBoss, check the documentation for your application server for instructions.

6. Open the Web project WebContent folder, right click on the schedule.jsp file, and invoke the **Run As ▸ Run on Server** command. WTP will start the server, deploy the application, and launch the browser to display the games (see Figure 9.14).

Derby Embedded Mode

Accessing the Derby database in a single-user embedded mode will work fine for the application in this example. However, if multiple applications need to access the same Derby database, or concurrent requests are made to the Web application, Derby must be used in the shared (networked) mode. Refer to the Derby documentation to use Derby in the shared mode. Change the JDBC URL to one that can connect to the networked database.

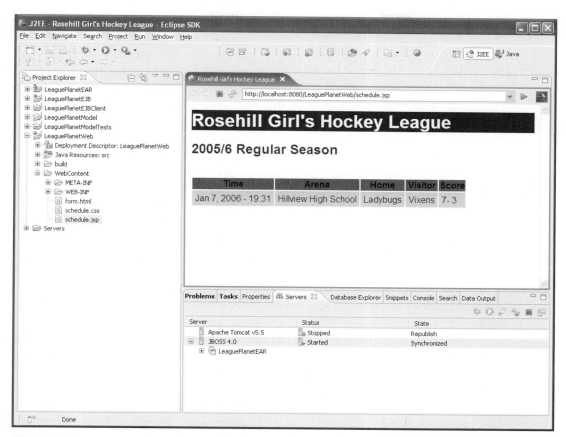

Figure 9.14 Game Schedule

Summary of Iteration 2

In this iteration you created a data access object that maps classes in the business tier to a database using the JDBC API. You replaced the persistence implementation from the previous chapter, which was an in-memory sample, with the new JDBC implementation without changing the business or the presentation tiers. You tested your code by executing the same Web application without any code change.

You are now ready to explore the use of entity beans for implementing your persistence tier.

Iteration 3: Entity Beans

This chapter presents different ways of building the persistence tier. The use of entity beans as defined by the EJB 2.1 specification created concerns due to their complexity of development and heavyweight infrastructure requirements. Despite these concerns, EJB persistence is still very useful for systems that need to be transactional and highly available. The complexity of writing all the classes needed for an entity bean can be reduced with powerful tools, such as those provided with WTP. At the end of the day, you tell the EJB container a few things about your model, and the EJB container performs all the mapping logic plus more. This can be better than hand coding.

Entity beans differ from session beans and MDBs in a few important ways: entity beans have persistent state that is meaningful for clients, they have identity, and they can be shared between different clients by exchanging handles. Entity beans model fine-grained business entities such as teams, games, and players, whereas session beans, like the LeagueFacade, are used to model coarse-grained business processes and services (see Chapter 8). **Game**, **Team**, or **League** classes can be implemented as entity beans because they have persistent state.

There are two types of entity beans: BMP and CMP. BMP beans contain handwritten SQL and JDBC code. In contrast, the EJB container automatically generates the necessary SQL and database calls for CMP beans, thereby making life easier for the developer.

An entity bean that is implemented according to the EJB 2.1 specification has all the familiar EJB component classes: remote interface, home interface, enterprise bean class, and deployment descriptors. In addition, an entity bean can have classes for the primary key (the object that is used to provide a unique id for the entity) and data holder classes.

An entity bean is an in-memory view of the database. The EJB container will create, delete, insert, and update records in the database when it is necessary. For example, when the home interface's create method, which corresponds to the ejbCreate method, is invoked, a new row will be inserted into the database. Similarly, when the remove method is invoked, the corresponding row will be deleted from the database. When you want to find an entity bean that is stored in a database, you invoke the the find methods from the home interface. Each find method is associated with a query coded with EJB Query Language (EJB-QL). When the find method is invoked, an SQL query is automatically executed to read the object into memory.

In this iteration, you will create a CMP bean to persist games in the database. You will use a Web application to add new games and list the game schedule. To do this you'll perform the following tasks:

- ○ Start Derby in client/server mode and add a Derby data source to JBoss for the League Planet database.

- ○ Configure XDoclet to generate CMP classes and generate JBoss-specific deployment descriptors.

- ○ Add a CMP bean for the games using WTP wizards.

- ○ Add custom methods to create and find games.

- ○ Extend the League Planet Web application to add new games and display the updated schedule.

Preparing JBoss, Derby, and XDoclet

You will use the JBoss application server, the Derby database, and XDoclet to develop CMP beans for League Planet. Do the following to prepare your environment:

1. Make sure that you have JBoss and Derby installed and XDoclet configured in your workspace. You can refer to Chapter 3 and/or Chapter 8 if you need more information.

2. Set up Derby to run in client/server mode. EJB containers typically access a database using pooled resources and data source objects. Data sources allow servers to share database resources efficiently so that multiple objects can connect concurrently to Derby over the network. Running Derby in networked mode is quite simple. On a Windows machine you can use the startup script shown in Example 9.6. To stop Derby, you can simply kill the process.

Example 9.6 Start Derby

```
set DERBY_INSTALL=C:\derby
call "%DERBY_INSTALL%"/frameworks/NetworkServer/bin/setNetworkServerCP.bat
call "%DERBY_INSTALL%"/frameworks/NetworkServer/bin/NetworkServerControl.bat
call "%DERBY_INSTALL%"/frameworks/NetworkServer/bin/startNetworkServer.bat
```

Derby will start as a server on the default port 1527 and will wait to accept connections. See the Derby documentation for more information on how to start and stop Derby as a server.

3. JBoss keeps default database configurations in the server deploy directory. Assuming you are working with defaults, this will be the JBOSS_HOME/ server/default/deploy directory under your JBoss installation. JBoss provides an example configuration for the Hypersonic database, which can be found in the file named hsqldb-ds.xml. Create a similar configuration for Derby in a file named derby-ds.xml (see Example 9.7).

Example 9.7 Derby Database Configuration

```
<?xml version="1.0" encoding="UTF-8"?>
<datasources>
    <local-tx-datasource>
        <jndi-name>LeagueDS</jndi-name>
        <connection-url>jdbc:derby://localhost:1527/leagueDB</connection-url>
        <driver-class>org.apache.derby.jdbc.ClientDriver</driver-class>
        <user-name>test</user-name>
        <password>test</password>
        <min-pool-size>5</min-pool-size>
        <max-pool-size>20</max-pool-size>
        <idle-timeout-minutes>5</idle-timeout-minutes>
    </local-tx-datasource>
</datasources>
```

JBoss will need a copy of derbyclient.jar, which contains the Derby JDBC drivers. Copy this file from the Derby installation folder into this JBoss directory: JBOSS_HOME/server/default/lib. When JBoss starts, it will automatically configure the connection to the League Planet database. Remember the name of the data source, LeagueDS, since you will need it to set up XDoclet.

4. In the **Project Explorer** view, locate the LeaguePlanetEJB project that was created previously (see Chapter 8). If you do not have the project, follow the instructions to create it now (see the Iteration 2: Developing Session EJBs section). Alternatively, you can import the project from the source code examples provided with the book.

5. Configure XDoclet CMP preferences for this project. Right click on the LeaguePlanetEJB project and open the project **Properties** dialog. Click on the **XDoclet** property. XDoclet is set up to use global workspace preferences by default. Uncheck **Use global xdoclet preferences** and click **Apply** (see Figure 9.15).

6. Click on the **ejbdoclet** item on the left side. XDoclet can generate JBoss-specific annotations and deployment descriptors. This example requires JBoss, so check JBoss and click **Apply** (see Figure 9.16).

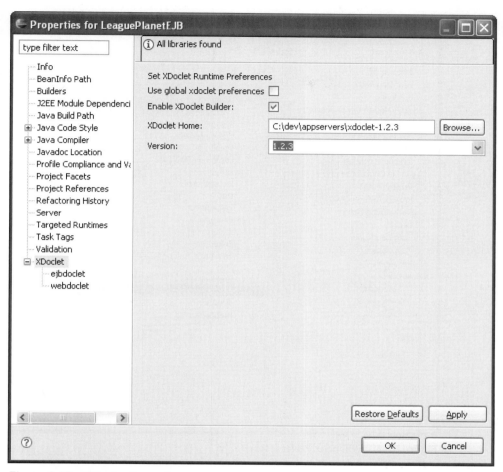

Figure 9.15   XDoclet Properties

7. While JBoss is selected, click on the **Edit** button. JBoss preferences provide default values for generated code. Later on, you can modify these values for each CMP. Enter java:/LeagueDS as the data source name and Derby as the default datasource mapping. Make sure that **createtable** and **altertable** are checked. These instruct the JBoss EJB container to automatically create or alter existing tables in the database (see Figure 9.17). Click **Finish**, and click **OK** to close the project properties window.

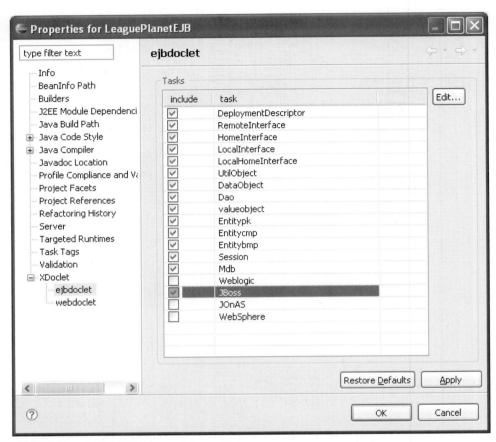

Figure 9.16   EJBDoclet Preferences

You have now completed the preparation of JBoss, Derby, XDoclet, and the EJB project. You can now proceed to the next step and add CMP beans.

Adding a CMP

Add a CMP to the LeaguePlanetEJB project as follows:

1. To create a CMP, select the LeaguePlanetEJB project in the **Project Explorer**. Right click and invoke the **New ▸ XDoclet Enterprise JavaBean** menu item. The **XDoclet EJB** wizard opens (see Figure 9.18).

2. Select **ContainerManagedEntityBean** and click **Next**.

   Enter

   ```
   com.leagueplanet.cmp
   ```

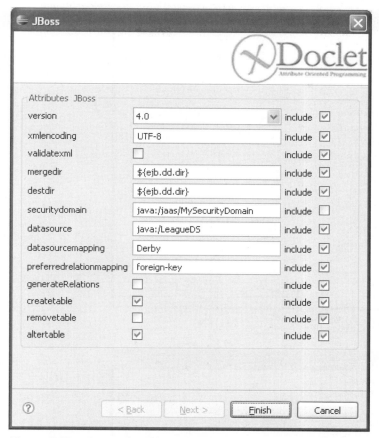

Figure 9.17   JBoss Preferences

as the Java package and `GameBean` as the class name. Remember that XDoclet needs you to use the suffix `Bean` for class names and avoid using other suffixes such as `Session`, `Entity`, `CMP`, or `BMP`. Leave the superclass as `Object` (see Figure 9.19).

3. Click the **Next** button. The next page allows you to enter initial attributes of the CMP bean. Leave the EJB name as `Game` and the schema name as `GameSCHEMA`. You can use the CMP wizard to define bean attributes from scratch or import attributes from an existing table in a database. When you import attributes from a database, the wizard will use the database connections previously defined (see Figure 9.20). You can also create a new connection. Leave all the default settings (see Figure 9.21).

4. Click the **Next** button. The next page allows you to review CMP attributes.

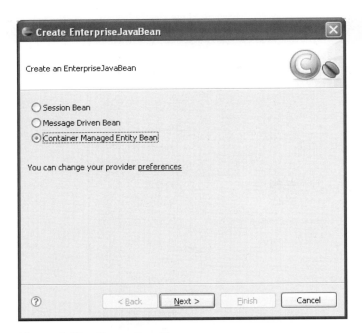

Figure 9.18   Choose Bean Type

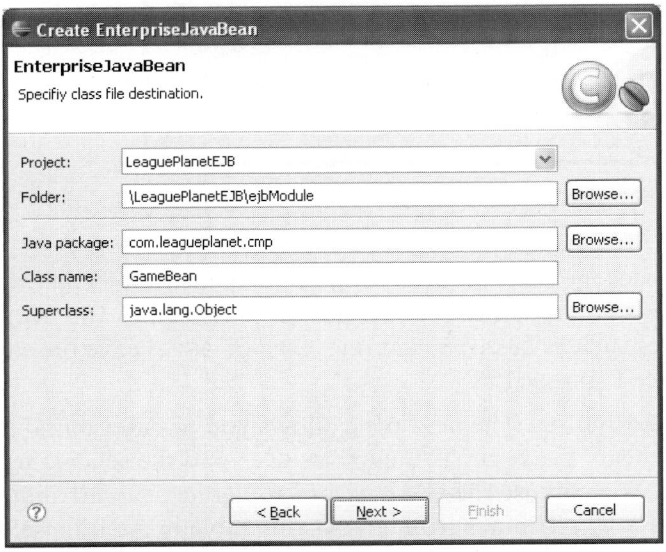

Figure 9.19   EJB Class Options

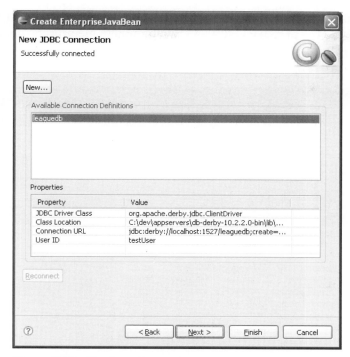

Figure 9.20 Database Connection

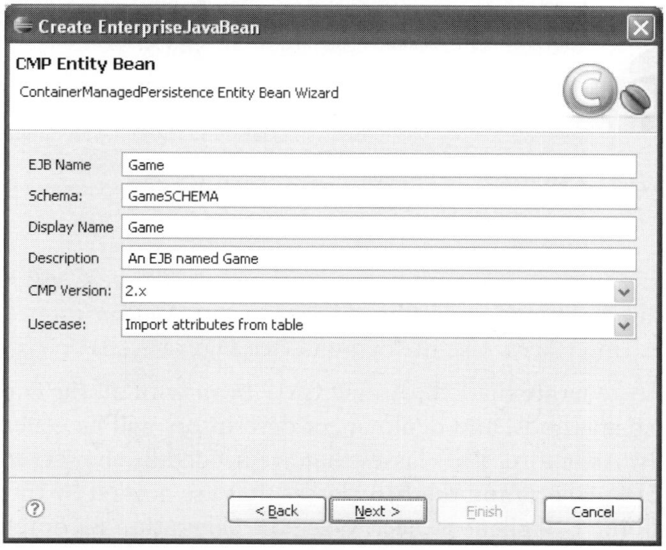

Figure 9.21 CMP Options

5. Select the table APP.GAME as the table name (see Figure 9.22). Select the id attribute to be the primary key, which will uniquely identify the game records in the table.

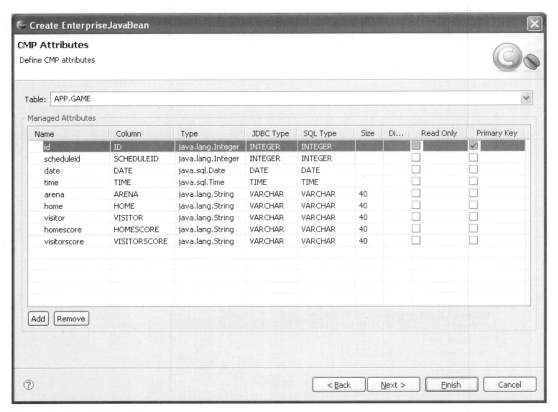

Figure 9.22 CMP Attributes

6. Click the **Next** button. The next page allows you to define CMP interfaces. An entity bean must implement the javax.ejb.EntityBean interface and other business interfaces. Use the defaults (see Figure 9.23).

7. Click **Finish** to generate the EJB. A new CMP bean with all the code for the EJB interfaces, methods, and deployment descriptors will be generated automatically. As before, EJB classes that are needed by the server are created in the EJB project, and the EJB classes that are needed by the clients are created in the EJB client project. Once the generation is complete you can browse these classes in the **Project Explorer**.

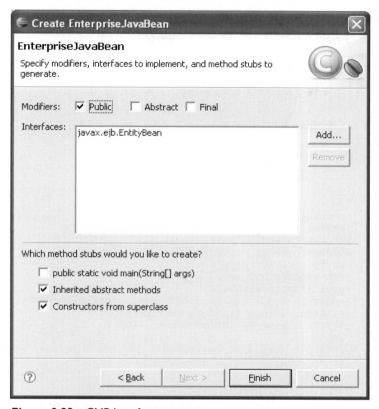

Figure 9.23 CMP Interfaces

Adding ejbCreate and finder Methods

Entity beans are responsible for inserting game objects into the database and running queries to find and read them. To do this you will need to add ejbCreate methods and finder queries. Clients of entity beans will use the create and find methods from the home interface, which correspond to the ejbCreate and ejbFind methods in the GameBean class. ejbFind methods run EJB-QL. You will use annotations for EJB-QL and let XDoclet generate the finder methods. Open the GameBean class and edit the code to make the following changes:

1. Add the ejbCreate method. The ejbCreate method replaces the role of a constructor for EJBs. Add the attributes of a game object as arguments to the ejbCreate method, and invoke the setMethods method of the CMP using these values.

For now, you will use a random number generator to create the primary key. The ejbCreate method must return null according to the EJB specification. Hit Ctrl+S to save the updated code.

XDoclet will automatically update the home interface. Example 9.8 provides the code snippet for the ejbCreate method.

Example 9.8 GameBean ejbCreate Method

```
public java.lang.Integer
    ejbCreate(int scheduleId,Date date,
                        Time time, String arena, String home, String visitor,
                        String hScore, String vScore)
                        throws javax.ejb.CreateException {

            setDate(date);
            setTime(time);
            setArena(arena);
            setHome(home);
            setVisitor(visitor);
            setHomescore(hScore);
            setVisitorscore(vScore);
            Random random = new Random(System.currentTimeMillis());
            setId(new Integer(random.nextInt()));
            setScheduleid(new Integer(scheduleId));

            //EJB 2.0 spec says return null for CMP ejbCreate methods.
            return null;
    }
```

2. Next, create the finders. EJB-QL, which is a part of the EJB 2.1 specification, is a standard language for writing CMP queries. EJB-QL can be used in finder methods. Add the annotation shown in Example 9.9 to the GameBean comment.

Example 9.9 GameBean finder Methods with EJB-QL

```
@ejb.finder
 query="SELECT OBJECT(a) FROM GameSCHEMA as a WHERE a.scheduleid = ?1"
 signature="java.util.Collection findScheduleGames(int scheduleid)"
```

3. This completes the CMP development. Save the code. XDoclet will update the necessary classes, such as the home interface, as usual. The complete code for the finished GameBean class is provided in Example 9.10.

Example 9.10   GameBean.java

```java
package com.leagueplanet.cmp;

import java.rmi.RemoteException;
import java.sql.Date;
import java.sql.Time;
import java.util.Random;

import javax.ejb.EJBException;
import javax.ejb.EntityContext;
import javax.ejb.RemoveException;

/**
 *   @ejb.bean name="Game"
 *   jndi-name="Game"
 *   type="CMP"
 *   primkey-field="id"
 *   schema="GameSCHEMA"
 *   cmp-version="2.x"
 *
 *   @ejb.persistence
 *     table-name="APP.GAME"
 *
 *   @ejb.finder
 *   query="SELECT OBJECT(a) FROM GameSCHEMA as a"
 *   signature="java.util.Collection findAll()"
 *
 *   @ejb.finder
 *   query="SELECT OBJECT(a) FROM GameSCHEMA as a WHERE a.scheduleid = ?1"
 *   signature="java.util.Collection findScheduleGames(int scheduleid)"
 *
 *   @ejb.pk class="java.lang.Integer"
 *
 *   @jboss. persistence
 *   datasource="java:/LeagueDS"
 *   datasource-mapping="Derby"
 *   table-name="APP.GAME"
 *   create-table="true"
 *   remove-table="false"
 *   alter-table="true"
 **/
public abstract class GameBean implements javax.ejb.EntityBean {

  /**
   *   @ejb.create-method
   */
  public java.lang.Integer ejbCreate(int scheduleId,Date date,
      Time time, String arena, String home, String visitor,
      String hScore, String vScore)
      throws javax.ejb.CreateException {
      setDate(date);
    setTime(time);
    setArena(arena);
    setHome(home);
    setVisitor(visitor);
```

```
  setHomescore(hScore);
  setVisitorscore(vScore);
  Random random = new Random(System.currentTimeMillis());
  setId(new Integer(random.nextInt()));
  setScheduleid(new Integer(scheduleId));
  //EJB 2.0 spec says return null for CMP ejbCreate methods.
  return null;
}

/**
 * @ejb.create-method
 */
public java.lang.Integer ejbCreate(int scheduleId,
              com.leagueplanet.model.Game game)
    throws javax.ejb.CreateException {
  setDate(new Date(game.getDateAndTime().getTimeInMillis()));
  setTime(new Time(game.getDateAndTime().getTimeInMillis()));
  setArena(game.getLocation().getName());
  setHome(game.getHome().getName());
  setVisitor(game.getVisitor().getName());
  setHomescore(""+game.getScore().getHome());
  setVisitorscore(""+game.getScore().getVisitor());
  Random random = new Random(System.currentTimeMillis());
  setId(new Integer(random.nextInt()));
  setScheduleid(new Integer(scheduleId));
  //EJB 2.0 spec says return null for CMP ejbCreate methods.
  return null;
}

public void ejbPostCreate() throws javax.ejb.CreateException {
}

/**
 *   @ejb.persistent-field
 *   @ejb.persistence
 *     column-name="ID"
 *     jdbc-type="INTEGER"
 *     sql-type="INTEGER"
 *     read-only="false"
 *   @ejb.pk-field
 *
 *   @ejb.interface-method
 */
public abstract java.lang.Integer getId();

/**
 *   @ejb.interface-method
 */
public abstract void setId(java.lang.Integer id);

/**
 *   @ejb.persistent-field
 *   @ejb.persistence
 *     column-name="SCHEDULEID"
 *       jdbc-type="INTEGER"
```

```
 *      sql-type="INTEGER"
 *      read-only="false"
 *
 *   @ejb.interface-method
 */
public abstract java.lang.Integer getScheduleid();

/**
 *   @ejb.interface-method
 */
public abstract void setScheduleid(java.lang.Integer scheduleid);

/**
 *   @ejb.persistent-field
 *   @ejb.persistence
 *     column-name="DATE"
 *     jdbc-type="DATE"
 *     sql-type="DATE"
 *     read-only="false"
 *
 *   @ejb.interface-method
 */
public abstract java.sql.Date getDate();

/**
 *   @ejb.interface-method
 */
public abstract void setDate(java.sql.Date date);

/**
 *   @ejb.persistent-field
 *   @ejb.persistence
 *     column-name="TIME"
 *     jdbc-type="TIME"
 *     sql-type="TIME"
 *     read-only="false"
 *
 *   @ejb.interface-method
 */
public abstract java.sql.Time getTime();

/**
 *   @ejb.interface-method
 */
public abstract void setTime(java.sql.Time time);

/**
 *   @ejb.persistent-field
 *   @ejb.persistence
 *     column-name="ARENA"
 *     jdbc-type="VARCHAR"
 *     sql-type="VARCHAR(40)"
 *     read-only="false"
 *
 *   @ejb.interface-method
 */
```

```java
    public abstract java.lang.String getArena();

    /**
     *  @ejb.interface-method
     */
    public abstract void setArena(java.lang.String arena);

    /**
     *  @ejb.persistent-field
     *  @ejb.persistence
     *    column-name="HOME"
     *    jdbc-type="VARCHAR"
     *    sql-type="VARCHAR(40)"
     *    read-only="false"
     *
     *  @ejb.interface-method
     */
    public abstract java.lang.String getHome();

    /**
     *  @ejb.interface-method
     */
    public abstract void setHome(java.lang.String home);

    /**
     *  @ejb.persistent-field
     *  @ejb.persistence
     *    column-name="VISITOR"
     *    jdbc-type="VARCHAR"
     *    sql-type="VARCHAR(40)"
     *    read-only="false"
     *
     *  @ejb.interface-method
     */
    public abstract java.lang.String getVisitor();

    /**
     *  @ejb.interface-method
     */
    public abstract void setVisitor(java.lang.String visitor);

    /**
     *  @ejb.persistent-field
     *  @ejb.persistence
     *    column-name="HOMESCORE"
     *    jdbc-type="VARCHAR"
     *    sql-type="VARCHAR(40)"
     *    read-only="false"
     *
     *  @ejb.interface-method
     */
    public abstract java.lang.String getHomescore();
```

```java
/**
 *  @ejb.interface-method
 */
public abstract void setHomescore(java.lang.String homescore);

/**
 *  @ejb.persistent-field
 *  @ejb.persistence
 *     column-name="VISITORSCORE"
 *     jdbc-type="VARCHAR"
 *     sql-type="VARCHAR(40)"
 *     read-only="false"
 *
 *  @ejb.interface-method
 */
public abstract java.lang.String getVisitorscore();

/**
 *  @ejb.interface-method
 */
public abstract void setVisitorscore(java.lang.String visitorscore);

public void ejbActivate() throws EJBException, RemoteException {
  // TODO Auto-generated method stub
}

public void ejbLoad() throws EJBException, RemoteException {
  // TODO Auto-generated method stub
}

public void ejbPassivate() throws EJBException, RemoteException {
  // TODO Auto-generated method stub
}

public void ejbRemove() throws RemoveException, EJBException,
    RemoteException {
  // TODO Auto-generated method stub
}

public void ejbStore() throws EJBException, RemoteException {
  // TODO Auto-generated method stub
}

public void setEntityContext(EntityContext arg0)
    throws EJBException, RemoteException {
}

public void unsetEntityContext() throws EJBException,
    RemoteException {
  // TODO Auto-generated method stub
}

}
```

You can now proceed to implement a new DAO that integrates CMP persistence into the League Planet application.

Adding the Ice Hockey CMP Data Access Object

In this section you will create a new DAO implementation for League Planet. Instead of using JDBC or in-memory objects, this DAO will use CMP entity beans. As before, you will simply swap the DAO implementation to replace the persistence tier with EJBs.

1. Start with mapping the games and leave others, such as schedules and leagues, incomplete. The new DAO class will refer to CMP beans, so you will create it as a part of the LeaguePlanetEJBClient project. Add a new package named com.leagueplanet.cmp to the EJB client project, and add a class named IceHockeyCMPDAOImpl that will implement the DAO interface (see the section The Data Access Layer). The code is provided in Example 9.11.

Example 9.11   Listing of IceHockeyCMPDAOImpl.java

```
package com.leagueplanet.cmp;

import java.rmi.RemoteException;
import java.sql.*;
import java.text.ParseException;
import java.util.*;

import com.leagueplanet.dao.LeagueDAO;
import com.leagueplanet.model.Game;
import com.leagueplanet.model.League;
import com.leagueplanet.model.Location;
import com.leagueplanet.model.Player;
import com.leagueplanet.model.Schedule;
import com.leagueplanet.model.Score;
import com.leagueplanet.model.Team;

public class IceHockeyCMPDAOImpl implements LeagueDAO {

  // singleton DAO
  private static IceHockeyCMPDAOImpl leagueDAO = null;

  public static LeagueDAO getLeagueDAO() {
    if (leagueDAO == null) {
      leagueDAO = new IceHockeyCMPDAOImpl();
    }
    return leagueDAO;
  }

  public League findLeague(long id) {
    // TODO: Add mappings for leagues and schedules
```

```
      League league=new League(id, "Rosehill Girl's Hockey League");
      league.getSchedules().add(findSchedule(1));
      return league;
   }
   public Schedule findSchedule(long id) {
      // TODO: Add mappings schedules
      Schedule schedule = new Schedule(id, "2005/6 Regular Season");
      try {
         Collection games = GameUtil.getHome().findScheduleGames(
            (int) id);
         Iterator iterator = games.iterator();
         while (iterator.hasNext()) {
            com.leagueplanet.cmp.Game cmp =
               (com.leagueplanet.cmp.Game) iterator.next();
            schedule.getEvents().add(createGameFromCMP(cmp));
         }
      } catch (Exception e) {
         e.printStackTrace();
      }
      return schedule;
   }

   private Game createGameFromCMP(com.leagueplanet.cmp.Game cmp)
         throws SQLException, ParseException, RemoteException {
      Game game = new Game();
      game.setId(cmp.getId().intValue());
      Calendar dateTime = Calendar.getInstance();
      dateTime.setTime(cmp.getDate());
      dateTime.set(Calendar.HOUR_OF_DAY,
         cmp.getTime().getHours() + 1);
      dateTime.set(Calendar.MINUTE, cmp.getTime().getMinutes() + 1);
      game.setDateAndTime(dateTime);
      game.setLocation(new Location(0, cmp.getArena()));
      Team homeTeam = new Team();
      homeTeam.setName(cmp.getHome());
      game.setHome(homeTeam);
      Team visitorTeam = new Team();
      visitorTeam.setName(cmp.getVisitor());
      game.setVisitor(visitorTeam);
      Score gameScore = new Score(Integer
         .parseInt(cmp.getHomescore()), Integer.parseInt(cmp
         .getVisitorscore()));
      game.setScore(gameScore);
      return game;
   }

   // TODO: Add mappings later
   public Set getSchedulesForLeague(String league) {
      return null;
   }

   public Set findLeaguesWithName(String name) {
      return null;
   }
```

```
    public void save(League newLeague) {
    }

    public Game findGame(long id) {
      return null;
    }

    public Location findLocation(long id) {
      return null;
    }

    public Team findTeam(long id) {
      return null;
    }

    public Player findPlayer(long id) {
      return null;
    }
}
```

2. Modify the session bean that was previously created (see the Iteration 2: Developing Session EJBs section in Chapter 8). Change `LeagueFacade` to use the CMP DAO just created. This change will be transparent to the business and presentation tiers. Open the session bean class named `com.leagueplanet.ejb.LeagueFacadeBean` in the Java editor and find the line in the `ejbCreate` method where the DAO is set. Replace it with the singleton from the new `IceHockeyCMPDAOImpl` class (see Example 9.12).

Example 9.12   Modified Listing of the LeagueFacadeBean ejbCreate Method

```
/**
 * @ejb.create-method view-type="remote"
 **/
public void ejbCreate() {
      LeagueFacadeImpl facadeImpl = new LeagueFacadeImpl();
      // point the facade at the dao for the ice hockey league
      LeagueDAO dao = IceHockeyCMPDAOImpl.getLeagueDAO();
      facadeImpl.setLeagueDAO(dao);
      leagueFacade = facadeImpl;

      // Reference to the old facade implementation
      //leagueFacade = IceHockeyFacade.getLeagueFacade();
}
```

Testing the CMP Implementation

Next, test the CMP-based persistence tier using the `LeaguePlanetWeb` Web application:

1. Open the Web application. Right click on the `schedule.jsp` file and invoke the **Run As** ▸ **Run on Server** menu item. The browser should display the same games (see Figure 9.14). The only difference is that the games were read using the new CMP.

2. Next, you will add new games to the schedule. To do this you will use a servlet to insert the new games in the database using your CMP. Create a new servlet named `GameServlet` in the `LeaguePlanetWeb` project. You will use this servlet to process an HTTP request coming from an HTML form named `gameForm.html`. You will need to define a servlet URL mapping in `web.xml` that directs requests sent with URI `/GameServlet` to this servlet.

   Use the **New Servlet** wizard as before to create the `GameServlet` class (see Figure 9.24).

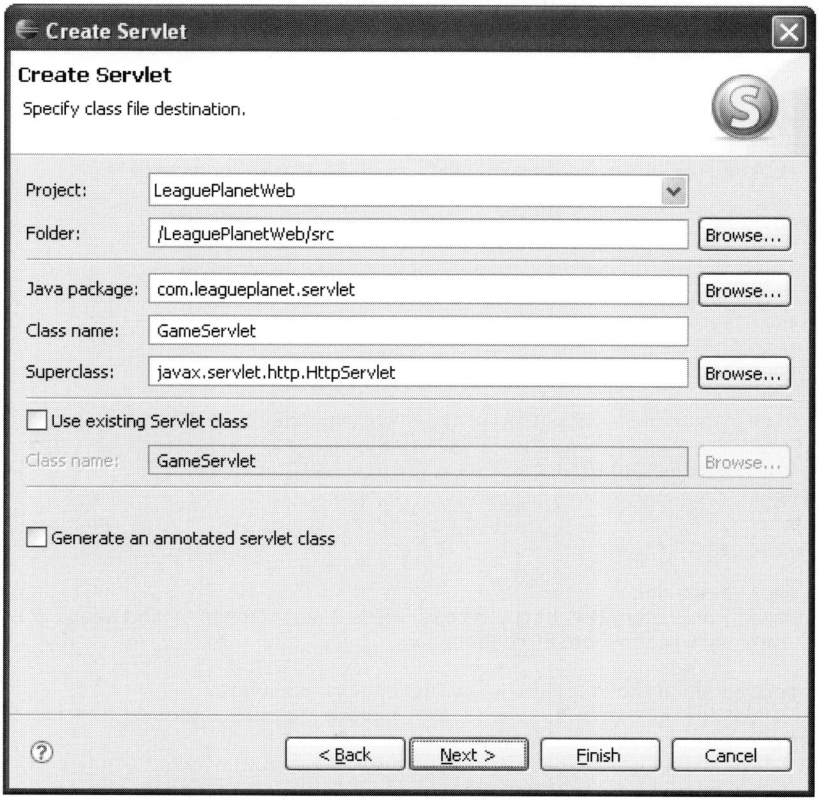

Figure 9.24 Create Servlet

3. Now add code to your servlet to get the form data from the request and call the CMP to create a new game. The EJB container will automatically save the game to the database. Finally, forward the response to `schedule.jsp`. Make sure that the code for your servlet looks like that shown in Example 9.13.

Example 9.13   Listing of GameServlet.java

```java
package com.leagueplanet.servlet;

import java.io.IOException;
import java.sql.Date;
import java.sql.Time;
import java.text.SimpleDateFormat;

import javax.servlet.ServletException;
import javax.servlet.http.HttpServletRequest;
import javax.servlet.http.HttpServletResponse;

import com.leagueplanet.cmp.GameUtil;

/**
 * Servlet implementation class for Servlet: GameServlet
 *
 * @web.servlet name="GameServlet" display-name="GameServlet"
 *
 * @web.servlet-mapping url-parrern="/GameServlet"
 */

public class GameServlet extends javax.servlet.http.HttpServlet implements
    javax.servlet.Servlet {
  /*
   * (non-Java-doc)
   *
   * @see javax.servlet.http.HttpServlet#HttpServlet()
   */
  public GameServlet() {
    super();
  }

  /*
   * (non-Java-doc)
   * @see javax.servlet.http.HttpServlet#doPost(HttpServletRequest request,
     HttpServletResponse response)
   */
  protected void doPost(HttpServletRequest request,
      HttpServletResponse response) throws ServletException, IOException {
    try {
      SimpleDateFormat dateFormat = new SimpleDateFormat("dd-MM-yyyy");
      SimpleDateFormat timeFormat = new SimpleDateFormat("hh:mm aaa");
      Date date = new Date(dateFormat.parse(request.getParameter("date"))
          .getTime());
```

```
        Time time = new Time(timeFormat.parse(request.getParameter("time"))
            .getTime());
        String arena = request.getParameter("arena");
        String home = request.getParameter("home");
        String visitor = request.getParameter("visitor");
        String homeScore = request.getParameter("homeScore");
        String visitorScore = request.getParameter("visitorScore");

        GameUtil.getLocalHome().create(1,date, time, arena, home, visitor,
            homeScore, visitorScore);
        this.getServletContext().getRequestDispatcher("/schedule.jsp")
            .forward(request, response);
      } catch (Exception e) {
      e.printStackTrace();
      }

    }

}
```

4. In the webContent folder, create an HTML file named gameForm.html and code a game data entry form in it (see Example 9.14). You will use this HTML form to submit game creation requests to the GameServlet.

Example 9.14 A Simple Game Form

```html
<!DOCTYPE HTML PUBLIC "-//W3C//DTD HTML 4.01 Transitional//EN">
<html>
<head>

<meta http-equiv="Content-Type" content="text/html; charset=ISO-8859-1">
<title>Insert title here</title>
</head>
<body>

<form action="/LeaguePlanetWeb/GameServlet" method="post">
<h1>Add a new game</h1>
<table>
  <tr>
    <td>date</td>
    <td><input type="text" name="date"></td>
  </tr>
  <tr>
    <td>time</td>
    <td><input type="text" name="time"></td>
  </tr>
  <tr>
    <td>arena</td>
    <td><input type="text" name="arena"></td>
  </tr>
  <tr>
    <td>home</td>
    <td><input type="text" name="home"></td>
  </tr>
```

```
<tr>
  <td>visitor</td>
  <td><input type="text" name="visitor"></td>
</tr>
<tr>
  <td>home score</td>
  <td><input type="text" name="homeScore"></td>
</tr>
<tr>
  <td>visitor score</td>
  <td><input type="text" name="visitorScore"></td>
</tr>
<tr>
  <td colspan="2"><input type="submit" name="Add" value="Add"></td>
</tr>

</table>


</form>
</body>
</html>
```

5. This completes the coding required for the iteration. Save your work, and publish the enterprise application to the JBoss server. To test your application, select gameForm.html and run it on the server. The form will be displayed in a Web browser. Enter some game data (see Figure 9.25) and click **Add**.

6. The updated schedule will appear in the browser (see Figure 9.26).

Developing JPA with WTP

WTP 1.5 does not have JPA tools. JPA support is being developed in the Dali incubator project, which will become available with WTP 2.0. With EJB 3.0, you can still build EJB 2.1 entity beans, but JPA is a much better alternative.

JPA is based on POJOs. There are no special EJB classes to deal with. For example, you can persist the classes in the business tier directly. As for EJB 3.0, deployment descriptors are optional with JPA. O/R mapping is done by adding JSR 175 annotations to the business model.

If you want to try JPA, you will need to use WTP 2.0 and do the following:

1. Use a JDK that is 1.5 and above (that is, Java 5), and choose this JDK as the Java runtime environment for projects and servers.

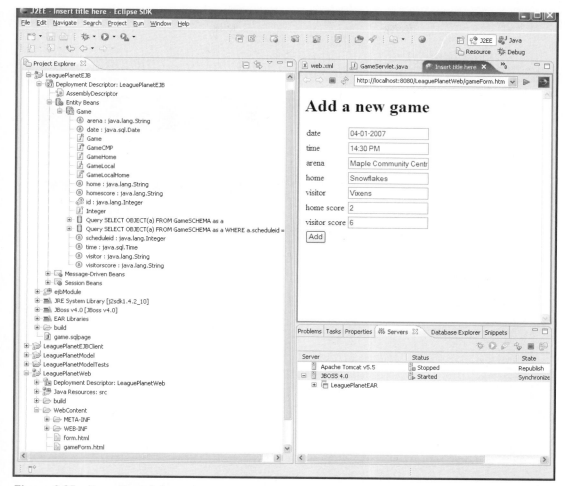

Figure 9.25 Enter Game Information

2. Use a server runtime environment that supports JPA. For example, Sun Microsystems provides GlassFish that can run EJB 3.0. GlassFish also provides WTP server adapter plug-ins.

3. You will need a JPA implementation, such as TOPLink essentials or Hibernate.

4. Download and use a WTP 2.0 stream build and Dali.

5. Add annotations to your classes so that they are marked as persistent and map your business objects (i.e., `LeaguePlanetModel`). For example, mapping the classes in the `com.leagueplanet.model` package with JPA annotations is quite easy (see Example 9.15).

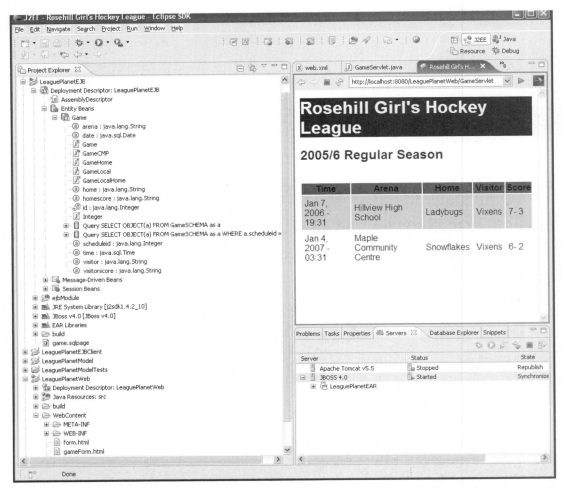

Figure 9.26   Game Schedule Information

Example 9.15   Game with JPA Annotations

```java
package com.leagueplanet.model;

import javax.persistence.*;

import java.io.Serializable;
import java.text.ParseException;
import java.util.Calendar;

@Entity
public class Game implements Serializable {

        private static final long serialVersionUID = 1L;
```

```
//Primary key
@Id
private long id;

private String name;
@OneToOne
private Location location;
private Calendar dateAndTime;

@OneToOne
private Team home;

@OneToOne
private Team visitor;

@OneToOne
private Score score = new Score();

public Game(long id, String name, Calendar dateAndTime) {
       setId(id);
       setName(name);
       setDateAndTime(dateAndTime);
}

public Game(long id, String name, String dateAndTime)
            throws ParseException {
            ...
}

public long getId() {
       return id;
}

public void setId(long id) {
       this.id = id;
}

public String getName() {
       return name;
}

public void setName(String name) {
       this.name = name;
}

public Location getLocation() {
       return location;
}

public void setLocation(Location location) {
       this.location = location;
}

public Team getHome() {
       return home;
}
```

```
public void setHome(Team home) {
        this.home = home;
}

public Score getScore() {
        return score;
}

public void setScore(Score score) {
        this.score = score;
}

public Team getVisitor() {
        return visitor;
}

public void setVisitor(Team visitor) {
        this.visitor = visitor;
}

public Calendar getDateAndTime() {
        return dateAndTime;
}
public void setDateAndTime(Calendar dateAndTime) {
        this.dateAndTime = dateAndTime;
}

}
```

6. Use the JPA `EntityManager` to save and load objects. Test them with or without an EJB container. You are done!

Summary of Iteration 3

In this iteration you learned about entity beans and used a CMP bean to implement a persistence tier. You added custom create and finder methods, and used EJB-QL. You created a new implementation of the DAO interface to integrate your persistence tier with the enterprise application.

Summary

In this chapter you covered the major functional areas of data tools and approaches to persistence tier development using WTP. You created a database and a table using the data tools, and you developed persistence tiers using two different approaches: JDBC and CMP entity beans. You used the classes in the data layer to make these changes transparently to the presentation and business tiers. You developed a Web application to view game information and create new games.

You are now ready to use the data tools and persistence in your own applications. For further details about the tools, consult the WTP Help and Web site.

The examples in this and the previous chapter used EJBs for remote access between the presentation and business tiers. Although RMI works well within an enterprise, it is limited to Java clients. In order to make your business tier accessible to non-Java clients, and to clients outside your enterprise, the best approach is to use Web services. In the next chapter, you will learn how to use WTP to create a Web service layer for your applications.

CHAPTER 10

Web Services

*"When I use a word," Humpty Dumpty said, in rather a scornful tone,
"it means just what I choose it to mean—neither more nor less."*

—Lewis Carroll

Web pages are a wonderful source of information, but it takes a human to understand what they mean. Wouldn't it be great if all the information on the Web was available in a form that could be easily used by other programs? Think of the amazing applications that you could build.

In the early days of the Web, application developers tried to programmatically mine information from Web pages by *screen scraping*, a technique where HTML is parsed and its meaning is inferred based on assumptions about page layout, table headings, and other clues. Of course, screen scraping is a lost cause because Web designers change page layout frequently to keep their sites interesting.

The best way to make your information available to other programs on the Web is to publish it in XML format. To implement this approach, you'll have to either define an XML vocabulary that describes your application data or use an industry standard vocabulary if a suitable one exists. Indeed the predominant activity following the publication of the XML specification was the definition of standard vocabularies such as Mathematical Markup Language (MathML), Chemical Markup Language (CML), and even Meat and Poultry Markup Language (mpXML)!

Although XML was initially touted as a "better HTML," it soon became apparent that the real sweet spot for XML was as a data interchange format. The term *Web service* was coined to describe a Web application that exchanged information in XML format. The combination of HTTP and XML was extremely potent. HTTP had become ubiquitous on the Internet. Firewalls allowed HTTP traffic on port 80 to pass through while other protocols and ports were shut out.

XML was textual and architecturally neutral so there was no confusion about low-level details such as the order of bytes in an integer. Although more verbose than binary formats, XML became universally supported. All platforms had XML parsers. At last there was a protocol, HTTP, and a format, XML, that applications on any platform could use to communicate. Web services became the *lingua franca* for application integration over the Internet.

The genesis of Web services was certainly in HTTP and XML, but today the term has been generalized to cover other protocols and formats. It is hard to come up with a definition of Web services that everyone would agree to. For an attempt at such a definition, see *Web Services Architecture* [WSARCH]. For the purposes of this book, a Web service is a Web application that is designed to be accessed by other Web applications rather than humans. Here, a Web application is simply any program that can be accessed using Web protocols, for example, HTTP, and that supports Web formats, for example, HTML and XML. Of course, a Web service will often use XML for data interchange, but it may also support other media types.

WSDL

One consequence of the requirement to be accessible by other applications is that a Web service must provide a well-defined interface and, in practice, this interface is specified using a Web Service Description Language (WSDL) document. WSDL 1.1 is currently the most prevalent way to describe the interface of Web services. WSDL 1.1 is, technically speaking, not actually a W3C standard. True W3C standards are the result of a rigorous development and review process and are called Recommendations. WSDL 1.1 is only a W3C Note, which means it was submitted to W3C by member organizations and made available to the industry under W3C licensing terms, which are generally *Royalty Free* (RF). The availability of a specification as a W3C Note promotes its adoption by the industry.

WSDL 2.0 is scheduled to become a W3C Recommendation in 2007. WSDL 1.1 and 2.0 are conceptually very similar, and in this book we'll refer to both simply as WSDL. However, WSDL 2.0 benefited from a long and careful review process, and it incorporates many new features that bring it better into line with Web architectural principles. The careful review and test process for WSDL 2.0 will undoubtedly also eliminate many of the interoperability problems that plagued WSDL 1.1. Of course, there is always inertia to overcome when a new specification like WSDL 2.0 seeks to replace a widely deployed incumbent like WSDL 1.1. WSDL 1.1 and WSDL 2.0 will coexist for a long time. New Web services that support Web architectural principles such as REST will probably be the first adopters of WSDL 2.0.

SOAP

The specification that really kick-started the Web services revolution was Simple Object Access Protocol (SOAP) 1.1, which defined an XML envelope for Web service messages, a processing model for Web service intermediaries, and an encoding algorithm for serializing objects as XML. The SOAP envelope was extremely simple, consisting of a *body* and an optional *header*. The SOAP body contained the application payload, and the SOAP header contained any other non-application data such as security, reliability, or transaction information. The separation of messages into a header and a body is a well-accepted design practice. The SOAP processing model specified how network intermediaries could process the SOAP header information before delivering the SOAP body to the Web service or client.

The SOAP envelope and processing model were fairly uncontentious and relatively easy to implement correctly. On the other hand, the SOAP encoding algorithm proved to be much more problematic. The root cause of the difficulty was that there is no universally accepted definition of objects. Each object-oriented programming language implements many common features of objects, but adds differences. For example, C++ supports multiple inheritance but Java only supports single inheritance. There is simply no way to faithfully interchange objects between arbitrary programming languages. The interoperability problems associated with SOAP encoding eventually led to its exclusion from the WS-I Basic Profile.

But even if there was a commonly accepted way to exchange objects, that would still be the wrong way to build robust distributed systems. If you look at a typical programming language object, it contains more than just state information. It also contains fields used to make navigation and other operations more efficient. For example, a linked list really just represents a sequence of objects, but it contains forward and backward pointers. There is no purpose in serializing these redundant fields in a Web service message. They increase the bulk of the message, and the receiving end may elect to represent the sequence in some other way, for example, as an array. Objects are wonderful for implementing applications but are really not a good basis for designing Web service interfaces. Furthermore, a Web service should support a wide variety of application types, not just object-oriented systems.

As the name SOAP suggests, SOAP encoding was motivated by a desire to create a distributed object technology for the Web. Earlier distributed object technologies such as CORBA, Java RMI, and DCOM failed to gain significant traction on the Internet. When XML emerged, Microsoft proposed that it could be used as an architecturally neutral way to serialize graphs of objects. SOAP was proposed as the carrier for these serialized object graphs and the serialization algorithm was dubbed *SOAP encoding*. The fact that XML was used as the serialization syntax was incidental. To use SOAP encoding, you had to have matching client and service implementations that understood the SOAP encoding algorithm. The client and the server were assumed to both be implemented in conventional object-oriented programming languages. The flaw in this approach is that exchanging objects is really not what the Web is all about. The Web is highly heterogeneous, and there are many types of clients and ways of processing XML. For example, XML can be processed using DOM, SAX, StAX, XPath, XSLT, and XQuery to name a few. In fact, one of the design principles behind XML is that it should be easily processable by a variety of applications. SOAP encoding clearly violates that principle.

A better approach to the design of Web service interfaces is to view Web service operations as document exchanges. After all, business in the real world is transacted by the exchange of documents. For example, I fill out a driver's license application form and the motor vehicle department sends me my driver's license. I do not remotely invoke the driver's license procedure or send the motor vehicle department a serialized driver's license application form object graph. Documents are very natural, and XML is an excellent way to represent them in information systems. XML Schema is the W3C standard type system for XML documents. But XML is really just a representation of a document, albeit a very convenient one for many purposes. In general, there may be other useful representations of documents. For example, if I just want to display the document to a human, then HTML or PDF is a better representation. Or if I want a highly interactive AJAX-based Web user interface to display the document, then perhaps JavaScript Object Notation (JSON) is a good representation. On the other hand, if I want to use the document in a Service-Oriented Architecture (SOA) application, then document/literal SOAP is probably the best representation.

REST

Web architecture teaches us that the way to design an application is to identify its important concepts, model them as *resources*, and assign them Uniform Resource Identifiers (URI). Software *agents*, such as Web browsers or Web applications, then request these resources, specifying their preferred representation formats. The Web server or service responds by transferring the *representation* of the resource to the agent in the format that most closely satisfies the request.

The selection of the best representation is referred to as *content negotiation*. The agent then transitions to its next *state* based on the content of the received resource, which typically contains hyperlinks to other resources. The hyperlinks are then used for subsequent requests, which cause the agent to transition to a new state. This architectural style is referred to as Representational State Transfer (REST), a term coined in Chapter 5 of the Ph.D. dissertation *Architectural Styles and the Design of Network-based Software Architectures* [Fielding2000], by Roy Fielding.

For example, consider League Planet. Its important concepts include leagues, schedules, games, teams, and locations. Each of these concepts is physically stored in a relational database and is identified by a unique number that acts as its primary key. This gives us a simple way to define URIs. Each row of the main *entity* tables corresponds to a URI. We create the URI by combining the table name and the primary key value; for example,

```
http://www.leagueplanet.com/resources/game/42
```

identifies game number 42.

There are a few other key ideas in Web architecture. One of the most important is the notion of *hyperlinking*. The representation of a resource will often contain links to other resources. An agent will typically follow these links to retrieve related information. In the context of Web services, this means that the messages exchanged will often contain references to other Web services. A full description of a Web service must also describe the interfaces of these references to other Web services. For example, it is not enough to know that the League Planet schedule Web service returns URIs to teams; it is also necessary to know that these URIs are in fact the endpoints of League Planet team Web services.

Another key idea in REST is the notion of *uniform interface*, which means that there is a standard set of *verbs* or *methods* that can be used to access any resource. In HTTP, the most common methods are PUT, GET, POST, and DELETE, which roughly correspond to the Create, Retrieve, Update, and Delete (CRUD) operations on databases. In practice, most Web applications just use GET and POST.

The proper use of GET has important performance benefits. GET should be used for operations that are *safe*, which means that they are *idempotent* and don't incur any obligations. *Idempotence* means that the result of performing the operation twice is the same as performing it once. For example, in banking, getting your account balance is idempotent, but withdrawing money from it is not. An obligation could be something like having your account charged for the operation. Safe operations admit certain optimizations such as prefetching and caching. For example, a Web browser could prefetch linked pages and cache the results to improve response time and reduce network traffic.

Finally, let's examine content negotiation. This is the mechanism by which an agent can specify the types of resource representation it prefers to receive in response to a request. For example, suppose a Web browser requests an HTML page. Part of the request is an HTTP Accept header that lists the image media types that the Web browser can render, with weightings that indicate its preferences. When the Web application receives the request, it inspects the Accept header and generates a Web page with links to the image media type that best fit the Web browser's preference. A similar mechanism can be used to specify the desired natural language of the response.

Content negotiation applies also to Web services. For example, an AJAX client may prefer a response encoded as JSON as its first choice, then plain XML, and then finally SOAP, since this is the order that minimizes its parsing time. The client includes an Accept header in its requests indicating that it accepts these three media types and then assigns them suitable preferences. In this way, the AJAX client receives the response in the format that is most efficient for it to process if the Web service provides it, but can still function if the Web service provides other acceptable formats. The nice thing about this architecture is that the Web service can be upgraded at a later date to improve performance and the clients will automatically benefit without any modification on their end. For example, suppose League Planet provides REST style Web services initially using plain XML, but then finds after reviewing the server logs that many clients prefer JSON. The service can then be upgraded to also provide JSON, and the existing clients will experience a performance boost without changing a line of their code.

REST Style Web Services

The REST architectural style is directly applicable to Web services. See *Building Web Services the REST Way* [Costello2002] by Roger Costello for an excellent description of this approach. Some vendors, such as Amazon, offer both SOAP and REST interfaces. The use of REST for Web services received a mindshare boost when, in the brief article "REST vs. SOAP at Amazon" [O'Reilly2003], Tim O'Reilly reported that Amazon was finding that 85 percent of their Web service usage was via the REST interface. This overwhelming preference for REST versus SOAP is undoubtedly due to the fact that the main use of the Amazon Web service is for providing product links on Web pages. Nevertheless, REST style interfaces are easier to use in this type of application and deserve to be given serious consideration when designing Web services in general.

Now let's briefly examine how well SOAP 1.1 and WSDL 1.1 align with REST principles. For starters, most SOAP 1.1 engines employ a single URL that acts like a router for service requests. The SOAP engine examines the request to determine the operation and then invokes the service implementation associated with it. Furthermore, SOAP 1.1 over HTTP always uses POST, so all operations are treated as unsafe. WSDL 1.1 is not much better. In addition to the SOAP 1.1 binding, WSDL 1.1 defines two HTTP bindings, one for GET and another for POST. This means you cannot describe a service that has a combination of safe and unsafe operations. Nor can you always use the correct HTTP method for any given operation since PUT, DELETE, and so forth are not supported. Finally, WSDL 1.1 provides no way to describe messages that refer to other Web services, that is, no support for hyperlinking.

So we see that SOAP 1.1 and WSDL 1.1 are somewhat REST-hostile. Nevertheless, these specifications do provide the basis for a large and rich set of additional specifications collectively referred to as WS-*. These include WS-Security, WS-Reliability, and WS-Addressing to name a few. The way to think about WS-* is that it defines a way to flow Web services messages over multiple transport hops involving a combination of protocols. For example, an enterprise Web service might receive a request over HTTP and then place it on a message queue. This is the domain of SOA.

Although SOA is undoubtedly useful in many contexts, it is overkill in others. For example, suppose you want to build an AJAX client. You need to get XML data from somewhere. Why not use a Web service? In this situation, you'd like the XML to be very easy to process, so SOAP encoding is ruled out. Document/literal style is much more appropriate. But maybe XML is even too complex here. Perhaps JSON is a better representation. Still, this is programmatic access, and even though you are not using SOAP or even XML, you'd like a well-defined interface you can program to.

Fortunately, the combination of SOAP 1.2 and WSDL 2.0 brings the world of Web services into much better alignment with REST architectural principles. SOAP 1.2 supports the use of GET for requests. WSDL 2.0 allows the description of safe operations, has a much improved HTTP binding, and includes support for describing messages that refer to other Web services; that is, hyperlinking between Web services can be described. As we enter the so-called Web 2.0 technology era, we could see a unification of WS-* and REST style Web services based on SOAP 1.2 and WSDL 2.0.

Overview of Iterations

Enough theory. It's time to write some code. In this chapter you'll add Web services to the League Planet site in the following iterations:

○ In Iteration 1 you develop a Web service that retrieves League Planet schedule information using the Top-Down approach. This means you create the description of the Web service interface first using the XSD and WSDL editors, and then generate its Java skeleton using the Web service wizard. You fill in the implementation of the Web service by writing Java code that accesses the League Planet business logic tier. Finally, you test the Web service using the Web Services Explorer.

❍ In Iteration 2 you develop a Web service that updates the game scores using the Bottom-Up approach. This means you write Java code that accesses the League Planet business logic tier first, and then use the Web service wizard to deploy the Java code as a Web service and generate its WSDL.

❍ In Iteration 3 you create a Web client that uses the update Web service. You use the Web service wizard to generate a Java client proxy from the WSDL of the Web service and a JSP test client that uses the proxy.

❍ In Iteration 4 you test your Web service for interoperability. You use the TCP/IP monitor and the WS-I test tools to test your Web service for compatibility with the WS-I profiles.

❍ In Iteration 5 you use your Web services in a Web application that displays schedules and updates game scores. The Web application accesses the Web services using Java client proxies.

❍ In Iteration 6 you use the Web Services Explorer to discover Web services in UDDI and WSIL registries. You also use the Web service wizard to publish WSIL documents that describe your Web services.

Iteration 1: Developing Web Services Top-Down

Top-Down development means designing the Web service interface first and then developing the implementation code. This approach yields the best interoperability because the underlying implementation details cannot "bleed through" into the interface. Top-Down development is required if the messages must use existing industry or corporate standard XML document formats. To perform Top-Down development you need to have XSD and WSDL design skills. Luckily, WTP has two great editors that make this task easier.

In this iteration, you'll perform the following tasks:

1. Use the XSD editor to describe the League Planet schedule format.

2. Use the WSDL editor to describe a Web service for querying schedules.

3. Use the Web service wizard to generate a Java skeleton for the service and deploy it to the Axis SOAP engine running on Tomcat.

4. Fill in the implementation of the Java skeleton by accessing the League Planet business logic tier.

5. Use the Web Services Explorer to test the schedule query service.

XSD

XML Schema Description (XSD) is the W3C Recommendation for describing the format or *schema* of XML documents, and is the preferred schema description language for use with Web services. XSD is far more expressive than its predecessor, DTD, and, like many specifications produced by industrial collaborations, is extremely feature rich. Fortunately, only a small portion of the XSD language is needed in practice to describe typical Web service messages. For an easily digestible overview of XSD, see Chapters 8 and 9 of *Essential XML Quick Reference* [Skonnard2002] by Aaron Skonnard and Martin Gudgin.

The definitive sources of information about XSD are, of course, the W3C specifications themselves. The best way to get started is to read *XML Schema Part 0: Primer* [XSD10-Part0], which gradually introduces all the major concepts and illustrates them using simple examples. The remaining parts, *XML Schema Part 1: Structures* [XSD10-Part1] and *XML Schema Part 2: Datatypes* [XSD10-Part2], provide normative definitions of the schema constructs and type system, but are very difficult to read. They are intended for people who need to build software that processes XSD. However, you might need to refer to these specifications in order to understand error messages produced by XSD processors. Be warned, though, this task is not for the faint-hearted.

WTP has a powerful XSD editor that includes both a source and a graphical view as well as an outline view and property sheets that greatly simplify the editing task. However, don't let the power of the XSD editor tempt you into using all the features of XSD when you design your Web service messages. You should keep the design simple to ensure that developers can understand it and that it will be consumable by the widest possible set of Web service toolkits. The initial toolkit support for the more exotic features of XSD was somewhat patchy, but the situation has steadily improved over time.

To create the schema for the League Planet schedule, do the following:

1. Create a new dynamic Web project named `IceHockeyService` to contain the Web service (see Figure 10.1).

2. League Planet has an XML format for schedules. Import

`IceHockeyService/schedule.xml`

for an example instance document (see Example 10.1). Your goal is to describe this format using XSD.

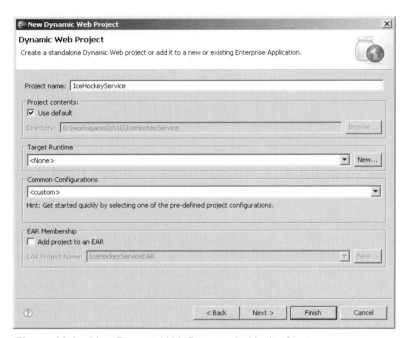

Figure 10.1   New Dynamic Web Project—IceHockeyService

Example 10.1   Listing of schedule.xml

```
<?xml version="1.0" encoding="UTF-8"?>
<schedule scheduleId="1"
  xmlns="http://leagueplanet.com/resource/schedule"
  xmlns:xsi="http://www.w3.org/2001/XMLSchema-instance"
  xsi:schemaLocation="http://leagueplanet.com/resource/schedule schedule.xsd">
  <name>2005-2006 Regular Season</name>
  <league leagueId="1">
    <name>Rosehill Girls Hockey League</name>
  </league>
  <games>
    <game gameId="1">
    <dateTime>2006-01-07T19:00:00-05:00</dateTime>
      <arena locationId="1">
        <name>Hillview High School</name>
        <timeZone>Canada/Eastern</timeZone>
      </arena>
      <visitor teamId="1">
        <name>Ladybugs</name>
      </visitor>
```

```
        <home teamId="2">
          <name>Vixens</name>
        </home>
        <score>
          <visitor>3</visitor>
          <home>7</home>
        </score>
      </game>
        .
        .
        .
      <game gameId="7">
        <dateTime>2006-01-22T19:30:00-05:00</dateTime>
        <arena locationId="2">
          <name>Maple Community Centre</name>
          <timeZone>Canada/Eastern</timeZone>
        </arena>
        <visitor teamId="3">
          <name>Snowflakes</name>
        </visitor>
        <home teamId="2">
          <name>Vixens</name>
        </home>
        <score>
          <visitor>2</visitor>
          <home>6</home>
        </score>
      </game>
    </games>
</schedule>
```

Note that in this format, the XML attributes are given names like `scheduleId` and `gameId` instead of `id`, which is the name of the corresponding property in the Java model. The reason is that the XML attribute `id` is often used to represent a unique identifier for elements within an XML document, which is not the case here. We therefore use different names to avoid confusion.

Also note that this XML format differs from the format you used earlier (see Example 7.9 in Chapter 7). Here you have refined the format to take advantage of the XSD type system. The date and time information is represented using the standard XSD date format instead of a pair of textual strings. The score information is represented using a pair of XSD integers instead of combined into a textual string. By using built-in XSD types, you are letting the XML parsers and validators do more work for you. You are also giving more precise information about the format of schedules to users of your Web service.

3. Create a new XML Schema file named `schedule.xsd` in `IceHockeyService` (see Figure 10.2).

Figure 10.2   New XML Schema File—schedule.xsd

4. In general, there are many equivalent ways to describe a given format using XSD. For Web services, it's a good practice to describe formats in a way that works well with XML data binding toolkits such as JAX-RPC and JAX-WS. Define complex types for the content model of each element. The XSD editor lets you edit in the source tab, the graphical tab, the outline view, and the property view. Try to develop `schedule.xsd` yourself. Import

    `IceHockeyService/schedule.xsd`

    before proceeding (see Example 10.2).

Example 10.2   Listing of schedule.xsd

```
<?xml version="1.0" encoding="UTF-8"?>
<schema xmlns="http://www.w3.org/2001/XMLSchema"
  targetNamespace="http://leagueplanet.com/resource/schedule"
  xmlns:tns="http://leagueplanet.com/resource/schedule"
  elementFormDefault="qualified">

  <element name="schedule" type="tns:ScheduleType" />

  <complexType name="ScheduleContent">
```

```
    <sequence>
      <element name="schedule" type="tns:ScheduleType" />
    </sequence>
  </complexType>

  <complexType name="ScheduleType">
    <sequence>
      <element name="name" type="string" />
      <element name="league" type="tns:LeagueResourceType" />
      <element name="games" type="tns:GamesType" />
    </sequence>
    <attribute name="scheduleId" type="long" />
  </complexType>

  <complexType name="LeagueResourceType">
    <sequence>
      <element name="name" type="string" />
    </sequence>
    <attribute name="leagueId" type="long" />
  </complexType>


  <complexType name="LocationResourceType">
    <sequence>
      <element name="name" type="string" />
      <element name="timeZone" type="string" />
    </sequence>
    <attribute name="locationId" type="long" />
  </complexType>

  <complexType name="TeamResourceType">
    <sequence>
      <element name="name" type="string" />
    </sequence>
    <attribute name="teamId" type="long" />
  </complexType>

  <complexType name="GamesType">
    <sequence>
      <element name="game" type="tns:GameType" minOccurs="0"
        maxOccurs="unbounded" />
    </sequence>
  </complexType>

  <complexType name="GameType">
    <sequence>
      <element name="dateTime" type="dateTime" />
      <element name="arena" type="tns:LocationResourceType" />
      <element name="visitor" type="tns:TeamResourceType" />
      <element name="home" type="tns:TeamResourceType" />
      <element name="score" type="tns:ScoreType" />
    </sequence>
    <attribute name="gameId" type="long" />
  </complexType>
```

```
<complexType name="ScoreType">
  <sequence>
    <element name="visitor" type="int" />
    <element name="home" type="int" />
  </sequence>
</complexType>

</schema>
```

5. The XSD editor provides two types of graphical views. The first is an overview of the entire schema. This view acts like a visual table of contents. It arranges the definitions in the schema into the main top-level categories such as global element declarations and type definitions. View schedule.xsd in the **Graph** tab of the XSD editor (see Figure 10.3).

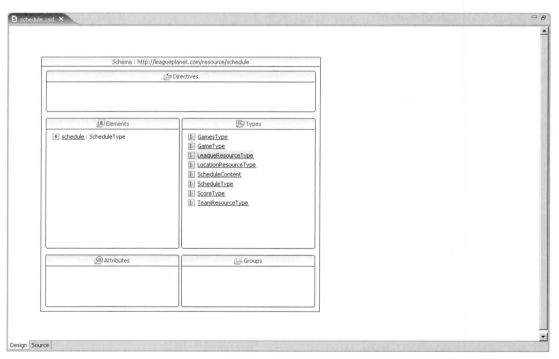

Figure 10.3   Graphical View of schedule.xsd

6. The second type of graphical view is the detailed structure of an element declaration or type definition. View the scheduleContent complex type definition in the **Graph** tab of the XSD editor (see Figure 10.4).

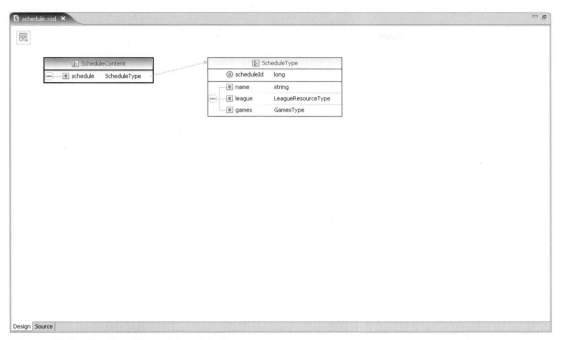

Figure 10.4 Graphical View of ScheduleContent

7. The XSD editor is linked to an outline view. You can edit the schema from this view. View `schedule.xsd` in the **Outline** view of XSD editor (see Figure 10.5).

WSDL

Now that you've described the message format using XSD, your next goal is to describe a Web service for retrieving it. For simplicity, the Web service will have a single operation named `getSchedule`. The operation will take the schedule id as input and return the corresponding schedule document as output.

1. Create a new WSDL file named `query.wsdl` in `IceHockeyService` (see Figure 10.6).

2. Enter the namespace

   `http://leagueplanet.com/ws/query/`

   for the WSDL and have the wizard generate a skeleton document for you using the SOAP binding and document/literal style (see Figure 10.7).

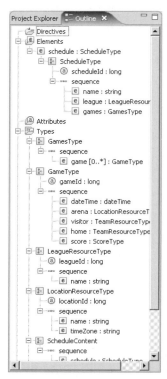

Figure 10.5   Outline View of schedule.xsd

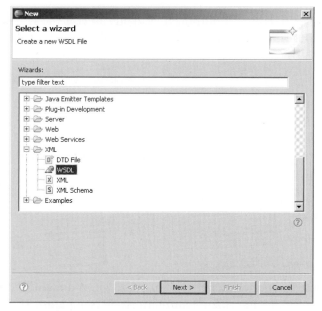

Figure 10.6   New WSDL File—query.wsdl

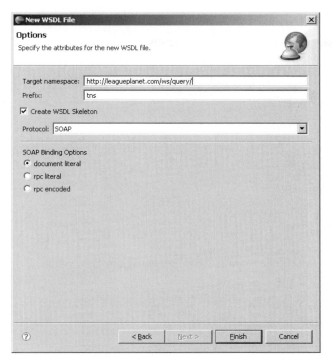

Figure 10.7 New WSDL File Options

3. You can edit the document in the graph tab, the source tab, the outline view, and the property view. WSDL describes Web services using a hierarchy of constructs: message, portType, binding, and service. The editor has a wizard that generates binding content for you. Try to develop `query.wsdl` yourself. Import

```
IceHockeyService/query.wsd
```

before proceeding (see Example 10.3).

Example 10.3 Listing of query.wsdl

```
<?xml version="1.0" encoding="UTF-8"?>
<wsdl:definitions xmlns:soap="http://schemas.xmlsoap.org/wsdl/soap/"
  xmlns:tns="http://leagueplanet.com/ws/query/"
  xmlns:schema="http://leagueplanet.com/message/query/"
  xmlns:wsdl="http://schemas.xmlsoap.org/wsdl/"
  xmlns:xsd="http://www.w3.org/2001/XMLSchema" name="query"
  targetNamespace="http://leagueplanet.com/ws/query/">
  <wsdl:types>
    <xsd:schema
      targetNamespace="http://leagueplanet.com/message/query/"
```

```
        xmlns:xsd="http://www.w3.org/2001/XMLSchema"
        xmlns:tns="http://leagueplanet.com/message/query/"
        xmlns:s="http://leagueplanet.com/resource/schedule">
        <xsd:import
          namespace="http://leagueplanet.com/resource/schedule"
          schemaLocation="schedule.xsd" />
        <xsd:element name="getScheduleRequest">
          <xsd:complexType>
            <xsd:sequence>
              <xsd:element name="scheduleId"
                type="xsd:long">
              </xsd:element>
            </xsd:sequence>
          </xsd:complexType>
        </xsd:element>
        <xsd:element name="getScheduleResponse"
          type="s:ScheduleContent" />
      </xsd:schema>
    </wsdl:types>
    <wsdl:message name="getScheduleInput">
      <wsdl:part element="schema:getScheduleRequest" name="request" />
    </wsdl:message>
    <wsdl:message name="getScheduleOutput">
      <wsdl:part element="schema:getScheduleResponse" name="response" />
    </wsdl:message>
    <wsdl:portType name="QueryInterface">
      <wsdl:operation name="getSchedule">
        <wsdl:input message="tns:getScheduleInput" />
        <wsdl:output message="tns:getScheduleOutput" />
      </wsdl:operation>
    </wsdl:portType>
    <wsdl:binding name="QuerySOAP" type="tns:QueryInterface">
      <soap:binding style="document"
        transport="http://schemas.xmlsoap.org/soap/http" />
      <wsdl:operation name="getSchedule">
        <soap:operation
          soapAction="http://www.leagueplanet.com/ws/query/getSchedule" />
        <wsdl:input>
          <soap:body use="literal" parts="request" />
        </wsdl:input>
        <wsdl:output>
          <soap:body use="literal" parts="response" />
        </wsdl:output>
      </wsdl:operation>
    </wsdl:binding>
    <wsdl:service name="QueryService">
      <wsdl:port binding="tns:QuerySOAP" name="QuerySOAPPort">
        <soap:address location="http://www.example.org/" />
      </wsdl:port>
    </wsdl:service>
  </wsdl:definitions>
```

4. View query.wsdl in the **Design** tab of the WSDL editor (see Figure 10.8).

5. View query.wsdl in the **Outline** view of the WSDL editor (see Figure 10.9).

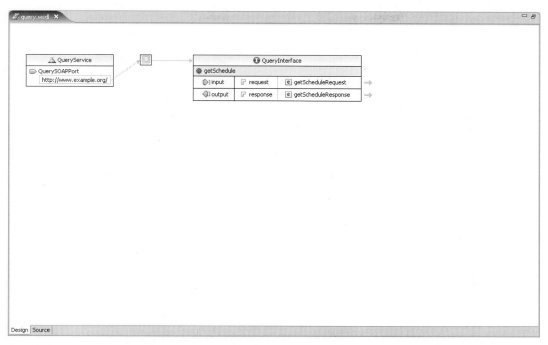

Figure 10.8 WSDL Editor Graph Tab—query.wsdl

Figure 10.9 WSDL Editor Outline View—query.wsdl

Deploying Web Services

WTP provides a Web service wizard to simplify the task of deploying Web services. In the Top-Down approach, the WSDL document is used to define a Java server skeleton that implements the Web service. The Java server skeleton is deployed in a Web application. The wizard also sets up the Web application, copies a SOAP engine into it, Apache Axis for example, and generates any required deployment descriptors. All you need to do then is fill in the implementation of the Java server skeleton with the business logic of the Web service.

1. You have now described the Web service. Your next goal is to deploy it. This step assumes you have previously installed Tomcat and added it to WTP. Select query.wsdl and execute the command **Web Services ▸ Generate Java bean skeleton**. This command launches the **Web service** wizard (see Figure 10.10).

   Pull the **Web service** slider up to the **Start service** position.

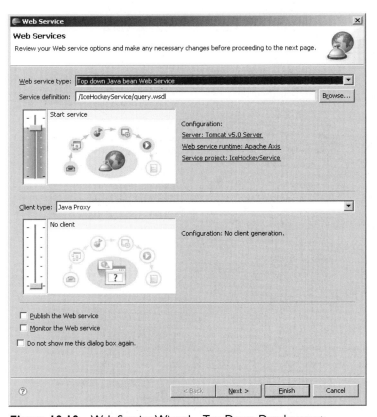

Figure 10.10   Web Service Wizard—Top-Down Development

2. Since you selected query.wsdl when you started the wizard, it appears as the **Service definition**. You can select a different WSDL file at this point by clicking the **Browse** button, which opens the **Select Service Definition** dialog (see Figure 10.11). Click the **OK** button to keep query.wsdl here.

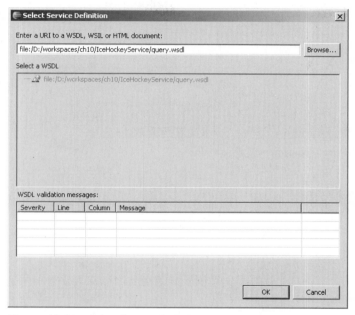

Figure 10.11   Select Service Definition

3. The wizard selects Axis and Tomcat by default, which is what you'll use here. To change these, click the **Server** or **Web service runtime** links, which open the **Service Deployment Configuration** dialog (see Figure 10.12). Click the **OK** button to dismiss the dialog and keep the current selections.

4. The wizard assumes that you are deploying the service to the same project as the WSDL file. To change this, click the **Service project** link, which opens the **Specify Service Project Settings** dialog (see Figure 10.13). Click the **OK** button to keep IceHockeyService.

5. Click the **Next** button to proceed. The wizard lets you select a source folder and change the package name for the generated Java skeleton (see Figure 10.14).

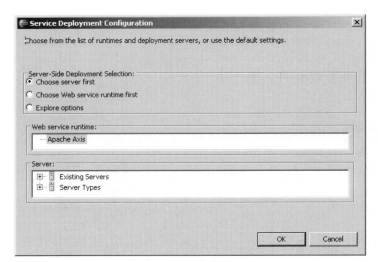

Figure 10.12   Service Deployment Configuration

Figure 10.13   Specify Service Project Settings

6. Click the **Next** button to proceed. The wizard is now ready to generate the code and deploy the Web service. The server must be started to complete this step (see Figure 10.15).

7. Click the **Start server** button, wait until the server starts, and then click **Next**. The Web service is now deployed. Finally, the wizard lets you publish the WSDL to UDDI (see Figure 10.16). Just click **Finish**.

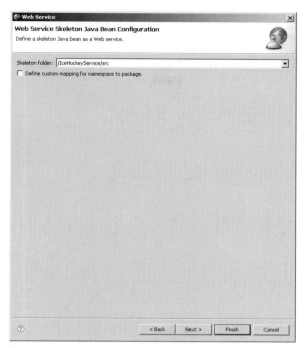

Figure 10.14 Web Service Skeleton Java Bean Configuration

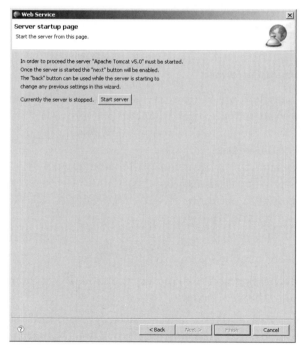

Figure 10.15 Web Service Wizard—Server startup page

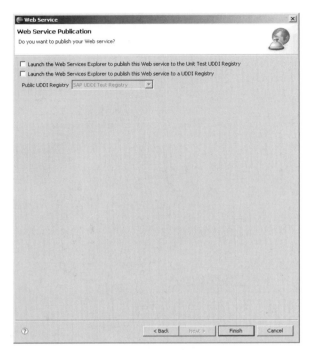

Figure 10.16　Web Service Publication

Steps the Web Service Wizard Performed

You probably noticed that there are a lot of steps involved in deploying a Web service. Fortunately, the **Web service** wizard handles all of these steps for you. In fact, if you are happy with the default behavior, you can simply click the **Finish** button on the first page of the wizard.

You can also avoid using the wizard altogether and use an Ant task that WTP provides instead. The Ant task is handy when you find yourself repeatedly using the wizard to redeploy a modified WSDL file. Consult the WTP Help system for more information about the Web service Ant tasks.

The **Web service** wizard:

1. installed the Axis SOAP engine in your dynamic Web project,

2. generated the Java bean skeleton for your service, and lots of Java XML data binding classes in the `src` folder,

3. copied `query.wsdl` to `WebContent/wsdl/QuerySOAPPort.wsdl` and set its endpoint address to your Web application (it also copied `schedule.xsd`),

4. created the Axis deployment descriptor `WebContent/WEB-INF/server-config.wsdd`,

5. created a couple of handy Axis files to deploy and undeploy your Web service in a subfolder of `WebContent/WEB-INF`, and

6. started Tomcat to make your Web service available.

   To verify that the Web service is actually deployed and running, do the following:

1. Use the **Project Explorer** view to examine the `IceHockeyService` project after the wizard completed (see Figure 10.17). Note that the Axis runtime includes a servlet named `AxisServlet`, which lists the deployed Web services. Select the `AxisServlet` servlet and execute the **Run As ▸ Run on Server** command.

Figure 10.17   Project Explorer—IceHockeyService Project

2. Running `AxisServlet` opens a Web browser with its URL. View the list of deployed Web services (see Figure 10.18). Note that `querySOAP` appears in the list.

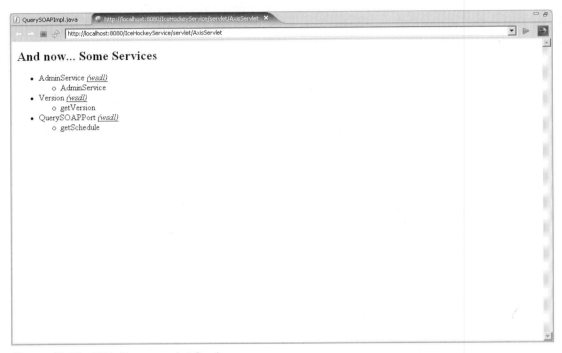

Figure 10.18   Web Browser—AxisServlet

Implementing the Web Service

The Web service is running but it just returns null at this point. Next, you need to fill in the implementation of the Java bean skeleton. The Web service needs to access the League Planet business logic tier.

1. If you have not previously done so, create a new J2EE utility project named `LeaguePlanetModel` and import the example source code from `LeaguePlanetModel/src` into it. Now, make this project available to the Web service as follows: Select the `IceHockeyService` project and open its **Properties** dialog. Add `LeaguePlanetModel` as a J2EE Module Dependency (see Figure 10.19).

2. View the module structure of the server in the **Servers** view (see Figure 10.20). Note that `LeaguePlanetModel` is shown as a dependent module of `IceHockeyService`.

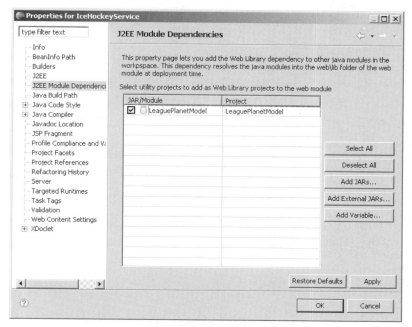

Figure 10.19 J2EE Module Dependencies—IceHockeyService Project

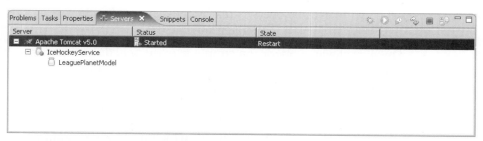

Figure 10.20 Servers View—IceHockeyService Project

3. You now have a Web service skeleton and access to the League Planet business logic tier. Your next goal is to implement the Web service. The generated skeleton class is

   `com.leagueplanet.ws.query.QuerySOAPImpl`

   Import

   `IceHockeyService/src/com/leagueplanet/ws/query/QuerySOAPImpl.java`

   now (see Example 10.4).

Example 10.4   Listing of QuerySOAPImpl.java

```
/**
 * QuerySOAPImpl.java
 *
 * This file was auto-generated from WSDL
 * by the Apache Axis 1.3 Oct 05, 2005 (05:23:37 EDT) WSDL2Java emitter.
 */

package com.leagueplanet.ws.query;

import com.leagueplanet.Query;
import com.leagueplanet.message.query.GetScheduleRequest;
import com.leagueplanet.resource.schedule.ScheduleContent;
import com.leagueplanet.ws.query.QueryInterface;
import java.rmi.RemoteException;

public class QuerySOAPImpl implements QueryInterface {
 public ScheduleContent getSchedule(GetScheduleRequest request)
     throws RemoteException {
   return new Query().getSchedule(request);
  }

}
```

4. This modified skeleton simply delegates to a new class

   `com.leagueplanet.Query`

   which will never be overwritten by the generated code. Create this new
   class now and try to implement it.

   The `getSchedule` operation simply gets the schedule object from the business tier and then copies it into an object required by the Web service.
   The Web service uses classes that were generated from `schedule.xsd`.
   This might seem like a waste of effort, but it has a couple of big advantages. First, the classes generated from `schedule.xsd` serialize precisely
   into the XML format you defined, which means that, unlike the situation
   for SOAP encoding, other programs can process it interoperably using a
   wide range of XML processing techniques. This is the main advantage of
   the document/literal approach. Second, you are now free to change the
   business tier model without breaking clients of your Web service. They
   are completely decoupled from your internal implementation. This is the
   meaning of loose coupling. Of course, if you change the business tier
   model, then you'll also have to update the Web service implementation.

   Import

   `IceHockeyService/src/com/leagueplanet/Query.java`

   before proceeding (see Example 10.5).

Example 10.5   Listing of Query.java

```java
/**
 * Query.java
 *
 * This class implements the query Web service.
 *
 * @author Arthur Ryman
 */

package com.leagueplanet;

import java.util.Arrays;
import java.util.Comparator;
import java.util.Iterator;
import java.util.Set;
import java.util.Vector;

import com.leagueplanet.message.query.GetScheduleRequest;
import com.leagueplanet.model.Game;
import com.leagueplanet.model.League;
import com.leagueplanet.model.Location;
import com.leagueplanet.model.Schedule;
import com.leagueplanet.model.Score;
import com.leagueplanet.model.Team;
import com.leagueplanet.resource.schedule.GameType;
import com.leagueplanet.resource.schedule.LeagueResourceType;
import com.leagueplanet.resource.schedule.LocationResourceType;
import com.leagueplanet.resource.schedule.ScheduleContent;
import com.leagueplanet.resource.schedule.ScheduleType;
import com.leagueplanet.resource.schedule.ScoreType;
import com.leagueplanet.resource.schedule.TeamResourceType;
import com.leagueplanet.services.IceHockeyFacade;
import com.leagueplanet.services.LeagueFacade;

public class Query {

  // use the ice hockey implementation for this service
  private LeagueFacade facade = IceHockeyFacade.getLeagueFacade();

  public ScheduleContent getSchedule(GetScheduleRequest request) {

    long scheduleId = request.getScheduleId();
    Schedule schedule = facade.findSchedule(scheduleId);

    ScheduleType scheduleType;
    if (schedule == null) {
      scheduleType = makeUnknownScheduleType(scheduleId);
    } else {
      scheduleType = makeScheduleType(schedule);
    }

    return new ScheduleContent(scheduleType);
  }
```

```java
private ScheduleType makeUnknownScheduleType(long scheduleId) {
  ScheduleType scheduleType = new ScheduleType();
  scheduleType.setScheduleId(scheduleId);
  scheduleType.setName("unknown schedule");
  scheduleType.setLeague(new LeagueResourceType("unknown league", 0));
  scheduleType.setGames(new GameType[0]);

  return scheduleType;
}

private ScheduleType makeScheduleType(Schedule schedule) {
  ScheduleType scheduleType = new ScheduleType();
  scheduleType.setScheduleId(schedule.getId());
  scheduleType.setName(schedule.getName());
  scheduleType.setLeague(makeResourceType(schedule.getLeague()));
  scheduleType.setGames(makeGamesType(schedule.getEvents()));

  return scheduleType;
}

private GameType[] makeGamesType(Set events) {
  Iterator eventIterator = events.iterator();
  Vector games = new Vector();
  while (eventIterator.hasNext()) {
    Object event = eventIterator.next();
    if (event instanceof Game) {
      Game game = (Game) event;
      GameType gameType = makeGameType(game);
      games.add(gameType);
    }
  }
  GameType[] gamesType = new GameType[games.size()];
  games.copyInto(gamesType);

  // sort the games by date
  Arrays.sort(gamesType, new Comparator() {
    public int compare(Object o1, Object o2) {
      long t1 = ((GameType) o1).getDateTime().getTimeInMillis();
      long t2 = ((GameType) o2).getDateTime().getTimeInMillis();
      if (t1 < t2)
        return -1;
      if (t1 > t2)
        return 1;
      return 0;
    }
  });

  return gamesType;
}

private GameType makeGameType(Game game) {
  GameType gameType = new GameType();
  gameType.setGameId(game.getId());
  gameType.setDateTime(game.toCalendar());
  gameType.setArena(makeResourceType(game.getLocation()));
```

```
        gameType.setVisitor(makeResourceType(game.getVisitor()));
        gameType.setHome(makeResourceType(game.getHome()));
        gameType.setScore(makeScoreType(game.getScore()));

        return gameType;
    }

    private ScoreType makeScoreType(Score score) {
        return new ScoreType(score.getVisitor(), score.getHome());
    }

    private TeamResourceType makeResourceType(Team team) {
        return new TeamResourceType(team.getName(), team.getId());
    }

    private LeagueResourceType makeResourceType(League league) {
        return new LeagueResourceType(league.getName(), league.getId());
    }

    private LocationResourceType makeResourceType(Location location) {
        return new LocationResourceType(location.getName(), location
            .getTimeZoneId(), location.getId());
    }

}
```

Testing with the Web Services Explorer

At this point the Web service is ready to test, and you will test it using the Web Services Explorer. The Web Services Explorer lets you test Web services without writing or generating any code. The Web Services Explorer accomplishes this by dynamically interpreting the WSDL for the Web service. You can test Web services that are deployed on your own machine or anywhere else on the Web.

The Web Services Explorer is itself a Web application. It runs in the embedded servlet container that Eclipse uses for displaying Help. The Web Services Explorer uses servlets and JSPs to generate its user interface, like any other Java Web application, but it is also integrated with Eclipse and can access the contents of your workspace.

Do the following to test your Web service:

1. Select

   ```
   IceHockeyService/WebContent/wsdl/QuerySOAPPort.wsdl
   ```

   and execute the command **Web Services ▸ Test with Web Services Explorer**. The Web Services Explorer will start and open a new Web browser in the editor area (see Figure 10.21).

   View `QuerySOAPPort.wsdl` in the Web Services Explorer. The Web Services Explorer user interface consists of three panes named **Navigation, Action,** and **Status**. The **Navigation** pane displays an object tree, which grows as you perform actions. The **Action** pane displays information about the currently selected object and lets you perform actions on it. The **Status** pane displays messages from the last performed action.

Click the **getSchedule** link in the **Action** pane to explore the getSchedule operation.

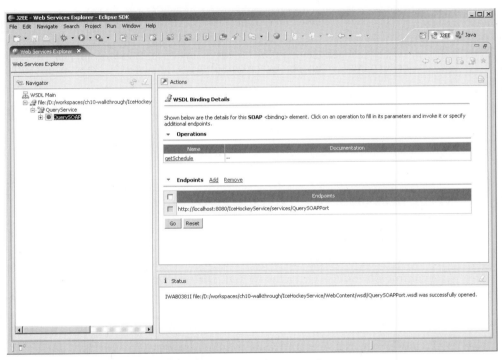

Figure 10.21   Web Services Explorer—QuerySOAPPort.wsdl

2. View the getSchedule operation (see Figure 10.22). To test the operation, enter 1 in the scheduleId field and click the **Go** button. The schedule is returned in the **Status** pane.

3. Double-click the **Status** pane title bar to maximize it (see Figure 10.23). The **Status** pane displays the response from the Web service formatted as a form that hides the XML detail. The request and response can also be displayed in raw source format. Click the **Source** link to view the messages as raw XML SOAP envelopes.

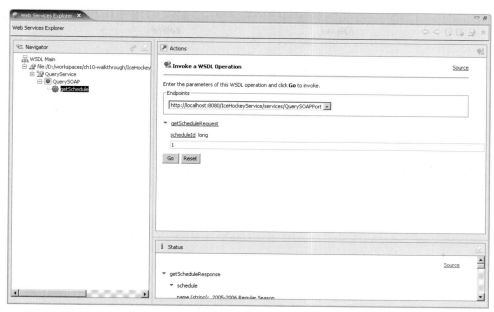

Figure 10.22 Web Services Explorer—getSchedule Operation

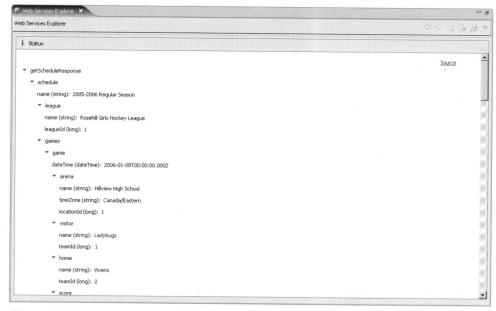

Figure 10.23 Message Form View—getSchedule Response

4. View the SOAP message source (see Figure 10.24). Click the **Form** link to return to the form display.

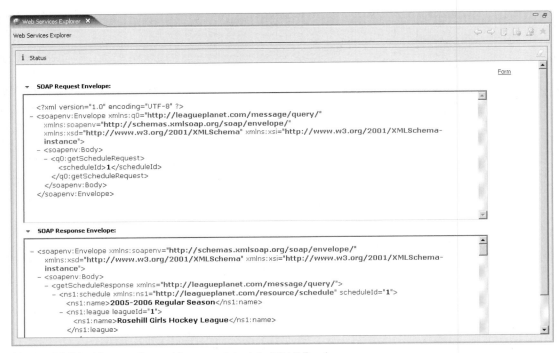

Figure 10.24 Message Source View—getSchedule SOAP Envelopes

Summary of Iteration 1

In this iteration you developed a Web service to retrieve League Planet schedules using the Top-Down approach. You designed an XML schema for the schedule using the XSD editor. You then used this schema in a Web service interface that you designed using the WSDL editor. You deployed the WSDL file to the Apache Axis SOAP engine using the Web service wizard and verified that it was running using the AxisServlet servlet. You then developed the implementation of the Web service using the League Planet business tier. Finally, you tested it, without creating any code, using the Web Services Explorer. You're now ready to design another Web service in iteration 2 using the Bottom-Up approach.

Iteration 2: Developing Web Services Bottom-Up

The Bottom-Up approach to Web service development begins with creation of a Java service class. The methods of the class define the operations of the Web service.

The argument lists and return types define the messages of the operations. After the service class is created, a tool is used to deploy it as a Web service and to generate the WSDL document that describes it. If changes are made to the interface of the class, the deployment and WSDL generation steps must be repeated.

The Bottom-Up approach lets Java developers become immediately productive at Web service development. No new XSD and WSDL design skills are required. Bottom-Up development results in good Web service interfaces when the Java service class uses simple data transfer objects as the inputs and outputs of its operations. However, if complex objects are used, then the resulting XSD may be hard to understand and less interoperable. There is also the risk of "bleed-through" from the implementation into the service interface, which results in undesirable coupling between the client and service. If the Web service interface changes whenever you change the implementation of the Java service class, then you will continually break your clients and largely defeat the benefits of Web services.

The best way to create a clean, stable, interoperable Web service interface is to design the XSD for the messages first, and use the Top-Down approach. The next best way is to design a simple data transfer object layer for use in the Java service class interface, and use the Bottom-Up approach. If you do use the Bottom-Up approach, be disciplined about not changing the method signatures of the Java service class. Confine your changes to the method implementations to avoid breaking your clients.

In this iteration, you'll do the following:

1. Develop a Java service class to get details about a game and to update its score.

2. Use the Web service wizard to deploy the service.

3. Use the WSDL editor to view the generated WSDL.

Develop the Java Service Implementation

1. The Java service implementation is in the `com.leagueplanet` package. Create this package now in the `IceHockeyService` project. You will create Java classes in the following steps. The complete source for these classes is available in the `IceHockeyService/src/com/leagueplanet` examples folder.

2. The `Update` Web service has two operations: `getGameDetail`, which retrieves the details of a game, and `updateScore`, which updates the score of a game. The `getGameDetail` operation takes as input the identifier of a game and returns as output the game detail. You therefore need to develop a simple data transfer class to store the game detail. Create the class

GameDetail and try your hand at designing it. Import GameDetail.java
before proceeding (see Example 10.6).

Example 10.6   Listing of GameDetail.java

```java
package com.leagueplanet;

import java.util.Calendar;

/**
 * This class contains detail about games. It is a simple JavaBean. It is
 * suitable for populating a data entry form.
 *
 * @author Arthur Ryman
 *
 */
public class GameDetail {
  private Calendar dateTime;
  .
  .

  .
  private int visitorScore;
  public Calendar getDateTime() {
    return dateTime;
  }
  public void setDateTime(Calendar dateTime) {
    this.dateTime = dateTime;
  }
  .
  .

  .
  public int getVisitorScore() {
    return visitorScore;
  }
  public void setVisitorScore(int visitorScore) {
    this.visitorScore = visitorScore;
  }
}
```

3. A well-designed Web service should carefully validate its inputs and throw
   informative exceptions if the inputs are invalid. Errors in inputs should be
   detected at the earliest possible opportunity to simplify the task of
   problem diagnosis. The operations of the Update Web service take the
   game identifier and score as inputs.

   Both the getGameDetail and updateScore operations take a game identifier as
   input. A game identifier is valid if it is the identifier of a game that exists in the
   database. Create the class GameException now and try to implement it. Import
   GameException.java before proceeding (see Example 10.7).

Example 10.7 Listing of GameException.java

```
package com.leagueplanet;

public class GameException extends Exception {

  private static final long serialVersionUID = 1L;

  private long gameId;

  public long getGameId() {
    return gameId;
  }

  public void setGameId(long gameId) {
    this.gameId = gameId;
  }

  public GameException(String message, long gameId) {
    super(message);
    setGameId(gameId);
  }
}
```

4. The updateScore operation takes as input the number of goals that the home and visitor teams score. The number of goals a team scores must be a non-negative integer. League Planet imposes the additional "mercy" rule that a hockey team cannot score more than 99 goals. Create the class ScoreException now and try to implement it. Import ScoreException.java before proceeding (see Example 10.8).

Example 10.8 Listing of ScoreException.java

```
package com.leagueplanet;

public class ScoreException extends Exception {

  private static final long serialVersionUID = 1L;

  private String team;

  private int score;

  public ScoreException(String message, String team, int score) {
    super(message);
    setTeam(team);
    setScore(score);
  }

  public int getScore() {
    return score;
  }
```

```
    public void setScore(int score) {
      this.score = score;
    }

    public String getTeam() {
      return team;
    }

    public void setTeam(String team) {
      this.team = team;
    }

}
```

5. Now that the data transfer object and exception classes are developed, you can move on to the service implementation. Create the `Update` class and design it as follows: Add `getGameDetail` and `updateScore` methods. The `getGameDetail` method takes as input a long `gameId` game identifier, throws a `GameException` exception, and returns as output a `GameDetail` data transfer object. The `updateScore` method takes as input a long `gameId` game identifier, int `visitorScore` and `homeScore` numbers of goals, throws both `GameException` and `ScoreException` exceptions, and returns nothing. The service accesses the League Planet business tier. Try to implement both methods. Import `Update.java` before proceeding (see Example 10.9). You've now developed all the required Java service implementation classes and are ready to deploy them using the Web service wizard.

Example 10.9 Listing of Update.java

```
/**
 * This class implements the update web service.
 *
 * @author Arthur Ryman
 */

package com.leagueplanet;

import com.leagueplanet.model.Game;
import com.leagueplanet.model.League;
import com.leagueplanet.model.Location;
import com.leagueplanet.model.Schedule;
import com.leagueplanet.model.Score;
import com.leagueplanet.model.Team;
import com.leagueplanet.services.IceHockeyFacade;
import com.leagueplanet.services.LeagueFacade;

public class Update {

  // use the ice hockey implementation for this service
  private LeagueFacade facade = IceHockeyFacade.getLeagueFacade();

  public void updateScore(long gameId, int visitorScore, int homeScore)
```

```
      throws GameException, ScoreException {
    Game game = facade.findGame(gameId);
    if (game == null)
      throw new GameException("Unknown game.", gameId);

    validateScore("visitor", visitorScore);
    validateScore("home", homeScore);

    game.getScore().setVisitor(visitorScore);
    game.getScore().setHome(homeScore);
  }

  private void validateScore(String team, int score) throws ScoreException
{
    if (score < 0 || score > 99)
      throw new ScoreException("Score must be between 0 and 99.", team,
          score);
  }

  public GameDetail getGameDetail(long gameId) throws GameException {
    Game game = facade.findGame(gameId);
    if (game == null)
      throw new GameException("Unknown game.", gameId);

    GameDetail gameDetail = new GameDetail();
    gameDetail.setGameId(gameId);
    gameDetail.setDateTime(game.toCalendar());

    Schedule schedule = game.getSchedule();
    gameDetail.setScheduleId(schedule.getId());
    gameDetail.setScheduleName(schedule.getName());

    League league = schedule.getLeague();
    gameDetail.setLeagueId(league.getId());
    gameDetail.setLeagueName(league.getName());

    Location location = game.getLocation();
    gameDetail.setLocationId(location.getId());
    gameDetail.setLocationName(location.getName());
    gameDetail.setLocationTimeZoneId(location.getTimeZoneId());

    Team visitor = game.getVisitor();
    gameDetail.setVisitorId(visitor.getId());
    gameDetail.setVisitorName(visitor.getName());

    Team home = game.getHome();
    gameDetail.setHomeId(home.getId());
    gameDetail.setHomeName(home.getName());

    Score score = game.getScore();
    gameDetail.setVisitorScore(score.getVisitor());
    gameDetail.setHomeScore(score.getHome());

    return gameDetail;
  }
}
```

Deploy the Service

Deploying a Java class as a Web service is the process of adding it to the SOAP engine's configuration. Some aspects of this process are standardized and others are implementation dependent. Fortunately, the Web service wizard makes deploying Java classes easy. You simply select the Java service class and run the wizard. The wizard lets you control many aspects of how the service is deployed, tested, and published. To deploy the Update class, do the following:

1. Select the Update class and execute the **Web Services ▸ Create Web service** command. The Web service wizard opens (see Figure 10.25). Note that the Web service type is **Bottom up Java bean Web Service** since the Update class was selected when you invoked the wizard.

   Ensure that the service slider is at the **Start service** position and that the client slider is at the **No client** position. You could click the **Finish** button at this point since the wizard picks sensible defaults. Instead, click the **Next** button to step through the wizard pages.

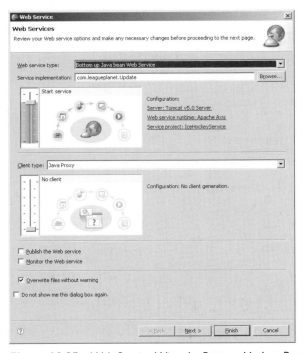

Figure 10.25   Web Service Wizard—Bottom Up Java Bean Web Service

2. The **Java Bean Identity** page appears (see Figure 10.26). The wizard lets you select the methods to include in the Web service interface. The wizard also lets you specify a name for the generated WSDL file and control several aspects of how the WSDL is generated.

One of the most important aspects of how the Web service is deployed is the *style/use* combination selected for the SOAP binding. The SOAP binding has *document* and *RPC* styles, and *literal* and *encoded* uses. *Document style* means that the SOAP body contains XML documents as children. *RPC style* means that the SOAP body conforms to a pattern that is used for remote procedure calls. *Literal use* means that the message content is literally described by the XML schema referenced by the WSDL document. *Encoded use* means that the message content conforms to the SOAP encoding specification and is only abstractly described by the XML schema referenced by the WSDL document.

Early SOAP implementations used the RPC/encoded combination, but this led to interoperability problems due to ambiguities in the SOAP encoding specification. The document/literal combination, with the additional WS-I recommendation that the SOAP body contain a single document child, is the preferred choice.

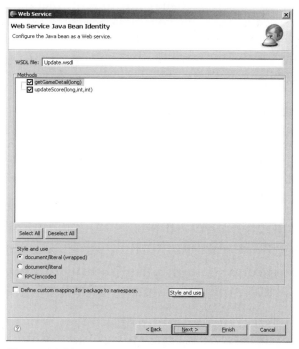

Figure 10.26   Web Service Wizard—Java Bean Identity

Although not formally specified anywhere, Microsoft introduced a pattern called *document/literal wrapped*, which can be used to generate a WS-I compliant document/literal WSDL document when deploying a service class in the Bottom-Up approach. In this pattern, the input message for an operation is composed of a document whose root element is the method name and whose child elements are the input parameters of the method. The output message is constructed similarly, except the root element is the concatenation of the method name and a `Response` string.

Use document/literal wrapped for the best possible interoperability and ease of consumption by clients. Toolkits that recognize this pattern can generate client proxies whose interfaces match the service interface. For a more complete discussion of the different styles and uses, see the highly informative article, "Which style of WSDL should I use?" [Butek2005] by Russell Butek.

The wizard also lets you explicitly specify the namespace of the generated WSDL document. Accept the defaults and click the **Finish** button. The wizard deploys the Web service and generates the WSDL. You're now ready to verify that the service has been properly deployed.

3. The `AxisServlet` servlet gives you a handy way to verify that the Web service wizard succeeded in deploying your class. Select the `AxisServlet` servlet in the **Project Navigator** and execute the **Run as ▸ Run on Server** command. The Web browser opens on the `AxisServlet` servlet (see Figure 10.27). Note that, as expected, the `Update` Web service is indeed now listed.

4. The wizard generated `Update.wsdl`, which is the WSDL document for the `Update` service. Open `Update.wsdl` in the WSDL editor and explore it (see Figure 10.28). Note that the interface for the Web service contains two operations that match the methods of the Java service class. Explore the XSD and look at the complex types generated for the `GameDetail` class and the exception classes.

Summary of Iteration 2

In this iteration you designed a Java service implementation, including data transfer object and exception classes, and then used the Web service wizard to deploy it as a Web service. This approach is called Bottom-Up Web service development. You used the `AxisServlet` servlet to verify that the Web service was deployed correctly. You also used the WSDL editor to explore the WSDL document generated by the Web service wizard.

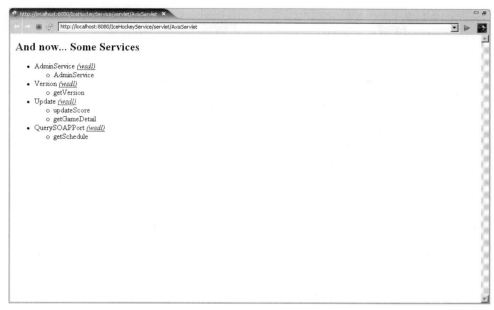

Figure 10.27 Web Browser—AxisServlet

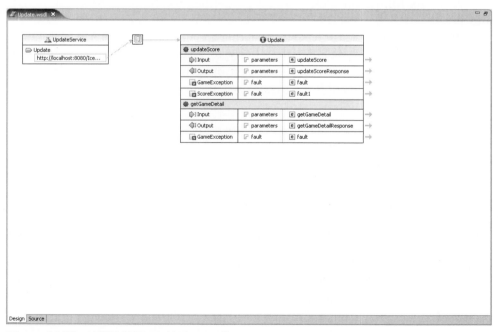

Figure 10.28 WSDL Editor—Update.wsdl

The Update service is now deployed and running. In the next iteration you'll use the Web service wizard to generate a Java client proxy that accesses the Update service.

Iteration 3: Generating Web Service Client Proxies

Web services can be invoked from programs written in many programming languages, including Java, C#, PHP, and JavaScript. Most languages have toolkits that support *dynamic invocation* of Web services and therefore do not require any code generation. Dynamic invocation is very useful for cases where the WSDL of the Web service is not known in advance. For example, the Web Services Explorer is a general-purpose tool that can dynamically invoke any Web service given its WSDL at runtime.

However, for most application development purposes, the interface of the Web service is known at development time, although the endpoint at which the service is deployed may not be known until runtime. Web service toolkits typically include a code generation program, for example, Axis WSDL2Java, that can generate a client proxy from a WSDL document. A client proxy simplifies Web service invocation by providing a class that resembles the service interface. In J2EE, client proxies are specified by the JAX-RPC specification as well as its follow-on JAX-WS, which defines the binding between WSDL and Java.

The Web service wizard lets you generate a client proxy from a WSDL document. The wizard also includes the ability to generate test clients so you can immediately test the proxy. You can inspect the generated test client source code and copy useful snippets of it into your own application. In this iteration, you'll do the following:

1. Use the Web service wizard to generate a Java client proxy and a JSP test client for the Update service.

2. Test the Update service using the JSP test client.

Generate a Java Client Proxy and JSP Test Client

The Web service wizard helps you access and test Web services. To access a Web service, you select its WSDL document and generate a client proxy for it. The wizard is extensible so that code generators for any language can be added. Here you'll use the WSDL2Java code generator that is part of Apache Axis. The wizard also has an extension point for test facilities. You've already seen the use of the Web Services Explorer for testing Web services. Here you'll use a code generator that creates a JSP test client that invokes the generated Java client proxy.

1. Select `Update.wsdl` and execute the **Web Services ► Generate Client** command. The **Web Service** wizard opens (see Figure 10.29). Pull the slider up to the **Test client** position and check the **Monitor** box.

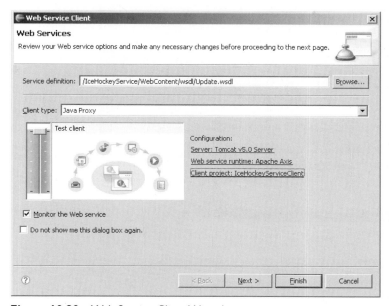

Figure 10.29   Web Service Client Wizard

2. You must generate the client proxy to a different project than the service to avoid filename conflicts. Click on the **Client project** link and set the output to be the project `IceHockeyServiceClient`.

> **Warning:**   Always generate the client proxy into a different project than the deployed service to avoid filename conflicts. If you generate the client to the same project as the service and the **Overwrite files without warning** checkbox is checked, then the wizard will silently overwrite the service, causing it to fail.

3. Click the **Next** button. The **Web Service Proxy Page** appears (see Figure 10.30). The wizard lets you change the source folder and package name for the generated client proxy code.

4. Click the **Next** button. The **Server startup page** appears (see Figure 10.31). Click the **Start server** button and wait until the server starts.

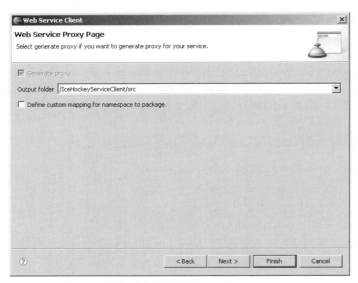

Figure 10.30 Web Service Proxy Page

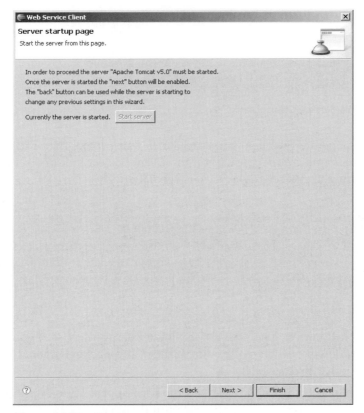

Figure 10.31 Server startup page

5. Click the **Next** button after the server has started. The **Web Service Client Test** page appears (see Figure 10.32). The wizard lets you select the operations to include in the generated JSP test client. Note that the `getGameDetail` and `updateScore` methods have the same names as the Web service operations. These methods let your application invoke the corresponding Web service operations.

The `getEndpoint` and `setEndpoint` methods let you modify the Web service endpoint at runtime. These methods come in handy if you have to change the port number so you can send messages through the TCP/IP monitor.

Finally, the `Update` method is used to access the underlying Web service. The wizard also lets you select a different output folder for the JSPs. Click the **Finish** button. The wizard now generates code and launches a Web browser on the test client.

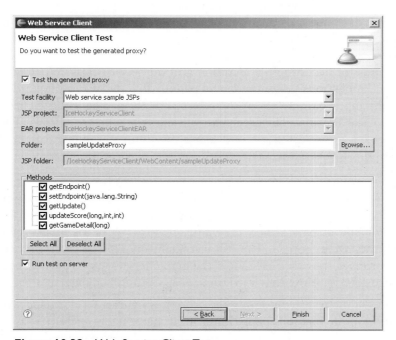

Figure 10.32   Web Service Client Test

Steps the Web Service Client Wizard Performed

The **Web service client** wizard did a lot of work for you. It:

1. created a new dynamic Web project named `IceHockeyServiceClient`,

2. installed the Axis runtime libraries in `IceHockeyServiceClient`,

3. generated Java proxy code, including XML data binding classes and exceptions, in the `src` folder of `IceHockeyServiceClient`,

4. generated JSP test client code in the new `sampleUpdateProxy` subfolder of the `webContent` folder of the `IceHockeyServiceClient` project,

5. started an instance of the TCP/IP Monitor and configured the JSP test client endpoint to use it, and

6. opened the JSP test client in a Web browser.

You are now ready to test the Web service.

Using the JSP Test Client

The JSP test client is a Web application that lets you test a Web service using a Java client proxy. The user interface of the JSP test client has a **Methods** pane, an **Inputs** pane, and a **Result** pane. The **Methods** pane lists the methods of the Java client proxy, which include the operations of the Web service and the convenience methods for accessing the endpoint and the service class. When you click a method in the **Methods** pane, the **Inputs** pane is updated to display a data entry form for the input parameters of the selected method. The **Inputs** pane contains **Invoke** and **Clear** buttons. The **Clear** button clears the data entry form. The **Invoke** button invokes the selected method using the input parameter values that are entered in the **Inputs** pane. The result of the invocation is displayed in the **Result** pane.

1. The Web service wizard opens the JSP test client in a Web browser. Start the test by getting the detail for a game. Click the `getGameDetail` method in the **Methods** pane. Enter the value `gameId = 1` in the **Inputs** pane and click the **Invoke** button. The JSP test client invokes the Web service and receives the response. View the game details in the **Result** pane (see Figure 10.33). Note that `visitorScore = 3` and `homeScore = 7`.

2. Continue the test by updating the score for a game. Click the `updateScore` method in the **Methods** pane. Enter input parameters `gameId = 1`, `visitorScore = 4`, and `homeScore = 2` in the **Inputs** pane and click the **Invoke** button. The operation returns an empty result (see Figure 10.34).

3. Finish the test by verifying that the score was updated correctly. Click the `getGameDetails` method in the **Methods** pane. Enter `gameId = 1` in the **Inputs** pane and click the **Invoke** button. View the updated score in the **Result** pane (see Figure 10.35). Now `visitorScore = 4` and `homeScore = 2`, as it should be after the update.

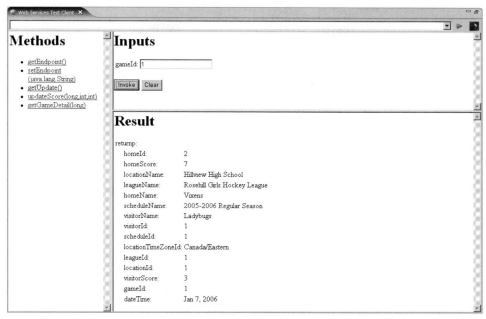

Figure 10.33 JSP Test Client—getGameDetail Before Update

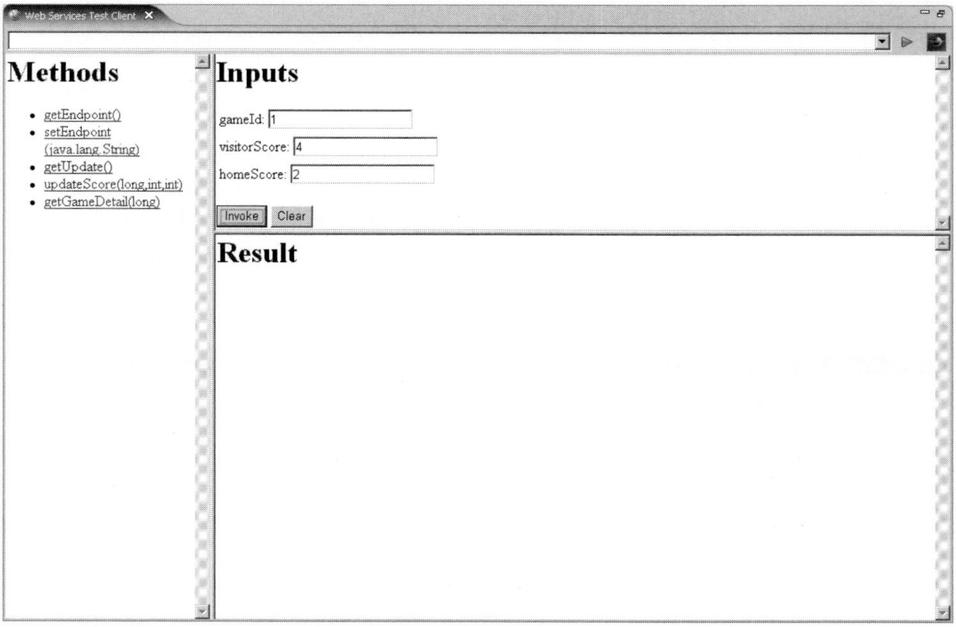

Figure 10.34 JSP Test Client—updateScore

Figure 10.35   JSP Test Client—getGameDetail After Update

Summary of Iteration 3

In this iteration, you used the Web service wizard to generate a Java client proxy to access the Update Web service. You also used the wizard to generate a JSP test client for the proxy. The wizard set up a TCP/IP monitor and configured the test client to use it. You then used the JSP test client to test the Web service.

All of the Web service messages that were exchanged during this testing session were captured by the TCP/IP monitor. You'll test these messages for compliance with the WS-I profiles in the next iteration.

Iteration 4: Testing Web Services for Interoperability

Web services are designed to enable heterogeneous systems to interoperate over the Web. For example, you may deploy a service on a J2EE application server and want both .NET desktop clients and PHP Web clients to be able to access it. Previous distributed computing technologies differed from Web services either because they were designed for homogeneous systems or they used proprietary protocols. For example, Java Remote Method Invocation (RMI) was designed to enable Java systems to interoperate, while Microsoft Distributed COM (DCOM) was designed for Windows to Windows communication. But the reality of the

Web is that there is no single dominant technology. The Web is composed of a highly heterogeneous combination of hardware, operating systems, and programming languages.

Web services achieve interoperability by using XML, which is an architecturally neutral text format. However, this interoperability comes at a price since textual formats are less efficient than binary alternatives. Therefore if Web services fail to interoperate in practice, then we have paid the performance penalty for nothing.

The interoperability of the first wave of Web services was, in fact, disappointing, largely due to ambiguities, errors, and omissions in the initial SOAP 1.1 and WSDL 1.1 specifications. These specifications did not go through the rigorous standards development processes established by the W3C. Instead, SOAP 1.1 and WSDL 1.1 were simply W3C Notes, which are specifications contributed by members. The follow-on specifications, SOAP 1.2 and WSDL 2.0, corrected these deficiencies. However, the industry could not wait for these revisions and instead created the Web Services Interoperability Organization (WS-I) to fix the problem. WS-I issued the Basic Profile (BP) 1.0 to establish interoperability guidelines. One of the key recommendations of BP 1.0 was to use the document/literal binding for SOAP. BP 1.0 was later split into two specifications, the Simple SOAP Binding Profile (SSBP) 1.0 and the Attachments Profile (AP) 1.0.

WTP includes WS-I Test Tools, which can validate HTTP SOAP messages and WSDL documents for WS-I compliance. These tools began life at WS-I as the reference Java implementation. They were then contributed to Eclipse as the Web Services Validation Tools (WSVT) Technology project. WSVT was created while the more comprehensive WTP top-level project proposal was being reviewed by the Eclipse Foundation. After WTP was approved, WSVT graduated into it.

Checking Messages for WS-I Compliance

The WS-I Test Tools include two main components. The first component is an extension to the WSDL validator. You can check a WSDL document for WS-I compliance by enabling the WS-I compliance preferences and then validating the document as usual. The second component is a message log validator. This component is integrated with the TCP/IP monitor. You can save the messages captured by the monitor into an XML log file and run the message log validator on it to check for WS-I compliance. You'll be validating messages for WS-I compliance in this iteration. The WSDL and message log validation and WS-I compliance levels are specified in the **Profile Compliance and Validation** preference page (see Figure 10.36).

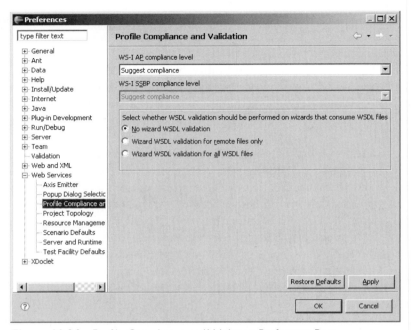

Figure 10.36   Profile Compliance and Validation Preference Page

1. Return to the Web browser with the JSP test client running in it, which
   you launched in the previous iteration. If you already closed the JSP test
   client, select the `TestClient.jsp` file in the *sampleUpdateProxy* subfolder of
   the `WebContent` folder in the `IceHockeyServiceClient` project, and execute
   the **Run as ▸ Run on Server** command to open it.

   Click the `getEndpoint` method in the **Methods** pane. Click the **Invoke** button in the **Inputs** pane. View the endpoint address in the **Result** pane. Note
   the port number on the endpoint URL, for example, 12302, instead of the
   usual 8080 for Tomcat (see Figure 10.37). This unusual port number is
   used by an instance of the TCP/IP monitor.

2. Open the **Preferences** dialog and select the **TCP/IP Monitor** page
   (see Figure 10.38). Note that the port number of the monitor matches the
   port number of the endpoint.

   You can use this **Preference** page to manage TCP/IP monitor instances. A
   TCP/IP monitor instance listens to some port on `localhost` and forwards
   the requests to another, possibly remote, host and port. You can manually
   configure the JSP test client endpoint address to use a TCP/IP monitor
   instance by getting the current endpoint using the `getEndpoint` method and
   setting it to match the TCP/IP monitor port using the `setEndpoint` method.

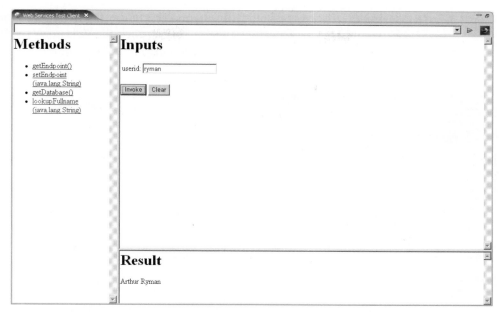

Figure 10.37   JSP Test Client—getEndpoint

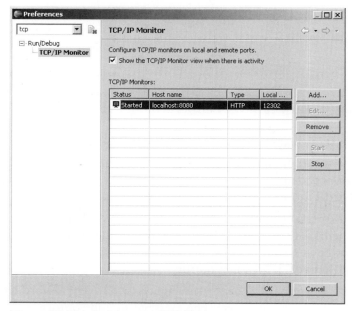

Figure 10.38   Preferences—TCP/IP Monitor

3. View the recorded messages from Iteration 3 in the **TCP/IP Monitor** view (see Figure 10.39). To validate the messages, click the **Validate WS-I Message Log File** icon ▤ (a document with checkmark) in the top right corner of the **TCP/IP Monitor** view.

Figure 10.39 TCP/IP Monitor—Update Web Service Messages

4. The **Validate WS-I Message Log File** wizard opens (see Figure 10.40). The messages are written into an XML log file. The wizard lets you select a folder to store the message log file. Select IceHockeyServiceClient and click the **Next** button.

5. The **Include WSDL File** page appears (see Figure 10.41). The wizard lets you optionally validate the message against a WSDL file. The messages should conform to the description in the Update.wsdl document. Select Update.wsdl and click the **Next** button.

6. The **WSDL Element** page appears (see Figure 10.42). The wizard lets you select the WSDL element to use. The message should conform to the description of the Update port element. Select the Update port and click the **Finish** button.

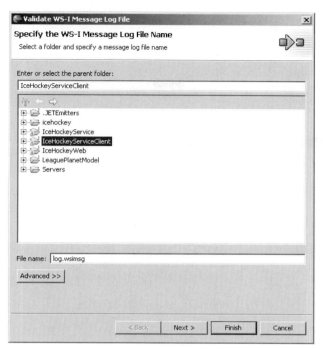

Figure 10.40 The Validate WS-I Message Log File

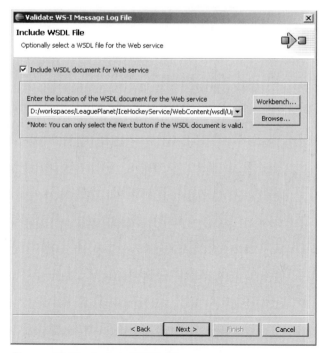

Figure 10.41 Include WSDL File

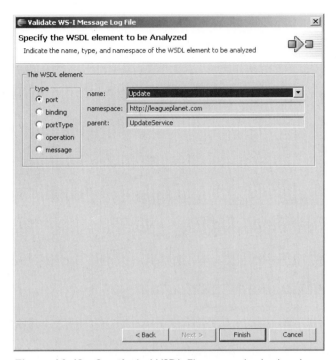

Figure 10.42   Specify the WSDL Element to be Analyzed

7. The wizard invokes the WS-I message log file validator and displays a success message since you selected WS-I compliant options when you deployed the Update class (see Figure 10.43). If the validator found errors, it would place markers in the generated log file and these would appear in the **Problems** view as usual.

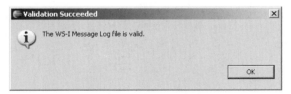

Figure 10.43   Validation Succeeded

Summary of Iteration 4

In this iteration you learned how to capture Web service messages using the TCP/IP monitor, control WS-I compliance levels and validation using preferences, and validate the message log file for WS-I compliance using the wizard. You now have a WS-I-compliant Update Web service running in the League Planet Web application and are ready to develop a client application that uses it.

Iteration 5: Using Web Services in Web Applications

Web services can be used in applications developed in many popular programming languages and technologies. You should adhere to the WS-I guidelines to ensure that your Web services are consumable by the widest possible range of clients. You should also design your Web services to use XML messages that can be processed by a variety of programming technologies such as JAXB, DOM, SAX, StAX, and XSLT.

Web services allow alternate user interfaces and applications to be developed. For example, even though League Planet provides a Web user interface to enter game information, a Web service interface lets other parties develop alternate, say, .NET desktop clients.

Web services also allow decoupling of the presentation and business tiers within an enterprise. For example, you could host the presentation and business tiers on different physical servers and drive the presentation tier off a Web service interface on the business tier. This decoupling allows the two tiers to be developed by different teams, at different times, using different programming technologies. For example, the business tier could be developed using J2EE, and the presentation tier could be developed using PHP or AJAX. The WSDL documents that describe the Web service interface on the business tier act like a contract between the tiers and insulate them from changes in implementation technology.

Java applications can use JAX-RPC or JAX-WS to access both Java and non-Java Web services. In this iteration, you'll develop a Java Web application for League Planet that accesses the Web service interface of its business tier.

In this iteration, you'll:

1. Generate a Java client proxy for the schedule Query Web service.

2. Develop a user interface based on JSPs and servlets.

3. Access the Web services from the servlets using the JAX-RPC programming model.

4. Run the Web application.

Generate the Query Web Service Client

Repeat the steps in Iteration 3 to generate a Java client proxy and JSP test client for QuerySOAPPort.wsdl. Run the JSP test client to verify that it is working correctly. You should now have two Java client proxies—one for updating scores and another for getting schedules—in the IceHockeyServiceClient project, which is where you will build the user interface for your Web application.

Create the Servlets

Your Web application will have two servlets, one to access the Update Web service and update the scores, and another to access the Query Web service and get the schedule information. Create these using the New Servlet wizard as follows:

1. Select the IceHockeyServiceClient project and invoke the New ▸ Servlet wizard. The class file destination page appears (see Figure 10.44). Create the servlet in the com.leagueplanet.ui package with UpdateScoreServlet as the class name. Click the Next button.

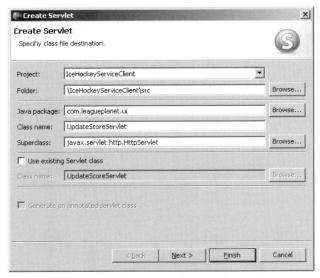

Figure 10.44   Create Servlet—Class File Destination Page

2. The deployment descriptor information page appears (see Figure 10.45). In the Description field enter Updates the score of a game.

   In the URL Mappings field enter /updateScore.

   In general, it's good planning to use URLs that don't reveal the implementation technology in case you want to change it later. See "Cool URIs don't change" [BernersLee1998] by Tim Berners-Lee for tips on how to evolve your Web site without breaking links.

   Click the Next button.

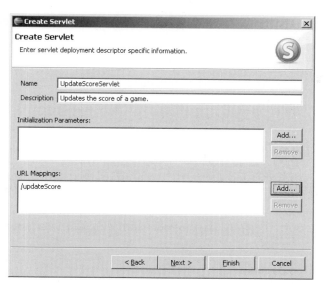

Figure 10.45 Create Servlet—Deployment Descriptor Information Page

3. The class structure page appears (see Figure 10.46). Check the doGet and doPost boxes. Click the **Finish** button. The wizard creates the servlet, updates the deployment descriptor, and opens a Java editor on the servlet class.

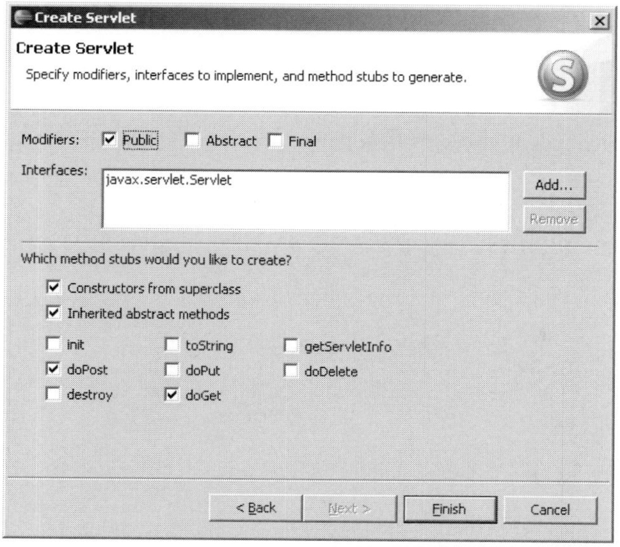

Figure 10.46 Create Servlet—Class Structure Page

4. Repeat these steps to create a schedule display servlet in the package
   `com.leagueplanet.ui`.

   Give the servlet the class name `ScheduleServlet`.

   Give it the description `Displays the schedule`.

   Give it the URL mapping `/schedule`.

Import the User Interface Code

The user interface is implemented using the techniques that were described in Chapter 7. The only notable new feature here is the use of the JAX-RPC programming model to access Web services, which we'll describe next. In this section, you'll simply import the fully developed example code into your project. Import the complete contents of the directory

`examples/ch10/iteration5/IceHockeyServiceClient`

into the project

`IceHockeyServiceClient`

The Java source code belongs to the package

`com.leagueplanet.ui`

and contains the following files:

- ❍ `GameForm.java`
- ❍ `ScheduleServlet.java`
- ❍ `UpdateScoreServlet.java`

The Web content is located in the subdirectory

`WebContent`

and contains the following files

- ❍ `schedule.css`
- ❍ `schedule.jsp`
- ❍ `score-confirmation.jsp`
- ❍ `score-form.jsp`
- ❍ `score-validator.js`
- ❍ `validator.css`

We'll discuss these files next.

UpdateScoreServlet.java

This servlet acts as a controller for the score form and confirmation JSPs. It also invokes the Update Web service (see Example 10.10; JAX-RPC programming model in bold font).

Example 10.10 Listing of UpdateScoreServlet.java

```java
package com.leagueplanet.ui;

import java.io.IOException;
.
.
.
public class UpdateScoreServlet extends javax.servlet.http.HttpServlet
    implements javax.servlet.Servlet {

  private static final long serialVersionUID = 1L;

  protected void doGet(HttpServletRequest request,
      HttpServletResponse response) throws ServletException, IOException {

    long gameId = getLongParam(request, "gameId", 0);
    forwardGameDetail(request, response, gameId, "/score-form.jsp");
  }

  protected void doPost(HttpServletRequest request,
      HttpServletResponse response) throws ServletException, IOException {

    long gameId = getLongParam(request, "gameId", 0);
    int visitorScore = (int) getLongParam(request, "visitorScore", -1);
    int homeScore = (int) getLongParam(request, "homeScore", -1);

    try {
      // call the Web service to update the game score
      UpdateService service = new UpdateServiceLocator();
      Update port = service.getUpdate();
      port.updateScore(gameId, visitorScore, homeScore);

      forwardGameDetail(request, response, gameId,
          "/score-confirmation.jsp");
    } catch (ServiceException e) {
      e.printStackTrace();
    }
  }

  private void forwardGameDetail(HttpServletRequest request,
      HttpServletResponse response, long gameId, String url)
      throws ServletException, IOException {
    try {
      // call the Web service to get the game details
      UpdateService service = new UpdateServiceLocator();
      Update port = service.getUpdate();
```

```
        GameDetail gameDetail = port.getGameDetail(gameId);

        // add the game details object to the session
        HttpSession session = request.getSession(true);
        session.setAttribute("gameDetail", gameDetail);

        // forward the request to the JSP
        ServletContext context = getServletContext();
        RequestDispatcher dispatcher = context.getRequestDispatcher(url);
        dispatcher.forward(request, response);

      } catch (ServiceException e) {
        e.printStackTrace();
      }
    }

    private long getLongParam(HttpServletRequest request, String name,
        long value) {

      String param = request.getParameter(name);
      if (param != null) {
        try {
          value = Long.parseLong(param);
        } catch (NumberFormatException e) {
        }
      }

      return value;
    }
  }
}
```

The doGet takes a gameId query parameter, calls the getGameDetail method of the Update service to get the game detail, puts the game detail object in the session, and then forwards the request to score-form.jsp, which displays a form.

The doPost takes gameId, visitorScore, and homeScore query parameters, calls the updateScore operation of the service to update the score, gets the new game detail, and then forwards the request to score-confirmation.jsp to confirm success.

Note the JAX-RPC client programming model in the doPost and forwardGameDetail methods. The UpdateServiceLocator class is instantiated to get an object that implements the UpdateService interface. This object represents an instance of the service. The getUpdate method returns an object that represents the Update port. This object has methods that correspond to the operations of the Web service.

score-form.jsp

This JSP lets you input the score (see Example 10.11).

Example 10.11 Listing of score-form.jsp

```
<%@ page language="java" contentType="text/html; charset=ISO-8859-1"
    pageEncoding="ISO-8859-1" session="true"%>
<!DOCTYPE HTML PUBLIC "-//W3C//DTD HTML 4.01 Transitional//EN">
<%@page import="com.leagueplanet.ui.GameFormat"%>
<html>
<head>
<jsp:useBean class="com.leagueplanet.GameDetail" id="gameDetail"
  scope="session"></jsp:useBean>
<title>Enter Score</title>
<link rel="stylesheet" href="schedule.css" type="text/css">
<link rel="stylesheet" href="validator.css" type="text/css">
<%
  GameFormat gameFormat = new GameFormat(gameDetail);

  long scheduleId = gameDetail.getScheduleId();
  String scheduleUrl = "schedule?scheduleId=" + scheduleId;
%>
</head>
<body onload="validateFields()">
<h1>Please enter the score for the game:</h1>

<script type="text/javascript" src="score-validator.js">
</script>

<form name="enterScore" action="updateScore" method="post"
  onsubmit="return submitScore()" onreset="resetValidators()"><input
  name="gameId" type="hidden"
  value="<jsp:getProperty name="gameDetail" property="gameId" />" />

<table>
  <tr>
    <th align="right">League:</th>
    <td><jsp:getProperty name="gameDetail" property="leagueName" />
    </td>
  </tr>

  <tr>
    <th align="right">Schedule:</th>
    <td><a href="<%= scheduleUrl %>"> <jsp:getProperty
      name="gameDetail" property="scheduleName" /></a></td>
  </tr>

  <tr>
    <th align="right">Date:</th>
    <td><%=gameFormat.getDateString()%></td>
  </tr>

  <tr>
    <th align="right">Time:</th>
    <td><%=gameFormat.getTimeString()%></td>
  </tr>
```

```
<tr>
  <th align="right">Arena:</th>
  <td><jsp:getProperty name="gameDetail" property="locationName" />
  </td>
</tr>

<tr>
  <th align="right">Visitor:</th>
  <td><input id="visitorId" name="visitorScore"
    value="<jsp:getProperty name="gameDetail" property="visitorScore" />"
    size="2" maxlength="2" onchange="validateVisitor()"> 
    <jsp:getProperty
    name="gameDetail" property="visitorName" /></td>
  <td><span id="visitorValidator" class="validator"></span></td>
</tr>

<tr>
  <th align="right">Home:</th>
  <td><input id="homeId" name="homeScore"
    value="<jsp:getProperty name="gameDetail" property="homeScore" />"
    size="2" maxlength="2" onchange="validateHome()"> 
    <jsp:getProperty
    name="gameDetail" property="homeName" /></td>
  <td><span id="homeValidator" class="validator"></span></td>
</tr>

<tr>
  <td colspan="2"> </td>
  <td>
  <button type="reset">Reset</button>
   
  <button type="submit">Submit</button>
  </td>
</tr>

</table>

</form>

</body>
</html>
```

The JSP has a **Submit** button to invoke the updateScore operation. It uses the CSS files you previously developed for League Planet to achieve a consistent look and feel for the application (see the Iteration 2: CSS section). It also uses the JavaScript validators you previously developed to check that the scores are valid (see the Data Entry Form Validation section). Note the hyperlink to the schedule display page. Also note the use of the GameFormat class. By putting the date, time, and score formatting in a Java class, it becomes reusable by other JSPs.

score-confirmation.jsp

This JSP confirms that the score update was successful (see Example 10.12).

Example 10.12   Listing of score-confirmation.jsp

```
<%@ page language="java" contentType="text/html; charset=ISO-8859-1"
    pageEncoding="ISO-8859-1" session="true"%>
<!DOCTYPE HTML PUBLIC "-//W3C//DTD HTML 4.01 Transitional//EN">
<%@page import="com.leagueplanet.ui.GameFormat"%>
<%<html>
<head>
<jsp:useBean class="com.leagueplanet.GameDetail" id="gameDetail"
  scope="session"></jsp:useBean>
<title>Confirmation</title>
<link rel="stylesheet" href="schedule.css" type="text/css">
<%
  GameFormat gameFormat = new GameFormat(gameDetail);

  long scheduleId = gameDetail.getScheduleId();
  String scheduleUrl = "schedule?scheduleId=" + scheduleId;
%>
</head>
<body>
<h1>The score has been updated successfully.</h1>

<form name="viewScore" action="updateScore" method="get"><input
  name="gameId" type="hidden"
  value="<jsp:getProperty name="gameDetail" property="gameId" />" />

<table>
  <tr>
    <th align="right">League:</th>
    <td><jsp:getProperty name="gameDetail" property="leagueName" />
    </td>
  </tr>

  <tr>
    <th align="right">Schedule:</th>
    <td><a href="<%= scheduleUrl %>"> <jsp:getProperty
      name="gameDetail" property="scheduleName" /></a></td>
  </tr>

  <tr>
    <th align="right">Date:</th>
    <td><%=gameFormat.getDateString()%></td>
  </tr>

  <tr>
    <th align="right">Time:</th>
    <td><%=gameFormat.getTimeString()%></td>
  </tr>
```

```
<tr>
  <th align="right">Arena:</th>
  <td><jsp:getProperty name="gameDetail" property="locationName" /></td>
</tr>

<tr>
  <th align="right">Visitor:</th>
  <td><jsp:getProperty name="gameDetail" property="visitorScore" />
    <jsp:getProperty name="gameDetail" property="visitorName" /></td>
</tr>

<tr>
  <th align="right">Home:</th>
  <td><jsp:getProperty name="gameDetail" property="homeScore" />
    <jsp:getProperty name="gameDetail" property="homeName" /></td>
</tr>

<tr>
  <td colspan="2"> </td>
  <td>
  <button type="submit">Edit</button>
  </td>
</tr>

</table>

</form>

</body>
</html>
```

It has an **Edit** button to let the user make further changes to the score. Note the hyperlink to the schedule display page.

ScheduleServlet.java

This servlet accesses the Query Web service to get the schedule information and forwards the result to the schedule JSP for display. It uses the Java convenience proxy generated by the Web service wizard to wrap the JAX-RPC programming model (see Example 10.13; Java convenience proxy is in bold font).

Example 10.13   Listing of ScheduleServlet.java

```
package com.leagueplanet.ui;

import java.io.IOException;
.
.
.

public class ScheduleServlet extends javax.servlet.http.HttpServlet implements
    javax.servlet.Servlet {
```

```java
    private static final long serialVersionUID = 1L;

    public ScheduleServlet() {
      super();
    }

    protected void doGet(HttpServletRequest request,
        HttpServletResponse response) throws ServletException, IOException {

      ScheduleType schedule = null;

      // get the schedule id from the request
      long scheduleId = 0;
      String param = request.getParameter("scheduleId");
      if (param != null) {
        try {
          scheduleId = Long.parseLong(param);
        } catch (NumberFormatException e) {
        }

      }

      // if the schedule id is valid, invoke the Web service
      if (scheduleId > 0) {
        try {
          QueryInterfaceProxy proxy = new QueryInterfaceProxy();

          GetScheduleRequest scheduleRequest = new GetScheduleRequest(
              scheduleId);
          ScheduleContent scheduleContent = proxy
              .getSchedule(scheduleRequest);
          schedule = scheduleContent.getSchedule();

        } catch (RemoteException e) {
          e.printStackTrace();
        }
      }

      if (schedule == null) {
        schedule = new ScheduleType();
      }

      // add the schedule object to the session
      HttpSession session = request.getSession(true);
      session.setAttribute("schedule", schedule);

      // forward the request to the schedule JSP
      ServletContext context = getServletContext();
      RequestDispatcher dispatcher = context
          .getRequestDispatcher("/schedule.jsp");
      dispatcher.forward(request, response);

    }
  }
```

schedule.jsp

This JSP displays the schedule information. Note the hyperlinks to the score update form (see Example 10.14).

Example 10.14   Listing of schedule.jsp

```jsp
<%@ page language="java" contentType="text/html; charset=ISO-8859-1"
  pageEncoding="ISO-8859-1" session="true"%>
<!DOCTYPE HTML PUBLIC "-//W3C//DTD HTML 4.01 Transitional//EN">
<%@page import="com.leagueplanet.resource.schedule.GameType"%>
<%@page import="com.leagueplanet.resource.schedule.LeagueResourceType"%>
<%@page import="com.leagueplanet.ui.GameFormat"%>
<jsp:useBean class="com.leagueplanet.resource.schedule.ScheduleType"
id="schedule" scope="session"></jsp:useBean>
<%
String name = schedule.getName();
LeagueResourceType league = schedule.getLeague();
GameType[] games = schedule.getGames();

String leagueName = league == null ? "unknown league" : league.getName();
String scheduleName = name == null ? "unknown schedule" : name;
String title = leagueName + " " + scheduleName;

int gameCount = games == null ? 0 : games.length;
%>
<html>
<head>
<meta http-equiv="Content-Type"
  content="text/html; charset=ISO-8859-1">
<title><%= title %></title>
<link rel="stylesheet" href="schedule.css" type="text/css">

</head>
<body>
<h1><%= leagueName %></h1>
<h2><%= scheduleName %></h2>

<% if (gameCount == 0) { %>
<p>There are no games in this schedule.</p>
<% } else { %>
<table>
  <thead>
    <tr>
      <th>Date</th>
      <th>Time</th>
      <th>Arena</th>
      <th>Visitor</th>
      <th>Home</th>
      <th>Score</th>
    </tr>
  </thead>
  <tbody>
```

```
<% for (int i = 0; i < gameCount; i++) {
  int row = i + 1;
  String rowClass = (row % 2) == 0 ? "even-row" : "odd-row";

  GameType game = games[i];
  GameFormat gameFormat = new GameFormat(game);
  long gameId = game.getGameId();
  String scoreUrl = "updateScore?gameId=" + gameId;
%>
    <tr class="<%= rowClass %>">
      <td><%= gameFormat.getDateString() %></td>
      <td><%= gameFormat.getTimeString() %></td>
      <td><%= gameFormat.getLocationName() %></td>
      <td><%= gameFormat.getVisitorName() %></td>
      <td><%= gameFormat.getHomeName() %></td>
      <td><a href="<%= scoreUrl %>"><%= gameFormat.getScoreString()
%></a></td>
    </tr>
<% } %>
  </tbody>
</table>
<% } %>
</body>
</html>
```

GameFormat.java

This class contains reusable formatting code for JSPs. It handles the game information returned from both Web services and applies consistent formatting rules to it (see Example 10.15).

Example 10.15   Listing of GameFormat.java

```
package com.leagueplanet.ui;

import java.text.SimpleDateFormat;
.
.
.
public class GameFormat {

  private String dateString;
  private String timeString;
  private String locationName;
  private String visitorName;
  private String homeName;
  private String scoreString;

  private final String DATE_PATTERN = "MMM d, yyyy";
  private final String TIME_PATTERN = "h:mm a";

  public GameFormat(GameType game) {
```

```
        LocationResourceType arena = game.getArena();
        String timeZoneId = arena.getTimeZone();
        TimeZone timeZone = TimeZone.getTimeZone(timeZoneId);
        dateString = formatDate(game.getDateTime(), timeZone, DATE_PATTERN);
        timeString = formatDate(game.getDateTime(), timeZone, TIME_PATTERN);

        locationName = game.getArena().getName();
        visitorName = game.getVisitor().getName();
        homeName = game.getHome().getName();

        ScoreType score = game.getScore();
        scoreString = score.getVisitor() + "-" + score.getHome();
    }

    public GameFormat (GameDetail game) {

        TimeZone timeZone = TimeZone.getTimeZone(game.getLocationTimeZoneId());
        dateString = formatDate(game.getDateTime(), timeZone, DATE_PATTERN);
        timeString = formatDate(game.getDateTime(), timeZone, TIME_PATTERN);

        locationName = game.getLocationName();
        visitorName = game.getVisitorName();
        homeName = game.getHomeName();

        scoreString = game.getVisitorScore() + "-" + game.getHomeScore();

    }

    private String formatDate(Calendar dateTime, TimeZone timeZone, String
pattern) {

        SimpleDateFormat dateFormat = new SimpleDateFormat(pattern);
        dateFormat.setTimeZone(timeZone);

        Date date = dateTime.getTime();

        return dateFormat.format(date);
    }

    .
    .
    .

}
```

schedule.css

This contains the previously developed CSS rules for the League Planet Web site (see Example 7.3).

validator.css

This contains the previously developed CSS rules for validation error messages (see Example 7.6).

score-validator.js

This contains the previously developed JavaScript score validation code (see Example 7.7).

Test the User Interface

1. Select the `schedule` servlet and execute the **Run As ▸ Run on Server** command. The Web browser displays a page titled "unknown league unknown schedule" because there was no `scheduleId` query parameter on the URL (see Figure 10.47).

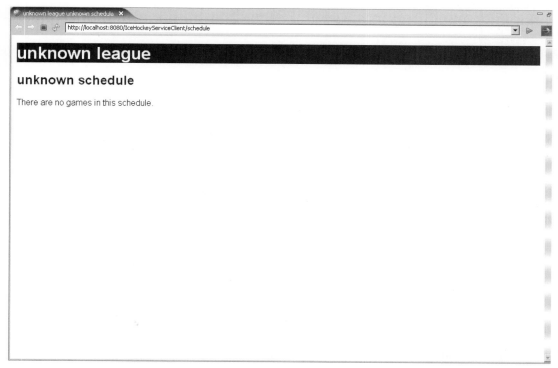

Figure 10.47 Unknown league unknown schedule

2. Append the query string `?scheduleId=1` to the URL in the Web browser and reload the page. This time the `schedule` servlet handles the GET request by calling the `getSchedule` operation of the `Query` Web service to get the schedule, adding the returned schedule object to the session, and then forwarding the request to `schedule.jsp` to display the result (see Figure 10.48).

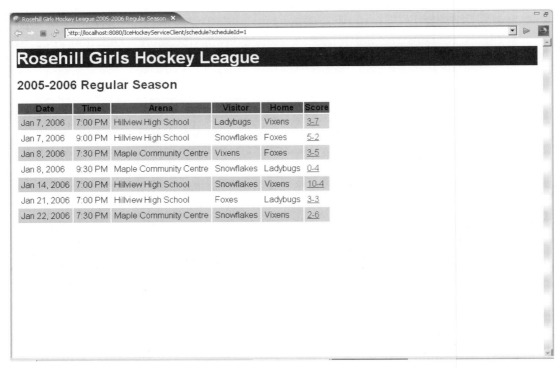

Figure 10.48   Ice Hockey Schedule

3. Note that the score for each game is hyperlinked. The score in the first
   row is currently 3-7. Click on the score to edit it. The updateScore servlet
   handles the GET action by calling the getGameDetail operation of the
   Update Web service to get the game detail, adding the returned game
   detail object to the session, and then forwarding the request to
   score-form.jsp.

   The score update form is displayed. Note that the schedule name is hyperlinked. If you click on it, you will be taken back to the schedule page.
   Change the score to 5-8 (see Figure 10.49).

4. Click the **Submit** button to update the score. The updateScore servlet handles
   the POST request by calling the updateScore operation of the Update Web
   service and then forwarding the request to score-confirmation.jsp to display
   the confirmation message (see Figure 10.50).

5. Click the schedule hyperlink to return to the schedule page. Note that the
   updated score, 5-8, is now displayed (see Figure 10.51).

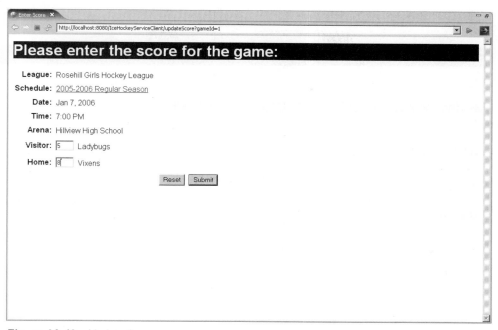

Figure 10.49 Update Score

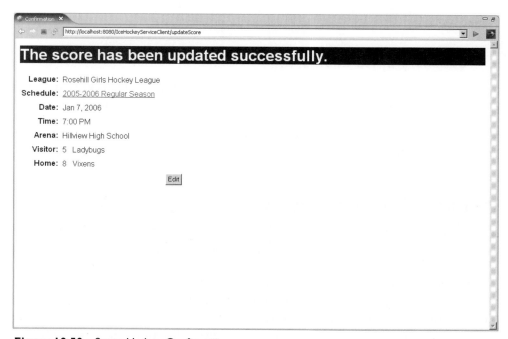

Figure 10.50 Score Update Confirmation

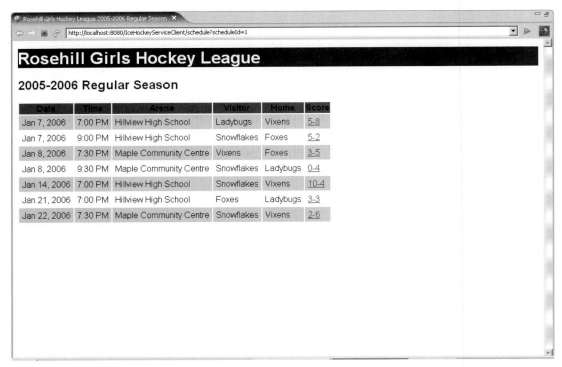

Figure 10.51   Ice Hockey Schedule with Updated Score

Summary of Iteration 5

In this iteration you created a client Java Web application that used the Query and Update Web services to display schedules and update game scores. You accessed the Web services using both the JAX-RPC client programming model and the convenience proxy generated by WTP. You are now ready to publish the League Planet Web services so that other application developers can easily find them.

Iteration 6: Discovering and Publishing Web Services

The Web started small. It was invented at CERN, a high-energy particle physics lab, as a way for scientists to share information. At first there was only a handful of Web sites, so finding what you were looking for was not a problem. Then the rest of the world discovered the Web and the number of sites exploded. The difficulty of finding information on the Web gave birth to indexers like Yahoo. Site owners entered descriptions of their content in a hierarchical classification scheme so Web surfers could do searches. This approach worked for a while, but as the number of sites grew and the rate of change of content accelerated, an automated approach was needed. Web crawlers such as Lycos were created to automatically transverse the Web and index the content of pages. Site owners could assist the Web crawlers by publishing metadata in `robots.txt` files, which listed the root pages to crawl. Today Google represents the pinnacle of Web-crawling technology. It's hard to imagine what the Web would be like without it.

This story is being replayed for Web services, although on a much smaller scale. Web service *discovery* is the task of locating Web services that perform a desired function and that satisfy other criteria such as quality of service or geographic location. For example, you may want to locate a flower delivery service that is located in Gladstone, Australia, so that you can send your mother-in-law roses on her birthday. Web service *publication* is the task of making information about a Web service available so that it can be indexed or searched.

In this iteration you will use two technologies for the discovery and publication of Web services: Universal Description, Discovery, and Integration (UDDI); and Web Service Inspection Language (WSIL), which is also referred to as WS-Inspection. UDDI is a registry technology that has programmatic interfaces for publishing and querying information about Web services. UDDI is therefore analogous to the original Yahoo index. WSIL is a simple XML file format for listing Web services. WSIL uses root XML files, named `inspection.wsil` by convention, that are analogous to the `robots.txt` files that guide Web crawlers. UDDI and WSIL are complementary in that a Web service crawler could automatically populate a UDDI registry using information retrieved from `inspection.wsil` files.

In this iteration, you will do the following:

1. Search a UDDI registry for Web services.

2. Browse a WSIL document that lists Web services.

3. Create a WSIL document to describe the League Planet Web services.

UDDI

The UDDI business registry standard was created in anticipation of the need to publish information about large numbers of Web services. With UDDI, Web service owners register and classify their services through a *publishing* interface. Developers or programmatic agents that are searching for Web services can then query UDDI registries through an *inquiry* interface. These interfaces are themselves made available as SOAP Web services.

UDDI registries typically provide a Web user interface that lets users manually publish and query Web service information. Developers can programmatically access UDDI registries through toolkits such as UDDI4J. The JAXR specification is the Java standard for access to UDDI and other registries. WTP provides the Web Services Explorer, which is a Web application based on UDDI4J that acts as a universal client to UDDI registries. The Web Services Explorer lets you flow Web service information seamlessly between UDDI registries and your Eclipse workspace.

It was further proposed that there would be a network of public UDDI registries, sometimes referred to as the *UDDI cloud*, that were linked to each other and that replicated information between each other. A Web service registered in one registry would be replicated to all other registries in the network. Therefore, any of the linked registries could be queried to locate any service no matter where it was initially registered.

Although the network of public UDDI registries was built, it did not achieve much market acceptance and has since been dismantled. Perhaps the number of publicly available Web services did not grow to the point where a registry was needed. Or perhaps the burden of registering services was too onerous. Maybe a scheme based on Web service crawlers would have succeeded. In any case, the use of UDDI now seems confined to within enterprises where it serves as a central place to register and locate in-house Web services.

Nevertheless, there is a very interesting publicly accessible UDDI registry at XMethods. This registry is not replicated with other registries, but it has become a place where many Web service developers advertise their work. To explore the XMethods UDDI registry, do the following:

1. Launch the Web Services Explorer by clicking its icon ▦ (the document) in the J2EE perspective or executing the Import ▸ Other ▸ Web Service command. The Web Services Explorer appears in a Web browser with the Open Registry page displayed (see Figure 10.52).

   The Web Services Explorer user interface is divided into Navigator, Actions, and Status panes. The Navigator pane displays an object history tree for either UDDI, WSIL, or WSDL. The Actions pane displays a form for the currently selected object. The Status pane displays the results of the last performed action.

   In the Actions pane, select the XMethods UDDI Registry and click the Go button.

2. The Registry Details page is displayed (see Figure 10.53). View the registry details. Click the Find link.

3. The Find page is displayed (see Figure 10.54). Enter Stock Quote Services as the name for the query. Search for Services. Enter a partial service name stock to search for and click the Go button.

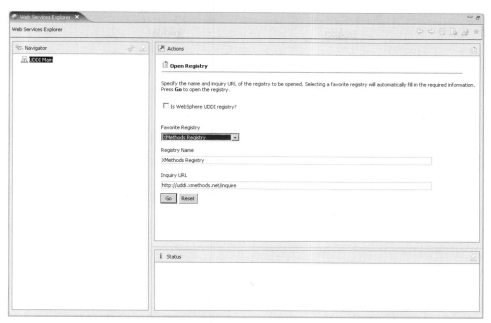

Figure 10.52   Web Services Explorer—Open Registry Page

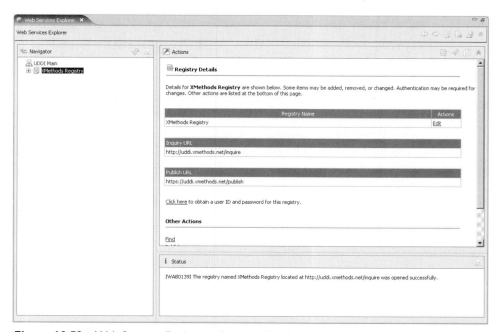

Figure 10.53   Web Services Explorer—Registry Details Page

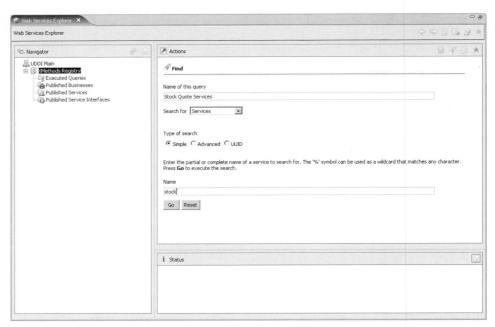

Figure 10.54 Web Services Explorer—Find Page

4. The **Query Results** page is displayed (see Figure 10.55). View the query results. Click the service links to explore the services. Click the link for the **Stock Quote** service and continue.

5. The **Service Details** page is displayed (see Figure 10.56). View the webservicex.com service details. Click the **Add to WSDL Page** icon (the one with the plus sign) in the top right corner of the **Actions** pane to explore the WSDL document for this service.

6. The **WSDL Service Details** page is displayed (see Figure 10.57). This page lists the bindings for the selected service. View the WSDL service details. Click the StockQuoteSOAP binding link.

7. The **WSDL Binding Details** page is displayed (see Figure 10.58). This page lists the operations for the selected binding. View the WSDL binding details. Click the GetQuote operation link.

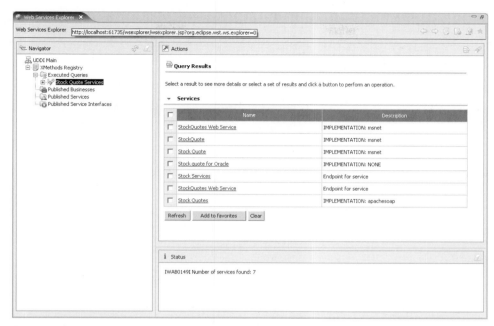

Figure 10.55   Web Services Explorer—Query Results Page

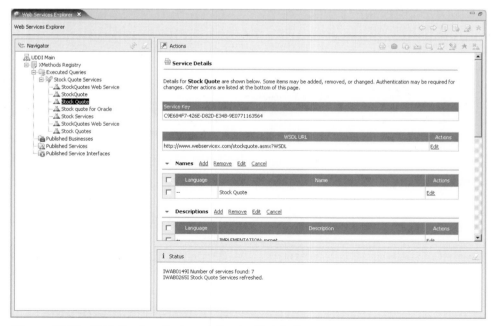

Figure 10.56   Web Services Explorer—Service Details Page

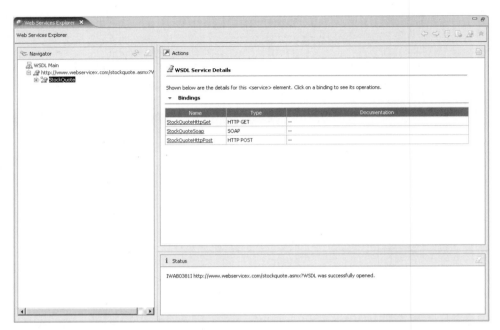

Figure 10.57   Web Services Explorer—WSDL Service Details Page

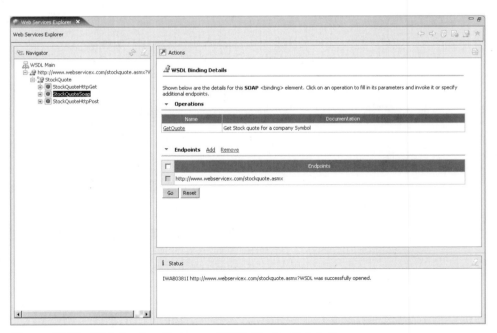

Figure 10.58   Web Services Explorer—WSDL Binding Details Page

8. The **Invoke a WSDL Operation** page is displayed (see Figure 10.59). This page lists the inputs for the selected operation. View the operation details. Click the **Add** link and enter a stock symbol. Click the **Go** button.

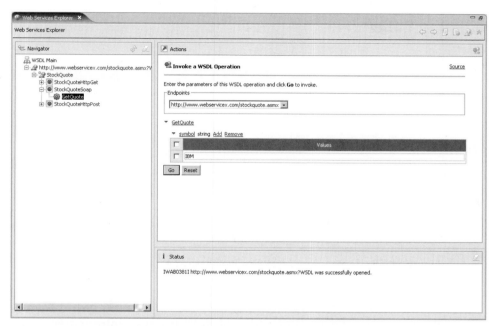

Figure 10.59 Web Services Explorer—Invoke a WSDL Operation Page

9. The Web Services Explorer invokes the operation and displays the result in the **Status** pane (see Figure 10.60). View the result of the operation in the **Status** pane. Double-click on the title of the **Status** pane to maximize it. Click the **Source** link to view the request and response SOAP messages.

WSIL

As you can see from the preceding exercise, UDDI is very complex. WSIL is a much simpler way to publish information about Web services. WSIL is an XML format that you publish on your Web site to advertise available Web services. WSIL documents can refer to WSDL, UDDI, and other WSIL documents. By convention, the root WSIL document for a Web site is named `inspection.wsil`. It can directly list all the Web services or point to subordinate WSIL documents. In the future, Web service crawlers might search the Web for `inspection.wsil` files and automatically index them in UDDI or other registries.

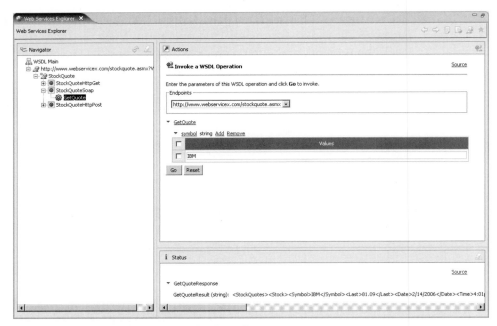

Figure 10.60   Services Explorer—GetQuoteResponse

WSIL was jointly developed by IBM and Microsoft, but Microsoft still uses the precursor DISCO format to publish Web service information. There is not a lot of WSIL deployed at present. However, XMethods supports it and several other Web service publication technologies.

In this part of the iteration you will use the Web Services Explorer to view a WSIL document published at XMethods. You will also use WTP to create your own WSIL document to publish the League Planet Web services. Do the following:

1. Open a Web browser and surf to

    http://www.xmethods.net

    The XMethods home page is displayed (see Figure 10.61). Look at the **Programmatic Interfaces** section, which lists UDDI, WS-Inspection, DISCO, RSS, and SOAP. These are the ways that XMethods publishes Web service information. Click the **Access** link.

2. The **Programmatic Interfaces to XMethods** page is displayed (see Figure 10.62). View the many access methods supported by XMethods. Copy the **WS-Inspection** link, which gives the URL to the inspection.wsil document.

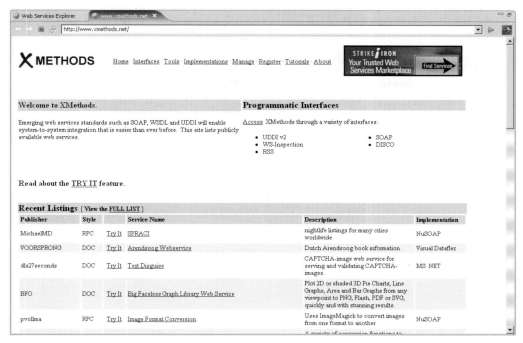

Figure 10.61   XMethods Home Page

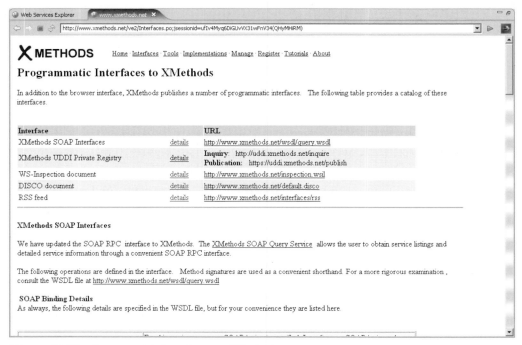

Figure 10.62   Programmatic Interfaces to XMethods

3. Click the **WSIL Page** icon 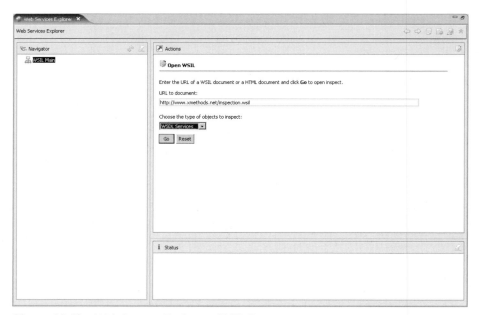 (the page with globe) at the top right corner of the Web Services Explorer to open the **WSIL** page in the **Navigator** pane (see Figure 10.63). Paste in the XMethods WSIL URL

   ```
   http://www.xmethods.net/inspection.wsil
   ```

   select **WSDL Services,** and click the **Go** button.

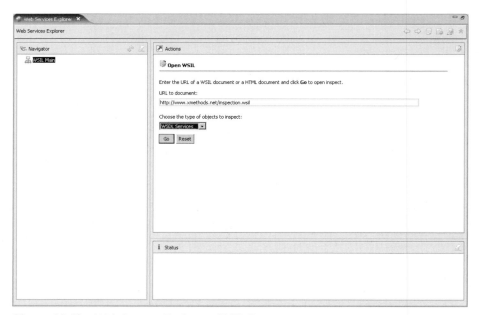

Figure 10.63   Web Services Explorer—WSIL Page

4. The **List All WSDL Services** page is displayed (see Figure 10.64). View the list of WSDL services registered at XMethods.

5. You are now going to create your own WSIL document for League Planet. Use the **New File** wizard to create a new `inspection.wsil` file in the `IceHockeyService/WebContent` folder (see Figure 10.65).

6. You will now use WTP to generate WSIL files for the two League Planet Web services and then merge them into the root `inspection.wsil` file. Select `QuerySOAPPort.wsdl` and execute the **Web Services ▶ Generate WSIL** command to create the `QuerySOAPPort.wsil` file. Repeat this for `Update.wsdl`. Merge the contents of these two generated WSIL files into `inspection.wsil` and add abstracts to describe them. Import

   ```
   IceHockeyService/WebContent/inspection.wsil
   ```

before proceeding (see Example 10.16). You now have a WSIL document for the League Planet Web site.

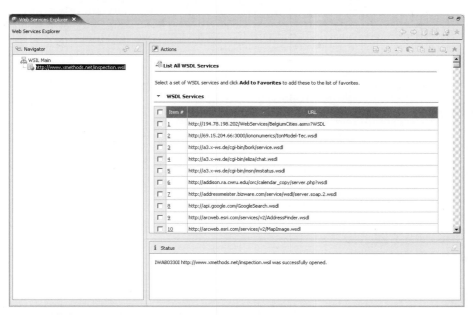

Figure 10.64   Web Services Explorer—List All WSDL Services Page

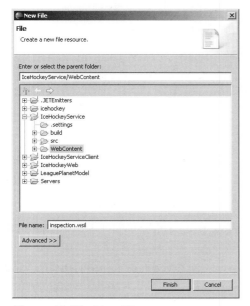

Figure 10.65   New File—inspection.wsil

Example 10.16   Listing of inspection.wsil

```
<?xml version="1.0" encoding="UTF-8"?>
<inspection xmlns="http://schemas.xmlsoap.org/ws/2001/10/inspection/"
  xmlns:wsilwsdl="http://schemas.xmlsoap.org/ws/2001/10/inspection/wsdl/"
  xmlns:wsiluddi="http://schemas.xmlsoap.org/ws/2001/10/inspection/uddi/"
  xmlns:uddi="urn:uddi-org:api">

  <service>
    <abstract xml:lang="en-US">
      This Web service lets you query the League Planet Web site
      for schedule information.
    </abstract>
    <description
      referencedNamespace="http://schemas.xmlsoap.org/wsdl/"
      location="wsdl/QuerySOAPPort.wsdl">
      <wsilwsdl:reference endpointPresent="true">
        <wsilwsdl:referencedService
          xmlns:impl="http://leagueplanet.com/ws/query/">
          impl:QueryService
        </wsilwsdl:referencedService>
      </wsilwsdl:reference>
    </description>
  </service>

  <service>
    <abstract xml:lang="en-US">
      This Web service lets you query the League Planet Web site
      for game details and update the scores.
    </abstract>
    <description
      referencedNamespace="http://schemas.xmlsoap.org/wsdl/"
      location="wsdl/Update.wsdl">
      <wsilwsdl:reference endpointPresent="true">
        <wsilwsdl:referencedService
          xmlns:impl="http://leagueplanet.com">
          impl:UpdateService
        </wsilwsdl:referencedService>
      </wsilwsdl:reference>
    </description>
  </service>

</inspection>
```

7. Enter the URL

   ```
   http://localhost:8080/IceHockeyService/inspection.wsil
   ```

   in the Web Services Explorer **WSIL** page, select **WSDL Services** and click **Go** (see Figure 10.66).

8. The **List All WSDL Services** page is displayed (see Figure 10.67). View the WSDL services available at League Planet. Click the `QuerySOAPPort.wsdl` link.

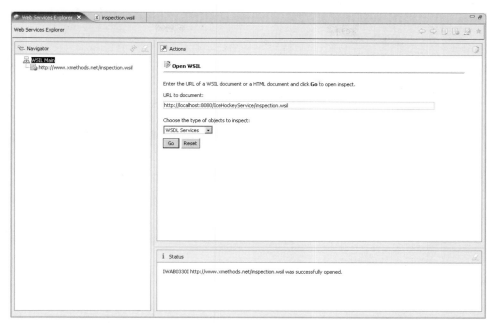

Figure 10.66 Web Services Explorer—Open WSIL for League Planet

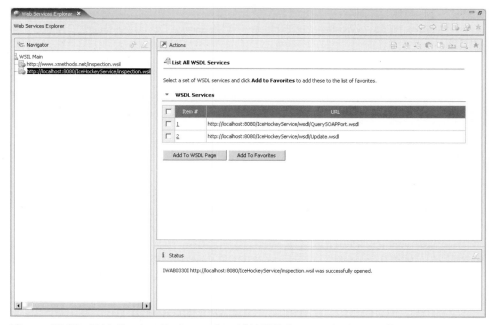

Figure 10.67 Web Services Explorer—List All WSDL Services for League Planet

9. The **WSIL Service Details** page is displayed (see Figure 10.68). View the `QuerySOAPPort.wsdl` details.

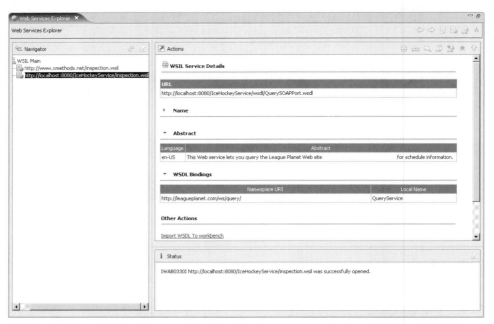

Figure 10.68   Web Services Explorer—WSIL Service Details for QuerySOAPPort.wsdl

Summary of Iteration 6

In this iteration you used the Web Services Explorer to view information published in a UDDI registry and in WSIL documents. You also used WTP to create a WSIL document for League Planet.

Summary

In this chapter you have covered all the major functional areas of Web service development that are available in WTP. You created Web services using both the Top-Down and Bottom-Up approaches, generated a Java client proxy to access a Web service, developed a Web application that invoked the client proxy using the JAX-RPC programming model, validated Web services for WS-I compliance, tested Web services using both the Web Services Explorer and the JSP test client, viewed information published in both UDDI and WSIL, and created your own WSIL. Your are now ready to use Web services in your own applications. For further details about the tools, consult the WTP Help and Web site.

CHAPTER 11

Testing

Quality is not an act, it is a habit.

—Aristotle

Your focus in the preceding chapters has been on getting the League Planet site up and running. In this chapter you'll switch gears and focus on testing it.

It seems that testing is one of those activities that most developers would rather avoid and that many simply do not perform. Those who do not test usually cite time constraints as the primary factor. Those who do test typically perform ad hoc testing by running through some quick, informal, manual tests to verify that their application works as designed. This methodology often breaks down because of the lack of breadth of test coverage and the difficulty in creating repeatable results. It's clear that, unfortunately, many developers do not see the value of testing. Refer to *JUnit Test Infected* [Beck2002] by Kent Beck, Erich Gamma, and David Saff for an excellent brief account of the importance of testing.

Testing should not be considered optional. Inadequate testing fails to uncover latent problems with your code that can have serious ramifications. In some safety-critical applications, poor testing is simply irresponsible since errors can be both dangerous and expensive. The Therac-25 radiation overdoses, Ariane 5 space shuttle explosion, and Airbus A320-211 plane crash were all caused by faulty software and led to fatalities [Dubrova2005].

Even without looking at dramatic examples, not testing your application tends to require more time than actually testing it in the first place. Maintenance now accounts for roughly half of a developer's time and more than half of the development budget [Stark1996]. Not having enough time is simply not a valid excuse. There are frameworks that provide the facility to easily automate your tests. These frameworks reduce the time requirements for testing and the weight of the "not enough time" argument against testing. And, as any seasoned developer will tell you, there is never enough time anyway regardless of the amount of it you spend testing.

Another misconception is that developers do not need to test because there are test teams. Test teams are very useful, and you should applaud the people on these teams for finding bugs in your code, but these teams do not excuse you from testing your own code. Test teams perform *blackbox* testing of your code. That is, they test it without knowing all the details of the internals. Test teams cannot test all of the key decisions you've made or defend all of your fixes because they simply do not have the background that you have.

Still not convinced? Running tests produces tangible results, including:

❍ Proof that your application is functioning correctly. A test exercises a specific part of your application, and regular passing results show that the part of your application under test is still working regardless of changes to it or other parts of the application.

❍ Recorded memory of decisions that you have made. It is generally very difficult to understand code that you wrote even shortly after you wrote it! Tests for your decisions will ensure that you don't inadvertently make a decision-breaking change in the future.

❍ Defense against regressions. This is similar to the previous benefit, but we've listed it separately to showcase the benefits for changes you have made to components you don't own. For example, when a contributor submits a fix to WTP, the contributor should also provide some automated tests that exercise the fix. These tests are run with each build and serve to defend the fix against possible future regression. Even though the contributor may not be able to regularly test the component himself, the contributed automated tests do get run frequently.

There are several types of tests that are useful for testing the League Planet site. These tests fall into two categories: those for functional requirements and those for nonfunctional requirements.

There are three types of functional requirements tests: unit, integration, and system. These three types of tests are commonly confused, likely because they can be implemented using the same tools and frameworks. Each of these tests focuses on a different conceptual level of the site. Unit tests exercise a specific piece of functionality, typically a method or a class. Integration tests focus on the interaction between components in your application, such as a servlet and the servlet container. System tests look at the entire site from an end user perspective and are generally driven by end-to-end scenarios. A comprehensive functional requirements test suite comprised of these three types of tests is enough to prove that the site is working properly.

Nonfunctional requirements tests are also system-level tests since they cover all aspects of the site—such as reliability, security, and speed—that are not covered by functional requirements tests. One type of nonfunctional test commonly performed for Web sites is performance testing. Performance tests are useful for a site like League Planet in order to measure its response time under an expected load. If the site is not performing as required, it can then be profiled in order to determine the source of the performance bottleneck.

Automated Testing

While automated test frameworks have been around for many years now, many developers continue to use

```
System.out.println()
```

or equivalent calls to test their code. Printing out variable values can work for small, manual test cases and debugging code but it is not a viable long-term testing solution. Not only does printing out values generally mean only one person understands the tests, but these tests cannot usually be run unattended with every build of your site since they rely on someone to manually verify their results. They also add a lot of clutter to your production code and are generally very brittle. For example, changes to the code can often move a test print statement, thereby changing the expected output value.

Automated testing allows you as a developer to assign the task of testing large parts of your application to the automated test harness. The extreme programming (XP) methodology even states that developers should create all of their tests up front, before the application is written. By creating tests in advance of your code, you confirm that your application is complete after all of your tests pass. Following the XP methodology, this chapter could have appeared much earlier in the book. However, because this book does not focus on XP, this chapter comes at the end of the development cycle as is typical for other development processes such as iterative design and waterfall. While you still must do some manual testing, especially of user interface components, much of your code can be reliably tested both quickly and often using automated tests.

Automated testing of your applications provides you with substantial benefits, including:

❍ *Robustness:* The test cases are separated from your development code and are therefore not subject to breakage caused by moving development code around.

❍ *Automation:* Your tests can be run on demand before you check in your code and as part of your build.

❍ *Readability:* The tests are located in separate classes with clear, measurable objectives. This not only keeps your development code clean and readable but also allows others to more easily understand your tests.

○ *Time Savings:* Automated tests save you time by reducing the amount of manual, labor-intensive testing you have to do. Having automated tests allows you to always do the safe thing and test your code before committing a change, even when under heavy time pressure.

○ *Simplicity:* Once you understand the automated test framework it is generally very easy to create and maintain your tests.

Overview of Iterations

In this chapter you'll test the League Planet site in the following iterations:

○ In Iteration 1 you develop a unit test for the `User.java` class with the JUnit test framework.

○ In Iteration 2 you develop an integration test for the `LoginServlet.java` servlet with the Cactus test framework.

○ In Iteration 3 you develop a system test for the League Planet site with the HttpUnit test framework.

○ In Iteration 4 you run a performance test on the update game results request mechanism of the League Planet site with the Eclipse Test and Performance Tools Platform (TPTP).

○ In Iteration 5 you profile the update score page of the League Planet site with TPTP.

Iteration 1: Unit Testing with JUnit

A unit test isolates and tests a small, defined piece of functionality. In Java this typically translates to a method of a class [Abran2004].

To unit test a method you create a series of tests that cover the interesting inputs. Interesting inputs test boundary or edge cases. For example, when testing a parameter that requires a String, along with testing expected input strings you should test the empty string and null. You then isolate each test by creating stub objects for any foreign objects referenced by your code. A good check to see if you have properly isolated a unit test is to count the number of classes the test imports. If the test imports classes from many other places in your code it is probably not a good unit test. Each test then asserts that the results returned and any exceptions thrown from the method are as expected for its inputs.

JUnit is the de facto standard automated test framework for Java. It is an Open Source framework hosted on SourceForge, bundled with the Eclipse IDE, and available from `http://www.junit.org`

The JUnit Web site describes JUnit as a "regression testing framework." We can't say it any more succinctly. JUnit is a powerful test harness that gives you a way to run automated, and therefore repeatable, tests of your Java code. It also simplifies test authoring, allowing you to quickly write new tests and contribute them to your existing test suite.

There are two main components in JUnit: test cases and test suites. Test cases contain the code for all of your unit tests. Test suites are collections of test cases. A test suite can contain individual test cases or other test suites.

When running your tests, you can either run a specific test case or a test suite. This is useful for debugging a single test failure since you do not have to run the entire suite, which may take some time. Typically a master test suite is created that contains all the other test cases and test suites for the application. This master test suite provides a convenient way to run all the tests for the application, which is useful when running the tests as part of your build. The JUnit Web site contains a list of articles that can assist you in configuring JUnit to run this master test suite in a variety of settings, including your build.

We've already established that your time is limited, so you will want to focus your testing effort on the most useful areas of your code. This means that simple methods such as getters and setters are not usually unit tested unless they do some special processing. And, specifically for Java Web applications, unit tests are not appropriate to test methods that interact with a servlet or Java EE 5 container. These classes should be tested by integration tests, as we'll discuss in the next iteration.

In this iteration, you will perform the following tasks:

1. Create and configure a separate test project in your workspace.

2. Create a JUnit test case that unit tests `User.java`.

3. Create a JUnit test suite that includes your test case.

Creating a Test Project

One of the benefits of automating your tests with JUnit is that you can keep your tests physically separated from your production code by storing them in a separate project. This eliminates the chance that the tests will be accidentally deployed along with your production code. Although your unit tests will not be deployed to a server, creating a new dynamic Web project to hold your tests will allow you to continue to work in the J2EE perspective.

Here you create a new test project by doing the following:

1. In the **Project Explorer** view, use the **New Dynamic Web Project** wizard to create a project named IceHockeyWebTest. For detailed information on creating Web projects, refer to the Creating Web Applications section in Chapter 6. Select None as the target runtime since you will not deploy this project to a server.

2. Click **Next**. The **Project Facets** page is displayed. The Java version set on the IceHockeyWebTest project needs to be the same as the version set on the IceHockeyWeb project. Ensure that the Java version is set to the same level as the IceHockeyWeb project. The level will be the same as the Tomcat JDK.

3. Accept defaults for other options and click **Finish**. WTP creates the project in your workspace.

4. To test the contents of the IceHockeyWeb project, you need to declare a dependency on that project. Right click on the IceHockeyWebTest project and select **Properties**. The **Properties** window for IceHockeyWebTest opens. Select Java Build Path from the menu on the left if it is not already selected. Select the **Projects** tab on the **Java Build Path** page. Click the **Add** button. The **Required Project Selection** dialog opens. Select the IceHockeyWeb project and click **OK**. The dependency is added to your project (see Figure 11.1).

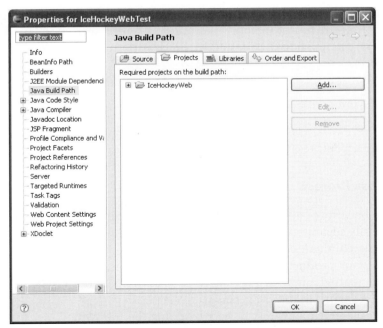

Figure 11.1   The IceHockeyWebTest Project Dependencies Page

5. Click **OK** in the properties window to close the window and save your changes.

You have now created a dynamic Web project named `IceHockeyWebTest` that will be used to house your tests. Next you'll add a JUnit test case to this project.

JUnit Test Case

You will now create a JUnit unit test for the class

`User.java`

that you have already created (see Example 7.13 in Chapter 7). To create the test, do the following:

1. In the **Project Explorer** view, right click on the `IceHockeyWebTest` project and select **New ▸ Other**. The **New** wizard opens. Select **Java ▸ JUnit ▸ JUnit Test Case** and click **Next**. The **New JUnit Test Case** wizard opens.

2. It is good practice to create tests in the same package as the class that is under test. This promotes well-structured test suites that are easy to understand and allows test classes access to protected methods and variables of the classes under test. It is a JUnit convention to name your test by appending `Test` to the name of the class under test. In this case you are testing the `User` class, so you will create a test class named `UserTest`. Specify the package `com.leagueplanet` and the class name `UserTest`.

3. JUnit provides two convenience methods for test cases: `setUp` and `tearDown`. The `setUp` method is run before each test method in the test case, and the `tearDown` method is run after each test method. Select the checkboxes for **setUp** and **tearDown** to create method stubs for both methods.

4. JUnit test cases require the JUnit libraries to be on your project's classpath. The **New JUnit Test Case** wizard provides you with a shortcut to add these libraries to your project's classpath. At the bottom of the wizard page there is a warning that states that JUnit 3.8.1 is not on the build path, and there is a link to add JUnit to the build path (see Figure 11.2). Click on the link. The **Properties** window for `IceHockeyWebTest` opens, showing that JUnit has been added to the project's libraries. Click **OK** to close the window.

5. Click **Finish** to close the wizard. The `UserTest` class is added to your project in the `com.leagueplanet` package and is opened in the Java source editor.

6. Edit `UserTest.java` (see Example 11.1).

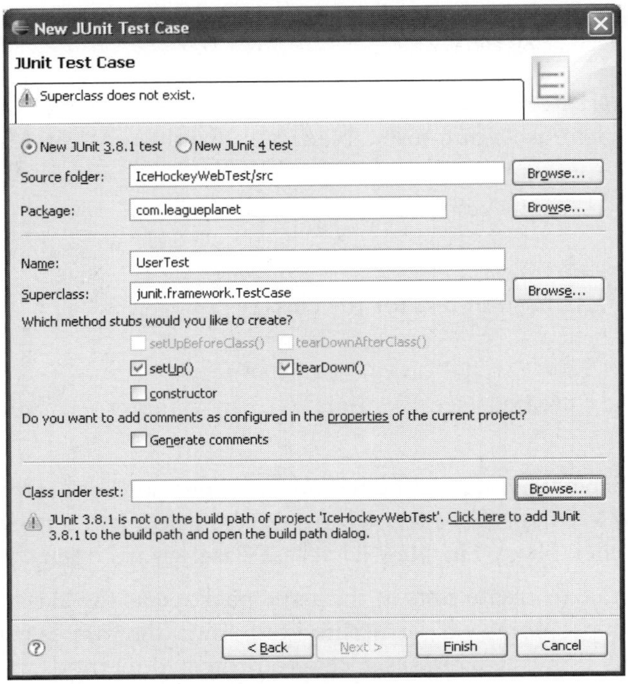

Figure 11.2   New JUnit Test Case Wizard

Example 11.1   Listing of UserTest.java

```java
package com.leagueplanet;

import junit.framework.TestCase;

public class UserTest extends TestCase {
  private User user;
  protected void setUp() throws Exception {
    user = new User();
  }

  protected void tearDown() throws Exception {
    user = null;
  }

  public void testLogInTypical() {
    user.logIn("userid");
    assertTrue("The user is not logged in.", user.isLoggedIn());
    assertNotNull("The user Id is null after logging in.",
                  user.getUserId());
  }

  public void testLogInEmpty() {
    user.logIn("");
    assertTrue("The user is not logged in.", user.isLoggedIn());
```

```
    assertNotNull("The user ID is null after logging in.",
                user.getUserId());
}
public void testLogInNull() {
  user.logIn(null);
  assertTrue("The user is not logged in.", user.isLoggedIn());
  assertNotNull("The user ID is null after logging in.",
                user.getUserId());
}
public void testLogOut() {
  user.logIn("userid");
  user.logOut();
  assertFalse("The user is logged in after logging out.",
                user.isLoggedIn());
  assertEquals("The user ID is not the empty string.", "",
                user.getUserId());
}
}
```

There are two methods in the User class that are tested: logIn and logOut. The rest of the methods are not tested since they have trivial implementations and are invoked by these methods.

The logIn method takes a String parameter as input. As we stated earlier, you should create tests for the boundaries or edge cases of the input parameters. In this case the userId parameter is tested in three separate tests with a typical value of userid, the empty string and null. In all cases, the tests assert that the user id set on the user object is not null and the logged in value is set to true.

The logOut method is simpler in that it does not have any parameters. For this method the test asserts that when a user is logged in, this method will successfully log the user out by changing the user name to the empty string and setting the logged in value to false.

As the test methods show, assert statements are used by JUnit to verify test results. One failing assertion will cause an entire test to fail. Each assert statement allows you to specify a description that will be displayed if the test fails. It is good practice to provide a description; otherwise, a failing test will only display its name and provide a stack trace, which may not be enough information to start debugging. UserTest employs the assertEquals, assertFalse, assertNotNull, and assertTrue methods. The JUnit framework provides many additional assert statements for various types of assertions.

UserTest also contains two convenience methods: setUp and tearDown. setUp is run before and tearDown is run after each test in the test case. They allow you to factor out common test configuration and initialization, and therefore help keep your test cases clean and easy to read. In UserTest these methods create a new user object before each test and destroy it when the test is complete.

7. The test class is now ready to run. Right click on the UserTest.java class and select **Run As ▸ JUnit Test**. The JUnit view opens with the test results (see Figure 11.3).

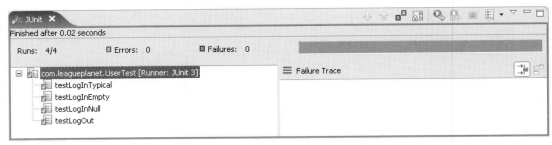

Figure 11.3   UserTest Results Displayed in the JUnit View

There are three types of results from a JUnit test: passed, failed, and error. Passed and failed are as you'd expect. Error indicates that there is a problem with the test case itself. The JUnit view will display a green bar if all tests pass and a red bar if there is even one failure or error. In this case the bar is green because all the tests passed.

You have now created a JUnit test case UserTest. Next you'll add this test case to a test suite.

JUnit Test Suite

JUnit test suites are a way to group related tests, such as those for a package or your entire application, so they may be run easily in one shot. To create a test suite for the IceHockeyWeb unit tests, do the following:

1. In the **Project Explorer** view, right click on the

   com.leagueplanet

   package in the IceHockeyWebTest project and select **New ▸ Other**. Select **Java ▸ JUnit ▸ JUnit Test Suite**. Click **Next**. The **New JUnit Test Suite** wizard opens.

2. The package field is prepopulated with the value com.leagueplanet, the name is set as AllTests, and the UserTest class is selected (see Figure 11.4). Accept all of these default values and click **Finish**.

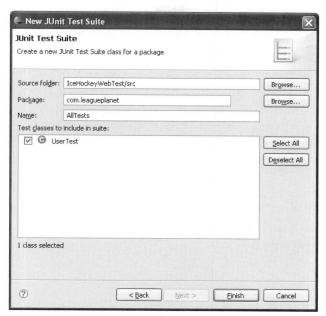

Figure 11.4 The New JUnit Test Suite Wizard

3. The AllTests.java class is added to your project and opened in the Java source editor (see Example 11.2).

Example 11.2 Listing of AllTests.java

```
package com.leagueplanet;

import junit.framework.Test;
import junit.framework.TestSuite;

public class AllTests {

  public static Test suite() {
    TestSuite suite = new TestSuite("Test for com.leagueplanet");
    //$JUnit-BEGIN$
    suite.addTestSuite(UserTest.class);
    //$JUnit-END$
    return suite;
  }
}
```

The generated class is very short. It contains one method, suite, that creates a new JUnit test suite; adds the UserTest class to the suite; and returns the suite. Adding test cases to this suite simply requires additional calls to the addTestSuite method on the suite object.

4. The test suite is now ready to run. Right click on the `AllTests.java` class and select **Run As ▸ JUnit Test**. The JUnit view opens with the test results (see Figure 11.5). These results look similar to the results displayed when running the test case, but are now grouped by test suite instead of only test case.

Figure 11.5   AllTests Results Displayed in the JUnit View

Summary of Iteration 1

In this iteration you created a new project to hold your tests. You then created a new JUnit test case to test the `User.java` class and a JUnit test suite to bundle your test case.

In the next iteration you'll create an integration test with Cactus for the project.

Iteration 2: Integration Testing with Cactus

Integration testing takes a step up from isolated test cases to concentrate on the interactions between two or more components. The preferred strategy for integration testing is usually an incremental strategy. In this way the interaction between two or a few components is tested first and additional components are added to the test mix after the current components under test have been proven to function correctly. The incremental test strategy is in contrast to the big bang test strategy where all the components are tested together at once [Abran2004].

JUnit supports testing stand-alone Java classes very well. When creating tests for Java EE 5 applications you have the added difficulty of ensuring that your code functions properly when run inside of a servlet or Java EE 5 container. (In this section, when we refer to a servlet container we mean either a servlet or a Java EE 5 container.) For example, you will have difficulty creating a JUnit test for

`com.leagueplanet.LoginServlet`

since JUnit provides no easy way to modify the session information or the information submitted to your servlet.

When using the incremental approach for integration testing it is often necessary to create stub or dummy objects for those components that have not yet been included in the test mix. When testing servlets, creating dummy objects can be a problem for two reasons. First, you may have to create many dummy objects to mimic the behavior of the servlet container. Creating many dummy objects can be very time consuming. Second, creating many dummy objects is itself error prone, which defeats the purpose of creating the dummy objects in the first place.

Cactus is an automated testing framework that extends JUnit and runs inside your servlet container. Like JUnit, Cactus is an Open Source project. It is hosted at Apache, bundled with WTP, and available from

```
http://jakarta.apache.org/cactus/
```

Cactus can be used to run unit tests on your servlet and functional tests on your application, but neither of these uses is a strength of the Cactus framework. For simplicity of your unit tests you are better off creating JUnit tests. For your functional tests you will find it easier to create the tests using a test framework, such as HttpUnit, that can handle end-to-end scenarios within your application. (We'll discuss HttpUnit in the next iteration.) Also, servlet tests that involve the servlet container are really integration tests since they test your code working with the servlet container module. Remember, integration testing your servlets still requires that you unit test the appropriate methods of your servlets. This will help you catch any integration problems with the servlet container, which you likely will not have written.

The benefit of the Cactus framework is that it allows your tests to interact with the artifacts produced by the servlet container. Cactus gives you access to several instance variables that a regular JUnit test does not have access to. These instance variables, detailed here, can be very useful when testing your servlet:

❍ The `request` instance variable gives your test access to and lets it set request parameters passed to your servlet. This variable allows you to mimic the input to your servlet from HTML forms or other requests. For example, using this variable your test can pass different login credentials to the League Planet login servlet.

The request object extends `javax.servlet.http.HttpServletRequest`. It has three additional methods that allow you to set its properties. Their function should be self-evident: `setRemoteIPAddress`, `setRemoteHostName`, and `setRemoteUser`.

○ The `response` instance variable gives your test access to the response object on which your servlet will set properties. You can use this variable to test the results returned by your servlet.

○ The `config` instance variable provides your test access to the servlet configuration and allows it to set additional configuration parameters. This allows your test to dynamically change the configuration of the servlet without restarting the application.

The `config` variable extends `javax.servlet.ServletConfig`. It has two additional methods that allow your test to set some of its properties: `setInitParameter` and `setServletName`.

In addition to these methods, when the `getServletConfig` method is called, a special servlet context is returned, which extends `javax.servlet.ServletContext`.

Like the `config` variable, this servlet context allows you to dynamically change the configuration of the servlet container without restarting the container. It contains two additional methods: `getLogs`, which returns the information logged by the `log` method, and `setInitParameter`, which sets a parameter as though it had been set in your application's deployment descriptor.

○ The `session` instance variable gives your test access to all the session properties for which your servlet has access. It extends `javax.servlet.http.HttpSession`.

Warning: If you are using an IBM 1.4.2 JDK, you may run into problems using Cactus. We recommend you use an IBM 1.5 SDK for the integration tests. You can download the 1.5 SDK from

```
http://www.ibm.com/developerworks/java/jdk/
```

After installing the runtime you will need to change the runtime of both your server and the `IceHockeyWeb` project. You can change the server runtime by editing the server on the **Server Preferences** page. The `IceHockeyWeb` runtime can be changed by right clicking on the project in the **Project Explorer** and selecting **Properties**. Select **Java Build Path**. Select the **Libraries** tab and then select the **JRE System Library** and click **Edit**.

In this iteration, you will create an integration test for `LoginServlet.java` in the `IceHockeyWeb` application (see Example 7.14 in Chapter 7). To create the test, do the following:

1. Cactus is both a server- and client-side framework. This means that your test will execute on the server side as well as the client side. Java Web applications have strict class loading rules, and therefore your tests cannot be separated into a different project as was the case with JUnit for unit tests. For servlet integration tests your test cases must be contained within the same Web module that contains the servlets. You will add the servlet test case to the IceHockeyWeb project that contains LoginServlet.java. However, you can still separate your test code from your production code by using a separate source folder for the servlet tests. This will allow you to easily remove the tests before deploying your application.

   In the **Project Explorer** view, right click on the IceHockeyWeb project and select **New ▸ Source Folder**. The **New Source Folder** wizard opens. Enter the folder name testsrc and click **Finish**. The testsrc source folder is added to the IceHockeyWeb project. This folder will be used to hold the IceHockeyWeb servlet integration tests.

2. Create a new servlet integration test by right clicking on the servlet to be tested, LoginServlet.java, and selecting **New ▸ Other**. The **New** wizard opens. Select **Java ▸ JUnit ▸ Servlet Test Case**.

   A question dialog opens indicating that the IceHockeyWeb project is missing the Cactus dependencies and asking if you want to add them. These dependencies are required to run Cactus tests. Click **Yes**. The Cactus libraries are added to the

   IceHockeyWeb/WebContent/WEB-INF/lib

   folder. Make a note of this folder. These libraries should be removed before deploying the IceHockeyWeb application into a production environment.

   The **New Cactus Test Case** wizard opens.

3. The **New Cactus Test Case** wizard is similar to the **New JUnit Test Case** wizard but has a couple of extra Cactus-specific options for generating beginXxx and endXxx method stubs. These methods work like the setUp and tearDown methods except they will be executed on the client side instead of the server side. You won't make use of these methods as your test does not require them.

   The source folder that's prepopulated is incorrect. You want to use the testsrc folder. Click **Browse** next to **Source folder** and select the testsrc folder.

As before, select to create the setUp and tearDown method stubs. You will once again use these methods to configure your test case.

The rest of the prepopulated entries are suitable for this test, so you do not need to change any of their values. Notice that the name of the test class follows the convention of appending Test to the servlet class name.

4. Click **Next**. The **Test Methods** wizard page is displayed (see Figure 11.6). This page allows you to select the methods that will be tested. The wizard will generate test method stubs for each selected method. Select getUser. Click **Finish** to complete the wizard. The wizard adds the new servlet test to the testsrc folder and opens it in the Java source editor.

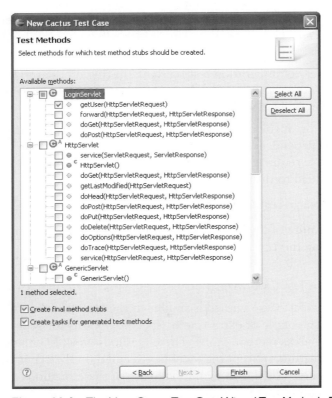

Figure 11.6   The New Cactus Test Case Wizard Test Methods Page

5. Edit LoginServletTest.java (see Example 11.3).

Example 11.3 Listing of LoginServletTest.java

```
package com.leagueplanet;

import org.apache.cactus.ServletTestCase;

public class LoginServletTest extends ServletTestCase {

  private LoginServlet servlet;

  public void setUp() throws Exception {
    servlet = new LoginServlet();
  }
  public void tearDown() throws Exception {
    servlet.destroy();
  }
  public void testGetUser() {
    assertNull("The user object has been set before getUser() " +
              "is called.", session.getAttribute("user"));
    User user = servlet.getUser(request);
    Object userObject = session.getAttribute("user");
    assertNotNull("The user object is null.", userObject);
    User retrievedUser = (User)userObject;
    assertEquals("The user object returned by getUser is not equal " +
                "to the object stored in the session.", user,
                retrievedUser);
  }
}
```

The test class was prepopulated with three methods: setUp, tearDown, and testGetUser.

As before, setUp and tearDown are used to configure each test case and clean up after each test case. In this case, a new instance of the LoginServlet is created before the test and destroyed after the test.

testGetUser contains the test logic. First it asserts that the user object has not been set before the test starts. This is a sanity check to ensure that the test has not been corrupted by an outside source. It then makes a call to the getUser method and retrieves the stored user object from the session object. Notice how Cactus grants the test implicit access to the session object from the servlet container. The test next asserts that the user object stored on the session is now set and that it is equal to the user object returned from the getUser method.

Remember, even though this test is at the method level, it is an integration test because it tests the interaction between a servlet and the servlet container.

6. Before you can run your test, there is one more configuration step you need to perform.

Cactus requires two entries to be added to the deployment descriptor: a Cactus servlet definition and a corresponding servlet mapping definition (see Example 11.4). In the **Project Explorer** view, double click on **Deployment Descriptor**. web.xml opens in the XML editor. Add the two entries and save the file. Remember, when editing your deployment descriptor, all servlet elements must be specified before all servlet-mapping elements.

Example 11.4   Listing of web.xml

```
<?xml version="1.0" encoding="UTF-8"?>
<web-app id="WebApp_ID" version="2.4"
  ...
  <servlet>
    <description></description>
    <display-name>LoginServlet</display-name>
    <servlet-name>LoginServlet</servlet-name>
    <servlet-class>
      com.leagueplanet.LoginServlet
    </servlet-class>
  </servlet>
  <!-- Begin Cactus Entries -->
  <servlet>
    <servlet-name>ServletRedirector</servlet-name>
    <servlet-class>
      org.apache.cactus.server.ServletTestRedirector
    </servlet-class>
  </servlet>
  <servlet-mapping>
    <servlet-name>ServletRedirector</servlet-name>
    <url-pattern>/ServletRedirector</url-pattern>
  </servlet-mapping>
  <!-- End Cactus Entries -->
  <servlet-mapping>
    <servlet-name>LoginServlet</servlet-name>
    <url-pattern>/login</url-pattern>
  </servlet-mapping>
  ...
</web-app>
```

Like the Cactus dependencies, these two Cactus entries should be removed before deploying your application into a production environment. We include comment delimiters around these entries to make it easy to distinguish them from the rest of the entries in the deployment descriptor.

7. Your test is now ready to run. Ensure that your server is started and is up to date. (Remember, the servlet test will run on the server.) Right click on LoginServletTest.java and select **Run As ▸ Run**. The **Run** wizard opens. Create a new JUnit test by right clicking on JUnit and selecting **New**. A new JUnit test configuration page opens.

The JUnit test runner that will control the tests and report the results needs to know where your server-side test is located. You need to specify the context URL of the IceHockeyWeb application to the test runner. To specify the context URL, change to the **Arguments** tab and add the following VM argument (see Figure 11.7):

```
-Dcactus.contextURL=http://localhost:8080/icehockey
```

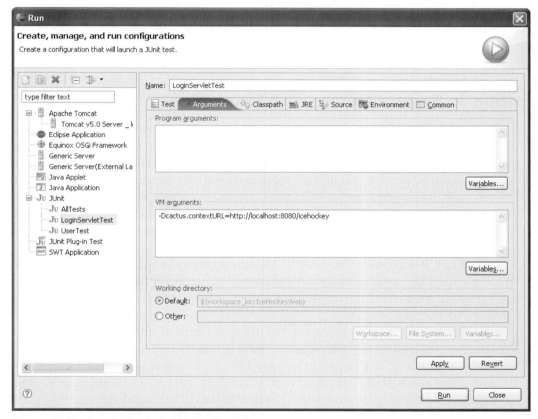

Figure 11.7   Specify the Context URL for Cactus Tests

Click **Run**. The test is run and the results are displayed in the JUnit view (see Figure 11.8), Again, the bar is green because the test passed.

Summary of Iteration 2

In this iteration you created a new test source folder in the IceHockeyWeb project. You then created a new Cactus servlet integration test for LoginServlet.java.

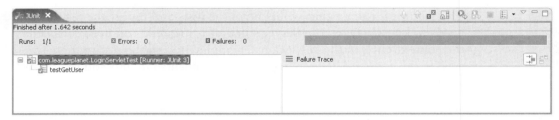

Figure 11.8   LoginServletTest Results Displayed in the JUnit View

In the next iteration you'll create a system test with HttpUnit for the IceHockeyWeb project.

Iteration 3: System Testing with HttpUnit

Unlike the previous types of tests, which focus on subsets of functionality, system tests aim to test the overall site. System tests are commonly performed using end-to-end user scenarios. When developing an end-to-end scenario it is important to keep in mind that these scenarios should exercise the system in the way that an end user will use the system. For example, an appropriate test of the League Planet site is to display the schedule, open a form to change the score of a game, change the score, return to the schedule, and review the change.

While JUnit and Cactus can be used to create system tests for Web applications, they are not a natural fit for these tests since JUnit has no built-in support for interacting with Web applications and Cactus focuses on individual servlets, not end-to-end scenarios.

Although it is typical for an end user to interact with a Web site using a browser, looking at the interaction from a technical perspective we see that it is really a matter of sending and receiving HTTP messages. Using this understanding of the interaction, you can create system tests that focus on the user interaction but do not require a browser. These tests will simply send and receive HTTP messages and verify that the returned results are correct.

Creating the necessary HTTP requests is a lot of work, and this isn't in and of itself a test of the site. All developers, including you, have precious little time, so instead of spending your time creating HTTP requests, you will use HttpUnit, a framework for interacting with Web applications.

HttpUnit is an Open Source SourceForge project but is not bundled with WTP. You will need to download and install it yourself (see the Getting HttpUnit sidebar).

Getting HttpUnit

HttpUnit is a framework for programmatically interacting with Web applications. Download HttpUnit from

http://www.httpunit.org/

Unzip HttpUnit to a directory such as `C:\HttpUnit`. Remember this location. You will need to refer to it when configuring your test project to use HttpUnit.

HttpUnit emulates a Web browser. It can send requests to and receive responses from a Web site. It can also parse the responses into one of three formats depending on what you determine is best for your test: plain text, an XML Document Object Model (DOM), or a container of Web page elements. When coupled with JUnit it is a powerful Web application system testing framework.

Of the three response formats, the container of Web page elements is the easiest to work with and is what you will use to implement the system test of the League Planet site. The plain text format does not assist you with any structure and is best if coupled with another parsing technology. The DOM format, which will be familiar to those who work with HTML or XML, is good for tests that need to walk the entire page. However, it is difficult to work with if you are not familiar with DOM.

The container of Web page elements is a Java model of a Web page. It is a collection of objects representing various parts of the page, such as forms, tables, and links, elements that will likely be of interest to you when writing your test. This collection makes it easy to retrieve specific elements from the page, especially if the page elements contain IDs or names.

In this iteration, you will create a system test for the `IceHockeyServiceClient` using HttpUnit and JUnit. The scenario for this test is:

1. A user is browsing the schedule page (see Figure 10.48 earlier) and notices that the score for a game was entered in reverse (that is, the home score was entered as the visitor score and vice versa).

2. The user clicks on the score. The Enter Score page is displayed (see Figure 10.49 earlier).

3. The user updates the score and clicks submit.

4. The Confirmation page is displayed (see Figure 10.50). The user clicks to return to the schedule page and confirms that the score has been updated.

To create the test do the following:

1. You will create the system test in the existing `IceHockeyWebTest` project. In order to use HttpUnit, you need to add HttpUnit and its required libraries to your project. Since the `IceHockeyWebTest` project is a dynamic Web project, you can simply place the libraries in the following folder, where they will automatically be picked up and registered for the project:

   `IceHockeyWebTest/WebContent/WEB-INF/lib`

   Copy the following libraries from the HttpUnit download (see the Getting HttpUnit sidebar) into the folder:
   - `lib/httpunit.jar`
   - `jar/js.jar`
   - `jar/nekohtml.jar`
   - `jar/xercesImpl.jar`
   - `jar/xmlParserAPIs.jar`

2. In the **Project Explorer**, right click on the `IceHockeyWebTest` project and select **New ▸ Other**. Select **Java ▸ JUnit ▸ JUnit Test Case** and click **Next**. The **New JUnit Test Case** wizard opens.

3. There are no special HttpUnit properties in this wizard. Create a JUnit test case as you did earlier. Enter a new package

   `com.leagueplanet.systemtest`

   to separate your system tests from your unit tests. Enter the name `UpdateScoreTest`. Deselect the `setUp` and `tearDown` method stubs as the system test will not make use of them. Click **Finish**. The wizard creates the new class and opens it in the Java source editor.

4. Edit `UpdateScoreTest.java` (see Example 11.5).

Example 11.5   Listing of UpdateScoreTest.java

```java
package com.leagueplanet.systemtest;

import junit.framework.TestCase;

import com.meterware.httpunit.TableCell;
import com.meterware.httpunit.WebConversation;
import com.meterware.httpunit.WebForm;
import com.meterware.httpunit.WebLink;
import com.meterware.httpunit.WebResponse;
import com.meterware.httpunit.WebTable;

public class UpdateScoreTest extends TestCase {
  public void testUpdateScore() {
```

```
try {
  WebConversation wc = new WebConversation();

  // Get the schedule page.
  WebResponse resp = wc
  .getResponse("http://localhost:8080/IceHockeyServiceClient/" +
               "schedule?scheduleId=1");

  // Get the schedule table.
  WebTable scheduleTable = resp.getTables()[0];
  // Find the score column.
  int numCols = scheduleTable.getColumnCount();
  int scoreCol = -1;
  for (int i = 0; i < numCols; i++) {
    if ("Score".equals(scheduleTable.getTableCell(0, i).getText())) {
      scoreCol = i;
      break;
    }
  }
  // Get and click the link to update the score for the first game.
  TableCell firstGameLinkCol =
    scheduleTable.getTableCell(1, scoreCol);
  String score = firstGameLinkCol.getText();
  WebLink editFirstGameLink = firstGameLinkCol.getLinks()[0];
  WebResponse editResp = editFirstGameLink.click();

  // Assert that the Enter Score page was returned.
  assertEquals("The Enter Score page was not returned when " +
               "selecting the edit score link.",
               "Enter Score", editResp.getTitle());

  // Reverse the score and submit.
  WebForm editForm = editResp.getFormWithName("enterScore");
  String visitorScore = editForm.getParameterValue("visitorScore");
  String homeScore = editForm.getParameterValue("homeScore");
  editForm.setParameter("visitorScore", homeScore);
  editForm.setParameter("homeScore", visitorScore);
  WebResponse submitResp = editForm.submit();

  // Assert that the Confirmation page was returned.
  assertEquals("The Confirmation page was not returned when " +
               "selecting the edit score link.",
               "Confirmation", submitResp.getTitle());

  // Get the link to the Schedule page and click it.
  WebLink scheduleLink = submitResp.getLinkWith("Regular Season");
  WebResponse scheduleResp = scheduleLink.click();

  // Assert that the Schedule page was returned.
  assertTrue("The Schedule page was not returned when selecting " +
             "the edit score link.",
             scheduleResp.getTitle()
             .startsWith("Rosehill Girls Hockey League"));
  assertTrue("The Schedule page was not returned when selecting " +
             "the edit score link.",
```

```
                    scheduleResp.getTitle()
                    .endsWith("Regular Season"));

        // Assert that the score has been updated.
        WebTable updatedScheduleTable = scheduleResp.getTables()[0];
        TableCell updatedFirstGameLinkCol = updatedScheduleTable
                                        .getTableCell(1, scoreCol);
        String updatedScore = updatedFirstGameLinkCol.getText();
        int scoreDiv = score.indexOf("-");
        String reverseScore = score.substring(scoreDiv + 1) + "-"
                            + score.substring(0,scoreDiv);
        assertEquals("The score was not set correctly.", reverseScore,
                    updatedScore);
    } catch (Exception e) {
        fail("Scenario did not complete successfully because: " + e);
    }
  }
}
```

UpdateScoreTest.java contains one method for the one system test. This method programmatically creates the page flow required of the end-to-end user scenario.

The test starts by retrieving the schedule page. This is done by creating a new WebConversation. It then retrieves the schedule table using the WebResponse and iterates through the header row to find the score column using the WebTable. Dynamically locating information on the page is preferred to hard coding the location to keep the test more nimble and responsive to future changes to the page. This test will still succeed if the columns in the table are reordered. With the score column in hand, the test then retrieves the score and clicks on the edit the score link.

The first assertion then checks that the page returned is the enter score page using the page title as the page identifier. This assertion will catch an incorrect link or a server error at this point.

Next the test retrieves the score values from the enter score page. Even though the score was previously retrieved from the schedule page it's best to work with the same information the end user has access to. The score is reversed and the form is then submitted.

The test asserts that the confirmation page is returned using the same method as before, and then selects the schedule link and clicks it.

The next two assertions check that the schedule page was returned by checking the beginning and end of the page title. The two assertions are required as the page name contains the year range 2005–2006 that will likely change the following season. Hard coding the year range will require the test to be updated the following year.

The test then retrieves the updated score and confirms that it is the reverse of the score that previously appeared on the page.

> **Tip:** An alternative method to assert that the correct page is returned is to use a unique page `id`. This requires the placement of an `id` in the page at development time, but will prevent problems due to page title changes.
>
> To use a page `id`, place an `id` attribute on the HTML element. Then assert that the element exists using the `WebResponse` object's `getElementWithID` method.

5. The system test is ready to run. Right click on the `UpdateScoreTest.java` class and select **Run As ▸ JUnit Test**. The JUnit view opens with the system test results (see Figure 11.9). Once again, the test succeeds and the bar is green.

Figure 11.9 UpdateScoreTest Results Displayed in the JUnit View

Summary of Iteration 3

In this iteration you configured your test project for HttpUnit. You then created a new system test for the `IceHockeyServiceClient` project. The test is based on an end-to-end user scenario and uses a combination of HttpUnit and JUnit.

In the next iteration you'll create a non-functional test that measures the performance of a portion of the League Planet site.

Iteration 4: Performance Testing with TPTP

There are many types of non-functional requirements, including, but not limited to, availability, reliability, security, speed, and stability. Non-functional requirements are not implemented in isolated modules. For example, an application may require security and have a security module, but for it to be secure the security architecture must percolate throughout the application. Likewise, it's not possible to write availability or reliability modules that can be tested in isolation as these features are woven throughout the application. In this iteration we shift the focus from functional tests to non-functional tests.

There are testing techniques and tools for many of these non-functional requirements, and each has its price that you must pay to implement it. The decision of which non-functional requirements to test and the degree to which testing will be performed should naturally depend on the specific requirements of your project.

In Iteration 3 you implemented a system test for the update game result scenario. Non-functional tests are often also referred to as system tests because they test attributes of the entire system.

When working with Web applications, it is common to create performance measurements because of the distributed nature of these applications. You will implement a page response time performance test for the same update game results scenario you implemented in Iteration 3. This test measures the response time of individual pages in your application and is useful for locating end user performance bottlenecks. To assess a test and produce a pass or fail result, you need to define the threshold. For the page response time test, the threshold is set to 0.04 seconds or less.

Tip: You've chosen an extremely low number for the threshold since all of your testing will occur on a single machine, bypassing the network. This number should not be taken as a good threshold for tests of your Web applications. Typical Web applications will take much longer than 0.04 seconds to respond to page requests.

Unlike the previous iterations, to implement and run this test you will use a manual test tool. The Eclipse Test and Performance Tools Platform (TPTP) (see the Installing TPTP sidebar) is a top-level Eclipse project like WTP that contains tools for executing Web application performance tests and generating reports to view the results.

In this iteration, you will perform the following tasks:

1. Create a new performance test project in your workspace.

2. Create and run an HTTP recording test.

3. Generate a report from the test and determine whether the page response time is above or below the set threshold.

Installing TPTP

TPTP is not part of WTP, but rather is a separate Eclipse top-level project that you will use to test and profile a Web application.

TPTP is available from

```
http://www.eclipse.org/tptp/
```

TPTP consists of two components that must be installed in order to use its test tools: the TPTP Eclipse tools and the TPTP agent controller.

❍ The simplest way to install the TPTP Eclipse tools is to use the Update Manager. Detailed instructions on installing updates via the update manager can be found in the Installation via Update Manager section in Chapter 4. Install the Testing and Performance features instead of the Web and J2EE Development features.

❍ **Note:** The following are very brief installation instructions that should get most installations up and running quickly. Detailed instructions for each platform the agent controller supports are available on the TPTP site.

To install the TPTP agent controller you will need to download it from the TPTP site. In your Web browser, go to the TPTP site and select Downloads. Select Agent Controller and download the runtime version for your platform.

Once downloaded, extract the agent controller to a directory such as

```
C:\AgentController
```

on Windows or

```
/opt/AgentController
```

on other platforms.

Ensure a JVM is present on the PATH environment variable. Run the

```
bin\SetConfig.bat
```

script on Windows or

```
bin/SetConfig.sh
```

script on other platforms located in the agent controller directory. Accept the default values for all the questions by pressing **Enter**.

Start the agent controller by running

```
bin\ACServer.exe
```

> on Windows or
>
> bin/RAStart.sh
>
> on most other platforms.
>
> To exit the agent controller on Windows, press **ctrl+C** and on other platforms run **bin/RAStop.sh**.

Creating a Performance Test Project

The performance tests will not be part of the automated test bucket created in Iteration 1 and will contain generated code. For these reasons you will create a new performance test project. Do the following:

> TPTP requires a Java project to store performance tests because it generates Java test code. In the **Project Explorer** view, use the **New Java Project** wizard to create a project named PerformanceTests. Create a project layout that contains separate source and output folders. If prompted, do not change to the Java perspective.

HTTP Recording Test

To create the performance test, you will create an HTTP recording test element. This element will be generated by recording your actions in a Web browser and can be used to play back those actions at a later time. You can configure your test to play back the actions simulating multiple users or, as you will do in your test, play back multiple times in sequence to test page response time for a single user. To create and run the test, do the following:

1. The HTTP recording test requires the TPTP agent controller. Ensure the controller is running before proceeding (see the Installing TPTP sidebar).

2. Switch to the **Test** perspective.

3. Create a new **HTTP Recording** test. Right click on the PerformanceTests project and select **New ▶ Test Element**. The **New** wizard opens. Select **Recording ▶ HTTP Recording**. Click **Next**. The **HTTP Recording** wizard opens.

4. Select the PerformanceTests project, enter the name ResponseTimeTest, and click **Finish**.

   The wizard starts the recorder and launches Internet Explorer (see Figure 11.10).

Figure 11.10 Recorder Control View

5. Perform the actions for the test. In the browser that opened, go to

   `http://localhost:8080/IceHockeyServiceClient/schedule?scheduleId=1`

   Click on the score for the first game in the schedule page.

   Click Submit on the enter score page. The specific game results are not important. The submission of game results is important.

   Click the regular season link on the confirmation page to return to the schedule page.

6. The actions for the test are complete. In Eclipse, click the stop button in the **Recorder Control** view. The recorder closes Internet Explorer, creates the test in your `PerformanceTests` project, and opens the test editor.

7. The test editor allows you to configure various properties of the test, including the number of iterations of the test. Set the number of iterations for a single user to 100. This will produce the average page response time.

   Change to the **Behavior** tab. Select `Loop1` in the **Behavior** list. `Loop1` contains a log of the actions you performed in Internet Explorer. Under **Detailed Properties** set the number of iterations to 100 (see Figure 11.11). Save the test.

8. The `ResponseTimeTest` file is not an executable test file. It is only a test description. In order to run this test you must generate the test class.

   Right click on `ResponseTimeTest` and select **Generate**. The **TPTP URL (JUnit) Test Definition Code Generation** wizard opens. Select the source folder

   `/PerformanceTests/src`

   and click **Finish**. The wizard generates the test class, which is hidden in the **Test** perspective but can be seen in the **Java** perspective.

Figure 11.11   ResponseTimeTest Editor Behavior Page

9. Your test is now ready to run. Right click on the ResponseTimeTest and select **Run As ▸ Test**. The test running time will depend on the speed of your machine, but it should take less than a minute. Upon completion, a new ResponseTimeTest file is created in the PerformanceTests project with the results of the test run. The file name will look something like this:

```
ResponseTimeTest[Jan 1, 2007 10:00:00 AM EST]
```

The results file is not very interesting on its own, so we won't discuss it any further here. This file is useful for generating reports.

You have created the page response time test, and you've run it to produce results. Next you will create a report from the results.

Generating a Report

With your results in hand you can now generate a report that provides an easy-to-understand view of the data. The report should help you to determine whether the test gets a passing or failing grade. To generate a report, do the following:

1. In the **Project Explorer** view, right click on the ResponseTimeTest (not on the results) and select **Report**. The **New Report** wizard opens (see Figure 11.12).

Figure 11.12   The New Report Wizard

2. Select an **HTTP Page Response Time** report and click **Next**.

3. Select the `PerformanceTests` project, enter the name `ResponseTimeTestReport` and click **Finish**. The wizard creates the `ResponseTimeTestReport` file in the `PerformanceTests` project.

4. To view the report, right click on the `ResponseTimeTestReport` file and select **Open With ▸ Web Browser**. The report is displayed (see Figure 11.13).

   The report shows that the average page response time for the `updateScore` page is 0.05 seconds. (Your performance measurements may not produce exactly the same number.) Even though the overall average page response time is less than 0.04 seconds, this single page fails this performance test.

Summary of Iteration 4

In this iteration you created a new test project for your non-functional performance tests. You created and ran an HTTP recording test, generated a report from the results using TPTP, and determined that the test failed.

In the next iteration you'll profile the League Planet application to determine the source of the performance test failure.

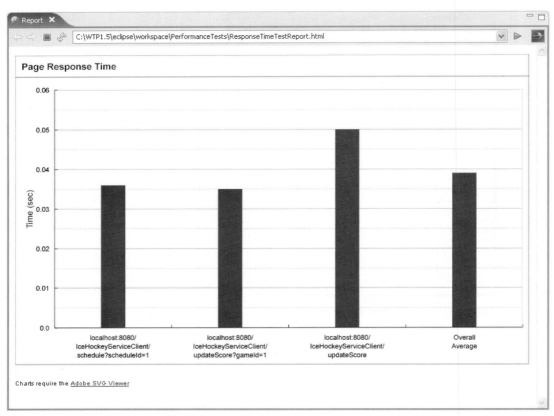

Figure 11.13   The Page Response Time Test Report

Iteration 5: Profiling with TPTP

One of the biggest problems with a failing performance test is that you know your application is not performing as required, but don't know why. Worse, you don't even know where in your code to start looking for the source of the problem. When solving a performance test failure, it is common to start taking educated guesses as to what may be causing the problem and working to resolve issues that you can find in your code. From our experience, manually searching through your code, even if you are a performance expert, is a good way to spend a lot of time and generally produce small, insignificant performance improvements. The problem with this method is that you just do not know that the problem you are fixing is the right problem.

Profiling is the odd man out in this chapter full of test methods because it isn't a test method at all. Profiling is a technique that you can use to identify potential sources of performance problems for a specific performance test.

Performance testing and profiling go hand in hand. It is not very useful to run a performance test if you cannot locate the source of a revealed problem and, similarly, it is not useful to profile your application to search for the source of problems that you do not know exist.

There are two common types of measurements that are taken when profiling: execution time and memory consumption. Profiling your application for execution time will result in reports that show the amount of time spent in each package, class, and method, and the number of times a method is called. Profiling the same application for memory consumption will result in reports that show the total number of instances, active instances, total size, and active size of packages and classes. Using these reports, you can determine the largest execution time or memory consumers in your application, and then target those for debugging and improvement.

TPTP includes profiling tools that integrate with WTP and allow you to easily profile server-side applications. In Iteration 4 you ran a performance test on a part of the League Planet site. The test failed because the following page took 0.05 seconds to respond:

```
http://localhost:8080/IceHockeyServiceClient/updateScore
```

In this iteration you will profile the updateScore page to take execution time measurements. You will use these measurements to identify the methods that are the largest execution time consumers, and therefore the best candidates for debugging and improvement. To profile the page, do the following:

1. You will use TPTP to profile the updateScore page. If you haven't done so already, install TPTP and run the agent controller (see the Installing TPTP sidebar).

2. To profile the page on the server, you need to start the server in profiling mode. If your server is running, shut it down. In the **Servers** view, right click on the server and select **Stop**.

   Now restart the server in profiling mode. Again in the **Servers** view, right click on the server and select **Profile**.

3. The **Profile on server** dialog opens (see Figure 11.14). Select the agent by clicking on it and selecting the top arrow button.

Tip: If no agent is listed, the agent controller may not be running.

4. Select the **Monitor** tab (see Figure 11.15). This tab lists the profiling measurements that can be recorded. Select **Execution Time Analysis**.

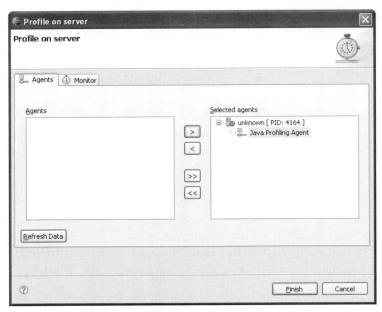

Figure 11.14 Profile on Server Agent Selection

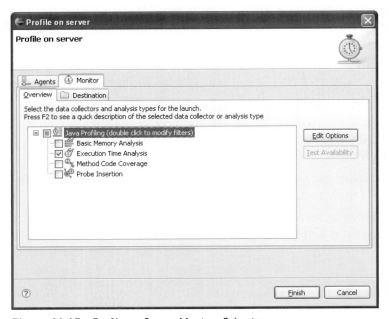

Figure 11.15 Profile on Server Monitor Selection

5. Profiling is a very intensive process. To allow the monitor to run effectively and to record useful results, it is a good idea to restrict the packages that are monitored.

Double click on **Java Profiling**. The **Edit Profiling Options** wizard opens. By default many common packages are excluded from monitoring. Include the League Planet packages. Click **Add** next to the filter sets. The **Add filter** dialog opens. Enter the package

```
com.leagueplanet.*
```

and click **OK**. The League Planet packages are added to the filter set list (see Figure 11.16). Click **Finish** to close the wizard.

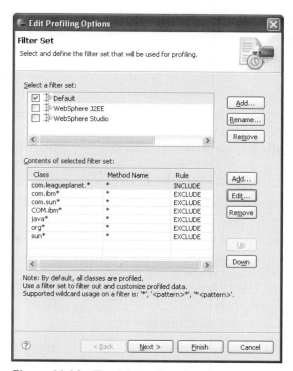

Figure 11.16   The Edit Profiling Options Wizard

6. The server is now configured for profiling. Click **Finish**. You are prompted to change perspectives to the **Profiling and Logging** perspective. Click **Yes** to change to this perspective.

7. The **Profiling and Logging** perspective is displayed, and you are presented with a tip stating that you must select to start monitoring. Click **OK** to close the tip.

8. Before starting the monitor you need to configure the test. Open your Web browser to

   `http://localhost:8080/IceHockeyServiceClient/updateScore?gameId=1`

   The test will involve clicking Submit on this page to make a request to the updateScore page, which failed the performance test. The handling of this request on the server is what will be monitored.

9. In the **Profiling Monitor** view in Eclipse, right click on **Profiling** and select **Start Monitoring**.

10. Return to your Web browser and click Submit to run the test. The updateScore page loads, completing the test.

11. Return to the **Profiling Monitor** view, right click on **Profiling**, and select **Pause Monitoring**. Selecting pause instead of terminate allows your server to continue to run.

12. Monitoring results are now available in the **Profiling Monitor** view. Double click on **Execution Time Analysis** to display the results. The **Execution Statistics** view opens, displaying execution statistics by package. Select the **Method** view by clicking on ⓜ (the blue circle containing the letter M) in the **Execution Statistics** view (see Figure 11.17).

    The method execution statistics view displays all of the collected information by method. There are three columns containing time information: **Base Time**, **Average Base Time**, and **Cumulative Time**. These three columns tell you the total time spent in a method, the average time spent in a method, and the cumulative time spent in a method tree (a method and every method it called). The **Calls** column tells you how many times a method was called. Together these four columns can be used to locate the method with the largest execution time.

13. Click on the **Base Time** column. The list is sorted by base time. Sorting by base time is usually a good way to identify methods with the worst performance. However, it's important to also look at the average base time. If the average base time of a method is much less than its base time, it's likely that this method is simply called many times. In this case, the problem is likely not with this method but with a method that calls this method. In your case, the top three methods have average base times similar to the base times and are only called once or twice.

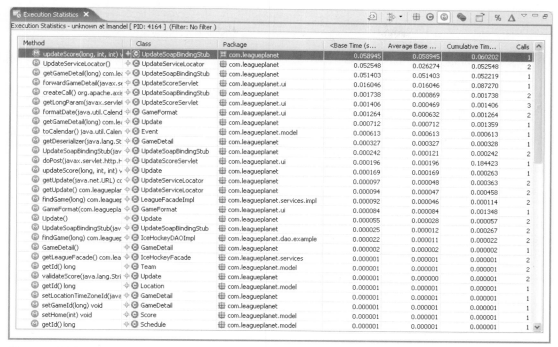

Figure 11.17   Method Execution Statistics View

14. When dealing with the execution numbers, it is often helpful to view them expressed as a percentage instead of as raw time. Select the percentage symbol % in the **Execution Statistics** view. Viewing the monitoring results by percentage (see Figure 11.18), it is clear that the top three methods are the only methods that take any significant amount of time. These three methods are the candidates for debugging and improvement.

Summary of Iteration 5

In this iteration you profiled the updateScore page on your server using TPTP. You identified three methods as candidates for debugging and improvement in order to fix the performance problem identified in Iteration 4.

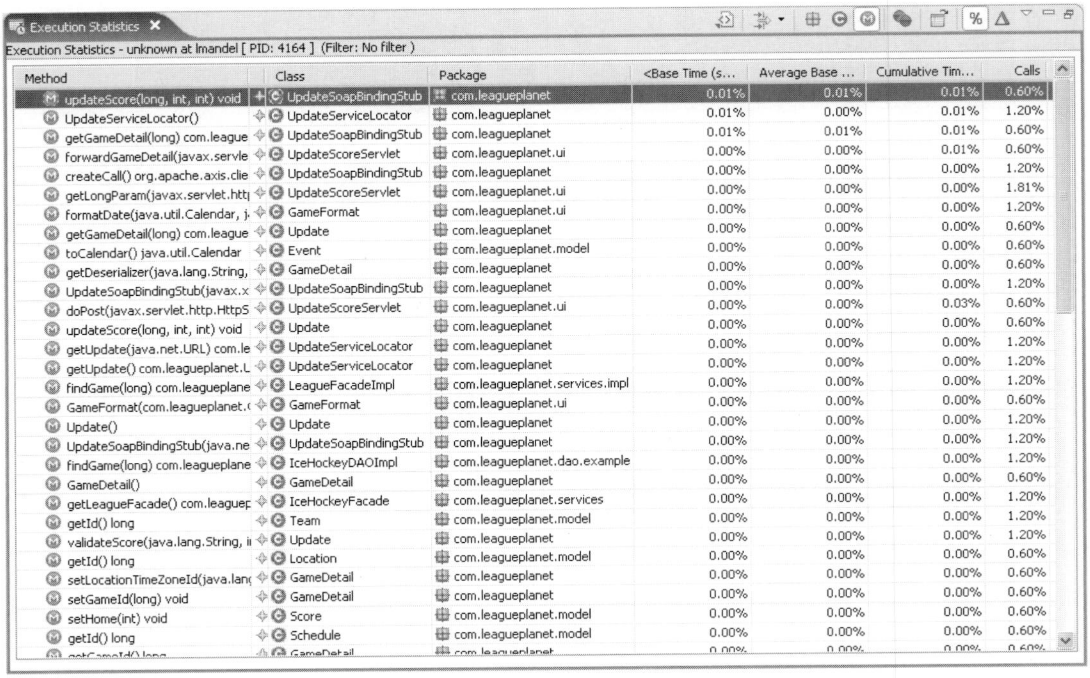

Figure 11.18 Method Execution Statistics View by Percentage

Summary

In this chapter you learned about the importance of testing and covered a range of tests for the League Planet site. You created a unit test with JUnit, a server-side integration test with Cactus, a Web application system test using a combination of HttpUnit and JUnit, and a performance test with TPTP based on an end-to-end user scenario. You also profiled a page of the League Planet site with TPTP and identified methods that will need to be investigated for their involvement in a performance problem. You are now ready to test many aspects of your own applications. We hope this chapter has inspired you to test your Web applications and that you will pursue the topic further to learn the techniques to test your application's requirements.

The completion of this chapter marks the end of Part II of this book in which you were walked through the development of the League Planet site. You learned about Web application architecture and design, and how to organize your development project. You implemented the presentation, business logic, and persistence tiers, you built Web services, and tested your application. This part of the book was written as a complete walkthrough, but it can also be used as a reference for the development of different sections of your own Web applications.

We hope you found Part II helpful. It will be a handy reference for you when creating your own Web applications and structuring your projects and code.

Next, Part III changes the focus from using WTP to extending WTP. There you'll learn about some of the many extension points in WTP and how to develop plug-ins that use them.

PART III

Extending WTP

As we explained in Chapter 2, About the Eclipse Web Tools Platform Project, WTP provides both Eclipse tools that can be used for Web application development and a platform that allows you to extend the tools. Our goal in this part of the book is to provide you with an overview of some of WTP's extension points.

One of the primary goals driving the development of WTP's APIs is that they must be of *platform* quality, which means that they are of high quality and are stable. Once an API is released, it will be maintained in future releases. Plug-ins that only use platforms APIs should work on future versions of WTP.

Throughout this section you will see that many of the extensions discussed use provisional APIs. A *provisional* API is not a platform API; rather, it is a possible API definition that has not yet been declared. As someone extending WTP, this means that the provisional APIs give you early access to extensions but do not give you a contract stating that the API definition will not change. The community's help is needed to finalize WTP's API. Through your feedback, many of the provisional APIs will be finalized and declared in future releases.

While this part of the book contains information about extending WTP, it is not an introduction to plug-in development. Furthermore, there are many extension points provided by the Eclipse platform that may interest you. These extension points allow you to contribute to many areas of the Eclipse workbench, including the menus, toolbars, views, filters, editors, and builders. If you're unfamiliar with plug-in development or are interested in working with the Eclipse platform extension points we suggest you take a look at other books in the Addison-Wesley *Eclipse Series*, such as *Eclipse: Building Commercial-Quality Plug-Ins* [Clayberg2006] by Eric Clayberg and Dan Rubel, *Contributing to Eclipse* [Gamma2003] by Erich Gamma and Kent Beck, and *Eclipse Rich Client Platform: Designing, Coding, and Packaging Java Applications* [McAffer2005] by Jeff McAffer and Jean-Michel Lemieux.

CHAPTER 12

Adding New Servers

When one has much to put into them, a day has a hundred pockets.

—Friedrich Nietzsche

A server is a software platform that provides the services and infrastructure required to develop, deploy, and run Web applications. WTP provides the tools to build these applications, and servers provide the runtime environment to execute them. This chapter describes how to add new server extensions to WTP. Once added, the new server extension will be listed in the **New Server Runtime** wizard and other dialogs, and it can be used like all the other servers to develop, deploy, test, and run Web applications. We'll start by defining some terms.

A *server runtime environment*, or just *runtime* for short, is a software application that is designed to execute as a server platform and support certain standards, such as J2EE. The runtime models the types of components that can run on the server, the standards that these components support, how the server is started and stopped, where it is installed, and other items.

A *server configuration*, or just a *server* for short, is an instance of a server runtime. A server configuration typically consists of a set of port numbers used by its services, such as HTTP, and a set of components, such as Web modules, that are deployed on it. A server models concepts such as the ports, locations of server configuration files, and the set of applications that are deployed. You can define many servers for a given runtime; for example, a single Tomcat runtime can have multiple server configurations on the same machine.

A *Web application,* or a *module* for short, is a stand-alone application that can be published and run on a server. You can publish multiple Web modules, such as LeaguePlanetWeb, EJBs, and EARs, on the same server. Another server in the workspace can have a different set of modules associated with it.

A *facet* is an aspect of a module that defines its runtime and development functionality. For example, by using facets, WTP can determine which server runtimes are compatible with a given module or create projects with advanced server-specific features. All Web projects are created with standard facets, such as J2EE, and some optional ones, such as JSF, that may only be supported by advanced server-specific features. For example, a Web module with the jst.web v2.4 facet is only compatible with a server runtime environment that supports the J2EE 1.4 and higher specifications. Each runtime specifies the facets that it supports, and modules are associated with facets that characterize them. This information is used to decide whether a module is compatible with a runtime. For example, if a runtime only supports jst.web facets, it cannot run a module that has a jst.ejb facet. Similarly, a runtime that supports jst.web v2.3 facets cannot run a module that has a jst.web v2.4 facet. The diagram in Figure 12.1 describes these relationships.

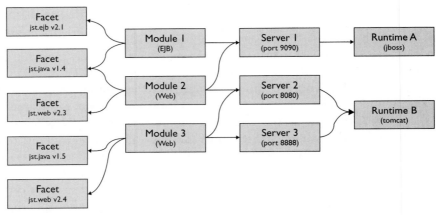

Figure 12.1   Runtimes, Servers, Modules, and Facets

A *server adapter* is a plug-in that extends WTP to add new server and runtime types. Server adapters are not limited to Java runtime environments. It is possible to build a server adapter for, say, the Apache Web Server.

Although server adapters are a WTP concept, the Web application code you develop is independent of WTP. After the development is complete, the application artifacts, such as Web and EJB modules, have no execution dependencies on the WTP tools and runtimes.

The server adapters provided by WTP are exemplary implementations for popular commercial and Open Source J2EE application servers. WTP has adapters for Open Source servers including Tomcat, JBoss, JOnAS, and Geronimo, and commercial servers including BEA WebLogic, IBM WebSphere, and Oracle Application Server. WTP encourages server vendors to develop and support adapters for their products. For example, the Apache Geronimo project hosts its own WTP server adapter. The Apache Geronimo adapter takes advantage of the WTP server installation extension point, which means you can easily install it via the **New Server Runtime** wizard.

The server tools and APIs are components of the WTP JST and WST subprojects. The server tools let you:

○ Develop Web applications for server runtime environments such as Tomcat, JBoss, and others

○ Start and stop servers in normal or debug modes

○ Target Web applications to specific servers

○ Add and remove projects from server configurations

○ Publish Web applications to servers

General and J2EE server tools plug-ins are found in the WST and JST projects, respectively. Server APIs and models are provided by the

`server.core.*`

plug-ins, whereas the API for server tools UI can be found in

`server.ui.*`

The UI plug-ins are for creating and configuring server views, wizards, preferences, and property pages (see Figure 12.2).

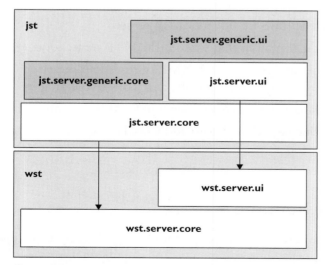

Figure 12.2 Server Tools

The JST project comes with a *generic server framework*, which is an extension of the server tools. The generic server framework simplifies the task of adding server adapters. It provides classes for runtime type and server type implementations, and a UI framework that can be configured with an XML server definition file. The JST project comes with exemplary implementations of the server tools for custom and generic server adapters. The Tomcat server plug-ins are excellent examples of full-scale implementations of server tools. You can find examples for the generic server adapter in server plug-ins for JBoss, JOnAS, BEA WebLogic, IBM WebSphere, and Oracle AS.

In the following sections we describe how you can:

❍ Build a server adapter plug-in using the generic server tools for the Sun Java System Application Server (SJSAS, aka GlassFish).

❍ Use the new adapter to develop, launch, and debug Web applications.

Overview of Adding a Generic Server Adapter

There are two ways to add a new J2EE server adapter to WTP: custom and generic. Writing a custom adapter requires plug-in and Java development skills. Writing a generic server adapter is easier because most of the Java code is already implemented, and you create the plug-in by providing the server definition as an XML file and the publishing task as an Ant script.

In this chapter you will build a generic server adapter for GlassFish by performing the following tasks:

1. Install the GlassFish Java EE 5 Application server.

2. Create a new Eclipse plug-in that extends the WTP server tools.

3. Add runtime types and server types, XML runtime and server definitions, Ant publisher scripts, wizard fragments, and icons to the plug-in.

4. Define GlassFish as a runtime component and add facet mappings.

5. Extend the runtime target handler to add GlassFish as a runtime target for Web projects.

6. Test your new server adapter with a Web application.

The GlassFish Server Runtime

You will develop a new generic server adapter for the Sun Java System Application Server developed by the GlassFish community. You can obtain it from

```
http://java.sun.com/javaee/glassfish
```

1. Download GlassFish and install it on your machine. GlassFish comes with an installation wizard. Installation involves running the wizard and following the steps (see Figure 12.3). If you need help, consult the GlassFish project documentation.

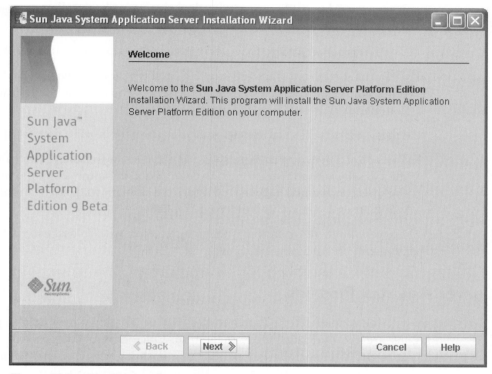

Figure 12.3   GlassFish Installer

You can accept most of the defaults. Make sure that the server is not added as a service. This will interfere with the development. In the following examples, we assume you installed GlassFish in this directory:

```
c:\dev\appservers
```

2. Once the installation is complete, you should find the GlassFish files and server configurations under a directory named

```
c:\dev\appservers\Sun\AppServer
```

GlassFish has an administrative concept called a *domain*. Each *domain* roughly corresponds to a WTP server configuration. A domain can have unique port numbers, a set of modules deployed, logs, and so forth. Each domain has a directory associated with it. The default domain named `domain1` is found in

```
C:\dev\appservers\Sun\AppServer\domains\domain1
```

To start a debuggable server for a domain, execute the following command using the GlassFish admin tool:

```
C:\dev\appservers\Sun\AppServer\bin>asadmin start-domain domain1
```

3. The admin tool can start and stop a GlassFish server as well as perform other administrative tasks. To stop the server you execute the following command:

```
C:\dev\appservers\Sun\AppServer\bin>asadmin stop-domain domain1
```

4. To deploy a new application, such as `LeaguePlanetWeb.war`, you can use the GlassFish administration console or tools, or simply copy the file to the directory named `autodeploy` under the domain folder. This information will be useful when you build your publisher.

This is enough information to get you started with GlassFish. In the next steps, you will create a new server plug-in.

Server Adapter Plug-ins

You will add a new server adapter to WTP by developing a new Eclipse plug-in. Plug-ins are the building blocks of Eclipse. Once developed, you can add the plug-in to any WTP installation by placing it in the subdirectory named `plugins`.

Every plug-in contains a manifest file named `plugin.xml` that describes the extensions to the Eclipse runtime. A plug-in also contains Java code and supporting resource files, such as the server definition, Ant scripts, icons, and properties files.

1. In the **Package Explorer** view, right click, and invoke the **New ▸ Plug-in Project** menu item. The **New Plug-in Project** wizard opens (see Figure 12.4).

2. Name the project

```
org.eclipsewtp.server.glassfish
```

and click **Next**. The **Plug-in Content** page opens.

3. Uncheck the **Generate an activator** and **This plug-in makes contributions to the UI** checkboxes. Click the **No** radio button in the **Rich Client Application** section (see Figure 12.5). Click **Finish** to create the plug-in project.

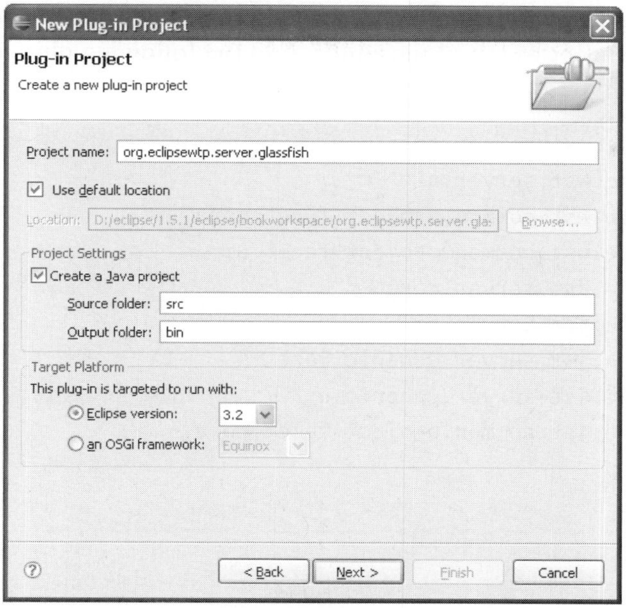

Figure 12.4 New Plug-in Project

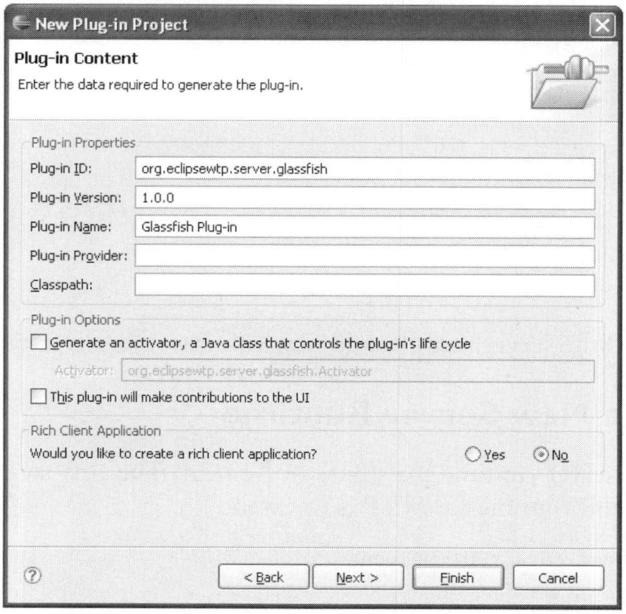

Figure 12.5 Plug-in Content

4. Eclipse creates the project and opens the plug-in descriptors in an editor. Select the **Dependencies** tab of the editor. Add the following plug-ins to the list of required plug-ins and save (see Figure 12.6).

- ○ `org.eclipse.wst.server.core`
- ○ `org.eclipse.wst.server.ui`
- ○ `org.eclipse.wst.common.project.facet.core`
- ○ `org.eclipse.wst.common.project.facet.ui`
- ○ `org.eclipse.jst.server.core`
- ○ `org.eclipse.jst.server.ui`
- ○ `org.eclipse.jst.server.generic.core`
- ○ `org.eclipse.jst.server.generic.ui`
- ○ `org.eclipse.jst.common.project.facet.core`

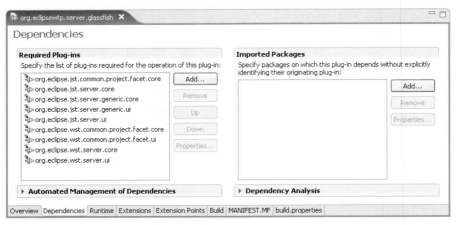

Figure 12.6   Required Plug-ins

Next you will extend the server tools to add new runtime and server types.

Adding Support for a New Server Runtime

GlassFish is a J2EE server runtime like JBoss or Tomcat. The first step in defining GlassFish as a valid runtime for WTP is to extend

`org.eclipse.wst.server.core.runtimeTypes`

1. In the plug-in editor, click **Extensions**. Click the **Add** button to add a new extension. The **New Extension** wizard opens.

2. Choose

   ```
   org.eclipse.wst.server.core.runtimeTypes
   ```

   from the list and click **Finish** (see Figure 12.7). The `runtimeType` extension is added to the list of extensions.

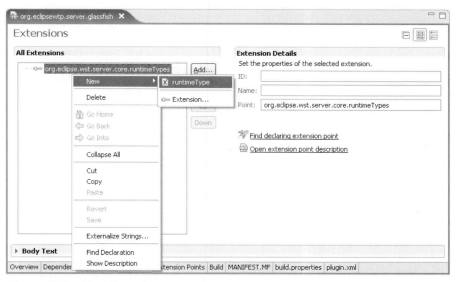

Figure 12.7   New Extension

3. Select the extension in the list, right click, and choose **New runtimeType**. This will add the new runtime type.

4. In the **Extension Element Details** form, enter

   ```
   org.eclipsewtp.server.glassfish.runtime
   ```

   as the id. Enter

   ```
   org.eclipse.jst.server.generic.core.internal.GenericServerRuntime
   ```

   as the runtime type class. Enter the rest of the fields and save the definition (see Figure 12.8).

5. Click on the **plugin.xml** tab. In this tab, you can view and edit the `plugin.xml` file in source form. Your code should look like Example 12.1.

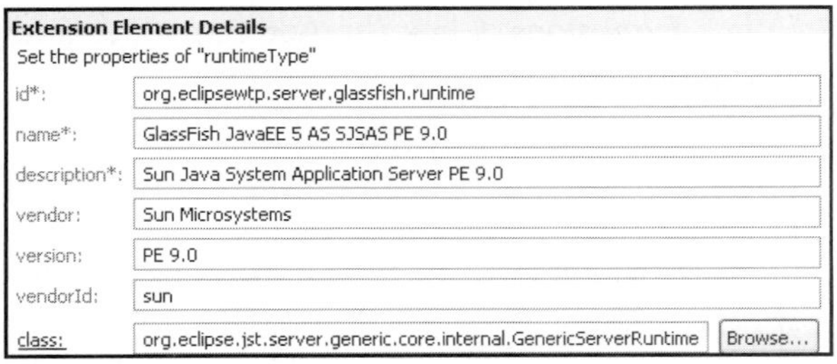

```
Extension Element Details
Set the properties of "runtimeType"
id*:          org.eclipsewtp.server.glassfish.runtime
name*:        GlassFish JavaEE 5 AS SJSAS PE 9.0
description*:  Sun Java System Application Server PE 9.0
vendor:       Sun Microsystems
version:      PE 9.0
vendorId:     sun
class:        org.eclipse.jst.server.generic.core.internal.GenericServerRuntime   [ Browse... ]
```

Figure 12.8   Runtime Element Details

Example 12.1   Runtime Type

```xml
<?xml version="1.0" encoding="UTF-8"?>
<?eclipse version="3.2"?>
<plugin>
  <extension
     point="org.eclipse.wst.server.core.runtimeTypes">
    <runtimeType
      class="org.eclipse.jst.server.generic.core.internal
                                       .GenericServerRuntime"
        description="GlassFish JavaEE 5 SJSAS PE 9.0"
        id="org.eclipsewtp.server.glassfish.runtime"
        name="GlassFish JavaEE 5 SJSAS PE 9.0"
        vendor="Sun Microsystems"
        vendorId="sun"
        version="PE 9.0">
    </runtimeType>
  </extension>
</plugin>
```

6. Add the J2EE modules supported by the GlassFish runtime to the runtime type extension. GlassFish is a Java EE 5 server. It supports all the latest versions of the Java EE modules as well as their earlier versions. Use the plug-in editor to add new moduleType elements to the runtimeType element (see Example 12.2).

Example 12.2   Module Types

```xml
<runtimeType
   class="org.eclipse.jst.server.generic.core.internal
                                       .GenericServerRuntime"
     description="Sun Java System Application Server PE 9.0"
     id="org.eclipsewtp.server.glassfish.runtime"
     name="GlassFish JavaEE 5 AS SJSAS PE 9.0"
     vendor="Sun Microsystems"
     vendorId="sun"
     version="PE 9.0">
     <moduleType types="jst.web" versions="2.2, 2.3, 2.4"/>
```

```
         <moduleType types="jst.ejb" versions="1.0, 1.1, 2.1, 3.0"/>
         <moduleType types="jst.ear" versions="1.2, 1.3, 1.4, 5.0"/>
         <moduleType types="jst.utility" versions="1.0"/>
         <moduleType types="jst.jca" versions="1.0, 1.5"/>
</runtimeType>
```

Now you have a new runtime type that supports jst.web, jst.ejb, jst.ear, jst.jca, and jst.utility module types. In the next step you will add server type extensions to this runtime.

Adding a New Server Type for a Runtime

A runtime must be associated with server configurations. Server configurations belong to runtime types. When you run a module on a server, it runs on an instance of the server. To define server types associated with the GlassFish runtime, you will need to extend:

```
org.eclipse.wst.server.core.serverTypes
```

1. Use the plug-in editor to add a new extension for a server type. Generic servers can start and stop servers by launching Java classes or by calling external programs. To start and stop GlassFish, you will call the external program adminas tool mentioned earlier.

2. The server implementation class will be GenericServer.

3. The server and launch behavior will be provided by the

   ```
   ExternalServerBehaviour
   ```

   and

   ```
   ExternalLaunchConfigurationType
   ```

   classes.

4. Enter the values for other attributes (see Example 12.3).

Example 12.3 Server Type

```
<extension
   point="org.eclipse.wst.server.core.serverTypes">
   <serverType
      id="org.eclipsewtp.server.glassfish.server"
      runtime="true"
      runtimeTypeId="org.eclipsewtp.server.glassfish.runtime"
      name="GlassFish JavaEE 5 SJSAS PE 9.0"
      description="GlassFish JavaEE 5 SJSAS PE 9.0"
      class="org.eclipse.jst.server.generic.core.internal.GenericServer"
```

```
        behaviourClass="org.eclipse.jst.server.generic.core.internal
                                            .ExternalServerBehaviour"
        hasConfiguration="false"
        initialState="stopped"
        launchConfigId="org.eclipse.jst.server.generic.core
                                    .ExternalLaunchConfigurationType"
        launchModes="run,debug"
        startBeforePublish="true"
        startTimeout="120000"
        stopTimeout="15000"
        supportsRemoteHosts="false"/>
</extension>
```

Next, you will define the runtime target handler.

Adding a New Runtime Target Handler

When a Web project is targeted to a runtime, WTP requests the runtime to pro-vide libraries that are needed for development of the project. This usually involves providing Java archives that contain J2EE API classes, Web service interfaces, and so forth. Since you will be using the generic server framework, these libraries will be defined in the server definition file. Later, you will do this by adding a `project` entry to the server definition file.

1. To add this behavior to the adapter, you will use an extension to provide an implementation of the runtime classpath provider. Use the plug-in editor to add a new extension for a classpath provider named

   `GenericServerRuntimeTargetHandler`

2. Make sure your extension looks like what you see in Example 12.4.

Example 12.4   Runtime Classpath Providers

```
<extension
   point="org.eclipse.jst.server.core.runtimeClasspathProviders">
   <runtimeClasspathProvider
      class="org.eclipse.jst.server.generic.core.internal
                                    .GenericServerRuntimeTargetHandler"
      id="org.eclipsewtp.jst.server.generic.glassfish
                                    .runtimeClasspathProvider"
      runtimeTypeIds="org.eclipsewtp.server.glassfish.*"/>
</extension>
```

Next, you will define the runtime components and facet mappings.

Facets and Runtime Components

WTP defines the concept of a runtime component to specify mappings between project facet versions and runtime environments. This allows tools to check compatibility of projects and runtimes automatically. For example, if a project has a facet such as jst.web v2.4, it can only be targeted to and run on a runtime component that has support for this module type and version. Runtime components are not limited to server runtimes but can include Java VMs or other aspects of the runtime. Runtime components are versioned, and facet versions can be mapped to either a specific runtime component version, a specific version or newer, or all versions.

To define new runtime components and facet mappings, you will extend

org.eclipse.wst.common.project.facet.core.runtimes

1. Use the plug-in editor to add a new extension for the facet core runtimes. First define a new runtime component and version as shown in Example 12.5.

Example 12.5 Runtime Component

```
<runtime-component-type
    id="org.eclipsewtp.server.glassfish"/>

<runtime-component-version
    type="org.eclipsewtp.server.glassfish"
    version="9.0"/>
```

2. Next, define the facets supported by this runtime component as shown in Example 12.6.

Example 12.6 Supported Facets

```
<supported>
  <runtime-component
    id="org.eclipsewtp.server.glassfish"
    version="9.0"/>
  <facet id="jst.web" version="2.2, 2.3, 2.4"/>
    .
    .
    .
</supported>
```

3. Then, you will map this runtime component to your server runtime type as shown in Example 12.7.

Example 12.7   Runtime Type to Runtime Component Mapping

```
<extension
   point="org.eclipse.jst.server.core.runtimeFacetMappings">
  <runtimeFacetMapping
     runtimeTypeId="org.eclipsewtp.server.glassfish.runtime"
     runtime-component="org.eclipsewtp.server.glassfish"
     version="9.0"/>
</extension>
```

4. The complete listing of this extension is provided in Example 12.8. Make sure your plugin.xml has the same content.

Example 12.8   Runtime Component Extension

```
<extension
   point="org.eclipse.wst.common.project.facet.core.runtimes">
  <runtime-component-type id="org.eclipsewtp.server.glassfish"/>
  <runtime-component-version
     type="org.eclipsewtp.server.glassfish"
     version="9.0"/>
  <adapter>
    <runtime-component id="org.eclipsewtp.server.glassfish" />
    <factory
       class="org.eclipse.jst.server.core.internal
                                    .RuntimeClasspathProvider$Factory"/>
    <type
       class="org.eclipse.jst.common.project.facet.core
                                          .IClasspathProvider"/>
  </adapter>
  <adapter>
    <runtime-component id="org.eclipsewtp.server.glassfish"/>
    <factory
       class="org.eclipse.jst.server.ui.internal
                                  .RuntimeLabelProvider$Factory"/>
    <type
       class="org.eclipse.wst.common.project.facet.ui
                                  .IRuntimeComponentLabelProvider"/>
  </adapter>
  <supported>
    <runtime-component
       id="org.eclipsewtp.server.glassfish"
       version="9.0"/>
    <facet id="jst.web" version="2.2, 2.3, 2.4"/>
    <facet id="jst.ejb" version="1.1, 2.0, 2.1"/>
    <facet id="jst.ear" version="1.2, 1.3, 1.4"/>
    <facet id="jst.connector" version="1.0, 1.5"/>
    <facet id="jst.appclient" version="1.2, 1.3, 1.4"/>
    <facet id="jst.utility" version="1.0"/>
  </supported>
</extension>

<extension
   point="org.eclipse.jst.server.core.runtimeFacetMappings">
  <runtimeFacetMapping
```

```
        runtimeTypeId="org.eclipsewtp.server.glassfish.runtime"
        runtime-component="org.eclipsewtp.server.glassfish"
        version="9.0"/>
</extension>
```

Next, you will define the UI components for the runtime and the server.

Extending the Server Tools UI

WTP uses views and wizards that are provided by the server adapters when a developer creates a new server or edits it. The best part of this step is that the UI will be generated dynamically. The generic server framework constructs views and wizards for generic servers and runtimes by using the server definitions. You will create this file soon.

1. In this step, all you need to do is create an extension to set the generic server UI components for GlassFish servers and runtimes. Use the plug-in editor to add a new extension for the wizard fragments and icons. You can use any 16x16 pixel icon to identify your server. The `glassfish.gif` icon is included in the sample code for this chapter. Make sure that your extensions look those in Example 12.9.

Example 12.9   Wizard Fragments and Icons

```
<extension
    point="org.eclipse.wst.server.ui.wizardFragments">
  <fragment
      id="org.eclipse.jst.server.generic.runtime"
      typeIds="org.eclipsewtp.server.glassfish.runtime"
      class="org.eclipse.jst.server.generic.ui.internal
                            .GenericServerRuntimeWizardFragment"/>
  <fragment
      id="org.eclipse.jst.server.generic.server"
      typeIds="org.eclipsewtp.server.glassfish.server"
      class="org.eclipse.jst.server.generic.ui.internal
                            .GenericServerWizardFragment"/>
</extension>
<extension
    point="org.eclipse.wst.server.ui.serverImages">
  <image
      id="org.eclipse.jst.server.generic.image"
      icon="icons/obj16/glassfish.gif"
      typeIds="org.eclipsewtp.server.glassfish.runtime"/>
  <image
      id="org.eclipse.jst.server.generic.image"
      icon="icons/obj16/glassfish.gif"
      typeIds="org.eclipsewtp.server.glassfish.server"/>
</extension>
<extension
    point="org.eclipse.wst.common.project.facet.ui.images">
```

```
<image
    runtime-component-type="org.eclipsewtp.server.glassfish"
    path="icons/obj16/glassfish.gif"/>
</extension>
```

2. Save the plug-in.

It is time to create the server definition file.

The Generic Server Definition

The generic server framework is a server adapter implementation that allows you to extend WTP with support for a new server without writing Java code. The behavior and definition for each distinct type of server is captured in a definition file. The framework classes use the definitions found in this file to start and stop a server, set the classpath of a project, publish a module to a server, and open a user interface to edit the properties of a server.

The server type definition is an XML file that contains information for the GlassFish runtime and server types. This file is validated against an XSD, which is located in the

```
org.eclipse.jst.server.generic.core
```

plug-in. The first part of the definition file contains user-defined server properties. These properties can be referred to in other parts of the server definition file. The values of the properties are edited with the server tools user interfaces. Each property has a context: server or runtime. A set of server properties is saved with each server configuration, and a set of runtime properties is saved with each runtime definition.

Properties also have types, each of which can be a string, boolean, file or directory. The type of the property, along with its label and default value, is also used to generate UI components. For example, consider the following property element:

```
<property
    id="serverRootDirectory"
    label="Server Directory"
    type="directory"
    context="runtime"
    default="/your_server_root/appservers"/>
```

The definition will result in the automatically generated UI component shown in Figure 12.9.

Figure 12.9   UI Component for a Server Property

You use the syntax ${serverRootDirectory} to refer to the variable with the id named serverRootDirectory in other parts of the definition file.

In addition to the properties, you also define the following server parameters using this file:

- ❍ module—type and publishing information for each of the supported modules
- ❍ project—classpath library that will be added to targeted applications
- ❍ start—executable, environment, and parameters that will be used to start the server
- ❍ stop—executable, environment, and parameters that will be used to stop the server
- ❍ publisher—type and properties needed for publishers to deploy modules to supported servers
- ❍ classpath—list of archives that make the entries of a classpath library

1. Define an extension to associate a server definition file with the GlassFish runtime in plugin.xml (see Example 12.10). The path for the server definition file must be relative to the root of the plug-in.

Example 12.10   Server Definition for a Runtime

```
<extension
    point="org.eclipse.jst.server.generic.core.serverdefinition">
  <serverdefinition
    id="org.eclipsewtp.server.glassfish.runtime"
    definitionfile="glassfish.serverdef"/>
</extension>
```

2. Create a new file named

   glassfish.serverdef

   at the root of your plug-in. Open the serverdef file using an XML editor. You will add properties for runtime and server attributes. These user-editable properties parameterize things like the location of the GlassFish installation, name of the domain, location of the auto-deploy directory, HTTP port, location of the asadmin executable, and so forth. Enter the complete contents of the server definition file (see Example 12.11).

Example 12.11   Listing of glassfish.serverdef

```
<?xml version="1.0" encoding="UTF-8"?>
<tns:ServerRuntime
    xmlns:tns=
"http://eclipse.org/jst/server/generic/ServerTypeDefinition"
```

```
  xmlns:xsi="http://www.w3.org/2001/XMLSchema-instance"
  xsi:schemaLocation=
"http://eclipse.org/jst/server/generic/ServerTypeDefinition
ServerTypeDefinitionSchema.xsd"
  name="GlassFish JavaEE 5 SJSAS PE 9.0" version="v9.0">
 <property id="serverRootDirectory"
    label="Runtime Directory"
    type="directory"
    context="runtime"
    default="/installdirectory/Sun/AppServer"/>
 <property id="domain"
    label="Domain Directory"
    type="directory"
    context="string"
    default="domain1"/>
 <property id="autoDeployDirectory"
    label="Auto Deploy Directory"
    type="directory"
    context="server"
    default="/installdirectory/Sun/AppServer/domains/domain1/autodeploy"/>
 <property id="adminScript"
    label="Start Script"
    type="file"
    context="server"
    default="/installdirectory/Sun/AppServer/bin/asadmin.bat"/>
 <property id="port"
    label="Server Port"
    type="string"
    context="server"
    default="8080"/>
 <property id="debugPort"
    label="Debug Port"
    type="string"
    context="server"
    default="9009"/>
<port>
  <no>${port}</no>
  <name>Http</name>
  <protocol>http</protocol>
  start
</port>
<module>
  <type>jst.web</type>
  <publishDir>${autoDeployDirectory}</publishDir>
  <publisherReference>
    org.eclipse.jst.server.generic.antpublisher
  </publisherReference>
</module>
<module>
  <type>jst.ejb</type>
  <publishDir>${autoDeployDirectory}</publishDir>
  <publisherReference>
    org.eclipse.jst.server.generic.antpublisher
  </publisherReference>
</module>
```

```
<module>
  <type>jst.ear</type>
  <publishDir>${autoDeployDirectory}</publishDir>
  <publisherReference>
    org.eclipse.jst.server.generic.antpublisher
  </publisherReference>
</module>
<project>
  <classpathReference>sjsas</classpathReference>
</project>
<start>
  <external>
    "${adminScript}"  "start-domain" --debug "${domain}"
  </external>
  <workingDirectory>${serverRootDirectory}/bin</workingDirectory>
  <debugPort>${debugPort}</debugPort>
</start>
<stop>
  <external>"${adminScript}"  "stop-domain" "${domain}"</external>
  <workingDirectory>${serverRootDirectory}/bin</workingDirectory>
</stop>
<publisher id="org.eclipse.jst.server.generic.antpublisher">
  <publisherdata>
    <dataname>build.file</dataname>
    <datavalue>sjsas.xml</datavalue>
  </publisherdata>
  <publisherdata>
    <dataname>target.publish.jst.web</dataname>
    <datavalue>deploy.j2ee.web</datavalue>
  </publisherdata>
  <publisherdata>
    <dataname>target.publish.jst.ejb</dataname>
    <datavalue>deploy.j2ee.ejb</datavalue>
  </publisherdata>
  <publisherdata>
    <dataname>target.unpublish.jst.web</dataname>
    <datavalue>undeploy.j2ee.web</datavalue>
  </publisherdata>
  <publisherdata>
    <dataname>target.unpublish.jst.ejb</dataname>
    <datavalue>undeploy.j2ee.ejb</datavalue>
  </publisherdata>
  <publisherdata>
    <dataname>target.publish.jst.ear</dataname>
    <datavalue>deploy.j2ee.ear</datavalue>
  </publisherdata>
  <publisherdata>
    <dataname>target.unpublish.jst.ear</dataname>
    <datavalue>undeploy.j2ee.ear</datavalue>
  </publisherdata>
</publisher>
<classpath id="sjsas">
  <archive path="${serverRootDirectory}/lib/javaee.jar"/>
</classpath>
<jndiConnection>
  <providerUrl>http://localhost:${port}</providerUrl>
```

```
<initialContextFactory>not.used</initialContextFactory>
<jndiProperty>
  <name></name>
  <value></value>
</jndiProperty>
</jndiConnection>
</tns:ServerRuntime>
```

In the next step you will create the Ant script that will be used to publish modules to the server.

Publishers

Generic publishers handle deployment of modules to servers. Generic servers provide an implementation of server publishing using Apache Ant. You already defined the publisher for all the modules to be the generic Ant publisher by setting their id to

```
org.eclipse.jst.server.generic.antpublisher
```

You also defined the name of the Ant target that will be invoked to publish or unpublish each module type. Now, you will write an Ant script to provide this publishing capability.

Enter the code shown in Example 12.12 to define an Ant script named sjsas.xml in the plug-in folder.

Example 12.12   Listing of sjsas.xml

```
<project
  name="deployextension"
  default="deploy.j2ee.web"
  basedir=".">
  <property name="newDeployPause" value="5"/>
  <property name="reDeployPause" value="5"/>
  <!-- only deploy if the archive does not exist in the auto deploy
       dir or the source is more recent -->
  <target name="deploy.j2ee.web"
    depends="-checkWebDeploy"
    unless="notNeeded">
    <jar destfile="${project.working.dir}/${module.name}.war">
      <zipfileset dir="${module.dir}">
        <include name="**/*.*"/>
        <exclude name="**/jsp_servlet/*.class"/>
        <exclude name="**/*.war"/>
      </zipfileset>
    </jar>
    <!-- set the pause to either the "new" or the "redeploy" value
         depending on whether the archive already exists in the
         autodeploy dir -->
    <available
      property="exists"
```

```
          file="${server.publish.dir}/${module.name}.war"/>
    <condition
        property="pause"
        value="${newDeployPause}">
      <not>
        <istrue value="${exists}"/>
      </not>
    </condition>
    <condition
        property="pause"
        value="${reDeployPause}">
      <istrue value="${exists}"/>
    </condition>
    <move
        file="${project.working.dir}/${module.name}.war"
        todir="${server.publish.dir}"/>
    <!-- delay in seconds to the server a chance to pick up the
         autodeployment -->
    <sleep seconds="${pause}"/>
  </target>
  <target name="-checkWebDeploy">
    <uptodate
        property="notNeeded"
        targetfile="${server.publish.dir}/${module.name}.war">
      <srcfiles dir="${module.dir}">
        <include name="**/*.*"/>
        <exclude name="**/jsp_servlet/*.class"/>
        <exclude name="**/*.war"/>
      </srcfiles>
    </uptodate>
  </target>
  <target name="deploy.j2ee.ejb"
      depends="-checkEJBDeploy"
      unless="notNeeded">
    <jar destfile="${project.working.dir}/${module.name}.jar">
      <zipfileset dir="${module.dir}">
        <include name="**/*.*"/>
        <exclude name="**/*.java"/>
      </zipfileset>
    </jar>
    <!-- set the pause to either the "new" or the "redeploy" value
         depending on whether the archive already exists in the
         autodeploy dir -->
    <available
        property="exists"
        file="${server.publish.dir}/${module.name}.jar"/>
    <condition
        property="pause"
        value="${newDeployPause}">
      <not>
        <istrue value="${exists}"/>
      </not>
    </condition>
    <condition
        property="pause"
        value="${reDeployPause}">
```

```xml
        <istrue value="${exists}"/>
      </condition>
      <move
        file="${project.working.dir}/${module.name}.jar"
        todir="${server.publish.dir}"/>
      <!-- delay in seconds to the server a chance to pick up the
           autodeployment -->
      <sleep seconds="${pause}"/>
  </target>
  <target name="-checkEJBDeploy">
    <uptodate
        property="notNeeded"
        targetfile="${server.publish.dir}/${module.name}.jar">
      <srcfiles dir="${module.dir}">
        <include name="**/*.*"/>
        <exclude name="**/*.java"/>
      </srcfiles>
    </uptodate>
  </target>
  <target name="deploy.j2ee.ear"
      depends="-checkJ2EEDeploy"
      unless="notNeeded">
    <jar destfile="${project.working.dir}/${module.name}.ear">
      <zipfileset dir="${module.dir}">
        <include name="**/*.*"/>
        <exclude name="**/*.java"/>
      </zipfileset>
    </jar>
    <!-- set the pause to either the "new" or the "redeploy" value
         depending on whether the archive already exists in the
         autodeploy dir -->
    <available
        property="exists"
        file="${server.publish.dir}/${module.name}.war"/>
    <condition
        property="pause"
        value="${newDeployPause}">
      <not>
        <istrue value="${exists}"/>
      </not>
    </condition>
    <condition
        property="pause"
        value="${reDeployPause}">
      <istrue value="${exists}"/>
    </condition>
    <move
        file="${project.working.dir}/${module.name}.ear"
        todir="${server.publish.dir}"/>
    <sleep seconds="${pause}"/>
  </target>
  <target name="-checkJ2EEDeploy">
    <uptodate
        property="notNeeded"
        targetfile="${server.publish.dir}/${module.name}.ear">
      <srcfiles dir="${module.dir}">
```

```
      <include name="**/*.*"/>
      <exclude name="**/*.java"/>
    </srcfiles>
  </uptodate>
</target>
<target name="undeploy.j2ee.web">
  <delete file="${server.publish.dir}/${module.name}.war"/>
</target>
<target name="undeploy.j2ee.ejb">
  <delete file="${server.publish.dir}/${module.name}.jar"/>
</target>
<target name="undeploy.j2ee.ear">
  <delete file="${server.publish.dir}/${module.name}.ear"/>
</target>
</project>
```

The Ant publisher defines variables, such as project.working.dir, module.dir, module.name, and server.publish.dir, before this script is invoked with the proper target. The publishing script simply archives the contents of a folder and copies the archive to the GlassFish server autodeploy folder. A pause is included to give the server a chance to detect the application.

This completes the development of the GlassFish server adapter plug-in. In the next iteration you will test it.

Testing the Server Adapter

The Eclipse Plug-in Development Environment (PDE) has a launcher that allows you to test and debug plug-ins. To accomplish this you will do the following:

○ Create and run a runtime workbench launch configuration for a second Eclipse instance that includes your server adapter plug-in and WTP.

○ Create a dynamic Web project that uses GlassFish.

1. Go the **Package Explorer** in the Eclipse workbench where you developed your server adapter plug-in, right click, and invoke the **Run As ▸ Run** to open the launch configuration dialog. Select **Eclipse Application**, right click, and invoke the **New** menu item. This will create a new runtime workbench configuration (see Figure 12.10).

2. Select the configuration named New_configuration and click **Run**. A new runtime Eclipse workbench will be launched, and you will see the familiar **Welcome** page.

3. Open the **Preferences** dialog, expand the **Servers** category, and select the **Installed Runtimes** preferences page. Click the **Add** button. The **New Server Runtime** wizard opens (see Figure 12.11). You will see the **GlassFish** runtime listed in the dialog under the **Sun Microsystems** category.

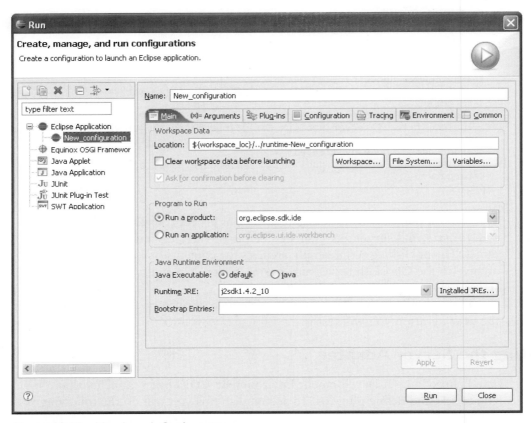

Figure 12.10   New Launch Configuration

4. You should see your GlassFish server adapter listed now. Select GlassFish and click the **Next** button. The **GlassFish Runtime** wizard opens (see Figure 12.12). Note how the wizard UI gets populated with form fields for the runtime properties you defined in the server definition file.

5. Specify the location of the GlassFish installation directory. Enter the location or select it using the **Browse** button. Note that a directory browse button has been provided because the type of the property was directory. Click the **Finish** button. The **Installed Runtimes** preference page now lists GlassFish (see Figure 12.13).

6. You have now added the GlassFish server runtime environment and are ready to use it for a new Web project. In the **Project Explorer** view, right click and select **New ▸ Dynamic Web Project**. The **New Dynamic Web Project** wizard opens (see Figure 12.14).

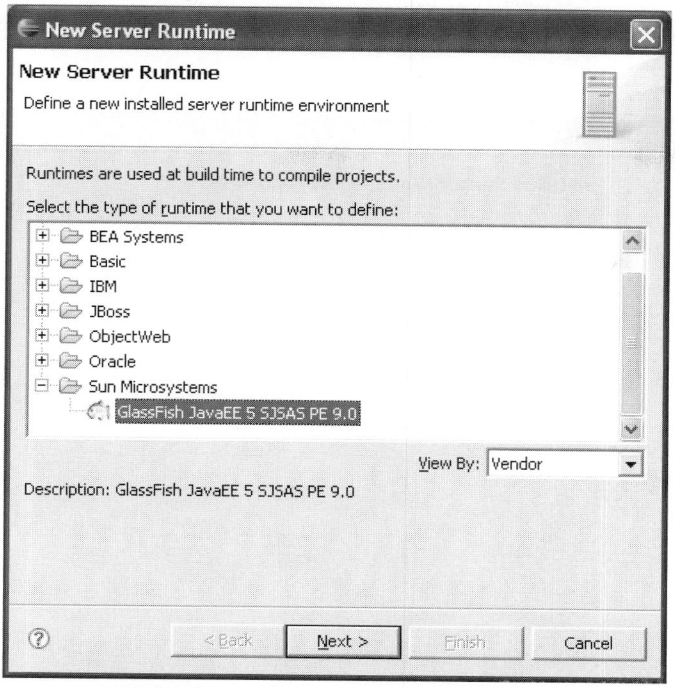

Figure 12.11   New Server Runtime

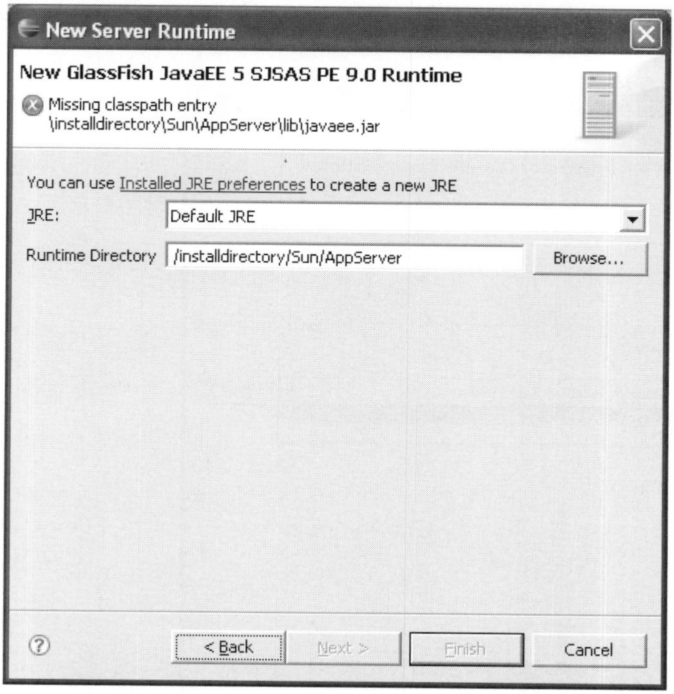

Figure 12.12   GlassFish Runtime

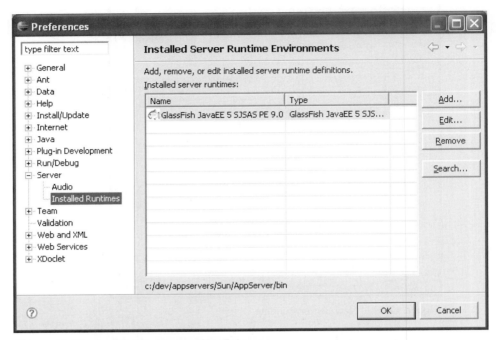

Figure 12.13   Installed Runtimes—GlassFish

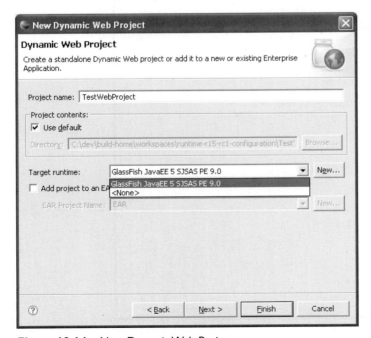

Figure 12.14   New Dynamic Web Project

7. Enter `TestWebProject` as the project name and select `GlassFish` as the target runtime. Click the **Next** button. The **Select Project Facets** page is displayed (see Figure 12.15).

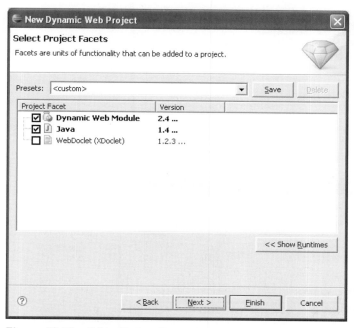

Figure 12.15   Select Project Facets

8. Notice how the set of supported facets matches the allowed values that were defined in `plugin.xml`. Accept the defaults for other properties. Click **Finish**. WTP creates the project. Notice that a GlassFish library gets added to the project as defined by the runtime classpath provider extension (see Figure 12.16).

9. Create a simple JSP named `index.jsp` in the `WebContent` folder. Add some simple content to it. This completes the project setup.

10. You are now ready to run the JSP on GlassFish. In the **Project Explorer**, select `index.jsp`, right click, and invoke the **Run As ▸ Run on Server** menu item. The **Run On Server** wizard opens (see Figure 12.17).

11. Create a new server configuration for the GlassFish runtime. Click **Next** to continue. You will see the server properties displayed (see Figure 12.18). These properties were also defined in the server definitions file. Enter the proper values.

12. Click **Next** to continue. The **Add and Remove Projects** page is displayed (see Figure 12.19).

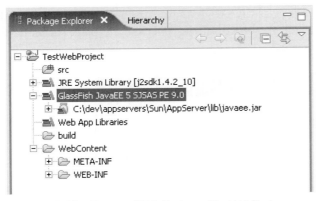

Figure 12.16   Dynamic Web Project—TestWebProject

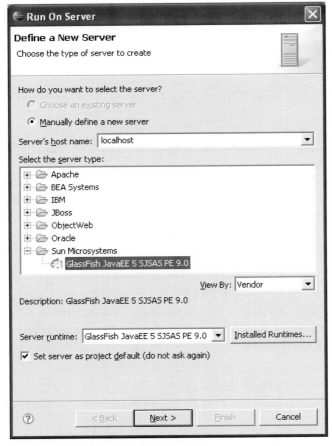

Figure 12.17   Define a New Server

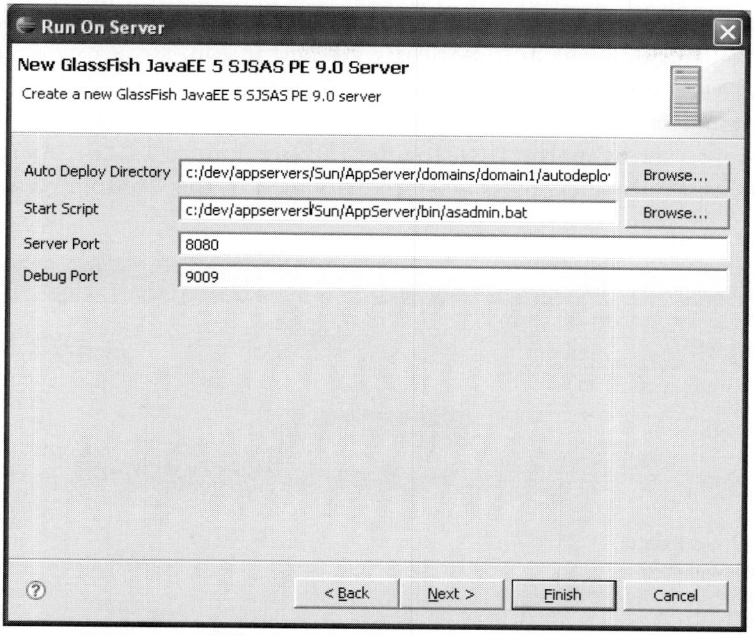

Figure 12.18 GlassFish Server

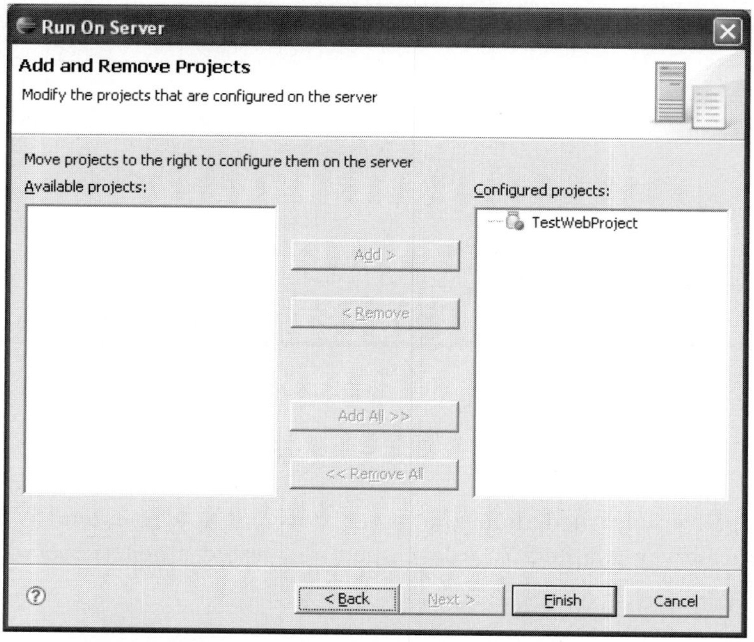

Figure 12.19 Add and Remove Projects

13. A server configuration includes the list of dynamic Web projects. TestWebProject was automatically added for you, so simply click the Finish button. The wizard creates the server, starts it, publishes the TestWebProject project to it using the Ant scripts, and launches the Web browser using the URL for the JSP (see Figure 12.20). As the server starts and publishes, messages are displayed in the Console view.

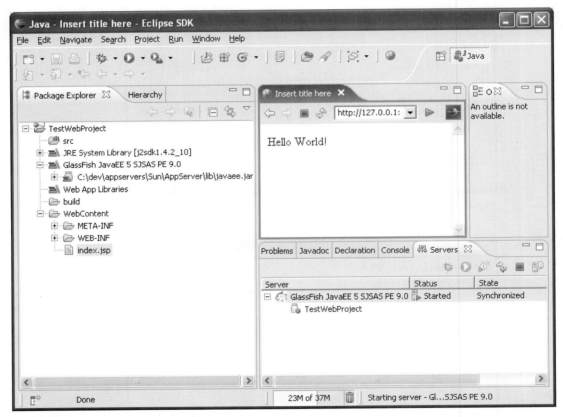

Figure 12.20   Run On Server—index.jsp

Summary

In this chapter you learned about the server tools and how to extend WTP with a new generic server adapter. You developed and tested a generic server adapter for GlassFish.

There is more to server tools than what was covered here. Generic server support is suitable for most purposes. However, you should also have a look at the custom adapters, such as the Tomcat plug-ins, to see how you can have full control over the server tools capability. If you would like to learn how to publish your server plug-ins as installable features, and provide links to your update sites, you should look at the Apache Geronimo plug-in.

CHAPTER 13

Supporting New File Types

The limits of my language mean the limits of my world.

—Ludwig Wittgenstein

At its core, an integrated development environment (IDE) assists a developer in working with various development artifacts. While some of the artifacts, such as server instances, may be intangible, most artifacts map to one or more files whose syntax is defined by programming languages. The IDE's job is to simplify the task of working with these languages.

There are a number of tools an IDE can provide to simplify development of language-specific files. A new file wizard handles tasks such as naming and placement of the file and can create a skeleton structure of the new file. A rich editor simplifies manual editing of the file with content assistance and syntax highlighting. Rich editors may also include a design or graphical view that provides an alternate visualization of the file. A validator, which will typically be integrated with the editor, checks the file to ensure it is compliant with the language specification. If a file requires compilation or some other form of transformation before it can be deployed, a facility for building the file should also be included.

DocBook is an XML language for authoring documents such as books, articles, and reference pages (see Example 13.1). It can be obtained from the DocBook Web site:

http://www.docbook.org

Example 13.1   Listing of article.docbook

```
<?xml version="1.0" encoding="UTF-8"?>
<article>
  <title>Supporting New File Types</title>
  <para>
    At its core, an integrated development environment (IDE) assists a
    developer in working with various development artifacts. While some
```

```
    of the artifacts, such as server instances, may be intangible, most
    artifacts map to a file or a variety of files defined by specific
    languages. The IDE's job is to simplify the task of working with
    specific languages.
  </para>
  <para>
    There are a number of tools an IDE can provide to simplify
    development of language-specific files. A new file wizard handles
    tasks such as naming and placement of the file and can create a
    skeleton structure of the new file. A rich editor simplifies
    manual editing of the file with content assistance and syntax
    highlighting. Rich editors may also include a design or graphical
    view that provides a different visualization of the file. A
    validator, which will typically be integrated with the editor,
    checks the file to ensure it is compliant with the
    language specification. If a file requires compilation or some
    other form of transformation before it can be deployed, a facility
    for building the file should also be included.
  </para>
</article>
```

Unlike many other authoring formats, DocBook documents contain no formatting or presentation information. Instead, a DocBook document contains tags (XML elements) that describe its content. The removal of presentation information from the source document solves the typical problem of inconsistent formatting and provides increased publishing flexibility (the ability to publish a document in multiple formats). Publishing flexibility is achieved by transforming the document after it has been authored into a desired format, such as HTML or PDF. In this way, DocBook is very much like a programming language in that you write the source and then transform it into a consumable form.

In this chapter you will add support for the DocBook language to Eclipse as follows:

❍ You create a DocBook validator for files with the .docbook extension.

Note that DocBook files typically use the .xml extension. The .docbook file extension is used in this chapter for illustrative purposes since WTP contains a number of tools, including a validator, for XML files.

❍ You define a DocBook marker type to allow end users to filter DocBook problems from the **Problems** view.

❍ You specify a DocBook content type that allows DocBook files to make use of all the XML-related tools, including the XML editor.

Warning: As of WTP 1.5, the WTP extension points and API shown in this chapter are not final. These extension points and API may change in future versions of WTP.

Creating the DocBook Extension Plug-in

As always, the first step in contributing DocBook support to Eclipse is to create a plug-in that will hold your DocBook-specific extensions. To create the DocBook extension plug-in, do the following:

1. Open the **Plug-in Development** perspective, create a new plug-in project using the **New Plug-in Project** wizard, and name it:

   ```
   org.eclipsewtp.docbook
   ```

2. The DocBook extensions you will contribute will not make any UI contributions or require an activator. Deselect the options **Generate an activator** and **This plug-in will make contributions to the UI** (see Figure 13.1).

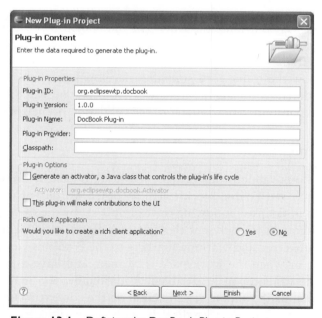

Figure 13.1   Defining the DocBook Plug-in Project

The DocBook Validator

Modern software development requires the use of many languages. Gone are the days when being an expert in one language was a career option. Many languages exist in the same space and, to effectively do their job, developers are often required to work with the many corresponding file types. For example, there are more than just a few languages available in the Web space, including ASP, CSS,

HTML, Java, JavaScript, Perl, PHP, Ruby, WSDL, XML, XSD, and XSL. While all of these languages are not required for every Web project, it is typical to use several of them. DocBook, which can be used to document Web and other applications, is just one more language in the mix.

With so many different languages, it can be difficult, and overwhelming, for developers to understand each one in the depth required to ensure that the files they are creating are correct according to the various specifications. DocBook contains a well-structured definition for documents. If a document does not comply with the DocBook structured definition, then it is not a DocBook document, and the behavior of DocBook tools when used with this document cannot be guaranteed to be correct. To solve this problem, you will contribute a DocBook validator to the Eclipse IDE. This validator will give developers the assurance that their DocBook files conform to the specification and remove the burden from them to be DocBook experts.

In this section you will contribute the DocBook validator to Eclipse using the WTP validation framework. The following sections will detail why and how you will use the validation framework. First, the benefits of the framework will be presented, highlighting how the framework simplifies development of the DocBook validator. After the rationale for using the framework is clear, you will then implement the DocBook validator and contribute it to the validation framework.

The WTP Validation Framework

Before creating a DocBook validator for Eclipse, you need to identify how the validator will interact with the Eclipse workbench. In other words, what will the DocBook validator do in Eclipse? Following the example set by the Java compiler (the JDT is typically thought to represent the best of Eclipse), the DocBook validator should contribute error and warning markers to the **Problems** view, be run automatically on save or when the workspace is cleaned, and have a preference defined that allows the validator to be disabled. Additionally, you may want to include an option to manually validate via an action on the context menu.

Although the validator can interact directly with the various pieces of the platform that provide the functionality outlined above, the validation framework provides a simplified method to consistently add the DocBook validator to Eclipse. Specifically, the validation framework will add errors and warnings reported by the validator to the **Problems** view, add a preference to disable the validator, and run the validator on save as part of the build and via the standard context menu **Validate** action. The validation framework allows you to focus on your core competency, which in this case is a deep understanding of DocBook, by handling these various pieces of Eclipse integration. It significantly reduces the learning curve and time required to add a validator to Eclipse.

Note that as of WTP 1.5, the validation framework does not support Eclipse content types. The WTP 1.5 support is limited to distinguishing resources based on file extension.

Implementing the DocBook Validator

In this section you implement the DocBook validator by doing the following:

1. For the DocBook validator to make use of the validation framework, you first must add a dependency on the validation framework to your plug-in. In your DocBook project, open the plug-in manifest editor, change to the dependencies tab, and add a dependency on

   `org.eclipse.wst.validation`

   The validation API depends on the core runtime plug-in for the scheduling of validation jobs and reporting validation status. Specify a second dependency on the plug-in

   `org.eclipse.core.runtime`

   The DocBook validator will make use of Eclipse file resources in order to validate them. In Eclipse, resources are represented by the `IResource` and `IFile` interfaces. Add a dependency on the following plug-in that contains these interfaces:

   `org.eclipse.core.resources`

2. With the dependencies declared, you can now create the extension that will declare the DocBook validator to the validation framework. Change to the **Extensions** tab and click **Add** to add a new extension.

   The validation framework defines this extension point:

   `org.eclipse.wst.validation.validator`

   You will use this extension point to register the DocBook validator with the framework. Select the extension point from the list and click **Finish**. The extensions page should now display the new extension point. Give the extension point the id `docbookvalidator` and the name `DocBook Validator`.

3. Next, right click on the extension point and select **New ▸ validator**. The `to` and `from` properties on the validator extension are used to migrate an existing validator to a new class while maintaining the existing marker affiliation with the validator. This means that when an old workspace is migrated to a newer version of WTP, markers that were created by a validator will not be stranded leaving the user with no way to remove

them. Because the DocBook validator is a new validator, these properties are not applicable.

4. The validator extension point requires three elements in order to specify the DocBook validator: the `run` element, the `helper` element, and the `filter` element.

The first element is the `run` element, which will be used to specify details about the validator class and how it should be used by the framework. Start by declaring the new validator using the `run` element. Right click on validator and select **New ▸ run**. You will use the `run` element's `class` attribute to specify the DocBook validator class to the validation framework, but first you will create the DocBook validator class.

Save your plug-in manifest and open the **New Java Class** wizard by selecting **File ▸ New ▸ Class**. Enter the class name `DocbookValidator` and the package

```
org.eclipsewtp.docbook
```

Add the following interface to the list of interfaces (see Figure 13.2):

```
org.eclipse.wst.validation.internal.provisional.core.IValidatorJob
```

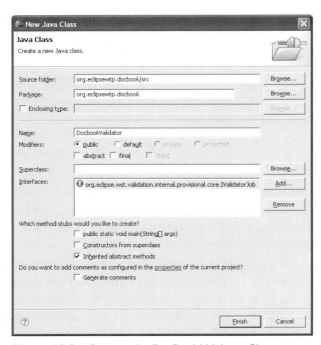

Figure 13.2 Creating the DocBook Validator Class

Click **Finish**. The `DocbookValidator` class opens in the Java source editor. You may see some warnings about discouraged access on your newly created class. These warnings are simply stating that you're not using API. You can ignore these warnings for now. (In general, these warnings alert you that you're in unsupported waters making use of code that has not been declared API.) Close the editor for now. You'll deal with the implementation details after you finish declaring the extension.

Now that you've created the class and know the fully qualified class name, return to your plug-in manifest editor and enter the following for the `run` element's `class` attribute:

```
org.eclipsewtp.docbook.DocbookValidator
```

There are three other boolean properties on the validator extension that are relevant for the DocBook validator (see Figure 13.3): `enabled`, `incremental`, and `fullBuild`. The fourth option, `async`, is deprecated. As the validator implements `IValidatorJob` it will be run asynchronously.

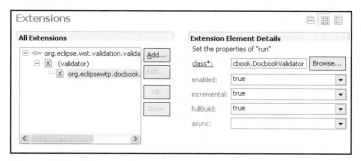

Figure 13.3   The run Extension

The `enabled` property specifies whether the DocBook validator should be enabled by default. You may want to disable a validator by default if there will be a significant performance penalty when the validator is enabled. The DocBook validator will be lightweight, so set this property to `true`.

The `incremental` property tells the validation framework whether the DocBook validator should be run as part of the incremental build. The incremental build runs when a resource is changed (typically when it is saved). One of the requirements for the DocBook validator is that it should validate on save. Set this option to `true`.

The `fullBuild` informs the validation framework whether or not the DocBook validator should run as part of a full build. A full build is run when users select to clean a project or their workspace (see Figure 13.4). Set this to `true` to allow users to clean DocBook files.

Figure 13.4   The Project ▶ Clean... Menu

5. The second element required by the validation framework is the `helper` element, which will be used to specify the class that handles model loading for the validator.

   Right click on validator and select **New ▶ helper**.

   The validation framework provides a list of resources that should be validated by passing a workbench context (also known as a helper) of type `IWorkbenchContext` to the validator. The validation framework requires that validators declare the implementation class of the `IWorkbenchContext` interface that they will use. The validation framework includes a default workbench context that can be used by client validators. The default workbench context provides the ability to load an `IFile` for each file that is to be validated. The DocBook validator will only support files; therefore, the default workbench context will suit its needs. Specify that the DocBook validator will use the default workbench context provided by the validation framework by setting the workbench context class as

   `org.eclipse.wst.validation.internal.operations.WorkbenchContext`

6. The third element that the validation framework requires is the `filter` element. This element is used to specify the resources for which the validator is enabled. As specified in the requirements, the DocBook validator will run for files with the extension .docbook.

To specify the filter, right click on the `validator` element and select
New ▸ filter. The `filter` element contains these three properties that you
need to specify: `objectClass`, `nameFilter`, and `caseSensitive`.

`objectClass` specifies the type of object that will be filtered. The DocBook
validator will validate files, so specify the `objectClass`

`org.eclipse.core.resources.IFile`

The `nameFilter` attribute specifies the name of the object. This property
accepts wildcards such as * and ?. For the DocBook validator, specify it as

`*.docbook`

`caseSensitive` is a boolean property that specifies whether the case of the
extension should be taken into account when matching names using the
`nameFilter`. The DocBook validator will disregard case, so set this property to `false`.

The `filter` element contains an optional fourth property, `action`, which
can be used to specify the specific actions for which the validator should
run. For example, you can specify that the validator should only run when
the **New** action is invoked. This will restrict the validator to running only
on file creation. The `action` property is not typically used with validators
as validators are generally defined for resources that will be edited.

7. You've now completed the DocBook extension declaration. Other extension contributions exist for the validator that allow further restrictions to
be placed on the condition for which it is enabled. These extensions allow
you to restrict the validator to certain project types or facets. For example,
if you were to define an authoring project nature, you may choose to
restrict the DocBook validator to only run on projects with this nature.
The DocBook validator will be enabled for all projects and facets, because
aside from the name filter no restrictions have been defined.

The manifest editor stores your extension declaration in `plugin.xml`. Take
a look at the extension by clicking on the **plugin.xml** tab (see
Example 13.2).

Example 13.2   Listing of the DocBook Validator Contribution to plugin.xml

```
<extension
  id="docbookValidator"
  name="DocBook Validator"
  point="org.eclipse.wst.validation.validator">
  <validator>
    <run
      class="org.eclipsewtp.docbook.DocbookValidator"
```

```
      enabled="true"
      fullBuild="true"
      incremental="true"/>
   <helper
      class="org.eclipse.wst.validation.internal.operations
                                        .workbenchContext"/>
   <filter
      caseSensitive="false"
      nameFilter="*.docbook"
      objectClass="org.eclipse.core.resources.IFile"/>
  </validator>
</extension>
```

8. With the DocBook validator declared to the validation framework, you can now move on to the implementation of the validator class. The validator class is where the validation logic for the DocBook validator will reside.

   Edit `DocbookValidator.java` (see Example 13.3).

Example 13.3 Listing of DocbookValidator.java

```java
package org.eclipsewtp.docbook;

import javax.xml.parsers.DocumentBuilder;
import javax.xml.parsers.DocumentBuilderFactory;

import org.eclipse.core.resources.IFile;
import org.eclipse.core.runtime.IStatus;
import org.eclipse.core.runtime.Status;
import org.eclipse.core.runtime.jobs.ISchedulingRule;
import org.eclipse.wst.validation.internal.core.ValidationException;
import org.eclipse.wst.validation.internal.operations.LocalizedMessage;
import org.eclipse.wst.validation.internal.provisional.core.IReporter;
import org.eclipse.wst.validation.....core.IValidationContext;
import org.eclipse.wst.validation.....core.IValidatorJob;
import org.w3c.dom.Document;
import org.w3c.dom.Element;
import org.xml.sax.SAXException;
import org.xml.sax.SAXParseException;

public class DocbookValidator implements IValidatorJob {

  public ISchedulingRule getSchedulingRule(IValidationContext helper) {
    return null;
  }

  public IStatus validateInJob(IValidationContext helper,
    IReporter reporter) throws ValidationException {
    final DocbookValidator validator = this;
    final IReporter theReporter = reporter;
    String[] uris = helper.getURIs();
    for (int i = 0; i < uris.length && !reporter.isCancelled(); i++) {
```

```java
        String filename = uris[i];
        filename = filename.substring(filename.indexOf("/", 1));
        Object[] parms = { filename };

        final IFile file = (IFile) helper.loadModel("getFile", parms);
        Document doc = null;
        try {
          DocumentBuilderFactory domFactory = DocumentBuilderFactory
            .newInstance();
          DocumentBuilder domBuilder = domFactory.newDocumentBuilder();
          domBuilder.setErrorHandler(new org.xml.sax.ErrorHandler() {
            public void error(SAXParseException e)
                throws SAXException {
              reportMessage(LocalizedMessage.NORMAL_SEVERITY,
                  e.getLocalizedMessage(), e.getLineNumber());
            }
            public void fatalError(SAXParseException e)
                throws SAXException {
              reportMessage(LocalizedMessage.HIGH_SEVERITY,
                  e.getLocalizedMessage(), e.getLineNumber());
            }
            public void warning(SAXParseException e)
                throws SAXException {
              reportMessage(LocalizedMessage.LOW_SEVERITY,
                  e.getLocalizedMessage(), e.getLineNumber());
            }
            private void reportMessage(int severity, String message,
                int lineno) {
              LocalizedMessage lMessage = new LocalizedMessage(
                  severity, message, file);
              lMessage.setLineNo(lineno);
              theReporter.addMessage(validator, lMessage);
            }
          });
          doc = domBuilder.parse(file.getRawLocation().toFile());
        }
        catch (Exception e) {
        }
        if (doc != null) {
          Element rootElem = doc.getDocumentElement();
          String rootName = rootElem.getNodeName();
          if (!"chapter".equals(rootName) && !"set".equals(rootName)
              && !"book".equals(rootName)
              && !"preface".equals(rootName)
              && !"appendix".equals(rootName)
              && !"glossary".equals(rootName)
              && !"bibliography".equals(rootName)
              && !"article".equals(rootName)) {
            LocalizedMessage message = new LocalizedMessage(
            LocalizedMessage.HIGH_SEVERITY,
                "DocBook documents must begin with one of the " +
                "following elements: appendix, article, bibliography, " +
                "book, chapter, glossary, preface or set.", file);
            message.setLineNo(1);
            reporter.addMessage(this, message);
          }
```

```
      }
    }
    return Status.OK_STATUS;
  }

  public void cleanup(IReporter reporter) {
    // There is no cleanup for the DocBook validator to perform.
  }

  public void validate(IValidationContext helper, IReporter reporter)
      throws ValidationException {
    // This method is for validators that do not run in jobs
    // and so is not implemented for the DocBook validator.
  }
}
```

The DocbookValidator contains four methods that we'll discuss in the following order: getSchedulingRule, validateInJob, validate, and cleanup.

The validation framework runs most validators as Eclipse jobs. For each job, a scheduling rule can be specified that the Eclipse jobs framework will use to determine when the job will be run. getSchedulingRule is used to specify a specific scheduling rule that the validation framework should use when running the validator job. This method is useful if your validator has scheduling requirements such as only running after another validator has completed. Returning null indicates that the validator will run with the default scheduling rule set by the validation framework. The DocBook validator does not require a special scheduling rule and therefore returns null. (For more about scheduling rules, see the Eclipse help topic Scheduling rules.)

As stated previously, most validators are run as jobs. This allows the validation framework to run multiple validators at the same time, can significantly reduce the amount of time required for all validators to complete, and allows the validators to run without blocking the Eclipse UI. To run a validator as a job, the validator must implement validateInJob with its validation logic. We'll discuss the DocBook validation logic after covering the last two methods in the validator.

The DocBook validator could alternatively be run without using a job. A validator should not be run as a job if it is not thread safe or has a specific scheduling requirement that cannot be met using Eclipse jobs. In this case, the validate method from the IValidator interface must be implemented instead of the validateInJob method. The DocBook validator will be run as a job and has therefore left the validate method empty. (You may be thinking that this part of the interface is a little clumsy in its current form. We agree. This is a candidate for refactoring.)

The `cleanup` method gives a validator a chance to clean up any artifacts produced during validation. As we will discuss next, the DocBook validator logic does not produce any artifacts that require clean up after validation completes, so this method remains empty.

As it stands, the only method that the DocBook validator needs to implement is the `validateInJob` method, which contains the validation logic.

The `validateInJob` method starts by requesting the list of file URIs to be validated from the helper. Only files applicable for the validator will be in the list, but it is the responsibility of the validator to iterate over the files and validate each one. This feature allows validators to implement specific logic for batch validation such as caching document models to improve performance.

The validator iterates over this list, validating each file. The exit criteria for the loop iterating over the files contains an additional check. The exit criteria contains the expression

```
!reporter.isCancelled()
```

This condition checks whether the validator has received a cancel request, such as that issued when a user selects to cancel validation, and terminates validation without validating the remaining files. To be a good citizen in the workbench and as part of the validation framework, a validator should check periodically to see if it has been canceled. (See the Validator Best Practices sidebar that follows for more about being a good validation citizen.)

The DocBook validation logic is then implemented as a two-step process:

❍ *Step 1:* DocBook is an XML language. The first step is to validate the document for XML conformance. Success in this step means the document is a well-formed XML document.

The DocBook validator uses the standard Java XML parsing (JAXP) interface to parse the DocBook document. Using JAXP serves two purposes. First, it has a validation option that performs XML conformance validation required by this step. Second, it parses the DocBook document into an easily traversable XML model, which will be used in step 2.

A custom error reporter is registered with the parser that allows the DocBook validator to report XML conformance errors using the validation framework. A `LocalizedMessage` object is used to hold an error, warning, or information message and is passed to the reporter to report the message to the workbench. `LocalizedMessage` is used both when reporting errors produced from XML conformance validation and when reporting custom DocBook error messages in step 2.

○ *Step 2:* DocBook contains specific rules beyond those defined for XML conformance. These rules are what differentiate a DocBook document from a generic XML document with no specified grammar. The second step is to validate the document according to the DocBook specific rule set.

To keep this example simple and focused on the validation extension, the DocBook validator only checks that the root element is one of the allowed elements. The allowed root elements are `appendix`, `article`, `bibliography`, `book`, `chapter`, `glossary`, `preface`, and `set`. Obviously, a complete validator will need to check a lot more than the root element.

Note that XML languages often define an XML schema or DTD, which can be used to perform most language-specific validation with the XML validator. DocBook does have an XML schema defined. This example does not make use of the schema to show the two stages of validation.

After all the files have been validated, the validator returns the OK status, signifying that validation has completed.

Tip: When implementing the DocBook validator you may see several restricted access warnings. These warnings appear because the validation framework API is still internal. To make it easier to work, you can disable these warnings by following these steps:

1. Right click on the DocBook plug-in project and select **Properties ▸ Java Compiler ▸ Errors/Warnings**. The **Errors/Warnings** page opens.

2. Select **Enable project specific settings**, expand the **Discouraged reference (access rules)** section and change the **Deprecated and restricted API Discouraged reference (access rules)** option to `Ignore`.

9. You've declared the minimum that's required to run the DocBook validator. Now is a good time to take a look at what you've accomplished thus far. Launch a runtime workbench. In the runtime workbench select **Window ▸ Preferences ▸ Validation**. The **Validation** preference page should

list the DocBook validator, indicating that the validator is registered with the validation framework (see Figure 13.5). Close the **Validation** preference page.

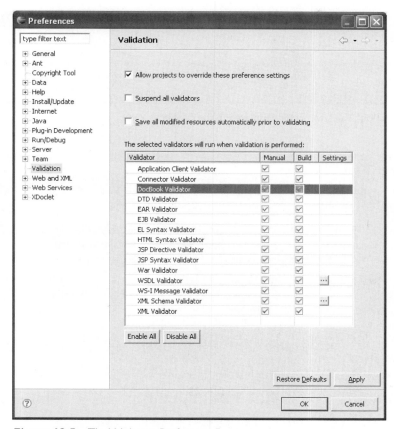

Figure 13.5 The Validation Preference Page

10. Open the **J2EE** perspective. Open the **New Project** wizard and create a new **General Project** named `Article`.

11. Open the **New File** wizard and create a new DocBook file with the name `article.docbook`.

12. Edit `article.docbook` as shown in Example 13.1.

13. In the **Project Explorer,** validate the file. Right click on it and select **Validate**. No errors are displayed in the **Problems** view.

14. Invalidate the file by changing the root element to `<eclipsearticle>`. Validate the file again. The **Problems** view displays an error that the DocBook validator produced (see Figure 13.6).

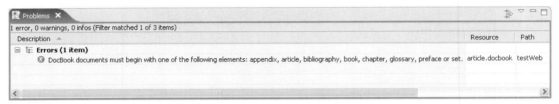

Figure 13.6   The DocBook Validator Error Displayed in the Problems View

---

Validator Best Practices

Given the nature of validators and their interaction with the Eclipse workbench, here are a few best practices when implementing your own validator:

1. As already mentioned, validators should check their canceled status and terminate early if they have been canceled. A failure to cancel when requested can lead to an unresponsive workbench.

2. A validator will likely not be run in isolation but rather as part of a group of validators and typically as part of the build. Validators should be lightweight and very fast to avoid introducing lags in build times.

3. A validator should not lock resources. Validators should only check for correctness of resources and should not try to fix or otherwise modify resources. Doing so can lead to deadlocks in the workbench or periods when the workbench is unresponsive.

Creating a Custom Marker Type

A marker is an annotation on a file that is used to represent information associated with the file, such as bookmarks, breakpoints, and problems. The DocBook validator reports error, warning, or information messages as markers. These markers are displayed in various places in the Eclipse workbench, most notably the **Problems** view, and the left margin of most editors. Each marker that is created is of a certain defined type. The views that display markers give users the ability to filter certain markers. For example, markers can be filtered in the **Problems** view by selecting Menu ▽ (down arrow) ▶ Configure Filters.

By default, all validators defined with the validation framework create markers of the type

`org.eclipse.wst.validation.problemmarker`

These markers can all be filtered from the **Problems** view by deselecting **Validation Message** in the **Filters** dialog. While this filter level may be fine for some validators, the DocBook validator should provide finer-grained filtering for users to improve the user experience. This finer-grained filtering can be achieved by specifying a custom marker type.

In this section you will create a custom DocBook marker type. To create the custom marker, do the following:

1. To specify the custom DocBook marker, you need to specify a new extension and add a contribution to the existing DocBook validator extension declaration.

   On the Extensions page of the manifest editor add the extension point

   `org.eclipse.core.resources.markers`

   Specify the id `validationMarker` and the name `DocBook Problem`.

2. The default marker defined by the validation framework specifies additions to the base marker type that are used by the framework. For the new DocBook marker to function properly it must extend the default validation marker.

   In the plug-in manifest editor's **Extensions** page, right click on the DocBook marker extension point and select a new `super`. Specify the type

   `org.eclipse.wst.validation.problemmarker`

3. With the DocBook marker type defined, the validation framework needs to be told to use this marker type when creating markers for the DocBook validator.

   Right click on the validate extension you created in the previous section and select a new `markerId`. Specify the `markerId` as the fully qualified id of the DocBook marker

   `org.eclipsewtp.docbook.validationMarker`

4. Save the plug-in manifest.

5. That's it. You've defined a DocBook marker type without writing any code. View your contribution to the plug-in manifest by selecting the **plugin.xml** tab in the manifest editor (see Example 13.4).

Example 13.4   Listing of the DocBook Marker Type Contribution to plugin.xml

```
<extension
    id="validationMarker"
    name="DocBook Problem"
    point="org.eclipse.core.resources.markers">
  <super
      type="org.eclipse.wst.validation.problemmarker"/>
</extension>
```

6. You have now configured the DocBook validator to use a custom DocBook marker type. Test your change by launching a runtime workbench. Invalidate `article.docbook` by changing the root element to `<eclipsearti-cle>` as you did in the previous section. Validate `article. docbook`. An error should appear in the **Problems** view (see Figure 13.6).

   In the **Problems** view, select **Menu** ▽ (down arrow) ▸ **Configure Filters**. The **Filters** dialog opens. Deselect the DocBook Problem (see Figure 13.7), and click **OK**. The **Filters** dialog closes and the **Problems** view is displayed without the DocBook error message.

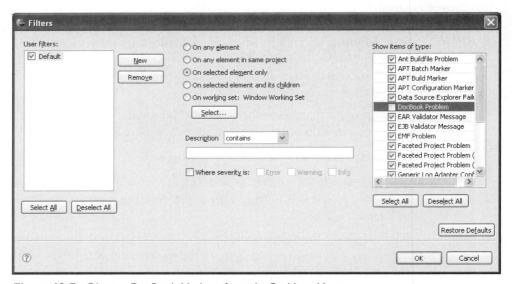

Figure 13.7   Filtering DocBook Markers from the Problems View

Tip: If you're having trouble with changes to plug-in manifests showing up in your runtime workbench, you may need to clear the configuration area when launching the runtime workbench. You can clear the configuration area on the **Configuration** tab of the **Run** dialog.

Declaring the DocBook Content Type

When adding a new language such as DocBook to Eclipse, it is a good idea to define the language to Eclipse. Defining the language allows Eclipse to handle the tools and operations that surround the language in a coordinated and unified fashion. For example, by defining the DocBook language with Eclipse it will allow editors, builders, and other tools to be defined specifically for the language.

The most effective way to inform Eclipse that you are adding a language is to specify a content type. By specifying a DocBook content type you are telling Eclipse what content it can expect to find in a DocBook file. You can specify a DocBook file simply by the file extension, but because a DocBook file is not tied to the file extension a content type is more flexible.

Getting a little more concrete, a content type has an id and a name for which you will specify DocBook specific entries. You can also specify the file extensions that are associated with the DocBook content type. Notice that we said *extensions*, not *extension*. Although in your case you will specify a single file extension, content types are not restricted to a single file extension. This flexibility can be exploited by Eclipse end users by customizing the content types in their workspace using a preferences page. You can also declare one or more base content types for the DocBook content type. Base content types represent more generic representations of the content type. For example, DocBook is an XML language. You will therefore specify that the DocBook content type has a base content type of XML. Specifying a base content type of XML will allow the DocBook content type to take advantage of all the tools and operations defined for the XML content type, such as the XML editor.

In this section you will define the DocBook content type to Eclipse by doing the following:

1. In the manifest editor, change to the **Extensions** tab and click **Add**. Add an extension of type

   ```
   org.eclipse.core.runtime.contentTypes
   ```

   The platform defines this extension point to specify content types to Eclipse.

2. Right click on the newly created content type extension and select **New ▸ content-type**. Specify an id of `contentType` and a name of `DocBook Content Type`. As discussed previously, you should specify that DocBook has a base content type of XML, so specify a base type of

   ```
   org.eclipse.core.runtime.xml
   ```

3. The `file-extensions` attribute accepts a list of the file extensions for which this content type is applicable. This is the default list, and more file extensions can be added later by other plug-ins or via Eclipse's preferences. Specify `file-extensions` as `docbook`.

4. It is also good practice to specify the default character set. In the case of XML and DocBook, this is UTF-8. Specify the `default-charset` as `UTF-8`. Save the manifest editor.

5. To take a look at your extension contribution to `plugin.xml`, switch to the source view of your plug-in manifest by clicking the **plugin.xml** tab (see Example 13.5).

Example 13.5 Listing of the DocBook Content Type Contribution to plugin.xml

```
<extension
    point="org.eclipse.core.runtime.contentTypes">
  <content-type
      base-type="org.eclipse.core.runtime.xml"
      default-charset="UTF-8"
      file-extensions="docbook"
      id="contentType"
      name="DocBook Content Type"
      priority="normal"/>
</extension>
```

6. Now take a look at what you've just done by launching the runtime workbench you created earlier. When the workbench is up, you should notice a couple of changes.

First, the `article.docbook` icon has been changed to the XML icon. The XML icon is displayed because the XML editor is now the default editor for DocBook files. The XML editor became the default editor for DocBook files when you specified the XML content type as a base content type for the DocBook content type. As should be expected, opening the file now opens the XML editor and populates the outline view. (You can also customize the XML editor for DocBook. See The Structured Source Editing (SSE) Framework sidebar.)

Second, the DocBook content type is now listed in the **Content Types** preferences page (see Figure 13.8). This listing allows users to declare other file extensions that represent DocBook files.

7. To show the power this content type grants an end user, you'll use it to specify that files with the extension *.dbk are DocBook files.

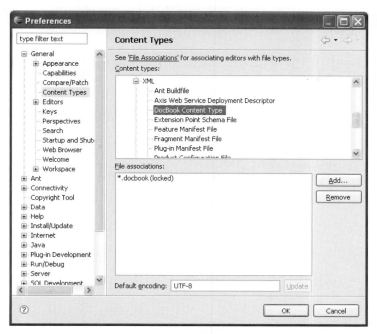

Figure 13.8   The Content Types Preference Page Featuring the DocBook Content Type

In the **Project Explorer**, rename `article.docbook` to `article.dbk`. Right click on `article.docbook` and select **Refactor ▸ Rename**. Specify the name `article.dbk` and click **OK**. The file's icon changes to the default text icon, and the XML editor no longer opens for the file.

Select **Window ▸ Preferences**. The **Preferences** dialog opens. Select **General ▸ Content Types**. On the **Content Types** page select **Text ▸ XML ▸ DocBook Content Type**. Click **Add** and specify the file type `*.dbk`. Click **OK**. `*.dbk` is associated with the DocBook content type (see Figure 13.9). The DocBook specific tools, including the XML icon and editor, are now enabled for the `*.dbk` extension.

In the case of the DocBook extension, a simple content type definition has provided some pretty significant benefits. The one limitation in this case is with the DocBook validator. The validator is not enabled for `*.dbk` files because it is associated with the `*.docbook` file extension and not with the DocBook content type.

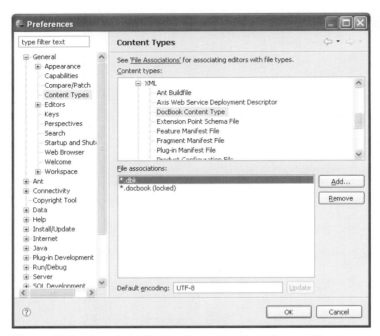

Figure 13.9   Associating *.dbk with the DocBook Content Type

The Structured Source Editing (SSE) Framework

When adding DocBook to Eclipse you simply enabled the XML editor to work for the DocBook content type. This is a very quick way to get improved functionality for XML-based languages with little effort, but there is a lot more customization that can be done.

The XML editor is part of a larger family of WTP editors known as the structured source editors. Many of WTP's editors, including the DTD, HTML, JavaScript, JSP, WSDL, and XML schema editors, are built on SSE. SSE provides enhancements on top of the text-editing framework. It is useful when creating editors for highly structured languages like XML, but really shines when used for editors that contain mixed content types such as JSPs and HTML. Mixed content types are those languages in which other languages can be embedded. For example, in JSP and HTML not only does the editor need to handle Java and HTML, it also needs to handle CSS and JavaScript.

SSE will assist you when you're ready to take the DocBook tooling to the next level by creating a custom DocBook source editor complete with content assistance and source validation—a project for another time.

Summary

In this chapter you added support for the DocBook language to Eclipse. You contributed a DocBook validator to the validation framework. You also contributed a custom DocBook marker and defined the DocBook content type, which allowed DocBook files to make use of the WTP XML tools such as the XML editor and outline view.

In the next chapter we'll focus on extending the WTP tooling for another language, WSDL.

CHAPTER 14

Creating WSDL Extensions

Our native language is like a second skin, so much a part of us we resist the idea that it is constantly changing, constantly being renewed.

—Casey Miller

Many languages are not static. They evolve and grow over time. For example, natural languages, such as English, continue to evolve and grow as new constructs, such as words, terms, and sentence structure, are added to the language or take on new meaning. Although all are written in English, Shakespeare's work is noticeably different from that of John Grisham or Margaret Atwood.

Just as natural languages may evolve, so too may computer languages. In the XML family of languages, the content of each element may be defined by a grammar, typically specified by a DTD or XML Schema (XSD). If the grammar limits the content to a fixed set of elements and attributes, the language is said to have a *closed content model*. For example, XSD itself has a closed content model. To add new content to XSD, you must put in it `annotation` elements.

In contrast, an XML language that allows new elements and attributes to be added is said to have an *open content model*. Web Service Description Language (WSDL) has an open content model. Elements and attributes may be added to the language at almost any level [WSDL11] (see Example 14.1).

Example 14.1 WSDL 1.1 Open Content Model

```
<wsdl:definitions name="nmtoken"? targetNamespace="uri"?>
  <import namespace="uri" location="uri"/>*
  <wsdl:documentation .... /> ?
  <wsdl:types> ?
    <wsdl:documentation .... />?
    <xsd:schema .... />*
    <-- extensibility element --> *
  </wsdl:types>
```

607

```
<wsdl:message name="nmtoken"> *
  <wsdl:documentation .... />?
  <part name="nmtoken" element="qname"? type="qname"?/> *
</wsdl:message>
<wsdl:portType name="nmtoken">*
  <wsdl:documentation .... />?
  <wsdl:operation name="nmtoken">*
    <wsdl:documentation .... /> ?
    <wsdl:input name="nmtoken"? message="qname">?
      <wsdl:documentation .... /> ?
    </wsdl:input>
    <wsdl:output name="nmtoken"? message="qname">?
      <wsdl:documentation .... /> ?
    </wsdl:output>
    <wsdl:fault name="nmtoken" message="qname"> *
      <wsdl:documentation .... /> ?
    </wsdl:fault>
  </wsdl:operation>
</wsdl:portType>
<wsdl:binding name="nmtoken" type="qname">*
  <wsdl:documentation .... />?
  <-- extensibility element --> *
  <wsdl:operation name="nmtoken">*
    <wsdl:documentation .... /> ?
    <-- extensibility element --> *
    <wsdl:input> ?
      <wsdl:documentation .... /> ?
      <-- extensibility element -->
    </wsdl:input>
    <wsdl:output> ?
      <wsdl:documentation .... /> ?
      <-- extensibility element --> *
    </wsdl:output>
    <wsdl:fault name="nmtoken"> *
      <wsdl:documentation .... /> ?
      <-- extensibility element --> *
    </wsdl:fault>
  </wsdl:operation>
</wsdl:binding>
<wsdl:service name="nmtoken"> *
  <wsdl:documentation .... />?
  <wsdl:port name="nmtoken" binding="qname"> *
    <wsdl:documentation .... /> ?
    <-- extensibility element -->
  </wsdl:port>
  <-- extensibility element -->
</wsdl:service>
<-- extensibility element --> *
</wsdl:definitions>
```

Extension attributes may be added on any element, and extension elements may be added anywhere in Example 14.1 where you see

```
<-- extensibility element -->
```

WSDL was created with an open content model to avoid placing restrictions on the technologies that may be used with Web services, most notably Web service bindings. New specifications for elements and attributes that describe additional technologies can be added to the language as the need arises. The WSDL 1.1 specification defines two such extensions: a binding for SOAP (see Example 14.2) and one for HTTP. (Okay, so really there is a third binding type defined for MIME, but it must be used in conjunction with SOAP or HTTP and as such is not a standalone binding.)

Example 14.2 SOAP Binding in WSDL 1.1

```
<wsdl:definitions...

  <wsdl:binding name="BindingSOAP" type="tns:portType">
    <soap:binding style="document"
                      transport="http://schemas.xmlsoap.org/soap/http"/>
    <wsdl:operation name="Operation1">
      <soap:operation soapAction="http://www.example.org/NewOperation"/>
      <wsdl:input>
        <soap:body use="literal" parts="OperationRequest"/>
      </wsdl:input>
      <wsdl:output>
        <soap:body use="literal" parts="OperationResponse"/>
      </wsdl:output>
    </wsdl:operation>
  </wsdl:binding>
  <wsdl:service name="Service">
    <wsdl:port name="ServiceSOAP" binding="tns:BindingSOAP">
      <soap:address location="http://www.example.org/"/>
    </wsdl:port>
  </wsdl:service>
</wsdl:definitions>
```

Just as WSDL is extensible so too are the WTP tools that allow you to develop WSDL documents. The tools define extension points and API that allow you to seamlessly integrate functionality for WSDL extensions into them. The tools can also be extended to allow for custom validation. This is useful when defining custom rules for WSDL documents such as those defined by your own organization or industry standard organizations like the Web Services Interoperability (WS-I).

In this chapter, let's suppose you've been given the task of customizing WTP's WSDL tools for your organization by adding support for the SOAP namespace and enforcing your organization's naming conventions for Web services.

Note that since SOAP 1.1 binding extensions are already defined in WTP, you will define SOAP bindings for the following artificial WTP SOAP namespace:

```
http://eclipsewtp.org/wsdl/soap/
```

instead of the actual SOAP namespace:

```
http://schemas.xmlsoap.org/wsdl/soap/
```

> ## The W3C WSDL 1.1 Binding for SOAP 1.2
>
> If you are ambitious, you might want to apply the following instructions to develop a realistic SOAP 1.2 binding as specified by the recent W3C Member Submission, *WSDL 1.1 Binding Extension for SOAP 1.2* [WSDL11SOAP12], which defines the namespace
>
> ```
> http://schemas.xmlsoap.org/wsdl/soap12/
> ```
>
> Such an extension would be a welcome contribution to WTP. You should send a note to the WTP developers list first to see if anyone else is already working on this. The WTP developers' mailing address is
>
> ```
> <wtp-dev@eclipse.org>
> ```

Your goal is to support WSDL documents such as that for the echo service (see Example 14.3). Before diving into this chapter, take a minute to familiarize yourself with the WSDL tools so you'll better understand the changes you will make. Launch a runtime workspace, create a new dynamic Web project, create the file `Echo.wsdl` in the project, and explore the WSDL editor, specifically the editor's representation of the WTP SOAP bindings.

Now that you've explored the WSDL editor, in this chapter you will:

○ Contribute binding extension elements for the WTP SOAP namespace to the WSDL editor

○ Contribute a validator for the WTP SOAP namespace to the WSDL validator

○ Contribute custom validation rules to enforce your organization's Web service naming conventions

Example 14.3   Listing of Echo.wsdl

```
<?xml version="1.0" encoding="UTF-8"?>
<wsdl:definitions name="Echo"
    targetNamespace="http://www.example.org/Echo/"
    xmlns:wtpsoap="http://eclipsewtp.org/wsdl/soap/"
    xmlns:tns="http://www.example.org/Echo/"
    xmlns:wsdl="http://schemas.xmlsoap.org/wsdl/"
    xmlns:xsd="http://www.w3.org/2001/XMLSchema">
```

```
<wsdl:types>
  <xsd:schema targetNamespace="http://www.example.org/Echo/">
    <xsd:element name="EchoResponse" type="xsd:string"/>
    <xsd:element name="EchoRequest" type="xsd:string"/>
  </xsd:schema>
</wsdl:types>
<wsdl:message name="EchoResponse">
  <wsdl:part element="tns:EchoResponse" name="EchoResponse"/>
</wsdl:message>
<wsdl:message name="EchoRequest">
  <wsdl:part element="tns:EchoRequest" name="EchoRequest"/>
</wsdl:message>
<wsdl:portType name="Echo">
  <wsdl:operation name="EchoOperation">
    <wsdl:input message="tns:EchoRequest"/>
    <wsdl:output message="tns:EchoResponse"/>
  </wsdl:operation>
</wsdl:portType>
<wsdl:binding name="EchoSOAP" type="tns:Echo">
  <wtpsoap:binding style="document"
      transport="http://schemas.xmlsoap.org/soap/http"/>
  <wsdl:operation name="EchoOperation">
    <wtpsoap:operation
        soapAction="http://www.example.org/Echo/NewOperation"/>
    <wsdl:input>
      <wtpsoap:body use="literal"/>
    </wsdl:input>
    <wsdl:output>
      <wtpsoap:body use="literal"/>
    </wsdl:output>
  </wsdl:operation>
</wsdl:binding>
<wsdl:service name="echo">
  <wsdl:port binding="tns:EchoSOAP" name="EchoSOAP">
    <wtpsoap:address
        location="http://www.eclipsewtp.org/services/Echo"/>
  </wsdl:port>
</wsdl:service>
</wsdl:definitions>
```

Warning: As of WTP 1.5, the WTP extension points and API shown in this chapter are not final. These extension points and API may change in future versions of WTP.

Tip: The WS-I validator will produce warnings for the WTP SOAP namespace because the namespace is not defined in the WS-I profiles. To remove these warnings, turn off the WS-I validator by navigating to the **Web Services ▶ Profile Compliance and Validation** preference page and setting both the WS-I AP and SSBP compliance levels to `Ignore Compliance`.

Creating the WSDL Extension Plug-in

As when adding any function to Eclipse, to use the WSDL extensions required of the tasks in this chapter you need to create a plug-in to hold the extension definitions and the associated Java classes. Create a new plug-in with the id

`org.eclipsewtp.wsdlextensions`

and the name WSDL Extensions Plug-in using the **New Plug-in Project** wizard (see Figure 14.1). Ensure the options **Generate an activator** and **This plug-in will make contributions to the UI** are selected.

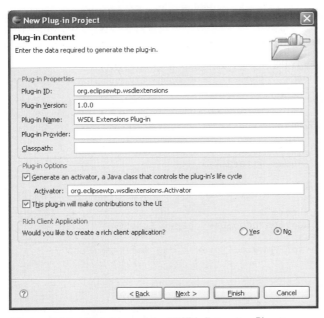

Figure 14.1   Definition of the WSDL Extension Plug-in

Extending the WSDL Editor

Like many description languages, WSDL 1.1 is complex. Taking the time to read and fully understand the specification and all of its intricacies is not always an option for developers who need to create Top-Down Web services. (For more on Top-Down Web services, see Chapter 10.) The WTP WSDL editor provides a way to visually author WSDL 1.1 documents. The editor provides a design overview of a WSDL document and assists in the editing process.

The WSDL editor comes with the logic for SOAP and HTTP bindings. It is possible to author WSDL documents that specify other bindings without extending the editor, but the editor will not provide any assistance for these types of bindings. In order for the editor to provide assistance and a non-generic visualization of other binding elements, it must be extended.

The WSDL editor consists of both source and design views. The source view is the same XML source editor you used for DocBook in Chapter 13. The XML source editor is simply reused in the WSDL editor. In order to extend the WSDL source editor to provide additional content assistance and context specific actions, you can provide extensions in the same way as for the XML source editor, or really for any Eclipse context menu, namely by contributing context actions for WSDL elements. The design view (see Figure 14.2) is what you will extend in this section. The design view can be extended to add first-class support for new namespaces. First-class support encompasses custom icons for the namespace's extensibility elements, such as those for new binding types, new extensibility element options, and context sensitive actions. In this section you will add a custom icon for the WTP SOAP binding, add the WTP SOAP extensibility elements to the editor's available list, and add a custom action to generate the WTP SOAP binding content.

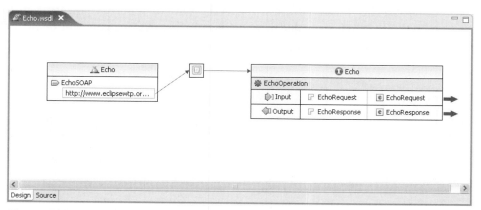

Figure 14.2   The WSDL Editor's Design View

WTP's WSDL Model

The WSDL editor extends the structured source editing (SSE) framework and is therefore based on a document object model (DOM). The editor makes use of the WTP Eclipse modeling framework (EMF) WSDL model. The WTP WSDL EMF model represents the specific structure of a WSDL document and is synchronized with the DOM used by SSE. Extending the editor does not require that the WSDL model be extended. Instead, when extending the WSDL editor you can simply use the built-in extensibility elements. You may, however, find it useful to extend the WSDL model when adding custom elements to the editor or when creating other Web service or WSDL tools that rely on the model. The discussion of extending the WSDL model does not fit in this chapter as it is not specific to WTP. Extending the WSDL model is very similar to extending any EMF-based model. EMF is a comprehensive, extremely useful, and complex framework. *Eclipse Modeling Framework: A Developer's Guide* [Budinsky2004] by Frank Budinsky, David Steinberg, Ed Merks, Raymond Ellersick, and Timothy Grosgs, the Eclipse series EMF book, can help you understand how to add custom elements to an EMF model, such as the WSDL one.

Customizing the Look of Extensibility Elements in the Editor's Design View

By default, the WSDL editor will display all elements, such as the WTP SOAP binding element, in the design view using a generic extensibility element (see Figure 14.3). This default representation of the WTP SOAP binding element does not differentiate it from other extension elements or indicate that it is a WTP SOAP binding element. For the WTP SOAP namespace to be truly integrated in the WSDL editor, it needs the same distinct visualization as the native WSDL elements. In order to provide this distinction, you will display a custom icon for the WTP SOAP binding element.

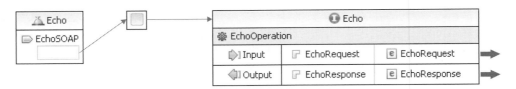

Figure 14.3   Default Visualization of a SOAP Binding

To display a custom icon, the WSDL editor needs to be told which icon to use for the WTP SOAP binding element. The editor defines the extension point

`org.eclipse.wst.xsd.ui.extensibillityNodeCustomizations`

This extension point allows you to tell the editor which icons to use for specific elements in a namespace.

> **Note:** As you may have noticed, the extension in use here is from an XML schema (XSD) plug-in. The WSDL and XML schema editors have several aspects in common and thus share this extension point.

Before you can make use of this extension point you need to create a dependency on the declaring plug-in, in this case the XML schema UI plug-in. Open the plug-in manifest editor and add a dependency on

`org.eclipse.wst.xsd.ui`

You can now define the extension. From the plug-in manifest editor's **Extensions** tab, add a new extension for the extension point

`org.eclipse.wst.xsd.ui.extensibilityNodeCustomizations`

Give the extension the id `soapLabelProvider` and the name `WTP SOAP Label Provider`. For this next part you'll once again have to venture into the XML representation of your extension. Select the **plugin.xml** tab. Create a new `nodeCustomization` element in the existing extension element with two attributes: a `namespace` attribute with the value

`http://eclipsewtp.org/wsdl/soap/`

and a `labelProviderClass` attribute with the value

`org.eclipsewtp.wsdlextensions.SOAPLabelProvider`

(see Example 14.4).

Example 14.4 SOAP Label Provider Extension
```
<extension
   id="soapLabelProvider"
   name="WTP SOAP Label Provider"
   point="org.eclipse.wst.xsd.ui.extensibilityNodeCustomizations">
  <nodeCustomization
     namespace="http://eclipsewtp.org/wsdl/soap/"
     labelProviderClass="org.eclipsewtp.wsdlextensions.SOAPLabelProvider"/>
</extension>
```

Now that you've defined the extension, you need to create the class you specified in the extension. Create the class

`org.eclipsewtp.wsdlextensions.SOAPLabelProvider`

using the **New Project** wizard. Ensure that the class extends

`org.eclipse.jface.viewers.LabelProvider`

The LabelProvider class contains two methods that you will override: getImage and dispose. Using the getImage method, you can specify your own icon and description instead of using the defaults (see Figure 14.3 earlier). Fill in the details of the class as shown in Example 14.5. You will associate the icon soapbinding.gif with the WTP SOAP binding element. This icon is available from the examples package from this book's accompanying Web site.

Example 14.5   Listing of SOAPLabelProvider.java

```
package org.eclipsewtp.wsdlextensions;

import org.eclipse.jface.viewers.LabelProvider;
import org.eclipse.swt.graphics.Image;
import org.w3c.dom.Node;

public class SOAPLabelProvider extends LabelProvider {
  private Image bindingImage = Activator.imageDescriptorFromPlugin(
      "org.eclipsewtp.wsdlextensions", "icons/soapbinding.gif")
      .createImage();

  public Image getImage(Object element) {
    Node node = (Node)element;
    String elementName = node.getLocalName();
    if("binding".equals(elementName))
      return bindingImage;
    return null;
  }

  public void dispose() {
    bindingImage.dispose();
  }
}
```

The implementation of the getImage method is pretty simple. First, a check is performed to see if the specified element is a WTP SOAP binding element. If so, the method returns the icon. If not, the method returns null, indicating that there is no custom icon to display for the element.

And what of the dispose method? Even though the implementation of this method is trivial, it simply disposes of the image; we can't stress enough the importance of properly disposing images you create.

> **Note:** Even in this simple example we advocate using responsible image handling by creating a single image object and ensuring that it is properly disposed. Allocating an image object results in a handle being allocated at the operating-system level. The operating system has a finite number of image handles, and this finite limit can realistically be hit.

Once the image handle limit is hit you will likely notice nasty side effects, such as the operating system deciding that your process is unstable and refusing to grant it more image handles.

Now is a good time to try out the customization of the WTP SOAP binding element you just implemented. Launch the same runtime workspace you created earlier and open `Echo.wsdl` (see Example 14.3 earlier) in the WSDL editor. Notice how the representation of the WTP SOAP binding has changed to use the custom icon you specified (see Figure 14.4).

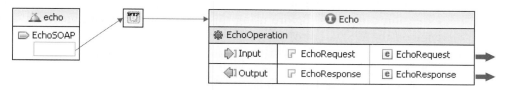

Figure 14.4   Configured Visualization of a WTP SOAP Binding

Adding Extensibility Elements to the Editor

The WSDL editor integrates with the Eclipse **Properties** view to allow users to set and configure the properties of specific elements. The **Properties** view for each WSDL element contains an **Extensions** tab. This tab allows users to add and remove extensibility elements and attributes from WSDL elements. The **Properties** view **Extensions** tab for the WSDL binding, shown in Figure 14.5, can be seen by right clicking on the binding, selecting **Show Properties** and selecting the **Extensions** tab in the **Properties** view that opens. Clicking on the **Add** button displays the **Add Extension Components** dialog. By default the editor makes available the extensions for HTTP, SOAP, and MIME. In this section you will contribute the WTP SOAP extensions to this list.

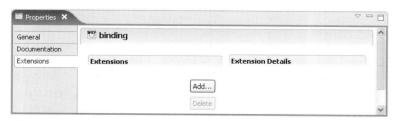

Figure 14.5   WTP Binding Properties View Extensions Tab

There are two tasks you must perform to add the WTP SOAP extensions to the extensibility elements list. First, you must contribute a new extensions category. This category will appear in the list and contain the extensibility elements for the WTP SOAP namespace. Second, you must provide an extensibility element filter. The filter will restrict the WTP SOAP extensibility elements to their allowed location in the document. Without the filter, a user will be able to add WTP SOAP extensibility elements anywhere in the document.

Start by contributing a new extensions category. The editor defines the extension point

```
org.eclipse.wst.wsdl.ui.extensionCategories
```

As you've likely guessed, this extension point allows you to define new extension categories. Before using this extension point you must add a dependency on the WSDL editor plug-in

```
org.eclipse.wst.wsdl.ui
```

With the dependency declared, change to the **Extensions** tab in your plug-in manifest editor and add the extension

```
org.eclipse.wst.wsdl.ui.extensionCategories
```

As before, you will need to customize the extension in the `plugin.xml` source view by selecting the **plugin.xml** tab. Add a category element to the new extension with a `displayName` attribute with the value `WTP SOAP` and a `namespaceURI` attribute with the value

```
http://eclipsewtp.org/wsdl/soap/
```

(see Example 14.6).

Example 14.6 Extensions Category Extension Declaration
```
<extension point="org.eclipse.wst.wsdl.ui.extensionCategories">
  <category
     displayName="WTP SOAP"
     namespaceURI="http://eclipsewtp.org/wsdl/soap/">
  </category>
</extension>
```

At this point you've declared the category. Launch a runtime workspace to take a look at the changes. The **Add Extension Components** dialog should now show the WTP SOAP category (see Figure 14.6). However, selecting the WTP SOAP category causes an error. This error occurs because the schema describing the WTP SOAP namespace cannot be located. To correct this error you need to add the schema to the XML catalog.

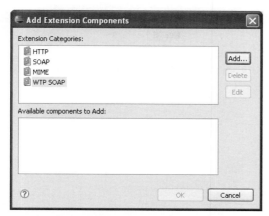

Figure 14.6 WTP SOAP Category in the Add Extension Components Dialog

The XML catalog, which you'll read more about in Chapter 15, provides the facility to register XML resources. It is most commonly used for XML schemas and DTDs. You can add the WTP SOAP schema to the XML catalog using the XML catalog preference page, or you can add it via an extension point. The advantage of the extension point, of course, is that the XML catalog will be preconfigured with your schema when Eclipse loads.

The following extension point is provided to add resources to the XML catalog:

```
org.eclipse.wst.xml.core.catalogContributions
```

Your first step is to add the schema to your plug-in. Create the file `wtpsoap.xsd` (see Example 14.7) in a `schemas` directory in your plug-in. Next, in your plug-in manifest editor, declare a dependency on the plug-in

```
org.eclipse.wst.xml.core
```

so you can make use of the XML catalog extension point. Select the **Extensions** tab and add a new extension for the extension point

```
org.eclipse.wst.xml.core.catalogContributions
```

Unlike the previous extensions, this one can be configured in the editor. Right click on the new extension and select **New ▸ catalogContribution**. Next, right click on the `catalogContribution` element and select **New ▸ uri**. Specify the name

```
http://eclipsewtp.org/wsdl/soap/
```

and the uri

```
schemas/wtpsoap.xsd
```

(see Figure 14.7). Change to the **plugin.xml** source view. Your extension should look like that shown in Example 14.8.

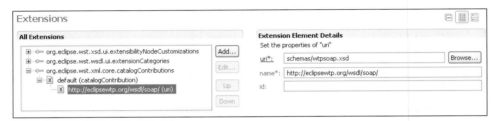

Figure 14.7   XML Catalog Extension Point to Contribute the WTP SOAP Schema

> **Note:** The `wtpsoap.xsd` schema shown in Example 14.7 is a very simplified SOAP schema. The industry standard SOAP schema can be found at:
>
> `http://schemas.xmlsoap.org/wsdl/soap/`

Example 14.7   Listing of wtpsoap.xsd

```
<?xml version="1.0" encoding="UTF-8" ?>
<xs:schema xmlns:xs="http://www.w3.org/2001/XMLSchema"
           xmlns:wsdl="http://schemas.xmlsoap.org/wsdl/"
           xmlns:wtpsoap="http://eclipsewtp.org/wsdl/soap/"
           targetNamespace="http://eclipsewtp.org/wsdl/soap/" >

  <xs:import namespace = "http://schemas.xmlsoap.org/wsdl/" />
  <xs:element name="binding" type="wtpsoap:wtpSOAPType" />
  <xs:element name="address" type="wtpsoap:wtpSOAPType" />
  <xs:element name="body" type="wtpsoap:wtpSOAPType" />
  <xs:element name="fault" type="wtpsoap:wtpSOAPType" />
  <xs:element name="header" type="wtpsoap:wtpSOAPType" />
  <xs:element name="headerfault" type="wtpsoap:wtpSOAPType" />
  <xs:element name="operation" type="wtpsoap:wtpSOAPType" />
  <xs:complexType name="wtpSOAPType" >
    <xs:complexContent>
      <xs:extension base="wsdl:tExtensibilityElement" >
        <xs:anyAttribute namespace="##any" processContents="lax"/>
      </xs:extension>
    </xs:complexContent>
  </xs:complexType>
</xs:schema>
```

Example 14.8   Listing of the Catalog Contribution Extension in plugin.xml

```
<extension
   point="org.eclipse.wst.xml.core.catalogContributions">
  <catalogContribution id="default">
    <uri
       name="http://eclipsewtp.org/wsdl/soap/"
       uri="schemas/wtpsoap.xsd"/>
  </catalogContribution>
</extension>
```

Now launch your runtime workspace and try out the **Add Extension Components** dialog again. This time selecting the WTP SOAP category should display a list of components (see Figure 14.8).

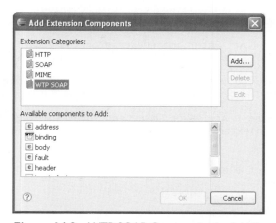

Figure 14.8   WTP SOAP Category in the Add Extension Components Dialog

There are two peculiarities with the component list shown in Figure 14.8: With the exception of the binding component, all the components are shown with the same icon, and the list contains many components that are not valid to add to a WSDL binding.

The icon problem is easy to fix. You just need to expand the SOAPLabel Provider class you created earlier. Copy the icons provided (see the examples package from this book's Web site) for the WTP SOAP namespace elements into the icons directory in your plug-in and expand the getImage method (see Example 14.9).

Example 14.9   Listing of SOAPLabelProvider.java

```java
package org.eclipsewtp.wsdlextensions;

import org.eclipse.jface.viewers.LabelProvider;
import org.eclipse.swt.graphics.Image;
import org.w3c.dom.Node;

public class SOAPLabelProvider extends LabelProvider {
  private Image bindingImage = Activator.imageDescriptorFromPlugin(
          "org.eclipsewtp.wsdlextensions", "icons/soapbinding.gif")
          .createImage();
  private Image addressImage = Activator.imageDescriptorFromPlugin(
          "org.eclipsewtp.wsdlextensions", "icons/soapaddress.gif")
          .createImage();
  private Image bodyImage = Activator.imageDescriptorFromPlugin(
          "org.eclipsewtp.wsdlextensions", "icons/soapbody.gif")
          .createImage();
  private Image faultImage = Activator.imageDescriptorFromPlugin(
          "org.eclipsewtp.wsdlextensions", "icons/soapfault.gif")
          .createImage();
  private Image headerImage = Activator.imageDescriptorFromPlugin(
          "org.eclipsewtp.wsdlextensions", "icons/soapheader.gif")
          .createImage();
  private Image headerfaultImage = Activator.imageDescriptorFromPlugin(
          "org.eclipsewtp.wsdlextensions", "icons/soapheaderfault.gif")
          .createImage();
  private Image operationImage = Activator.imageDescriptorFromPlugin(
          "org.eclipsewtp.wsdlextensions", "icons/soapoperation.gif")
          .createImage();

  public Image getImage(Object element) {
    Node node = (Node)element;
    String elementName = node.getLocalName();
    if("binding".equals(elementName))
      return bindingImage;
    else if("address".equals(elementName))
      return addressImage;
    else if("body".equals(elementName))
      return bodyImage;
    else if("fault".equals(elementName))
      return faultImage;
    else if("header".equals(elementName))
      return headerImage;
    else if("headerfault".equals(elementName))
      return headerfaultImage;
    else if("operation".equals(elementName))
      return operationImage;
    return null;
  }

  public void dispose() {
    bindingImage.dispose();
    addressImage.dispose();
    bodyImage.dispose();
```

```
        faultImage.dispose();
        headerImage.dispose();
        headerfaultImage.dispose();
        operationImage.dispose();
    }
}
```

The different component icons should now appear in the components list (see Figure 14.9).

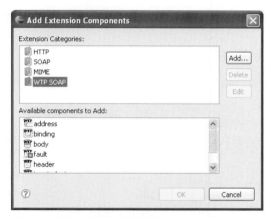

Figure 14.9 WTP SOAP Category with Icons Specified

On to the second problem: The component list contains components from the WTP SOAP namespace that are not valid to add to the WSDL binding element. (The same list also appears when using content assist in the WSDL source editor—try it out!) All the components for the WTP SOAP namespace are included in the component list because the editor does not know that only a subset of the elements is valid. To configure the editor, you need to provide a filter for the WTP SOAP namespace. You want to restrict the elements that appear in the components list to those that are valid to add to the selected WSDL element. This restriction will help prevent users from creating invalid WSDL documents.

The WSDL editor provides the following extension point that will allow you to define a filter for the WTP SOAP namespace:

```
org.eclipse.wst.wsdl.ui.extensibilityElementFilter
```

Your next action is to add a filter to the WSDL editor for the WTP SOAP namespace.

Select the plug-in manifest editor's **Extensions** tab and create a new extension for the extension point

`org.eclipse.wst.wsdl.ui.extensibilityElementFilter`

Give the extension the id `soapExtensibilityElementFilter` and the name `WTP SOAP Extensibility Element Filter`.

Once again, change to the `plugin.xml` tab and create a new `extensibilityElementFilter` element in the `extensibilityElementFilter` extension you just created. Assign the extension element a `namespace` attribute with the value

`http://eclipsewtp.org/wsdl/soap/`

Assign a second attribute with the name `class` and the value

`org.eclipsewtp.wsdlextensions.SOAPExtensibilityElementFilter`

(see Example 14.10).

Example 14.10   Listing of the WTP SOAP Extensibility Element Filter Extension in plugin.xml

```
<extension
   id="soapExtensibilityElementFilter"
   name="WTP SOAP Extensibility Element Filter"
   point="org.eclipse.wst.wsdl.ui.extensibilityElementFilter">
  <extensibilityElementFilter
     class="org.eclipsewtp.wsdlextensions.SOAPExtensibilityElementFilter"
     namespace="http://eclipsewtp.org/wsdl/soap/"/>
</extension>
```

Next you need to create the filter class. Create the class:

`org.eclipsewtp.wsdlextensions.SOAPExtensibilityElementFilter`

Ensure that the class implements

`org.eclipse.wst.wsdl.ui.internal.filter.ExtensibilityElementFilter`

The filter class contains one method that you need to implement: `isValidContext`. As the method name indicates, this method will determine whether the current context allows specific elements from the WTP SOAP namespace. The current context is based on the parent element. The logic you will implement in this method will determine the elements in the WTP SOAP namespace that can be added as children of the current parent element. `isValidContext` provides two parameters: `parentElement`, which is the parent element context of the extensibility element, and `localName`, which is the local name of the extensibility element. (The namespace of the extensibility element—in your case the WTP SOAP namespace—is not provided as the filter will only be called for the namespace that you specify in your extension declaration.) Returning `true` indicates that the element is valid in this context and should be available in the Components list and from content assist in the source editor. To implement this method you will perform simple checks for each element in the WTP SOAP namespace to check if the context is valid. The valid context for each element in the WTP SOAP namespace is shown in Table 14.1

Table 14.1 WTP SOAP Namespace Element Contexts

WTP SOAP Element	Valid Context
Address	WSDL Port element
Binding	WSDL Binding element
Body	WSDL Binding Input/Output element
Fault	WSDL Binding Fault element
Header	WSDL Binding Input/Output element
HeaderFault	WTP SOAP Header element
Operation	WSDL Binding Operation element

Implement the method as shown in Example 14.11.

Example 14.11 Listing of SOAPExtensibilityElementFilter.java

```
package org.eclipsewtp.wsdlextensions;
import org.eclipse.wst.wsdl.ui.....filter.ExtensibilityElementFilter;
import org.w3c.dom.Element;

public class SOAPExtensibilityElementFilter
    implements ExtensiblityElementFilter {

  private static final String WSDL_NAMESPACE
    = "http://schemas.xmlsoap.org/wsdl/";
  private static final String WTP_SOAP_NAMESPACE
    = "http://eclipsewtp.org/wsdl/soap/";

  public boolean isValidContext(Element parentElement,
      String localName) {
    String parentElementName = parentElement.getLocalName();
    String parentElementNamespace = parentElement.getNamespaceURI();
    if(WSDL_NAMESPACE.equals(parentElementNamespace)) {
      if("port".equals(parentElementName)) {
        return "address".equals(localName);
      }
```

```
        else if("binding".equals(parentElementName)) {
          return "binding".equals(localName);
        }
        else if("binding".equals(parentElement.getParentNode()
            .getLocalName())) {
          if("operation".equals(parentElementName)) {
            return "operation".equals(localName);
          }
        }
        else if("operation".equals(parentElement.getParentNode()
            .getLocalName())) {
          if("binding".equals(parentElement.getParentNode()
              .getParentNode().getLocalName())) {
            if("input".equals(parentElementName)) {
              return "body".equals(localName) ||
                      "header".equals(localName);
            }
            else if("output".equals(parentElementName)) {
              return "body".equals(localName) ||
                      "header".equals(localName);
            }
            else if("fault".equals(parentElementName)) {
              return "fault".equals(localName);
            }
          }
        }
      }
      else if(WTP_SOAP_NAMESPACE.equals(parentElementNamespace)) {
        if("header".equals(parentElementName)) {
          return "headerfault".equals(localName);
        }
      }
      return false;
    }
}
```

The implementation of the isValidContext method consists of a series of
tests. Looking specifically at the WTP SOAP binding, there are two tests that
must be performed to determine whether the WTP SOAP binding element
should be available for a given element context. The first test checks that the parent element is the binding element. The WTP SOAP binding element should only
be available for inclusion within a binding element. The second test checks that
the element specified is the WTP SOAP binding element. Both tests are performed by checking that the name of the element is binding. The first test also
requires a test for the namespace because any element in the WSDL model that
allows extensibility elements may be passed in as the parent element. The tests
for the other elements in the WTP SOAP namespace are very similar to this one
specific example.

With the extensibility element filter implemented, your extension for the WTP SOAP binding namespace is complete. Try out the changes you just made by launching a runtime workspace and returning to the **Add Extension Components** dialog for the WSDL binding element. You should now only see the WTP SOAP binding component as an available option (see Figure 14.10). Select other WSDL binding elements, such as operation or body, and because of the filter you added, you will see the available WTP SOAP binding components change depending on the element selected. (Hint: Double click on the binding element in the design view to reveal its operation, input, and output elements.)

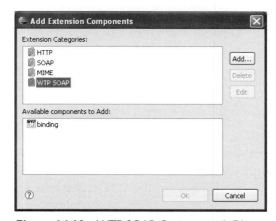

Figure 14.10 WTP SOAP Category with Filtering

Adding Custom Actions to the WSDL Editor Design View

Right click on any element in the WSDL editor design view and you will see that there are several menu items available. These menu items allow users to perform actions relevant to the element, such as adding specific child elements, generating content, and specifying references to other elements in the WSDL document structure. The menu items available for the WSDL binding element are shown in Figure 14.11. You can add your own menu items that will add your own elements, generate your own content, specify your own references, and perform any other action that you need.

A typical use case when authoring WSDL documents is to define an abstract portType and then create a corresponding concrete binding for the portType, such as a SOAP binding. As bindings generally contain very similar content, an option to generate the bindings for a specific portType will likely be useful to users of the editor because it will simplify the task. Next you will add a custom menu item that allows users to generate WTP SOAP binding content for a WSDL binding.

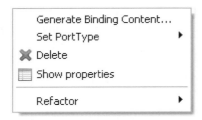

Figure 14.11   Binding Menu Items

Adding custom menu items to the context menus in the WSDL editor is no different from adding custom menu items to any other context menu in Eclipse. To contribute a menu item, you extend the platform extension point

`org.eclipse.ui.popupMenus`

This extension point allows you to contribute a menu item for a specific type of object. Next, you will contribute a **Generate WTP SOAP Binding** menu item and action for the WSDL binding element.

The WSDL editor specifies a facade layer for the WSDL elements displayed in the design editor. To contribute context menu actions to the editor's design view, you will need to know the representation of the element in the facade layer. The element representations in the facade (some of which are shown in Table 14.2, can be found in the

`org.eclipse.wst.wsdl.ui.internal.asd.facade`

package in the plug-in

`org.eclipse.wst.wsdl.ui`

The interface in the facade that corresponds to the WSDL binding element is

`org.eclipse.wst.wsdl.ui.internal.asd.facade.IBinding`

Table 14.2   WSDL Elements and Corresponding Representation in the Facade Layer

WSDL Element	**Class in Facade Layer**
Binding	IBinding
Binding Operation	IBindingOperation

WSDL Element	Class in Facade Layer
Description	IDescription
Message	IMessage
Operation	IOperation
PortType	IInterface
Service	IService
Types	IType

Before adding a custom menu item, you must again ensure your plug-in has the required dependencies. To contribute a menu item, your plug-in must declare a dependency on the plug-in

`org.eclipse.ui`

This dependency has already been declared because you checked the **will make contributions to the UI** checkbox when you created your plug-in with the **New Plug-in** wizard. Your plug-in also already depends on the plug-in

`org.eclipse.wst.wsdl.ui`

which contains the WSDL editor facade layer. You need to add dependencies on the plug-ins

`org.eclipse.wst.wsdl`

`org.wsdl4j`

`org.eclipse.emf.ecore`

which contain the WSDL model.

From the plug-in manifest editor's **Extensions** tab, extend the extension point

`org.eclipse.ui.popupMenus`

Give the extension point the id `bindingGeneration` and the name `WTP SOAP Binding Generation`. Create a new **objectContribution** extension for the class

`org.eclipse.wst.wsdl.ui.internal.asd.facade.IBinding`

with the id `bindingContribution`. The **objectContribution** tells Eclipse for which object, in your case the WSDL binding element, you want to contribute a menu item. Now create a new action for the contribution. Specify an id of `binding GenerationAction`, a label of `Generate WTP SOAP Binding`, and a class of:

`org.eclipsewtp.wsdlextensions.BindingGenerationAction`

The action specified by the class `BindingGenerationAction` will be performed when your menu item is selected and the label is the name of your menu item. The contribution in the manifest editor's extensions page can be seen in Figure 14.12, and the contribution to `plugin.xml` can be seen in Example 14.12.

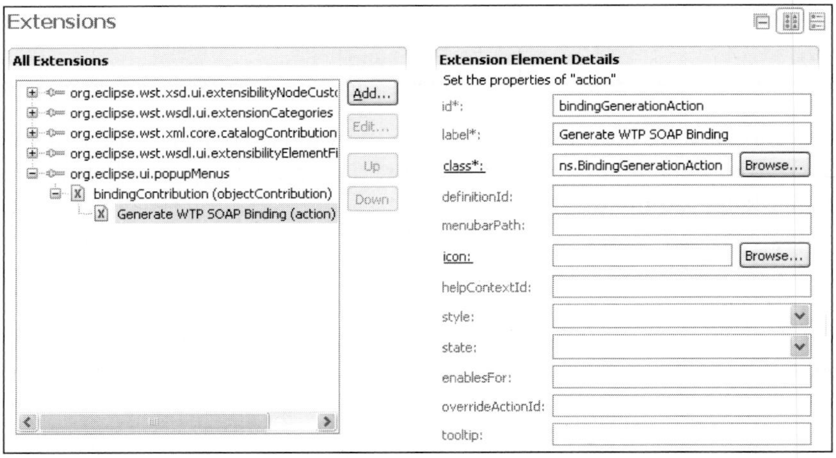

Figure 14.12   Generate WTP SOAP Binding Extension

Example 14.12   Listing of the WTP SOAP Binding Generation Extension in plugin.xml

```
<extension
   id="bindingGeneration"
   name="WTP SOAP Binding Generation"
   point="org.eclipse.ui.popupMenus">
  <objectContribution
     adaptable="false"
     id="bindingContribution"
     objectClass="org.eclipse.wst.wsdl.ui.internal.asd.facade.IBinding">
    <action
       class="org.eclipsewtp.wsdlextensions.BindingGenerationAction"
       id="bindingGenerationAction"
       label="Generate WTP SOAP Binding"/>
  </objectContribution>
</extension>
```

You've now defined the generate binding menu item. Try out the changes to your plug-in by launching a runtime workspace. You should see that the menu item **Generate WTP SOAP Binding** is available for the binding element (see Figure 14.13).

Figure 14.13   Generate WTP SOAP Binding Menu Item

So, you have defined the menu item and have seen that it appears in the context menu for the binding element. Selecting this action should generate the WTP SOAP binding content, including creating WTP SOAP binding, operation, and body elements. However, if you try to select the menu item you will receive an error stating that the current action is not available. The action is not available as you have not yet created the logic that supports it. Your next step is to create the action.

In the plug-in manifest editor's extension page, click on the action's class property. The **New Java Class** wizard will appear. Ensure the class implements

`org.eclipse.ui.IObjectActionDelegate`

and click **Finish** to create the class.

The generated class contains three methods, two of which are applicable for the action. Leave the implementation of `setActivePart` empty. This method can be used to change the enablement of the action depending on the workbench context in which an action is called. In this case you want the action to run the same regardless of whether it was called from the WSDL editor or the outline view. (That's right. By contributing this action to the **IBinding** interface, the action will be available from both the editor design view and the outline view.) The two methods you will implement are `run` and `selectionChanged`.

The `selectionChanged` method will be called when a user hovers over the menu item. This method provides two parameters, `action` and `selection`. The `action` parameter allows you to change the enablement of the generate binding action. The generate binding action should always be enabled so you will not make use of this parameter. (You could also have chosen to disable the action if, for example, the WTP SOAP binding elements already exist.) The `selection` parameter provides you with the object for which the context menu was selected. In this case, because you specified in your extension definition that the action should only be available for objects of the type

```
org.eclipse.wst.wsdl.ui.internal.asd.facade.IBinding
```

the selection will always contain the binding element. Store the selection so you can retrieve the binding element when the action is run.

The guts of your action are performed in the run method. This is where you will modify the model, adding the WTP SOAP binding content. This method again provides the action parameter so you can change the enablement. As before, you can disregard the action parameter.

Implement the BindingGenerationAction class as shown in Example 14.13.

Example 14.13   Listing of GenerateBindingAction.java

```java
package org.eclipsewtp.wsdlextensions;

import org.eclipse.emf.common.notify.Adapter;
import org.eclipse.jface.action.IAction;
import org.eclipse.jface.viewers.ISelection;
import org.eclipse.jface.viewers.StructuredSelection;
import org.eclipse.ui.IObjectActionDelegate;
import org.eclipse.ui.IWorkbenchPart;
import org.eclipse.wst.wsdl.Binding;
import org.eclipse.wst.wsdl.ui.internal.asd.facade.IBinding;
import org.w3c.dom.Document;
import org.w3c.dom.Element;
import org.w3c.dom.Node;
import org.w3c.dom.NodeList;

public class BindingGenerationAction implements IObjectActionDelegate {
  private StructuredSelection selection = null;

  public BindingGenerationAction() {
    super();
  }

  public void setActivePart(IAction action, IWorkbenchPart targetPart) {
    // Do nothing.
  }

  public void run(IAction action) {
    Object obj = ((StructuredSelection)selection).getFirstElement();
    if(obj instanceof IBinding) {
      Binding bindingModelObj = (Binding)((Adapter)obj).getTarget();
      Element domBindingElement = bindingModelObj.getElement();

      Document doc = domBindingElement.getOwnerDocument();
      Element docElem = doc.getDocumentElement();
      docElem.setAttribute("xmlns:wtpsoap",
                      "http://eclipsewtp.org/wsdl/soap/");
      Element soapBinding =
        doc.createElementNS("http://eclipsewtp.org/wsdl/soap/",
                      "wtpsoap:binding");
      soapBinding.setAttribute("style", "document");
```

```
soapBinding.setAttribute("transport",
                    "http://schemas.xmlsoap.org/soap/http");
Node firstBindingChild = domBindingElement.getFirstChild();
if(firstBindingChild == null) {
  domBindingElement.appendChild(soapBinding);
}
else {
  domBindingElement.insertBefore(soapBinding, firstBindingChild);
}

NodeList operations =
  domBindingElement.getElementsByTagNameNS(
      "http://schemas.xmlsoap.org/wsdl/", "operation");
int numOperations = operations.getLength();
for(int i = 0; i < numOperations; i++) {
  Element operation = (Element)operations.item(i);
  String operationName = operation.getAttribute("name");
  Element soapOperation =
    doc.createElementNS("http://eclipsewtp.org/wsdl/soap/",
                        "wtpsoap:operation");
  String soapAction = docElem.getAttribute("targetNamespace");
  if(!soapAction.endsWith("/"))
    soapAction += "/";
  soapAction += operationName;
  soapOperation.setAttribute("soapAction", soapAction);

  Node firstOperationChild = operation.getFirstChild();
  if(firstOperationChild == null) {
    operation.appendChild(soapOperation);
  }
  else {
    operation.insertBefore(soapOperation, firstOperationChild);
  }

  NodeList inputs =
    domBindingElement.getElementsByTagNameNS(
        "http://schemas.xmlsoap.org/wsdl/", "input");
  int numInputs = inputs.getLength();
  for(int j = 0; j < numInputs; j++) {
    Element input = (Element)inputs.item(i);

    Element soapBody =
      doc.createElementNS("http://eclipsewtp.org/wsdl/soap/",
                          "wtpsoap:body");
    soapBody.setAttribute("use", "literal");

    Node firstInputChild = input.getFirstChild();
    if(firstInputChild == null) {
      input.appendChild(soapBody);
    }
    else {
      input.insertBefore(soapBody, firstInputChild);
    }
  }
}
```

```
          NodeList outputs =
            domBindingElement.getElementsByTagNameNS(
                "http://schemas.xmlsoap.org/wsdl/", "output");
          int numOutputs = outputs.getLength();
          for(int j = 0; j < numOutputs; j++) {
            Element output = (Element)outputs.item(i);

            Element soapBody =
              doc.createElementNS("http://eclipsewtp.org/wsdl/soap/",
                                  "wtpsoap:body");
            soapBody.setAttribute("use", "literal");

            Node firstOutputChild = output.getFirstChild();
            if(firstOutputChild == null) {
              output.appendChild(soapBody);
            }
            else {
              output.insertBefore(soapBody, firstOutputChild);
            }
          }
        }
      }
    }
  }

  public void selectionChanged(IAction action, ISelection selection) {
    if(selection instanceof StructuredSelection) {
      this.selection = (StructuredSelection)selection;
    }
  }
}
```

As the implementation shows, the `selectionChanged` method stores the selection. Only `StructuredSelections` are stored as they are the only type of selections that contain the object for which the action will run. The `run` method in turn checks that the object is indeed an

`org.eclipse.wst.wsdl.ui.internal.asd.facade.IBinding`

element. If so, a few actions are performed. First, in order to contribute to the model, you need to access the WSDL binding element. Accessing the model binding element requires that you jump though a few hoops, as shown in lines 3 and 4 of the `run` method. You need to cast the structured selection object to an EMF adapter, get the target of the adapter, and cast that to the model binding element. Then, to work with the DOM model (which can be easier and more flexible than working with the WSDL model), you need to get the DOM element from the WSDL element. Once you have the model element, adding the required WTP SOAP binding elements simply requires that you create new elements for the WSDL binding, binding operation, and input and output elements. The method iterates through all of the binding operation and input and output elements as WTP SOAP elements need to be added to all elements in the binding. It also adds the WTP SOAP namespace to the WSDL definitions element in case it is not already present.

With the action implemented, go ahead and try it out. Launch a runtime workbench and select the menu item. (Remove the WTP SOAP elements from the WSDL document if they are already present.) This time the menu item does not tell you that it can't run as you've now defined the action. The action runs and adds the WTP SOAP elements to the WSDL document.

There are of course many more enhancements you can make to the generate binding action, such as checking if a WTP SOAP binding or other binding element already exists, using the existing namespace declaration instead of declaring a new one, formatting the WTP SOAP element additions in the document, and providing a way for users to specify their own values for the `style` and `transport` attributes. The rest of these enhancements require additional logic and UI changes and are left up to you to implement as an exercise.

Extending WSDL Validation

At this point you've configured the WSDL editor to handle SOAP binding elements in the WTP SOAP namespace. However, the ability to add WTP SOAP binding elements to WSDL documents using the editor does not stop a user from using the WTP SOAP binding elements in an invalid way. Although this is typically a larger concern when working in the source editor, it is also possible to create an invalid WSDL document using the design editor. Furthermore, you've been given the task of ensuring that WSDL documents follow your organization's naming conventions, and there is no way to ensure that they do using the current tools. This is where the extensible WSDL validator fits in.

WTP's WSDL validator is extensible, allowing the addition of validation logic for specific WSDL extension namespaces and custom validation logic not bound by one specific namespace. WSDL validation is really a three-stage process, as shown in Figure 14.14. Stage 1 simply checks that the document structure is well-formed XML (that is, that all elements are nested and closed properly). Stage 2 performs WSDL 1.1 validation, that is, validation according to the WSDL 1.1 specification; and WSDL extension namespace validation, that is, validation according to extension WSDL specifications such as those for SOAP, HTTP, and MIME. Stage 3 performs any custom validation that is not part of the WSDL 1.1 specification and does not extend the WSDL 1.1 specification. Custom validation is typically validation that spans several namespaces, such as that for the WS-I profiles, which specify additional rules and constraints for WSDL documents and the bindings that may be used when describing a service. Validation of a given stage does not occur unless validation of the proceeding stage concluded that the document is valid.

Contributing to WSDL 1.1 Validation

WSDL 1.1 validation is included in WTP, but out of the box does not know how to validate all possible extension elements declared in extension namespaces, like the WTP SOAP namespace, and for good reason. The WSDL extensions were not known at the time the specification was written. If all the extensions were known at that time, there would not have been a need to create an open content model. To complete the editing experience, you will need to extend WSDL validation to test the WTP SOAP binding elements. Because you declared the WTP SOAP schema in the XML catalog, you will get partial validation for free from XML schema validation. Schema validation does not completely cover the requirements of the WTP SOAP namespace, specified in the WSDL 1.1 specification, so you will need to implement a custom WTP SOAP validator. In order to keep the example simple, you will only check one constraint. According to the WSDL 1.1 specification, every SOAP binding element must specify a `transport` attribute. This means a WTP SOAP binding element must contain a `transport` attribute with a non-empty value.

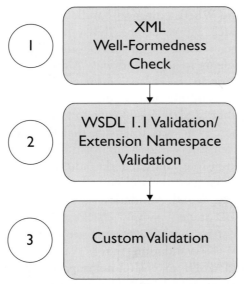

Figure 14.14   The Three Stages of WSDL Validation

Tip: The meaning of the `transport` attribute is not relevant here. All you need to know is that it is required on every WTP SOAP binding element.

WTP's WSDL validator defines the following extension point:

```
org.eclipse.wst.wsdl.validation.wsdl11validator
```

This extension point allows validation logic for a WSDL 1.1 extension namespace, in your case:

```
http://eclipsewtp.org/wsdl/soap/
```

to be contributed to stage 2 of WSDL validation. To extend the WSDL validator you must first create a dependency on the WSDL validator plug-in. In the plug-in manifest editor, select the **Dependencies** tab and add the following dependency on the plug-in:

```
org.eclipse.wst.wsdl.validation
```

A dependency, which you added in the previous section, is also required for the plug-in

```
org.wsdl4j
```

a lightweight WSDL model used in WTP for validation.

Next, extend the WSDL validator extension point shown above by adding a new extension on the **Extensions** tab. Right click on the extension and create a new **validator** (see Figure 14.15). The validator requires that two pieces of information be specified: `namespace` and `class`. The namespace is that of the extension elements that will be validated, in your case:

```
http://eclipsewtp.org/wsdl/soap/
```

Figure 14.15   WTP SOAP Validator Declaration

The class is the class that implements

```
org.eclipse.wst.wsdl.validation.internal.wsdl11.IWSDL11Validator
```

and provides the validation logic for the elements. In your case, specify the class

```
org.eclipsewtp.wsdlextensions.SOAPValidator
```

Your contribution to `plugin.xml` can be seen in Example 14.14.

Example 14.14   Listing of the WTP SOAP Validator Extension in plugin.xml

```
<extension
    point="org.eclipse.wst.wsdl.validation.wsdl11validator">
  <validator
      class="org.eclipsewtp.wsdlextensions.SOAPValidator"
      namespace="http://eclipsewtp.org/wsdl/soap/"/>
</extension>
```

As said above, the class that implements the validation logic must implement `IWSDL11Validator` (see Example 14.15). This interface contains a single method, `validate`. The `validate` method is where the validation logic for the validator resides. In your case, this is where the test of the WTP SOAP binding element will be performed.

This `validate` method will be called for each element in the namespace that is encountered in the WSDL document. The three parameters, `element`, `parents`, and `valInfo`, contain the element to validate, a list of the parent elements of the element to validate, and a validation information object that is used for reporting errors and warnings.

Example 14.15   Listing of IWSDL11Validator.java

```
package org.eclipse.wst.wsdl.validation.internal.wsdl11;
import java.util.List;

public interface IWSDL11Validator {

  public void validate(Object element, List parents,
      IWSDL11ValidationInfo valInfo);
}
```

With the extension defined, you should now create the class containing the validation logic. Create the class

```
org.eclipsewtp.wsdlextensions.SOAPValidator
```

by clicking on the `class` property for the validator extension declaration. Ensure the class implements this interface:

```
org.eclipse.wst.wsdl.validation.internal.wsdl11.IWSDL11Validator
```

Implement the test for the SOAP binding transport as shown in Example 14.16.

Example 14.16   Listing of SOAPValidator.java

```
package org.eclipsewtp.wsdlextensions;
import java.util.List;

import javax.wsdl.extensions.UnknownExtensibilityElement;
import javax.xml.namespace.QName;

import org.eclipse.wst.wsdl.validation.....wsdl11.IWSDL11ValidationInfo;
import org.eclipse.wst.wsdl.validation.....wsdl11.IWSDL11Validator;

public class SOAPValidator implements IWSDL11Validator
{
  public void validate(Object element, List parents,
                       IWSDL11ValidationInfo valInfo) {
    if(element instanceof UnknownExtensibilityElement) {
      UnknownExtensibilityElement soapElem =
        (UnknownExtensibilityElement)element;
      QName name = soapElem.getElementType();
      if(name.getLocalPart().equals("binding")) {
        String transport = soapElem.getElement()
                          .getAttribute("transport");
        if(transport == null || transport.equals("")) {
          valInfo.addError("A transport must be specified for the " +
                    "WTP SOAP binding element.", element);
        }
      }
    }
  }
}
```

The test shown in the `validate` method first checks whether the element is a SOAP binding element. If so, its `transport` attribute is retrieved and checked to ensure it is not null and not empty. If the transport contains a value, the method returns. If not, an error is added to the `IWSDL11ValidationInfo` object. The `addError` method on the `IWSDL11ValidationInfo` interface takes a string error message and the element the message was found on. The element will be used to determine the line and column location information for the error message. You can set these values yourself using the alternate `addError` method that accepts the line and column numbers and the URI of the file containing the element.

Now is a good time to test what you've just completed. Launch your runtime workbench and validate the valid `Echo.wsdl` WSDL document by right clicking on the file in the **Project Explorer** and selecting **Validate**. Change the value of the SOAP binding transport to an empty string to see the error message produced by your WTP SOAP validator displayed in the **Problems** view (see Figure 14.16).

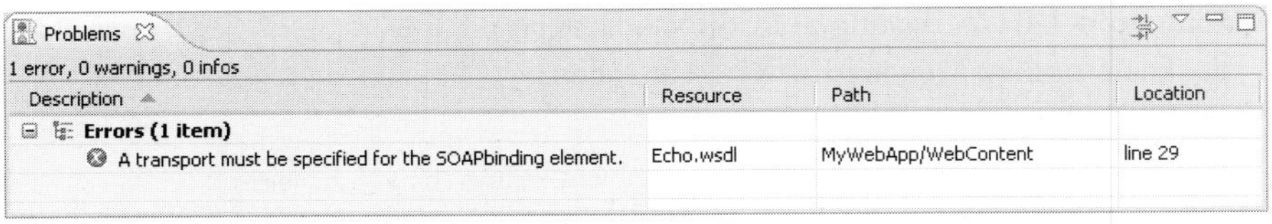

Figure 14.16   Binding Transport Error Message Shown in the Problems View

Tip: You can see a complete implementation of a WSDL 1.1 SOAP validator in the class

```
org.eclipse.wst.wsdl.validation.internal.wsdl11.soap.SOAPValidator
```

in the WTP plug-in

```
org.eclipse.wst.wsdl.validation
```

Contributing Custom Validation Rules

With the WTP SOAP validation rules in place, it's now time to take a look at implementing validation for your organization's naming conventions. The validation logic for the naming conventions differs from that in the previous section. In the previous section you contributed a validator for an extension WSDL namespace. The validator was run during stage 2 of WSDL validation. The validation logic you will now contribute is for an entire WSDL document, can span namespaces, and is not an extension of WSDL but rather a new set of rules governing WSDL documents for your organization. Also, custom validation rules typically require a valid WSDL document to validate. Stage 3 validators will only be invoked if the WSDL document is deemed valid by all stage 2 WSDL validators.

Your organization's WSDL naming conventions are simple but illustrative. The naming conventions are simply that all element names in a WSDL document begin with a capital letter. This means names such as `mybinding` and `2006binding` are not allowed.

WTP's WSDL validator defines the following extension point:

```
org.eclipse.wst.wsdl.validation.extvalidator
```

This extension point allows validation logic for a custom validator to be contributed to stage 3 of WSDL validation. As for all extensions, the extension validator must be defined in your plug-in manifest. This extension point also requires that two pieces of information be specified: `namespace` and `class`. In this case, the namespace corresponds with the version of WSDL to be validated. Currently only WSDL 1.1 is supported by the validator. The class is a class that implements

`org.eclipse.wst.wsdl.validation.internal.IWSDLValidator`

and provides the validation logic for the elements.

Add the extension by selecting the **Extensions** tab in your plug-in manifest editor. On your plug-in manifest's **Extensions** tab, select **Add** and create a new extension for the extension point

`org.eclipse.wst.wsdl.validation.extvalidator`

Right click on the extension and select **New** ▸ **extvalidator**. Set the namespace to the WSDL 1.1 namespace, that is,

`http://schemas.xmlsoap.org/wsdl/`

and set the class as

`org.eclipsewtp.wsdlextensions.NamingConventionValidator`

(see Figure 14.17). Your contribution to `plugin.xml` can be seen in Example 14.17.

Figure 14.17   WSDL Naming Convention Validator Declaration

Example 14.17   Listing of the WSDL Naming Convention Validator Extension in plugin.xml

```
<extension
  point="org.eclipse.wst.wsdl.validation.extvalidator">
  <extvalidator
    class="org.eclipsewtp.wsdlextensions.NamingConventionValidator"
    namespace="http://schemas.xmlsoap.org/wsdl/"/>
</extension>
```

The class that implements the validation logic must implement the `IWSDLValidator` interface (see Example 14.18). This interface is similar to the

`IWSDL11Validator` interface in that it contains the one method, `validate`. However, this `validate` method takes different parameters. The `validate` method takes two parameters: `domModel` and `valInfo`. The `valInfo` parameter serves the same purpose as before. The `domModel` is a DOM representation of the WSDL document. This raw form of the WSDL document provides the freedom to access all aspects of the XML document.

Example 14.18   Listing of IWSDLValidator.java

```
package org.eclipse.wst.wsdl.validation.internal;

import org.eclipse.wst.wsdl.....exception.ValidateWSDLException;
import org.w3c.dom.Document;

public interface IWSDLValidator {

  public void validate(Document domModel, IValidationInfo valInfo)
    throws ValidateWSDLException;
}
```

The validation logic for the naming convention validator is very simple. It simply iterates over every element in the WSDL model, and for each element that has a `name` attribute it ensures that the first character is a capital letter, and if not it creates an error message.

Create the class

```
org.eclipsewtp.wsdlextensions.NamingConventionValidator
```

by clicking on the `class` property on the **extvalidator** declaration page. Ensure that the class implements

```
org.eclipse.wst.wsdl.validation.internal.IWSDLValidator
```

Implement the naming convention test as shown in Example 14.19.

Example 14.19   Listing of NamingConventionValidator.java

```
package org.eclipsewtp.wsdlextensions;

import org.apache.xerces.dom.ElementImpl;
import org.eclipse.wst.wsdl.validation.internal.IValidationInfo;
import org.eclipse.wst.wsdl.validation.internal.IWSDLValidator;
import org.eclipse.wst.wsdl.....exception.ValidateWSDLException;
import org.eclipse.wst.wsdl.validation.internal.xml.ElementLocation;
import org.w3c.dom.Document;
import org.w3c.dom.Element;
import org.w3c.dom.Node;
import org.w3c.dom.NodeList;
```

```
public class NamingConventionValidator implements IWSDLValidator {
  public void validate(Document domModel, IValidationInfo valInfo)
      throws ValidateWSDLException {
    Element rootElem = domModel.getDocumentElement();
    checkNames(rootElem, valInfo);
  }

  private void checkNames(Element element, IValidationInfo valInfo) {
    String name = element.getAttribute("name");
    if(name != null && name.length() > 0 &&
       !Character.isUpperCase(name.charAt(0))) {
      ElementLocation loc = (ElementLocation)((ElementImpl)element)
        .getUserData();
      valInfo.addError("The name of this element must begin with a " +
          "capital letter.", loc.getLineNumber(),
          loc.getColumnNumber(), valInfo.getFileURI());
    }

    NodeList childNodes = element.getChildNodes();
    int numChildNodes = childNodes.getLength();
    for(int i = 0; i < numChildNodes; i++) {
      Node child = childNodes.item(i);
      if(child instanceof Element) {
        checkNames((Element)child, valInfo);
      }
    }
  }
}
```

You can now test your naming convention validator as you did for your
WTP SOAP validator. Launch a runtime workspace and validate the Echo.wsdl
file. (You will need to correct the transport attribute error if the attribute is still
invalid from the previous section.) A new error should appear on the WSDL
service element because the name of the element does not start with a capital letter. The error message will once again be displayed in the **Problems** view (see
Figure 14.18). Change the name to start with a capital letter and validate again.
The error should disappear.

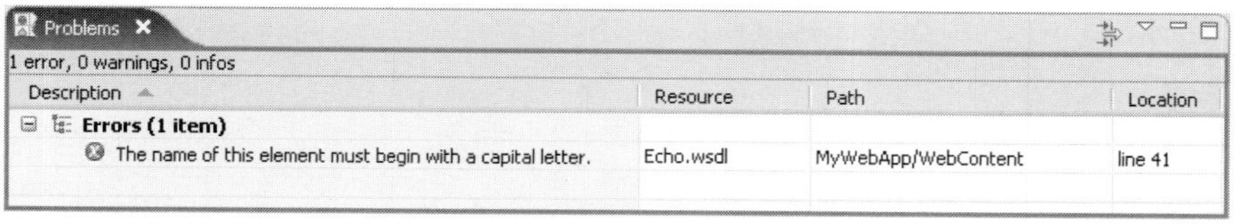

Figure 14.18   Service Element Naming Error Message Shown in the Problems View

Although this example contained simple naming conventions, we hope you
can see that it should be easy to replace the simple naming conventions with

more complex naming conventions such as camel casing or requiring the use of specific prefixes for every name.

> **Note:** Changing the name of an element in the WSDL document that is referenced by another element, such as a message name, may cause a WSDL validation error to display instead of the naming error. Remember that the document must pass the first two stages of validation before the third stage will run.

Summary

WTP's WSDL extension points are used for customizing the WSDL authoring experience in Eclipse. In this chapter you used the WSDL extension points to add extensibility elements for the WTP SOAP namespace to the WSDL editor and validator. Specifically, you added custom icons, a category, a custom binding generation action, and validation for the WTP SOAP namespace. You also added custom validation rules to the WSDL validator that ensure a WSDL document complies with your organization's naming conventions. You now have the tools you need to create your own customizations for WTP's WSDL tools.

In the next chapter you'll further customize these tools and other tools by altering WTP's URI resolution strategies.

CHAPTER 15

Customizing Resource Resolution

Any problem in computer science can be solved with another layer of indirection.

—David Wheeler

When a WTP tool processes an XML document, it often encounters references to other documents. For example, the grammar of the document might be specified by a DTD or XML Schema (XSD). This is the case with J2EE deployment descriptors, such as `web.xml` (see Example 15.1). Another common case is when one document refers to the contents of other documents. For example, Web Service Description Language (WSDL) documents refer to components defined in other WSDL and XSD documents.

Example 15.1 Listing of web.xml

```
<?xml version="1.0" encoding="UTF-8"?>
<web-app id="WebApp_ID"
   version="2.4"
   xmlns="http://java.sun.com/xml/ns/j2ee"
   xmlns:xsi="http://www.w3.org/2001/XMLSchema-instance"
   xsi:schemaLocation="http://java.sun.com/xml/ns/j2ee
                       http://java.sun.com/xml/ns/j2ee/web-app_2_4.xsd">
  <display-name>
    leagueplanet.com
  </display-name>
  <welcome-file-list>
    <welcome-file>index.html</welcome-file>
    <welcome-file>index.htm</welcome-file>
    <welcome-file>index.jsp</welcome-file>
    <welcome-file>default.html</welcome-file>
    <welcome-file>default.htm</welcome-file>
    <welcome-file>default.jsp</welcome-file>
  </welcome-file-list>
</web-app>
```

Web documents are generally referred to as *resources*, and the process of locating them as *resource resolution*. A *resource resolution strategy* is the way in which a resource is located. Resource resolution is the act of locating some resource using one or more resource resolution strategies. This means that in any given scenario there may be many resource resolution strategies all employed for the same resource resolution action.

Let's briefly examine how resource resolution works in WTP for `web.xml`. We'll discuss resource resolution in much more detail below. Here the XSD grammar is specified by the namespace URI

```
http://java.sun.com/xml/ns/j2ee
```

WTP processes any Web deployment descriptor and tries to locate the XSD document that defines the grammar for its namespace. In this example, the document itself provides a hint as to where the XSD can be found. The hint is provided in the `xsi:schemaLocation` attribute, which tells any processor that a copy of the XSD is located at

```
http://java.sun.com/xml/ns/j2ee/web-app_2_4.xsd
```

However, the rules of XML processing allow a processor to ignore this hint and obtain the XSD from elsewhere, for example, a locally cached copy. In fact, WTP does not redistribute copies of the J2EE deployment descriptor schemas. The first time you create a Web project in a new workspace, WTP attempts to retrieve the XSD from the Web and you are prompted to agree to the licensing terms for J2EE. WTP caches this copy for future use so you can work offline and are not repeatedly asked to agree to the license.

When it comes to Web development, many Web resources are stand-alone, which means that they do not rely on any other resources. Editing and validating stand-alone Web resources is generally straightforward as there is no need to access other resources. Web resources that depend on other resources are generally more difficult for tools to deal with. Dependent Web resources, including XML files that depend on grammars from type systems such as XSD and DTD, add complexity to tools that handle them, such as editors, validators, and generators. The added complexity comes from the need of these tools to locate dependent resources using some resource resolution strategy.

Many tools have resource resolution embedded right into them. For stand-alone or simple tools there is nothing wrong with this approach. Problems start to arise when your project has multiple tools that require consistent resource resolution. Embedding resource resolution in each of the tools may lead to inconsistency problems, requires duplicate code and maintenance, and does not allow third parties to easily follow or change the resource resolution strategy employed by your tools.

To solve these problems, WTP includes the *URI resolution framework*. This framework serves two key purposes. First, if your tools use it, it ensures that the resource resolution strategy employed by your tools will be consistent with the strategy defined by WTP. This both removes the burden from you of mimicking the resource resolution strategy of the platform and allows your tools to better integrate with the platform. Second, the framework allows you to extend it with any custom resource resolution strategy you need. By using the framework in this way, your tools and all WTP tools will follow your defined resolution strategy and consistently resolve the location of resources.

In this chapter, you play the role of a plug-in developer for an organization that has decided to use WTP as the standard tool set for Web and J2EE development. Unfortunately, (for legal reasons) WTP does not bundle either the J2EE schemas and DTDs or your own organization's proprietary schemas used for Java Web applications. Every WTP installation must therefore download and cache the schemas and DTDs itself. You've been assigned the task of coming up with and implementing a way to prevent this installation step.

In this chapter you will:

○ Contribute the J2EE schemas and DTDs to the WTP XML catalog, a type of URI resolver that provides a specific resource resolution strategy

○ Create a custom URI resolver with your own resource resolution strategy for locating your organization's proprietary schemas

> **Warning:** As of WTP 1.5, the WTP extension points and API shown in this chapter are not final. These extension points and API may change in future versions of WTP.

Creating the Resource Resolution Extension Plug-in

Once again, the first step in making use of the resource resolution extensions required of the tasks in this chapter is to create a plug-in to hold the extension definitions and the associated Java classes. Create a new plug-in with the id

`org.eclipsewtp.resourceresolution`

and name it `Resource Resolution Extensions Plug-in` using the **New Plug-in Project** wizard (see Figure 15.1). As your plug-in will not contain any UI components and will have nothing to activate, deselect the options for **Generate an activator** and **This plug-in will make contributions to the UI**.

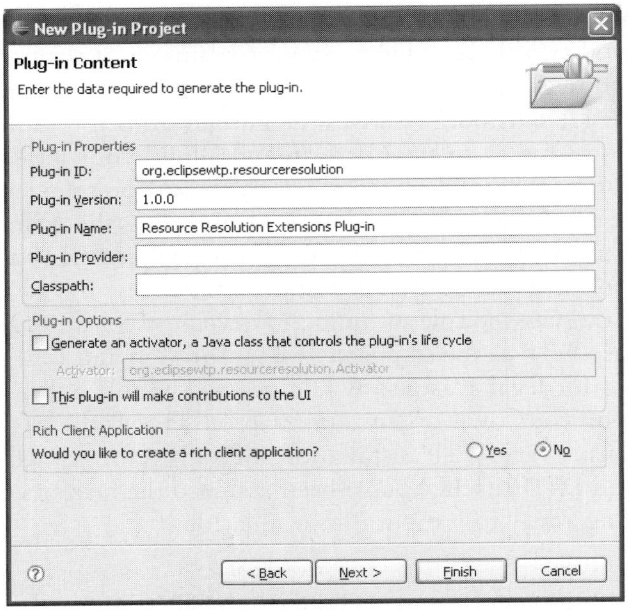

Figure 15.1   Definition of the Resource Resolution Extensions Plug-in

Contributing Resources to the XML Catalog

As we stated in the introduction, your organization has decided to use WTP as the standard tool set for Web and J2EE development. It is your job to bundle the J2EE schemas and DTDs with WTP for distribution within your organization. There are a number of reasons why you've been asked to complete this task. Before getting to the task, we'll take a minute to discuss the importance of schemas and DTDs.

Much in the same way that natural languages such as English and French define specific grammars for their respective languages, a schema or DTD represents a grammar for a specific XML language. This grammar defines the elements that may appear in the language and the structure that the elements must take in order to conform with the language's requirements. Because these files contain detailed information about a language, they are very useful for authoring tools (think of editors and the tools that surround them). Authoring tools can use a schema or DTD to provide validation of a given instance of the language (typically a file), inline editor syntax highlighting, and content assistance based on the rules the grammar defines.

In order for an XML file to specify its grammar, it must reference the grammar in some way. There are two types of identifiers that allow an XML file to reference a schema or DTD: public and system.

A public identifier (or `publicId`) provides no hint as to the actual location of a schema or DTD but instead provides a unique identifier for the artifact that you can use to determine the location by some other means (such as the XML catalog). A schema's public identifier is its namespace, such as

```
http://java.sun.com/xml/ns/j2ee
```

and is typically specified by declaring a namespace in an XML document (see line 4 in Example 15.1 earlier). A DTD's public identifier, typically specified in a comment in the DTD, is specified in an XML file by using the PUBLIC keyword in a DOCTYPE statement (see Example 15.2).

Example 15.2 J2EE 1.3 PUBLIC DOCTYPE

```
<!DOCTYPE web-app PUBLIC
    "-//Sun Microsystems, Inc.//DTD Web Application 2.3//EN"
    "http://java.sun.com/dtd/web-app_2_3.dtd">
```

A system identifier (or `systemId`) provides a hint as to the actual location of a schema or DTD. A schema system identifier, typically a URL, is specified in an XML file using the `xsi:schemaLocation` attribute. This attribute contains a list of paired items, where the first item is the schema namespace and the second item is the system identifier (see lines 6 and 7 in Example 15.1 earlier). A DTD system identifier, also typically a URL, is specified in an XML file using the SYSTEM keyword in a DOCTYPE statement (see Example 15.3).

Example 15.3 J2EE 1.3 SYSTEM DOCTYPE

```
<!DOCTYPE web-app SYSTEM
    "http://java.sun.com/dtd/web-app_2_3.dtd">
```

Every J2EE Web application contains the XML file `web.xml`, known as the deployment descriptor (see Example 15.1), which holds configuration details for the application, such as servlet mappings. The deployment descriptor is located in the `web-inf` folder in each application.

The deployment descriptor specifies the specific J2EE grammar it requires by declaring a system identifier. For J2EE 1.4 the system identifier is

```
http://java.sun.com/xml/ns/j2ee/web-app_2_4.xsd
```

(There are different grammars for the different parts and versions of the J2EE specification.) As mentioned earlier, having access to the file containing the J2EE grammar will allow WTP's tools to provide enhanced function for validation and content assistance for `web.xml`.

By default, WTP will attempt to retrieve remote schemas and DTDs from the Web and cache them using a cache resource resolution strategy. In the case of J2EE, this allows WTP users to get the enhanced function even though the J2EE schemas and DTDs are not bundled with WTP. Although this solution generally works well, it does have a number of drawbacks for new users.

❍ New users must use WTP while connected to the Internet in order to download these schemas and DTDs. This adds an extra configuration step to the WTP install process and can lead to problems if the servers are not visible (due to server outage, proxy configuration or some other problem) when attempting to download the files.

❍ Creation of the first Web application will take longer than subsequent Web applications as the user has to accept license agreements and download the schemas and DTDs.

❍ Every new user must perform this operation. This reduces the efficiency of your organization by placing a burden on all developers that use WTP, increases bandwidth consumption, and may lead to an increase in support calls if there are any network difficulties.

For these reasons you will bundle the J2EE schemas and DTDs with the version of WTP your organization distributes internally, preventing the need for WTP to retrieve the files remotely. In the following sections you will contribute the J2EE schemas to WTP using WTP's XML catalog.

The XML Catalog

WTP's XML catalog allows you to register schemas and DTDs for use in resource resolution. (The catalog can actually register any resource that can be specified with a URI, such as a WSDL document. See the online documentation on the WTP Web site for more about registering any resource.) Typically the XML catalog is used in the way you are going to make use of it, to specify the location of local schemas and DTDs. To put this function in resource resolution terminology, the XML catalog implements a resource resolution strategy that retrieves a specific resource from a catalog of resources using a key. In fact, the XML catalog is a URI resolver that has been contributed to the URI resolution framework, which you will make direct use of later in this chapter.

The XML catalog includes a graphical user interface (see Figure 15.2) that allows you to easily contribute resources to it. Resources can be contributed through the XML catalog preferences page, found under **Window ▶ Preferences ▶ Web and XML ▶ XML Catalog**. While this preferences page is a good way for users to customize their workspace, it still requires user interaction and therefore will not completely solve your problem. To bundle the J2EE schemas with WTP, you will need to contribute them to the XML catalog using the XML catalog's defined extension point.

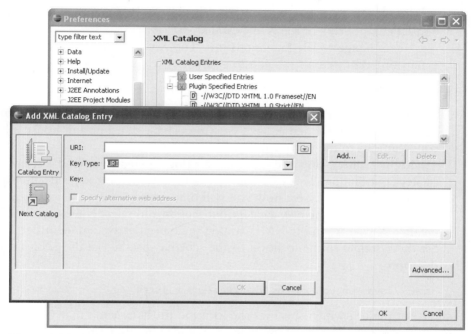

Figure 15.2 Add XML Catalog Entry

Adding a Single Resource to the XML Catalog

As you saw earlier in Example 15.1, the J2EE deployment descriptor for a J2EE 1.4 application specifies the following location for its grammar:

```
http://java.sun.com/xml/ns/j2ee/web-app_2_4.xsd
```

Open this location in your Web browser. You will see that this location is that of the J2EE schema. It is this file that you want to bundle with WTP.

The J2EE schema contains license terms in a documentation block at the top. These are the terms that restrict WTP from bundling this schema. As long as you accept the terms (perhaps schools should start teaching software developers licensing law, as we frequently seem to be in positions that require us to understand licensing terms), download the schema and save it in your plug-in in a folder named `j2eeschemas`.

With the J2EE schema stored locally in your plug-in, you are ready to contribute it to the XML catalog. Open your plug-in manifest editor and change to the **Dependencies** tab. Add a dependency on

```
org.eclipse.wst.xml.core
```

The XML core plug-in contains non-UI XML functionality, including the non-UI components of the XML catalog.

Next change to the **Extensions** tab. The XML catalog defines the following extension point that allows you to add your own entries to the catalog:

```
org.eclipse.wst.xml.core.catalogContributions
```

Add a new `catalogContributions` extension. Give your new extension the id `j2eecatalog` and the name `J2EE Catalog`. This extension will house all of your contributions to the XML catalog.

Right click on the XML catalog extension and select **New ▶ catalogContribution**. This extension element allows you to specify multiple catalog contributions, but for now you will only specify one.

Right click on the new **catalogContribution** and select **New ▶ system**. This will create a new entry in the XML catalog that specifies system identifier as the key. Set the **systemId** to the location of the schema specified in the J2EE deployment descriptor:

```
http://java.sun.com/xml/ns/j2ee/web-app_2_4.xsd
```

Set the **uri**, which specifies the location of the schema that you want to use, to the relative location of the schema in your plug-in, namely

```
j2eeschemas/web-app_2_4.xsd
```

(You can also click **Browse** to select the location.) The effect of adding this entry to the XML catalog is that when the J2EE schema location is requested, it will return the local location of the schema from your plug-in. Save your plug-in manifest. Change to the **plugin.xml** source view and view the extension declaration (see Example 15.4).

Example 15.4 Listing of Catalog Extension

```
<extension
   id="org.eclipsewtp.resourceresolution.j2eecatalog"
   name="J2EE Catalog"
   point="org.eclipse.wst.xml.core.catalogContributions">
  <catalogContribution>
   <system
      systemId="http://java.sun.com/xml/ns/j2ee/web-app_2_4.xsd"
      uri="j2eeschemas/web-app_2_4.xsd"/>
  </catalogContribution>
</extension>
```

Time to try out your changes. Launch a runtime workspace. When the workspace is open, navigate to the XML catalog preference page. The J2EE schema should now be listed in the catalog (see Figure 15.3). So far, so good.

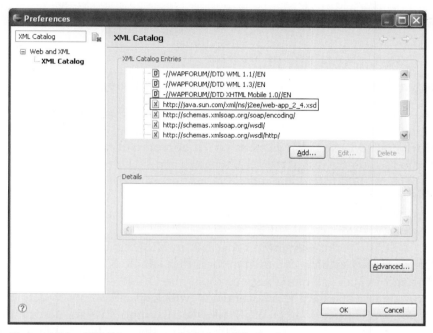

Figure 15.3 J2EE Schema Entry Added to XML Catalog

Next create a new dynamic Web project. You can name the project anything you like. Accept all the default settings and click **Finish** in the **New Dynamic Web Project** wizard. The license dialog does not appear (good) and your new project shows an error (bad). What went wrong? The error has occurred because the J2EE schema is not a stand-alone schema. It requires other schemas that cannot be resolved by the validator now that the schema is included in the XML catalog. In the next section you will add the rest of the J2EE schemas to the XML catalog.

Tip: In this section you added a location for a schema system identifier to the XML catalog. There is only one step you need to change in order to add a catalog entry specifying a location for a schema's public identifier (its namespace). Simply use the `public` element instead of the `system` element and the `publicId` attribute instead of the `systemId` attribute as follows:

```
<public
    publicId="http://java.sun.com/xml/ns/j2ee"
    uri="j2eeschemas/web-app_2_4.xsd"/>
```

You can also add entries to the catalog for DTD public and system identifiers using the same method used for a schema by replacing the values of the `publicId` and `systemId` attributes with DTD public and system identifiers.

Adding a Catalog of Resources to the XML Catalog

The method of adding an entry to the XML catalog that you used in the previous section can be used to add many entries to the catalog. For each entry you simply provide a new extension element of the appropriate type. So, you can use this method to add the rest of the J2EE schemas and DTDs to the XML catalog.

The method for adding individual resources to the XML catalog works well in many situations. However, one notable limitation is that it restricts the catalog you create to Eclipse. This restricts who you can share your catalog with and how others can make use of it.

WTP is not the only project that has an XML catalog implementation. This type of facility is fairly common in tools that handle XML artifacts. To facilitate sharing of catalogs among various tools, the OASIS standards body created an XML catalog standard [XMLCatalogs], which specifies how to define an XML catalog representation in an XML file. (See Example 15.5 for an example.) This standard allows you to create XML catalogs that can be used in any tool that supports the OASIS standard. As you've probably guessed by now, WTP supports the OASIS standard.

Example 15.5 Listing of OASIS XML Catalog File

```
<catalog xmlns="urn:oasis:names:tc:entity:xmlns:xml:catalog">
  <system uri="web-app_2_4.xsd"
      systemId="http://java.sun.com/xml/ns/j2ee/web-app_2_4.xsd"/>
  <system uri="j2ee_1_4.xsd"
      systemId="j2ee_1_4.xsd"/>
  <system uri="jsp_2_0.xsd"
      systemId="jsp_2_0.xsd"/>
  <system uri="j2ee_web_services_client_1_1.xsd"
      systemId=
"http://www.ibm.com/webservices/xsd/j2ee_web_services_client_1_1.xsd"/>
  <public uri="web-app_2_3.dtd"
      publicId="-//Sun Microsystems, Inc.//DTD Web Application 2.3//EN"/>
  <public uri="web-app_2_2.dtd"
      publicId="-//Sun Microsystems, Inc.//DTD Web Application 2.2//EN"/>
</catalog>
```

For your J2EE catalog to be reusable within your organization, you will create the OASIS XML catalog shown in Example 15.5 and contribute it to the WTP XML catalog.

Before you create your J2EE OASIS XML catalog, you need to download the rest of the J2EE schemas and DTDs. The J2EE 1.4 schemas are listed at

`http://java.sun.com/xml/ns/j2ee/`

You've already downloaded `web-app_2_4.xsd`, and

`http://www.w3.org/2001/xml.xsd`

is already bundled with WTP. The rest of the schemas that you need for a J2EE 1.4 Web application are `jsp_2_0.xsd`, `j2ee_1_4.xsd`, and `j2ee_web_services_client_1_1.xsd`, which is listed as

`http://www.ibm.com/webservices/xsd/j2ee_web_services_client_1_1.xsd`

Download these schemas and place them in the `j2eeschemas` folder in your plug-in.

Next you need the J2EE 1.3 DTD, `web-app_2_3.dtd`, which is available from

`http://java.sun.com/dtd/`

Download this file and place it in the `j2eeschemas` folder.

The last resource you need to obtain is the J2EE 1.2 DTD, `web-app_2_2.dtd`, which is available from

`http://java.sun.com/j2ee/dtds/`

Download this file as well and place it in the `j2eeschemas` folder.

> **Note:** The J2EE schema and DTD pages contain listings for many other schemas besides those that you have downloaded. These other schemas and DTDs are used for other parts of the J2EE specification and are not needed for your immediate purpose, although depending on your use you may find it beneficial to place these in your catalog as well.

Now that you have all of your required resources you can create your OASIS XML catalog. Create a new XML file in the `j2eeschemas` folder named `j2eeschemacatalog.xml` to hold your catalog entries. Add the entries in the catalog (see Example 15.5 previously). The OASIS XML catalog standard and the WTP XML catalog extension point are very similar by design, so your OASIS catalog entries will be similar to the entry that you contributed in the previous section (although, unlike the extension point, WTP does not contain a GUI to create OASIS XML catalogs).

With your J2EE OASIS XML catalog complete, all that's left is to contribute it to WTP. Contributing an OASIS XML catalog to the WTP XML catalog is very similar to contributing an individual entry. Open your plug-in manifest to the **Extensions** tab. Right click on the existing `catalogContribution` and select **New ▸ nextCatalog**. Enter the location `j2eeschemas/j2eeschemacatalog.xml` for the catalog or select your catalog with the **Browse** button. Save your plug-in manifest and you're done. Change to the **plugin.xml** source view to view your extension (see Example 15.6).

Example 15.6 Listing of nextCatalog Extension

```
<extension
   id="j2eeCatalog"
   name="J2EE Catalog"
   point="org.eclipse.wst.xml.core.catalogContributions">
  <catalogContribution>
    <system
       systemId="http://java.sun.com/xml/ns/j2ee/web-app_2_4.xsd"
       uri="j2eeschemas/web-app_2_4.xsd"/>
    <nextCatalog
       catalog="j2eeschemas/j2eeschemacatalog.xml"/>
  </catalogContribution>
</extension>
```

You've made it to the fun part. Try out your changes by launching a new runtime workspace. Once the new workspace is up, open the **XML Catalog** preferences page. The preferences page should now contain a catalog entry that you can expand to reveal the entries contained within that catalog (see Figure 15.4). This demonstrates another benefit of using OASIS XML catalogs. Using these catalogs allows you to group related entries together in the WTP **XML Catalog** preferences page.

Exit the preferences page and return to your dynamic Web project that displayed an error after you completed the previous section. Validate your project by right clicking on it and selecting **Validate**. The error is removed as the required schemas can now be resolved by the XML catalog. Try creating new J2EE 1.3 and 1.2 Web projects by changing the **Dynamic Web Module** facet on page two of the **New Dynamic Web Project** wizard.

Note: At the time of writing this book, there was a bug in WTP that resulted in all of the entries within an OASIS catalog being displayed with an error marker, and this may result in those entries not being used in resource resolution.

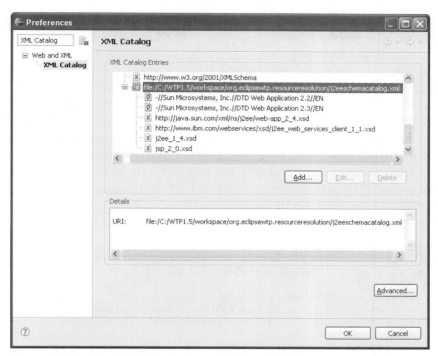

Figure 15.4 J2EE OASIS Catalog Entry Added to XML Catalog

Implementing a Custom Resource Resolution Strategy

There are many ways in which a resource can be resolved. In the previous section you contributed resources to the XML catalog. The XML catalog is a resource resolution strategy that allows you to contribute individual resources. In order to customize the resource resolution employed by WTP's tools, you need to add a strategy to the URI resolution framework, which provides the facility to implement any strategy you need. (We'll discuss this framework in detail in the next section.)

The second part of your task is to include your company's proprietary schemas in WTP. Here's a little more background about your task.

Your company uses schemas to define the grammar for many types of XML documents, including those that hold employee information. An example of an employee information document is shown in Example 15.7 and the corresponding schema is shown in Example 15.8. These schemas are used by employees to author XML documents. There is already a process in place within your company that automatically downloads the latest version of your company schemas onto all employee machines and stores them in c:\schemas. (Yes, all employees of your company use Windows.) This process was put in place to ensure that every employee has up-to-date copies of all of the company's schemas.

Management wants the latest version of these schemas incorporated into WTP. The benefits of including your company's schemas in WTP are the same as those of including the J2EE schemas and DTDs. Your company wants all employees to be able to use content assistance and validation in order to minimize the amount of mistakes in these important documents.

As the schemas may change and new schemas may be added to the collection, the XML catalog is not suitable for this task. To incorporate your company's schemas in WTP, you will create a custom URI resolver and contribute it to the URI resolution framework. In the next two sections we'll start with an overview of the URI resolution framework and then you'll implement your custom URI resolver.

Example 15.7   Listing of a Sample Employee XML Document

```
<?xml version="1.0" encoding="UTF-8"?>
<tns:employee
   xmlns:tns="http://www.leagueplanet.com/employee/"
   xmlns:xsi="http://www.w3.org/2001/XMLSchema-instance"
   xsi:schemaLocation="http://www.leagueplanet.com/employee/employee.xsd">
   <id>11111111</id>
   <firstname>Lawrence</firstname>
   <surname>Mandel</surname>
   <busaddress>
     <street>8200 Warden Ave</street>
     <city>Markham</city>
     <state>Ontario</state>
     <zipcode>L6G1C7</zipcode>
     <country>Canada</country>
   </busaddress>
   <position>Software Developer</position>
   <department>Eclipse Web Tools</department>
   <company>IBM</company>
</tns:employee>
```

Example 15.8   Listing of employee.xsd

```
<?xml version="1.0" encoding="UTF-8"?>
<schema
   xmlns="http://www.w3.org/2001/XMLSchema"
   targetNamespace="http://www.leagueplanet.com/employee/"
   xmlns:tns="http://www.leagueplanet.com/employee/">
   <element name="employee" type="tns:employeeInfo"/>
     <complexType name="employeeInfo">
     <sequence>
     <element name="id" type="int"/>
     <element name="firstname" type="string"/>
     <element name="surname" type="string"/>
     <element name="busaddress" type="tns:address"/>
     <element name="position" type="string"/>
```

```
        <element name="department" type="string"/>
        <element name="company" type="string"/>
      </sequence>
    </complexType>
    <complexType name="address">
      <sequence>
        <element name="street" type="string"/>
        <element name="city" type="string"/>
        <element name="state" type="string"/>
        <element name="zipcode" type="string"/>
        <element name="country" type="string"/>
      </sequence>
    </complexType>
  </schema>
```

The URI Resolution Framework

The pluggable URI resolution framework allows custom URI resolvers that implement specific resource resolution strategies to be inserted in the resource resolution strategy employed by WTP's tools. More concretely, this means that you can insert your custom URI resolver into the URI resolution framework and change the resource resolution employed by tools like the XML editor. In fact, all of WTP's tools make use of the URI resolution framework, so contributing your own resolver will consistently change the way resource resolution is performed across all of WTP. (To get the same benefit in your tools, see the Using the URI Resolution Framework in Your Tools sidebar.)

Consistency is generally a good thing, but there are scenarios in which you do not want every URI resolver to run. The prime reason for this is performance. Looking up a resource from many tools may take a nontrivial amount of time. You may therefore want to limit the instances in which your tool runs. For example, if your URI resolver looks up the location of a schema that will only be used in the context of Java projects, you should restrict it to being employed for Java projects.

You can customize the overall resource resolution strategy in a couple of ways. First, you can specify the project natures for which your resolver will be invoked. For the previous example, you would restrict your resolver to running on projects with the nature

```
org.eclipse.jdt.core.javanature
```

Specifying no project natures implicitly means that your resolver will be invoked for all project natures. Second, you can specify the priority of your resolver relative to other resolvers. The URI resolution framework will run all of the resolvers for a given scenario in a chained way (see Figure 15.5), setting the output of the first resolver as the input to the second, and so on. If you determine that your resolver should be run before the existing WTP resolvers—for example, if you want the results of your resolver to be resolved by the XML catalog resolver—you can specify a high priority to ensure that your resolver is run before all resolvers with normal and low priorities.

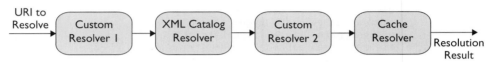

Figure 15.5 URI Resolution Resolver Chaining

Taking the concept of priority a step further, there are two types of resolvers, logical and physical, both of which implement the same interface. The difference lies in the intended use.

Logical resolvers resolve the location of a URI, but the location does not necessarily map to a physical location. Practically, this typically means that the resolver does not check that the location exists. For example, if your resolver has a mapping for a DTD public identifier to a URL but does not fetch the contents of the URL, it is a logical resolver.

Physical resolvers resolve the location of a URI and ensure that the location exists. For example, the WTP cache resolver will retrieve remote resources from the Internet before returning their location.

The distinction between logical and physical resolvers is made as physical resolvers are generally heavier weight than logical resolvers, meaning that they perform a slow retrieval of a URI in order to verify the location. Therefore, for performance reasons, client tools are given the choice of whether to run physical resolution or not. (Physical resolution may not be necessary if your tool simply wants to resolve an identifier and display the result.)

Using the URI Resolution Framework in Your Tools

As you read at the beginning of this chapter, using the URI resolution framework in your tools will allow them to follow the same resource resolution strategy as the WTP tools and any other tools that use the framework. Using it also means that your tools provide an extensible way for others to modify their resource resolution strategy, reducing the amount of resolution code that you have to maintain and modify.

But which of your tools should make use of the URI resolution framework? The simple answer is any tool that needs to locate resources—files, folders, machines, or simply identifiers—can benefit from the URI resolution framework. The tools in WTP tend to use the framework to locate files and to resolve identifiers, and the available WTP resolvers reflect these requirements.

Using the URI resolution framework in your Eclipse tools is very straightforward. To use the URI resolution framework, follow these steps:

1. Add the following dependency to your plug-in:

   ```
   org.eclipse.wst.common.uriresolver
   ```

2. Replace the custom resolution code in your plug-in with the following for logical URI resolution:

   ```
   URIResolver resolver = URIResolverPlugin.createResolver();
   String logicalResult =
     resolver.resolve(baseLocation, publicId, systemId);
   ```

   and the following for physical URI resolution:

   ```
   URIResolver resolver = URIResolverPlugin.createResolver();
   String logicalResult =
     resolver.resolve(baseLocation, publicId, systemId);
   String physicalResult =
     resolver.resolvePhysicalLocation(baseLocation,
                             publicId, logicalResult);
   ```

For physical resolution, it is typical to perform logical resolution first and use the result in the physical resolution.

There is nothing more to it. The URI resolution framework is just simple and powerful. It automatically handles resolution based on project type, file type, and any other resource resolution strategy determinant. Nothing else needs to be added to your code.

Creating the Folder URI Resolver

The previous section stated the requirements of your custom URI resolver. We'll summarize them here so that the task is clear.

❍ The schemas must reside in `c:\schemas` in order to reuse the existing distribution mechanism that is in place.

❍ The existing schemas must be able to be updated, and new schemas must be able to be added without restarting Eclipse.

❍ No restrictions have been mentioned with respect to tools or project types, so initially your resolver should run for all project types.

As your custom URI resolver will retrieve all of your company's schemas from a specific folder, we've dubbed this resolver the Folder URI Resolver. Now, on with your task.

Start by declaring a dependency for your plug-in on

```
org.eclipse.wst.common.uriresolver
```

This plug-in contains the URI resolution framework. URI resolvers also require the

```
org.eclipse.core.resources
```

plug-in, so declare a dependency on this plug-in as well.

The URI resolution framework defines the following extension point:

```
org.eclipse.wst.common.uriresolver.resolverExtensions
```

This extension point allows you to contribute your custom resolver to the framework. Add a new extension of this type to your plug-in. Specify the id as `folderUriResolver` and the name as `Folder URI Resolver`. At the time of writing there is no extension point schema, which specifies to the plug-in manifest editor how to construct an extension, in place for this extension. So, to specify the rest of your extension, you will have to manually edit the `plugin.xml` file.

Change to the **plugin.xml** tab. This tab displays the source XML of your extension declarations. The extension you just added will be listed with no child elements. To contribute your resolver, add a child element named `resolverExtension`. There are two attributes you need to set on this element: `class` and `stage`. The `class` attribute specifies your custom URI resolver class. You will create a class named `FolderUriResolver` in the package

```
org.eclipsewtp.resourceresolution
```

so specify the `class` value here as

```
org.eclipsewtp.resourceresolution.FolderUriResolver
```

The basic action of your resolver will be to locate the schemas in the folder `c:\schemas` and ensure that they exist. According to our previous description, your resolver is a physical one, so specify a value of `physical` for the `stage` attribute (see Example 15.9). Save your plug-in manifest.

Example 15.9   Listing of Folder URI Resolver Extension

```
<extension
   id="folderUriResolver"
   name="Folder URI Resolver"
   point="org.eclipse.wst.common.uriresolver.resolverExtensions">
  <resolverExtension
```

```
          class="org.eclipsewtp.resourceresolution.FolderUriResolver"
          stage="physical"/>
</extension>
```

With your extension declared you now need to implement your resolver. Create a new class with the name `FolderUriResolver` in the package

`org.eclipsewtp.resourceresolution`

This class must implement the interface

`org.eclipse.wst.common.uriresolver.internal.provisional.URIResolverExtension`

The `URIResolverExtension` interface (see Example 15.10) specifies one method to implement: `resolve`. The `resolve` method provides four parameters to your resolver.

❍ `file` represents the in-workspace resource that is attempting to resolve the resource specified by the `publicId` and `systemId` parameters, if one exists.

❍ `baseLocation` represents the location of the resource that is attempting to locate the resource specified by the `publicId` and `systemId` parameters as an absolute URL. This value will exist if there is a base resource, regardless of whether or not that resource is in the workspace.

❍ `publicId` represents an optional public identifier of the resource to be resolved. For a DTD, this is the PUBLIC identifier and for a schema this is the namespace of the schema. There is not typically a value for other types of resources.

❍ `systemId` represents the relative or absolute location of the resource to be resolved if there is any hint to the location. DTDs and schemas may not provide this information, although at least a relative location is typically available.

Example 15.10   Listing of URIResolverExtension.java

```
package org.eclipse.wst.common.uriresolver.internal.provisional;
import org.eclipse.core.resources.IFile;

public interface URIResolverExtension {

  public String resolve(IFile file, String baseLocation,
      String publicId, String systemId);
}
```

The implementation of your resolver is pretty straightforward and does not contain a lot of code. Because you're creating a physical resolver, you will only be concerned with the value passed in by the `systemId`. The `publicId` should already have been handled by any logical resolvers that were applicable for the current scenario. Implement logic for your resolver as follows: Take the filename portion of the systemId, prepend C:\schemas, and see if the file exists. If it does, your resolver will return the properly formatted URI containing the location. If not, your resolver will return null.

An implementation of the Folder URI Resolver can be seen in Example 15.11. The first few lines determine the segment of the systemId that contains the file name based on the last '/' in the string. Once the file name is obtained, C:\schemas is prepended and the new location is checked to see if it exists.

Example 15.11   Listing of FolderUriResolver.java

```
package org.eclipsewtp.resourceresolution;

import java.io.File;
import org.eclipse.core.resources.IFile;
import org.eclipse.wst.common.uriresolver.....URIResolverExtension;

public class FolderUriResolver implements URIResolverExtension {

  private static String folderLoc = "C:/schemas/";

  public String resolve(IFile file, String baselocation,
                        String publicId, String systemId) {
    String result = null;
    if(systemId != null) {
      String filename = systemId.replace("\\", "/");
      int lastSlashLoc = systemId.lastIndexOf('/');
      if(lastSlashLoc != -1) {
        filename = filename.substring(lastSlashLoc+1);
      }
      filename = folderLoc + filename;
      File localFile = new File(filename);
      if(localFile.exists()) {
        result = "file:///" + filename;
      }
    }
    return result;
  }
}
```

You've now completed your Folder URI Resolver. Now it's time to try it out. Launch a runtime workspace, create a new project, and create a file like that shown in Example 15.7 earlier. Try changing an element name. For example, change state to province. No errors are reported as the schema cannot be located. Create the folder C:\schemas and create the file employee.xsd in the folder with the contents shown earlier in Example 15.8. (If you're not running Windows you can create a folder such as /usr/schemas—or something appropriate for your platform—and change the folderLoc in your implementation.)

Try changing the element names again. Notice how the file is flagged with errors because it no longer conforms to the schema and the schema can now be located. Your Folder URI Resolver provided the location of the schema to the XML editor and validator, allowing it to read the schema and flag the errors.

Summary

In this chapter we introduced the XML catalog and the URI resolution framework. You contributed the J2EE schemas and DTDs to the XML catalog using the individual entry and OASIS catalog approaches. You also created a custom Folder URI Resolver to implement a resource resolution strategy that locates resources in a specific folder. The URI resolution framework applied the results of your changes uniformly to the WTP XML tools, removing the need for you to modify each tool individually.

This chapter concludes the discussion of developing plug-ins for WTP. We hope you found these examples informative. You should now have some confidence about your ability to extend WTP and be ready to dive into the code to learn more about the many available extension points. If you come up with a cool extension, please consider contributing it to WTP or writing an article about your experiences to help your fellow members of the WTP development community.

In Part IV, you'll learn about other commercial and Open Source products that are based on WTP and what's on the horizon for the next major release, WTP 2.0.

PART IV

Products and Plans

Our goal in this final part of the book is to discuss life beyond WTP 1.5. We begin with a discussion of the many commercial and Open Source products that are based on WTP and that can be used in conjunction with WTP. If WTP itself does not meet all your development tool needs, then it is very likely that one of the products we describe here will. We conclude this part, and the book as a whole, with our best attempt at predicting what will be included in the next major release, WTP 2.0. Of course, it is very difficult to predict what will be included in a future release of any software project. Watch the WTP Web site for the latest information.

CHAPTER 16

Other Web Tools Based on Eclipse

Whenever you are asked if you can do a job, tell 'em, 'Certainly, I can!' Then get busy and find out how to do it.

—Theodore Roosevelt

Most IDEs, even the great ones, are limited in the tools that can be reasonably included and as such cannot solve every development tooling need of every software developer. One of the great benefits of using Eclipse as your IDE is the extensible nature of the platform. This benefit, while not listed in terms of tools that you can use, provides you with the ability to customize your IDE to suit your needs by plugging in any Eclipse tool.

WTP has currently limited its scope to a subset of Java Web application development tools. However, because WTP is an Eclipse project, you can further customize your Web development IDE to suit your additional Web development needs. This chapter showcases other Eclipse-based Web tools that can help beef up your Web development IDE. Some of the tools that we will cover in this chapter extend WTP, providing additional functionality for the existing tools. Others do not integrate with WTP directly but can be used alongside WTP in Eclipse to create broader Web-based development coverage in your IDE.

To allow you to focus your reading on the tools that you need, we will present the tools in this chapter by the language that they support. In the following sections we will cover Web development tools for Java, Perl, PHP, Python, and Ruby.

Java Web Tools

Given Eclipse's Java heritage it should come as no surprise that there are a number of Java Web application development tools for Eclipse. In this section we'll cover nine different tools you can use to enhance your Java Web application development IDE, many of which extend WTP.

BEA Workshop

Because BEA is a collaborator on WTP, it should be expected that their tools extend WTP, and they do. BEA Workshop is available in several configurations, some free and some commercial. Workshop adds specific support for the WebLogic Platform and SOA as well as server support for Resin and Jetty. It also has tools for JSF, EJB 3.0, Spring, Hibernate, Struts, and Tiles, and it includes WYSIWYG editors and BEA AppXRay for checking and validating your Web application. For more, see

```
http://workshopstudio.bea.com
```

CodeGear JBuilder

CodeGear is Borland's developer tools group. Their Java EE product, JBuilder—which comes in Developer, Professional, and Enterprise versions—extends the WTP toolset, adding visual tools for EJB and JPA projects. This tool focuses on team-based development by supporting the configuration of the IDE for various Open Source project tools, such as those for version control, bug tracking, and builds. JBuilder also supports performance tuning via Borland Optimizeit, URL modeling, and code quality tools. For more, see

```
http://www.codegear.com/jbuilder
```

Exadel Studio

Exadel Studio, built on WTP, provides enhancements and other tools to the WTP platform. This free download adds support to WTP for JSF, Struts, Spring, and Hibernate, and it includes visual editors such as a Struts Web application flow editor.

Exadel Studio is also available in a Pro version that adds additional support on top of that provided by the free Studio. The Pro version will cost you, but it includes support for MyFaces, Oracle ADF, Struts Shale, and Facelets. It also includes a WYSIWYG JSP editor and more wizards to assist in development tasks. For more, see

```
http://www.exadel.com/web/portal/products/ExadelStudio
```

IBM Rational Application Developer for WebSphere Software

Much of WTP's current code base was donated by IBM from Rational Application Developer (RAD) for WebSphere, shown in Figure 16.1. RAD, the follow-on product to WebSphere Studio Application Developer, contains significantly more features than the other projects and products featured in this chapter. RAD allows developers to—in many cases visually—design, develop, analyze, test, profile, and deploy Web, Web services, Java, J2EE, portal, and SOA applications. Although there are too many features to list here, some of the notable ones include XSL, EJB, JSF, Struts, and modeling support using UML. Developers can also use RAD to improve their code quality with tools for automated code quality reviews and build interactive reports with Crystal Reports. RAD is optimized for WebSphere Application Server but supports multiple vendor application runtimes. For more, see

```
http://www.ibm.com/software/awdtools/developer/application
```

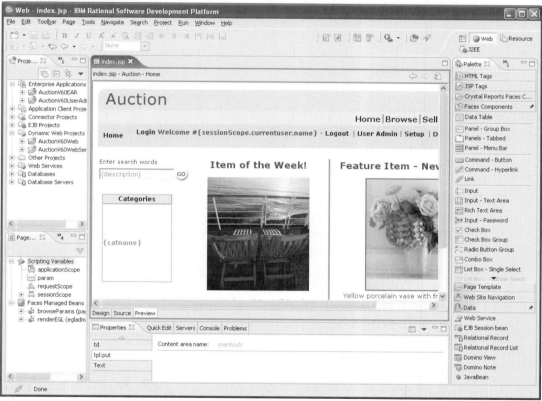

Figure 16.1 RAD's WYSIWYG JSP Editor

JBoss IDE for Eclipse

JBoss, best known for the Open Source JBoss Application Server, also provides the Open Source JBoss IDE for Eclipse. The JBoss IDE extends WTP by adding tools that support developing for the JBoss Enterprise Middleware System (JEMS), which includes the JBoss Application Server. The added tools include tools for EJB 3.0, Hibernate, and control of the JBoss Application Server. For more, see

```
http://labs.jboss.com/portal/jbosside
```

MyEclipse

MyEclipse, a commercial Web development IDE, is only one of three IDEs discussed in this chapter that also features modeling capabilities such as UML diagram editors and UML to Java code generation. MyEclipse extends WTP and adds support for a variety of Web technologies including JSF, EJB, Hibernate, and Struts. It also includes a WYSIWYG HTML/JSP editor, Hibernate configuration tools, visual Struts and JSF designers, and support for additional server types including Geronimo, GlassFish, Jetty, JRun, Orion, and Resin. For more, see

```
http://www.myeclipseide.com
```

ObjectWeb Lomboz

The code base from the Open Source Lomboz was one of the original two used to seed WTP. It should therefore be no surprise that recent versions of Lomboz build on the WTP platform. Lomboz adds features for Enterprise Portals and Service-Oriented Architectures (SOA), and supports development of Apache Struts applications and SCA-based SOA modules that run on Apache Tuscany. It also includes tools that simplify development for the JOnAS and JBoss Application servers. In fact, simplifying development is a Lomboz theme that is evident in the project workspace coming preconfigured with a runtime environment and with the additional tutorials and cheat sheets for Web, EJB, and Web service development. For more, see

```
http://lomboz.objectweb.org
```

SAP NetWeaver Developer Studio

SAP NetWeaver Developer Studio is a commercial IDE that supports the development of J2EE applications. NetWeaver includes support for Web services, J2EE, enhanced Java debugging, and model-driven design of user interfaces. It also includes persistence and development infrastructure perspectives. The persistence perspective allows you to manipulate data objects such as tables and indexes. The development infrastructure perspective allows you to manage the development of your project, including its source code, build, and deployment. For more, see

```
http://www.sap.com/platform/netweaver/components/developerstudio
```

W4T Eclipse

W4T Eclipse differs from the other tools presented in this section. W4T Eclipse provides a visual development environment for Java Web applications. This commercial product from Innoopract does not focus on the Java Web technologies in use, but instead aims to simplify Java Web development. To that end, it provides developers the ability to implement the Web UI by dragging and dropping Web UI components onto a canvas, configure the properties of their application in views, and see a real-time view of their newly constructed user interface (see Figure 16.2). This visual creation of Web applications is accomplished by building on top of Innoopract's W4 Toolkit, which is also part of the Eclipse Rich Ajax Platform Project. Although the IDE's development focus is not on specific technologies, W4T Eclipse and the W4 Toolkit are built on Java standards such as Java beans and servlets. W4T Eclipse also includes support for Hibernate and EJB based applications. For more, see

```
http://www.innoopract.com/w4teclipse
```

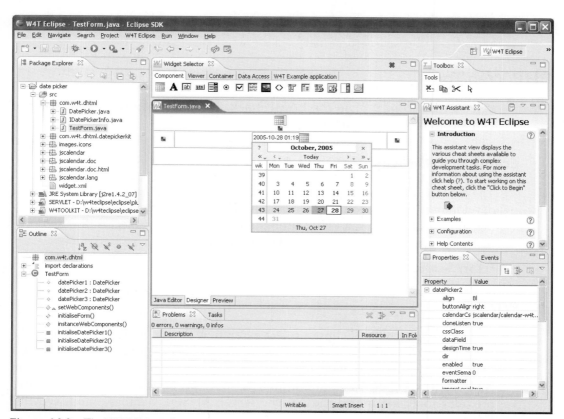

Figure 16.2 The W4T Eclipse Perspective

Perl Web Tools

Perl is the original "P" in the LAMP acronym, which represents a common Open Source stack for Web applications (LAMP = Linux Apache MySQL Perl/PHP/Python). In this section we will cover a project that provides support for Perl to Eclipse.

EPIC

The EPIC Open Source project provides Perl support for Eclipse. The main contributions of this project are a Perl editor that includes many nice features that you've likely come to expect from Eclipse tools, such as syntax highlighting, validation and content assistance, and a full-featured debugger. The project also includes an integrated Web browser for testing your Web application's Perl scripts within Eclipse. For more, see

```
http://e-p-i-c.sourceforge.net
```

PHP Web Tools

PHP is the second "P" in the LAMP stack. In this section we'll highlight two PHP projects that you can use in Eclipse.

Eclipse PHP Development Tools Project

The Eclipse PHP Development Tools project is a fully featured PHP IDE for developing PHP-based Web applications. This project extends WTP by providing, among other tools, a PHP editor and debugger. This project is discussed further in Chapter 17, which follows. For more, see

```
http://www.eclipse.org/pdt
```

PHPEclipse

The Open Source PHPEclipse project extends WTP and adds PHP tools to the Eclipse IDE. Specifically, PHPEclipse adds a PHP perspective, which includes a PHP editor with code completion and outline view, PHP, Smarty, HTML and XML syntax highlighting, and a Web browser preview view. The perspective provides tools to control the Apache server, MySQL database, and XAMPP. For more, see

```
http://www.phpeclipse.net
```

Python Web Tools

The third "P" in the LAMP stack is Python. While the one Python project we will cover in this section is not itself a Web development project, we think it warrants inclusion in this chapter because Python is a popular Web development language, and you can create a pretty useful Python Web development IDE by coupling a Python IDE with WTP.

PyDev

Although not specifically a Web development project, PyDev is an Open Source project that contains advanced Python and Jython tools for the Eclipse IDE. The list of advanced tools is limited in scope to those tools that support the languages themselves. These tools include an editor with syntax highlighting, content assistance, validation, and refactoring (and more), as well as a fully featured debugger. For more, see

```
http://pydev.sourceforge.net
```

Ruby Web Tools

Over the past few years Ruby has been gaining popularity as a language due in large part to the Ruby on Rails Web application framework. In this section we'll introduce you to an Eclipse-based Ruby on Rails IDE.

RadRails

RadRails is an open source Ruby on Rails IDE built on Eclipse. This IDE, which can run stand-alone as a rich client application or as part of an existing Eclipse install, adds the following list of tools to Eclipse: a Ruby editor with syntax highlighting, content assistance, and validation; CSS and JavaScript editors; server control for the WEBrick, Mongrel, and LightTPD servers; and a data perspective that includes an SQL query builder. For more, see

```
http://www.radrails.org
```

Summary

In this chapter we covered some of the Eclipse-based Web tools you can use alongside WTP to create a Web IDE customized for your specific requirements. Some of the tools are commercial; others are Open Source or freely available. You should now have a good sense of the Eclipse Web development tool landscape and how you can start customizing your IDE.

CHAPTER 17

The Road Ahead

If you don't know where you're going, you'll probably end up somewhere else.

—Yogi Berra

Now that you've had a close look at WTP 1.5, you're probably wondering what's coming in the next release. The answer to that question depends on many factors, such as where the industry is heading, what the user community is asking for, and the level of resources that WTP contributors are prepared to make available to do the work. As Yogi says, "It's tough to make predictions, especially about the future." It's even tougher to make predictions about the future of software. Nevertheless, we'll review the currently published plans and make some inferences about what you're likely to see in WTP 2.0. Of course, the WTP Web site is the ultimate authority on what is committed for the 2.0 release.

The WTP PMC decided to name the next major release 2.0. Why not simply up the number to 1.6 to indicate that it is fully compatible with WTP 1.5? WTP 2.0 will certainly preserve all the APIs published in the 1.0 and 1.5 releases; however, it will also include some major new function. A larger release number increment was therefore appropriate.

The choice of 2.0 also resonates with the so-called Web 2.0 platform, which includes the next wave of Web technologies such as AJAX and the new Web service standards. These include SOAP 1.2, WSDL 2.0, and Apache Axis2. The project goal is to make WTP 2.0 the preferred tool set for developing Web 2.0 applications.

The following list is based on the best information available at the time of writing about what will appear in WTP 2.0. For the most current information, consult the *Web Tools Platform 2.0 Plan* Wiki at

```
http://wiki.eclipse.org/index.php/Web_Tools_Platform_2.0_Plan
```

Each of these items will be discussed in more detail below:

○ Migration to the Eclipse Data Tools Platform Project

○ Maturation of the Eclipse JavaServer Faces Tools Incubator Project

○ Maturation of the Eclipse Dali JPA Tools Incubator Project

○ Maturation of the Eclipse AJAX Tools Framework Incubator Project

○ Support for Java Enterprise Edition 5

○ Support for Apache Axis2 and W3C WSDL 2.0

○ Integration with the Eclipse PHP Tools Project

○ Integration with the Eclipse SOA Tools Platform Project

Eclipse Data Tools Platform (DTP) Project

The initial charter of WTP included Data tools. Although SQL is not a Web technology, WTP included it because database access is an essential part of most Web applications and no other Eclipse project provided the needed capability. However, shortly before the release of WTP 0.7, Sybase proposed the creation of the DTP project to focus on this important aspect of application development. IBM and several other vendors supported the proposal, and the WTP PMC agreed to move its Data tools into the DTP project. The original plan was for WTP 1.5 to use DTP 1.0, but due to differences between the WTP Data tools and DTP, this move was deferred to WTP 2.0. As previously stated, it's tough to make predictions about software.

DTP contains many improvements over the WTP Data tools, including a much more capable SQL editor. However, the underlying relational database models in DTP are the same as those in WTP, so the migration should be straightforward. WTP 2.0 will not reship its Data tools. Adopters will be required to migrate.

Eclipse JavaServer Faces (JSF) Tools Project

The JSF Tools project was proposed by Oracle and began life as an incubator in WTP. It released a Technology Preview with WTP 1.5. The JSF project includes a source editor for JSP-JSF files, a JSF component registry, and a graphical editor for page flow (`faces-config.xml`). Future plans include a visual editor for JSP-JSF pages.

JSF is part of Java EE 5 and is the standards-based successor to the popular Apache Struts framework. WTP 2.0 will include the 1.0 release of the JSF tools as part of its comprehensive support for Java EE 5.

Eclipse Dali Java Persistence Architecture (JPA) Tools Project

The Dali project began life as an incubator in the Technology project and graduated into the WTP project as part of the WTP 1.5 release, which contains a Technology Preview of it. The Dali project contains the new object-relational mapping tools that are specified in JSR 220 EJB 3.0 Persistence. The official name for this technology is Java Persistence Architecture (JPA). Although part of the EJB 3.0 specification, JPA can be used outside an EJB container.

The Dali project is in fact a merger of two Technology projects that were proposed by Oracle and Versant to build development tools for JSR 220 object-relational mapping. The name "Dali" was chosen in honor of Salvador Dali, the Spanish surrealist, who painted the masterpiece *The Persistence of Memory*, which is currently hanging in the Louvre.

WTP 2.0 will contain the 1.0 release of Dali as part of its comprehensive support for Java EE 5.

Eclipse AJAX Tools Framework (ATF) Project

The ATF project was proposed by IBM and is currently an incubator of WTP. It will graduate in WTP 2.0. The ATF project will provide a framework for adding AJAX libraries to Web projects. It will also significantly improve the current WTP JavaScript source editor, and it will add a sorely needed JavaScript debugger.

Java Enterprise Edition 5

Perhaps the biggest new feature in WTP 2.0 is support for Java EE 5, which includes JSF, JPA, and revisions of many existing specifications, including JAX-WS for Web services. JAX-WS will include support for SOAP 1.2. All of the WTP J2EE models will be upgraded to the new specification levels.

The most exciting aspect of Java EE 5 for programmers is its simplification of the programming model and its use of attribute-based programming. Code attributes were introduced into the Java programming language by JSR 175. Attributes for Web services were defined in JSR 181. Both JSR 175 and 181 are part of Java EE 5. In addition, code attributes for EJBs and JPA are defined in JSR 220, which is also part of Java EE 5.

Of course, a new specification is rather dull until there are implementations of it. Sun is leading the development of a Java EE 5 reference implementation at the Open Source java.net GlassFish project. WTP 1.5 users can already use GlassFish by virtue of the server adapter available at the GlassFish Plug-ins project. Other Open Source Java EE 5 server implementations such as Apache Geronimo and JBoss are likely to be available for use with WTP 2.0.

Apache Axis2 and W3C WSDL 2.0

Web service standards are also undergoing significant change. During the last few years, many new specifications have been developed. The original SOAP 1.1 and WSDL 1.1 specifications, which were member submissions and published as W3C Notes, entered the W3C Recommendation Track. SOAP 1.2 is now a W3C Recommendation, and WSDL 2.0 is a W3C Candidate Recommendation. In addition to these core specifications, there are many Web service specifications that cover advanced protocol features. These include Web Service Security, Web Service Reliable Messaging, Web Service Addressing, Web Service Policy, and many more. In fact, the large number of new Web service specifications has given rise to the term WS-*. There seems to be a new Web service specification for every conceivable aspect of distributed computing. Many of the specifications will never be implemented, but many of them are being implemented and will be available for use in production soon.

Microsoft is one of the main proponents of the WS-* stack and has delivered implementations of them in the *Windows Communication Framework* (WCF), which is part of the Vista release of the Windows operating system. Beta versions of WCF have been available for some time. In the Java Open Source world, Apache Axis2 is leading the way. Axis2 Version 1.1.1 was released on January 9, 2007. Major J2EE vendors are likely to adopt Axis2 as their core Web services engine. WTP plans to upgrade its current Axis support to include Axis2.

In the area of WSDL 2.0 support, the Apache Woden project is developing a reference implementation of a validating parser. This code is being integrated into Axis2, which will include WSDL2Java and Java2WSDL code generators. WTP plans to integrate Woden into its WSDL tools, including the WSDL editor, validator, explorer, and wizard.

Support for the combination of SOAP 1.2 and WSDL 2.0 will help bridge the current gap between the WS-* stack and REST style Web services. With its support for HTTP GET requests, SOAP 1.2 will make it possible to implement REST style Web services that play well with the WS-* stack. Similarly, with its improved HTTP binding, SOAP 1.2 support, and ability to describe safe operations and messages that contain references to Web services, WSDL 2.0 now is a suitable description language for REST style Web services.

Eclipse PHP Development Tools Project

PHP is one of the most widely used scripting languages for dynamically generating Web pages. Although PHP is technically similar in many respects to JSP and ASP.NET, its huge popularity derives in part from its tight association with the Apache Web server. PHP is an Open Source technology and there is a PHP module available for the Apache Web server. Most sites that use the Apache Web server, which according to the Netcraft surveys hold in excess of a 60 percent market share, also include the PHP module. This means that the path of least resistance for including dynamic content in your Web site is to use PHP. This translates to a large PHP development community.

Zend, the creator of PHP, and IBM recently created the Eclipse PHP Development Tools project. PHP is outside the scope of the WTP Web Standard Tools (WST) project because PHP is not governed by a standards body. It is a de facto standard. However, it is a stated goal of WST to be extendable to support other technologies, including PHP, and that is precisely what the PHP project has done. Zend and IBM in fact demonstrated the PHP tools running on top of WST at EclipseCon 2006. The two main integration points with WST are a server adapter for the Apache Web server, which uses the Server Tools API, and a PHP source editor, which uses the Structured Source Editor (SSE) API. The Apache Web server adapter is, of course, not specific to PHP developers and is likely to be contributed to WST.

Eclipse SOA Tools Platform (STP) Project

At the end of 2005, IONA led the creation of the Eclipse STP project. Web services are a key enabling technology behind Service Oriented Architecture (SOA), but the concept of service is much broader and includes many enterprise technologies, especially message-oriented middleware and the so-called *Enterprise Service Bus* (ESB). The Apache Tuscany project is developing an Open Source reference implementation for emerging SOA specifications including Service Component Architecture (SOA).

The STP project will require additional support for key specifications such as WS Security and WS Policy. Although plans are not firm yet, we expect there to be fruitful interaction and cross-over between WTP and STP. At a minimum, the STP project will adopt relevant Web service components and APIs from WTP, and provide WTP with new requirements. In the best case, STP developers will actively contribute to WTP and add support for the relevant Web service standards.

Conclusion

As you can see, WTP is an extremely active project. There are many exciting developments going on in the industry. The Web is still a source of great technical innovation, and WTP is the focal point for Web development tools at Eclipse.

WTP 1.5 currently provides a core set of tools that are forming the basis for commercial products and other Open Source projects, both at Eclipse and elsewhere. In addition to technical advances, we can also expect to see new business models emerge around the Open Source tools space. The free availability of cool tools is wonderful for developers, but in order for this bonanza to continue, the companies who are currently funding it must come up with sustainable business models.

You, as a user of Open Source tools, can play an important part in keeping this grand experiment going. Although WTP may not cost you any money, it's not really free. As a user, you have a moral obligation to contribute to the community. Be a good Open Source citizen. Help your fellow users, report those bugs, submit those patches, and contribute that next cool feature. Happy coding, and stayed tuned for WTP 2.0!

Glossary

API

See Application Programming Interface.

Application Programming Interface

A contract that specifies programming services provided by a platform to application clients. An API consists of the syntactic definition of the programmatic interfaces and file formats provided to the application client, the semantics of their behavior, and possibly additional restrictions and limitations on their use. The goal of an API is to isolate application clients from changes to the implementation of the platform.

Black Box Testing

The type of testing in which the tester has access to and tests the application using the public parts of the application, including the API and user interface, and has no knowledge of the internal workings of the application.

DAO

See Data Access Object.

Data Access Object

An object used to access a datastore. A DAO hides the persistence mechanism used to store the object.

Eclipse Management Organization

The body that governs the Eclipse Foundation.

EJB

See Enterprise Java Bean.

EMO

See Eclipse Management Organization.

Enterprise Java Bean

The component model defined by J2EE for business objects. An EJB is a managed component that is hosted in an EJB container. The container provides a variety of services including transactions, access control, and life cycle management. EJBs are further divided into Session Beans, Entity Beans, and Message-Driven Beans (MDB).

J2EE

See Java 2 Enterprise Edition.

J2EE Standard Tools

The subproject of WTP whose scope is tools that implement J2EE standards defined by the JCP.

Java 2 Enterprise Edition

A set of JCP APIs and formats that define standards for Java-based enterprise applications. There are several versions of J2EE, which are referred to as J2EE 1.2, J2EE 1.3, J2EE 1.4, and Java EE 5.0. Note that starting with version 5.0, the standard is referred to as Java Enterprise Edition.

Java Community Process

The organization that defines the standards for the Java platform. A Java standard is referred to as a JSR. *See also* Java Specification Request.

Java EE

See Java 2 Enterprise Edition.

Java Specification Request

A formal standard issued by the JCP that defines part of the Java platform. A JSR typically defines a Java API. It may also define a file format, often using XML. *See also* Java Community Process.

JSR

See Java Specification Request.

JST

See J2EE Standard Tools.

LAMP

See Linux, Apache, MySQL, PHP/Perl/Python.

Linux, Apache, MySQL, PHP/Perl/Python

The pure Open Source Web application development platform based on the Linux operating system, the Apache Web server, the MySQL database, and the PHP, Perl, and Python programming languages.

Maven

An Apache project for build automation. For more information, *see*

http://maven.apache.org

Plain Old Java Object

An ordinary Java class that is not based on an advanced component model such as EJB.

Plain Old XML

Used to describe a Web service message that omits a SOAP envelope.

PMC

See Project Management Committee.

POJO

See Plain Old Java Object.

POM

See Project Object Model.

POX

See Plain Old XML.

Project Management Committee

The body that governs each top-level project in the Eclipse Foundation. The PMC typically has a leader and includes the leads of the subprojects and the leads of various committees such as Architecture, Planning, and Requirements.

Project Object Model

A model used by Maven that describes the structure of a project.

Representational State Transfer

The architectural style of the Web. This term was coined by Roy Fielding, who described it in his Ph.D. dissertation. *See* [Fielding2002].

REST

See Representational State Transfer.

SOAP

An XML vocabulary for Web service message envelopes and rules for processing them by network intermediaries. It is formally defined by W3C. *See*

```
http://www.w3.org/2000/xp/Group/
```

UDDI

See Universal Description, Discovery, and Integration.

Uniform Resource Locator

A character string that specifies the location of a resource, such as a Web page, on the Internet. It is formally defined by IETF RFC 1738. *See*

```
http://www.ietf.org/rfc/rfc1738.txt
```

Universal Description, Discovery, and Integration

A registry specification for publishing and discovering Web services. It is formally defined by OASIS. *See*

```
http://uddi.org
```

URL

See Uniform Resource Locator.

Web Service Description Language

An XML vocabulary for describing Web services. It is formally defined by W3C. *See*

```
http://www.w3.org/2002/ws/desc/
```

Web Standard Tools

The subproject of WTP whose scope is tools that implement open Web standards defined by organizations such as W3C, IEFT, OASIS, WS-I, and ECMA.

WSDL

See Web Service Description Language.

WST

See Web Standard Tools.

References

Articles

[Anderson2006] "Apache Derby Fortune Server Tutorial." Jean Anderson. April 21, 2006. Apache Software Foundation.
`http://db.apache.org/derby/papers/fortune_tut.html`

[Bader2004] "Integrating Cloudscape and Tomcat." Lance Bader. August 3, 2004. IBM developerWorks.
`http://www-128.ibm.com/developerworks/db2/library/techarticle/dm-0408bader/`

[Beck2002] "JUnit Test Infected. Programmers Love Writing Tests." Kent Beck, Erich Gamma, and David Saff. April 7, 2002. JUnit Documentation.
`http://junit.sourceforge.net/doc/testinfected/testing.htm`

[BernersLee1998] "Cool URIs don't change." Tim Berners-Lee. 1998. W3C.
`http://www.w3.org/Provider/Style/URI`

[Butek2005] "Which style of WSDL should I use?" Russell Butek. May 24, 2005. IBM developerWorks.
`http://www-128.ibm.com/developerworks/webservices/library/ws-whichwsdl/`

[Costello2002] "Building Web Services the REST Way." Roger L. Costello. July 3, 2002. XFront.
`http://www.xfront.com/REST-Web-Services.html`

[Dubrova2005] "Structural Testing Based on Minimum Kernels." Elena Dubrova. Proceedings of the Design, Automation and Test in Europe Conference and Exhibition (DATE'05) March 7–11, 2005. IEEE Software. 2005. 1168–1173.

[Garrett2005] "Ajax: A New Approach to Web Applications." Jesse James Garrett. February 18, 2005. Adaptive Path.
`http://www.adaptivepath.com/publications/essays/archives/000385.php`

[Hutchinson2005] "Developing the WTP with Eclipse." Mark Hutchinson. February 21, 2005. Eclipse Web Tools Platform Project.
`http://www.eclipse.org/webtools/community/tutorials/DevelopingWTP/`
`DevelopingWTp.html`

[Knight2002] "Objects and the Web." Alan Knight and Naci Dai. IEEE Software. April 2002. 51–59.

[Kusakov2006] "Develop HTML widgets with Dojo." Igor Kusakov. October 31, 2006. IBM developerWorks.
`http://www-128.ibm.com/developerworks/edu/wa-dw-wa-dojowidgets.html`

[Murray2005] "Asynchronous JavaScript Technology and XML (AJAX) With Java 2 Platform, Enterprise Edition." Greg Murray. June 9, 2005. Sun Microsystems.
`http://java.sun.com/developer/technicalArticles/J2EE/AJAX/`

[OReilly2003] "REST vs. SOAP at Amazon." Tim O'Reilly. April 3, 2003. O'Reilly xml.com.
`http://www.oreillynet.com/pub/wlg/3005`

[Stark1996] "Measurements for Managing Software Maintenance." George E. Stark. IEEE Software. 1996. 152–161.

Books

[Abran2004] *Guide to the Software Engineering Body of Knowledge (SWEBOK®)*. Alain Abran, James W. Moore, Pierre Bourque, and Robert Dupuis. IEEE Computer Society, 2004. ISBN: 0-7695-2330-7.

[Alur2003] *Core J2EE Patterns: Best Practices and Design Strategies*. Deepak Alur, Dan Malks, and John Crupi. Prentice Hall, 2003. ISBN: 0-13-142246-4.

[Booch1994] *Object-Oriented Analysis and Design with Applications, Second Edition*. Grady Booch. Benjamin/Cummings, 1994. ISBN: 0-8053-5340-2.

[Brown2001] *Enterprise Java™ Programming with IBM® WebSphere®*. Kyle Brown, Dr. Gary Craig, Greg Hester, Jaime Niswonger, David Pitt, and Russell Stinehour. Addison-Wesley, 2001. ISBN: 0-201-61617-3.

[Brunner2002] *Java™ Web Services Unleashed*. Robert J. Brunner, Frank Cohen, Francisco Curbera, Darren Govoni, Steven Haines, Matthias Kloppmann, Benoît Marchal, K. Scott Morrison, Arthur Ryman, Joseph Weber, and Mark Wutka. Sams, 2002. ISBN: 0-672-32363-X.

[Budinsky2004] *Eclipse Modeling Framework: A Developer's Guide.* Frank Budinsky, David Steinberg, Ed Merks, Raymond Ellersick, and Timothy J. Gross. Addison-Wesley. 2004. ISBN: 0-13-142542-0.

[Burd2001] *JSP™: JavaServer Pages™.* Barry Burd. M&T Books, 2001, ISBN: 0-7645-3535-8.

[Cagle2001] *Professional XSL.* Kurt Cagle, Michael Corning, Jason Diamond, Teun Duynstee, Oli Gauti Gudmundsson, Michael Mason, Jon Pinnock, Paul Spencer, Jeff Tang, and Andrew Watt. Wrox Press, 2001. ISBN: 1-861003-57-9.

[Callaway1999] *Inside Servlets: Server-Side Programming for the Java Platform.* Dustin R. Callaway. Addison-Wesley, 1999. ISBN: 0-201-37963-5.

[Clayberg2006] *Eclipse: Building Commercial-Quality Plug-Ins, Second Edition.* Eric Clayberg and Dan Rubel. Addison-Wesley, 2006. ISBN: 0-321-42672-X.

[Cooper2004] *The Inmates are Running the Asylum. Why High-Tech Products Drive Us Crazy and How to Restore the Sanity.* Alan Cooper. Sams, 2004. ISBN: 0-672-32614-0.

[Cox1986] *Object-Oriented Programming: An Evolutionary Approach.* Brad J. Cox. Addison-Wesley, 1986. ISBN: 0-201-10393-1.

[DeMarco1982] *Controlling Software Projects: Management, Measurement, & Estimation.* Tom DeMarco. Yourdon Press, 1982. ISBN: 0-917072-32-4.

[Fielding2000] *Architectural Styles and the Design of Network-based Software Architectures.* Roy Thomas Fielding. University of California, Irvine, 2000. http://www.ics.uci.edu/~fielding/pubs/dissertation/top.htm

[Flanders1996] *Web Pages That Suck. Learn Good Design by Looking at Bad Design.* Vincent Flanders and Michael Willis. Sybex, 1996. ISBN: 0-7821-2187-X.

[Flannagan2002] *JavaScript: The Definitive Guide, Fourth Edition.* David Flannagan. O'Reilly, 2002. ISBN: 0-596-00048-0.

[Fogel2001] *Open Source Development with CVS.* Karl Fogel and Moshe Bar. Coriolis, 2001. ISBN: 1-58880-173-X.

[Fowler2003] *Patterns of Enterprise Application Architecture.* Martin Fowler. Addison-Wesley, 2003. ISBN: 0-321-12742-0.

[Francis2003] *Professional IBM WebSphere 5.0 Application Server: A Guide to Building J2EE Applications from IBM WebSphere Architects.* Tim Francis, Eric Herness, Rob High, Jr., Jim Knutson, Kim Rochat, and Chris Vignola. Wrox Press, 2003. ISBN: 1-86100-581-4.

[Franciscus2005] *Struts Recipes. Strategies for Building Business Applications.* George Franciscus and Danilo Gurovich. Manning, 2005. ISBN: 1932394249.

[Fung2005] *An Introduction to IBM Rational Application Developers. A Guided Tour.* J. Fung, C. Yu, C. Lau, E. McKay, G. Flood, J. Hunter, T. deBoer, V. Birsan, Y. Lu, P. Walker, J. Winchester, and Dr. G. Mendel. IBM Press, 2005. ISBN: 1-931182-22-1.

[Gamma1995] *Design Patterns: Elements of Reusable Object-Oriented Software.* Erich Gamma, Richard Helm, Ralph Johnson, and John Vlissides. Addison-Wesley, 1995. ISBN: 0-201-63361-2.

[Gamma2003] *Contributing to Eclipse: Principles, Patterns, and Plug-Ins.* Erich Gamma and Kent Beck. Addison-Wesley, 2003. ISBN: 0-321-20575-8.

[Goldfarb1990] *The SGML Handbook.* Charles F. Goldfarb. Clarendon Press, 1990. ISBN: 0-19-853737-9.

[Gosling1996a] *The Java™ Application Programming Interface, Volume 1: Core Packages.* James Gosling, Frank Yellin, and The Java™ Team. Addison-Wesley, 1996. ISBN: 0-201-63453-8.

[Gosling1996b] *The Java™ Application Programming Interface, Volume 2: Window Toolkit and Applets.* James Gosling, Frank Yellin, and The Java™ Team. Addison-Wesley, 1996. ISBN: 0-201-63459-7.

[Graham1995] *The HTML Sourcebook. A Complete Guide to HTML.* Ian S. Graham. John Wiley & Sons, 1995. ISBN: 0-471-11849-4.

[Groff1990] *Using SQL.* James R. Groff and Paul N. Weinberg. Osborne McGraw-Hill, 1990. ISBN: 0-07-881524-X.

[Hightower2002] *Java Tools for Extreme Programming. Mastering Open Source Tools including Ant, JUnit, and Cactus.* Richard Hightower and Nicholas Lesiecki. John Wiley & Sons, Inc., 2002. ISBN: 0-471-20708-X.

[Holzner2005] *Ant: The Definitive Guide, Second Edition.* Steve Holzner. O'Reilly, 2005. ISBN: 0-596-00609-8.

[Johnson2004] *Expert One-on-One J2EE Development without EJB.* Rod Johnson and Juergen Hoeller. Wrox, 2004. ISBN: 0764558315.

[Judd2005] *Pro Eclipse JST. Plug-ins for J2EE Development.* Christopher M. Judd and Kakeem Shittu. Apress, 2005. ISBN: 1-59059-493-2.

[Kay2001] *XSLT Programmer's Reference, Second Edition.* Michael Kay. Wrox Press, 2001. ISBN: 1-861005-06-7.

[Laurie1999] *Apache: The Definitive Guide, Second Edition: Vital Information for Apache Programmers & Administrators*. Ben Laurie and Peter Laurie. O'Reilly, February 1999. ISBN: 1-56592-528-9.

[Lerdorf2002] *Programming PHP: Creating Dynamic Web Pages*. Rasmus Lerdorf and Kevin Tatroe. O'Reilly, 2002. ISBN: 1-56592-610-2.

[Marinescu2003] *EJB Design Patterns: Advanced Patterns, Processes, and Idioms*. Floyd Marinescu. John Wiley & Sons, Inc, 2002. ISBN: 0-471-20831-0.

[Massol2004] *JUnit in Action*. Vincent Massol and Ted Husted. Manning, 2004. ISBN: 1-930110-99-5.

[Massol2005] *Maven: A Developer's Notebook*. Vincent Massol and Timothy O'Brien. O'Reilly, 2005. ISBN: 0-596-00750-7.

[McAffer2005] *Eclipse Rich Client Platform: Designing, Coding, and Packaging Java Applications*. Jeff McAffer and Jean-Michel Lemieux. Addison-Wesley, 2005. ISBN: 0-321-33461-2.

[Melton1993] *Understanding the New SQL: A Complete Guide*. Jim Melton and Alan R. Simon. Morgan Kaufmann, 1993. ISBN: 1-55860-245-3.

[Monson-Haefel1999] *Enterprise JavaBeans™*. Richard Monson-Haefel. O'Reilly, 1999. ISBN: 1-56592-605-6.

[Nic2000] *XSLT Reference*. Miloslav Nic. 2000. ZVON.org.
`http://www.zvon.org/xxl/XSLTreference/Output/`

[Niederst1999] *Web Design in a Nutshell: A Desktop Quick Reference*. Jennifer Niederst. O'Reilly, 1999. ISBN: 1-56592-515-7.

[Pawson2002] *Naked Objects*. Richard Pawson and Robert Matthews. John Wiley and Sons Ltd., 2002. ISBN: 0-470-84420-5.

[Raymond2001] *The Cathedral and the Bazaar: Musings on Linux and Open Source by an Accidental Revolutionary*. Eric S. Raymond. O'Reilly, 2001. ISBN: 0-596-00131-2.

[Roman2005] *Mastering Enterprise JavaBeans, Third Edition*. Ed Roman, Rima Patel Sriganesh, and Gerald Brose. Wiley Publishing, Inc., 2005. ISBN: 0-7645-7682-8.

[Rumbaugh1991] *Object-Oriented Modelling and Design*. James Rumbaugh, Michael Blaha, William Premerlani, Frederick Eddy, and William Lorensen. Prentice Hall, 1991. ISBN: 0-13-629841-9.

[Sessions1997] *COM and DCOM: Microsoft's Vision for Distributed Objects*. Roger Sessions. John Wiley & Sons, Inc., 1997. ISBN: 0-471-19381-X.

[Shavor2003] *The Java™ Developer's Guide to Eclipse.* Sherry Shavor, Jim D'Anjou, Scott Fairbrother, Dan Kehn, John Kellerman, and Pat McCarthy. Addison-Wesley, 2003. ISBN: 0-321-15964-0.

[Singh2002] *Designing Enterprise Applications with the J2EE™ Platform, Second Edition.* Inderjeet Singh, Beth Stearns, Mark Johnson, and the Enterprise Team. Sun Microsystems, 2002.
`http://java.sun.com/blueprints/guidelines/designing_enterprise_applications_2e/`

[Sklar2002] *PHP Cookbook: Solution & Examples for PHP Programmers.* David Sklar and Adam Trachtenberg. O'Reilly. 2002. ISBN: 1-56592-681-1.

[Skonnard2002] *Essential XML Quick Reference: A Programmer's Reference to XML, XPath, XSLT, XML Schema, SOAP, and More.* Aaron Skonnard and Martin Gudgin. Addison-Wesley, 2002. ISBN: 0-201-74095-8.

[Spainhour1996] *Webmaster in a Nutshell: A Desktop Quick Reference.* Stephen Spainhour and Valerie Querica. O'Reilly, October 1996. ISBN: 1-56592-229-8.

[StLaurent1998a] *Cookies.* Simon St. Laurent. McGraw-Hill, 1998. ISBN: 0-07-05498-9.

[StLaurent1998b] *XML: A Primer.* Simon St. Laurent. MIS:Press, 1998. ISBN: 1-55828-592-X.

[Thomas2004] *Pragmatic Version Control with CVS: The Pragmatic Starter Kit—Volume I.* David Thomas and Andrew Hunt. The Pragmatic Bookshelf, 2004. ISBN: 0-9745140-0-4.

[Tidwell2001] *XSLT: Mastering XML Transformations.* Doug Tidwell. O'Reilly, 2001. ISBN: 0-596-00053-7.

[Tidwell2005] *Designing Interfaces.* Jennifer Tidwell. O'Reilly, 2005. ISBN: 0-596-00803-1.

[Whitehead2001] *JavaServer Pages™: Your Visual Blueprint for Designing Dynamic Content with JSP™.* Paul Whitehead. Hungry Minds, 2001. ISBN: 0-7645-3542-0.

[Williams1994] *The Non-Designer's Design Book: Design and Typographic Principles for the Visual Novice.* Robin Williams. Peachpit Press, 1994. ISBN: 1-56609-159-4.

[Williams1998] *The Non-Designer's Web Book: An Easy Guide to Creating, Designing, and Posting Your Own Web Site.* Robin Williams and John Tollert. Peachpit Press, 1998. ISBN: 0-201-68859-X.

[Williamson2005] *IBM® WebSphere® System Administration.* Leigh Williamson, Lavena Chan, Roger Cundiff, Shawn Lauzon, and Christopher C. Mitchell. Prentice Hall, 2005. ISBN: 0-13-144604-5.

[Yourdon1979] *Classics in Software Engineering*. Edward Nash Yourdon. Yourdon Press, 1979. ISBN: 0-917072-14-6.

[Zikopoulos2005] *Apache Derby—Off to the Races: Includes Details of IBM Cloudscape*. Paul C. Zikopoulos, George Baklarz, and Dan Scott. IBM Press, 2005. ISBN: 0-13-185525-5.

[Zimmermann2003] *Perspectives on Web Services: Applying SOAP, WSDL, and UDDI to Real-World Projects*. Olaf Zimmermann, Mark Tomlinson, and Stefan Peuser. Springer, 2003. ISBN: 3-540-00914-0.

Standards

[CSS2] *Cascading Style Sheets, level 2, CSS2 Specification*. Bert Bos, Håkon Wium Lie, Chris Lilley, and Ian Jacobs. May 12, 1998. W3C.
http://www.w3.org/TR/REC-CSS2/

[HTML401] *HTML 4.01 Specification*. Dave Raggett, Arnaud Le Hors, and Ian Jacobs. December 24, 1999. W3C.
http://www.w3.org/TR/html401/

[JSR31] JSR 31: *XML Data Binding Specification: The Java™ Architecture for XML Binding (JAXB)*. Joe Fialli and Sekhar Vajjhala. March 4, 2003. JCP.
http://www.jcp.org/en/jsr/detail?id=31

[JSR45] JSR 45: *Debugging Support for Other Languages*. Robert Field. November 24, 2003. JCP.
http://www.jcp.org/en/jsr/detail?id=45

[JSR63] JSR 63: *Java API for XML Processing (JAXP) Version 1.2 Final Release*. Rajiv Mordani and Scott Boag. September 6, 2002. JCP.
http://www.jcp.org/en/jsr/detail?id=63

[JSR77] JSR 77: *J2EE™ Management*. JCP.
http://www.jcp.org/en/jsr/detail?id=77

[JSR88] JSR 88: *Java™ EE Application Deployment*. JCP.
http://www.jcp.org/en/jsr/detail?id=88

[JSR127] JSR 127: *JavaServer Faces*. JCP.
http://www.jcp.org/en/jsr/detail?id=127

[JSR175] JSR 175: *A Metadata Facility for the Java™ Programming Language*. JCP.
http://www.jcp.org/en/jsr/detail?id=175

[JSR181] JSR 181: *Web Services Metadata for the Java™ Platform*. JCP.
http://www.jcp.org/en/jsr/detail?id=181

[WSARCH] *Web Services Architecture*. W3C Web Services Architecture Working Group.
February 11, 2004. W3C.
http://www.w3.org/TR/ws-arch/

[WSDL11] *Web Services Description Language (WSDL) 1.1*. W3C Note. March 15, 2001.
W3C.
http://www.w3.org/TR/wsdl

[WSDL11SOAP12] *WSDL 1.1 Binding Extension for SOAP 1.2*. W3C Member Submission. April 5, 2006. W3C.
http://www.w3.org/Submission/wsdl11soap12/

[XHTML10] *XHTML™ 1.0 The Extensible HyperText Markup Language, Second Edition*. W3C HTML Working Group. August 1, 2002. W3C.
http://www.w3.org/TR/xhtml1/

[XMLCatalogs] *XML Catalogs*. Norman Walsh. August 6, 2001. OASIS.
http://www.oasis-open.org/committees/entity/spec.html

[XML10] *Extensible Markup Language (XML) 1.0, Third Edition*. Tim Bray, Jean Paoli,
C. M. Sperberg-McQueen, Eve Maler, and François Yergeau. February 24, 2004.
W3C.
http://www.w3.org/TR/REC-xml/

[XSD10-Part0] *XML Schema Part 0: Primer, Second Edition*. David C. Fallside and Priscilla
Walmsley. October 28, 2004. W3C.
http://www.w3.org/TR/xmlschema-0/

[XSD10-Part1] *XML Schema Part 1: Structures, Second Edition*. Henry S. Thompson, David
Beech, Murray Maloney, and Noah Mendelsohn. October 28, 2004. W3C.
http://www.w3.org/TR/xmlschema-1/

[XSD10-Part2] *XML Schema Part 2: Datatypes, Second Edition*. Paul V. Biron and Ashok
Malhotra. October 28, 2004. W3C.
http://www.w3.org/TR/xmlschema-2/

[XSLT10] *XSL Transformations (XSLT) Version 1.0*. James Clark. November 16, 1999.
W3C.
http://www.w3.org/TR/xslt

Index